THE ROUGH GUIDE TO
BELGIUM
& LUXEMBOURG

ROUGH
GUIDES

This eighth edition was updated by

Phil Lee

Contents

Introduction to
Belgium & Luxembourg

We bet you a beer – heavens, make that two – that Belgium will exceed your expectations. Rumours of a drab, flat land famous only for its fries and EU bureaucracy are massively false. The country's highlights range from the ancient and quirky to the oh-so-cool: you can bank on centuries-old castles and boisterous carnivals as well as home-grown haute couture, comic book museums and street art. And thanks to its compact geography, travellers can flit from the historic to the hip with a quick train ride. You might spend the morning touring one of Flanders' culture-rich cities – Brussels, Bruges, Antwerp and Ghent – and lunching in a Michelin-starred restaurant, before whiling away the afternoon exploring a time-forgotten Ardennes village, where the pubs – known as *estaminets* – dish up hearty dinners of beer-soaked rabbit stews.

If you overindulge, you'll be able to work it off cycling poplar-lined **canals**, hiking hilly **moors** and canoeing or kayaking along dinking **rivers**, all the while trying to wrap your tongue around the country's **three official languages** – French, Dutch and German. What's more, Belgium is one vast, immersive history lesson: it was here that Napoleon was finally defeated at the **Battle of Waterloo**, and here, too, that some of the bloodiest battles of both **world wars** played out.

Meanwhile, **Luxembourg** isn't reserved for bankers and diplomats. Its **UNESCO**-listed capital, perched on a plateau above green gorges, will instantly charm travellers; its regional **wines** will tickle the taste buds, while its **thermal spas** will unwind every last knot. So much more than convenient targets for a weekend break or cross-Channel booze run, Belgium and Luxembourg are central to Europe's cultural identity – EU or no EU.

GHENT'S CAFÉ CULTURE

Where to go

The beauty of bijou Belgium is that you can see a lot in a short amount of time. Divided into **three regions** – Flanders, the Dutch-speaking north; Wallonia, the French-speaking south; and Brussels, a bilingual island stranded in the south of Flanders – almost all the major towns are connected by a speedy and comprehensive **rail network**.

Brussels has myriad personalities thanks to the numerous nationalities that call the city home. This demographic mix is as fascinating as the city's odd blend of modern business districts, characterful **old towns** and open green spaces. The vast selection of hotels, from boutique to budget, makes Brussels a good base to explore surrounding towns on day-trips. However, be sure to allocate a good few days to the capital itself, particularly for its **world-class museums** and countless atmospheric **bars**.

FACT FILE
- **Belgium** is one of Europe's smallest nations
- It has three official **languages**
- The world's first weekly **newspaper** was printed in Antwerp in 1605
- Belgium produces more than 173,000 tonnes of **chocolate** per year
- The Belgian coastal **tram** route is the longest in the world at 68km
- Founded in 1830, Belgium is one of the youngest countries in Europe
- Most Luxembourgers speak **Luxembourgish** (a dialect of German), yet all official business is carried out in French
- Luxembourg has won the **Eurovision Song Contest** five times
- Luxembourg City is the seat of the **European Court of Justice**

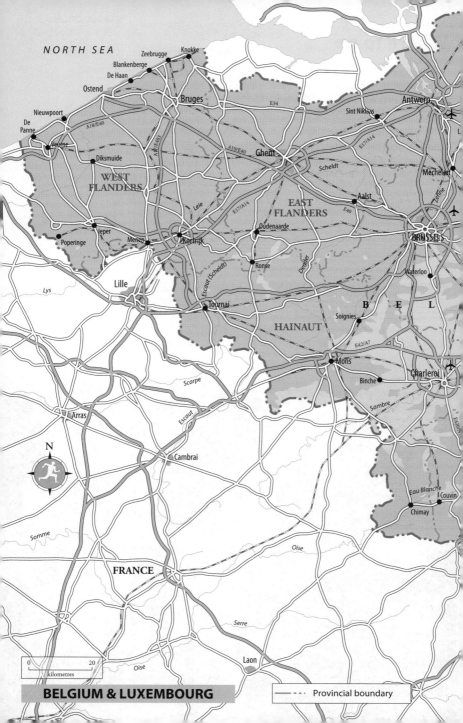

BELGIUM & LUXEMBOURG

Provincial boundary

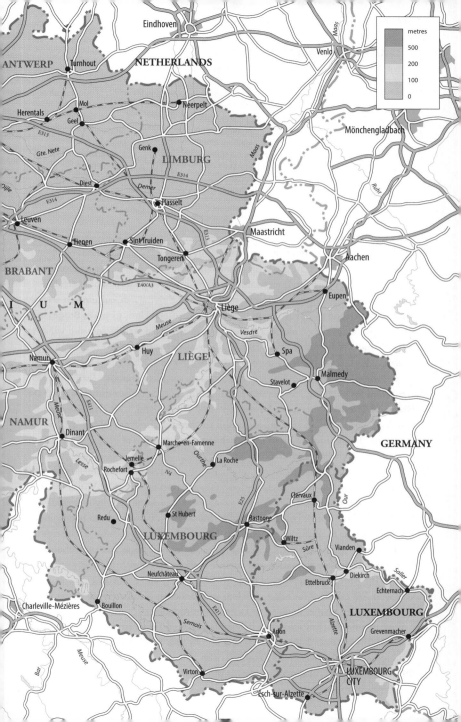

CHOCOLATE: A BELGIAN ART FORM

The Belgians picked up their love of **chocolate** via the most circuitous of historical routes. The Aztecs of Mexico were drinking chocolate, which they believed gave them wisdom when Hernando Cortéz's Spanish conquistadors turned up in 1519. Cortéz liked the stuff and brought cocoa beans back to Spain as a novelty gift for **Emperor Charles V** in 1528. Within a few years, its consumption had spread across Charles's empire, including today's Belgium and Luxembourg. At first, chocolate-making was confined to a few Spanish monasteries, but eventually, Belgians got in on the act and now produce what is generally regarded as the world's finest chocolates. Even the smallest town will have at least one **chocolate shop**, and although some brands are everywhere – Leonidas, Godiva and Neuhaus are three big players – try to seek out **independent producers** such as Wittamer or Pierre Marcolini in Brussels (see page 90) or The Chocolate Line in Bruges (see page 117), as their chocolates are usually that bit better.

Northern **Flanders** – made up of the provinces of West and East Flanders, Antwerp, Limburg and the top half of Brabant – is mainly flat but features a wealth of vibrant, forward-thinking cities. At the helm is **Antwerp**, a bustling old port famed for its nightlife and high fashion, but try and build in time to visit **Mechelen**, which lies just to the south – hugely underrated, the city has a thriving café culture and several top-notch attractions. Further west are the great medieval cloth towns of **Bruges** and **Ghent**, with a stunning concentration of Flemish art, listed architecture and winding canals. Bruges is undoubtedly touristy in summer, but you shouldn't miss it on this account. Beyond lie the sandy shores of the **Belgian coast**, which are easily accessible via the world's longest tram line and renowned for excellent seafood. The North Sea is too cold for anything other than a brave toe dip, but the rolling dunes near the **De Haan** and **Ostend** resorts make for a lovely walk. Back inland, it's worth spending a couple of days in and around **Ieper** (Ypres), the heart of the World War I battlefields and an ideal base from which to explore the vast, sad acreages of cemeteries and first-class museums dedicated to the conflict.

To the east of Brussels lies the old university city of **Leuven**, where you'll find Belgium's largest *begijnhof* (originally a beguinage), now a UNESCO World Heritage Site. Moving south, the Walloon province of **Hainaut** is dominated by industrial **Charleroi** and the more obviously appealing **Mons**, but it's also home to handsome **Tournai**, with its magnificent cathedral. To the east lies Belgium's most scenic region, the **Ardennes**, spread across the three provinces of **Namur**, **Liège** and **Luxembourg**, the first two of which are also cities – try to visit both, as they're rich in history and good eating. The Ardennes is an area of deep, wooded valleys and heath-laden plateaus, often very wild and excellent for hiking, cycling and canoeing. Namur makes a great base; alternatively, try smaller **Bouillon** or **La Roche-en-Ardenne**.

The Ardennes reaches across the Belgian border into the northern part of the **Grand Duchy of Luxembourg**, a landscape of hills and wooded ravines topped with tumbledown castles overlooking rushing rivers. The two best centres for touring the countryside are the quiet little towns of **Vianden** and **Echternach**, featuring an

MAS (MUSEUM AT THE STREAM), ANTWERP

SHEER BEER BLISS

No other country in the world produces more **beers** than Belgium – around **eight hundred** and counting. There are strong, dark brews from a handful of **Trappist monasteries**, light wheat beers perfect for a hot summer's day and fruity **lambic beers** bottled and corked like champagne, not to mention unusual concoctions that date back to medieval times. In the 'Contexts' section (see box, page 343), we've listed a selection of the best and most common to get you started, but the joy is in experimenting with new brews. Any decent establishment will have a beer menu and the **glasses** to go with them – no Belgian bar worth its salt would dare to serve a beer in anything other than its proper glass.

---

extravagantly picturesque castle and a splendid abbey, respectively. Indeed, despite its feeble reputation, the Duchy – or rather its northern reaches – packs more scenic highlights into its tight borders than many other, more renowned holiday spots and is perfect for hiking and, at a pinch, mountain biking. The Ardennes fizzles out into the **Moselle Valley**, whose slopes are lined with vines, while in the south, **Luxembourg City**'s bastions and bulwarks recall the days when this was one of the strongest fortresses in Europe.

When to go

Weather-wise, Belgium and Luxembourg are on par with the **south of England**: they're both temperate countries with warm summers and moderately cold winters – with the occasional brutal blast of snow and ice in January and February. The threat of **rain** is undeniably omnipresent, but at least it keeps things green. Generally speaking, **temperatures** rise the further south you go, with Wallonia a couple of degrees warmer than Flanders for most of the year.

Both countries can be visited **year-round** but are at their best from spring to late summer (**April–Sept**) when the weather is calmer and the nights longer. That said, there is one main **exception**: Bruges is inundated with tourists during the high season, so it's best to visit in winter or at least the autumn or spring, whilst the contrary applies in the Ardennes, which tends to go into hibernation in winter with many sites closing. Finally, December and early January can also be a lovely time to visit, thanks to the legendary **Christmas markets** in all the major towns.

MONTHLY TEMPERATURES AND RAINFALL

	Jan	Feb	Mar	Apr	May	Jun	Jul	Aug	Sep	Oct	Nov	Dec
BRUSSELS												
max/min (ºC)	6/-1	8/0	11/4	14/6	19/10	22/11	23/14	23/14	21/11	15/8	9/3	6/0
rainfall (mm)	66	61	53	60	55	76	95	80	63	83	75	88
LUXEMBOURG CITY												
max/min (ºC)	2/-2	4/-2	8/1	12/3	17/7	20/10	23/12	22/12	19/10	13/6	7/1	3/-1
rainfall (mm)	71	62	70	61	81	82	68	72	70	75	83	80

Author picks

Our author has scaled belfry towers, hiked hidden paths and slurped on bowls of *paling in 't groen* (a sort of eel stew) to bring you the best recommendations. Here are some of his personal favourites.

A beer pilgrimage Pay a visit to Brussels' *À La Mort Subite*, one of the capital's most famous bars, where you can limber up for a night on the town (see page 86).

Canal cycling tour Take a leisurely cycle ride out from Bruges along a poplar-lined canal to enjoy lunch at tiny Damme (see page 113).

Sample unusual chocolates Pop into *The Chocolate Line* (see page 117), Bruges' best chocolatier, famed for its lip-smackingly unusual recipes; try the tequila chocolate shots.

Strike a pose Visit the boutiques of Antwerp's leading clothes designers (see page 188), and don't miss the superb exhibitions at MoMu (see page 178).

Belgium's largest flea and antiques market Tongeren's town centre is taken over every Sunday by bric-a-brac and antique traders, as well as browsers and buyers, from far and wide (see page 205).

Taste Liège waffles A visit to Liège wouldn't be complete without savouring some crispy, sweet waffles from artisan maker *Une Gaufrette Saperlipopette* (see page 254). Unmissable.

Max out your memory card Take postcard-worthy photos of Luxembourg's prettiest hamlet by climbing the hill above Esch-Sur-Sûre (see page 293) – locals can point you towards the trail.

Romantic room with a view *De Hofkamers* in Ostend is a cosy three-star boutique hotel with four-poster beds and a view of the sea from the sixth floor (see page 122).

Our author recommendations don't end here. We've flagged up our favourite places – a perfectly sited hotel, an atmospheric café, a special restaurant – throughout the Guide, highlighted with the ★ symbol.

ENJOYING BELGIAN BEER
MOMU - MUSEUM OF FASHION, ANTWERP

15

things not to miss

It's impossible to see everything that Belgium and Luxembourg offer in one trip – and we don't suggest you try. In no particular order, the following is a selective and subjective taste of the two countries' highlights, from fantastic food and striking Gothic architecture to handsome forested hills. All highlights are colour-coded by chapter and have a page reference to take you straight into the guide, where you can find out more.

1

1 ADORATION OF THE MYSTIC LAMB, GHENT
See page 149

Ghent's pride and joy; this altarpiece is one of the most astonishing paintings in the medieval world.

2 MOSELLE VALLEY, LUXEMBOURG
See page 298

Sip through a glass or three of crémant, Luxembourg's incredibly quaffable, sparkling white wine.

3 GRAND-PLACE, BRUSSELS
See page 48

Take a seat at a café terrace, order a beer and admire the intricate UNESCO-listed guild houses of this world-famous cobbled square.

4 THE HAUTES FAGNES, ARDENNES
See page 259

The Ardennes' windswept expanse of moorland and woodland offers fabulous hiking.

5 OSTEND BEACH
See page 119

The pearl of the Belgian coastline – expect art installations, the freshest seafood and beach-chic hotels.

6

7

8

6 MAGRITTE, BRUSSELS
See pages 64 & 76
Two museums – the unmissable Musée Magritte and the outlying Musée René Magritte – powerfully evoke the legacy of Belgium's most famous modern artist.

7 MENIN GATE, IEPER
See page 134
The many thousands of soldiers' names inscribed on the hulking Menin Gate recall the slaughter of World War I as played out in Flanders.

8 THE BURG, BRUGES
See page 99
Bruges' medieval heart is home to one of Christendom's holiest relics – the Basilica of the Holy Blood.

9 MOULES-FRITES
See page 30
Belgian food is among the world's best; no trip is complete without tucking into a steaming pot of locally caught mussels and freshly cooked fries.

10 BRUSSELS' ART NOUVEAU
See page 73
The capital's middle class took to this style of architecture like ducks to water – Victor Horta is the main name to look out for.

11 MUSEÉS ROYAUX DES BEAUX ARTS, BRUSSELS
See page 62
Quite simply one of the best-stocked art galleries in Europe: feast your eyes on works of art by Bosch, Bruegel, Ensor and many more.

12 VIANDEN CASTLE, LUXEMBOURG
See page 295
Luxembourg's prettiest hilltop castle is the staging ground for an immersive summertime medieval festival.

13 STAVELOT CARNIVAL
See page 256
Give in to a beating with dried pig's bladders by the hooded Blancs Moussis at this annual carnival, celebrated for over five hundred years.

14 BEER
See page 343
With an inexhaustible range of brews, picking your way through the beer menus of Belgium's many cosy bars and cafés is one of the country's great pleasures.

15 KAYAKING IN THE ARDENNES
See pages 263 & 270
Paddle through picturesque valleys on the calm, cool waters of the River Lesse – no previous experience required.

Itineraries

Belgium and Luxembourg may be small, but they're jam-packed with things to do. The urban centres are a major draw, as are the historical sites of World War I and the region's wealth of outdoor activities.

THE GRAND TOUR

Allow a minimum of one week for this highlights tour, which takes in the main towns and cities.

❶ **Ostend** Kick off your trip in Ostend, a good base from which to explore the North Sea coastline. Ride the longest tram line and tuck into a plate of ultra-fresh *moules-frites*. See page 117

❷ **Bruges** From Ostend, it's a short train journey to Belgium's most famous city. Explore the maze of cobbled streets, see fabulous Flemish artworks in the Groeninge Museum and St-Janshospitaal, visit the *begijnhof* and take a boat trip on the canals. See page 97

❸ **Ghent** Head southeast to this buzzing university town, filled with waterways and ancient architecture, and home to the masterful *Adoration of the Mystic Lamb altarpiece*. See page 145

❹ **Antwerp** Go east across the country to Belgium's second-largest city for superb nightlife, cutting-edge fashion and all things related to the painter Rubens. See page 166

❺ **Brussels** Spend a few days touring the dynamic capital. Sip a beer in a time-forgotten *estaminet*, visit the world-class art galleries and take a selfie with the diminutive Manneken Pis. See page 44

❻ **Namur** Hop on a train south into French-speaking Wallonia, about an hour southeast, to visit the magnificent citadel. In town, marvel at the medieval gold and metalwork known as the Trésor d'Oignies. See page 238

❼ **Liège** From Namur, it's an easy train or car journey east to the university city of Liège, where you can visit the new La Boverie fine arts museum and drink some award-winning craft beer at charming *Brasserie Curtius*. See page 247

❽ **Luxembourg City** Drive or take the train south through the verdant, rolling hills of the Ardennes to one of Europe's most spectacularly sited capitals. Check out the underground casemates hidden beneath the Old Town and the laid-back bars of the leafy Grund. See page 282

WORLD WAR I SITES

Travellers commemorating World War I might trace the following route at a relaxed pace. Allow a week for this tour.

❶ **Ieper (Ypres)** This handsome town in West Flanders is home to the In Flanders Fields Museum, an excellent introduction to World War I, and is also the site of the Menin Gate, a moving memorial to the thousands of British and Imperial soldiers. See page 131

Create your own itinerary with Rough Guides. Whether you're after adventure or a family-friendly holiday, we have a trip for you, with all the activities you enjoy doing and the sights you want to see. All our trips are devised by local experts who get the most out of the destination. Visit **www.roughguides.com/trips** to chat with one of our travel agents.

❷ The Ypres Salient By bike or car, explore this area just north and east of Ieper, whose gentle ridges and woods witnessed bitter fighting during World War I. Be sure to visit Tyne Cot, a substantial British cemetery; Langemark, a German one; and Entry Point South, where a footpath follows the route of the front line. See page 135

❸ Poperinge Ten minutes by train west of Ieper, just beyond the range of the German artillery, Poperinge was where British and Imperial soldiers licked their psychological wounds at the Talbot House. See page 138

❹ Diksmuide From Poperinge, it's a half-hour drive north to unassuming Diksmuide, famous for its Ijzertoren – a towering monument and war museum – and the nearby Dodengang (Trench of Death). See page 129

❺ Nieuwpoort At the Westfront Nieuwpoort Museum up on the coast (accessible by car or bus from Diksmuide), see the ring of sluices that saved Belgium from total occupation and how the flooding was executed. See page 125

❻ Ostend Northeast of Nieuwpoort, the well-preserved concrete gun emplacements of the Atlantikwall line up along the coast just outside Ostend. Most are from World War II. See page 117

HIKING, BIKING AND KAYAKING

Flat in the north, hilly in the south and riddled with rivers, parts of Belgium and Luxembourg are an outdoor enthusiast's playground. This route can be enjoyed in four or five days.

❶ Tongeren Get warmed up with a gentle bike ride through the fruit orchards and small villages of the Haspengouw, between Tongeren and St-Truiden. See page 204

❷ The Hautes Fagnes Drive south into the Ardennes (public transport is thin on the ground) to the wild national park Hautes Fagnes and hike to Belgium's highest point – Signal de Botrange. See page 259

❸ La Roche-en-Ardenne From the Hautes Fagnes, it's about an hour's drive southwest through dense forests to this popular town for a family-friendly kayaking session along the River Lesse. See page 266

❹ Mullerthal Trail Lace up the hiking boots once more and, driving southeast from La Roche for about an hour and a half, cross the border into Luxembourg to tackle this 112km trail littered with impressive rock formations. See page 302

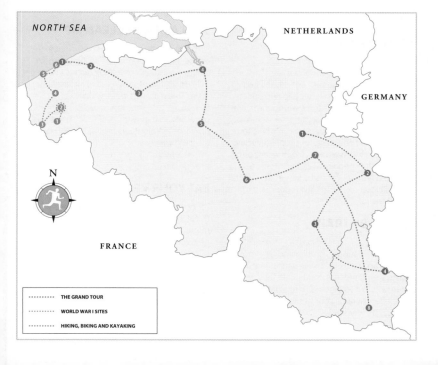

THE GRAND TOUR

WORLD WAR I SITES

HIKING, BIKING AND KAYAKING

Sustainable travel

Climate change has made many travellers more conscious of tourism's environmental impact, and Belgium and Luxembourg are emerging as top destinations for low-impact travel.

Regarding the environment, Belgium is in a quandary: it's one of the most heavily populated countries in the world, yet the pollution this entails now engages a gaggle of political leaders struggling to adjust to climate change. The capital's Green politicians wield considerable influence, but only after citizens acted together was the Brussels city council persuaded to pedestrianise much of the city centre.

HOP ON A BICYCLE

Belgium is almost universally flat, making cycling a feasible proposition for most visitors. Even better, cycle lanes are well-signposted and well-maintained, whilst cycle-hire outlets are ubiquitous. Belgian and Luxembourg trains carry bicycles at super-bargain rates, and many train stations offer inexpensive cycle hire, too. Visitors needn't cough up for specialist cycling gear – the Belgians almost always wear normal clothes as they peddle away. Cyclists are also protected from motorists by law: in the event of a cycle/auto crash, the law is designed to protect the former.

TRAVEL BY TRAIN

Belgium has an outstanding rail network covering the country's bulk, including almost all its towns and cities. Trains are almost invariably punctual and frequent. Neither are they expensive, so if you intend to explore a fair slice of the country, rail is your best bet, especially as driving is usually slower – before counting the

train's environmental advantages. Where the train network fizzles out, buses and sometimes trams take over, and even in the far south, the Ardennes can be reached easily by train and explored by bus. Luxembourg has a more modest train network, and here, the emphasis is more on the bus, but as a bonus, public transport is free right across the Grand Duchy.

JOIN A BEACH CLEAN-UP

Surprisingly, few visitors to Belgium seem to realise that the country has a long seaboard, where a scattering of seaside resorts intercepts mile upon mile of pristine sandy beach and dune. This seaboard looks out onto one of Europe's busiest shipping lanes, so it's unsurprising that all sorts of rubbish get washed up onshore. Volunteers mount a beach clean-up campaign every spring. If you are interested in volunteering, major tourist offices will be able to provide details.

EAT YOUR VEG

Far be it for *Rough Guides* to tell anyone what to eat, but even the most dedicated carnivore might balk (environmentally) at some of the items on offer at the average Belgian and Luxembourger restaurant, from king prawns flown in from Asia to beef from Argentina. The good news is that an increasing number of local restaurants have adapted to the environmental concerns of their fellow citizens by emphasising local, seasonal ingredients. Furthermore, if

CYCLING IS A GREAT WAY TO SIGHTSEE

you want to avoid meat altogether, there are now tasty vegetarian options at most good restaurants, with many dishes featuring local crops like asparagus, beetroot, sprouts, peas and, of course, the good old potato.

DAY-TRIPPING

Unless you want to experience the effects of excessive tourism, it's best to avoid visiting Bruges in the summertime as the place heaves with visitors. In fairness, Bruges city council has begun to impose restrictions to limit the numbers, but in the meantime, if you want to visit this popular and beautiful city, go out of season. You might also consider swapping the most popular tourist destinations for nearby cities where your money may be more appreciated – Oudenaarde for Ghent, Mechelen for Antwerp and Ostend for Bruges.

TO FLY OR NOT TO FLY

Shocking and environmentally senseless as it is, it's often cheaper to fly from a UK airport to Brussels than it is to travel by any other means. Hopefully, this will change in the future, but in the meantime, if you have the money and are keen to do what you can for the environment, then stick to getting there by train. What's more, you'll probably save yourself time.

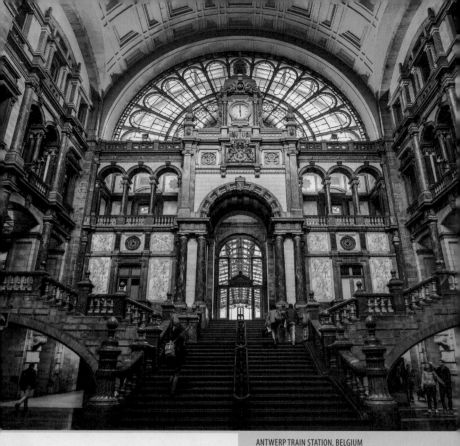

ANTWERP TRAIN STATION, BELGIUM

Basics

Getting there

UK travellers are spoilt for choice when it comes to getting to Belgium. There are flights to Brussels from London and a string of regional airports; direct Eurostar trains from London to Brussels; car ferries from Hull to the Netherlands near Antwerp; Eurotunnel services from Folkestone to Calais, a short drive from the Belgian coast; and frequent international buses from London to Brussels and Antwerp. Buses are usually the least expensive means of transport, but the train is faster and often not much pricier, and there are great deals on flights, too. Luxembourg is also easy to get to: there are flights from London, but it's just three hours by train from Brussels to Luxembourg City.

The main decision for travellers arriving from North America is whether to fly directly to Brussels – though the options are limited – or via another European city, probably London. Australians, New Zealanders and South Africans will have to route through another city – there are no nonstop flights.

Flights from the UK

From the **UK**, Belgium's major airport – **Brussels Airport** – is readily reached from London and a number of regional airports. There's also Brussels South Charleroi Airport (informally Brussels-Charleroi Airport), though the name is somewhat deceptive – it's actually on the edge of Charleroi, about 50km south of the capital. **Luxembourg City** Airport, the third choice, is just a short bus ride from Luxembourg City. The **airline** with the broadest selection of flights from the UK to Belgium is Brussels Airlines (Ⓦ brusselsairlines.com). **Flying times** are insignificant: no more than an hour and a half from London or regional airports to Brussels and Luxembourg.

Whichever route and carrier you choose, it's hard to say precisely what you'll pay at any given time – there are too many variables. That said, flying to Brussels from the UK with one of the low-cost airlines, a reasonable **average fare** would be about £200 return (including taxes), though you can pay as little as £70 and as much as £400.

Flights from Ireland

If you are flying from **Ireland**, Dublin is likely to be the fastest and cheapest option, with **nonstop flights** to both Brussels and Luxembourg City. Flying from Shannon or Cork will require a connecting flight. **Prices** vary considerably but begin at about €110 for a return flight from Dublin to Brussels (flights to Luxembourg City are in a similar ballpark). **Flying times** are modest, too: under two hours.

Flights from the US and Canada

From the **US**, you can **fly directly** to Brussels from New York City and several other big cities, but you'll often find cheaper deals if you're prepared to **stop once**, either in the US or in mainland Europe. Return **fares** to Brussels from New York can be found for as little as $900, but $1,500 is a more normal fare. There are no nonstop flights from the **West Coast**, but plenty of carriers will get you to Brussels with one stop for as little as $1,200 return. There are no nonstop flights from the US to Luxembourg.

From **Canada**, Brussels Airlines (Ⓦ brusselsairlines.com) flies directly from Toronto to Brussels, while Air Canada (Ⓦ aircanada.com) flies **nonstop** from Montreal to Brussels. Return **fares** from Toronto to Brussels start at around CA$1,300.

Flights from Australia and New Zealand

There are no non-stop flights from **Australia** or **New Zealand** to Brussels or Luxembourg City. Most itineraries will involve **two changes**: one in the Far East – Singapore, Bangkok or Kuala Lumpur – and another in the gateway city of the airline you're flying with (most commonly Paris, Amsterdam or London).

Fares to Brussels from Sydney or Melbourne are in the AU$1,500–2,000 range; from Auckland, the figure is NZ$2,000–2,500.

Flights from South Africa

There are no nonstop flights from **South Africa** to Belgium or Luxembourg City, but KLM offers nonstop flights to Amsterdam, a short train ride away from Belgium, from Cape Town and Johannesburg. With other airlines, you must change to a gateway city – for example, Lufthansa via Frankfurt – but this can often be more economical. As for sample **fares**, nonstop return flights with KLM from South Africa begin at about R7,000. The **flight time** is about eleven hours.

By train from the UK

Eurostar trains (ⓦeurostar.com) departing from London St Pancras reach Brussels via the Channel Tunnel in a few hours. In Brussels, trains arrive at **Bruxelles-Midi/Brussel-Zuid** station. Eurostar operates around **ten services a day**, and **fares** vary enormously, depending on the day, time, flexibility and ticket category – either Standard, Standard Premier or Business Premier; the least expensive returns cost in the region of £180, but you can pay much, much more; booking early is essential to get the best deals. Eurostar tickets valid for onward train travel from Brussels across the rest of Belgium cost extra. They may or may not be good value for money, given that Belgian train travel is inexpensive.

By train from continental Europe

Belgium and Luxembourg have borders with France, Germany and the Netherlands. A raft of rail lines runs into Belgium from its neighbours – and Luxembourg has good international connections, too. It's a little confusing, but most international (high-speed) trains are operated by companies acting as offshoots of one national operator or another. The main ones are ICE (mainly to and from Germany; ⓦint.bahn. de/en/), SNCB International (ⓦb-europe.com), NS International (ⓦnsinternational.com/en), and Eurostar (ⓦeurostar.com). Predictably, express trains are almost always **more expensive** than ordinary services.

Rail passes

If you're planning on travelling around Belgium and/or Luxembourg as part of a more extensive European tour, it may be worth considering an **Interrail Global Pass** (ⓦmyinterrail.com), which is valid for 5 to 31 days of travel within one month in 33 countries. **Rail Europe** (ⓦraileurope.com), the umbrella company for all international passes, operates a comprehensive website detailing all the options and prices. Rail Europe also has details of the similar **Eurail Global Pass** for US and Canadian citizens. Note in particular that some passes have to be bought before leaving home.

By bus from the UK

Travelling by **long-distance bus** is generally the cheapest way of reaching Belgium from the UK, but it is very time-consuming. **FlixBus** (ⓦflixbus.co.uk) has daily departures from London's Victoria coach station to Brussels, with a journey time of upwards of nine hours. Return tickets start at as little as £60 in summer if you book well in advance. There are also regular FlixBus services to several other Belgian cities, including Bruges, Ghent and Antwerp.

Driving from the UK

To reach Belgium **by car or motorbike from the UK**, take a **car ferry** (see below) or use the shuttle train operated by **Eurotunnel** (ⓦeurotunnel.com) through the Channel Tunnel from Folkestone to Calais. **Fares** are charged per vehicle, including passengers, depending on the time of year, time of day and length of stay; the journey takes just over half an hour. For example, a five-day return fare in the summer starts at around £230. Book well in advance. Note that the Eurotunnel only carries cars (including occupants) and motorbikes, not foot passengers. From the Eurotunnel exit in Calais, it's just 50km or so to De Panne on the Belgian coast, 120km to Bruges and 200km to Brussels.

By ferry from the UK

At the time of writing, there are no **car ferries** offering direct services from the UK to Belgium, but there are sailings from Hull to Rotterdam, just 100km from Antwerp. The operator is **P&O Ferries** (ⓦpoferries. com), and the sailing time is approximately thirteen hours. Alternatively, Stena Line (ⓦstenaline.co.uk) operates car ferries from Harwich to the Hook of Holland, 125km from Antwerp; the sailing time is just under seven hours. **Tariffs** vary enormously, depending on when you leave, how long you stay, what size your vehicle is and how many passengers are in it; there is also the cost of a cabin to consider. Booking ahead is strongly recommended and essential in summer.

Getting around

Travelling around Belgium is almost always easy: it's a small country with a well-organised – and reasonably priced – public transport system, with an extensive train network supplemented by (and tied in with) many local bus services. The main exception is the Ardennes, where, ideally, you'll have a car to explore with. Luxembourg is, of course, even smaller. Still, matters are not quite so straightforward here: the train network is limited, and public transport is based mainly around buses, whose timetables can demand scrutiny.

Travel **between Belgium and Luxembourg** is seamless, with no border controls and routine through-ticketing by train and bus. **Two main rail lines** link the two countries: the first runs from Brussels to Luxembourg City via Namur and Arlon, and the second links Liège with Luxembourg City. **Journey times** are insignificant – Brussels to Luxembourg City takes under three hours – and services are frequent. Note also that in addition to the domestic deals and discounts mentioned below, there is a host of pan-European rail passes (see page 24).

By train

Belgium

The best way to get around Belgium is by train. The system, operated by the **Société Nationale des Chemins de Fer Belges/Belgische Spoorwegen** (Belgian Railways; ⓦ belgiantrain.be), is one of the best in Europe: trains are fast, frequent and very punctual; the network of lines is comprehensive; and **fares** are relatively low. For example, a standard, second-class ticket (*billet ordinaire/gewone biljet*) from Bruges to Arlon, one of the longest domestic train journeys you can make, costs just €25 one-way, while the forty-minute trip from Ghent to Brussels costs €10.80. Standard return tickets are twice the cost of single, but same-day return tickets knock about 10 percent off the price. First-class fares cost about 50 percent on top of the regular fare. There are substantial **discounts** for children and seniors (65+) and other discount tickets and deals that reward off-peak travelling and repeat journeys. Best of all are the **special weekend returns**, which can knock up to 50 percent off. With any ticket, you can **break your journey** anywhere en route and continue later that day, but you're not allowed to backtrack. You can **buy tickets** via the company's compendious website,

via the NMBS/SNCB smartphone app (details on the website), and at any train station, either at the ticket office or at the automatic ticket machines installed at all major stations, though note that these only accept credit cards (not debit cards).

Luxembourg

In Luxembourg, trains are run by the **Société Nationale des Chemins de Fer Luxembourgeois** (CFL; ⓦ cfl.lu). The network comprises just a handful of lines, with the principal route cutting north-south down the middle of the country from Belgium's Liège to Luxembourg City via Clervaux and Ettelbruck. Trains are fast and efficient, and most operate hourly. A free **diagrammatic plan** of the country's bus and train network is online and available at most train stations, as are individual train and bus **timetables**. All public transport in the Grand Duchy – including trains – is free.

By bus

Belgium

With so much of the country covered by the rail network, Belgian **buses** are mainly used for short distances, and wherever there's a choice of transport, the train is quicker and not much more expensive. Indeed, to all intents and purposes, buses essentially supplement the trains, with services radiating out from the train station and/or connecting different rail lines. Local buses are invaluable in some parts of rural Belgium, like the **Botte de Hainaut** and **the Ardennes**, where the train network fizzles out. Three bus companies provide nationwide coverage: **De Lijn** (ⓦ delijn.be) in the Flemish-speaking areas, STIB (ⓦ stib-mivb.be) in Brussels, and **TEC** (ⓦ letec.be) in Wallonia.

Luxembourg

In Luxembourg, the sparseness of the rail system means that **buses** are much more important than in Belgium, though again, bus and train services are **fully integrated**. A free diagrammatic plan of the Grand Duchy's bus and train network is available at major bus and train stations, as are individual bus timetables; you can also get detailed information online (ⓦ cfl.lu).

By car

For the most part, **driving** around Belgium and Luxembourg is pretty much what you would hope: smooth, easy and quick. Both countries have a good road network, with most of the major towns linked by some kind of motorway or dual carriageway, though snarl-ups are far from rare, especially in Belgium. That said, big-city driving, where congestion and one-way systems are the norm, is almost always problematic, particularly as drivers in Belgium are generally considered some of the most pugnacious in Europe. One problem peculiar to Belgium, however, is **signage**. In most cases, the French and Flemish names are similar – or at least mutually recognisable – but in others, they do not resemble each other (see box, page 27). In Brussels and its environs, all the road signs are bilingual. Still, elsewhere it's either French or Flemish, and, as you cross **Belgium's language divide** (see page 335), the name you've been following on the road signs can simply disappear, with, for example, 'Liège' suddenly transformed into 'Luik'.

Rules of the road are straightforward: you drive on the right, and speed limits are 20km/h in built-up areas, 70km/h outside, and 120km/h on motorways; note that speed cameras are commonplace. Drivers and passengers are required by law to wear seatbelts, and penalties for drunk driving are always severe. Remember also that trams have the right of way over any other vehicle and that, unless indicated otherwise, motorists must give way to traffic merging from the right. There are no toll roads, and although **fuel** is pretty expensive, the short distances involved mean this isn't too much of an issue.

Most **foreign driving licences**, including EU/ EEA, Australian, New Zealand, US and Canadian, are honoured in Belgium and Luxembourg. If you're **bringing your car**, you must have adequate insurance, preferably covering legal costs. Having an appropriate breakdown policy from your home motoring organisation is also advisable.

Renting a car

All the major **international car rental agencies** are represented in Belgium and Luxembourg. To **rent a car**, you'll have to be 21 or over (and have been driving for at least a year), and you'll need a credit card – though some local agencies will accept a hefty cash deposit instead. **Rental charges** are reasonable, beginning around €200 per week for unlimited mileage in the smallest vehicle, and (should) include collision damage waiver and vehicle (but not personal) insurance. To cut costs, book in advance and online. Compare prices at ⓦtravelsupermarket. com. If you go to a smaller, **local company** (of which there are many), you should proceed with care: in particular, check the policy for the excess applied to claims and ensure that it includes a collision damage waiver (applicable if an accident is your fault) as well as adequate levels of financial cover. If

you **break down** in a rented car, you'll get roadside assistance from the repair company the rental firm has contracted. The same principle works with your own vehicle's breakdown policy providing you have coverage abroad.

Taxis

Taxis are easy to find in the major towns and cities, with fares starting at around €2.40–4.40 and then €2.50–3 per km. However, it's a different story in the wilds of the Ardennes, where there might only be one taxi driver in a particular area. The local tourist offices will be able to advise you, and you'll probably need to book ahead of time for travel.

By bike

Belgium

Cycling is something of a national passion in Belgium, and it's also – given the short distances and essentially flat terrain – a viable and fairly effortless way of getting around. But you have to be selective: cycling on most trunk roads – where separate cycle lanes are far from ubiquitous – is precarious, verging on the suicidal. On the other hand, once you've reached the countryside, there are dozens of **clearly signposted cycle routes** to follow – and local tourist offices will invariably have maps and route descriptions, which you can supplement with the relevant **IGN (NGI) map** (see page 38). The logic of all this means that most Belgian cyclists – from Eddy Merckx lookalikes to families on an afternoon's pedal – carry their bikes to their chosen cycling location by car or train. Train operators transport bicycles with the minimum of fuss and at minimal cost, but the same isn't true for bus operators – it's not usually allowed.

If you haven't brought your own, you can **rent bikes** from innumerable train stations nationwide (mostly in Flanders) under the **Blue Bike scheme** (ⓦblue-bike.be) for just €2.50–3.50 per day (depending on location) plus an initial registration fee of €12. It's a good idea to reserve your bike ahead of time during the summer. Otherwise, local bike rental shops are commonplace – reckon on €20 per day for basic/ no-frills models.

Luxembourg

Luxembourg is popular with cyclists and has over 600km of **cycle tracks**, many following old railway lines. You can **rent bikes** at an assortment of campsites, hostels, hotels and tourist offices for around €20 a day (€30 for a mountain bike); tourist

FRENCH AND FLEMISH PLACE NAMES

The list below provides the **French and Flemish names** of some of the more important towns in Belgium, where the difference may cause confusion. The official name comes first, and the alternative comes afterwards, except in the case of Brussels, where both languages have equal standing.

FRENCH–FLEMISH

Bruxelles – Brussel
Ath – Aat
Liège – Luik
Mons – Bergen

Namur – Namen
Nivelles – Nijvel
Soignies – Zinnik
Tournai – Doornik

FLEMISH–FRENCH

Antwerpen – Anvers
Brugge – Bruges
De Haan – Le Coq
Gent – Gand
Ieper – Ypres
Kortrijk – Courtrai
Leuven – Louvain
Mechelen – Malines

Oostende – Ostende
Oudenaarde – Audenarde
Ronse – Renaix
Sint Truiden – St-Trond
Tienen – Tirlemont
Tongeren – Tongres
Veurne – Furnes
Zoutleeuw – Léau

offices also have comprehensive lists of local bike rental outlets. Also, bear in mind that you can take your bike on trains (but not buses) for free. For further details, consult the website of the Luxembourg National Tourist Office (see page 40).

Accommodation

Inevitably, hotel accommodation is one of the significant expenses incurred on a trip to Belgium and Luxembourg. Indeed, if you're after a degree of comfort, it will be the costliest factor by far. There are budget alternatives, however, beginning with the no-frills end of the hotel market, some B&Bs and rented rooms in private accommodation via online booking agencies such as Airbnb. Even more of a bargain are the youth hostels, be they Hostelling International-affiliated or 'unofficial' (private) ones located in both countries' larger cities and/or main tourist spots. Note that it is advisable to book in advance no matter where or when you're going.

Hotels

The majority of **hotels** in Belgium and Luxembourg are graded according to the pan-European **Hotelstars**

Union (🌐 hotelstars.eu/belgium). By necessity, this system measures easily identifiable criteria – lifts, toilets, room service, etc – rather than aesthetics, specific location or even cost. **Prices** fluctuate wildly with demand and not necessarily with the season – summer is bargain time in Brussels. One-star and no-star hotels are rare, and prices for two-star establishments start at around €80 for a double room without a private bath or shower and €90 for en-suite facilities. Three-star hotels cost upwards of about €120; for four- and five-star places, you'll pay €180-plus. Note also that hotel foyers can be deceptively plush compared with the rooms beyond, and you only begin to hit the real comfort zone at three stars.

B&Bs

Primarily as a result of COVID-19, the number of **Belgian B&Bs** (*chambres d'hôtes/gastenkamers*) has fallen in recent years, but even so, 'B&B' is perhaps something of a misnomer as guests rarely have much contact with their hosts – it's more like a **rented room in a private house**. The **average rate** for a B&B in both Belgium and Luxembourg works out at €100 per double per night, a tad more in Brussels and Bruges. The only common snag is that many B&Bs are **inconveniently situated** far from the respective town or city centre – be sure to check out the location before you accept a room. Note, too, that as the owners often don't live on the premises, access has to be arranged

ACCOMMODATION PRICE CODES

All the **accommodation** detailed in this guide have been graded according to the four price categories listed below. These represent how much you can expect to pay in each establishment for the **least expensive double or twin room with breakfast in high season**, barring special deals and discounts; for a single room, expect to pay around 80 percent of the price of a double. Our categories are simply a guide to prices and do not indicate the facilities you might expect; they differ from the star system the tourist authorities apply. At **hostels**, we usually give two prices – the price of a double room, if available, and of a dormitory bed. For **campsites**, prices are based on two adults and a tent pitch.

€ = €50–100
€€ = €100–150
€€€ = €150–230
€€€€ = €230-plus

beforehand. In most places, the tourist office has a list of local B&Bs, which it will issue to visitors, but in the more popular destinations, for instance, Bruges and Ghent, B&Bs are publicised alongside hotels. In **Luxembourg**, B&Bs are less of a feature, though again, local tourist offices have the details.

Hostels

If you're travelling on a tight budget, a **hostel** may well be your accommodation of choice – whether you're youthful or not. They can often be extremely good value, offering clean and comfortable **dorm beds** and a selection of **private rooms** (doubles and sometimes singles) for around €80–90. Both city and country locations can get full between June and August when you should book in advance. If you plan to spend several nights in **HI-affiliated** hostels, joining your home HI organisation before you leave makes sense to avoid paying surcharges. However, you can participate at the first local hostel where you stay instead.

Belgium

Belgium has around thirty HI-affiliated hostels (*auberges de jeunesse/jeugdherbergen*) operated by two separate organizations, **Vlaamse Jeugdher-bergen** (🌐jeugdherbergen.be/en), covering the Flemish region, and **Les Auberges de Jeunesse de Wallonie** (🌐lesaubergesdejeunesse.be) for Wallonia. Both run hostels in Brussels. **Dorm beds** cost about €30–40 per person per night, including breakfast; no age restrictions exist. Most hostels have **single- and double-bedded rooms**, which rise to €40–60 per person per night. **Meals** are often available, and some hostels have **self-catering facilities** too. Some of Belgium's larger cities – primarily Antwerp, Bruges and Brussels – have several **private hostels** (sometimes referred to as *logements pour jeunes/jeugdlogies*),

offering dormitory accommodation and, invariably, double- and triple-bedded rooms, at broadly similar prices, though standards vary enormously.

Luxembourg

Luxembourg has nine youth hostels, all members of the **Centrale des Auberges de Jeunesse Luxem-bourgeoises** (CAJL; 🌐youthhostels.lu). The prices for HI members are around €35 per person for a **dorm bed** and €20 per person in a **double room**, with breakfast included; some places also serve meals.

Camping

Camping is a popular pastime in both Belgium and Luxembourg. There are hundreds of campsites in Belgium, from a field with a few pitches to extensive complexes with all mod cons. The country's campsites are regulated by two governmental agencies – one for Flanders and one for Wallonia – each produces camping booklets and operates a **website**: 🌐camping. be for Flanders; 🌐campingbelgique.be for Wallonia. Many Belgian campsites are situated with the motorist in mind, occupying key locations beside main roads, and they are all classified within a **one- to five-star matrix**. The majority are two- and three-star estab-lishments. **Luxembourg** has around ninety registered campsites, all detailed on 🌐camping.lu. Luxembourg does not now enforce the Benelux star system (though individual campsites can register if they wish), and the best campsites are now awarded the **Luxembourg Quality Label**; environmentally friendly sites can opt for the **Luxembourg EcoLabel** instead.

Farm and rural holidays

In Belgium and Luxembourg, the tourist authorities coordinate farm and rural holidays, ranging from family accommodation in a farmhouse to renting rural apartments and country dwellings. In Wallonia and Luxembourg, there are also **gîtes d'étapes** – dormitory-style lodgings situated in relatively remote parts of the country – which can house anywhere between ten and one hundred people per establishment. You can often rent just part of the *gîte d'étape* or stay on a bed-and-breakfast basis. Some of the larger *gîtes d'étape* (or *gîtes de groupes*) cater for large groups only, accepting bookings for a minimum of 25 people. In all cases, booking is essential, and **prices**, naturally enough, vary widely depending on the quality of accommodation, the length of stay and the season. For example, a high-season (mid-June– Aug), week-long booking of a pleasantly situated and comfortable farmhouse for four adults and three children might cost you in the region of €450, whereas a ten-person *gîte d'étape* might cost €400. For further details, check out Ⓦlogereninvlaanderen-vakantieland.be for Flanders; Ⓦgitesdewallonie.be for Wallonia; and Ⓦgites.lu for Luxembourg.

Food and drink

Belgian cuisine, particularly that of Brussels and Wallonia, is held in high regard worldwide and, in most of Europe, is seen as second only to French in quality. Indeed, many feel it's of equal standing. There's a surprising amount of regional diversity for such a small country. Still, it's generally true that pork, beef, game, fish and seafood – especially mussels – are staple items, often cooked with butter, cream and herbs, or sometimes beer – which is, after all, Belgium's national drink. Soup is also common, a hearty stew-like affair offered in a huge tureen from which you can help yourself. The better Belgian chefs are often eclectic, dipping into many other cuisines, especially those of the Mediterranean, and borrowing freely from across their own country's cultural/ linguistic divide.

Luxembourg cuisine doesn't rise to quite such giddy heights, though it's still of an excellent standard. The food here borrows extensively from the **Ardennes** but, as you might expect, has more Germanic influences, with sausages and sauerkraut featuring on menus alongside pork, game and river fish. As for **drink**, one of the real delights of Belgium is its **beer**, and Luxembourg produces some very drinkable **white wines** from the vineyards along the west bank of the River Moselle.

For a **menu reader** in both French and Flemish (Dutch), see pages 341 & 337.

Food

In Belgium and Luxembourg, the least expensive places to eat are **cafés and bars** – though the distinction between the two is typically blurred, hence the large number of **café-bars**. Several of these establishments will flank the main square of every small and medium-sized town you visit, offering basic dishes such as pasta, soups, croque-monsieurs (a toasted ham and cheese sandwich served with salad) and chicken or steak with chips. **Prices** are usually reasonable – reckon on about €15–20 for the more modest dishes, €20–30 for the more substantial – though, of course, you will often pay more in the most popular tourist destinations. In general – and especially in Wallonia – the quality of these dishes will regularly be excellent, and portions will be characteristically substantial. In the big cities, these café-bars play second fiddle to more specialist – and equally inexpensive – places: primarily pasta and pizza joints, cafés that cater for the shopper (and specialise in cakes and pastries), ethnic café-restaurants and so forth.

Though there's often a thin dividing line between the café and the **restaurant**, the latter is mostly a little more formal and, not surprisingly, somewhat

---

EATING OUT PRICE CODES

All the **restaurants** detailed in this guide have been graded according to the four price categories listed below. These represent how much you can expect to pay in each establishment for a **two-course meal for one, including a glass of wine** and excluding special deals and discounts.

€ = €15–25
€€ = €25–35
€€€ = €35–50
€€€€ = €50-plus

more expensive. Even in the cheapest restaurant, a main course rarely costs under €20, with a more usual figure between €25 and €30. Restaurants are usually open at lunchtime (noon–2pm), but the main focus is in the evening. In addition, many restaurants close one day a week, often Monday or Tuesday, and in the smaller towns, kitchens start to wind down around 9.30/10pm. Many bars, cafés and restaurants offer a good-value plat du jour (*dagschotel*), usually for around €20, which frequently includes a drink. **Vegetarians** may, however, not be so enamoured: Belgian and Luxembourg cuisine is essentially fish- and meat-based, which means vegetarians can be in for a difficult time, though all of the larger towns do have at least a couple of vegetarian places, even if these tend to operate limited opening hours.

Breakfast, lunch and snacks

In most parts of Belgium and Luxembourg, **breakfast** comprises a cup of coffee and a roll or croissant. However, the more expensive hotels usually offer sumptuous banquet-like breakfasts with cereals, fruit, hams and cheeses. Everywhere, **coffee** is almost always first-rate – aromatic and strong, but rarely bitter; in Brussels and the south, it's often accompanied by hot milk (café au lait), but throughout Belgium, there's a tendency to serve it in the Dutch fashion, with a small tub of evaporated rather than fresh milk.

Later in the day, the most common **snack** is *frites* (chips) – served everywhere in Belgium from *friture/frituur* stands or parked vans, with salt or mayonnaise, or more exotic dressings (see box, page 337). More wholesome are the filled **baguettes** (*broodjes*) that many bakeries and cafés prepare on the spot – imaginative, tasty creations that make a meal in themselves. Many fish shops, especially on the coast, also do an appetising line in seafood baguettes, while **street vendors** in the north sell various sorts of toxic-looking sausage (*worst*), especially black pudding (*bloedworst*).

Mussels (*moules/mosselen*), cooked in a variety of ways and served with chips, are a national favourite at lunch or dinner – indeed, it's effectively Belgium's national dish. Traditionally, mussels are only served in season – when there is an 'r' in the month (Sept–April) – and are best eaten the time-honoured way, served in a vast pot with chips and mayonnaise on the side, either *à la marinière* (steamed with white wine, shallots and parsley or celery) or *à la crème* (steamed with the same ingredients but thickened with cream and flour).

Lapin à la gueuze (rabbit cooked in beer) is another **favourite** countrywide. So, too, is *filet americain*

(highly seasoned steak tartare or raw minced beef), especially delicious with frites. Wherever you are, you'll usually find *tomates aux crevettes* (tomatoes stuffed with tiny, deliciously sweet grey shrimp) on the menu.

Although it has nothing like the variety of France, Belgium boasts some decent **cheeses**, among which Herve, from the Liège province town of the same name, is one of the best and most common. It's a rind cheese, a bit like the French Pont l'Evêque, but stronger. Others, like Chimay, are made by monks in the Trappist monasteries, where the cheese-making tradition still exists alongside brewing.

Wallonian cuisine

Wallonian cuisine is broadly similar to French, based upon a fondness for rich sauces and fresh ingredients. From the Walloons come *truite à l'Ardennaise* (trout cooked in a wine sauce); *chicorées gratinées au four* (chicory with ham and cheese); *fricassée Liègeoise* (basically, fried eggs, bacon and sausage or blood pudding); *fricadelles à la bière* (meatballs in beer); *boulets liégois* (meatballs doused in a sweet, syrupy sauce); and *carbonnades de porc Bruxelloises* (pork with a tarragon and tomato sauce).

The **Ardennes**, in particular, is well known for its cured **ham** (similar to Italian Parma ham) and, of course, its **pâté**, made from pork, beef, liver and kidney – though it often takes a particular name from an additional ingredient, for example, *pâté de faisan* (pheasant) or *pâté de lièvre* (hare). Unsurprisingly, **game** (*gibier*) features heavily on most Ardennes menus. Among the many **salads** you'll find are *salade de Liège* (made from beans and potatoes) and *salade wallonie* (a warm salad of lettuce, fried potatoes and bits of bacon).

Flemish cuisine

In **Flanders**, the food is akin to that of the Netherlands, characteristically plainer and simpler than that of Wallonia. Indeed, for decades, traditional Flemish cuisine was regarded with much disdain as crude and unsubtle. However, in recent years, there's been a dramatic revival of its fortunes, and nowadays, Flemish specialities appear on most menus in the north, and there are dozens of speciality Flemish restaurants, too. **Typical dishes** include *waterzooi* (a soup-cum-stew consisting of chicken or fish boiled with fresh vegetables); *konijn met pruimen* (an old Flemish standby of rabbit with prunes); *paling in 't groen* (eel braised in a spinach sauce with herbs); *stoofvlees* (beef marinated in beer and cooked with herbs and onions); *stoemp* (mashed potato mixed with vegetable and/or meat purée); and *hutsepot* (literally 'hotchpotch', a mixed stew of mutton, beef and pork).

Luxembourg cuisine

Favourite **dishes in Luxembourg** include pike in green sauce (*hiecht mat kraïderzooss*), jugged hare (*huesenziwwi*), black pudding (*boudin*) served with apple sauce and mashed potatoes, tripe (*kuddelfleck*), nettle soup (*brennesselszopp*), buckwheat dumplings (*stäerzelen*) and smoked collar of pork with broad beans (*judd mat gaardebou'nen*), which is virtually the national dish. Along the **Moselle River**, many restaurants serve *friture de la Moselle*, a small fried fish. At many annual celebrations and fairs, lots of restaurants serve *fesch*, which is fried whole fish in batter.

Cakes, pastries and chocolate

Belgium and Luxembourg heave with **patisseries**, where you can pick up freshly baked bread, cakes and pastries – from mousse slices to raspberry tarts and beyond. Belgium is, of course, famous for its **chocolates** and on average, each Belgian eats a prodigious 12.5kg of the stuff annually. The big Belgian **chocolatiers** – Neuhaus, Godiva and Leonidas – have stores in all the main towns and cities, but many consider their products too sugary – one of the reasons why all of Belgium's cities now boast at least a couple of small, **independent chocolate makers**. These almost invariably charge more than their bigger rivals, but few would deny the difference in taste.

Drink

No trip to **Belgium** would be complete without sampling its **beer**, which is always good, almost always reasonably priced and comes in an amazing variety of brews (see box, page 343). There's a **bar** on nearly every corner, and most serve at least twenty types of beer; in some, the 'menu' runs into the hundreds. Traditionally, Belgian bars are cosy, unpretentious places, the walls stained brown by years of tobacco smoke. Still, in recent years, many have been decorated in anything from a sort of potty medievalism (wooden beams, etc) to Art Nouveau and a frugal post-modernist style, which is especially fashionable in the big cities. Many bars also serve simple food, while many pride themselves on first-rate dishes from a small but well-conceived menu.

Luxembourg also has a good supply of bars, with imported Belgian beers commonplace alongside the fairly modest lagers of the country's three dominant **breweries** – Brasserie Nationale (producing Bofferding and Battin), Brasserie de Luxembourg (producing Diekirch and Mousel) and Brasserie Simon (producing

WAFFLES

Right across Belgium, there are stands selling **waffles** (*gaufres/wafels*), a mixture of butter, flour, eggs, and sugar grilled on deep-ridged waffle irons and served steaming hot with jam, honey, whipped cream, ice cream, chocolate, or fruit. There are two main types of waffle: the **Liège version**, sweet, caramelised, and with the corners squared off, and the larger, fluffier **Brussels waffle**, the latter needs a topping to give added flavour.

Simon and Ourdaller) – and the white wines from the west bank of the River Moselle.

Wines and spirits

In **Belgium**, beer very much overshadows **wine**, but the latter is widely available, with four **AOPs** in Flanders – Hageland, Hapsengouw, Heuvelland and Vlaamse Mousserende Kwaliteitswijn (sparkling wine) – and one in Wallonia – Côtes de Sambre et Meuse. In **Luxembourg**, the duchy's pleasant whites are worth sampling; they are fruitier and drier than the average French wine and are more akin to the vintages of Germany. A Luxembourg speciality is **crémant**, a sparkling, Champagne-like wine – very palatable and reasonably priced: try the St-Martin brand, which is excellent and dry. All the premium Luxembourg wines are marked with the appellation 'Marque Nationale' to guarantee quality.

There's no one national Belgian **spirit**, but the Flemings have a penchant – like their Dutch neighbours – for **jenever**, which is similar to gin, made from grain spirit and flavoured by juniper berries. It's available in most ordinary and specialist bars, selling as many as several hundred varieties. Broadly speaking, jenever comes in **two types**: young (*jonge*) and old (*oude*), the latter characteristically pale yellow and smoother than the former; both are served ice-cold. In Luxembourg, you'll come across locally produced bottles of **eau de vie** – distilled from various fruits and around 50 percent alcohol by volume – head-thumping stuff.

The media

British newspapers and magazines are easy to get hold of on the day of publication in Belgium and Luxembourg, and there is not much difficulty in finding some

American publications. As far as British TV is concerned, BBC1 and BBC2 television channels are on many hotel-room TVs in Belgium and some in Luxembourg. Access to cable and satellite channels is commonplace in hotels and bars across both countries. Frequencies and schedules for the BBC World Service (@bbc.co.uk/worldservice), Radio Canada (@rcinet.ca) and Voice of America (@voanews.com) are listed on their respective websites.

Newspapers and magazines

Several national and regional daily and weekly newspapers in French and Dutch are published in Belgium, and French and German are published in Luxembourg. The leading English-language (online) publications in Belgium are The Bulletin (@xpats.com), Flanders Today (@flanderstoday.eu) and the Brussels Times (@brusselstimes.com); in Luxembourg, it's the Chronicle (@chronicle.lu), Delano (@delano.lu) and Wort (@wort.lu).

TV and radio

Domestic TV is largely uninspiring, though the Flemish-language TV1 and Kanaal 2 usually run English-language films with subtitles, whereas the main Wallonian channels – RTBF 1 and ARTE – mainly dub; Luxembourg's RTL channel does both. Belgium's English-language radio station is Radio X (@radioguide.fm); in Luxembourg it's Ara City Radio (@aracityradio.com).

Festivals

Belgium and Luxembourg are big on festivals – everything from religious processions to cinema, fairs and contemporary music binges. These are spread throughout the year, though, as you might expect, most tourist-oriented festivals take place in the summer.

Belgium

Belgium's annual carnivals (carnavals), held in February and early March, are original, colourful and boisterous in equal measure. One of the most renowned is held in February at Binche, in Hainaut, when there's a procession involving some 1,500 extravagantly dressed dancers called Gilles. There are also carnivals in Ostend and Aalst and in Eupen, where the action lasts over the weekend before Shrove Tuesday and culminates with Rosenmontag on Easter Monday – a pageant of costumed groups and floats parading through the town centre. Most remarkable is Stavelot's carnival, where the streets are overtaken by so-called Blancs Moussis, townsfolk clothed in white hooded costumes and equipped with long red noses.

Nominally commemorating the arrival by boat of a miraculous statue of the Virgin Mary from Antwerp in the fourteenth century, the Brussels Ommegang is the best-known of the festivals with a religious inspiration; a largely secular event these days, it's held on the first Tuesday and Thursday of July. However, if you want to see anything on the Grand-Place, where most of the action is, you must reserve seats months in advance. Among the other religious events, perhaps the most notable is the Heilig-Bloed-processie (Procession of the Holy Blood), held in Bruges on Ascension Day, when the shrine encasing the medieval phial, which supposedly contains a few drops of the blood of Christ, is carried solemnly through the streets.

Among any number of folkloric events and fairs, one of the biggest is the Gentse Feesten, a nine-day knees-up held in Ghent in late July. It includes all sorts of events, from music and theatre to fireworks and fairs.

Luxembourg

Carnival is a big deal in Luxembourg, too, with most communities having some celebration. If nothing else, almost every patisserie sells small doughnut-like cakes, knudd, during the days beforehand. On Ash Wednesday, a great straw doll is set alight and then dropped off the Moselle bridge in Remich with much whooping-it-up, while on the first Sunday after Carnival, bonfires are lit on hilltops all over the country on Buurgbrennen. Mid-Lent sees Bretzelsonndeg (Pretzel Sunday) when pretzels are sold in all the duchy's bakeries, and there are lots of processions. At Easter, no church bells are rung in the whole of the country between Maundy Thursday and Easter Saturday – folklore asserts that the bells fly off to Rome for confession – and their place is taken by children, who walk the streets with rattles announcing the Masses from about 6am onwards. On Easter Monday morning, with the bells 'back', the children call on every house to collect their reward – brightly coloured Easter eggs.

Every village in Luxembourg has an annual fair – kermess – which varies in scale and duration according to the size of the village, ranging from a stand selling fries and hot dogs to a full-scale funfair. The **Schueberfouer** in Luxembourg City – over the first three weeks of September – is one of the biggest mobile fairs in Europe, held since 1340 (it started life as a sheep market) and traditionally opened by the royal family. On the middle of Sunday, in the Hammelsmarsch, shepherds bring their sheep to town, accompanied by a band, and then work their way around the bars.

Luxembourg's **National Day** is on 23 June. On the previous evening, at 11pm or so, there's an enormous fireworks display off the Pont Adolphe in the capital, and all the bars and cafés were open most of the night. On 23 June, parades and celebrations will occur across most of the country.

Festival calendar

FEBRUARY

Brussels: Anima, the International Animation Film Festival, ten days in early Feb; Ⓦ animafestival.be. First-rate animation festival, which screens over a hundred new and old cartoons from around the world at the Flagey cultural centre in Ixelles.

Eupen: Carnival, Shrove Tues and the preceding four or five days; Ⓦ eupen.be. Eupen Carnaval kicks off with the appearance of His Madness the Prince and climaxes with the Rosenmontag (Rose Monday) procession.

Malmedy: Carnival, Shrove Tues and the preceding four or five days; Ⓦ malmedy.be. In Malmedy, Carnival is called Cwarmê, and on the Sunday, groups of Haguètes, masked figures in colourful robes and plumed hats, wander around, nipping passers-by with wooden pincers.

Aalst: Carnival, Shrove Tues and the preceding two days; Ⓦ aalstcarnaval.be. Aalst Carnaval begins on the Sunday with a parade of the giants and floats, often with a contemporary/satirical theme.

Binche: Carnival, Shrove Tues and the preceding two days; Ⓦ carnavaldebinche.be. Binche Carnaval builds up to the parade of the Gilles, locals dressed in fancy gear complete with ostrich-feather hats.

Luxembourg: Carnival, Sun preceding Shrove Tues; Ⓦ visitluxembourg.com. Carnival parades take place in several Luxembourg towns, including Diekirch and Remich.

Luxembourg: Buergbrennen (Bonfire Day), first Sun after Carnival (between late Feb and early March); Ⓦ visitluxembourg.com. Bonfires plus hot-food stalls all over Luxembourg, but especially in Luxembourg City.

MARCH

Stavelot: Carnival, Refreshment Sun (fourth Sun in Lent); Ⓦ laetare-stavelot.be. Stavelot Carnaval features the famous parade of the Blancs Moussis, all hoods and long red noses. See page 256.

FESTIVAL VAN VLAANDEREN (JUNE–DEC)

The extraordinarily ambitious **Festival van Vlaanderen** (Flanders Festival; Ⓦ festival. be) offers over five hundred classical music concerts in churches, castles and other historic venues in over eighty Flemish towns, cities and villages. Each big **Flemish-speaking** city – Antwerp, Mechelen, Ghent and Bruges – gets a fair crack of the cultural whip, as does Brussels, with the festival celebrated for about two weeks in each city before moving on to the next.

APRIL

Brussels: International Fantastic Film Festival, two weeks in mid-April; Ⓦ bifff.net. This well-established festival is a favourite with cult film lovers. It has become the place to see all those entertainingly dreadful B-movies, as well as more modern sci-fi classics, horror, thrillers and fantasy epics.

Sint-Truiden: Bloesemfeesten (Blossom Festival), late April; Ⓦ sint-truiden.be. Blessing of the blossoms in Sint-Truiden, at the heart of the Haspengouw fruit-growing region.

MAY

Brussels: Concours Musical International Reine Elisabeth de Belgique, early May to early June; Ⓦ concoursreineelisabeth.be. A world-famous classical music competition established over fifty years ago by Belgium's violin-playing Queen Elisabeth. The categories change annually, rotating piano, voice and violin.

Mechelen: Hanswijkprocessie (Procession of our Lady of Hanswijk), Sun before Ascension Day; Ⓦ hanswijkprocessie. be. Large and ancient procession held in the centre of Mechelen. Traditionally, it focused on the veneration of the Virgin Mary, but it is more of a historical pageant today.

Bruges: Heilig Bloedprocessie (Procession of the Holy Blood), Ascension Day, forty days after Easter; Ⓦ holyblood. com. One of medieval Christendom's holiest relics, the phial of the Holy Blood, is carried through the centre of Bruges once every year.

Brussels: Jazz Marathon, three days in May; Ⓦ brussels.be/brussels-jazz-weekend. Hep cats can listen to nonstop jazz around the city for three whole days (which changes each year – check the website), and the quality of the music is usually very high. Entrance fees vary depending on the venue, but you can buy a three-day pass, and there are free concerts, too.

Echternach, Luxembourg: Springprozession, Whit Tues; Ⓦ springprozession.com. Ancient and somewhat eccentric dancing procession commemorating the eighth-century English missionary St Willibrord.

JUNE

Brussels: Brussels Film Festival, eight days in late June & early July; ⓦ brff.be. Something of a movable feast, this festival promotes the work of young film directors from across Europe. The festival takes place in the capital's Flagey arts centre, in Ixelles.

Luxembourg: Luxembourg National Day, 23 June. Expect fireworks in the capital and celebrations – including much flag-waving – all over the Grand Duchy.

Middelkerke and the coast: Sand sculptures, end June to mid-Sept; ⓦ zandsculpturenfestival.com/en. Sand sculpture competitions are popular along the Belgian coast throughout the summer, but Middelkerke features some of the best, with everything from the bizarre to the surreal, and beyond.

JULY

Knokke-Heist: Internationaal cartoon festival, early July to late Aug; ⓦ knokke-heist.be/cartoonfestival-knokke-heist. Established in the 1960s, this summer-season festival in the seaside resort of Knokke-Heist showcases several hundred world-class cartoons from around the globe.

Werchter, near Leuven: Rock Werchter Festival, four days in early July; ⓦ rockwerchter.be. Belgium's premier rock and pop festival and one of Europe's largest open-air music events. There are special festival buses from Leuven train station to the festival site.

Brussels: Ommegang, first Wed & Fri of July; ⓦ ommegang.be. This grand procession cuts a colourful course from place du Grand Sablon to the Grand-Place. Begun in the fourteenth century as a religious event to celebrate the arrival of a miracle-working statue of the Virgin from Antwerp; nowadays, it's almost entirely secular, with a whole gaggle of locals dressed up in period costumes. It all finishes with a traditional dance on the Grand-Place and has proved so popular that it's now held twice a year (originally it was just once). To secure a seat on the Grand-Place for the finale, you must reserve at least six months ahead.

Bruges: Cactusfestival, three days over the second weekend of July; ⓦ cactusfestival. Going strong for over twenty years, the Cactusfestival is something of a classic. Known for its amiable atmosphere, it proudly pushes against the musical mainstream with rock, reggae, rap, roots and R&B all rolling together from domestic and foreign artists.

Ghent: Gentse Feesten (Ghent Festival), mid- to late July, but always including 21 July; ⓦ gentsefeesten.be. Ghent gets stuck into partying for ten days every July, pretty much around the clock. Local bands perform free open-air gigs throughout the city, and street performers turn up everywhere, including fire-eaters, buskers, comedians, actors, puppeteers and so forth. There's also an outdoor market selling everything from jenever (gin) to handmade crafts.

Boechout, Antwerp: Sfinks, last weekend in July; ⓦ sfinks.be. Sfinks is Belgium's best world music festival. It is held outdoors in the suburb of Boechout, about 10km southeast of downtown Antwerp.

Veurne: Boetprocessie (Penitents' Procession), last Sun in July; ⓦ boetprocessie.be. Although this event is now a good deal cheerier than it used to be, with lots of townsfolk dressed up in fancy historical gear, it's still got a gloomy heart with a couple of hundred participants dressed in the brown cowls of the Capuchins, some walking along dragging heavy crosses behind them. See box, page 127.

AUGUST

Bruges: International Competition Musica Antiqua, ten days in early Aug; ⓦ mafestival.be. Part of the Festival van Vlaanderen (see box, page 116), this well-regarded international competition of medieval music offers an extensive programme of live performances at a host of historic venues in Bruges.

Brussels: Flower Carpet, four days in mid-Aug; ⓦ flowercarpet. brussels/en/. Grand-Place is brought to life every two years with a colourful carpet of half a million begonias.

Dinant: International Bathtub Regatta, 15 Aug; ⓦ lesbaignoires.be. Dozens of pimped-up bathtubs float down the River Meuse, attracting thousands of onlookers.

Kiewit, just outside Hasselt: Pukkelpop, five days in mid-Aug; ⓦ pukkelpop.be. Large-scale progressive music festival running the gamut from indie through R&B to house.

Ath: La Ducasse, four days at the end of Aug; ⓦ ducasse-ath. be. Dating back to the thirteenth century, this festival has all sorts of parades and parties. Still, the star turn is the giant figures – or goliaths – that make their ungainly way around town, representing historical and folkloric characters.

Luxembourg City: Schueberfouer, three weeks from the last week of Aug; ⓦ vdl.lu/en/. A former shepherds' market, this is now the capital's largest funfair.

SEPTEMBER

Tournai: La Grande Procession de Tournai, second Sun in Sept; ⓦ grandeprocessiontournai.org. This procession dates back to the eleventh century. It is part secular shindig in historical costume and part religious ceremony involving carrying the reliquary of St Eleuthère through the city's streets.

Namur: Fêtes de Wallonie, third weekend in Sept; ⓦ fetesdewallonie.be. City-wide festival celebrating Wallonian culture, featuring stilt walkers, a funfair, regional food and lots of drinking.

Nivelles: Le Tour Sainte-Gertrude de Nivelles, last Sun in Sept or first Sun in Oct; ⓦ toursaintegertrude.be. Beginning in the centre of Nivelles, this is a religious procession in which the reliquary of St Gertrude is escorted on a circular, 15km route out into the countryside surrounding the town.

OCTOBER

Ghent: Ghent Film Festival, eleven days in Oct; ⓦ filmfestival. be. The Ghent Film Festival is one of Europe's foremost cinematic events. Every year, the city's cinemas combine to present around two hundred feature films and a hundred shorts from all over the world, screening Belgian films and the best of world cinema well before they hit the international circuit.

NOVEMBER

Brussels: Ars Musica, all month; ⓦarsmusica.be. This biannual contemporary classical music festival has an impressive international reputation and regularly features world-renowned composers.

Vianden, Luxembourg: Miertchen (St Martin's Fire), mid-Nov. A celebration of the end of the harvest (and formerly the payment of the levy to the feudal lord), with bonfires and a giant open-air market.

DECEMBER

Nationwide: The Arrival of St Nicholas (aka Santa Klaus), 6 Dec. The arrival of St Nicholas from his long sojourn abroad is celebrated by processions and the giving of sweets to children across Belgium and Luxembourg. In Luxembourg, he's traditionally accompanied by 'Père Fouettard' (the bogey-man), dressed in black and carrying a whip to punish unruly children.

Sports and outdoor activities

Most visitors to Belgium confine their exercise to cycling and walking, both of which are ideally suited to the flatness of the terrain and, for that matter, the excellence of the public transport system. The same applies to Luxembourg, except the land is much hillier and often more scenic. Both also offer all the sporting facilities you would expect of prosperous European countries, from golf to gyms, swimming pools to horse riding, and, in the Ardennes, canoeing, kayaking, skiing and mountaineering. There are now five national parks in Belgium, but the wildest and most diverting is the Hoge Kempen National Park (ⓦnationaalpark hogekempen.be/en) in the Province of Limburg.

Football

The chief spectator sport is **football,** and the sixteen teams that make up the top division of the country's national league attract a fiercely loyal following. Big-deal clubs include RSC Anderlecht of Brussels (ⓦrsca.be), Club Brugge (ⓦclubbrugge.be) and Standard Liège (ⓦstandard.be). The **national team** (known as 'The Red Devils') has enjoyed considerable success in recent years, topping the FIFA World

Rankings for the first time in November 2015. Football season runs from early August to May, with a break over Christmas.

Local sports

More distinctive offerings include **korfbal** (ⓦkorfbal. be), a homegrown sport cobbled together from netball, basketball and volleyball and played with mixed teams and a high basket popular in the Netherlands and Flemish-speaking Belgium; and canal ice skating, again in the Flemish-speaking areas, though this depends on the weather being cold enough.

Travel essentials

Accessible travel

In all the major cities, the most obvious difficulty facing people with **mobility problems** is negotiating the cobbled streets and narrow, often broken pavements of the older districts, where the key sights are mainly located. Similarly, the provision for people with disabilities in the public transport system is only average, although it is improving – many new buses, for instance, are now wheelchair accessible. While it can be challenging to get around, practically all **public buildings** – museums, theatres, cinemas, concert halls and hotels – are obliged to provide access. Hotels, hostels and campsites that have been certified wheelchair-accessible carry the **International Accessibility Symbol (ISA)**. Bear in mind, however, that many older, narrower hotels are not allowed to install lifts for conservation reasons, so check first.

Addresses

In the **French-speaking part of Belgium and Luxembourg, addresses are usually written in** a standard format. The first line begins with the category of the street or thoroughfare (rue, boulevard, etc), followed by the name and then the number; the second line gives the area – or zip code, followed by the town or area. Common abbreviations include 'bld' or 'bd' for *boulevard*, 'av' for *avenue*, 'pl' for *place* (square) and 'ch' for *chaussée*. The hyphenated Grand-Place (main square) is an exception, written in full. In the **Flemish-speaking** areas, the first line gives the street's name, followed by (and joined to) its category – hence, Krakeelplein is Krakeel square, Krakeelstraat is Krakeel street; the number comes next. The second line gives the area – or zip code followed by the town or area. Consequently, Flemish abbreviations occur at the end of words, 'Hofstr' for *Hofstraat*, for instance. An exception is Grote Markt (main square), which is not abbreviated. Common categories include *plein* for square, *plaats* for place, *laan* or *weg* for avenue, *kaai* for quay, and *straat* for street. In **bilingual Brussels**, all signs give both the French and Flemish versions. In many cases, this is pretty straightforward as they are either the same or similar, but sometimes it's incredibly confusing (see box, page 27), most notoriously in the name of one of the three principal train stations – in French, Bruxelles-Midi; in Flemish Brussel-Zuid.

Costs

The minimum expenditure for a couple travelling on public transport, self-catering and camping is in the region of £50 each a day, rising to around £65 per person if you stay at hostels and eat the odd meal out. Staying at budget B&Bs, eating at unpretentious restaurants and visiting the odd tourist attraction means spending at least £90 each per day. If you're renting a car, staying in comfortable B&Bs or hotels and eating well, you should reckon on at least £130 a day per person. Note that there are **concessionary rates** on public transport and at most attractions for the young and the old (65+). The standard rate of **VAT** in Belgium is 21 percent; citizens of non-EU countries may be eligible for a refund, so check out the rules and conditions on ⓦ finance.belgium.be.

Crime and personal safety

By comparison with other parts of Europe, both Belgium and (even more so) Luxembourg are relatively **free of crime**, so there's little reason why you should ever come into contact with either country's police force. However, there is more **street crime** in Belgium than there used to be, especially in Brussels (the area

around the Gare du Midi is especially dodgy) and Antwerp, so it's advisable to be on your guard against petty theft. Using **public transport**, even late at night, isn't usually a problem, but if in doubt take a taxi. If you are robbed, you'll need to go to a **police station** to report it, not least because your insurance company will require a police report; remember to note the report number – or, better still, ask for a copy of the statement itself. Don't expect a great deal of concern if your loss is relatively small – and don't be surprised if completing forms and formalities takes ages.

Electricity

The **current** is 220 volts AC, with standard European-style two-pin plugs. British equipment needs only a plug adaptor; American apparatus requires a transformer and an adaptor.

Entry requirements

Citizens of the EU/EEA and the UK, Australia, New Zealand, Canada and the US do not need a visa to enter Belgium or Luxembourg if staying for ninety days or less. However, they do need a current **passport** (or **EU national identity card**) whose validity exceeds the length of their stay by at least three months. Travellers from **South Africa**, on the other hand, need a passport and a tourist visa for less than ninety-day visits; visas must be obtained before departure and are available from the appropriate embassy (see box, page 36).

EU/EEA residents will have a few problems with staying **longer than ninety days**, but everyone else needs a mix of **visas** and **permits**. In all cases, consult the appropriate embassy at home before departure.

Health

Under reciprocal healthcare arrangements, all EU (European Union) and EEA (European Economic Area)

BELGIAN EMBASSIES ABROAD

For further information, consult ⓦ diplomatie.belgium.be/en

Australia ⓦ australia.diplomatie.belgium.be/en
Canada ⓦ canada.diplomatie.belgium.be/en
Ireland ⓦ ireland.diplomatie.belgium.be/en
Luxembourg ⓦ luxembourg.diplomatie.belgium.be

New Zealand No embassy – see Australia
South Africa ⓦ southafrica.diplomatie.belgium.be/en
UK ⓦ unitedkingdom.diplomatie.belgium.be/en
US ⓦ unitedstates.diplomatie.belgium.be/en

LUXEMBOURG EMBASSIES ABROAD

For further information, consult ⓦ gouvernement.lu/en

Belgium ⓦ bruxelles.mae.lu

UK ⓦ londres.mae.lu/en
US ⓦ washington.mae.lu/en

citizens are entitled to subsidised medical treatment within Belgium and Luxembourg's public healthcare system. The UK is, of course, no longer part of the EU. However, its citizens are still entitled to limited **and subsidised** access to Belgium and Luxembourg's public healthcare system if they have a **GHIC** (Global Health Insurance Card), which replaces the **EHIC** (European Health Insurance Card). Other non-EU/EEA nationals are not generally entitled to free treatment and should take out medical insurance. That said, EU/EEA/UK citizens may also want to consider **private health insurance** to cover the cost of items not within the EU/EEA/UK schemes, such as dental treatment and repatriation on medical grounds. No **inoculations** are currently required for Belgium and Luxembourg.

The **public healthcare system** in Belgium and Luxembourg is of an excellent standard and widely available, with clinics and hospitals in all the cities and larger towns. If you're seeking treatment **under GHIC reciprocal health arrangements**, check that the medic who treats you is seeing you as a patient of the public system so that you receive (subsidised) treatment just as the locals do. You may be asked to show your passport and GHIC to prove you are eligible for EU/EEA/UK healthcare. Sometimes, no one bothers, but you should always have it with you just in case.

If you have an insurance policy covering **medical expenses**, you can seek treatment in either the public or private health sectors; the main issue is whether – at least in major cases – you have to pay the costs upfront and then wait for reimbursement. Note that in all the larger towns and cities, your hotel will probably be able to arrange an appointment with an **English-speaking doctor**, who will almost certainly see you as a private patient.

Minor ailments can often be remedied at a **pharmacy** (French *pharmacie*, Flemish *apotheek*): pharmacists are highly trained, able to give advice (often in English), and authorised to dispense many drugs which would only be available on prescription in many other countries. Pharmacies are easy to come across everywhere.

Note also that **mosquitoes** thrive in the country's canals and can be a real handful (or mouthful) if you are camping. An antihistamine cream such as Phenergan is the best antidote, although this can be difficult to find – in which case preventative sticks (Autan; Citronella) alongside repellant sprays are the best bet.

Insurance

Even if you are eligible for the EU/EEA healthcare privileges in Belgium and Luxembourg, taking out an insurance policy to cover theft, loss, illness or injury is

---

EMERGENCY CALLS

In Belgium and Luxembourg, call ☎112 for police, fire brigade and emergency medical assistance.

---

still a good idea. For non-EU/EEA citizens, insurance is a must. A typical policy usually covers the loss of baggage, tickets and – up to a specific limit – cash, as well as cancellation or curtailment of your journey. Private health insurance also covers the cost of items not included in the EU medical scheme, such as dental treatment and repatriation on medical grounds. In the case of major expenses, the more worthwhile policies promise to sort matters out before you pay rather than after, but if you do have to pay upfront, make sure you keep full doctors' reports, signed prescription details and all receipts. In the event that you have anything stolen, you must obtain an official statement from the police if you intend to claim.

Internet and email

In Belgium and Luxembourg, almost all hotels, B&Bs and hostels provide wi-fi and/or **internet access** for their guests at no charge, as do most cafés. Every major library offers internet access too – free but almost invariably time-limited.

LGBTQ+

Gay and **lesbian** life in both Belgium and Luxembourg does not have a high international profile, especially in comparison with the Netherlands next door. Nonetheless, there's still a vibrant gay scene in **Brussels** (see page 89) and **Antwerp** (see page 187) and at least a couple of gay bars and clubs in most major towns. In both countries, the gay/lesbian scene is left largely unmolested by the rest of society, a pragmatic tolerance – or intolerance soaked in indifference – that has provided opportunities for **legislative change**. In 1998, Belgium passed a law granting certain rights to cohabiting couples irrespective of their sex, and civil unions for same-sex couples were legalised after much huffing and puffing by the political right. In 2003, Luxembourg legalised same-sex civil unions in 2004. The legal **age of consent** for men and women is 16 in Belgium and Luxembourg.

Mail

Both Belgium and Luxembourg have efficient **postal systems**. **Post offices** are now few and far between,

ROUGH GUIDES TRAVEL INSURANCE

Looking for travel insurance? Rough Guides partners with top providers worldwide to offer you the best coverage. Policies are available to residents of anywhere in the world, with a range of options whether you are looking for single-trip, multi-country or long-stay insurance. There's coverage for a wide range of adventure sports, 24-hour emergency assistance, high levels of medical and evacuation cover and a stream of travel safety information. Even better, roughguides.com users can take advantage of these policies online 24/7, from anywhere in the world – even if you're already travelling. To make the most of your travels and ensure a smoother experience, it's always good to be prepared for when things don't go according to plan. For more information go to ⓦ roughguides.com/travel-insurance.

but **stamps** are sold at a wide range of outlets, including many shops and hotels. Mail to the US takes seven days or so, and within Europe, two to three days. **Mailboxes** are painted red in Belgium and yellow in Luxembourg.

Maps

The **maps** provided in this guide should be sufficient for most purposes, but drivers will need to buy a good road map, and prospective hikers will need specialist hiking maps. One good-value **national road map** is the clear and easy-to-use Michelin *Belgium and Luxembourg* (1:350,000) map, which comes complete with an index. Michelin (ⓦ viamichelin.co.uk) also publishes an excellent **Benelux road map** in book form at 1:150,000; this comes with 67 city maps, though the **free city maps** issued by the tourist offices in all the major towns are even better and have more detail.

Belgium's Institut Géographique National/Nationaal Geografisch Instituut (IGN/NGI; ⓦ ngi.be) produces the most authoritative **hiking maps** (1:10,000, 1:20,000, 1:50,000) covering the whole country. The equivalent organisation in Luxembourg, Luxembourg Survey (ⓦ act.public.lu), does a similarly thorough job in Luxembourg with two series of Ordnance Survey maps, one at 1:50,000 (two sheets), the other at 1:20,000 (thirty sheets).

All the maps mentioned above should be easy enough to track down in Belgium or Luxembourg, but to be sure (and to check what's currently on the market), you might consider ordering from a leading **bookseller** before departure – ⓦ stanfords.co.uk is hard to beat. Finally, in both countries, **GPS navigation** is easy and straightforward both for hikers and drivers.

Money and exchange

In Luxembourg and Belgium, the **currency** is the **euro** (€). Each euro is made up of 100 cents. There are

seven euro **notes** – in denominations of €500, €200, €100, €50, €20, €10 and €5 – and eight different **coins**, specifically €2 and €1, then 50, 20, 10, 5, 2 and 1 cents. Euro notes and coins feature a standard EU design on one face but different country-specific designs on the other. Note also that many retailers will not touch the €500 and €200 notes with a bargepole – you'll have to break them down into smaller denominations at the bank. At the time of writing, the **exchange rate** for €1 is US\$1.07 and £0.85. For the most up-to-date rates, check the currency converter website ⓦ xe. com. You can change **foreign currency** into euros at most banks, which are ubiquitous; **banking hours** are usually Monday to Friday from 9am to 3.30/4pm, with a few banks also open on Saturday mornings.

ATMs are liberally distributed around every city, town and major village in Belgium and Luxembourg – and they accept a host of **debit cards**. **Credit cards** can be used in ATMs too. Credit and debit cards can be used for **contactless payment** in a host of places. In the UK, check out ⓦ moneysupermarket.com for the best credit cards to use abroad.

Opening hours and public holidays

Business hours (office hours) generally run from Monday to Friday, from 9.30/10am to 4.30/5pm. Normal **shopping hours** are Monday to Saturday, 10am to 5.30/6pm, though many smaller shops open late Monday morning and/or close a tad earlier on Saturdays. In addition, in some of the smaller towns and villages, many places close at lunchtime (noon–2pm) and for the half-day on Wednesdays or Thursdays. At the other extreme, larger establishments – primarily supermarkets and department stores – are increasingly likely to have extended hours, often on Fridays when many remain open till 9pm. In the big cities, **convenience stores** (*magasins de nuit/avondwinkels*) stay open all night or until 1am or 2am daily.

PUBLIC HOLIDAYS IN BELGIUM AND LUXEMBOURG

Note that if any of the below falls on a Sunday, the next day becomes a holiday.

New Year's Day (1 Jan)
Easter Monday
Labour Day (1 May)
Ascension Day (forty days after Easter)
Whit Monday
Luxembourg National Day (23 June)
Flemish Day (Flemish-speaking Belgium only; 11 July)
Belgium National Day (21 July)
Assumption (mid-Aug)
Walloon Day (French-speaking Belgium only; 27 Sept)
All Saints' Day (1 Nov)
Armistice Day (Belgium only; 11 Nov)
Christmas Day (25 Dec)
St Stephen's Day/Boxing Day (only an official holiday in Luxembourg; 26 Dec)

Belgium has ten national **public holidays** (see box, page 39) per year and two regional holidays, one each for Wallonia and Flanders. Luxembourg has the same public holidays with a couple of exceptions. For the most part, these holidays are keenly observed, with most businesses and many attractions closed and public transport reduced to a Sunday service.

Phones

All but the remotest parts of Belgium and Luxembourg are on the mobile phone (cell phone) network at GSM900/1800, the band common to the rest of Europe, Australia and New Zealand. Mobile/cell phones bought in North America will need to be able to adjust to this GSM band. If you intend to use your own **mobile/cell phone** in Belgium and Luxembourg, note that **call** and data roaming charges can be excruciating – particularly irritating is the supplementary charge that you often have to pay on incoming calls – so check with your provider before you depart. Travellers from outside the EU may find buying a **local SIM card** cheaper, though this can get complicated: many mobiles/cells will not permit you to swap SIM cards, and the connection instructions for the replacement SIM card may not be in English. If you overcome these problems, you can buy local SIM cards at high-street phone companies, which offer myriad deals beginning at about €5 per SIM card. **Text messages**, on the other hand, are typically charged at ordinary or at least bearable rates – and with your existing SIM card in place. And, of course, you can use the free text and photo service available on **Whatsapp** on local wi-fi.

There are **no area codes** in either Belgium or Luxembourg. Belgian numbers mostly begin with a zero, a relic of former area codes that have been incorporated into the numbers. Telephone numbers starting with ☎0900 or ☎070 are premium-rated, and ☎0800 are toll-free. Within both countries, there's no distinction between local and national calls – in other words, calling Ostend from Brussels costs the same as calling a number in Brussels.

INTERNATIONAL CALLS

PHONING HOME FROM BELGIUM AND LUXEMBOURG

To make an international phone call from Belgium or Luxembourg, dial the appropriate international access code below, then the number you require, omitting the initial zero where there is one.
Australia ☎0061
Canada ☎001
Republic of Ireland ☎00353
New Zealand ☎0064
South Africa ☎0027
UK ☎0044
US ☎001

PHONING BELGIUM AND LUXEMBOURG FROM ABROAD

To call a number in Belgium or Luxembourg, dial the local international access code, then ☎32 for Belgium or ☎352 for Luxembourg, followed by the number you require, omitting the initial zero where there is one.

Shopping

When it comes to **shopping**, chocolates and beer are on most tourists' radar, but it's worth seeking out the local **open-air markets**: most towns and large villages have a market day once a week, where you can sample all manner of **local delicacies**. The cities have fresh produce markets, sprawling flea markets, flower markets, antique markets and bird markets (though these are not to everyone's taste).

Time zones

Belgium and Luxembourg are on **Central European Time** (CET): one hour ahead of Greenwich Mean Time, six hours ahead of US Eastern Standard Time, nine hours ahead of US Pacific Standard Time, nine hours behind Australian Eastern Standard Time, and eleven hours behind New Zealand. There are, however, minor variations during the changeover periods involved in **daylight saving**. Belgium and Luxembourg operate daylight saving time, moving their clocks forward one hour in the spring and one hour back in autumn.

Tipping

Tipping is unnecessary when there's a service charge, but restaurant waitpersons anticipate a 10 to 15 percent tip when there isn't. Tipping is neither required nor expected in taxis, but people often round up the fare.

Tourist information

Belgium has two official tourist boards, one covering the French-speaking areas and the other the Flemish-speaking regions; they share responsibility for Brussels. These boards are the **Office de Promotion du** Tourisme de Wallonie et Bruxelles (OPT; Ⓦ visitwallonia.com) and **Toerisme Vlaanderen** (Visit Flanders; Ⓦ visitflanders.com). Their websites cover everything from hotels and campsites to forthcoming events. Both also publish a wide range of glossy, free booklets of both a general and specific nature, available at tourist offices throughout Belgium. A similarly excellent set of services is provided by the **Office National du Tourisme Luxembourg** (Luxembourg National Tourist Office; Ⓦ visitluxembourg.com).

In Belgium and Luxembourg, there are tourist offices in every large village, town and city (typically located on or near the main square).

Travelling with children

In general terms, the Belgian and Luxembourg tourist industry is at least sympathetic to those travelling with children: extra beds in hotel rooms are usually easy to arrange; many restaurants (but not the smartest) have children's menus; and baby-changing stations are commonplace. Breastfeeding in public is perfectly acceptable.

Concessions for children are the rule, from public transport to museums. Rates vary, but usually, children under 5 go free, and kids over 5 and under 15/16 get a substantial discount; family ticket deals are also commonplace. Attractions that are especially child-friendly include the Centre Belge de la Bande Dessinée (see page 57); the Muséum des Sciences Naturelles with its dinosaurs (see page 69); the Atomium (see page 78); and the Euro Space Center in St-Hubert (see page 266). There are also numerous beaches, boat trips, caves and castles around the country. Note that **pharmacists** carry all the kiddy stuff you would expect – nappies, baby food and so forth.

Brussels

THE GRAND-PLACE AT NIGHT

1 Brussels

Wherever else you go in Belgium, allow time for Brussels, which is anything but the dull centre of EU bureaucracy, some would have you believe: in postwar years, the city has become a thriving, cosmopolitan metropolis with top-flight museums and architecture, a superb restaurant scene and an energetic nightlife. Moreover, most of the key attractions are crowded into a well-preserved late seventeenth-century centre that is small enough to be absorbed over a few days, its boundaries largely defined by a ring of boulevards – the 'petit ring' or, less colloquially, the 'petite ceinture'.

First-time visitors to Brussels are often surprised by the raw vitality of the **city centre**. It isn't neat and tidy; many old tenement houses are shabby, but there's a buzz about the place that's hard to resist. The larger, westerly portion of the centre comprises the **Lower Town**, fanning out from the marvellous **Grand-Place**, with its exquisite guild houses and town hall, while up above, on a ridge to the east, lies the much smaller **Upper Town**, home to the finest art collection in the country at the **Musées Royaux des Beaux Arts**.

Since the eleventh century, the ruling elite has lived in the Upper Town – a state of affairs that still in part remains, though, in recent times, this class division has been complicated by discord between Belgium's two main linguistic groups, the **Walloons** (the French speakers) and the **Flemings** (the Dutch or Flemish speakers). To add to the communal stew, these two groups now share their city with many others, including EU civil servants and **immigrants** from North and Central Africa, Turkey and the Mediterranean. Brussels' compact nature heightens the contrasts: in five minutes, you can walk from a chichi shopping mall into an African bazaar or from a depressed slum quarter to a resplendent square peppered with antique shops and exclusive cafés. This increases the city's allure, not least because of the sheer variety of affordable **cafés and restaurants**. Brussels is a wonderful place to eat, and its gastronomic reputation perhaps exceeds that of Paris. It's also a great place to drink, with **bars** ranging from designer chic to rough-and-ready, plus everything in between.

The city's **specialist shops** are another pleasure. Everyone knows about Belgian chocolates, but here in the capital, there are substantial open-air markets and contemporary art galleries, not to mention shops devoted to everything from comic books to costume jewellery and club-land fashion. Furthermore, Belgium is such a small country, and the rail network is so fast and efficient that Brussels also makes the perfect base for a wide range of **day-trips** – from Ghent and Bruges in the north through to the French-speaking cities of the south principally Tournai and Mons.

Brief history

Brussels takes its name from Broekzele, or 'village of the marsh', a community which grew up beside the wide and shallow River Senne in the sixth century, allegedly around a chapel built here by **St Géry**, a French bishop turned missionary. An insignificant part

BILINGUAL BRUSSELS

As a cumbersome compromise between Belgium's French- and Flemish-speaking communities, Brussels is the country's only officially **bilingual region**. This means that every instance of the written word, from road signs and street names to adverts, has by law to appear in both languages. Visitors soon adjust, but for simplicity, we've used the French version of street names, sights, etc, throughout this chapter.

MUSÉE VICTOR HORTA

Highlights

❶ The Grand-Place Extraordinarily beautiful, this is one of Europe's most perfectly preserved Gothic-Baroque squares. See page 48

❷ Fondation Jacques Brel Devotees of chanson should make a beeline to this museum to hear Brel in full – and very anguished – voice. See page 58

❸ Musée Old Masters Holds an exquisite sample of early Flemish paintings. See page 62

❹ Musée Victor Horta A fascinating museum set in the old house and studio of Victor Horta,

the leading exponent of Art Nouveau. See page 72

❺ Bars Brussels has some wonderful bars; two of the oldest and most atmospheric are *À l'Imaige de Nostre-Dame* and *Au Bon Vieux Temps*. See page 86

❻ Comic strips Belgians love their comics, and the Brüsel comic shop has the best range in the city. See page 90

❼ Flea markets The pick of the bunch is held daily at place du Jeu de Balle. See page 90

HIGHLIGHTS ARE MARKED ON THE MAPS ON PAGES 49, 54 AND 74

1

of Charlemagne's empire at the end of the eighth century, Brussels was subsequently inherited by the dukes of **Lower Lorraine** (roughly Wallonia and northeast France), who constructed a fortress here in 979. Protected, the village benefited from its position on the trade route between Cologne and the burgeoning towns of Bruges and Ghent, which allowed it to become a significant trading centre in its own right. The surrounding marshes were drained to allow for further expansion, and in 1229, the city was granted its first charter by the **dukes of Brabant**, the feudal overlords who controlled things here, on and off, for around two hundred years. In the early fifteenth

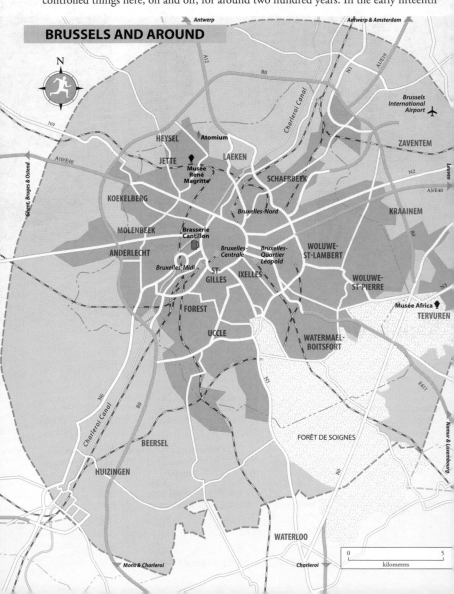

BRUSSELS AND AROUND

1

THE BRUSSELS CARD

The good-value **Brussels Card** (⌨ brusselscard.be) provides free access to 49 of the city's museums and discounts of up to 25 percent at specified restaurants, bars and shops. There are **three versions**: 24-hour (€32), 48-hour (€44) and 72-hour (€50). You can add 'hop on, hop off' bus tours or free travel on public transport for additional fees. The card is on sale **online** via the website and at the main **tourist office** (see page 81); there are no concessionary rates for seniors or children. If you purchase in person, it's issued with a free city map and a booklet detailing all the benefits.

century, marriage merged the interests of the Duchy of Brabant with that of Burgundy, whose territories passed to the **Habsburgs** in 1482.

The first Habsburg rulers had close ties with Brussels. Emperor **Charles V** ran his vast kingdom from the city for over a decade, making it wealthy and politically important in equal measure. By contrast, his successor, **Philip II**, lived in Spain and ruled through a governor resident in Brussels. Horrified by the Protestant leanings of many of his Low Country subjects, the king imposed a series of anti-Protestant edicts. When these provoked extensive **rioting**, he dispatched an army of ten thousand men – led by a hardline reactionary, the Duke of Alba – to crush his opponents in Brussels. Alba quickly restored order and set about the rioters with gusto with the help of the Inquisition; his Commission of Civil Unrest was soon nicknamed the '**Council of Blood**' after its habit of executing those it examined. Brussels, along with much of the Low Countries, exploded in revolt. In 1577, the one-time protégé of the Habsburgs, **William the Silent**, made a triumphant entry into the city and installed a Calvinist government. Protestant control lasted for just eight years before Philip's armies recaptured Brussels. Seeing which way the religious wind was blowing, hundreds of Protestants left the city, and the economy slumped. However, complete catastrophe was averted by the conspicuous consumption of the (Brussels-based) Habsburg elite, whose high spending kept hundreds of workers in employment. Brussels also benefited from digging the **Willebroek Canal** in 1561, which linked it to the sea for the first time.

By the 1580s, the Habsburgs had lost control of the northern part of the Low Countries (now the Netherlands), and Brussels was confirmed as the capital of the remainder, the **Spanish Netherlands** – broadly modern Belgium. Brussels prospered more than the rest of the country. Still, it was always prey to the dynastic squabbling between France and Spain: in 1695, for example, **Louis XIV** bombarded Brussels for 36 hours merely to teach his rivals a lesson through the **guilds**, those associations of skilled merchants and workers who were crucial to the economy of Brussels, rebuilt their devastated city in double time, and it's this version of the Grand-Place that survives today.

In 1700, Charles II, the last of the Spanish Habsburgs, died without issue. The ensuing **War of the Spanish Succession** dragged on for over a decade. Eventually, the Spanish Netherlands was passed to the Austrian Habsburgs, who ruled – as had their predecessors – through a governor based in Brussels. It was during this period as capital of the **Austrian Netherlands** (1713–94) that most of the monumental buildings of the Upper Town were constructed and its Neoclassical avenues and boulevards laid out – grand extravagance in the context of an increasingly industrialised city crammed with a desperately poor working class.

The **French Revolutionary Army** brushed the Austrians aside in 1794 and, a year later, annexed the Austrian Netherlands to France. When Napoleon was defeated in 1815, Brussels was absorbed into the new Kingdom of the Netherlands, and the city took turns with The Hague to be the capital. In 1830, a Brussels-led rebellion removed the Dutch and led to the creation of an independent Belgium with Brussels becomming the capital.

1

The **nineteenth century** was a period of modernisation and expansion, during which the city achieved all the attributes of a modern European capital under the guidance of Burgomaster Anspach and **King Léopold II**. New boulevards were built; the Senne – an open sewer by then – was covered in the city centre; many slum areas were cleared; and a series of grand buildings were erected. The whole enterprise culminated in the golden jubilee exhibition celebrating the founding of the Belgian state in the newly inaugurated Parc du Cinquantenaire. Following the **German occupation** of Belgium in World War II, the modernisation of Brussels has proceeded inexorably, with many major development projects refashioning the city and reflecting its elevated status as the headquarters of both NATO and the EU.

The Grand-Place

The obvious place to begin any tour of Brussels is the **Grand-Place**, one of Europe's most beautiful squares, which sits at the centre of the Lower Town and has long been a UNESCO World Heritage Site. Originally marshland, the Grand-Place was drained in the twelfth century and became a market, cementing its role as the commercial hub of the emergent city when the city's guilds built their headquarters on the square. In the fifteenth century, it also assumed a civic and political function with the construction of the **Hôtel de Ville**. The ruling dukes visited the square to meet the people or show off in tournaments, and it was here that official decrees and pronouncements were proclaimed. During the religious wars of the sixteenth century, the Grand-Place became as much a place of public execution as of trade, but after that, it resumed its former role as a marketplace. Of the square's medieval buildings, only parts of the Hôtel de Ville and one or two **guild houses** have survived, the consequence of an early example of the precepts of total war: a 36-hour French artillery bombardment pretty much razed Brussels to the ground in 1695. After the French withdrew, the city's guildsmen dusted themselves down. They speedily rebuilt their headquarters, adopting the distinctive and flamboyant **Baroque style** that characterises the square today – a set of slender, gilded facades swirling with exuberant, self-publicising carvings and sculptures. Each guild house has a name, usually derived from one of the statues, symbols or architectural quirks decorating its facade. Inevitably, such an outstanding attraction draws tourists and expats in their droves, but there's no better place to get a taste of Brussels' past and Eurocapital present.

Hôtel de Ville

South side of the Grand-Place • Charge • Ⓦ brussels.be/city-hall

The scrubbed and polished **Hôtel de Ville** (town hall) dominates the Grand-Place, its 96m **spire** soaring high above two long series of robust windows, whose straight lines are mitigated by fancy tracery and an arcaded gallery. The building dates from the beginning of the fifteenth century, when the town council decided to build itself a mansion that adequately reflected its wealth and power. The first part to be completed was the **east wing** – the original entrance is marked by the twin lions of the Lion Staircase, though the animals were only added in 1770. Work started on the **west wing** in 1444 and continued until 1480. Despite the gap, the wings are of very similar style, and you have to look hard to notice that the latter one is slightly shorter than its neighbour, allegedly at the insistence of Charles the Bold, who, for some unknown reason, refused to have the adjacent rue de la Tête d'Or narrowed. The niches were left empty, and the **statues** on view today, which represent leading figures from the city's past, were added as part of a nineteenth-century refurbishment.

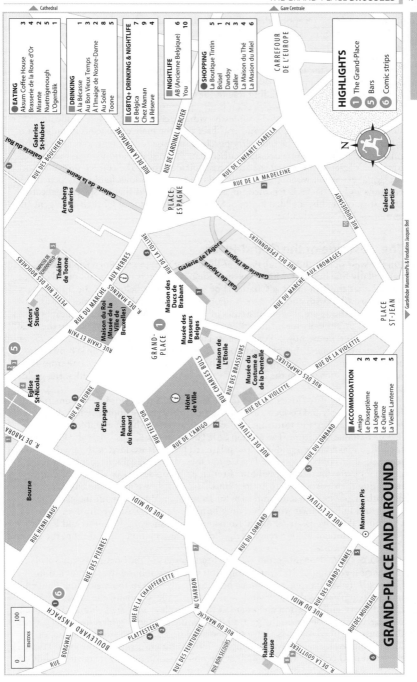

● EATING	
Aksum Coffee House	3
Brasserie de la Roue d'Or	4
Mirante	2
Nuetnigenough	5
L'Ogenblik	1

■ DRINKING	
À la Bécasse	1
Au Bon Vieux Temps	3
À l'Image de Nostre-Dame	2
Au Soleil	8
Toone	5

■ LGBTQ+ DRINKING & NIGHTLIFE	
Le Belgica	7
Chez Maman	9
La Réserve	4

■ NIGHTLIFE	
AB (Ancienne Belgique)	6
You	10

● SHOPPING	
La Boutique Tintin	5
Brüsel	1
Dandoy	2
Galler	3
La Maison du Thé	4
La Maison du Miel	6

HIGHLIGHTS	
1	The Grand-Place
5	Bars
6	Comic strips

■ ACCOMMODATION	
Amigo	2
Le Dixseptième	3
La Légende	4
Le Quinze	1
La Vieille Lanterne	5

GRAND-PLACE AND AROUND

1

Tours start at the reception desk of the interior quadrangle and take in a string of lavish official rooms used for receptions and council meetings, plus parts of the tower.

The tower

By any standard, the **tower** of the Hôtel de Ville is quite extraordinary, its remarkably slender appearance the work of **Jan van Ruysbroeck**, the leading spire specialist of the day, who also played a leading role in the building of the cathedral (see page 60). Ruysbroeck had the lower section built square to support the weight above, choosing a design that blended seamlessly with the elaborately carved facade on either side – or almost: look carefully, and you'll see that the **main entrance** is slightly out of kilter. Ruysbroeck used the old belfry porch as the base for the new tower, hence the misalignment, a deliberate decision rather than the miscalculation which (according to popular legend) prompted the architect's suicide. Above the **cornice** protrudes an octagonal extension where the basic design of narrow windows flanked by pencil-thin columns and pinnacles is repeated up as far as the pyramid-shaped **spire**, a delicate affair surmounted by a gilded figure of **St Michael**, protector of Christians in general and of soldiers in particular.

The west side of the Grand-Place

On the west side of the Grand-Place, at the end of the row, the **Roi d'Espagne** is a particularly fine building which was once the headquarters of the guild of bakers; it's named after the bust of King Charles II of Spain (see box below) on the upper storey, flanked by a Moorish and a Native American prisoner, symbolic trophies of war. On the balustrade are allegorical statues of Energy, Fire, Water, Wind, Wheat and Prudence, presumably meant to represent the elements necessary for baking the ideal loaf. The guild house now holds the most famous of the square's bars, *Le Roy d'Espagne*; however, many prefer the café next door, *La Brouette*, in **La Maison de la Brouette** at **Nos 2–3**, once the tallow makers' guild house – though it takes its name from the wheelbarrows etched into the cartouches. The figure at the top is St Gilles, the guild's patron saint.

Next door, the three lower storeys of the **Maison du Sac**, at **No. 4**, were constructed for the carpenters and coopers, with the upper storeys being appropriately designed by a cabinet-maker and featuring pilasters and caryatids which resemble the ornate legs of Baroque furniture. The **Maison de la Louve**, at **No. 5**, was originally home to the influential archers' guild, and the pilastered facade is studded with sanctimonious representations of concepts like Peace and Discord; the medallions just beneath the pediment carry the likenesses of four Roman emperors set above allegorical motifs indicating their particular attributes. Thus, Trajan is shown above the Sun, a symbol of Truth; Tiberius with a net and cage for Falsehood; Augustus with the globe of Peace; and Julius Caesar with a bleeding heart for Disunity. Above the door, there's a charming, if dusty, bas-relief of the Roman she-wolf suckling Romulus and Remus, while the pediment holds a relief of Apollo firing at a python; right on top, the Phoenix rises from the ashes.

At **No. 6**, the **Maison du Cornet** was the headquarters of the boatmen's guild and is a fanciful creation of 1697, sporting a top storey resembling the stern of a ship. Charles II makes another appearance here, too – his head in the medallion, flanked by representations of the four winds and a pair of sailors. Finally, the house of the haberdashers' guild, **Maison du Renard** at **No. 7**, displays animated cherubs in bas-relief playing at haberdashery on the ground floor, while a scrawny gilded fox – after which the house is named – squats above the door. Up on the second storey, a statue of Justice, flanked by figures symbolising the four continents, suggests the guild's designs on world markets – an aim to which St Nicholas, patron saint of merchants, glinting above, clearly gives his blessing.

THE HEALTH OF CHARLES II

Philip IV of Spain (1605–65) had no fewer than fourteen children, but only one of his sons – **Charles II** (1661–1700) – reached his twenties. With women banned from the succession, the sickly Charles became king at 4 years old and, much to everyone's surprise, survived to adulthood. After his first marriage in 1679, there were great hopes that he would sire an **heir**, but none arrived. Twenty years later, a second marriage was equally fruitless. As it became increasingly clear that Charles could not procreate, Europe focused on what would happen when Charles died, and the Spanish royal line died out. Every ambassador to the Spanish court wrote long missives home about the health of Charles, none more so than the English representative, **Stanhope**, who painted an especially gloomy picture: 'He has a ravenous stomach, and swallows all he eats whole, for his nether jaw stands so much out, that his two rows of teeth cannot meet'. In the autumn of 1700, it was clear that Charles was dying, and his doctors went to work in earnest, replacing his pillows with freshly killed pigeons and covering his chest with animal entrails. Not surprisingly, this didn't work, and Charles died on 1 November, an event which triggered the **War of the Spanish Succession** (see page 47).

The south side of the Grand-Place

Beside the Hôtel de Ville, the arcaded **Maison de l'Étoile**, at **No. 8**, is a nineteenth-century reconstruction of the medieval home of the city magistrate. In the arcaded gallery, the exploits of city magistrate **Everard 't Serclaes** are commemorated. In 1356, the Francophile Count of Flanders attempted to seize power from the Duke of Brabant, occupying the magistrate's house and flying his standard from the roof. Everard 't Serclaes scaled the building, replaced the count's standard with that of the Duke of Brabant, and went on to lead the recapturing of the city. The events that unfolded are represented in bas-relief above a reclining **statue** of 't Serclaes. His effigy is polished smooth from the long-standing superstition that good luck will come to those who stroke it – surprising as he was hunted down and hacked to death by the count's men in 1388.

Next door, the **Maison du Cygne**, at **No. 9**, takes its name from the ostentatious swan on the facade but is more noteworthy for its connection with **Karl Marx**. Historically a tavern, legend has it, Marx and fellow revolutionary Friedrich Engels penned the *Communist Manifesto* here – its publication in London in January 1848 prompted Marx's expulsion from Belgium as a political undesirable the following month. The Belgian Workers' Party was also founded here in 1885, though nowadays, the building houses one of the city's more exclusive restaurants.

The adjacent **Maison des Brasseurs**, at **No. 10**, is the only house on the Grand-Place still to be owned by a guild – the brewers' – not that the equestrian figure stuck on top gives any clues: the original effigy (of one of the city's Habsburg governors) dropped off, and the present statue, picturing the eighteenth-century aristocrat Charles of Lorraine, was moved here simply to fill the gap. Inside is a small and mundane brewery museum, the **Musée des Brasseurs Belges** (Charge; ⓦbeermuseum.be/en).

The east side of the Grand-Place

The seven guild houses (**Nos 13–19**) that fill out the **east side** of the Grand-Place have been subsumed within one grand facade, whose slender symmetries are set off by a curved pediment and narrow pilasters, sporting nineteen busts of the dukes of Brabant. More than any other building on the Grand-Place, **Maison des Ducs de Brabant** has the flavour of the aristocracy – as distinct from the bourgeoisie – and was much admired by the city's Habsburg governors.

1

The north side of the Grand-Place

Other than the **Maison du Roi** (see below), the guild houses and private mansions (**Nos 20–39**) running along the north side of the Grand-Place are not as distinguished as their neighbours. That said, the former painters' guild house, **Maison du Pigeon**, at **Nos 26–27**, bears four unusual mascaron and literary cachet in the shape of **Victor Hugo** – the poet and writer lived here for a time in the 1850s after he was forced into exile from France. The adjacent **Maison des Tailleurs**, at **Nos 24–25**, the old headquarters of the tailors' guild, is appealing too, adorned by a pious bust of St Barbara, their patron saint.

Maison du Roi: Musée de la Ville de Bruxelles
Grand-Place • Charge • ⓦ brusselscitymuseum.brussels

Much of the north side of the Grand-Place is taken up by the late nineteenth-century **Maison du Roi**, a relatively faithful reconstruction of the palatial Gothic structure commissioned by Charles V in 1515. The emperor had a point to make: the Hôtel de Ville (see page 48) was an assertion of municipal independence, and Charles wanted to emphasise imperial power by constructing his building directly opposite. Despite its name, no sovereign ever lived here permanently, though this is where the Habsburgs held their more important **prisoners** – the counts of Egmont and Hoorn (see page 66) spent their last night here before being beheaded just outside. The building now houses the **Musée de la Ville de Bruxelles**, which holds a wide-ranging collection; the best sections feature medieval fine and applied art.

The museum

Inside, the museum's **first room,** just to the right of the entrance, showcases several superb **retables**, altarpieces that were a speciality of the city from the end of the fourteenth century until the economic slump of the 1640s – most of them comprised of a series of mini-tableaux illustrating biblical scenes, with the characters wearing medieval gear in a medieval landscape. It's the extraordinary detail that impresses: look closely at the niche carvings on the whopping **Saluzzo altarpiece** (*The Life of the Virgin and the Infant Christ*) of 1505, and you'll spy candlesticks, an embroidered pillowcase and a carefully draped coverlet in Mary's bedroom in the *Annunciation* scene. Up above and to the right, in a swirling, phantasmagorical landscape of what looks like climbing toadstools, is the *Shepherds Hear the Good News*. Also in this room is **Pieter Bruegel the Elder**'s *Wedding Procession*, a good-natured scene with country folk walking to church to the accompaniment of bagpipes. The **second room** to the right is devoted to another municipal speciality: large and richly coloured **tapestries** dating from the sixteenth and seventeenth centuries and depicting folkloric events and tales of derring-do. Upstairs, the first floor has **scale models** of the city and sections devoted to various aspects of its history; the second floor continues in the same vein.

The Lower Town

Cramped and populous, the **Lower Town** fans out from the Grand-Place in all directions, bisected by one major **north-south boulevard**, variously named Adolphe Max, Anspach and Lemonnier. Setting aside the boulevard – which was ploughed through in the nineteenth century – the **layout** of the Lower Town remains essentially medieval, a skein of narrow, cobbled lanes and alleys in which almost every street is crimped by tall and angular townhouses. There's nothing neat and tidy about any of this, and it's this that gives Brussels its appeal – dilapidated terraces stand next to prestigious mansions and the whole district is dotted with **superb buildings**, everything from beautiful Baroque churches through to Art Nouveau department stores.

These days, arguably the most attractive part of the area is **northwest** of the Grand-Place, where the **church of Ste-Catherine** stands on its café-studded square, and not far away, **place St-Géry** is a secondary hub of activity. The streets immediately **north** of the Grand-Place are of less immediate appeal, with dreary **rue Neuve** – a pedestrianised main drag that's home to the city's mainstream shops and stores – leading up to the clumping skyscrapers that surround the **place Rogier** and the **Gare du Nord** – although relief is at hand in the precise Habsburg symmetries of the **place des Martyrs** and the Art Nouveau **Centre Belge de la Bande Dessinée**. You'll also want to stroll in the elegant **Galeries St-Hubert**, though nearby **rue des Bouchers** is not the restaurant haven it cracks itself up to be. To the **south** of the Grand-Place, almost everyone makes a beeline for the city's mascot, the **Manneken Pis**, but more enjoyable is the museum dedicated to Belgium's most celebrated chansonnier, **Jacques Brel**, and the lively, increasingly gentrified but still resolutely working-class **Marolles** district.

St-Nicolas

rue au Beurre 1 • Free • ☎ 0486 05 82 47

Walking **northwest** out of the Grand-Place along rue au Beurre, you soon reach the **church of St-Nicolas**, dedicated to St Nicholas of Bari, the patron saint of sailors or, as he's better known, Santa Claus. The church dates from the twelfth century but has been heavily restored on several occasions, most recently in the 1950s when parts of the outer shell were reconstructed in a plain Gothic style. The **interior** hardly sets the pulse racing, although – among a scattering of objets d'art – there is a handsome **reliquary shrine** near the entrance. Of gilded copper, the shrine was made in Germany in the nineteenth century to honour a group of Catholics martyred by Protestants in the Netherlands in 1572.

Bourse

pl de la Bourse • Free

Opposite the church of St-Nicolas rises the grandiose **Bourse**, formerly the home of the city's stock exchange, a Neoclassical structure of 1873 caked with fruit, fronds, languishing nudes and frolicking putti. This breezily self-confident structure sports a host of allegorical figures (Industry, Navigation, Asia, Africa, etc) that both reflect the preoccupations of the nineteenth-century Belgian bourgeoisie and, in their easy self-satisfaction, imply that wealth and pleasure are synonymous. The building now hosts a restaurant, meeting rooms and the uninspiring **Belgian Beer World** (charge; ⓦbelgianbeerworld.be/en).

Rue Antoine Dansaert and Place St-Géry

In front of the Bourse, **place de la Bourse** marks the start of an agreeable part of the city, car-free and including **rue Antoine Dansaert**, where several of the most innovative and stylish of the city's fashion designers have set up shop among the dilapidated old townhouses that stretch up to **place du Nouveau Marché aux Grains**. At No. 10, you'll find **MAD** (Mode & Design Center; ⓦmad.brussels), which has been set up to promote fashion and design in the city and is open to the public for temporary exhibitions. Off the left side of rue Dansaert is the tiny place **St-Géry**, crowded by high-sided tenements whose stone balconies and wrought-iron grilles hark back to ritzier days. The square is thought to occupy the site of the sixth-century chapel from which the medieval city grew and has one specific attraction in the refurbished, late nineteenth-century covered market, the **Halles St-Géry** (ⓦhallessaintgery.be), an airy glass, brick and iron edifice now used for temporary, free exhibitions of art and photography. The square is also

1

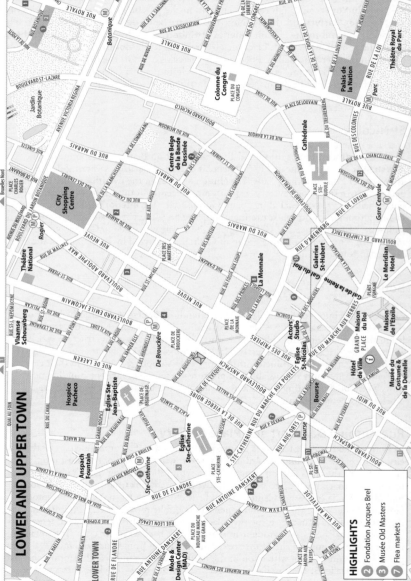

LOWER AND UPPER TOWN

LOWER TOWN

Bruxelles Nord

HIGHLIGHTS

2 Fondation Jacques Brel
3 Musée Old Masters
7 Flea markets

1

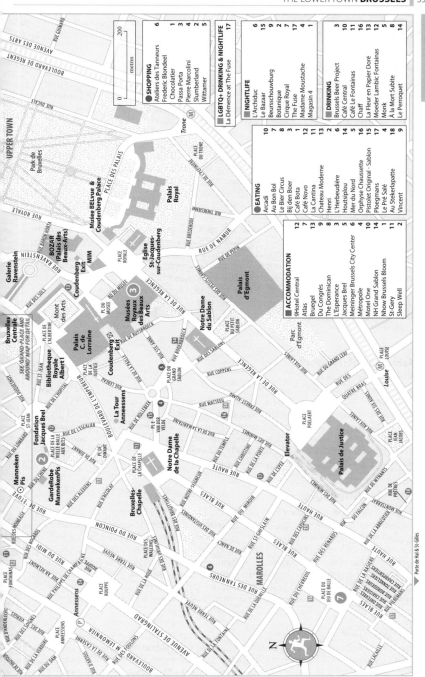

● SHOPPING

Ateliers des Tanneurs	6
Frederic Blondeel Chocolatier	1
Passa Porta	3
Pierre Marcolini	4
Slumberland	5
Wittamer	2

■ LGBTQ+ DRINKING & NIGHTLIFE

La Démence at The Fuse	17

■ NIGHTLIFE

L'Archiduc	6
Le Bazaar	15
Beursschouwburg	9
Botanique	2
Cirque Royal	7
The Fuse	17
Madame Moustache	4
Magasin 4	1

■ DRINKING

Brussels Beer Project	3
Café Central	10
Café Le Fontainas	11
Chaff	16
La Fleur en Papier Doré	13
Moeder Lambic Fontainas	12
Monk	5
À la Mort Subite	18
Le Perroquet	14

● EATING

Arcadi	10
Au Bon Bol	7
Le Bier Circus	8
Bij den Boer	3
Café Bota	1
Café Novo	12
La Cantina	4
Chateau Moderne	11
Henri	13
L'Herbeudière	2
Houtsiplou	6
Mer du Nord	14
Orphyse Chaussette	5
Pistolet Original - Sablon	16
Ploegmans	15
Le Pré Salé	17
Au Stekerlapatte	18
Vincent	9

■ ACCOMMODATION

9Hotel Central	12
Atlas	7
Bruegel	13
The Dominican	9
Du Congrès	8
L'Esperance	3
Jacques Brel	5
Meininger Brussels City Center	6
Métropole	10
Motel One	14
NH Grand Sablon	1
Nhow Brussels Bloom	4
St-Gery	11
Sleep Well	2

home to some of the trendiest **bars** and most boisterous terraces in town, such as *Café Central* (see page 86).

Place Ste-Catherine

Just off rue Antoine Dansaert, tree-shaded **place Ste-Catherine** lies at the heart of one of the city's most fashionable districts. It's named for the large **church of Ste-Catherine** (free), a battered nineteenth-century replacement for the Baroque original, of which the creamy, curvy **belfry** beside the west end of the church is the solitary survivor. Venture inside, and behind the glass screen that closes off most of the nave, you'll spy a fourteenth-century **Black Madonna and Child**, a sensually carved stone statuette that was chucked into the Senne by Protestants but fished out while floating on a fortuitous clod of peat. The real attraction here and in the adjacent **place du Vieux Marche-aux-Grains** is the buzzy **cafés** that spread their tables across the two squares.

The Quais

Quai aux Briques and the parallel **quai au Bois à Brûler** extend northwest from the place Ste-Catherine on either side of a vast and open area, which was the most central part of the city's main **dock** until it was filled in. Strolling along this open area, you'll pass a motley assortment of old houses, warehouses, shops and restaurants, which together maintain an appealing canal-side feel – an impression heightened in the early morning when the streets are choked with lorries bearing trays of fish for local restaurants. The fanciful **Anspach water fountain** at the end of the old quays, with its lizards and dolphins, honours Burgomaster Anspach, a galvanising force in the 1880s drive to modernise the city.

Galeries St-Hubert

Northeast corner of the Grand-Place

Handsome and elegant, the trio of glass-vaulted galleries that comprise the **Galeries St-Hubert** – **du Roi**, **de la Reine** and the smaller **des Princes** – date from 1847, making them one of Europe's first indoor **shopping arcades**. Even today, it's a grand place to escape the weather or have a coffee, and the pastel-painted walls, classical pilasters and cameo sculptures retain an air of genteel sophistication. Try *Arcadi* (see page 84) at the far end for snacks and lunches, while *l'Ogenblik* (see page 85), just off the main gallery, is good for high-end slap-up dinners.

Rue des Bouchers

Halfway down, **rue des Bouchers** divides the Galeries St-Hubert in two and is the city's best-known restaurant ghetto, where the narrow cobblestone lanes are transformed at night into fairy-lit tunnels flanked by elaborate displays of dull-eyed fish and glistening molluscs; it's all very tempting, but these restaurants have a reputation for charging way over the odds and are best avoided. A small side alley, **Impasse de la Fidélité**, is home to a number of rowdy drinking joints centred on the *Delirium Café*, the heart of the Brussels drinking scene for young tourists. It's far better, though, to head for the rather wonderful bar of the nearby puppet theatre **Théâtre Royal de Toone** (see page 88).

La Monnaie

It's a short walk from rue des Bouchers to **place de la Monnaie**, a dreary modern square that's overshadowed by the huge shopping and office complex of Centre Monnaie. The **Théâtre Royal de la Monnaie** (nowadays known as **La Monnaie**), Brussels' prestigious opera house, provides some aesthetic relief. A grand Neoclassical structure, it was built in 1819 with an interior added in 1856 to a design by Poelaert, the architect of the Palais de Justice (see page 67). The theatre's main claim to fame, however, is as the starting point of the revolution against the Dutch in 1830: a nationalistic libretto in Auber's *The Mute Girl of Portici* sent the audience wild, and they poured out into the streets to raise the flag of Brabant, signalling the start of the rebellion. Given that the opera tells the tale of an Italian uprising against the Spanish, with lines such as 'To my country I owe my life, to me it will owe its liberty', one of the Dutch censors – of whom there were many – should have seen what was coming, as a furious King William I pointed out.

Rue Neuve and the Place des Martyrs

From place de la Monnaie, Brussels' principal shopping street, pedestrianised **rue Neuve**, forges north as far as the boulevards of the petit ring. About halfway up, on the right, the **place des Martyrs** is a cool, rational square superimposed on the city by the Habsburgs in the 1770s. There's no mistaking the architectural elegance of the ensemble. The imposing centrepiece, the **Pro Patria Monument** (Monument to the Fatherland), is a later addition: a stone plinth surmounted by a representation of the Fatherland Crowned that rises from an arcaded gallery inscribed with the names of those 445 rebels who died in the Belgian Revolution of 1830.

Centre Belge de la Bande Dessinée

rue des Sables 20 • Charge • ⓦ cbbd.be

Just east of the place des Martyrs, Brussels' only surviving **Horta**-designed department store, the **Grand Magasin Waucquez**, dating from 1906, exhibits all the classic features of Victor Horta's work (see box, page 73), from the soft lines of the ornamentation to the handsome frame of the metal grilles, exposed girders and balustrades. It's now home to the **Centre Belge de la Bande Dessinée**, which incorporates a café, reference library and bookshop downstairs and the enjoyable **Belgian Comic Strip Center** on the floors above. Among much else, there are examples of work from all the leading practitioners: **Tintin** creator Georges Remi; Jijé (the Western feature *Jerry Spring*); Peyo (best known for *The Smurfs*); and Edgar P. Jacobs, whose theatrical compositions and fluent combination of genres – science fiction, fantasy and crime – are seen to good effect in his Blake and Mortimer series.

Manneken Pis

Walking south from the Grand-Place, it's the briefest of strolls to Brussels' best-known tourist attraction, the **Manneken Pis**, a diminutive statue of a pissing urchin stuck high up in a shrine-like affair that's protected from the crowds by an iron fence. There are all sorts of folkloric tales about the origins of the lad, from lost aristocratic children recovered when they were taking a pee to peasant boys putting out dangerous fires and – least likely of the lot – kids slashing on the city's enemies from the trees and putting them to flight. More reliably, it seems that Jerome Duquesnoy, who cast the original bronze statue in the 1600s, intended the Manneken to embody the 'irreverent spirit' of the city; indeed, its popularity blossomed during the sombre, priest-dominated years following the Thirty Years' War. The statue may have been Duquesnoy's idea or replaced an earlier stone version of ancient provenance. Still, whatever the truth, it has certainly attracted the attention of thieves, notably in 1817 when a French ex-convict swiped it before breaking it into pieces. The thief and the smashed Manneken were apprehended, the former publicly branded on the Grand-Place and sentenced to a life of forced labour, while the fragments of the latter were used to create the mould in

1

which the present-day Manneken was cast. It's long been the custom for visiting VIPs to donate a **costume**, and the little chap is regularly kitted out in different tackle – often military or folkloric gear, but sometimes something more incongruous such as golfers' plus fours or Mickey Mouse outfits. To view his wardrobe, head to the nearby **Garde-Robe MannekenPis** (rue du Chêne 19; charge; ⓦmannekenpis.brussels/en). You can also see the Manneken's equally irreverent though rather more modern sister – **Jeanneke Pis** – squatting in a niche opposite the *Delirium Café*.

Fondation Jacques Brel

place de la Vieille-Halle aux Blés 11 • Charge • ⓦ fondationbrel.be

Five minutes' walk from the Grand-Place, the **Fondation Jacques Brel** is a small but inventive museum celebrating the life and times of the Belgian singer **Jacques Brel** (1929–78), who was born and raised in Schaarbeek, a suburb of Brussels. A legend in his musical lifetime, Brel became famous in the 1960s as the gravelly-voiced singer of mournful chansons about death, loss, desire and love, all of which he wrote himself (see box below). He died in 1978 at 49 in Paris (having spent his final years in the Marquesas Islands, where he is buried). A proud Belgian to the end, this museum goes some way to explaining the man and his relationship with his homeland through family reminiscences, film and music, with the help of a free audio tour: Brel's monologue on the charms and tedium of Belgian life – 'The Doctor' – is especially sharp-witted. You can also don another headset and set off on a Jacques Brel **city-centre tour**, which was put together – like the museum – by the songwriter's widow and daughters, strolling the streets of Brussels to his songs and stopping off at sights meaningful to Brel along the way, such as the spot on the Grand-Place where he conceived the song, 'Jef'.

Notre Dame de la Chapelle

pl de la Chapelle 15 • Free

Founded in 1134, the sprawling, broadly Gothic **Notre Dame de la Chapelle** is the city's oldest church. However, the attractive Baroque bell tower was only added after the French artillery bombardment of 1695. Inside, heavyweight columns with curly capitals support a well-proportioned **nave**, whose central aisle is bathed in light from the soaring windows. Among the assorted furniture and fittings, the **pulpit** is the most arresting, an intricately carved hunk of wood featuring the Old Testament prophet Elijah stuck out in the wilderness. The prophet looks mightily fed up, but then he doesn't realise that there's an angel beside him with a loaf of bread (manna). The church's main claim to fame is the **memorial to Pieter Bruegel the Elder**, high up on the wall of the south aisle's fourth chapel. The painting – a copy of a Rubens showing St Peter being given the keys to heaven – is the work of Pieter's son Jan, while the other plaque and bronze effigy in the chapel were added in the 1930s. Pieter is thought to have lived and died just down the street at rue Haute 132.

The Quartier Marolles

South of Notre Dame de la Chapelle, **rue Blaes**, together with the parallel **rue Haute**, form the double spine of the **Quartier Marolles**, which was home to artisans working on the nearby mansions of the Sablon (see page 66) in the seventeenth-century. Industrialised in the eighteenth century, it remained a thriving working-class district until the 1870s, when the paving over of the Senne led to the riverside factories closing down and moving to the suburbs. The workers and their families followed, initiating a long process of decline, which turned the district into an impoverished **slum**. Things finally started to change in the late 1980s, when

JACQUES BREL PLAYLIST

If you like what you hear at the **Fondation Jacques Brel** (see page 58), you might want to check out some songs from the **playlist** below, which covers the very best of Brel's work:

'Amsterdam' One of Brel's most intense live numbers, this deliberately repetitive, climactic tale of sailors in seedy ports is a fantastically evocative song.

'Au suivant' A satirical, biting rant against war, militarism and middle-class bourgeois values.

'Les Bonbons' Brel at his wittiest and most unforgiving, poking fun at 1960s hippies.

'La Chanson de Jacky' The songwriter in autobiographical mode, looking back in fantastically rumbustious fashion on his career and forward to his future.

'Je suis un soir d'été' A late and very atmospheric study of summer ennui in small-town Belgium; it ranks among Brel's most beautiful creations.

'Mathilde' One of Brel's greatest love songs, brilliantly covered by Scott Walker.

'Le Moribond' This tormented yet curiously upbeat lament of a dying man gave rise to Terry Jacks' hit of 1974.

'Ne me quitte pas' Brel's heartbreaking 'hymn to the cowardice of men', most memorably covered by Nina Simone.

'Quand on n'a que l'amour' One of Brel's earliest songs and his first hit single.

'La Quête' Covered by just about everyone but never bettered, this is quite rightly one of Brel's best-known songs.

outsiders began to snaffle up property here, and although the *quartier* still has its rougher moments, the two main streets, **rue Haute** and **rue Blaes** – or at least those parts from Notre-Dame de la Chapelle to place du Jeu de Balle – are now lined with antique and interior-design shops, and the odd decent restaurant. Place du Jeu de Balle, at the heart of Marolles, is also the appropriately earthy location of the city's most famous **flea market** (daily 6am–2pm), which is at its hectic best on Sunday mornings.

It's worth knowing that a **public elevator** (daily 7am–11.30pm; free), just off rue Haute on rue Notre-Dame de Graces, can whisk you up to the Palais de Justice in the Upper Town – a helpful shortcut.

The Upper Town

From the heights of the **Upper Town**, the Francophile ruling class long kept a beady eye on the proletarians down below. It was here they built their mansions and palaces, and the wide avenues and grand architecture of this aristocratic quarter – the bulk of which dates from the late eighteenth and nineteenth centuries – have survived pretty much intact, lending a stately, dignified feel that's markedly different from the tatty confusion of the Lower Town.

The Upper Town begins at the foot of the sharp slope which runs north to south from one end of the city centre to the other, its course marked – in general terms at least – by a wide **boulevard** that's variously named Berlaimont, L'Impératrice and L'Empereur. Above here, the **rue Royale** and **rue de la Régence** together make up the Upper Town's spine, on and around which is the outstanding **Musées Royaux des Beaux Arts**, the pick of Belgium's many fine art collections; the low-key **Palais Royal**; and the entertaining **Musée des Instruments de Musique** (MIM). A short walk south, rue de la Régence soon leads to the well-heeled **Sablon** neighbourhood, whose antique shops, chic bars and cafés fan out from the medieval church of **Notre Dame du Sablon**. Beyond this is the monstrous late nineteenth-century **Palais de Justice**, traditionally one of the city's most disliked buildings.

1

Cathedral of St Michael and St Gudula

pl Ste-Gudule • **Cathedral** Free • **Treasury** Charge • ⓦ cathedralisbruxellensis.be

It only takes a couple of minutes to walk from the Grand-Place to the east end of rue de la Montagne, where a short slope climbs up to the city's **cathedral**, a splendid Gothic edifice whose commanding position is only slightly compromised by the modern office blocks either side. Begun in 1215 and three hundred years in the making, the cathedral is dedicated jointly to the **patron and patroness of Brussels**, respectively St Michael the Archangel and St Gudula, the latter a vague seventh-century figure whose reputation was based on her gentle determination – despite all sorts of shenanigans, the devil could never make her think an uncharitable thought.

The cathedral sports a striking, twin-towered, **white stone facade**, with the central double doorway trimmed by fanciful tracery and statues of the Apostles and – on the central column – the Three Wise Men. The facade was erected in the fifteenth century in the High Gothic style. Still, the intensity of the decoration fades away inside with the cavernous triple-aisled nave completed a century before. Other parts of the interior illustrate several phases of Gothic design, the **chancel** being the oldest part of the church, built in stages between 1215 and 1280 in the Early Gothic style.

The interior is short on **furnishings and fittings**, reflecting the combined efforts of Protestants and the French Republican Army, but the massive oak **pulpit** survives, an extravagant chunk of frippery by the Antwerp sculptor Hendrik Verbruggen, featuring Adam and Eve being chased from the Garden of Eden, while up above the Virgin Mary and some helpful cherubs stamp on the head of the serpent-dragon.

The stained-glass windows

The cathedral also boasts some superb sixteenth-century **stained-glass windows**, beginning above the main doors with the hurly-burly of the *Last Judgement*. Look closely; you'll spot the donor in the lower foreground with an angel on one side and a woman with long blonde hair (symbolising Faith) on the other. Each main colour has a symbolic meaning: green represents hope, yellow eternal glory and light blue heaven. There's more remarkable work in the **transepts**: in the **north**, Charles V kneels alongside his wife beneath a vast triumphal arch as their patron saints present them to God the Father; his sister, Marie, and her husband, King Louis of Hungary, play out a similar scenario in the **south**. Both windows were designed by **Bernard van Orley** (1490–1541), a long-time favourite of the royal family and the leading Brussels artist of his day.

Chapel of the Blessed Sacrament and treasury

Just beyond the north transept, flanking the choir is the Flamboyant Gothic **Chapel of the Blessed Sacrament**, named after an anti-Semitic legend that featured a Jew from a small Flemish town stealing the consecrated Host from his local church. Thereafter, the thief witnesses the Host being stabbed with daggers by his fellow Jews before it's rescued by his wife and brought to the cathedral, thereby saving her soul. The chapel was built to display the retrieved Host in the 1530s, and its four **stained-glass windows** retell the tale in a strip cartoon that unfolds above representations of the aristocrats who paid for the windows. Based on designs by Bernard van Orley and his one-time apprentice Michiel van Coxie (1499–1592), the artistry is delightful, but the story is perfectly shameful.

Also displayed in the chapel is the cathedral **treasury**, one of whose highlights is a splendid Anglo-Saxon reliquary of the **True Cross**, recently winkled out of the ornate, seventeenth-century, gilded silver reliquary Cross (Item 4) that was made to hold it. There are also two flowing sixteenth-century **altar paintings** to look out for in the chapel – *The Legend of St Gudula* and *The Last Supper* by Michiel van Coxie – and, behind the chapel's high altar, the ghoulish **skull** of St Elizabeth of Hungary (1207–31), a faithful wife, a devoted mother and a loyal servant of the church – hence her beatification.

Galerie Ravenstein and the Palais des Beaux Arts

Across the road from **Gare Centrale**, dug deep into the slope where the Lower and Upper Town meet, the **Galerie Ravenstein** shopping arcade clambers up to rue Ravenstein – a classic piece of 1950s design, sporting bright and cheerful tiling and an airy atrium equipped with a (defunct) water fountain. At the far end, on rue Ravenstein, stands the **Palais des Beaux Arts** or **BOZAR** (see page 88), a severe, low-lying edifice designed by Horta during the 1920s (see box, page 73). The building holds a theatre and concert hall and hosts numerous temporary exhibitions, primarily contemporary art and photography. From here, you can climb the steps up to rue Royale or follow the street to the top of the Mont des Arts and the Musée des Instruments de Musique.

Mont des Arts

The most prominent feature of the slope between the Lower and Upper Towns is the **Mont des Arts**, a name bestowed by Léopold II in anticipation of a fine art museum he intended to build. However, the project was never completed, and the land was only properly built on in the 1950s. At the bottom, **place de l'Albertine** is overlooked by a large and imposing equestrian statue of Belgium's most popular king, **Albert I** (1875–1934), gazing out at a modest statue of Albert's popular queen, **Elizabeth**, just across the street. From here, a wide stone **stairway** clambers up to a **piazza** equipped with water fountains, footpaths and carefully manicured shrubbery, and eventually to the Upper Town proper and the Musée des Instruments de Musique and Musées Royaux des Beaux Arts. Not surprisingly, there are lovely views from the top and a decent restaurant – *Château Moderne* (see page 84) – from which to enjoy them.

Musée des Instruments de Musique (MIM)

rue Montaigne de la Cour 2 • Charge • Ⓦ mim.be

Near the top of the Mont des Arts, the **Old England building** is a whimsical Art Nouveau confection – all glass and wrought iron – that started as a store built by the eponymous British company as its Brussels headquarters in 1899. Cleverly recycled, it now houses the entertaining **Musée des Instruments de Musique**, whose permanent collection, featuring several hundred musical instruments, spreads over four main floors. The special feature here is the **infrared headphones**, which are cued to play music to match the type of instrument you're looking at. This is really good fun, especially in the folk-music section, where you can listen, for example, to a Tibetan temple trumpet, Congolese drums, a veritable battery of bagpipes and a medieval cornemuse, as featured in the paintings of Pieter Bruegel the Younger.

Place Royale and St-Jacques-sur-Coudenberg

Composed and self-assured, **place Royale** forms a fitting climax to rue Royale, the dead-straight backbone of the Upper Town, which runs 2km north to the Turkish neighbourhood of St-Josse. Precisely symmetrical, the square is framed by late eighteenth-century mansions, each an exercise in architectural restraint, though there's no mistaking their size or the probable cost of their construction. Pushing into this understated opulence is the facade of the church of **St-Jacques-sur-Coudenberg** (free), a fanciful 1780s version of a Roman temple, with a colourfully frescoed pediment representing Our Lady as Comforter of the Depressed. Indeed, the building was so secular in appearance that the French Revolutionary Army had no hesitation in renaming it the Temple of Reason, though they did destroy the **statue** of the Habsburg governor that once stood in front of the church; its

1

replacement – a dashing equestrian representation of **Godfrey de Bouillon**, one of the leaders of the first Crusade – dates from the 1840s. It was an appropriate choice, as this was the spot where Godfrey was supposed to have exhorted his subjects to enlist for the Crusade, rounding off his appeal with a thunderous '*Dieu li volt*' (God wills it).

Musées Royaux des Beaux Arts

rue de la Régence 3 • Charge • Ⓦ fine-arts-museum.be

On the edge of the place Royale, the **Musées Royaux des Beaux Arts** holds Belgium's best all-around fine art collection. This vast hoard is currently exhibited in two interconnected museums: the **Musée Old Masters**, which has art from the Renaissance to the early nineteenth century, and the **Musée Magritte**, which is devoted solely to the work of the Belgian surrealist. The museum also hosts a prestigious programme of **temporary exhibitions** for which a supplementary admission fee is usually required. Be sure to pick up a gallery plan at reception. A third interconnected museum, formerly the **Musée Fin-de-Siècle**, covering art from the mid-nineteenth to the early twentieth century, is closed for refurbishment and reorganisation until 2026, maybe later.

Musée Old Masters

The galleries of the **Musée Old Masters** kick off with paintings from the fifteenth and sixteenth centuries, including the Flemish primitives and the Bruegels. Later galleries focus on paintings from the seventeenth and eighteenth centuries, including the work of Rubens and his contemporaries.

The fifteenth century

The museum's collection begins with several paintings by **Rogier van der Weyden** (1399–1464), who moved to Brussels from his home town of Tournai in the 1430s, becoming the city's official painter shortly afterwards. When it came to portraiture, Weyden's favourite technique was to highlight his subject's features – and tokens of rank – against a black background. His *Portrait of Antoine de Bourgogne* is a case in point, with Anthony, the illegitimate son of Philip the Good, casting a haughty, tight-lipped stare to his right while wearing the chain of the Order of the Golden Fleece and clasping an arrow, the emblem of the guild of archers.

Weyden's contemporary, Leuven-based **Dieric Bouts** (1410–75) is well represented by the two panels of his *Justice of the Emperor Otto*. The story was well known: the empress accuses a nobleman of attempting to seduce her in revenge for refusing her advances. He is executed, but the man's wife remains convinced of his innocence and subsequently proves her point using an ordeal by fire – hence the red-hot iron bar she's holding. The empress then receives her just desserts, being burnt on the hill in the background.

Moving on, the anonymous artist known as the **Master of the Legend of St Lucy** weighs in with a finely detailed, richly allegorical *Madonna with Saints* where, with the city of Bruges in the background, the Madonna presents the infant Jesus for the adoration of eleven holy women. Decked out in elaborate medieval attire, the women have blank, almost expressionless faces, but each bears a token of her sainthood, which a medieval congregation would have easily recognised: St Lucy, whose assistance was sought by those with sight problems, holds two eyeballs in a dish.

Beyond here is a beautifully coloured, clear and precise Lamentation by **Petrus Christus** (1410–75), and several fine portraits by **Hans Memling** (1430–94), plus his softly hued *Martyrdom of St Sebastian*, which was commissioned by the guild of archers in Bruges around 1470 and shows the trussed-up saint serenely indifferent to the arrows of the firing squad.

The sixteenth century

One of the museum's most interesting paintings is a copy of *Temptations of St Anthony*, the original of which, by **Hieronymus Bosch** (1450–1516), is in Lisbon's Museu Nacional. No one is quite sure who painted this triptych – it may or may not have been one of Bosch's apprentices – but it was undoubtedly produced in Holland in the late fifteenth or early sixteenth century and shows an inconspicuous saint sticking desperately to his prayers surrounded by all manner of fiendish phantoms. On the right panel, Anthony is tempted by lust and greed; on the left, his companions help him back to his shelter after he's been transported through the skies by weird-looking demons. Another leading Flemish artist, **Quinten Matsys** (1465–1530), is well represented, not only by his *Triptych of the Holy Kindred*, which abandons the realistic interiors and landscapes of his Flemish predecessors in favour of the grand columns and porticoes of the Renaissance, but also by a loving and sensitive *Virgin and Child*. There's also a beautifully composed *Adoration of the Magi* by **Gerard David** (1460–1523).

Beyond here are paintings by the German painters **Lucas Cranach the Younger and Elder** and the museum's superb collection of works by the Bruegel family, notably **Pieter the Elder** (1527–69), who moved to Brussels in the early 1560s. He preferred to paint in the Netherlandish tradition, and his works often depict crowded Flemish scenes in which are embedded religious or mythical stories, a sympathetic portrayal of everyday life that revelled in the seasons and was worked in muted browns, greys and bluish greens with red or yellow highlights. Typifying this approach are two particularly absorbing works, the *Adoration of the Magi* and the *Census at Bethlehem* – a scene that **Pieter** (1564–1638), his son, repeated on several occasions. The versatile **Pieter the Elder** also dabbled with the lurid imagery of Bosch, whose influence is seen most clearly in the *Fall of the Rebel Angels*. This frantic panel painting had been attributed to Bosch until Bruegel's signature was discovered hidden under the frame. The *Fall of Icarus* is, however, his most haunting work, its mood perfectly captured by W.H. Auden in his poem 'Musée des Beaux Arts':

In Bruegel's Icarus, for instance how everything turns away
Quite leisurely from the disaster; the ploughman may
Have heard the splash, the forsaken cry,
But for him it was not an important failure; the sun shone
As it had to on the white legs disappearing into the green
Water; and the expensive delicate ship that must have seen
Something amazing, a boy falling out of the sky,
Had somewhere to get to and sailed calmly on.

The seventeenth century

The larger works of another of the museum's significant painters, **Peter-Paul Rubens** (1577–1640), are gathered together in one room, as are the works of his contemporary **Jacob Jordaens** (1593–1678), whose big and brassy canvases perfectly suit the space. Like Rubens, Jordaens had a bulging order book, and for years, he and his apprentices churned out paintings by the cartload. His best work is generally agreed to have been completed early on – between about 1620 and 1640 – and there's evidence here in the two versions of the *Satyr and the Peasant*; the earlier work is clever and inventive, the second a hastily cobbled-together piece that verges on buffoonery. As for **Rubens**, the museum holds a broad sample of his work, including the *Ascent to Calvary*, an intensely physical painting, capturing the confusion, agony and strain as Christ struggles on hands and knees under the weight of the cross and the bloodcurdling *Martyrdom of St Lieven*, whose cruel torture – his tongue has just been ripped out and fed to a dog – is watched from on high by cherubs and angels. In another room, there are more paintings by Rubens, among them depictions of Archdukes Albert and Isabella and the

1

wonderfully observed *Four Studies of the Head of a Negro*, a preparation for the Black magus in the *Adoration of the Magi*, a luminous work that hangs in the same room. From the same era, there are also works by the skilled portraitist **Anthony van Dyck** (1599–1641), who is well represented by depictions of St Anthony and St Francis and figures of an old man and an old woman. There are also portraits by the Dutchmen **Rembrandt** and **Frans Hals**, among a variety of other Dutch works.

The eighteenth century

The museum has a scattering of eighteenth-century paintings, the main highlight of which by far is the much-celebrated *Death of Marat* by **Jacques-Louis David** (1748–1825), a propagandist piece of 1793 showing Jean-Paul Marat, the French Revolutionary hero, dying in his bath after being stabbed by Charlotte Corday. David has given Marat a perfectly proportioned, classical torso and a face which looks almost Christ-like with its large hooded eyes, the effect heightened by the composition's flatness and the background's emptiness. The dead man clasps a quill in one hand and the letter given him by Corday in the other, inscribed, 'My deepest grief is all it takes to be entitled to your benevolence'. As a counterpoint, to emphasise the depth of Corday's betrayal, David has added another note on the wooden chest, written by Marat beginning, 'You will give this warrant to that mother with the five children, whose husband died for his country'. The painting was David's paean to a fellow revolutionary, for, like Marat, he was a Jacobin – the deadly rivals of the Girondins, supported by Corday. David was also a leading light of the Neoclassical movement and became the new regime's Superintendent of the Fine Arts. He did well under Napoleon until Waterloo, after which he was exiled, along with all the other regicides, ending his days in Brussels.

Musée Magritte

From the ground floor of the Musée d'Art Ancien, a passageway leads through to the **Musée Magritte**, whose four floors are devoted to the life, times and work of **René Magritte** (see box, page 65). Beginning on the top floor, the museum trawls through Magritte's life chronologically, with original documents, old photos and snatches of film, quotations and a decent sample of his paintings (though sadly not many of his most famous works, which are scattered around the galleries of the world). There is an early sketch of his wife Georgette, early Cubist efforts, and the later surrealist works he became best known for – often perplexing pieces whose weird, almost photographically realised images and bizarre juxtapositions aim to disconcert. There are posters by Magritte (an accomplished graphic artist) advertising drinks, films and commercial products, plus a selection of the more Impressionistic works he produced in the 1940s.

Palais Royal

pl des Palais • Free • ⓦ monarchie.be

Around the corner from place Royale, the long and somewhat cumbersome **Palais Royal** is something of a disappointment, consisting of a stodgy nineteenth-century conversion of late eighteenth-century townhouses, begun by King William I, the Dutch royal who ruled both Belgium and the Netherlands from 1815 to 1830. The Belgian Revolution of 1830 polished off the joint kingdom, and since then, the kings of independent Belgium haven't spent much time here. Indeed, although it remains their official residence, the royals have lived in Laeken (see page 77) for decades. It's hardly surprising, therefore, that the **palace interior** is formal and rather unwelcoming. It comprises little more than a predictable sequence of opulent rooms, all gilt trimmings, parquet floors and endless royal portraits, though three features make a guided tour (summer only) just about worthwhile: the tapestries designed by **Goya**, the magnificent chandeliers of the **Throne Room** and the Mirror Room's **iridescent ceiling** –

RENÉ MAGRITTE

René Magritte (1898–1967) is the most famous of Belgium's modern artists, and his disconcerting, strangely haunting images are a familiar part of popular culture. Born in a small town just outside Charleroi, he entered the Royal Academy of Fine Arts in Brussels in 1915 and was a sporadic student until 1920. Initially, Magritte worked in a broadly **Cubist** manner, but in 1925, influenced by the Italian painter Giorgio de Chirico, he switched to Surrealism. He almost immediately stumbled upon the themes and images that would preoccupy him for decades. His work incorporated startling comparisons between the ordinary and the extraordinary, with the occasional erotic element thrown in. **Favourite images** included men in bowler hats, metamorphic figures, enormous rocks floating in the sky and juxtapositions of night and day. He also dabbled in word paintings, mislabelling familiar forms to illustrate the arbitrariness of linguistics. His canvases were devoid of emotion, deadpan images that were easy to recognise but perplexing because of their setting. At times, he broke with this characteristic style, most famously in 1948 to revenge long years of neglect by the French artistic establishment: hundreds turned up to see Magritte's first **Paris exhibition** only to be confronted with crass and crude paintings of childlike simplicity. These so-called **Vache paintings** created a furore, and Magritte beat a hasty artistic retreat. Despite this, Magritte was picked up and popularised by an American art dealer, Alexander Iolas, who made him rich and famous.

Magritte and his family lived in Jette, a suburb of Brussels, until the late 1950s, and the house is now the **Musée René Magritte** (see page 64). He died in 1967, shortly after a major retrospective of his work at the Museum of Modern Art in New York cemented his reputation as one of the twentieth century's great artists.

Heaven of Delight, a contemporary work by the Belgian artist Jan Fabre (b.1958), made up of more than a million wing cases of the Thai jewel beetle.

Musée BELvue

pl des Palais, corner of rue Royale · Charge · ⓦ belvue.be

The **Hôtel Bellevue** was once part of the palace but has been turned into the **Musée BELvue**, which aims to help visitors understand Belgium and Belgian society. It's professionally done, with interactive displays on seven themes: democracy, prosperity, solidarity, pluralism, migration, language and Europe. A gallery of around two hundred objects, including a lithograph by Magritte and a football signed by the Belgium national football team, gives an insight into daily life and popular culture in the country since the nineteenth century. It's a fascinating exhibition, not least thanks to the filmed interviews with the locals on different subjects. It's an appropriate location for the museum, too, as it was in this very building that the rebellious Belgians fired at the Dutch army, which was trying to reach the city centre via the Parc de Bruxelles (see page 66) in 1830.

Coudenberg Palace

pl des Palais, corner of rue Royale · Charge · ⓦ coudenberg.brussels/en

Dating from the 1770s, the Hôtel Bellevue was built on top of the subterranean remains of the **Coudenberg Palace**, which stretched right across to what is now place Royale. A castle was first built on this site in the eleventh century and was enlarged on several subsequent occasions. It was severely damaged by fire in 1731, and the site was cleared forty years later, leaving only the foundations. These have now been cleared of debris, revealing a labyrinth of tunnels that can only be reached via the Musée BELvue. Visitors can wander around these foundations, the most notable feature of which is the **Aula Magna**, the great hall built by Philip the Good in the 1450s. You emerge on the

1

other side of the street at the so-called **Hoogstraten House**, which displays a collection of objects found on the site, and then exit onto an alley next door to the Musical Instruments Museum (see page 61).

Parc de Bruxelles

Set between the Palais Royal and the Belgian Parliament building, the **Parc de Bruxelles** is the most central of the city's main parks, along whose tree-shaded footpaths civil servants and office workers stroll at lunchtime or race to catch the métro in the evenings. They might well wish the greenery was a bit more interesting. Laid out in the **formal French style** in 1780, the park undoubtedly suited the courtly – and courting – rituals of the times, but today, the straight footpaths and long lines of trees seem a little tedious, though the classical statues and large **fountain** in the centre do cheer things up a tad.

Place du Trône

From the east side of the royal palace, rue Ducale leads to **place du Trône**, its conspicuous equestrian statue of Léopold II is the work of Thomas Vinçotte, whose skills were much used by the king – look out for Vinçotte's chariot on top of the Parc du Cinquantenaire's triumphal arch (see page 71).

Place du Petit Sablon

Just off the eastern side of busy rue de la Régence, the peaceful rectangle of **place du Petit Sablon** was laid out as a public garden in 1890 after previous use as a horse market. The wrought-iron fence surrounding the garden is decorated with 48 **statuettes** representing the medieval guilds; inside, near the top of the slope, are ten slightly larger statues honouring some of the country's leading sixteenth-century figures. The ten are hardly household names in Belgium, never mind anywhere else. Still, one or two may ring a few bells – Mercator, the sixteenth-century geographer and cartographer responsible for the most common representation of the earth's surface, and William the Silent (see page 310), to all intents and purposes, the founder of the Netherlands. Here also, on top of the fountain, are the figures of the counts **Egmont and Hoorn**, beheaded on the Grand-Place for their opposition to the Habsburgs in 1568.

Notre Dame du Sablon

pl du Grand Sablon • Free • ⓦ fondsamiseglisesablon.be

The fifteenth-century church of **Notre Dame du Sablon** began life as a chapel for the guild of archers in 1304. Its fortunes were, however, transformed when a **statue of Mary**, purportedly with healing powers, was brought here from Antwerp in 1348. The chapel soon became a pilgrimage centre, and a High Gothic church was built to accommodate visitors. The church endured some inappropriate tinkering at the end of the nineteenth century, but overall, it is a handsome structure, the sandy hues of its exterior stonework enhanced by slender buttresses and a forest of prickly pinnacles. The **interior** no longer holds the statue of Mary – the Protestants chopped it up in 1565 – but two carvings of a **boat** with its passengers and holy cargo recall its story, one located in the nave, the other above the inside of the rue de la Régence door. The woman in the boat is one Béatrice Sodkens, the pious creature whose visions prompted her to procure the statue and bring it here. The occasion of its arrival in Brussels is still celebrated annually in July by the **Ommegang**, the historic-heritage procession from the Sablon to the Grand-Place.

1

Place du Grand Sablon

Behind the church of Notre Dame du Sablon, the sloping wedge of the **place du Grand Sablon** serves as the centre of the **Sablon** neighbourhood, which is one of the city's wealthiest districts – as evidenced by the luxury stores and chocolate shops (see page 90) that sit around its fringes. The square is busiest at weekends when it hosts an antique **market**. You could easily spend an hour or so browsing the market and surrounding shops or soak up the atmosphere in one of Sablon's several cafés.

Palais de Justice

pl Poelaert • Free

From place du Grand Sablon, it's a brief walk south to place Poelaert, named after the architect who designed the immense **Palais de Justice**, which anchors the end of rue de la Régence. Whatever Poelaert's intentions, it's a monstrous Greco-Roman wedding cake of a building that dwarfs the square and everything around it. It's possible to wander into the building's sepulchral **main hall**; the size alone impresses – not that it pleased the several thousand townsfolk who were forcibly evicted so the place could be built. Poelaert became one of the most **hated men** in the capital, so much so that when he went insane and died in 1879, it was widely believed a *steekes* (witch) from the Marolles had been sticking pins into an effigy of him.

Place Louise

A stone's throw from the Palais de Justice, **place Louise** – part square, part traffic junction – heralds the edge of perhaps the city's most exclusive shopping district, home to a good proportion of Brussels' designer boutiques, jewellers and glossy shopping malls, which spread east along boulevard de Waterloo and south down the first part of avenue Louise.

The EU Quarter and Le Cinquantenaire

By no means does Brussels end at the **petit ring**. King Léopold II pushed the city limits out beyond the course of the old walls, grabbing land from the surrounding *communes* to create the irregular boundaries that survive today. To the **east**, he sequestered a rough rectangle of land, across which he ploughed two wide boulevards to link the city centre with **Le Cinquantenaire**, a self-glorifying and markedly grandiose monument erected to celebrate the golden jubilee of Belgian independence and one that now houses three sprawling museums, including the large **Musée du Cinquantenaire**. In recent decades, the grandeur of Léopold's design has been overlaid with the uncompromising office blocks of the EU, which coalesce on and around rue de la Loi to form the loosely defined **EU Quarter** – not a particularly enjoyable area to explore. However, there are a handful of appealing parks and squares, while the flashy **EU Parliament building** is of passing interest, as are the other EU institutions.

EU Parliament

Rue Wiertz 60 • Free • ⓦ visiting.europarl.europa.eu/en

The sprawling **EU Parliament** complex fronts the busy rectangle of **place du Luxembourg**, a wide and attractive square framed on three sides by late nineteenth-century townhouses. The Parliament's central structure, the **Spaak building**, was completed in 1997; a glass, stone and steel behemoth equipped with a horseshoe-shaped debating chamber and a curved glass roof that rises to a height of 70m. It has admirers but is known locally as the '*caprice des dieux*', a wry comment on the EU's

1

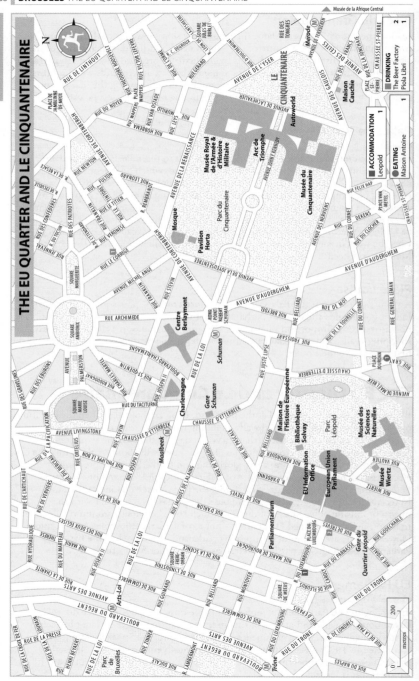

THE EU QUARTER AND LE CINQUANTENAIRE

Musée de l'Afrique Central

ACCOMMODATION	
Leopold	1

EATING	
Maison Antoine	1

DRINKING	
The Beer Factory	2
Piola Libri	1

1

sense of its own importance. Behind, the **Spinelli building**, connected by a footbridge, was completed in 1992 and houses MEPs' offices and those of the various political groupings. The half-hour **tours** of the Spaak building (report to the visitors' entrance 15min in advance and be sure to take a photo ID) are fairly cursory affairs, more or less a look at the debating chamber and the stairwell outside, with headphones that take you through the whole thing and explain how the EU works. It's not exactly essential viewing, but you do learn something of the purpose of the building – which, amazingly enough, is here less for the debating chamber than to house the Parliament's various committees.

The other way to get the lowdown on the EU Parliament is in the **Parliamentarium exhibition**, housed in a separate building on the left side of the main plaza. This series of interactive displays, around which an audio guide guides you, traces the origins of the European vision, taking you through the EU's evolution from the Schuman Agreement of 1950 to its current 27 member states. It's a slick presentation and gives a crash course on the workings of the EU Parliament and its other institutions, with screens on which you can find out about any of the 705 MEPs. There are displays of the various political groupings and their agendas and a mock parliamentary chamber that takes you through the (excruciating) decision-making processes via a series of short films. You can also take a mini-tour around the continent, discover various European initiatives, and relax in comfy chairs while listening to European citizens describe their daily lives. It's all good stuff, but inevitably a touch worthy – and above all, a giant slice of propaganda for the EU.

Musée Wiertz

rue Vautier 62 • Free • ⓦ fine-arts-museum.be/en/museums/musee-wiertz-museum

Hidden away near the grandiose buildings of the EU Parliament, the pocket-sized **Musée Wiertz** is devoted to the works of one of the city's most distinctive nineteenth-century artists, **Antoine-Joseph Wiertz** (1806–65). Barely remembered today, Wiertz was once a popular painter – so much so that no less a figure than Thomas Hardy could write of Wiertz's 'staring and ghastly attitudes'. The museum is housed in the artist's former **studio**, built for him by the Belgian state on the understanding that on his death, he bequeath both it and his oeuvre to the nation – and he obliged. **Wiertz** painted mainly religious and mythological canvases featuring gory hells and strapping nudes, as well as fearsome scenes of human madness and suffering. There are also a number of elegantly painted quasi-erotic pieces featuring coy nudes, a colossal *Triumph of Christ*, a small but especially gruesome *Suicide* – not for the squeamish – and macabre works such as *The Thoughts and Visions of a Severed Head* and *Hunger, Folly, Crime* in which a madwoman is pictured shortly after hacking off her child's leg and throwing it into the cooking pot. Mercifully, there is some relief with a few conventional portraits, but few would pretend that Wiertz was one of the greatest painters who ever lived – as he believed.

Muséum des Sciences Naturelles

rue Vautier 29 • Charge • ⓦ naturalsciences.be

Follow rue Vautier up the hill from the Wiertz museum, and you will soon reach the **Muséum des Sciences Naturelles**, which holds the city's natural history collection. It's a large, sprawling, somewhat disorientating museum with wide-ranging displays in a mixture of late nineteenth-century and 1960s galleries. There are sections devoted to crystals and rocks, rodents and mammals, insects and crustaceans; a whale gallery featuring the enormous remains of a blue whale; and, most impressive of the lot, a capacious **dinosaur gallery** with a superb selection of **dinosaur fossils** discovered in the coal mines of Hainaut in the late nineteenth century. The most striking are those of

1

THE EU IN BRUSSELS

The three leading institutions of the **European Union** operate mainly, though not exclusively, from Brussels. The **European Parliament** carries out its committee work and most of its business in Brussels, heading off for Strasbourg for around a dozen three-day plenary sessions annually. It's the only EU institution to meet and debate publicly and has been directly elected since 1979. There are currently 705 **MEPs**, and they sit in political blocks made up of like-minded parties rather than national delegations; members are very restricted on speaking time, and debates tend to be well-mannered, consensual affairs controlled by the **president**, who is elected for five years by Parliament itself – although this mandate is often split in two and shared by the two biggest political groups. The **Conference of Presidents** – the president of the Parliament and leaders of all the political groups – meet to plan future parliamentary business. Supporting and advising this political edifice is a complex network of committees from agriculture to human rights.

The **European Council** consists of the heads of government of each member state and the **president of the European Commission**; they meet twice every six months in the much-publicised 'European Summits'. However, between these meetings, ministers responsible for different issues meet in the **Council of the European Union**, the main decision-making structure alongside the European Parliament. There are complex rules regarding decision-making: some subjects require only a simple majority, others need unanimous support, some can be decided by the Council alone, others need the agreement of Parliament; and overall, in a bid to make the EU more democratic, the power of the Parliament has been strengthened in recent years. This political structure is underpinned by scores of Brussels-based committees and working parties made up of both civil servants and political appointees.

The **European Commission** acts as the EU's executive arm and board of control, managing funds and monitoring all manner of agreements. The 27 Commissioners are political appointees nominated by their home countries, but their tenure has to be agreed upon by the European Parliament, and they remain accountable to the MEPs. The European Parliament elects the president of the European Commission for five years of office. Over twenty thousand civil servants work for the Commission, whose headquarters are in Brussels, mainly in the Berlaymont and adjacent Charlemagne building on rue de la Loi, as well as other buildings in the area.

a whole herd of **iguanodons**, whose skeletons are raised on two legs, though, in fact, these herbivores may well have been four-legged. In December 2017, the museum showed its first new dinosaur fossil in more than one hundred years – a 210 million-year-old Plateosaurus called 'Ben', discovered in Switzerland.

Parc Léopold

On rue Vautier, almost opposite the Musée Wiertz, a back entrance leads into the rear of **Parc Léopold**, a green and hilly enclave landscaped around a **lake**. The park is pleasant enough, but its open spaces were encroached upon years ago when the industrialist Ernest Solvay began constructing a prototype science centre's educational and research facilities here. The result is a string of big, old buildings spreading along the park's western periphery. The most interesting to visit is the **Bibliothèque Solvay** (rue Belliard 137; ⓦedificio.be/bibliotheque-solvay), a splendid barrel-vaulted structure with magnificent mahogany panelling overlaying a cast-iron frame, which is now an events venue. On the northern edge of the park is the **Maison de l'Histoire Européenne** (rue Belliard 135; free; ⓦvisiting.europarl.europa.eu/en), which has a permanent exhibition on the history of Europe from the nineteenth century and explores the union's future.

Parc du Cinquantenaire

The wide and leafy lawns and tree-lined avenues of the **Parc du Cinquantenaire** slope up towards a gargantuan arch surmounted by a huge and bombastic bronze entitled *Brabant Raising the National Flag*. The arch, along with the two heavyweight stone buildings it connects, comprise **Le Cinquantenaire**, which Léopold II erected for an exhibition to mark the golden jubilee of the Belgian state in 1880. The buildings contain **three extensive collections**: art and applied art, weapons, and cars – displayed in separate museums but sometimes clumped together as the **Musées du Cinquantenaire**.

Musée Art et Histoire

South side of the south wing of Cinquantenaire complex • Charge • Ⓦ kmkg-mrah.be

The **Musée Art et Histoire** is made up of a maddening maze of pottery, carvings, furniture, tapestries, glassware and paintings from around the world. There's almost too much to absorb in even a couple of visits, and there doesn't seem to be much of a plan, which makes it harder to select the bits that interest you most. There are, for example, enormous galleries of early Greek, Egyptian and Roman artefacts, an assortment of Far Eastern art and textiles, medieval and Renaissance carving and religious artefacts, and a wide collection of glasswork from all eras.

To the right of the entrance hall, set in part around the museum's neo-Gothic cloister, the European decorative arts galleries perhaps have the most immediacy. Highlights include some striking fifteenth- and sixteenth-century **altarpieces** from Antwerp, a prime collection of Brussels **tapestries** dating from the middle of the sixteenth century (the heyday of the city's tapestry industry), and an intriguing selection of scientific and precision instruments from the sixteenth century onwards. On the other side of the entrance hall, the **European collection** continues with turn-of-the-twentieth-century furnishings and an **Art Nouveau** section (Victor Horta designed the display cases for a firm of jewellers). Here, you'll find the celebrated *Mysterious Sphinx*, an ivory bust of archetypal Art Nouveau design – the work of Charles van der Stappen in 1897. On the same side of the museum, seek out the **Greek and Roman sections**. Among various statuary, pottery and other artefacts, you'll come across a fabulous mosaic depicting hunting scenes dating from the fifth century AD, which you can view from a balcony above. There's also a bronze of an emperor and a wonderful scale model of ancient Rome, again viewable from above. Nearby, a lovely gallery displays artefacts from the **Islamic world**, including Persian and Ottoman ceramics, carpets, manuscripts and all sorts of beautiful objects.

Autoworld

South wing of Le Cinquantenaire • Charge • Ⓦ autoworld.be

Housed in a vast hangar-like building, **Autoworld** is a chronological stroll through the short history of the automobile, with a huge display of **vintage vehicles** that begins with turn-of-the-twentieth-century motorised cycles and Model T Fords. European varieties predominate, with Peugeot, Renault and Benz well represented, and there are home-grown vehicles, too, including a Minerva from 1925 that once belonged to the Belgian monarch. American cars include early Cadillacs, a Lincoln from 1965 owned by the Belgian royals, and some gangster-style Oldsmobiles. Among the British brands, there's a mint-condition Rolls-Royce Silver Ghost from 1921, one of the first Austins and, from the modern era, the short-lived DeLorean sports car. Upstairs, you'll find a mishmash of assorted vehicles that don't fit into the main exhibition: early Porsches and Volvos, classic 1960s Jaguars and even a tuk-tuk from Thailand.

Musée Royal de l'Armée et d'Histoire Militaire

North wing of Le Cinquantenaire • Charge • Ⓦ klm-mra.be

The **Musée Royal de l'Armée et d'Histoire Militaire** traces the history of the 'Belgian' army from the late eighteenth century to the present day via a vast hoard of weapons,

1

armaments and uniforms. The **first part** of the collection is enjoyably old-fashioned, with a long series of glass cases holding a small army of life-sized model soldiers, with assorted rifles, swords and muskets nailed to the walls above. The sections dealing with 'Belgian' regiments in the Austrian and Napoleonic armies and the volunteers who formed the nucleus of the 1830 revolution are particularly interesting. Elsewhere, there's an excellent **World War I** display, with uniforms and kits from every nationality involved in the conflict and a fearsome array of field guns, artillery pieces and very primitive early tanks. A second, larger hall covers **World War II**, including the Belgian experience of collaboration and resistance, all illustrated by a superb selection of blown-up period photographs. The **courtyard** outside has a large collection of World War II tanks, armoured cars and artillery pieces – British, American and German. A third large **hall** dedicated to aviation holds an array of aircraft, some of which you can clamber aboard.

The outer neighbourhoods

Often neglected, the city's **outer neighbourhoods**, beyond the petit ring, hold a veritable platoon of alluring attractions. To the southeast, cobwebbed by tiny squares and narrow streets, the **St-Gilles** and **Ixelles** areas make a great escape from the razzmatazz of the city centre. **St-Gilles**, the smaller of the two *communes*, has patches of inner-city decay but is nicer the further east you go, its run-down streets giving way to attractive avenues and some of the city's best **Art Nouveau buildings**, including Victor Horta's own house and studio, now the glorious **Musée Victor Horta** (a UNESCO World Heritage Site). **Ixelles**, meanwhile, is one of the capital's most interesting and exciting neighbourhoods, with a diverse street life and an arty, bohemian vibe that has long drawn artists, writers and intellectuals – Karl Marx, Auguste Rodin and Alexandre Dumas all lived here. Ixelles is split in two by **avenue Louise**, a prosperous corridor laid out by Léopold II in the 1840s named after his eldest daughter. Some of Brussels' premier hotels, shops and boutiques flank the northern reaches of the avenue; further along it lies the enjoyable **Musée Constantin Meunier**, sited in the sculptor's old house. Northwest of the **Gare du Midi**, flanking the southwestern edge of the city centre, **Anderlecht** is best known for its football team. It remains a working-class neighbourhood, with one enjoyable, very Brussels attraction in the **Cantillon Brewery**. Northwest of the petit ring, **Jette** is a well-heeled suburb that might not merit a second glance if it weren't for the former home of René Magritte, now turned into the engaging **Musée René Magritte**, which pays detailed tribute to the artist, his family and friends. Just east of Jette and immediately north of the city centre, leafy **Laeken** is where the Belgian royal family hunker down. A short distance northwest of here lies **Heysel** with its trademark **Atomium** – a hand-me-down from the 1958 World's Fair. Finally, if you've got an insatiable appetite for the monuments of the Belgian royal family, then you should venture out east of the city to **Tervuren**, where King Léopold II built the massive **Musée Royal de l'Afrique Centrale** on the edge of the woods of the Forêt de Soignes. The museum was built to trumpet Belgium's colonial 'achievements' in the Congo and has been pushed to change its whole approach in recent years, rebranding itself as the **Africa Museum**.

Musée Victor Horta

rue Americaine 25 • Tues–Fri 2–5.30pm, Sat & Sun 11am–5.30pm • Charge • ⓦ hortamuseum.be • Tram Nos 92 or 97 to Janson

The principal sight in the **St-Gilles** neighbourhood is the delightful **Musée Victor Horta**, which occupies the two houses Horta designed as his home and studio at the end of the nineteenth century and was where he lived until 1919. The **exterior** sets the tone, a striking reworking of what was originally a modest terraced structure, the design fluidly incorporating knotted and twisted ironwork. Yet it is for his interiors that Horta is particularly famous, and **inside** is a sunny, sensuous dwelling exhibiting all the architect's favourite flourishes – wrought iron, stained glass, ornate furniture and panelling made from several different types of timber. The main unifying feature is the **staircase**, a dainty spiralling affair, which runs through the centre of the house illuminated by a large skylight. Decorated with painted motifs and surrounded by mirrors, it remains one of Horta's most magnificent and ingenious creations, giving access to a sequence of wide, bright rooms. Also of interest is the modest but enjoyable selection of **paintings**, many of which were given to Horta by friends and colleagues, including works by Félicien Rops and Joseph Heymans.

Musée Constantin Meunier

rue de l'Abbaye 59 • Free • ⊕ fine-arts-museum.be/en • Tram No. 93 from pl Louise to Abbaye

The **Musée Constantin Meunier** is housed on the ground floor of the former home and studio of Brussels-born artist **Constantin Meunier** (1831–1905), who lived here for the

HORTA'S PROGRESS

The son of a shoemaker, **Victor Horta** (1861–1947) was born in Ghent, where he failed in his first career and was expelled from the city's music conservatory for indiscipline. He promptly moved to Paris to study **architecture**, returning to Belgium in 1880 to complete his internship in Brussels with Alphonse Balat, architect to King Léopold II. Balat was a traditionalist, partly responsible for the classical facades of the Palais Royal – among many other prestigious projects – and Horta looked elsewhere for inspiration. He found it in the work of **William Morris**, the leading figure of the English Arts and Crafts movement, whose designs were key to the development of **Art Nouveau**. Taking its name from the Maison de l'Art Nouveau, a Parisian shop which sold items of modern design, Art Nouveau rejected the imitative architectures which were popular at the time – Neoclassical and neo-Gothic – in favour of an innovative style characterised by **sinuous, flowing lines**. In England, Morris and his colleagues had focused on book illustrations and furnishings, but Horta extrapolated the new style into architecture, experimenting with new building materials such as steel and concrete and traditional stone, glass and wood.

In 1893, Horta completed the curvaceous **Hôtel Tassel**, just off avenue Louise, Brussels' first Art Nouveau building (*hôtel* meaning 'townhouse'). Inevitably, there were howls of protest from the traditionalists, but no matter what his opponents said, Horta never lacked work again. The following years – roughly 1893 to 1905 – were Horta's most inventive and prolific. He designed over forty buildings, including the **Hôtel Solvay** (see page 70), the **Hôtel Max Hallet**, and his own beautifully decorated house and studio, now the **Musée Victor Horta**. The delight Horta took in his work is obvious, especially when employed on private houses, and his enthusiasm was all-encompassing – he almost always designed everything from the blueprints to the wallpaper and carpets. He never kept a straight line or sharp angle where he could deploy a curve, and his **use of light** was revolutionary, often filtering through from above, with skylights and as many windows as possible. Horta felt that the architect was as much an artist as the painter or sculptor, so he insisted on complete stylistic freedom. Curiously, he also believed that originality was born of **frustration**, so he deliberately created architectural difficulties, pushing himself to find harmonious solutions. His value system allied him with the **political Left** – as he wrote, 'My friends and I were reds, without however having thought about Marx or his theories.' Completed in 1906, the **Grand Magasin Waucquez** (see page 57) department store was a transitional building signalling the end of Horta's Art Nouveau period. His later works were more **Modernist** constructions, whose understated lines were a far cry from the ornateness of his earlier work. In Brussels, the best example is the **Palais des Beaux Arts** (BOZAR) of 1928 (see pages 61 and 88).

ST-GILLES, AVENUE LOUISE AND IXELLES

ACCOMMODATION
Argus	1
Made in Louise	4
Steigenberger Wiltcher's	2
Zoom	3

EATING
Dolma	3
La Quincaillerie	5
Sale Pepe Rosmarino	2
Volle Gas	1
Le Waterloo	4

DRINKING
Brasserie Verschueren	5
Café Belga	6
Café Maison du Peuple	4
Moeder Lambic	8
La Porteuse d'Eau	3
L'Ultime Atome	1

NIGHTLIFE
Flagey	7
Sounds Jazz Club	2

SHOPPING
Beer Mania	1

– – – Commune Boundaries

1

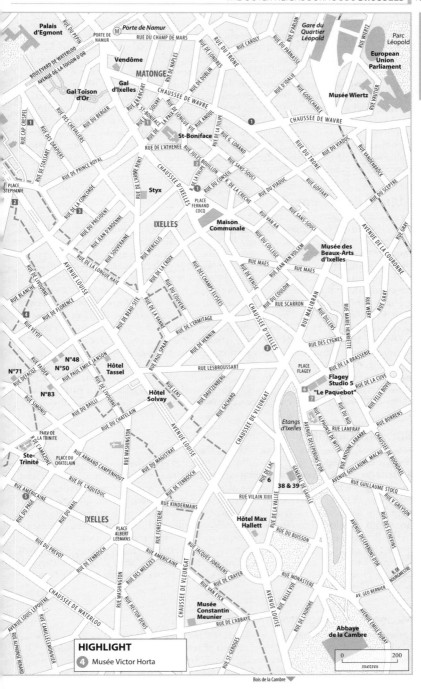

Palais d'Egmont
Porte de Namur
Gare du Quartier Léopold
Parc Léopold
PORTE DE NAMUR
RUE DU CHAMP DE MARS
European Union Parliament
BOULEVARD DE WATERLOO
AVENUE DE LA TOISON D'OR
Vendôme
RUE DE NAPLES
RUE DE DUBLIN
RUE DE LONDRES
RUE DU TRONE
RUE CAROLY
RUE DU PARNASSE
RUE DJARON
RUE WIERTZ
RUE VAUTIER
MATONGE
Gal Toison d'Or
Gal d'Ixelles
CHAUSSEE DE WAVRE
RUE D'IDALIE
RUE GODECHARLE
Musée Wiertz
RUE CAP CRESPEL
RUE DES CHEVALIERS
RUE DU BERGER
RUE ERNANCART
RUE ST-BONIFACE
RUE SOLVAY
RUE DE LONGUE VIE
RUE ANOUL
CHAUSSEE DE WAVRE
St-Boniface
RUE DE LA TULIPE
RUE G. LORAND
RUE DU VIADUC
RUE VANDERMOCK
RUE DU SCEPTRE
RUE DES DRAPIERS
RUE DE STASSART
RUE DE PRINCE ROYAL
RUE DE L'ATHENEE
RUE JULES BOUILLON
RUE DE LA PAIX
RUE SANS-SOUCI
RUE DU TRONE
PLACE STEPHANIE
RUE DE LA CONCORDE
RUE DE L'ARBRE BENIT
Styx
CHAUSSEE D'IXELLES
RUE DE LA TULIPE
RUE DU CONSEIL
K. DE LA CRECHE
RUE DU VIADUC
RUE GOFFART
RUE DU PRESIDENT
PLACE FERNAND COCQ
RUE VAN AA
RUE SANS-SOUCI
AVENUE DE LA COURONNE
RUE GRAY
IXELLES
Maison Communale
RUE DU COLLEGE
RUE JEAN VAN VOLSEM
Musée des Beaux-Arts d'Ixelles
RUE JEAN D'ARDENNE
RUE MERCELIS
RUE DE LA CROIX
RUE MAES
RUE MAES
RUE DE LA LONGUE HAIE
AVENUE LOUISE
RUE DE LA VANNE
RUE DES CHAMPS-ELYSEES
RUE DE VENISE
RUE DU COULOIR
RUE SCARRON
RUE MALIBRAN
RUE DILLENS
RUE MARIE HENRIETTE
RUE WERY
RUE GRAY
RUE BLANCHE
RUE L'IVOIRNE
RUE DE FLORENCE
RUE DE BEAU-SITE
RUE DU COUVENT
RUE DE L'ERMITAGE
CHAUSSEE D'IXELLES
RUE DES CYGNES
RUE DE LA BRASSERIE
RUE VEYDT
RUE DE HENNIN
RUE PAUL SPAAK
RUE LESBROUSSART
PLACE FLAGEY
RUE FLAGEY
RUE DE LA CUVE
Flagey Studio 5
"Le Paquebot"
N°71
N°48
N°50
RUE PAUL EMILE JANSON
Hôtel Tassel
RUE FAIDER
RUE DEFACQZ
RUE DE L'IVOIRNE
RUE DAUTZENBERG
RUE LENS
RUE DU NID
RUE ELLA BORTE
RUE BORRENS
N°83
RUE SIMONIS
RUE DU BAILLI
Hôtel Solvay
RUE GACHARD
Etangs d'Ixelles
RUE LANFRAY
PARV DE LA TRINITE
RUE DU CHATELAIN
RUE L'AMAZONE
AVENUE LOUISE
CHAUSSEE DE VLEURGAT
AVENUE ALPHONSE DE WITTE
AVENUE ANTOINE LABARRE
CHAUSSEE DE BOONDAEL
Ste-Trinité
RUE ARMAND CAMPENHOUT
PLACE DU CHATELAIN
RUE DU MAGISTRAT
AVENUE DESPERONS D'OR
AVENUE GUILLAUME MACAU
RUE GUILLAUME STOCQ
RUE DE L'AQUEDUC
RUE DE TENBOSCH
6
RUE DE LAC
38 & 39
GENERAL DE GAULLE
RUE V GREYSON
RUE AMERICAINE
RUE KINDERMANS
RUE VILAIN XIIII
RUE DU PAGE
RUE DU MAIL
IXELLES
PLACE ALBERT LEEMANS
RUE FORESTIERE
Hôtel Max Hallett
RUE DU BUISSON
AVENUE DESPERONS D'OR
RUE DES ECHEVINS
RUE DU PREVOT
RUE DE TENBOSCH
RUE AMERICAINE
RUE JACQUES JORDAENS
RUE MONASTERE
RUE DE BOURGMESTRE
CHAUSSEE DE WATERLOO
RUE WASHINGTON
RUE HECTOR DENIS
RUE DES MELEZES
CHAUSSEE DE VLEURGAT
RUE DE CRAYER
RUE VAN EYCK
AVENUE LOUISE
RUE BELLE VUE
RUE DE L'AURORE
AV. GEO BERNIER
AVENUE LOUIS LEPOUTRE
Musée Constantin Meunier
RUE DE L'ABBAYE
Abbaye de la Cambre
AVENUE EMILE DURAY
RUE ST-GEORGES

HIGHLIGHT

4 Musée Victor Horta

0 ___ 200
metres

1

last six years of his life. Meunier began as a painter, but it's as a sculptor that he's best remembered, and the museum has a substantial collection of his dark and brooding bronzes. The largest and most important pieces are in the old studio at the back, where a series of **life-size bronzes** of muscular men with purposeful faces stand around looking heroic – *Le Faucheur* (The Reaper), *Un Semeur* (A Sower) and *Le Marteleur* (The Metalworker) – and **oil paintings** depict gritty industrial scenes like the coalfield of *Black Country Borinage* and the gloomy dockside of *The Port*, one of Meunier's most forceful works. Meunier was angered by the dreadful living conditions of Belgium's working class, particularly (like Van Gogh before him) the harsh life of the coal miners of the Borinage. This anger fuelled his art, which asserted the dignity of the worker in a style that was to be copied by the Social Realists of his and later generations. According to historian Eric Hobsbawm's *Age of Empire*, 'Meunier invented the international stereotype of the sculptured proletarian'.

Abbaye de la Cambre

Av E Duray/Av de Mot • Free • Tram No. 93 to Abbaye

The postcard-pretty **Abbaye de la Cambre** nestles in a lovely little wooded dell just to the east of avenue Louise and not far from the Meunier Museum. Of medieval foundation, the abbey was suppressed by the French Revolutionary Army at the beginning of the nineteenth century; however, its eighteenth-century brick buildings survived pretty much untouched and, after much toing and froing, ended up as **government offices**. An extensive complex, the main courtyard is especially attractive and serves as the main entrance to the charming **Notre-Dame de l'Abbaye church**, whose nave, with its barrel vaulting and rough stone walls, is an exercise in simplicity. The church is an amalgamation of styles, but Gothic predominates except in the furnishings of the nave, where carefully carved **Art Deco** wooden panelling frames a set of religious paintings of the Stations of the Cross. The church also holds **Albert Bouts**' tiny *Mocking of Christ*, a marvellous, early sixteenth-century **painting** in the left aisle that depicts a mournful, blood-spattered Jesus. A small cloister is attached to the church, and lovely walled, terraced gardens surround the abbey buildings – an oasis of peace away from the hubbub of avenue Louise.

Brasserie Cantillon

rue Gheude 56 • Charge • ⓦ cantillon.be • Métro Nos 2 or 6 to Clemenceau

A short walk north of the Gare du Midi, in the heart of the working-class district of **Anderlecht**, the **Brasserie Cantillon** is one of the city's more popular attractions and the only place in Brussels that still makes the local brew according to traditional methods. The beer concerned – otherwise known as **lambic beer** or **gueuze** (see box, page 343) – is a sour, almost cidery concoction made only with water, barley and hops, and it's allowed to ferment naturally, reacting with the natural yeasts present in the Brussels air; it's also bottled two years before it is ready to drink. You can do a quick **tour** of the mustily atmospheric brewery (best outside summer months when they make the beer) and taste afterwards in the comfy bar area. Plus, of course, you can buy bottles to take home; there is perhaps no better souvenir of Brussels than a bottle of Cantillon gueuze.

Musée René Magritte

rue Esseghem 135, Jette • Charge • ⓦ magrittemuseum.be • Tram No. 51 from the city centre to the Woeste stop, then a 5min walk

Northwest of the city centre, in the suburb of **Jette**, the enthralling **Musée René Magritte** holds many of the Surrealist's paraphernalia and a limited collection of his early **paintings** and **sketches**. Magritte (see box, page 65) lived with his wife

Georgette on the ground floor of this modest house for 24 years from 1930, an idiosyncratic location for what was effectively the **headquarters** of the **Surrealist** movement in Belgium, most of whose leading lights met here every Saturday to concoct a battery of subversive books, magazines and images.

The ground floor

The **ground floor** has been faithfully restored to re-create the artist's studio and living quarters, using mostly original ornaments and furniture, with the remainder carefully replicated from photographs; the famous **bowler hat** which crops up in several of Magritte's paintings is hung near the indoor studio. Many features of the house itself also appear in a number of his works: the sash window, for instance, framed the painting entitled *The Human Condition*, while the glass doors to the sitting room and bedroom appeared in *The Invisible World*. Magritte built himself a studio – which he named **Dongo** – in the garden, and it was here that he produced his bread-and-butter work, such as graphics and posters, though he was usually unhappy when working on such mundane projects, and his real passions were painted in the **dining-room studio**, where he displayed just one work by another artist – a photo by Man Ray – which is there again today.

The first and second floors

You have to don shoe covers to visit the **first and second floors** of the house, which were separate apartments when the Magrittes lived here but are now taken up by letters, photos, telegrams, lithographs, posters and sketches pertaining to the artist, all displayed in chronological order. There are two fine posters announcing the international film and fine arts festivals which took place in Brussels in 1947 and 1949, as well as Magritte's **first painting**, a naive landscape which he produced at the tender age of 12, the blue rug he had made for the bedroom and work by other Surrealists. Finally, there are a number of **personal objects** displayed in the **attic** (which he rented), including the easel he used at the end of his life. Overall, it's a fascinating glimpse into the life of one of the most influential artists of the twentieth century.

Musée d'Art Abstrait

rue Esseghem 137, Jette • Charge • ⓦ magrittemuseum.be • Tram No. 51 from the city centre to the Woeste stop, then a 5min walk

Next door to the Musée René Magritte, the mildly engaging **Musée d'Art Abstrait** (Abstract Art Museum) holds a substantial collection of abstract paintings – about 250 are on display at any one time. Most of the paintings are by Belgians, with the likes of Servranckx, Vantongerloo, Alechinsky, Rets and Delahaut leading the way.

Laeken

Serres Royales av du Parc Royal 61 • Charge • ⓦ monarchie.be • Métro No. 6 to Bockstael then bus No. 53 to Serres Royales

To the north of Brussels' city centre, **Laeken** is home to the Belgian royal family, who hunker down at the **Château Royal**. Built in 1790, its most famous occupant was Napoleon, who stayed several times and signed the declaration of war against Russia here in 1812. You can't visit the palace itself, but for three weeks every year, they open up the **Serres Royales** (royal greenhouses) for public visits (reservations required) – worth doing not just for the plants but for the magnificent structures themselves. Be warned, though, that the queues can be lengthy at weekends. Opposite the front of the royal palace, a wide **footpath** leads up to the fanciful neo-Gothic **monument** erected in honour of Léopold I, the focal point of the pretty **Parc de Laeken**. The park's glorious woods, grassy meadows, lawns and wooded thickets extend northwest for a couple of kilometres towards Heysel. They are well worth a stroll and a picnic, particularly if you're en route to the Atomium.

1

The Atomium

pl de l'Atomium • Charge • ⓦ atomium.be • Métro Heysel

Most visitors come to the northern peripheries of Brussels to see the **Atomium**, a curious model of a molecule expanded 165 billion times. Built for the 1958 World's Fair in Brussels, it has never quite become the symbol of the city it was intended to be, but after restoration a few years ago, it is looking better than it has for some time. **Visits** are in two parts: the lift whizzes you up to the top sphere for the views, you descend and then make your way back up to take in the other three spheres, which are reached by a mixture of escalators and stairs. It's all pleasingly retro – the Atomium was quite a feat of technology in its day (its elevator was the world's fastest, the escalator connecting the spheres the world's longest), and its construction is remembered by apposite photos. There's not much to see – the spheres are mainly given over to **temporary exhibitions**, and trudging up and down the stairs and escalators can turn into a bit of a slog – but it's an undeniably impressive sight overall. The views from the top are as panoramic as you would expect (enhanced by computer screens pointing out what you're looking at). While you're here, it's worth checking out the **Design Museum** on place de Belgique (charge; ⓦdesignmuseum. brussels), which celebrates plastic art and design of the twentieth century and holds interesting temporary exhibitions.

Musée Africa

Leuvensesteenweg 13 • Charge • ⓦ africamuseum.be/en • Tram No. 44 (1–2 hourly; 25min) from Métro Montgomery; the museum is a 2min walk from the tram terminus – and some 10km east of the Parc du Cinquantenaire along av de Tervueren

The **Musée Africa** occupies grandiose premises in the well-heeled suburb of Tervuren, on the edge of the vast expanse of the **Forêt de Soignies**. A monument to Belgium's colonial past, the museum started as the **Musée Royal de l'Afrique Centrale**, a pet project of that most savage of Belgian colonialists, **King Léopold II**, who was personally presented with the vast **Congo River basin** by a conference of the European Powers in 1885. Léopold's initial attempts to secure control of the area were aided and abetted by the explorer – and ex-Confederate soldier – **Henry Stanley**, who went to the Congo on a five-year fact-finding mission in 1879, just a few years after he had famously found the missionary David Livingstone (1813–73). Léopold made the most of his colonial assets, becoming one of the world's wealthiest men. However, even by the standards of the colonial powers of the day, his Congo regime was too chaotic and extraordinarily cruel to countenance. In the event, a British diplomat by the name of **Roger Casement** (1864–1916) played a leading role in exposing the barbarity and banditry of Léopold's Congo – the same Casement whom the British hanged for his involvement in the Easter Rising of 1916 (an armed revolt against the British government in Ireland). In 1908, the Belgian government was finally shamed into taking over the territory and installed a marginally more efficient state bureaucracy. Nonetheless, when the Belgian Congo gained independence as the **Republic of Congo** in 1960, it was poorly prepared, and its subsequent history (as both Zaire and the Republic of Congo) has been one of the most bloodstained in Africa.

Some of the booty looted from the Congo by Léopold II was brought back to the Musée Royal de L'Afrique Centrale, where it was presented in a colonialist and racist manner until a long-warranted 2013–18 refit brought the museum a more enlightened approach. It's an undeniably rich collection, part ethnographic and part natural history, that covers many aspects of domestic Congolese life. There are displays on clothing, furniture, tools and musical instruments, plus an impressive array of dope pipes and a superb 60m long dugout canoe that is some three hundred years old. Other displays get to grips with Congolese culture and ritual, with nail sculptures, masks, sculptures and busts, whilst others tell the sad and bitter story of colonisation through photos, maps and documents. There are ancient shots of Stanley and later ones of Baudouin, the Belgian king, visiting Leopoldville for the independence celebrations when his ill-conceived speech infuriated several Congolese leaders.

ARRIVAL AND DEPARTURE   BRUSSELS

Brussels is served by Belgium's busiest international airport and is on the main routes heading inland from the Channel ports via Flanders. Eurostar trains arrive here directly from London, and the city is a convenient stop on the fast train line between France and Holland. The city has an excellent transport system that puts all the main points of arrival – its airport, train and bus stations – within easy reach of the centre.

BY PLANE

BRUSSELS AIRPORT
Most flights to Brussels land at the city's international airport (ⓦ brusselsairport.be) – known as Brussels International – in the satellite suburb of Zaventem, 14km northeast of the city centre. Trains run from Brussels International to the city's three main stations (4 hourly, 5.30am–midnight); the journey to Bruxelles-Centrale takes just over a quarter of an hour and costs about €10.80 each way. There are also direct buses into the city centre from the airport's bus station, located one floor below the arrivals hall. The most useful service is the hourly No. 12 (Mon–Fri 5.40am–7.48pm), which runs to pl de Luxembourg in the EU Quarter, stopping off at Schuman and other métro stops along the way, though note that on weekends, and during the week after 8pm, this becomes the slower bus No. 21. Outside of these times, you'll need to take a taxi to the city centre (20min), for which you'll pay around €55, though less if you order one in advance.

BRUSSELS-CHARLEROI AIRPORT
Some airlines – principally Ryanair – fly to Brussels-Charleroi Airport (ⓦ brussels-charleroi-airport.com/en/), sometimes called Brussels South, though it is some 50km south of central Brussels. This secondary airport is rapidly expanding and has a reasonable range of facilities. From the airport, there is a shuttle bus service to the city centre (every 30min, 7.50am–11.59pm; 1hr; ⓦ flibco.com/en), departing from outside the terminal building and dropping off at the bus stop on the west side of Bruxelles-Midi train station at the junction of rue de France and rue de l'Instruction. Alternatively, you can take a local bus (every 30min; 20min) from the airport to Charleroi Sud train station, where there are regular services to all three of Brussels' main stations (every 30min, hourly on Sat & Sun; 50min). A taxi into Brussels city centre will cost around €90.

BY TRAIN
Stations Brussels has three main stations (see box, page 79). Most domestic trains stop at all three, but many international services only stop at Bruxelles-Midi, including Eurostar trains from London and express trains from Amsterdam, Paris, Cologne and Aachen. Bruxelles-Centrale is, as its name suggests, the most central of the stations, located a short walk from the Grand-Place; Bruxelles-Nord lies among the bristling tower blocks of the business area just north of the main ring road; and Bruxelles-Midi is situated in a slightly depressed area on the southern edge of the city centre.

Transfers If you need to transfer from one of the three main train stations to another, simply jump on the next available main line train; services between them run every 10min or so, the journey only takes minutes, and all you'll have to do (at most) is swap platforms. You can find lots of information in English on the Belgian Railways (SNCB/NMBS) website (ⓦ belgianrail.be).

Destinations Amsterdam Centraal Station (hourly; 2hr 30min); Antwerp (every 20min; 40min); Bruges (every 20min; 1hr); Charleroi (every 20min; 50min); Ghent (every 20min; 35min); Mechelen (every 15min; 25min); Leuven (every 15min; 25min); Liège (every 30min; 1hr 20min); Luxembourg (every 30min; 3hr); Mons (every 30min; 50min); Namur (several hourly; 1hr); Ostend (every 20min; 1hr 20min).

TRAIN STATION NAMES
When you first arrive, the city's **bilingual signage** can be confusing, especially with regard to the names of the **three main train stations**: Bruxelles-Nord (in Flemish Brussel-Noord), Bruxelles-Centrale (Brussel-Centraal) and, most bewildering of the lot, Bruxelles-Midi (Brussel-Zuid). To add to the puzzle, each of the three adjoins a **métro station** – respectively, the Gare du Nord (Noord station), Gare Centrale (Centraal Station) and Gare du Midi (Zuid station). And in an extra twist of unhelpfulness, note that on **bus timetables** and **maps of the city transit system** (including the one in this book), Bruxelles-Nord usually appears as 'Gare du Nord', Bruxelles-Centrale as 'Gare Centrale' and Bruxelles-Midi as 'Gare du Midi', taking the names of their respective métro stops.

1

BRUSSELS MÉTRO AND PRÉMÉTRO

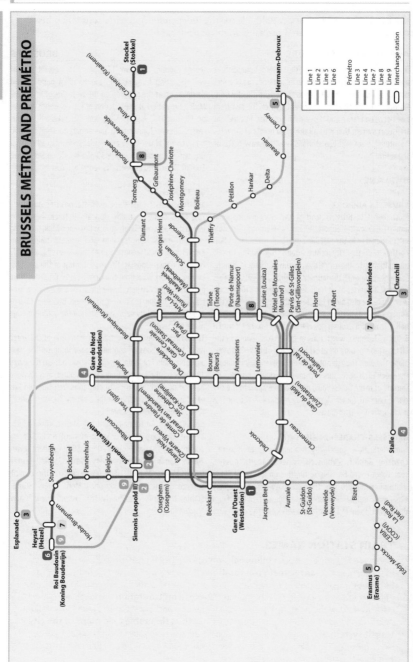

BY BUS

Most international bus services to Brussels, including FlixBus from Britain, use the Bruxelles-Nord station complex as their terminus. Belgium's comprehensive rail network means that it's unlikely that you'll arrive in the city by long-distance domestic bus, but if you do, then Bruxelles-Nord is the main terminal for these services, too.

GETTING AROUND

Operated by STIB-MIVB (Ⓦ stib-mivb.be; information line ☎ 070 23 2000), the city's **public transport** system comprises an integrated mixture of **bus**, **tram**, **underground tram** and **métro** lines that cover the city comprehensively. It's a user-friendly network, with every métro station carrying métro system diagrams, **route maps** available online and free from most major métro stations, and **timetables** posted or signed at most bus and tram stops.

Tickets Valid on any part of the STIB system; paper tickets (single/€2.50; 24hr/€8) are available from métro kiosks, automatic machines at métro stations and from newsagents displaying the STIB-MIVB sign. At the beginning of each journey, you're trusted to stamp tickets yourself, using one of the machines on every métro station concourse or inside every tram and bus. After that, the ticket is valid for an hour, during which you can get on and off as many trams, métros and buses as you like.

Fares and travel cards The most convenient way to travel if you're around for more than a day or so is to invest in a MOBIB card, a credit-card-style pass that you can purchase at any métro station for €5 plus as much credit as you want. You can then add credit to it using the machines and, at the end of your visit, either keep the card or return it and get your €5 back. Travelling with a MOBIB card is a little cheaper than travelling with a paper ticket.

BY MÉTRO, PRÉMÉTRO OR TRAM

The métro system consists of six partly underground lines, though to a considerable extent they overlap. The city also has a substantial tram system serving the centre and its suburbs. These trams are at their speediest when they go underground to form what is sometimes called the prémétro, which runs as lines Nos 3 and 4 right beneath the heart of the city from Bruxelles-Nord, through De Brouckère and Bourse to Bruxelles-Midi, Porte de Hal and on into St-Gilles. Times of operation and frequency vary considerably, but key parts of the system operate from 6am until midnight.

BY BUS

Trams and the métro are supplemented by a network of buses, particularly a limited night bus service on major routes. Again, timetable info is available in real-time on the STIB website. In addition, De Lijn (Ⓦ delijn.be) runs buses from the city to the Flemish-speaking communities surrounding the capital, while TEC (Ⓦ letec.be) operates services to the French-speaking areas. Most of these buses run from, or at least call in at, the Gare du Nord complex.

BY LOCAL TRAIN

Local trains, run by Belgian Railways (Ⓦ belgianrail.be), supplement the STIB network. They shuttle in and out of the city's seven train stations, connecting parts of the inner city and the outskirts. However, unless you live and work in the city, you most likely won't need to use them.

BY BICYCLE

The city council operates an excellent public bicycle scheme (Ⓦ villo.be) in which bikes can be taken from stands dotted across the city centre and returned after use to another. There are 350 stands in total, and rates are very reasonable.

BY TAXI

Taxis don't cruise the streets but can be picked up at stands around the city, notably outside the main train stations. The fixed tariff consists of two main elements: a fixed charge of €5 (more at night) and the price per kilometre (€1.94 inside the city). If you can't find a taxi, phone Taxis Verts on ☎ 02 349 49 49 or Taxis Bleus on ☎ 02 268 00 00.

INFORMATION

At the **international airport**, you'll find a tourist information desk (daily 8am–9pm) in the arrivals hall, with a reasonable range of blurbs on the city, including free maps. The city's main tourist office is in the **Hôtel de Ville** on the Grand-Place (daily 9am–6pm; Ⓦ visit.brussels). They issue free city and transport **maps**, have details of forthcoming events and concerts, make reservations on **guided tours** (see box, page 82) and sell the **Brussels Card** (see box, page 47). If you're heading off into Flemish-speaking Belgium you can pick up oodles of information at **Tourism Flanders**, metres from the Grand-Place at rue du Marché aux Herbes 61 (Mon–Sat daily 9am–5pm; Ⓦ visitflanders.com).

ACCOMMODATION

With approaching one hundred **hotels** dotted within its central ring of boulevards, Brussels has no shortage of convenient places to stay. Even so, finding accommodation can still prove challenging, particularly in the **spring** and **autumn**, when the capital enjoys what amounts to its **high seasons**, during which it's essential to book ahead

1

of time. Hotel prices vary hugely, but as the accommodation scene is dominated by business, you can almost always expect rates to be much **lower at weekends** – many of the city's higher-end hotels half their rates. In **high summer**, they're much cheaper during the week when the EU pretty much shuts up shop.

THE LOWER AND UPPER TOWN, SEE MAPS PAGES 49 AND 54

9Hotel Central rue des Colonies 10 w 9-hotel-central-brussels.be; Métro Gare Centrale. This hip hotel boasts white, minimalist rooms with exposed brickwork. Rooms are equipped with beverage trays, and the beds are particularly comfortable. There's also a 24hr bar and co-working space. Check out the weekend and summer offers online, which include breakfast. €€€

★ **Amigo** rue de l'Amigo 1–3 w roccofortehotels.com; Métro Gare Centrale or Bourse. This lavish five-star Rocco Forte hotel must be Brussels' most desirable place to stay, with impeccable service and a fabulous location just around the corner from the Grand-Place. The building dates from the sixteenth century and has seen several incarnations, including the town prison, only becoming a hotel in the 1950s. Rooms are tasteful and contemporary in all-natural hues enhanced with splashes of colour. The superb *Bocconi* restaurant serves some of the best Italian food in Brussels. €€€

Atlas rue du Vieux Marché-aux-Grains 30 w atlas-hotel.be/en/; Métro Ste-Catherine. Inserted behind the handsome stone facade of a nineteenth-century mansion in the heart of the Ste-Catherine district, this modern three-star hotel is within an easy walk of the Grand-Palace. The 88 rooms are a (slight) cut above those of the average chain. Wheelchair accessible. €€€

Bruegel rue du Saint-Esprit 2 w jeugdherbergen.be/en; Métro Gare Centrale. This official HI hostel, which occupies a functional modern building in a good location by the church of Notre-Dame de la Chapelle, is a popular spot, boasting both dorms and private rooms with bunks. A basic breakfast is included. Dorms €, doubles €

Du Congrès rue du Congrès 42 w hotelducongres.be; Métro Madou. Pleasant mid-range hotel occupying a set of attractive late nineteenth-century townhouses in an appealing corner of the Upper Town. Each of the 67 en-suite rooms is spacious and decorated in an unfussy style. €€€

★ **Le Dixseptième** rue de la Madeleine 25 w le dixseptieme.be; Métro Gare Centrale. This place tries hard to be central Brussels' most elegant boutique hotel, with just 24 deluxe rooms and suites, and more or less pulls it off. Half are in the tastefully renovated seventeenth-century mansion at the front, the remainder in the new extension behind. There's a lovely downstairs sitting room and bar with comfy sofas to sink into, and the rooms themselves have a grand yet homely feel – all very soothing and a real antidote to the mayhem outside. It's much less expensive than you might expect. €€€

The Dominican rue Léopold 9 w thedominican.be; Métro De Brouckère or Bourse. This deluxe four-star boasts a prime location close to the Grand-Place and a claim to fame as the place where the painter Jacques-Louis David drew his last breath in 1825 – look for the plaque on the facade. The spacious foyer sets the funky, stylish tone, as do the generous banquettes in the courtyard-style breakfast/restaurant area behind. Beyond, all 150 rooms are well-appointed and stylishly kitted out with wooden floors and earthy tones. Breakfast included. €€€

L'Esperance rue du Finistère 1 w hotel-esperance.be; Métro De Brouckere. This pleasant Art Deco bar has seventeen en-suite rooms upstairs, all very nicely furnished in a fresh style, with flatscreen TVs and lovely big bathrooms with walk-in power showers. They also put on a decent buffet breakfast. Extremely good value. €€

Jacques Brel rue de la Sablonnière 30 w lesaubergesde jeunesse.be; Métro Madou or Botanique. This official HI hostel is modern and comfortable, with a hotel-like atmosphere. All the rooms have showers, and breakfast is included in the price. There's no curfew, and inexpensive meals can be bought at the café. Reservations advised. Dorms €, doubles €

La Légende rue du Lombard 35 w hotellalegende.com; Métro Bourse. Set around a small courtyard, this old mansion is centrally located but enjoys a pleasant, tucked-away feel. All 26 rooms have en-suite facilities and TVs, and the decor, albeit a bit bland, is crisp and modern. €€

★ **Meininger Brussels City Center** quai de Hainaut 33 w meininger-hotels.com; Métro Comte de Flandre. Housed in a former brewery next to the canal, a short walk west of fashionable rue Antoine Dansaert, this hip hostel is an excellent budget option. Its 750 beds are set over four floors in bright, contemporary dorms and rooms. The bar is a popular meeting place, plus there's a games zone, too. Dorms €, doubles €€

Métropole pl de Brouckère 31 ⓦ metropolehotel.com; Métro De Brouckère. Dating from 1895, this grand five-star has long been one of Brussels' finest hotels, famous for the exquisite Art Nouveau decor in its public areas. At the time of writing, the *Métropole* is closed for a thoroughgoing revamp, with a grand reopening promised for 2025. €€€€

★ **Motel One** rue Royale 120 ⓦ motel-one.com; Métro Park. Very popular budget design hotel a 10min walk northeast of Grand-Place. The minimalist white rooms have turquoise and chocolate-coloured furnishings and are comfortable enough for a few days. There's an outdoor terrace, a stylish bar and a copious breakfast buffet. It is probably the overall best-value hotel in the centre; book well ahead. €€

NH Grand Sablon rue Bodenbroek 2–4 ⓦ nh-hotels. com; Métro Gare Centrale or Porte de Namur. Perfectly situated in the Sablon neighbourhood and a bigger hotel than you might think from the outside, with nearly two hundred rooms, the *Grand Sablon* is comfy and welcoming, with stylish, modern rooms. The café serves tapas, while the restaurant, *Hispania*, specialises in avant-garde Spanish cuisine. €€€

nhow Brussels Bloom rue Royale 250 ⓦ nh-hotels. com; Métro Botanique. This is a good-value business hotel with a self-consciously cool vibe. Its three hundred rooms are furnished with a clean, modern feel and incorporate nice touches, such as the hand-drawn mural behind each bed. They have a great breakfast buffet (you can make waffles if you're inclined), and the restaurant offers a good-value three-course lunch menu. €€€

Le Quinze Grand-Place 15 ⓦ hotel-le-quinze-grand-place.be; Métro Bourse. The only hotel to look out over the Grand-Place, this small, friendly establishment occupies an old guild house on the square's east side. Formerly the *Hôtel St Michel*, the fifteen rooms have been given a contemporary makeover with a Fifties feel. Breakfast is taken downstairs at the *'t Kelderke* café. If you're not a light sleeper (the revellers on the Grand-Place can make a real racket), treat yourself to one of the slightly more expensive rooms at the back. €€€

Sleep Well rue du Damier 23 ⓦ sleepwell.be; Métro Rogier. Bright and breezy hostel close to the city centre and only a 5min walk from pl Rogier. Hotel-style facilities plus a kitchen, bike rental and free walking tours. The 'Star' rooms have TVs and fridges, and there are 'Duplex' rooms for families. Dorms €, doubles €

★ **St-Géry** pl St-Géry 29–32 ⓦ hotelstgery.com; Métro Bourse. Situated right on pl St-Géry, so arguably enjoying one of the coolest locations in Brussels, this tall townhouse has 24 rooms, each done out with edgy, arty decor. They vary quite a lot in size and shape, and the ones at the front can inevitably be a bit noisy at weekends, but all are well-furnished and sleek, and most have baths. There's a restaurant and bar here too. €€€

La Vieille Lanterne rue des Grands Carmes 29 ⓦ la vieillelanterne.com; Métro Bourse. This tiny, family-run, one-star *pension*, tucked away above a souvenir shop overlooking the Manneken Pis, is perhaps the cheapest place to stay in the centre. It's certainly nothing special, but its handful of boxy rooms are perfectly adequate. Simply furnished, each comes with a shower and TV. There's free wi-fi throughout, and breakfast – included in the price – is brought up to your room. €€

ST GILLES, AVENUE LOUISE AND IXELLES, SEE MAP PAGE 74

Argus rue Capitaine Crespel 6 ⓦ argus-hotel-brussels. com; Métro Louise. This pleasant and straightforward three-star hotel has a good location, just to the south of the boulevards of the petit ring. The forty-or-so modest guest rooms can be a bit on the small side, but they're cosy enough, and the service is impeccable. It is a nice alternative to the gargantuan, expensive hotels that pepper this district. Breakfast included. €€

★ **Made in Louise** rue Veydt 40 ⓦ madeinlouise. com; Métro Louise. Very nice family-run boutique hotel in an early twentieth-century townhouse in an Art Nouveau district, about a 10min walk southwest of pl Louise. The high-ceilinged rooms are bright and airy; some have fireplaces. There's a courtyard with a giant chess set, and the bar serves organic Belgian beers and has a pool table. Delicious home-made breakfasts are served in the conservatory. €€€

Steigenberger Wiltcher's av Louise 71 ⓦ steigenberger.com; Métro Louise. Formerly the *Conrad*, this remains one of the capital's top hotels and the choice of many a visiting VIP. Housed in an immaculate tower block with all sorts of retro flourishes, it boasts 267 large and lavish rooms, comprehensive facilities and impeccable service. €€€€

★ **Zoom** rue de la Concorde 59 ⓦ zoomhotel.be; Métro Louise. Hip boutique hotel in an old townhouse on a quiet side street near the top of av Louise. The 37 'industrial chic' rooms come in two sizes: opt for a larger one with a metal four-poster. All rooms feature photos of Brussels created by a local artist. There's a good spread at breakfast, and the bar has more than fifty Belgian beers on the menu and, pleasingly, chocolates. €€

EU QUARTER, SEE MAP PAGE 68

Leopold rue du Luxembourg 35 ⓦ hotel-leopold.be; Métro Trône. If you're staying in the EU Quarter, it's easy to get stuck beside a thundering boulevard, but this neat and trim, family-run four-star hotel has a first-rate location on a quiet(ish) side street, a brief walk from pl du Luxembourg. There are over a hundred guest rooms, all in a no-nonsense, modern style. €€€

1

EATING

Brussels can lay a fair claim to being one of Europe's best dining destinations, regardless of your taste, price range or preferred cuisine. In particular, it's worth seeking out typically **Bruxellois** dishes, canny amalgamations of Walloon and Flemish ingredients and cooking styles, whether rabbit cooked in beer (usually Gueuze), *poulet à la Bruxelles*, fish or chicken *waterzooi*, or just plain *saucisses à la stoemp*. As for **where** to eat, as in the rest of Belgium, the distinction between the city's cafés, café-bars and restaurants is pretty elastic: there are particular concentrations of bars and restaurants on and around pl Ste-Catherine and pl St-Géry in the **Lower Town**, but there are decent places to eat everywhere.

THE LOWER AND UPPER TOWN, SEE MAPS PAGES 49 AND 54

★ **Aksum Coffee House** Galerie du Roi 3, Galeries St-Hubert ⓦ facebook.com/AksumCoffee; Métro Gare Centrale. A short walk from the Grand-Place, this little café is regarded as serving the best coffee in town: Ethiopian coffee made from single-origin beans, to be exact. Noted for its excellent cappuccinos, the café also serves herbal teas, baobab drinks, beer and wine from various African countries. The yummy cakes, though – try their famous passion fruit tart – are made locally. €

Arcadi rue d'Arenberg 1B ⓦ arcadi.be; Métro Gare Centrale. At the north end of the Galeries St-Hubert, this busy café's long opening hours make it a perfect spot for breakfast, lunch, afternoon tea or a bite before the cinema. The menu offers lots of choices, but the salads, quiches and fruit tarts are particularly delicious. It can get a little too crowded for comfort at lunchtime. €

Au Bon Bol rue Paul Devaux 9 ⓦ bonbol.be/en; Métro Bourse. You could walk right past this Chinese place and not notice it, but the vegetables are as fresh as they come, the noodles are made on the premises, and the portions are more than generous. It's cheap, too, but not the place to come for a big night out – your food is brought quickly, and you're not encouraged to linger. €

Le Bier Circus rue de l'Enseignement 57 ⓦ bier-circus. be; Métro Parc. One of a number of restaurants on this popular Upper Town street, this place has – as you might expect from the name – a great choice of beers, but it also offers lots of dishes cooked in them, including spaghetti bolognese made with Chimay. Belgian classics too: meatballs in tomato sauce, *carbonnades flamandes*, fish *waterzooi*, etc. €€

★ **Bij den Boer** quai aux Briques 60 ⓦ bijdenboer. com; Métro Ste-Catherine. This atmospheric, bistro-style place with tiled floors and old wall posters is the best of the fish and seafood restaurants that line the Quais. €€€

Brasserie de la Roue d'Or rue des Chapeliers 26 ☎ 02 514 25 54; Métro Gare Centrale. This eminently appealing old brasserie with wood panelling, stained glass and brass fittings lies just south of the Grand-Place. It serves generous portions of Belgian regional specialities. €€

Café Bota rue Royale 236 ⓦ botanique.be/en/; Métro Botanique. Part of the Botanique arts centre (see page 88), this is a perfect spot for a bite to eat before a concert, particularly if you sit out on the terrace overlooking the city's skyscrapers, a very atmospheric spot at sunset. The food is straightforward, tasty, and excellently priced Italian. The heaped antipasti plate is a winner, with good veggie options. €€

Café Novo pl de la Vieille Halle aux Blés 37 ⓦ cafenovo. be; Métro Anneessens. Bright, quirky café with lots of original touches, from the menus in old books to the colourful selection of chairs on the square out front and in the secluded back garden. Simple food – burgers, salads, fish and chips – is available at lunchtime and in the evening, and there's a wide selection of newspapers and books. €

La Cantina rue du Jardin des Olives 13–15 ☎ 02 513 42 76; Métro Anneessens. Brazilian warmth and exuberance at this colourful restaurant just west of the Grand-Place. The menu is short but awash with exotic ingredients, and naturally, there are one or two cocktails to wash everything down. The buffet is available at lunchtime when you pay by weight. €€

Château Moderne Mont des Arts 1 ⓦ chateau-moderne.be/en; Métro Gare. This smart, airy café-restaurant at the top of the Mont des Arts steps has nice views over the Lower Town and a real buzz about it, both at lunchtime and in the evening. The menu is largely Belgian, with a few contemporary and international twists. €€

Henri rue de Flandre 113–115 ⓦ restohenri.be; Métro Ste-Catherine. Belgo-French fusion with everything made on site, right down to the stock cubes. The menu changes regularly, dishes are always seasonal, and the ingredients are top-notch. There's a set menu at lunchtime, while the evening is à la carte – or rather from the blackboard. Reservations are recommended at all times. €€€

L'Herbeudière pl de la Liberté 9 ☎ 02 218 77 13; Métro Madou. Well-established Breton creperie in a lovely little square up near the Cirque Royale (see page 88). There is a long list of tasty, sweet, or savoury fillings for the pancakes prepared on the restaurant counter. Omelettes and salads, too. The prim-and-proper decor is a good fit for this low-key, family-run café. €

Houtsiplou pl Rouppe 9 ⓦ houtsiplou.be; Métro Anneessens. This ode to Belgium features walls covered in cartoons depicting the country's history in true Surrealist style. An equally colourful menu offers home-made burgers with a plant pot of chips, a few Belgian classics, generous, delicious salads and a kids' menu. €€

Mer du Nord rue Ste-Catherine 45 ⓦ noordzeemer dunord.be; Métro Ste-Catherine. This legendary, stand-up seafood joint is a Ste-Catherine landmark. You have to stand (at piles of fish crates), but the seafood selection is large and tasty, and you can eat inside or out on the street. Salads, sandwiches and all manner of fish and seafood goodies: succulent pieces of haddock, tuna, herring and tiny prawns. All come served with a big bowl of bread and salad. Beer and wine, too, if you want it. €

Mirante Plattesteen 13 ⓦ pizzeriarestaurantmirante. be; Métro Bourse. This small Italian restaurant serves the best pizza in the city, cooked in its wood-fired oven, along with all sorts of good and authentic Italian regional specialities. There are always a few daily specials on offer. €€

Nuetnigenough rue de Lombard 25 ⓦ nuetnigenough. be; Métro Bourse. You can't book at this small, unpretentious restaurant. Still, it's worth a short wait – the Belgian food and beer are excellent and reasonably priced, and they tend to turn tables around quickly anyway. Lots of dishes are cooked in beer – including rabbit *à la Kriek* – and all come served with generous helpings of *stoemp* or fries and a salad. It has a good beer list, too. €€

L'Ogenblik galerie des Princes 1 ⓦ ogenblik.be; Métro Gare Centrale. In the Galeries St-Hubert, this outstanding Franco-Belgian restaurant is kitted out in antique bistro style, right down to the ancient cash till, and serves a well-judged, wide-ranging menu that includes the basics – steak and chips with wild mushrooms, for instance – but also aims higher. €€

Orphyse Chaussette rue Charles Hanssens 5 ⓦ orphyse chaussette.be; Poelaert tram stop. Chef and owner Philippe Renoux prides himself on original dishes with quality ingredients, and this cosy restaurant doesn't disappoint. There's always a non-meat dish available on the short, predominantly French menu, too. The setting is candlelit and intimate, and the staff are willing to help you navigate your way around the extensive wine menu. €€€€

Pistolet Original - Sablon rue Joseph Stevens 26 ⓦ pistolet-original.be; Métro Louise. In Belgium, a *pistolet* is a crisp-crust bread roll, and this place specialises in, you guessed it, gourmet sandwiches – and very tasty they are, too. €

Ploegmans rue Haute 148 ⓦ ploegmans.be; Métro Gare Centrale. Situated right in the heart of the Marolles, this is one of Brussels' most authentic old brasseries, with lots of traditional grub, including meatballs or carbonades with fries, steaks and *rognons de veau* (veal kidneys), and lots of hearty starters too. €€

★ **Le Pré Salé** rue de Flandre 20 ⓦ lepresale.be; Métro Ste-Catherine. Agreeable and typically Bruxellois neighbourhood restaurant, just off pl Ste-Catherine, providing an appealing alternative to the swankier places nearby. The plain cream tiled interior dates from when it used to be a chip shop, but now the menu features great mussels, fish dishes such as *anguilles au vert* (eels in a herb sauce) and other Belgian specialities. It's always crowded, so it's not a place for a quiet dinner. €€€

Au Stekerlapatte rue des Prêtres 4 ⓦ austekerlapatte. be; Métro Hôtel des Monnaies. On a side street tucked away behind the Palais de Justice, this long-established brasserie serves Franco-Belgian cuisine in a bustling atmosphere – great carbonades, *stoemp*, steaks and other classics. €€€

Vincent rue des Dominicains 8–10 ⓦ restaurantvincent. be/en; Métro Bourse. This long-standing restaurant was a favourite with Jacques Brel and his cronies, who used to drink at the bar next door when it was called *Chez Stans*. The food is still good, and you still have to walk through the kitchen to get to your table, which gives you a good view of the action. Belgo-French cuisine, with meat and seafood dishes that are a cut above what you'll find on nearby rue des Bouchers. €€€

ST GILLES, AVENUE LOUISE AND IXELLES, SEE MAP PAGE 74

Dolma ch d'Ixelles 329 ⓦ restaurant.dolma.be; Métro Flagey. This new-age veggie joint is popular with the locals for the all-you-can-eat buffet lunch and dinner. It offers different set of menus each day, and although it's not the most refined vegetarian cuisine, it's tasty and excellent value. €

La Quincaillerie rue du Page 45 ⓦ quincaillerie.be. Mouthwatering Franco-Belgian cuisine in this delightful restaurant, one of the longest-established in the ultra-cool Châtelain area. Set in an imaginatively converted old hardware shop with splendid Art Nouveau flourishes, it serves great fish and seafood (particularly oysters) and fabulous steaks, duck and chicken. Reservations are advised, especially when the local market is open. €€€

Sale, Pepe, Rosmarino rue Berckmans 98 ❶ 02 538 90 63; Métro Hôtel des Monnaies. Authentic, delicious Italian cuisine, where even the excellent pizzas are outdone by the frequently superb pasta and meat dishes, which change regularly according to the creative influence of owners Aurelio and Antonio. Reservations are essential. €€€

Volle Gas pl Fernand Cocq 21 ⓦ restaurant-volle-gas-bruxelles.be; Métro Port de Namur. This traditional, wood-panelled bar-brasserie serves classic Belgian cuisine in a friendly, family atmosphere. The Brussels specialities include the delicious *carbonnades de boeuf à la Gueuze*, *waterzooi* and *lapin à la Kriek*, but there are also pasta and salads. €€€

Le Waterloo ch de Waterloo 217 ⓦ lewaterloo.be; Métro Horta. This is the quintessential small neighbourhood restaurant with wooden benches and exhibitions by local artists. The three-course weekday lunch is excellent value, while the à la carte menu features traditional dishes. €€

THE EU QUARTER, SEE MAP PAGE 68

Maison Antoine 1 pl Jourdan ⓦ maisonantoine.be; Métro Schuman. Opened in 1948, this kiosk in a square

1

to the southeast of Parc Léopold serves what is generally regarded as the best fries in town. There are about thirty sauces and a wide range of snacks to accompany them, including meatballs, burgers and croquettes. Unfortunately, there's no seating, so you'll have to find a bench. €

DRINKING

Drinking in Brussels, as in the rest of the country, is a joy. The city boasts an enormous variety of **bars**: sumptuous Art Nouveau establishments, traditional joints with ceilings stained brown by a century's smoke, speciality beer bars with literally hundreds of different varieties of ale and, of course, more modern hangouts. Many of the more distinctive bars are handily located within a few minutes' walk of the Grand-Place and in **Ixelles**, but you'll be spoilt for choice. Belgians make little – or no – distinction between their bars and cafés: both serve alcohol, many stay open late (until 1am or even 2am), and most sell food. What you won't find (thank goodness) are lots of the coffee-house chains that beleaguers so many big cities.

THE LOWER AND UPPER TOWN, SEE MAPS PAGES 49 AND 54

À la Bécasse rue de Tabora 11 ⓦ alabecasse.com; Métro Bourse. Situated just northwest of the Grand-Place, this old-fashioned, wood-panelled bar has long wooden benches and ancient blue-and-white wall tiles. Authentic lambic and Gueuze beer is served in earthenware jugs. Lots of snacks to go with your drink, too.

Au Bon Vieux Temps rue du Marché aux Herbes 12 ☎ 02 217 26 26; Métro Bourse. An ancient little place tucked away down an alley near the Grand-Place, the bar has all sorts of old bric-a-brac, including a stained-glass window salvaged from the local parish church. Popular with British service members just after the end of World War II, the bar still has old-fashioned signs advertising Mackenzie's port and Bass pale ale.

★ **Brussels Beer Project** rue Antoine Dansaert 188 ⓦ beerproject.be; Métro Ste-Catherine. Opened in 2013 in Brussels' fashion district, this crowd-funded micro-brewery aims to mix Belgian beer-making know-how with international influences. For example, similar brews from Ireland and New Zealand influenced their Babeleir de Bretagne oyster stout, made with Brittany oysters. There are several regular beers on tap and around twenty 'pop-ups'.

Café Central rue Borgwal 14 ☎ 02 513 73 08; Métro Bourse. DJs, concerts and film screenings pack the agenda at this cool bar just off pl St-Géry. You sometimes have to battle at the bar for a drink, but there's a great atmosphere and clientele.

Café Le Fontainas rue Marché au Charbon 91 ⓦ le fontainas.be; Métro Anneessens. This popular bar has a retro feel and a low-key gay affiliation. It's one of the nicest on this busy stretch, with Vedett on draught and many outside tables – but don't wait for a waitperson as service is at the bar, making English folk feel very at home. DJs on Sun 4–8pm.

Chaff pl du Jeu de Balle 21, Marolles ☎ 02 502 58 48; Métro Gare du Midi. There's no better place to take in the hustle and bustle of the city's biggest and best flea market than at this amenable café-bar. Weekday evenings see the place become a hub for live music (Mon) and chess (Thurs), and you can also get good bistro food here.

★ **La Fleur en Papier Doré** rue des Alexiens 53 ⓦ goudblommekeinpapier.be; Métro Gare Centrale. This cosy bar was reopened by a group of enthusiasts keen to preserve this slice of Brussels heritage: *La Fleur* was one of the preferred watering holes of René Magritte, while novelist Hugo Claus apparently held his wedding reception here. Idiosyncratic antique decor, a good choice of beers, excellent house wine and classic Belgian food.

À l'Imaige de Nostre-Dame Impasse des Cadeaux, rue du Marché aux Herbes 6 ☎ 02 219 42 49; Métro Bourse. Set at the end of a narrow alley, this welcoming, quirky little bar is decorated like an old Dutch kitchen. It serves a good range of speciality beers, including seven on tap.

Moeder Lambic Fontainas pl Fontainas 8 ⓦ moeder lambic.com; Métro Anneessens. Local beer enthusiasts have given a new lease of life to this small square off bd Anspach, opening a sister bar to the original behind the St Gilles town hall. Forty beers on tap and trained staff to give guidance and recommendations are temptation enough – particularly as these are not your run-of-the-mill beers, with small Belgian brewers such as Dupont, Val-Dieu and Cantillon from across the way in Anderlecht all on offer.

Monk quai aux Briques 22 ⓦ monk.be; Métro Ste-Catherine. Named after the jazz musician Thelonious Monk, this big and popular Ste-Catherine bar is probably the nicest place to drink in the area. It has a few tables outside and a large, airy interior that attracts a young and largely Flemish-speaking crowd. Service is at the bar, and they serve lots of nice, thoroughly Belgian snacks – cheese, sausage, meatballs – and spaghetti dishes in the dining room at the back.

À la Mort Subite rue Montagne aux Herbes Potagères 7 ⓦ alamortsubite.com; Métro Gare Centrale. This notorious/famous 1920s bar loaned its name to a popular bottled beer. It occupies a long, narrow room with nicotine-stained walls, long tables and lots of mirrors. On a good night, it's inhabited by a dissolute arty clientele, but large groups of teenage tourists on others. Snacks are served, or you can just order a plate of cheese cubes to accompany your beer.

Le Perroquet rue Watteeu 31 ☎ 02 512 99 22; Métro Gare Central. Housed in attractive Art Nouveau premises on a pleasant street corner, this busy, semicircular café-bar offers an imaginative range of stuffed pittas, salads and other tasty snacks. It has an excellent beer menu, too. A fair warning: you'll find it difficult to get a seat on Fri or Sat night.

Au Soleil rue Marché au Charbon 86 ☎ 02 512 34 30; Métro Anneessens. A short walk west from the Grand-Place, this popular bar, formerly a men's clothing shop, quenches the thirst of a young and arty Brussels clientele. Inexpensive bar snacks are available, and there's a pavement terrace where you can while away the day over a coffee or something stronger. It's generally laid-back, but it's often difficult to get a seat come nightfall.

Toone impasse Schuddeveld 6 ⓦ www.toone.be. The café-cum-bar of the famous Toone puppet theatre (see page 88), squeezed down a tight alley that most people walk straight by, is the perfect city-centre venue to enjoy a quiet beer and some good chat with a cat curled up next to you, overlooked by the puppets on the wall.

ST GILLES, AVENUE LOUISE AND IXELLES, SEE MAP PAGE 74

Brasserie Verschueren parvis de St-Gilles 11–13 ⓦ verschu.be; Métro Parvis de St-Gilles. Art Deco neighbourhood bar with a laid-back atmosphere and football league results on the wall – essential in the days before television – serves a good range of Belgian beers and food (meatballs, spaghetti, *croques*, etc).

Café Belga pl Flagey 18 ☎ 02 640 35 08; Métro Flagey. This is a bar for any time of day: coffee and croissants on the terrace after the market, buffet lunches or an evening nibble before a film or concert at the cultural centre next door, and boozing into the early hours with the mixed crowd who flock here from all over the city.

★ **Café Maison du Peuple** parvis de St-Gilles 39 ⓦ cafemdp.be; Métro Parvis de St-Gilles. Built in 1907 for the education and entertainment of the workers, the

'People's House' of St-Gilles is nowadays a spacious café hosting DJs and concerts, exhibiting local artists and providing a perfect spot for breakfast or lunch while visiting the market. It's worth checking the website to see what's on.

Moeder Lambic rue de Savoie 68 ⓦ moederlambic. com; Métro Albert. This small and very popular bar, just behind the Hôtel de Ville in St-Gilles, has over a thousand beers available, including five hundred or so Belgian varieties, mostly bottled. For a broader selection on draught, check out its sister bar in the Lower Town.

La Porteuse d'Eau av Jean Volders 48a ⓦ laporteuse. eu/en; Métro Porte de Hal. Refurbished Art Nouveau café on the corner of rue Vanderschrick, near the Porte de Hal. The food isn't up to much, but the beer menu is excellent, and the ornate interior is well worth the price of a glass.

L'Ultime Atome rue St-Boniface 14 ⓦ ultimeatome.be; Métro Porte de Namur. The large selection of beers and wines, simple but tasty food and late opening hours make this hip café-bar a hit with the fashionable Ixelles crowd on weekdays and weekends. Its location, in the appealing pl St-Boniface, also makes it a great place to sit outside with a newspaper in the summer.

THE EU QUARTER, SEE MAP PAGE 68

The Beer Factory pl du Luxembourg 6 ⓦ brasserie-beer-factory.be; Métro Trône. A recent addition to the bevy of bars on this appealing square, metres from the European Parliament and the chosen haunt of Eurocrats for after-work hobnobbing, its centrepiece bar is made of an old beer vat. As the name suggests, there's a good range of beers alongside some pretty decent food – *stoemp-saucisses*, carbonades, burgers and the like.

Piola Libri rue Franklin 66–68 ⓦ piolalibri.be; Métro Trône. Popular with EU workers, particularly Italians, this Italian bookshop and bar is perfect for an aperitivo. The counter offers a selection of tasty antipasti to go with your glass of wine or prosecco.

NIGHTLIFE

The city has a decent nightlife scene, including a number of established **clubs**, but most of the action revolves around nights with moveable locations – pick up flyers in bars and clubs for the latest and best events. Brussels is also a good place to catch **live music**, with a couple of central, well-established venues and festivals, plus a strong jazz scene. For details of listings and ticket sales, see page 88.

CLUBS

Le Bazaar rue des Capucins 63, Marolles ⓦ bazaar brussels.be; Métro Gare Centrale; see map page 54. Formerly a restaurant with music, this is now primarily a club, with two spaces for live music, DJs and dancing.

The Fuse rue Blaes 208, Marolles ⓦ fuse.be; Métro Gare du Midi; see map page 54. Widely recognised

as the finest techno club in Belgium, this pulsating venue has hosted some of Europe's top DJs. It has three floors of techno, house, and occasional hip-hop, as well as the usual chill-out rooms and visuals. Ticket prices go up if there's a big-name DJ.

★ **Madame Moustache** quai aux Bruler 5–7 ⓦ madame moustache.be; Métro Ste-Catherine; see map page 54. This centrally located bar and club hosts live bands – indie, grunge, garage – and has regular themed evenings, from rock'n'roll to funk and soul.

You rue du Duquesnoy 18 ⓦ leyou.be; Métro Gare Centrale; see map page 49. A short walk southeast of the Grand-Place, *You* is one of the city's most notorious (snooty) clubs, with an interior designed by Miguel Câncio Martins (the man behind the *Buddha Bar* in Paris) and

1

famously choosy door attendants. It is set over two levels, with comfy couches in the bar lounge. DJs play everything from funk and disco to electro and house. There are gay tea dances on Sun, too.

LIVE MUSIC

AB (Ancienne Belgique) bd Anspach 110 Ⓦ abconcerts. be; Métro Bourse; see map page 49. International underground artists perform at the capital's leading rock venue in the main auditorium or the smaller space on the first floor. There's usually a gig every night.

★ **L'Archiduc** rue Antoine Dansaert 6 Ⓦ archiduc.net; Métro Bourse; see map page 54. Art Deco jazz bar with live sets on Mon and at the weekend, including a free concert every Sat and Sun afternoon. Great cocktails, too.

Beursschouwburg rue Auguste Orts 20–28 Ⓦ beursschouwburg.be; Métro Bourse; see map page 54. Occupying a handsomely restored building from 1885, this fine-arts venue makes the most of its different spaces, from the cellar to the stairs, the theatre to the café. Features DJs of all genres, plus an eclectic live music programme catering to a wide range of tastes.

Botanique rue Royale 236 Ⓦ botanique.be; Métro Botanique; see map page 54. The Francophone cultural centre hosts exhibitions and regular live music – look out especially for Les Nuits Botanique in May to hear lots of new bands in a festival atmosphere.

Cirque Royal rue de l'Enseignement 81 Ⓦ cirque royalbruxelles.be; Métro Madou; see map page 54. Formerly an indoor circus, the Upper Town's Cirque Royal works in tandem with the Botanique. The larger venue of the two is a regular on the roster of big-name rock, pop and jazz tours.

Flagey pl Sainte-Croix, Ixelles Ⓦ flagey.be; Métro Flagey; see map page 74. Pl Flagey's wonderful Art Deco cultural centre hosts a regular roster of eclectic live music from world to orchestral to jazz. Invariably, there will be something interesting going on.

Forest National av Victor Rousseau 208 Ⓦ forest-national.be; tram No. 32 from the city centre, No. 82 from Gare du Midi; get off at stop Zaman. This large arena, with space for around eleven thousand people, is Brussels' main venue for big-name international concerts.

Sounds Jazz Club rue de la Tulipe 28, Ixelles Ⓦ sounds. brussels; Métro Porte de Namur; see map page 74. Off pl Fernand Cocq, this atmospheric café has showcased local and internationally acclaimed jazz acts for over twenty years. Live music every night (from around 9.30pm).

ENTERTAINMENT

The websites Ⓦ bruzz.be and Ⓦ agenda.brussels have comprehensive **listings** of concerts and events. **Tickets** for most concerts are available at Fnac in the City 2 shopping complex on rue Neuve or direct from the venue websites listed below.

THEATRE AND OPERA

BOZAR rue Ravenstein 23 Ⓦ bozar.be; Métro Gare Centrale. This well-regarded venue presents an innovative programme of events, including theatre, world music, and themed cultural nights, in its two-thousand-seater Art Deco concert hall and several smaller auditoria. It also hosts the internationally renowned Orchestre National de Belgique (Ⓦ nationalorchestra.be).

La Monnaie pl de la Monnaie Ⓦ lamonnaiedemunt. be; Métro De Brouckère. Belgium's premier opera house consistently earns glowing reviews and is much lauded for its adventurous repertoire. It nurtures promising singers rather than casting the more established stars. It is home to Brussels' main dance venue, hosts classical concerts and chamber music recitals, and has a reputation for contemporary interpretations of classic operas and an eclectic repertoire. Book well in advance.

Théâtre Royal de Toone Impasse Schuddeveld 6 Ⓦ toone.be; Métro Bourse or Gare Centrale. This puppet theatre with a long and distinguished pedigree offers four

---

FESTIVALS IN BRUSSELS

As you might expect of a European capital, there's always something going on in Brussels, and the city hosts a vast number of cultural and arts events throughout the year. The city's **Gay Pride** (Ⓦ pride.be) takes place in May and attracts big crowds, whilst the **Vendôme cinema** (see page 89) hosts Belgium's annual gay and lesbian film festival in January or February. Other **film festivals** include the Flagey Cinema's Brussels Short Film Festival, focusing on European cinema, in the last week of April and the first week of May (Ⓦ flagey.be/bsff) and April's Brussels International Fantastic Film Festival (Ⓦ bifff.net) dedicated to horror and science fiction. **Music festivals** include the internationally acclaimed Jazz Marathon Weekend held every May (Ⓦ brussels.be/brussels-jazz-weekend); the biennial Ars Musica festival of contemporary classical music held in November (Ⓦ arsmusica.be); and May's prestigious Concours Musical Reine Elisabeth violin competition (Ⓦ concoursreineelisabeth.be).

FOOTBALL IN BRUSSELS

1

Brussels has several soccer teams, of which **Royal Sporting Club (RSC) Anderlecht** (w rsca. be) is by far the best known. They play in the Belgian Pro League, and their stadium is the Lotto Park, formerly the Stade Constant Vanden Stock, at av Théo Verbeeck 2. The stadium is within comfortable walking distance of Métro St-Guidon and has a capacity of 21,000. Tickets for home games are reasonably priced, though fair warning, games are frequently sold out.

or five performances every week, mainly in French but sometimes in the traditional Bruxellois dialect known as Brusselse Sproek or Marollien – a colourful, ribald brand of Flemish that is in danger of dying out.

CINEMA

In Brussels, most films are shown in the original language and subtitled in French and/or Flemish (coded 'VO', *version originale*). The main exception is in a few multiscreen cinemas, where some films, especially kids' movies, are likely to be dubbed into French (look out for 'VF', *version française*). Brussels has an excellent range of small cinemas, which consistently undercut prices at the multiscreen, though you are expected to tip the usher who checks your ticket – 50 cents will do. The city's annual film festivals are highly recommended (see box, page 88). Cinemas usually change their programmes on Wed.

Actors' Studio petite rue des Bouchers 16 w actorsstudio.

cinenews.be; Métro Bourse or Gare Centrale. This small cinema is a good place to catch art-house or independent films. It's cheaper than its more commercial rivals and has the added advantage that you can buy a beer or a coffee from outside and take it in with you.

Flagey Cinema pl Sainte-Croix, Ixelles w flagey.be; Métro Flagey. Part of place Flagey's Art Deco cultural centre (see page 88), this studio cinema showcases an impressive range of films, usually focusing on a particular genre or director, and is the main host to the Brussels Film Festival in June (see box, page 88).

Vendôme ch de Wavre 18, Ixelles w cinema-vendome. be; Métro Porte de Namur. This five-screen cinema is well known for its wide selection of art films as well as more mainstream flicks but also hosts several film festivals dedicated to short films, plus Latin American, Korean and movies made by women (see box, page 89). They offer multiple ticket deals, too.

LGBTQ+ DRINKING AND NIGHTLIFE

The city's scene focuses on the Rainbow House at rue Marché au Charbon 42 (w rainbowhouse.be), in the heart of Brussels' gay area, where you can pick up all sorts of up-to-date information. They also help to organise the city's Gay Pride festival (see box, page 88).

Le Belgica rue Marché au Charbon 32 w lebelgica.be; Métro Bourse; see map page 49. Perhaps the most popular gay bar and pick-up joint in the capital. It's a tad run-down, with Formica tables and dilapidated chairs that have seen better days, but if you're out for a lively, friendly atmosphere, you could do a lot worse. Come at the weekend when the place is heaving – all are welcome, whether male, female, gay or straight – and be sure to slam back a few of the house speciality lemon-vodka 'Belgica' shots.

Chez Maman rue des Grands Carmes 7 w chezmaman. be; Métro Anneessens; see map page 49. Not a lesbian place per se, but this tiny bar has achieved cult-like status for the transvestite cabaret of the proprietor, Maman, with

crowds flocking in from all corners of Brussels to see him and his protégés strut up and down. Jam-packed every weekend – occasional lesbian nights.

La Démence at The Fuse rue Blaes 208, Marolles w lademence.com; Métro Gare du Midi; see map page 54. The city's most popular gay party night is held monthly on two floors in The Fuse (see page 87) – cutting-edge techno and bus-loads of guys from Amsterdam, Cologne and Paris. The crowd's a bit difficult to pigeonhole – expect to find a hybrid mix of muscle men, transsexuals and out-and-out ravers. Check the website for dates – usually, a couple of nights over one weekend a month.

La Réserve petite rue au Beurre 2A w la-reserve.brussels; Métro De Brouckère; see map page 49. This traditional café is probably the oldest gay bar in town, with a good selection of beers. The clientele is a mix of locals and tourists, young and old(er) – occasional parties and theme nights.

SHOPPING

Brussels has a supreme selection of small, **independent shops**, a good range of **open-air markets** and several **charming galleries** – covered shopping 'streets' dating back to the nineteenth century. The main downtown shopping street, **rue Neuve**, is dominated by chain stores.

The Galeries St-Hubert, near the Grand-Place, are much more distinctive, accommodating a smattering of upmarket shops and stores, while the nearby **Galerie Agora** peddles bargain-basement leather jackets, incense, jewellery and ethnic goods. Behind the Bourse, rue Antoine Dansaert

1

caters for the young and fashionable, housing the stores of **upcoming designers**, and nearby streets like rue des Riches Claires and rue du Marché au Charbon are good for **streetwear**. Av Louise and around is home to the big **international designers**. More than anything else, however, Brussels is famous for three things: **comic strips**, **chocolate** and **beer**, and shops all over the city centre sell all three – pl du Grand Sablon alone has at least half a dozen chocolate shops.

BOOKS AND COMICS

La Boutique Tintin rue de la Colline 13 ⓦ boutique. tintin.com; Métro Gare Centrale; see map page 49. Tintinarama, from comics to all sorts of branded goods – postcards, stationery, figurines, T-shirts and sweaters. Geared up for the tourist trade, it's just off the Grand-Place.

★ **Brüsel** bd Anspach 100 ⓦ brusel.com; Métro Bourse; see map page 49. This well-known comic shop stocks more than eight thousand new issues and specialises in French underground editions – *Association*, *Amok*, and *Bill*, to name but three. You'll also find the complete works of Belgian comic-book artist Schuiten, most popularly known for his controversial comic *Brüsel*, which depicts the architectural destruction of a city (guess which one) in the 1960s. There is also a Mega Tintin collection and a small English section.

Passa Porta rue Antoine Dansaert 46 ⓦ passaporta bookshop.be; Métro Ste-Catherine; see map page 54. The manager of this book-lovers haven practises his theory that you wouldn't buy clothes without first trying them on – and the same goes for books – hence the readings and regular events in all languages here, with guest authors and an increasingly popular biennial literary festival. About 10 percent of the total stock is in English.

Slumberland rue des Sables 20 ⓦ slumberlandbdworld. com; Métro Botanique; see map page 54. Based in the Centre Belge de la Bande Dessinée (see page 57), it's worth a visit whether or not you're visiting the museum, with one of the city's best selections of comics and graphic novels.

CHOCOLATES

★ **Frederic Blondeel Chocolatier** rue de Ganshoren 39, Koekelberg ⓦ frederic-blondeel.be; Métro Étangs Noirs; see map page 54. This factory-cum-shop from the renowned Flanders chocolatier is a paradise for chocolate connoisseurs. All the chocolate is made on site, beautifully displayed and reasonably priced, while the café's Madagascan chocolate and Tahitian vanilla ice cream in a chocolate-filled cone may well be a foretaste of paradise.

Galler rue au Beurre 44 ⓦ galler.com; Métro Bourse; see map page 49. Galler is the chocolatier to the king – and therefore the holder of the Royal Warrant – but it is still less well known than many of its rivals and rarely seen outside Belgium, so it is a good choice for a special present.

It offers excellent dark chocolate – its 70g bar comes in all sorts of inventive flavours.

Pierre Marcolini rue des Minimes 1 ⓦ marcolini.be; Métro Louise; see map page 54. Pierre Marcolini is a true master of his art – classy service, beautiful packaging and a mouthwatering choice of chocolate cakes. A glass of hot chocolate at the shop's small bar is the perfect antidote to a winter evening.

Wittamer pl du Grand Sablon 6 ⓦ wittamer.com; Métro Louise; see map page 54. Brussels' most famous patisserie and chocolate shop, established in 1910 and still run by the Wittamer family, sells gorgeous (if expensive) light pastries, cakes, mousses and chocolates. The shop also serves speciality teas and coffees in its tearoom at No. 12.

FOOD AND DRINK

Beer Mania ch de Wavre 174–176, Ixelles ⓦ beermania. be; Métro Trone; see map page 74. A drinker's heaven, this shop stocks more than four hundred different types of beer, and you can even buy the correct glass to match your favourite. It's one of the few places to get the elusive Trappist beer from Westvleteren, usually only for sale at the abbey gates. There's a small bar where you can taste before you buy. The owner's brew, Mea Culpa, includes ten different herbs and is served in an impressive Bohemian glass.

Dandoy rue au Beurre 31 ⓦ maisondandoy.com; Métro Bourse; see map page 49. Biscuits have been made at this famous shop just off the Grand-Place since 1858, so it's no surprise they have it down to a fine art. The main speciality is known locally as 'speculoos', a kind of hard gingerbread which comes in every size and shape imaginable – the largest is the size of a small child and costs as much as €50. Be warned that gingerbread can wreak havoc on loose fillings.

La Maison du Miel rue du Midi 121 ⓦ lamaisondumiel. be; Métro Bourse; see map page 49. As the name suggests, this tiny, family-run shop is stacked high with jar upon jar of honey and its multifarious by-products, from soap to candles, plus a number of curious honeypots and receptacles.

La Maison du Thé Plattesteen 11 ⓦ comptoirflorian. be; Métro Bourse; see map page 49. This shop is dedicated to the good old cuppa. A far cry from the average English brew, floor-to-ceiling tins harbour scores of teas to smell, taste and buy. There is also lots of tea-related paraphernalia.

MARKETS

Ateliers des Tanneurs rue de Tanneurs 60, Marolles; Métro Gare du Midi; see map page 54. Indoor organic food market in a good-looking Art Nouveau building on the west side of the Marolles quarter. Good prices for high-quality products, mostly from local producers, plus a café that serves an excellent brunch buffet on Sun (11am–3pm).

Gare du Midi Métro Gare du Midi; see map page 74. One of Brussels' largest and most colourful food markets is held outside the main station every Sun, with traders crammed under the railway bridge and spilling into the surrounding streets. Among the vegetables and cheap clothes, numerous stands sell pitta, olives, North African raï music cassettes, spices and herbs. There's a first-rate flower and plant section, too.

Place du Grand Sablon Métro Louise; see map page 74. The swankiest antiques and collectables market in town is located here, and there are plenty of pricey antique shops in the surrounding streets, too.

Place du Jeu de Balle Marolles; Métro Gare du Midi; see map page 74. This sprawling flea market opens every morning, but it's at its biggest and best on the weekend when an eccentric muddle of colonial spoils, quirky odds and ends, and domestic and ecclesiastical bric-a-brac gives an impression of a century's fads and fancies.

DIRECTORY

Banks and exchange There are ATMs dotted right across the city centre.

Embassies Australia, av des Arts 56 ☎ 02 286 05 00; Canada, av des Arts 58 ☎ 02 741 06 11; Ireland, rue Froissart 50 ☎ 02 282 34 00; New Zealand, av des Nerviens 9–31 ☎ 02 512 10 40; UK, av d'Auderghem 10 ☎ 02 287 62 11; US, bd du Régent 27 ☎ 02 811 40 00.

Emergencies Phone ☎ 112.

Left luggage There are coin-operated lockers at all three main train stations.

Pharmacies Multipharma, near the Grand-Place at rue du Marché aux Poulets 37 (☎ 02 511 35 90). Details of 24hr pharmacies are available on ⊛ pharmacie.be, and details of duty pharmacies are usually posted on every pharmacy's front door.

Police Brussels Central Police Station, rue du Marché au Charbon 30.

Post Post office counters are located in many supermarkets.

Flanders

A SUMMER'S DAY IN BRUGES

Flanders

The Flemish-speaking provinces of West Vlaanderen and Oost Vlaanderen (West Flanders and East Flanders) roll east from the North Sea coast, stretching out towards Brussels and Antwerp. Except for the range of low hills around Oudenaarde and the sea dunes along the coast, Flanders is well-nigh pancake-flat, a wide-skied landscape seen at its best in its quieter recesses, where poplar trees and whitewashed farmhouses decorate sluggish canals. There are also many reminders of Flanders' medieval greatness, beginning with the ancient and fascinating cloth cities of Bruges and Ghent, which hold equally marvellous collections of early Flemish art.

Less familiar is the region's clutch of intriguing smaller towns, most memorably **Oudenaarde**, which has a delightful town hall and is famed for its tapestries; **Kortrijk**, with its classic small-town charms; and **Veurne**, whose main square is framed by a beguiling medley of fine old buildings. There is also, of course, the legacy of **World War I**. By 1915, the trenches extended from the North Sea coast to Switzerland, cutting across West Flanders via **Diksmuide** and Ieper, and many of the key engagements of the war were fought here. Every year, hundreds of visitors head for **Ieper** (formerly called Ypres) to see the numerous cemeteries and monuments in and around the town, poignant reminders of what proved to be a desperately pointless conflict.

Not far from the battlefields, the **Belgian coast** is **beach** territory, an almost continuous stretch of golden sand crowded with locals and tourists every summer. An excellent **tram** service connects all the major seaside resorts, and although a lot of the development has been somewhat crass, cosy **De Haan** has kept much of its late nineteenth-century charm. The largest town on the coast is **Ostend**, a lively seaside resort sprinkled with popular bars and restaurants, the pick of which sells a wonderful range of seafood.

Brief history

As early as the thirteenth century, **Flanders** was one of the most prosperous parts of Europe, with an advanced, integrated economy dependent on the **cloth trade** with England. The boom lasted a couple of centuries, but the region was in decline by the sixteenth century, with trade slipping north towards the Netherlands and England's cloth manufacturers beginning to undermine Flanders' economic base. The speed of the collapse was accelerated by **religious wars**, for though the great Flemish towns were by inclination Protestant, their counts, kings and queens were Catholic. Flanders sank into poverty and decay, a static, priest-ridden and traditional society where nearly every aspect of life was controlled by decree, and only 3 percent of the population could read or write.

With precious little say in the matter, the Flemish peasantry of the seventeenth and eighteenth centuries saw their lands crossed and re-crossed by the armies of the Great Powers, for it was here that the relative fortunes of dynasties and nations were decided. Only with **Belgian independence** did the situation begin to change: the towns started to industrialise, tariffs protected the cloth industry, Zeebrugge was built, and Ostend was modernised, all in a flurry of activity that shook Flanders from its centuries-old torpor. This steady progress was severely interrupted by the German occupations of both world wars, but Flanders emerged prosperous, with its citizens maintaining a distinctive cultural and linguistic identity, often in sharp opposition to their Walloon (French-speaking) neighbours.

TYNE COT CEMETERY, IEPER

Highlights

❶ Bruges By any measure, Bruges is one of Western Europe's most beautiful cities, with its jangle of ancient houses overlooking a cobweb of picturesque canals. See page 97

❷ Ostend beach The Belgian coast boasts a first-rate sandy beach, of which Ostend has an especially fine slice. See page 119

❸ Ieper Flanders witnessed some of the worst battles of World War I, and the attractive little

town of Ieper is dotted with sad and mournful reminders. See page 131

❹ Flemish tapestries Small-town Oudenaarde was once famous for its tapestries; a superb selection is on display there today. See page 144

❺ Ghent's Adoration of the Mystic Lamb This wonderful Jan van Eyck painting is unmissable. See page 150

HIGHLIGHTS ARE MARKED ON THE MAP ON PAGE 96

Bruges

Passing through **BRUGES** in 1820, William Wordsworth declared that this was where he discovered 'a deeper peace than in deserts found'. Perhaps inevitably, crowds tend to overwhelm the place today – its reputation as a perfectly preserved medieval city has made it the most popular tourist destination in Belgium – but you'd be mad to come to Flanders and miss it: the museums of Bruges hold some of the country's finest collections of Flemish art, and is intimate, winding streets, woven around a skein of narrow canals and lined with gorgeous ancient buildings, live up to even the most inflated hype.

Wordsworth was neither the first nor the last Victorian to fall in love with Bruges; by the 1840s, there was a substantial **British colony** here, its members enraptured by the city's medieval architecture and air of lost splendour. Neither were the expatriates slow to exercise their economic muscle, applying an architectural **Gothic Revival** brush to parts of the city that weren't 'medieval' enough. Time and again, they intervened in municipal planning decisions, allying themselves with like-minded Flemings in a movement that changed, or at least modified, the face of the city. Thus, Bruges is not the perfectly preserved medieval city of much tourist literature but a clever, frequently seamless combination of medieval original and nineteenth- and sometimes twentieth-century additions.

The obvious place to start an exploration of the city is the two principal squares: the **Markt**, overlooked by the mighty **belfry**, and the **Burg**, flanked by the city's most impressive architectural ensemble. Almost within shouting distance are the three main museums, the pick of them being the **Groeninge**, which offers a wonderful sample of early Flemish art. Another short hop brings you to the **St-Janshospitaalmuseum** and the important paintings of the fifteenth-century artist **Hans Memling**, as well as Bruges' most impressive churches, the **Onze Lieve Vrouwekerk** and **St-Salvatorskathedraal**. Further afield, the gentle canals and maze-like cobbled streets of eastern Bruges – stretching out from **Jan van Eyckplein** – are extraordinarily pretty. As elsewhere in the centre, the most characteristic **architectural feature** is the crow-step gable, popular from the fourteenth to the eighteenth century and revived by the restorers of the 1880s, but there are also expansive Classical-style mansions and humble, homely cottages. Time and again, the eye is surprised by the subtle variety of the cityscape, featuring everything from intimate arched doorways and bendy tiled roofs to wonky chimneys and a bevy of discreet shrines and miniature statues.

Brief history

Bruges started as a ninth-century fortress built by the warlike first count of Flanders, **Baldwin Iron Arm**, who was intent on defending the Flemish coast from Viking attack. The settlement prospered, and by the fourteenth century, it shared effective control of the **cloth trade** with its two great rivals, Ghent and Ypres (now Ieper), turning high-quality English wool into clothing that was exported worldwide. An immensely profitable business, it made the city a focus of international trade. At its peak, the town was a key member of – and showcase for the products of – the **Hanseatic League**, the most powerful economic alliance in medieval Europe. Through the harbours and docks of Bruges, Flemish cloth and Hansa goods were exchanged for hogs from Denmark, spices from Venice, hides from Ireland, wax from Russia, gold and silver from Poland and furs from Bulgaria. No fewer than 21 consulates protected the business of these foreign traders, and the city developed a wide range of support services, including banking, money-changing and maritime insurance.

Trouble and strife

Despite (or because of) this lucrative state of affairs, Bruges was dogged by **war**. Its weavers and merchants were dependent on the goodwill of the **kings of England** for the proper functioning of the wool trade, but their feudal overlords, the counts of Flanders, and their successors, the dukes of Burgundy (from 1384), were vassals of the rival **king of France**. Although some dukes and counts were strong enough to defy their king, most felt obliged to obey his orders and thus take his side against the English when the two countries were at war. This conflict of interests was compounded by the designs the French monarchy had on the independence of Bruges itself. Time and again, the French sought to assert control over the cities of West Flanders, but more often than not, they encountered armed rebellion. In Bruges, **Philip the Fair** precipitated the most famous insurrection at the beginning of the fourteenth century. Philip and his wife, Joanna of Navarre, had held a grand reception in Bruges, but it had only served to feed their envy. In the face of the city's splendour, Joanna moaned, 'I thought that I alone was Queen, but here in this place, I have six hundred rivals.' The opportunity to flex royal muscles came shortly after when the city's guildsmen refused to pay a new round of taxes. Enraged, Philip dispatched an army to restore order and garrison the town, but at dawn on Friday, 18 May 1302, a rebellious force of Flemings crept into the city and massacred Philip's sleepy army – an occasion later known as the **Bruges Matins**: anyone who couldn't correctly pronounce the Flemish shibboleth *schild en vriend* (shield and friend) was put to the sword. There is a statue celebrating the leaders of the revolt – Jan Breydel and Pieter de Coninck – in the Markt (see page 98).

Decline and revival

The **Habsburgs**, who inherited Flanders – as well as the rest of present-day Belgium and the Netherlands in 1482 – chipped away at the power of the Flemish cities, no one more so than the **Emperor Charles V**. As part of his policy, Charles favoured Antwerp at the expense of Flanders and, to make matters worse, the Flemish cloth industry began its long decline in the 1480s. Bruges was especially badly hit and, as a sign of its decline, failed to dredge the silted-up estuary of the **River Zwin**, the town's trading lifeline to the North Sea. By the 1510s, the stretch of water between Sluis and Damme was only navigable by smaller ships, and by the 1530s, the city's sea trade had collapsed completely. Bruges withered away, its canals empty, and its money spirited north with the merchants. Some four centuries later, **Georges Rodenbach**'s novel *Bruges-la-Morte* alerted well-heeled Europeans to the town's aged, quiet charms. Escaping damage in both world wars, Bruges exerts just as much appeal today.

The Markt

At the heart of Bruges is the **Markt**, an airy open space edged on three sides by rows of gabled buildings and horse-drawn buggies clattering over the cobbles. The burghers of nineteenth-century Bruges were keen to put something suitably civic in the middle of the square, and the result was the conspicuous **monument** to the leaders of the Bruges Matins (see page 98): Pieter de Coninck of the guild of weavers and Jan Breydel, dean of the guild of butchers. Standing close together, they clutch the hilt of the same sword; their faces turned to the south in slightly absurd poses of heroic determination.

The biscuit-tin buildings flanking much of the Markt form a charming architectural ensemble, their mellow, ruddy-brown brick shaped into a long series of crow-step gables, each slightly different from its neighbour. Most are late nineteenth- or even early twentieth-century re-creations – or re-inventions – of older buildings, though the old **provincial courthouse** hogging the east side of the square breaks aesthetic ranks, its thunderous neo-Gothic facade of 1878 announced by a brace of stone lions; it's scheduled to become an information centre in the near future.

Belfort

Markt • Charge • ⓦ visitbruges.be • Entry via the Hallen

Filling out the south side of the Markt, the mighty **Belfort** was long a potent symbol of civic pride and municipal independence, its distinctive octagonal lantern visible far and wide across the surrounding polders. The Belfort was begun in the thirteenth century when the town was at its richest and most extravagant, but it has had a blighted history. The original wooden version was struck by lightning and burned to the ground in 1280. Its brick replacement received its octagonal stone lantern and a second wooden spire in the 1480s, but the new spire was lost to a thunderstorm a few years later. Undeterred, the Flemings promptly added a third spire, though when this went up in smoke in 1741, the locals gave up, settling for the present structure with the addition of a stone parapet in 1822. Few would say the Belfort is good-looking – it's large and rather clumsy – but it does have a certain ungainly charm, though this was lost on G.K. Chesterton, who described it as 'an unnaturally long-necked animal, like a giraffe'.

2

The **belfry staircase** begins innocuously enough, but it gets steeper and much narrower as it nears the top. On the way up, it passes several mildly interesting chambers, starting with the **Treasury Room**, where the town charters and money chest were locked for safekeeping. Here also is an iron trumpet with which a watchman could warn the town of a fire outbreak – though given the size of the instrument, it's hard to believe this was very effective. Further up is the **Carillon Chamber**, where you can observe the slow turning of the large spiked drum that controls the 47 bells of the municipal carillon. The city still employs a full-time bell-ringer – you're likely to see him fiddling around in the Carillon Chamber – who puts on regular **carillon concerts** (Wed, Sat & Sun at 11am; plus mid-June to mid-Sept Mon & Wed at 9pm). A few stairs up from here, you emerge onto the **roof**, which offers fabulous views, especially in the late afternoon when the warm colours of the city are at their deepest.

Hallen

Markt • Free

Now used for temporary exhibitions, the **Hallen** at the foot of the belfry is another much-restored thirteenth-century edifice, its style and structure modelled on the Lakenhalle in Ieper (see page 131). In the middle, overlooked by a long line of galleries, is a rectangular courtyard, which originally served as the city's principal market, its cobblestones once crammed with merchants and their wares. Up a flight of steps, the belfry's entrance is on the courtyard's north side.

The Burg

From the east side of the Markt, Breidelstraat leads through to the city's other main square, the **Burg**, named after the fortress built here by the first count of Flanders, Baldwin Iron Arm, in the ninth century. The fortress disappeared centuries ago, but the Burg long remained the centre of political and ecclesiastical power, with the **Stadhuis** (which has survived) on one side and **St-Donaaskathedraal** (which hasn't) on the other. The French army destroyed the cathedral in 1799, and although the foundations were laid bare in the 1950s, they were promptly re-interred – they lie in front of and underneath the *Crowne Plaza Hotel*.

Heilig Bloed Basiliek

Burg • **Basilica** Free • **Treasury** Charge • Ⓦ holyblood.com

The southern half of the Burg is overseen by the city's finest group of buildings, beginning on the right with the **Heilig Bloed Basiliek** (Basilica of the Holy Blood), named after the holy relic that found its way here in the Middle Ages. The church is divided into two parts. Tucked away in the corner, the **lower chapel** is a shadowy, crypt-like affair, originally built at the beginning of the twelfth century to shelter another relic, that of St Basil, one of the great figures of the early Greek Church. The chapel's heavy and simple Romanesque lines are decorated with just one relief, carved

N9

2

Damme

BRUGES

KLOOSTERMUUR
EDESTRAAT
W. LANYNSTR
KAROUILERSTR
Kruispoort
DELAPLACESTR
SPORTSTRAAT
NOOLSTCN
DAMPOORTSTR
ZUIDERVAARTJE
PARADIJSSTR

BUITEN KRUISVEST R30

DAMPOORT

St-Janshuis-
molen
KRUISVEST
VERRIESTSTR
STIJN STREUVELSSTRAAT
JOS. NIJS
RODESTRAAT
BALSEMBOOMSTRAAT
KWEERSTR
LANGESTRAAT

FORT LAPIN

NOORWEEGSE KAAI
BRUGES SURE EURO
DAMSE VAART ZUID

PETERSEELIESTRAAT

Potteriemuseum

G. Gezelle
Museum

Engels
Klooster

Kantcentrum

Adornesdomein &
Jeruzalemkerk
PEPERSTRAAT

2

MOLENWEERSTR
WIELINGENSTRAAT
VERBRANDE

POTTERIEREI
LANGEREI
'S GRAVENSTRAAT
KOMVEST
Handelskom

SASPLEIN

DUINENABDIJSTR
OLIEBAAN

Volkskundemuseum
BALSTRAAT

ROPEERDSTR
RIJKEPIJNDERSSTR
E. ZORGHESTR
SNAGGAARDSTRAAT
CARMERSSTRAAT
JERUZALEMSTR
BLEKERSSTR
ST-ANNAREI
VERVERSDIJK
BOOMGAARDSTR
RIDDERSTR

WALWEINSTRAAT

Vlotkom

KOMVEST

ST-CLARADREEF

CALVARIEBERGSTRAAT

J. EN M. SABBESTRAAT

LANGEREI
POTTERIEREI
C. MANSIONSTR
BALIESTRAAT
ANNUNTIATENSTRAAT
LANGE RA AMSTRAAT
GOUDEN-HANDSTR
GOUDEN-HANDREI
GOUDEN HANDREI
SPEYE-REI
SPAANSE-REI
KONINGSTR
ENGELSE STR
ST-JANSSTRAAT

ST-PIETERSKAAI

KONWEST

ST-CLARADREEF

IJZERSTRAAT
DIKSMUIDESTRAAT

W. GISTELHOF
HOEDENMAKERSTR
SPANJAARDSTR
AUGUSTIJNENREI
KLOMMERSTR
VLAMINGSTRAAT
KUIPERSSTRAAT
AL DOENSTRAAT
ST-JAKOBS STR

BIDDERSTRAAT

JAN MIRAELSTR
ST-JORISSTRAAT

KONINGIN ELISABETHLAAN

GOMBERTSTRAAT
KARD MERCIERSTRAAT
WERF-
PLEIN
WERFSTRAAT

VLAMINGDAM

ST-CLARASTRAAT

Ezelpoort

ST-Jakobskerk

ZAKSE-POTTERIJNSTRAAT
GRAUWWERKERSSTRAAT

EZELSTRAAT
RAAMSTRAAT
ROZENDAL
EEKHOUTSTRAAT
OUDE ZAK
BEENHOUWERSTR

GULDEN-VLIESLAAN

LEOPOLD II-LAAN

SCHEERSDALELAAN

FLIPS DE GOEDELAAN
KEIZER KARELSTRAAT
GOUDEN-BOOMSTRAAT

Graaf
Visart-
park

KOLHHAAI

SPEELMANSREI OOSTENDESE STEENWEG N9
STEENKAAI

LAUWERSTRAAT
KAREL DE STOUTELAAN
MARIA VAN BOURGONDIELAAN
KEIZER KARELSTRAAT
LEOPOLD I-LAAN
N351
BEVRIJDINGSLAAN

2

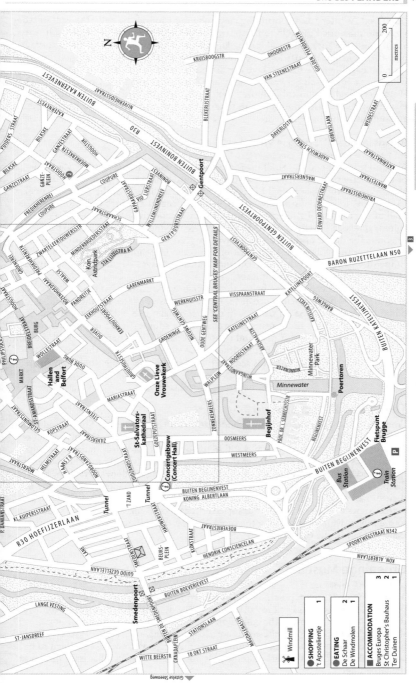

N

0 — 200 metres

KRUISBOOGSTR
DHOORESTR
VAN STEENESTRAAT
NIJVERHEIDSSTRAAT
BUITEN KAZERNEVEST
BLEKERIJSTRAAT
GULDEN PEERDENSTR
BLOKKERSSTRAAT
VUDERS STRAAT
BILSKSE
GANZESTRAAT
HOOGSTUK
MOERKERKERSTR
GANZE-PLEIN
BILSKSE
GANZESTRAAT
HOOGSTRAAT
PREDIKHERENREI
COUPURE
COUPURE
WILLEMUNEDREEF
DANVERLOSTR
RUBENSLAAN
HADEWIJCH STRAAT
WANTESTRAAT
KATERINASTRAAT
WEIRDSTRAAT
WAGNERSTRAAT
EDWARD DEDRECKSTRAAT
VRIJHEIDSSTRAAT
BUITEN BONINVEST
R30
Gentpoort
BONINVEST
OUA
LIERSTRAAT
SCHAARSTRAAT
GENTPOORTSTRAAT
BUITEN GENTPOORTVEST
BARON RUZETTELAAN N50
BUITEN KATELIJNEVEST

MINDERBROEDERSSTRAAT
ZWARTELEERTOUWERSSTR
Kon. Astridpark
STALIJZERSTRA AT
GENTPOORTVEST

GROENEREI
PREDIKHERENREI
ROZENDDRAAL
PANDREITJE
EEKHOUTSTRAAT
WAALSE
GARENMARKT
WERKHUISSTR
VISSPAANSTRAAT
KATELINEPOORT
BARGEWEG
KATELIJNEVEST
HOOGSTRAAT
BREIDELSTRAAT
BURG
OUDE BURG
DWETER
EEKHOUTSTRAAT/POORT
MINIEM. GENTWEG
OUDE GENTWEG
KATELIJNSTRAAT
ASSEBROEKSTRAAT
NOORDSTRAAT
KATELIJNVEST
PHILIPSTOCKSTR
MARKT
WOLLESTRAAT
GRUUTHUSSTR
GROENINGE
WIJNGAARDSTRAAT
WIJNGAANDPLAATS
MINNEWATER
Minnewater Park
Poortoren

SEE 'CENTRAL BRUGES' MAP FOR DETAILS

Hallen and Belfort

MARIASTRAAT
ST-AMANDSSTRAAT
GELDMUNTSTRAAT
STEENSTRAAT
ZILVERSTRAAT
Onze Lieve Vrouwekerk
WALPLEIN
ZONNEKEMEERS
PROF. DR. J. SEBRECHTSSTR
Minnewater
BEGIJNEVEST

St-Salvators-kathedraal
GOEZEPUTSTRAAT
Begijnhof

KOPSTRAAT
MOERSTRAAT
HELMSTRAAT
H. STR
OUDE ZANDSTRAAT
ZUIDZANDSTRAAT
Concertgebouw (Concert Hall)
OOSMEERS
WESTMEERS

Fietspunt Brugge
P

BUITEN BEGIJNENVEST
Bus Station
i **Train Station**

'T ZAND
Tunnel
Tunnel
BUITEN BEGIJNENVEST
KONING ALBERTLAAN

P. DAMIAANS TRAAT
KL. KUIPERSSTRAAT
R30 HOEFIJZERLAAN
HAUWERSTRAAT
BEURS-PLEIN
BOEVERIESTRAAT
KLOMSTRAAT
HENDRIK CONSCIENCELAN
SPOORTWEGSTRAAT N342

Smedenpoort
GUIDO GEZELLELAAN
BUITEN BOEVERIEVEST
BUITEN DE SMEDENPOORT

LANGE VESTING
STATIONSLAAN
KON. ALBERTLAAN

ST-JANSDREEF
WITTE BEERSTR
CANADAPLEIN
18 OKT STRAAT

Gistelse Steenweg

✦ Windmill		
● **SHOPPING**		
't Apostelientje	1	
● **EATING**		
De Schaar	2	
De Windmolen	1	
■ **ACCOMMODATION**		
Bruges Europa	3	
St Christopher's Bauhaus	2	
Ter Duinen	1	

2

(inscribed 'Winter') and continuing clockwise right round the hall. The wall **frescoes** were commissioned in 1895 to illustrate the history of the town – or rather, history as the council wanted to recall it. The largest scene, commemorating the victory over the French at the Battle of the Golden Spurs in 1302, has lots of noble knights hurrahing, though it's hard to take this seriously when you look at the dogs, one of which has a mismatch between its body and head. Adjoining the Gothic Hall is the **Historische zaal** (Historical Room), which features an intriguing audio-visual display exploring the city's relationship with the sea – and the endless cycle of dredging and embankment this has entailed.

Renaissancezaal 't Brugse Vrije
Burg 11A • Charge, includes Stadhuis • ⓦ visitbruges.be

Next door but one to the Stadhuis is the **Landhuis van het Brugse Vrije** (Mansion of the Liberty of Bruges), a comparatively demure building where just one room has survived from the original fifteenth-century structure. This, the Schepenkamer (Aldermen's Room), now known as the **Renaissancezaal 't Brugse Vrije** (Renaissance Hall of the Liberty of Bruges), is dominated by an enormous marble and oak **chimneypiece**, a superb example of Renaissance carving completed in 1531 to celebrate the defeat of the French at Pavia six years earlier and the advantageous Treaty of Cambrai that followed. A paean of praise to the Habsburgs, the work features Emperor Charles V and his Austrian and Spanish relatives – humorously equipped with eye-catching bulbous **codpieces**.

The **alabaster frieze** running below the carvings was a caution for the Liberty's magistrates, who held their courts here. In four panels, it relates the then-familiar biblical story of **Susanna**, in which – in the first panel – two old men surprise her bathing in her garden and threaten to accuse her of adultery if she resists their advances. Susanna does just that, and the second panel shows her in court. In the third panel, Susanna is about to be put to death, but Daniel interrogates the two men and uncovers their perjury. Susanna is acquitted, and in the final scene, the two men are stoned to death.

The Vismarkt and around

From the arch beside the Stadhuis, **Blinde Ezelstraat** (Blind Donkey Street) leads south across one of the city's canals to the sombre nineteenth-century Doric colonnades of the **Vismarkt** (fish market), which is still in use by a handful of fish traders, though knick-knack sellers now outnumber them. The fish sellers have done rather better than the tanners and dyers who used to work in neighbouring **Huidenvettersplein**. Both disappeared long ago and nowadays, tourists converge on this picturesque square in their droves, holing up in its bars and restaurants and snapping away at the postcard-perfect views of the belfry from the adjacent **Rozenhoedkaai**. From here, it's footsteps to the **Dijver**, which tracks along the canal, passing the path to the first of the city's main museums, the **Groeninge**.

Groeninge Museum
Dijver 12 • Charge • ⓦ visitbruges.be

The **Groeninge Museum** possesses one of the world's finest samples of early Flemish paintings, from Jan van Eyck to Jan Provoost. The description below details some of the most important works. The collection is regularly rotated, but most, if not all, should be on display. Note, the city is currently building a lavish, new arts complex – **BRUSK** – on the neighbouring Garenmarkt; at this stage, with work scheduled to be completed in 2025/6, it's hard to know if or how this will affect what is on display at the Groeninge.

CENTRAL BRUGES

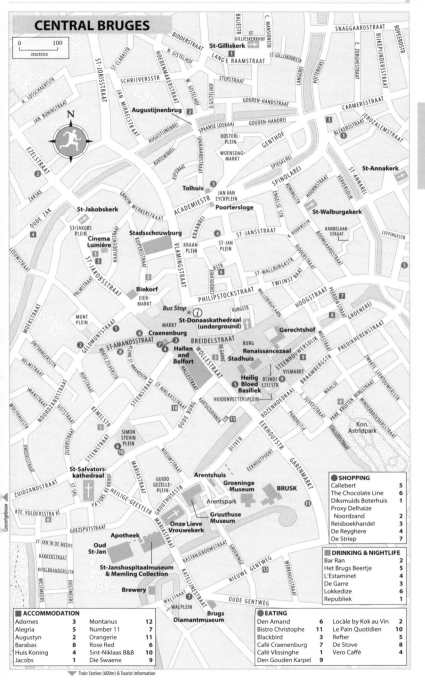

0 — 100 metres

N

St-Gilliskerk **1**

Augustijnenbrug **2**

Tolhuis **3**

St-Jakobskerk

Poortersloge

St-Annakerk

St-Walburgakerk

Cinema Lumière **1** **5**

Stadsschouwburg

Biekorf

Bus Stop

St-Donaaskathedraal (underground)

Craenenburg **3**

Hallen and Belfort **4**

Gerechtshof

Renaissancezaal

Stadhuis

Heilig Bloed Basiliek

St-Salvators-kathedraal

Arentshuis

Groeninge Museum

BRUSK

Arentspark

Gruuthuse Museum

Apotheek

Oud St-Jan

Onze Lieve Vrouwekerk

St-Janshospitaalmuseum & Memling Collection

Brewery

Brugs Diamantmuseum

● **SHOPPING**

Callebert	5
The Chocolate Line	6
Diksmuids Boterhuis	1
Proxy Delhaize Noordzand	2
Reisboekhandel	3
De Reyghere	4
De Striep	7

■ **DRINKING & NIGHTLIFE**

Bar Ran	2
Het Brugs Beertje	5
L'Estaminet	4
De Garre	3
Lokkedize	6
Republiek	1

■ **ACCOMMODATION**

Adornes	3	Montanus	12
Alegria	5	Number 11	7
Augustyn	2	Orangerie	11
Barabas	8	Rose Red	6
Huis Koning	4	Sint-Niklaas B&B	10
Jacobs	1	Die Swaene	9

● **EATING**

Den Amand	6	Locàle by Kok au Vin	2
Bistro Christophe	11	Le Pain Quotidien	10
Blackbird	3	Refter	5
Café Craenenburg	7	De Stove	8
Café Vlissinghe	1	Vero Caffè	4
Den Gouden Karpel	9		

Train Station (600m) & Tourist information

Jan van Eyck

Arguably, the greatest of the early Flemish masters, **Jan van Eyck** (1385–1441), lived and worked in Bruges from 1430 until his death eleven years later. He was a key figure in the development of oil painting, modulating its tones to create paintings of extraordinary clarity and realism. The Groeninge has two gorgeous examples of his work, beginning with the miniature portrait of his wife, *Margareta van Eyck*, painted in 1439 and bearing his motto, *als ich can* (the best I can do). The painting is a private picture with no commercial value, marking a step away from the sponsored art and religious preoccupations of previous Flemish artists. The second van Eyck painting is the remarkable *Madonna and Child with Canon George van der Paele*, a glowing and richly symbolic work with three figures surrounding the Madonna and Child: the kneeling canon, St George (his patron saint) and St Donatian. St George doffs his helmet to salute the infant Christ and speaks by means of the Hebrew word *Adonai* (Lord) inscribed on his armour's chin-strap, while Jesus replies through the green parrot he holds: folklore asserted that this type of parrot was fond of saying *ave*, the Latin for 'welcome' or 'hail'. The canon's face is exquisitely executed, down to the sagging jowls and the bulging blood vessels at his temple, while the glasses and book in his hand add to his air of deep contemplation. Audaciously, van Eyck broke with tradition by painting the canon among the saints rather than as a lesser figure – a distinct nod to the humanism that was gathering pace in contemporary Bruges.

Rogier van der Weyden

The Groeninge possesses two fine and roughly contemporaneous copies of paintings by **Rogier van der Weyden** (1399–1464), one-time official city painter to Brussels. The first is a tiny *Portrait of Philip the Good*, in which the pallor of the duke's aquiline features, along with the brightness of his hatpin and chain of office, is skilfully balanced by the sombre cloak and hat. The second and much larger painting, *St Luke painting the Portrait of Our Lady*, is a rendering of a popular if highly improbable legend that Luke painted Mary – thereby becoming the patron saint of painters. The painting is notable for the detail of its Flemish background and the cheeky-chappie smile of the baby Christ.

Hugo van der Goes

One of the most gifted of the early Flemish artists, **Hugo van der Goes** (d.1482), is a shadowy figure, though it is known that he became master of the painters' guild in Ghent in 1467. Eight years later, he entered a Ghent priory as a lay brother, perhaps on account of the prolonged bouts of depression that afflicted him. Few of his paintings have survived, but these exhibit a superb compositional balance and a keen observational eye – as in his last work, the luminescent *Death of Our Lady*. Sticking to religious legend, the Apostles have been miraculously transported to Mary's deathbed, where, in a state of agitation, they surround the prostrate woman. Mary is dressed in blue, but there are no signs of luxury, reflecting both van der Goes's asceticism and his polemic – the artist may well have been appalled by the church's love of glitter and gold.

Hans Memling

Hans Memling (1430–94) is represented by a pair of *Annunciation* panels from a triptych – gentle, romantic representations of an angel and Mary in contrasting shades of grey. Here also is Memling's *Moreel Triptych*, in which the formality of the design is offset by the warm colours and the gentleness of the detail – St Giles strokes the fawn, and the knight's hand lies on the donor's shoulder. The central panel depicts three saints – two monkish figures on either side of St Christopher, who carries the infant Jesus – and the side panels show the donors and their sixteen children. There are more Memling paintings in Bruges at the St-Janshospitaalmuseum (see page 108).

Hieronymus Bosch

The Groeninge also holds a *Last Judgement* by **Hieronymus Bosch** (1450–1516), comprising a trio of oak panels crammed with mysterious beasts, microscopic mutants and scenes of awful cruelty – men boiled in a pit or cut in half by a giant knife. It looks like an unbridled fantasy, but the scenes are read as symbols, a sort of strip cartoon of legend, proverb and tradition. Indeed, Bosch's religious orthodoxy is confirmed by the appeal his work had for the most Catholic of Spanish kings, Philip II.

Jan Provoost

There's more grim symbolism in **Jan Provoost**'s (1465–1529) striking *The Miser and Death*, which portrays the merchant with his money in one panel, trying desperately to pass a promissory note to the grinning skeleton in the next. Provoost's career was typical of many of the early sixteenth-century Flemish artists. Initially, he worked in the Flemish manner, his style greatly influenced by Gerard David, but from about 1521, his work was reinvigorated by contact with the German painter and engraver Albrecht Dürer, who had himself been inspired by the artists of the early Italian Renaissance. Provoost moved around, too, working in Valenciennes and Antwerp before settling in Bruges in 1494.

Gerard David

Born near Gouda in the Netherlands, **Gerard David** (*c.*1460–1523) moved to Bruges in his early twenties. Soon admitted to the local painters' guild, he quickly rose through the ranks, becoming the city's leading artistic light after the death of Memling. Official commissions rained in on David, mostly for religious paintings, which he approached formally but with a fine eye for detail. The Groeninge holds two fine examples of his work, starting with the *Baptism of Christ Triptych*, where a boyish, lightly bearded Christ is depicted as part of the Holy Trinity in the central panel. One of David's few secular ventures is the intriguing *Judgement of Cambyses*, painted on two large oak panels. Based on a Persian legend related by Herodotus, the first panel's background shows the corrupt judge Sisamnes accepting a bribe, with his subsequent arrest by grim-faced aldermen filling the rest of the panel. The aldermen crowd in on Sisamnes with a palpable sense of menace, and as the king sentences him to be flayed alive, a sweaty look of fear sweeps over the judge's face. In the gruesome second panel, the king's servants carry out the judgement, applying themselves to the task with clinical detachment. Behind, in the top right corner, the fable is completed with the judge's son dispensing justice from his father's old chair, now draped with Sisamnes's flayed skin. Completed in 1498, the city burghers hung the painting in the council chamber to encourage honesty among its magistrates.

Pieter Pourbus

The Groeninge's collection of late sixteenth- and seventeenth-century paintings isn't especially strong. Still, there's enough to discern the period's watering down of religious themes in favour of more secular preoccupations. For example, **Pieter Pourbus** (1523–84) is well represented by a series of austere and often surprisingly unflattering portraits of the movers and shakers of his day. There's also his *Last Judgement*, a much larger but atypical work, crammed with muscular men and fleshy women; completed in 1551, its inspiration came from Michelangelo's Sistine Chapel. Born in Gouda, Pourbus moved to Bruges in his early twenties, becoming the leading local portraitist of his day, as well as squeezing in work as a civil engineer and cartographer.

The Symbolists

There is a small but significant collection of nineteenth- and early twentieth-century Belgian art at the Groeninge. One obvious highlight is the work of the Symbolist **Fernand Khnopff** (1858–1921), who is represented by *Secret Reflections*, not perhaps one of his better paintings, but interesting in so far as its lower panel – showing St Janshospitaal reflected in a canal – confirms one of the movement's favourite conceits: 'Bruges the dead city'. This was inspired by Georges Rodenbach's novel *Bruges-la-Morte*, a highly stylised muse on love and obsession first published in 1892. The book boosted the craze for visiting Bruges, the so-called 'dead city' where the novel's action unfolds. The upper panel of Khnopff's painting is a play on appearance and desire, but it's pretty feeble, unlike his later attempts, in which he painted his sister, Marguerite, again and again, using her refined, almost plastic beauty to stir a vague sense of passion – for him she was desirable and unobtainable in equal measure.

The Expressionists

The museum has a healthy sample of the work of the talented **Constant Permeke** (1886–1952). Wounded in World War I, Permeke's grim wartime experiences helped him develop a distinctive **Expressionist** style in which his subjects – usually agricultural workers, fishermen and so forth – were monumental in form but invested with sombre, sometimes threatening emotion. His charcoal drawing, the *Angelus*, is a typically dark and earthy representation of Belgian peasant life dated to 1934. The enormous *Last Supper* by Gustave van de Woestijne (1881–1947) is another excellent example of Belgian Expressionism, with Jesus and the disciples, all elliptical eyes and restrained movement, trapped within prison-like walls.

The Surrealists

The Groeninge owns a clutch of works by the inventive **Marcel Broodthaers** (1924–76), most notably his tongue-in-cheek (and very Belgian) *Les Animaux de la Ferme*. **René Magritte** (1898–1967; see page 65) appears too, in his characteristically unnerving *The Assault*, while **Paul Delvaux** (1897–1994) features in the spookily stark Surrealism of his *Serenity*. Delvaux has a museum all to himself in St-Idesbald (see page 126).

Arentspark

The **Arentshuis**, close to the Groeninge at Dijver 16, is a rather grand eighteenth-century mansion with a stately porticoed entrance. Formerly a museum, it stands in the north corner of the pocket-sized **Arentspark**, whose pair of forlorn **stone columns** are all that remains of the Waterhalle. This large trading hall once straddled the most central of the city's canals but was demolished in 1787 after the canal was covered over. Also in the Arentspark is the tiniest of humpbacked bridges – **St Bonifaciusbrug** – whose stonework is framed against a tumble of antique brick houses. One of Bruges' most picturesque (and photographed) spots, the bridge looks like the epitome of everything medieval, but it was built in 1910. It takes its name from an eighth-century Anglo-Saxon missionary who successfully Christianised the Germans before being stabbed to death by the more obdurate Frisians.

Gruuthuse Museum

Dijver 17 • Charge • ⓦ visitbruges.be

The **Gruuthuse Museum** is located inside a rambling mansion from the fifteenth century. The building is a fine example of civil Gothic architecture, and it takes its name from the house owners' historical right to tax the *gruit*, the dried herb and flower mixture once added to barley during the beer-brewing process to improve the flavour. The last lord of the Gruuthuse died in 1492. After many twists and turns, the mansion was turned into a museum to hold a hotchpotch of Flemish fine, applied and decorative arts, mainly from the medieval and early modern periods. The museum's most famous artefact is a polychromatic terracotta **bust** of a youthful Emperor Charles V, and its most unusual feature is the oak-panelled **oratory** that juts out from the first floor to overlook the altar of the Onze Lieve Vrouwekerk next door. A curiously intimate room, the oratory allowed the lords of the *gruit* to worship without leaving home – a real social coup.

Onze Lieve Vrouwekerk

Mariastraat • Free • **South aisle** & **chancel** Charge • Ⓦ visitbruges.be

The **Onze Lieve Vrouwekerk** (Church of Our Lady) is a rambling shambles of a building, a clamour of different dates and styles whose spire is – at 115.50m – the highest brick tower in Belgium. Entered from the north, the **nave** was three hundred years in the making, an architecturally discordant affair, whose thirteenth-century grey-stone central aisle is the oldest part of the church. The central aisle blends in with the south aisle, but the later, fourteenth-century north aisle doesn't mesh at all – even the columns aren't aligned. The result of changing fashions, not slapdash work: the High Gothic north aisle was intended to start a complete remodelling of the church, but the money ran out before the project was finished. The church's most acclaimed objet d'art is a delicate marble *Madonna and Child* by Michelangelo in the **south aisle**. Purchased by a Bruges merchant, this was the only one of Michelangelo's works to leave Italy during the artist's lifetime, and it had a significant influence on the painters then working in Bruges, though its present setting – beneath gloomy stone walls and set within a gaudy Baroque altar – is hardly prepossessing.

The chancel

The most interesting part of the church is the **chancel**, beyond the heavy-duty black and white marble rood screen. Here, you'll find the **mausoleums** of Charles the Bold and his daughter Mary of Burgundy (see box, page 108), two exquisite examples of Renaissance artistry, their side panels decorated with coats of arms connected by the most intricate floral designs. The royal figures are enhanced in detail, from the helmet and gauntlets placed gracefully by Charles' side to the pair of watchful dogs nestled at Mary's feet. Oddly enough, the **hole** dug by archaeologists beneath the mausoleums during the 1970s to discover who was buried here was never filled in, so you can see the burial vaults of several unknown medieval dignitaries, three of which have now been moved across to the Lanchals Chapel.

Lanchals Chapel

Just across the ambulatory from the mausoleums is the **Lanchals Chapel**, which holds the imposing Baroque gravestone of Pieter Lanchals, a one-time Habsburg official who had his head lopped off by the citizens of Bruges for corruption in 1488. In front of the Lanchals gravestone are three relocated **medieval burial vaults** moved here from beneath the mausoleums, each plastered with lime mortar. The inside walls of the vaults sport brightly coloured **grave frescoes**, a type of art which flourished hereabouts from the late thirteenth to the middle of the fifteenth century. The iconography is fairly consistent, with the long sides mostly bearing one, sometimes two, angels apiece, and most of the angels are shown swinging thuribles (the vessels in which incense is burnt during religious ceremonies). Typically, the short sides show the Crucifixion and a Virgin and Child. The background decoration is more varied, with crosses, stars and dots all appearing, and two main sorts of flowers – roses and bluebells. The frescoes were painted freehand and executed at great speed – Flemings were then buried on the day they died – hence the delightful immediacy of the work.

St-Janshospitaal

Mariastraat • **Apotheek** Charge • **Oud St-Jan** Free • Ⓦ visitbruges.be

Across the street from the Onze Lieve Vrouwekerk is **St-Janshospitaal**, a sprawling complex that sheltered the sick of mind and body until well into the nineteenth

2

THE EARTHLY REMAINS OF CHARLES THE BOLD AND MARY OF BURGUNDY

The last independent rulers of Flanders were **Charles the Bold**, the Duke of Burgundy, and his daughter **Mary of Burgundy**. Both died in unfortunate circumstances: Charles during the siege of the French city of Nancy in 1477 and Mary after a riding accident in 1482. Mary was married to **Maximilian**, a Habsburg prince and future Holy Roman Emperor, who inherited her territories on her death. Thus, at a dynastic stroke, Flanders was incorporated into the Habsburg Empire with all the dreadful consequences that would entail.

In the sixteenth century, the **Habsburgs** relocated to Spain, but they were keen to emphasise their connections with, and historical authority over, Flanders. Nothing did this quite as well as the ceremonial burial – or reburial – of bits of the royal body. Mary was safely ensconced in Bruges's Onze Lieve Vrouwekerk, but the body of Charles was in a makeshift grave in **Nancy**. The **Emperor Charles V**, the great-grandson of Charles the Bold, had this body exhumed and carried to Bruges, where it was reinterred next to Mary. Or at least he thought he had: there were persistent rumours that the French – the traditional enemies of the Habsburgs – had deliberately handed over a dud skeleton. In the 1970s, **archaeologists** had a bash at solving the mystery by digging beneath Charles and Mary's mausoleums in the Onze Lieve Vrouwekerk. However, among the assorted tombs, they failed to authoritatively identify either the body or even the tomb of Charles. Things ran more smoothly in Mary's case, with her skeleton confirming the details of her hunting accident. Moreover, buried alongside her was the **urn** that contained her son, Philip the Fair's heart, placed here in 1506. More archaeological harrumphing over the remains of poor old Charles is likely at some point or another.

century. The oldest part – at the front on Mariastraat, behind two church-like gable ends – has been turned into the excellent **St-Janshospitaalmuseum**, while the nineteenth-century annexe, reached along a narrow passageway on the north side of the museum, has been converted into a rather mundane events and exhibition centre called – somewhat confusingly – **Oud St-Jan**. As you stroll down the path to **Oud St-Jan**, you pass the old **Apotheek** (Apothecary), where one room holds dozens of ex-votos, the other an ancient dispensing counter flanked by dozens of vintage apothecary's jars.

St-Janshospitaalmuseum

Mariastraat 38 • Charge • ⓦ visitbruges.be

St-Janshospitaalmuseum occupies three distinct spaces: the old, stone-arched hospital ward, an adjoining chapel, and a modern floor that was added much later. The first part of the museum, in the old hospital ward, looks at care and caring over the centuries and explores the historical background of the hospital through documents, paintings and religious objets d'art. Highlights include an enlarged photo of the hospital's nuns in their full and fancy habits as of 1858 and a pair of sedan chairs used to carry the infirm to the hospital in emergencies. There's also Jan Beerblock's *The Wards of St Janshospitaal*, a minutely detailed painting of the hospital ward as it was in the late eighteenth century, the patients tucked away in row upon row of tiny, cupboard-like beds. There were 150 beds divided into three sections: one for women, one for men and the third for the dying. The nuns had a fine reputation for the quality of their ministrations, but presumably, being moved to the dying beds was some cause of alarm.

The Memling collection

The museum holds six wonderful works by **Hans Memling** (1433–94). Born near Frankfurt, Memling spent most of his working life in Bruges, where Rogier van der Weyden (see page 104) instructed him. He adopted much of his tutor's style and stuck to the detailed symbolism of his contemporaries, but his painterly manner was distinctly restrained and often pious and grave. Graceful and warmly coloured, his figures also had a velvet-like quality that greatly appealed to the city's burghers, whose enthusiasm made Memling a rich man – in 1480, he was listed among the town's major moneylenders.

Reliquary of St Ursula and two Memling triptychs

The most unusual of the Memling works on display is the **reliquary of St Ursula**, comprising a miniature wooden Gothic church painted with the story of St Ursula. Memling condensed the legend into six panels, with Ursula and her ten companions landing at Cologne and Basle before reaching Rome at the end of their pilgrimage. Things go badly wrong on the way back: they leave Basle in good order but are then – in the last two panels – massacred by Huns as they pass through Germany. Memling had a religious point, but today, it is the mass of incidental detail which makes the reliquary so enchanting, providing an intriguing evocation of the late medieval world. Close by are two triptychs, a *Lamentation* and an *Adoration of the Magi*, in which there's a gentle nervousness in the approach of the Magi, who are shown as the kings of Spain, Arabia and Ethiopia.

Triptych of St John the Baptist and St John the Evangelist

The delightful **Mystical Marriage of St Catherine** is the **middle panel** of a large triptych. St Catherine, who represents contemplation, is shown receiving a ring from the baby Jesus to seal their spiritual union. The complementary **side panels** depict the beheading of St John the Baptist and a visionary St John the Evangelist writing the Book of Revelation on the bare and rocky island of Patmos. Again, the detail impresses: between the inner and outer rainbows above the Evangelist, for instance, the prophets play music on tiny instruments – look closely, and you'll spy a lute, a flute, a harp and a hurdy-gurdy.

Virgin and Martin van Nieuwenhove

The **Virgin and Martin van Nieuwenhove** diptych depicts the eponymous merchant in the full flush of youth and with a hint of arrogance: his lips pout, his hair cascades down to his shoulders, and he is dressed in the most fashionable of doublets. By the middle of the 1480s, when the portrait was commissioned, no Bruges merchant wanted to appear too pious. Opposite, the Virgin gets the full stereotypical treatment from the oval face and almond-shaped eyes through to full cheeks, a thin nose and a bunched lower lip.

Portrait of a Young Woman

Memling's skill as a portraitist is demonstrated to exquisite effect in his **Portrait of a Young Woman**, where the richly dressed subject stares dreamily into the middle distance, her hands – in a superb optical illusion – seeming to clasp the picture frame. The lighting is subtle and sensuous, with the woman set against a dark background, her gauze veil dappling the side of her face. A high forehead was then considered a sign of great womanly beauty, so her hair is pulled back and was probably plucked – as are her eyebrows. There's no knowing who the woman was, but in the seventeenth century, her fancy headgear convinced observers that she was one of the legendary sibyls who predicted Christ's birth; so convinced were they that they added the cartouche in the top left-hand corner, describing her as *Sibylla Sambetha* – and the painting is often referred to by this name.

St-Salvatorskathedraal

Steenstraat • Free • ⓦ sintsalvatorskathedraal.be

The high and mighty **St-Salvatorskathedraal** (Holy Saviour Cathedral) is a bulky Gothic edifice that mostly dates from the late thirteenth century – the ambulatory was added some two centuries later. A parish church for most of its history, it was only made a cathedral in 1834 following the destruction of St Donatian's by the French (see page 99). This change of status prompted lots of ecclesiastical rumblings: nearby Onze Lieve Vrouwekerk (see page 107) was bigger and its spire higher, so when part of St Salvator's went up in smoke in 1839, the opportunity was taken to make its tower higher and grander in a romantic rendition of the Romanesque style.

The nave and porch

The cathedral **nave** may recently have emerged from a thoroughgoing restoration, but it remains a cheerless, cavernous affair despite the lashings of cream paint. Nevertheless, it possesses a star turn in the **eight paintings** by Jan van Orley displayed in the transepts. Commissioned in the 1730s, the paintings were used to manufacture a matching set of **tapestries** from a Brussels workshop; remarkably enough, these have survived and hang in sequence in the choir. Each of the eight scenes is a fluent, dramatic composition featuring a familiar episode from the life of Christ – from the Nativity to the Resurrection – complete with a handful of animals, including a remarkably determined Palm Sunday donkey. The tapestries are mirror images of the paintings as the weavers worked with the rear of the tapestries uppermost on their looms; the weavers also had sight of the tapestry paintings – or rather cartoon copies, as the originals were too valuable to be kept beside the looms. Adjoining the nave, in the floor of the **porch** behind the old main doors, look out also for the six excavated tombs, whose interior walls are decorated with **grave frescoes** that follow the same design as those in the Lanchals Chapel (see page 107).

The treasury

The cathedral **treasury** (Schatkamer) occupies the adjoining neo-Gothic chapterhouse, whose cloistered rooms are packed with ecclesiastical bits and pieces, from religious paintings and statues to an assortment of reliquaries, vestments and croziers. The labelling is poor, however, so it's a good idea to pick up the English-language mini-guide at the entrance. **Room B** holds the treasury's finest painting, a gruesome, oak-panel triptych, *The Martyrdom of St Hippolytus*, by **Dieric Bouts** (1410–75) and **Hugo van der Goes** (d. 1482). The right panel depicts the Roman Emperor Decius, a notorious persecutor of Christians, trying to persuade the priest Hippolytus to abjure his faith. He fails, and in the central panel, Hippolytus is pulled to pieces by four horses.

The Begijnhof

Begijnhof • Free • ⓦ visitbruges.be

Bruges' tourist throng zeroes in on the **Begijnhof**, just south of the centre, where a rough circle of old and infinitely pretty whitewashed houses surrounds a central green, which looks a treat in spring when a carpet of daffodils pushes up between the elms. There were once *begijnhoven* all over Belgium, and this is one of the few to have survived in good nick. They date back to the twelfth century when a Liège priest – a certain Lambert le Bègue – encouraged widows and unmarried women to live in communities, the better to do pious acts, especially caring for the sick. These communities differed from convents in that the inhabitants – the **Beguines** (*begijnen*) – did not have to take conventual vows and had the right to return to the secular world if they wished. Margaret, Countess of Flanders, founded Bruges' *begijnhof* in 1245. Although most houses now date from the eighteenth century, the medieval layout has survived intact, preserving the impression of the *begijnhof* as a self-contained village, with access controlled through two large gates. Almost all of the houses are still in private hands. With the Beguines long gone, they're now occupied by a mixture of single, elderly women and Benedictine nuns, whom you'll see flitting around in their habits, mostly on their way to and from the **Begijnhofkerk**, a surprisingly large church with a set of gaudy altarpieces.

Minnewater

Facing the more southerly of the *begijnhof*'s two gates is the **Minnewater**, often hyped as the city's 'Lake of Love'. The tag certainly gets the canoodlers going, but the lake – more a large pond – started life as a city harbour. The distinctive stone **lock house** at the head of the Minnewater recalls its earlier function, though it's a fanciful nineteenth-century reconstruction of the medieval original. The **Poertoren**, on the west bank at the far end of the lake, is more authentic; its brown brickwork dates back to 1398 and once formed part of the city wall. This is where the city kept its gunpowder – hence the name 'powder tower'. Beside the Poertoren, a footbridge spans the southern end of the Minnewater to reach the leafy expanse of **Minnewaterpark** – or you can keep on going along the footpath that threads its way along the old city **ramparts**, now pleasantly wooded.

Jan van Eyckplein and around

Jan van Eyckplein, a five-minute walk north of the Markt, is one of the prettier squares in Bruges, its cobbles backdropped by the easy sweep of the Spiegelrei canal. The centrepiece of the square is an earnest **statue of Jan van Eyck**, erected in 1878, while on the north side is the **Tolhuis**, whose fancy Renaissance entrance is decorated with the coat of arms of the dukes of Luxembourg, who long levied tolls here. The Tolhuis dates from the late fifteenth century but was extensively remodelled in medieval style in the 1870s, as was the **Poortersloge** (Merchants' Lodge; no public entry), whose slender tower pokes up above the rooftops on the west side of the square. Theoretically, any city merchant was entitled to be a member of the Poortersloge, but in fact, membership was restricted to the richest and most powerful. An informal alternative to the Stadhuis, it was here that key political and economic decisions were taken – and this was also where local bigwigs could drink and gamble discreetly.

Spiegelrei canal

Running east from Jan van Eyckplein, the **Spiegelrei canal** was once the heart of the foreign merchants' quarter, its frenetic quays overlooked by the trade missions of many of the city's trading partners. The medieval buildings were demolished long ago, but they have been replaced by an exquisite medley of architectural styles, from expansive Classical mansions to pirouetting crow-step gables.

Gouden Handrei and around

At the far end of Spiegelrei, a left turn brings you onto one of the city's loveliest streets, **Gouden-Handrei**, which – along with its continuation, **Spaanse Loskaai** – was once the focus of the Spanish merchants' quarter. The west end of Spaanse Loskaai is marked by the **Augustijnenbrug**, the city's oldest surviving bridge, a sturdy three-arched structure dating from 1391. The bridge was built to help the monks of a nearby (and long demolished) Augustinian monastery get into the city centre speedily; the benches set into the parapet were cut to allow itinerant tradesmen to display their goods here.

Spanjaardstraat

Running south from Augustijnenbrug is **Spanjaardstraat**, another part of the old Spanish enclave. It was here, at No. 9, in a house formerly known as **De Pijnappel** (The Fir Cone), that the founder of the Jesuits, Ignatius Loyola (1491–1556), spent his holidays while he was a student in Paris – unfortunately, the town's liberality failed to dent Loyola's nascent fanaticism.

2

The Adornesdomein

Peperstraat 3 • Charge • ⓦ adornes.org

Beyond the east end of the Spiegelrei canal is an old working-class district whose simple brick cottages surround the **Adornesdomein**, a substantial complex of buildings belonging to the wealthy Adornes family, who migrated here from Genoa in the thirteenth century and made a fortune from a special sort of dye fastener. A visit to the *domein* begins towards the rear of the complex, where a set of humble brick almshouses hold a small **museum**, which gives the historical low-down on the family. The most interesting figure was the much-travelled **Anselm Adornes** (1424–83), whose roller-coaster career included high-power diplomatic missions to Scotland and being punished for alleged corruption – he was fined and paraded through Bruges dressed only in his underwear.

The Jeruzalemkerk

Anselm Adornes and several of his kinfolk made pilgrimages to the Holy Land, and one result is the idiosyncratic **Jeruzalemkerk** (Jerusalem Church), the main feature of the *domein* and an approximate copy of the Church of the Holy Sepulchre in Jerusalem. The church's interior is on **two levels**: the lower one is dominated by a large and ghoulish **altarpiece** decorated with skulls and ladders, in front of which is the black marble **mausoleum** of Anselm Adornes and his wife Margaretha – though the only part of Anselm held here is his heart: Anselm was murdered in Scotland, which is where he was buried, but his heart was sent back here to Bruges. There's more grisliness at the back of the church, where a vaulted chapel holds a **replica of Christ's tomb** with an imitation body – it's down a narrow tunnel behind the iron grating. To either side of the main altar, steps ascend to the choir, right below the eccentric, onion-domed lantern **tower**.

Kantcentrum

Balstraat 16 • Charge • ⓦ kantcentrum.eu

The ground floor of the **Kantcentrum** (Lace Centre), just metres from the Adornesdomein, traces the history of the industry here in Bruges and displays a substantial sample of antique handmade lace. The earliest major piece is an exquisite, seventeenth-century Lenten veil with scenes from the life of Ignatius of Loyola, the founder of the Jesuits, and there are also intricate collars, ruffs, fans and sample books – the most fanciful pieces – Chantilly lace, especially – mostly date from the late nineteenth century. Belgian lace – or **Flanders lace** as it was formerly known – was renowned for the fineness of its thread and beautiful motifs, and it was once worn in the courts of Brussels, Paris, Madrid and London, with Bruges the centre of its production. **Handmade lace** peaked in the early nineteenth century when hundreds of Bruges women and girls worked as home-based lace-makers. The industry was, however, transformed by the arrival of **machine-made lace** in the 1840s and by the end of the century, handmade lace had been largely supplanted, with the lace-makers obliged to work in factories. This highly mechanised industry collapsed after World War I when lace, a symbol of an old and discredited order, suddenly had no place in most women's wardrobes. Most **lace shops in Bruges** sell lace manufactured in the Far East, especially China, but upstairs at the Kantcentrum, there are **demonstrations** of handmade lace-making. You can buy pieces here, too – or stroll along the street to 't Apostelientje (see page 117).

ARRIVAL AND DEPARTURE BRUGES

By train & bus The train and adjacent bus station are about 2km southwest of the city centre. Local buses Nos 1 and 2 depart for the Dijver, near the Markt, from outside the train station (every 5min).

Destinations by train Brussels (every 20min; 1hr); Ghent (every 20min; 20min); Ostend (every 20min; 15min). Destinations by bus Damme (No. 43 Mon–Fri 1 or 2 daily; 30min).

2

CYCLING AROUND BRUGES

Beginning about 2.5km northeast of the Markt, the country lanes on either side of the **Brugge-Sluis canal** cut across a pretty parcel of land that extends as far as the E34/N49 motorway, about 12km further to the northeast. This rural backwater is ideal **cycling country**, its green fields crisscrossed by drowsy canals and causeways, each shadowed by poplar trees that quiver and rustle in the prevailing westerly winds. An obvious itinerary – of about 28km – takes in the quaint village of **DAMME**, which was, in medieval times, Bruges's main seaport. After that, the Brugge-Sluis carries on east as far as tiny **HOEKE**, where, just over the bridge and on the north side of the canal, you turn hard left for the narrow causeway – the **Krinkeldijk** – that wanders back in the direction of Bruges. Just over 3km long, the Krinkeldijk drifts across a beguiling landscape of whitewashed farmhouses and deep-green grassy fields before reaching an intersection where you turn left to regain the Brugge–Sluis waterway.

If you prefer **maps to phones**, the **Fietsnetwerk Brugse Ommeland** (1:50,000) is available from any major bookshop.

By car The E40, running northwest from Brussels to Ostend, skirts Bruges. Bruges is signed from the E40, and its oval-shaped centre is encircled by the R30 ring road.
Parking In the centre can be a real tribulation; the best and most economical option is to use the 24/7 car park by the train station, particularly as the price – €6.10 per day – includes the cost of the bus ride to and from the centre.

GETTING AROUND

By bus Local buses are operated by De Lijn (ⓦ delijn.be). A standard one-way fare costs €2.50. Tickets are valid for an hour and can be purchased at automatic ticket machines. A city transport pass, the Dagpas (24hr), costs €7.50. There's a De Lijn information kiosk outside the train station (Mon–Fri 7.30am–5.45pm, Sat 9am–5pm & Sun 10am–5pm).
By bike Flat as a pancake, Bruges and its environs are a great place to cycle (see box, page 113), especially as there are cycle lanes on many of the roads and cycle racks dotted across the centre. There are about a dozen bike rental places in town – tourist information has the full list. The largest is Fietspunt Brugge, beside the train station (April–Sept: Mon–Fri 7am–7pm, Sat & Sun 10am–9pm; Oct–March: Mon–Fri 7am–7pm; ☏ 050 39 68 26).
By taxi Bruges has several taxi ranks, including one on the Markt and another outside the train station. Fares are metered – and the most common journey, from the train station to the centre, costs about €12.

INFORMATION

Tourist information There are three tourist information offices: a small one at the train station (daily 10am–5pm); another in the Concertgebouw (Concert Hall) complex, on the west side of the city centre on 't Zand (Mon–Sat 10am–5pm, Sun 10am–2pm); and a third on the Markt (daily 10am–5pm), in the same building as the ghastly Historium where, allegedly, you can 'Experience the magic of the medieval period'. They have a common phone line and website (☏ 050 44 46 46, ⓦ visitbruges.be).

City passes A splurge of new (and occasionally tawdry) attractions made Bruges's old CityCard pass increasingly hard to co-ordinate, and as a consequence, it was abandoned in 2016. It may or may not be revived, but in the meantime, what you can do is the Museum Bruges Card (Musea Brugge Card; ⓦ museabrugge.be) , which is valid for three days, covers entry to all the main museums and costs €33 (12–25-year-olds €25)

ACCOMMODATION   SEE MAPS PAGES 100 AND 103

Bruges has over a hundred hotels, almost two hundred B&Bs, and several youth hostels. However, it still can't accommodate all its visitors at busy times, especially in the high season (roughly late June to early Sept) and at Christmas, so you'd be well advised to book ahead. Most of the city's hotels are small – twenty rooms, often fewer – and few are chains. Standards are generally high among the hotels and B&Bs, whereas the city's hostels are more inconsistent.

HOTELS

★ **Adornes** St Annarei 26 ⓦ adornes.be. Medium-sized three-star in two tastefully converted old Flemish townhouses. Both the public areas and the comfortable bedrooms are decorated in attractive pastel shades, emphasising the place's antique charm. The location's great – at the junction of two canals near the east end of Spiegelrei – and the breakfasts are delicious. Also very child-friendly. **€€€**

2

GUIDED TOURS AND BOAT TRIPS IN AND AROUND BRUGES

Guided tours are big business in Bruges. Tourist information (see page 113) has comprehensive details, but among the many options, one long-standing favourite is a **horse-drawn carriage ride**. Carriages hold a maximum of five and line up on the Markt (daily 10am–10pm; 30min; €70 per carriage) to offer a short canter around town; demand can outstrip supply, so expect to queue at the weekend. A second favourite is half-hour **boat trips** along the city's central canals with boats departing from a number of jetties south of the Burg (March–Nov: daily 10am–6pm; €12). Boats leave every few minutes, but long queues still build up during the high season, with few visitors seemingly concerned by the canned commentary. In winter (Dec–Feb), there's only a spasmodic service at weekends.

Quasimodo Tours ⓦ quasimodo.be. Bruges has a small army of tour operators, but this is one of the best. It runs a first-rate programme of excursions both in and around Bruges and out into Flanders. Their 'Flanders Field Battlefield' minibus tour of the World War I battlefields near Ieper is highly recommended. This includes a picnic lunch and lasts about eight hours. Reservations are required; hotel or train station pick-up can be arranged.

Quasimundo Predikherenstraat 28 ⓦ quasimundo. com. Quasimundo runs several bike tours, starting from the Burg. Their 'Bruges by Bike' excursion (March–Oct: 1 daily; 2.5hr) zips around the main sights and then explores less-visited parts of the city, while their 'Border by Bike' tour (March–Oct: 1 daily; 4hr) is a 25km ride out along the poplar-lined canals to the north of Bruges, visiting Damme and Oostkerke with stops and stories along the way. Both are good fun, and the price includes mountain bike and rain-jacket hire; reservations are required.

★ **Alegria** St-Jakobsstraat 34 ⓦ alegria-hotel.com. Formerly a B&B, this appealing, family-run three-star has a dozen or so large and well-appointed rooms, each decorated in attractive shades of brown, cream and white. The rooms at the back, overlooking the garden, are quieter than those at the front. The owner is a mine of information about where and what to eat, and the hotel is in a central location near the Markt. €€

Augustyn Augustijnenrei 18 ⓦ hotelaugustyn.com. In a great location, in one of the prettiest parts of the city, this smart, modern hotel occupies a late-nineteenth-century townhouse overlooking a canal just minutes' walk north of the Burg. Competitively priced with a variety of room categories – including an apartment. €€€

Jacobs Baliestraat 1 ⓦ hoteljacobs.be. A good budget option, this three-star hotel in a quiet, central location occupies a pleasantly modernised old brick building with a precipitous crow-step gable. The twenty-odd rooms are decorated in a crisp, modern style, though some are a little small. €€

Montanus Nieuwe Gentweg 76 ⓦ denheerd.be. This four-star hotel occupies a big old house that has been sympathetically modernised with little of the decorative over-elaboration of many rivals. The twelve rooms here are large, comfortable and modern – and there are twelve more at the back, in chalet-like accommodation at the far end of the large garden. There's also an especially appealing room in what amounts to a (cosy and luxurious) garden shed. The garden also accommodates an up-market restaurant. €€

Orangerie Kartuizerinnenstraat 10 ⓦ hotelorangerie. be. In a former convent and one-time bakery, this classy, family-owned four-star hotel has twenty guest rooms, the pick of which are kitted out in an exuberant version of country-house style. The wood-panelled lounge oozes a relaxed and demure charm – as does the breakfast room – and a tunnel leads down to a canal-side terrace. Great central location, too. €€€€

Rose Red Cordoeaniersstraat 18 ⓦ hotelrosered.be/en. This medium-sized, family-run, two-star hotel is handily located on a narrow side street a few minutes' walk north of the Burg. Mosquitoes can be a problem here, but the 22 rooms are neat, trim and modern. €€

Die Swaene Steenhouwersdijk 1 ⓦ dieswaene.com. In a perfect location, beside a particularly pretty and peaceful section of the canal close to the Burg, this long-established four-star hotel has thirty guest rooms decorated in an individual and rather sumptuous antique style. There's also a heated pool and sauna. €€€

★ **Ter Duinen** Langerei 52 ⓦ terduinen.eu. Charming four-star hotel in a lovely part of the city, beside the Langerei canal, a 15min walk from the Markt. Occupies a beautifully maintained eighteenth-century villa, with period public areas and charming modern rooms. Superb breakfasts, too. €€€

B&BS

Barabas Hertsbergestraat 8–10 ⓦ barabas.be. Deluxe affair in a pair of handsome – and handsomely restored – eighteenth-century houses, with four large guest rooms/ suites kitted out in grand period style down to the vast, flowing drapes. Central location: the garden backs onto a canal. €€€

Huis Koning Oude Zak 25 ⓦ huiskoning.be. A plushly renovated B&B in a seventeenth-century, step-gable terraced house with a pleasant canal-side garden. The four en-suite guest rooms are decorated in a fresh-feeling modern style, and two have canal views. €€€

Number 11 Peerdenstraat 11 ⓦnumber11.be. In the heart of old Bruges, on a traffic-free side street, this first-rate B&B in an ancient terrace house has just four lavish guest rooms: all wooden floors, beamed ceilings and expensive wallpaper. Every comfort is laid on – and smashing breakfasts, too. €€€

Sint-Niklaas B&B St-Niklaasstraat 18 ⓦsintnik.be. In a good-looking, three-storey, eighteenth-century townhouse on a side street near the Markt, this well-kept B&B has three modern, en-suite guest rooms. One has a lovely view of the Belfort. €€

HOSTELS

Bruges Europa Baron Ruzettelaan 143 ⓦjeugdher bergen.be/en. Big and looking like a school, this HI hostel is set on its own grounds a (dreary) 2km south of the centre in the suburb of Assebroek. There are over two hundred beds in a mixture of rooms from doubles through to six-bed dorms, most en suite. Breakfast is included in the price, and there are security lockers, wi-fi, free parking, a bar and a lounge. City bus Nos 4 or 6 from outside Bruges train station, go within 300m – ask the driver to let you off at the Wantestraat bus stop. Dorms €, doubles €

St Christopher's Bauhaus Langestraat 133–137 ⓦbauhaus.be. This lively, laid-back hostel, a 15min walk east of the Burg, has a boho air and offers a mishmash of rooms accommodating two and six bunks each, some with pod beds. Bike rentals, lockers, a bar and a café are also available. Dorms €, doubles €

EATING

SEE MAPS PAGES 100 AND 103

There are scores of **cafés**, **café-bars**, and restaurants in Bruges, but mercifully, few of them are chains. Many are indeed geared up for the day-trippers, with variable results, but there's also a slew of first-rate places that take their reputations seriously – and these range from the expensive to the affordable. Most waiters speak at least a modicum of **English** – many are fluent – and multilingual menus are the norm.

CAFÉS AND CAFÉ-BARS

★ **Blackbird** Jan van Eyckplein 7 ⓦblackbird-bruges. com. Infinitely cosy café with a lively eye as to its decor. They throw a wide gastronomic net here – from breakfasts featuring all manner of healthy options to sandwiches, plus superb lunchtime salads, heaped high and fresh. €

Café Craenenburg Markt 16 ⓦcraenenburg.be. Unlike Markt's other tourist-dominated café-restaurants, this old-fashioned place still attracts a loyal local clientele. With its leather and wood panelling, wooden benches and mullion windows, the *Craenenburg* has the flavour of old Flanders. Although the daytime-only food is routine, it has a good range of beers, including a locally produced, tangy brown ale called Brugse Tripel. €

★ **Café Vlissinghe** Blekersstraat 2 ⓦcafevlissinghe. be. With its wood panelling, antique paintings and long wooden tables, this is one of the oldest and most distinctive bars in Bruges, thought to date from 1515. The atmosphere is relaxed and easy-going, emphasising quiet conversation – there are certainly no jukeboxes here – and the café-style food is Flemish. There's a pleasant garden terrace too. €

Le Pain Quotidien Simon Stevinplein 15 ⓦlepain quotidien.be. This popular café, part of a chain, occupies a grand old building on one of the city's busiest squares and has a large terrace at the back. Much of the chain's success is built upon its bread and whole food, baked in every which way. A substantial menu clocks up salads, light bites and cakes, and they also make an excellent home-made soup and bread, which makes a meal in itself. €

Vero Caffè St-Jansplein 9 ☎0484 76 41 10. A decorated café with whitewashed brick walls where local hipsters and students rub shoulders to enjoy a great cup of coffee. There are home-baked cakes, too, but the tastiest vanish early. Its location on a quiet square is pleasantly removed from the hubbub of central Bruges. €

De Windmolen Carmersstraat 135 ☎050 33 97 39. This amiable neighbourhood café-bar, in an old brick house at the east end of Carmersstraat, is a pick for its setting – away from the crowds and next to the grassy bank that marks the course of the old city wall. It has a competent beer menu and a reasonably decent line of inexpensive snacks – keep to the simpler offerings. Has a pleasant outside terrace and an interior dotted with folksy knick-knacks. €

RESTAURANTS

Den Amand St-Amandstraat 4 ⓦdenamand.be. This small and informal, family-run restaurant offers an inventive range of dishes combining Flemish, Italian and Asian cuisines. Mains from the limited but well-chosen menu – for instance, brill in coconut milk – average a reasonable €25. It's a small place, so booking a few hours in advance is best. €€

Bistro Christophe Garenmarkt 34 ⓦchristophe-brugge.be. Rural chic furnishings and fittings make for a relaxing atmosphere at this little bistro, where a Franco-Flemish menu is especially strong on meat. One exception is the excellent bouillabaisse. €€€

Den Gouden Karpel Vismarkt 9 ⓦdengoudenkarpel.be. Since its opening, this seafood restaurant has garnered rave reviews for its simple and straightforward approach to wet fish and shellfish. The restaurant comprises just a handful of plain modern chairs and tables behind the fish shop and counter. The menu varies depending on the day's catch. €€€

Locàle by Kok au Vin Ezelstraat 21 ⓦlocale.be/en. Smart restaurant occupying tastefully modernised

2

old premises on the north side of the city centre. A well-considered and ambitious menu covers all the Franco-Belgian bases and then some. Try the signature dish – coq au vin. Reservations are essential. €€€

Refter Molenmeers 2 ⓦbistrorefter.com. Fashionable bistro restaurant with über-cool decor where the emphasis is on classic Flemish dishes using local, seasonal ingredients – try the meatballs in a tarragon sauce. It is competitively priced too, especially at lunchtime. Outside terrace for summertime dining; one criticism: the tables are too close together. €€€

De Schaar Hooistraat 2 ⓦbistrodeschaar.be. In the cosiest of terrace houses, complete with a stepped gable, this appealing restaurant sits prettily beside the Coupure Canal. The speciality here is grilled meat – for example, a rack of lamb with wok vegetables and mustard sauce – but there are other gastronomic delights, such as duck with a raspberry sauce. All are nicely served and presented. €€€

De Stove Kleine St-Amandsstraat 4 ⓦrestaurant destove.be. This small Franco-Belgian restaurant is recommended by just about everyone. The menu is carefully constructed, with both fish and meat dishes given equal prominence. A la carte mains, but the big deal is the three-course set menu. Reservations are essential. €€€

DRINKING AND NIGHTLIFE
SEE MAP PAGE 103

Few would say Bruges' **bars** are cutting-edge, but neither are they staid and dull. Indeed, **drinking** in the city can be an absolute pleasure and one of the potential highlights of any visit. As for the **club scene**, Bruges struggles to make a real fist of it, though a couple of places are enjoyable enough.

Bar Ran Kuipersstraat 4 ⓦbarranbrugge.com. Locally run, with an amiable neighbourhood vibe, this is probably the best cocktail bar in the city. The decor is great – though staying on one of the stools can be a challenge – and the cocktails are fabulous; for something different, try the King Kong Milk Punch.

Het Brugs Beertje Kemelstraat 5 ⓦbrugsbeertje.be. This small and friendly speciality beer bar claims a stock of three hundred brews (plus guest beers on draught), which aficionados reckon is one of the best selections in Belgium. On the (backpacker) tourist trail, there are also tasty snacks, such as cheeses and toasties.

★ **L'Estaminet** Park 5 ⓦestaminet-brugge.be. Groovy café-bar with a relaxed neighbourhood feel and (for Bruges) a diverse and cosmopolitan clientele. Drink in the dark, almost mysterious interior or outside on the large, sheltered terrace. It has a well-chosen beer menu, which skilfully picks its way through Belgium's vast resources.

★ **De Garre** De Garre 1 ⓦdegarre.be. Down a narrow alley off Breidelstraat, between the Markt and the Burg, this cramped but charming and ancient tavern offers an outstanding range of Belgian beers and tasty snacks. Classical music adds to the relaxing atmosphere.

Lokkedize Korte Vuldersstraat 33 ⓦbistrolokkedize. be. This popular café-bar is atmospheric, with subdued lighting and soft sounds. It also regularly features live music, everything from jazz and chanson to R&B.

Republiek St-Jacobsstraat 36 ⓦrepubliekbrugge.be. One of the most fashionable spots in town, this large and darkly lit café-bar attracts an arty, mostly youthful clientele. Very reasonably priced snacks, including vegetarian and pasta dishes, plus the occasional gig. Terrace at the back for summertime drinking.

ENTERTAINMENT

Bruges puts on a varied programme of **performing arts**, mostly as part of its annual schedule of festivals and special events (see box, page 116). As for **film**, Bruges has an excellent art-house cinema, where movies are usually shown in the original language, with Dutch/Flemish subtitles as required. For details of **upcoming events**, consult the tourist information website (ⓦvisitbruges.be) or pick up their free monthly events calendar.

Cinema Lumière St-Jacobstraat 36 ⓦlumierecinema. be. Bruges' premier venue for alternative, cult, foreign and art-house movies, with three screens.

Concertgebouw 't Zand 34 ☎078 15 20 20 (ticket line), ⓦconcertgebouw.be. Built in 2002 to celebrate Bruges' year as a European Capital of Culture, the venue now hosts all the performing arts, from opera and classical music to big-name bands.

FESTIVALS AND EVENTS IN BRUGES

Leading **festivals** in Bruges' crowded calendar include the **Musica Antiqua** festival of medieval music at the beginning of August, though this is but one small part of the more generalised **Festival van Vlaanderen** (Flanders Festival; March–Oct; ⓦfestival.be), which comprises over five hundred classical concerts distributed among the big Flemish-speaking cities, including Bruges. Bruges also hosts one big-deal music festival, the **Cactusfestival** (ⓦcactusfestival.be) of rock, reggae, rap and roots, spread over three days on the second weekend of July.

Stadsschouwburg Vlamingstraat 29 ⓦccbrugge.be. Occupying a big neo-Renaissance building from 1869, the

Stadsschouwburg's wide-ranging programme includes theatre, dance, musicals, concerts and opera.

SHOPPING

SEE MAPS PAGES 100 AND 103

't Apostelientje Balstraat 11 ⓦapostelientje.be. Footsteps from the Kantcentrum (see page 112), this small shop sells a charming variety of handmade lace pieces of both modern and traditional designs; it's easily the best lace shop in Bruges.

Callebert Wollestraat 25 ⓦcallebert.be. Bruges's top contemporary homeware, ceramics, and furniture shop features leading brands such as Alessi and Bodum alongside some less familiar names. It also stocks everything from bags, watches, and jewellery to household utensils, textiles and tableware.

The Chocolate Line Simon Stevinplein 19 ⓦthe chocolateline.be. The best chocolate shop in town – and there's some serious competition – with everything handmade using natural ingredients. Truffles and pralines are two specialities. Boxes of mixed chocolates are sold in various sizes: a 250g box costs €20.

Diksmuids Boterhuis Geldmuntstraat 23 ⓦdiksmuids boterhuis.be. One of the few traditional food shops to have survived in central Bruges, this Aladdin's cave of a place specialises in cooked meats, bread, butter and Belgian cheeses.

Proxy Delhaize Noordzand Noordzandstraat 4 ⓦdelhaize.be. Ordinary shops have all but disappeared from central Bruges, but there are a couple of smallish supermarkets – and this is probably the best.

Reisboekhandel Markt 12 ⓦdereyghere.be. Travel specialist with a wide selection of travel guides, many in English, plus road and city maps. The shop also sells hiking and cycling maps of Bruges and its surroundings and stocks travel-related English-language magazines. It's up the stairs, above its sister shop, *De Reyghere*.

De Reyghere Markt 12 ⓦdereyghere.be. Founded over a century ago, De Reyghere is a local institution and a meeting place for every book lover in town. The shop stocks a wide range of domestic and foreign literature, art and reference books, and it is also good for international newspapers, magazines, and periodicals.

De Striep Katelijnestraat 42 ⓦstripweb.be. Comics are a Belgian speciality (remember *Tintin*), but this is the only comic-strip specialist in Bruges. It stocks everything from run-of-the-mill cheapies to collectors' items in Flemish, French, and even English.

DIRECTORY

ATMs ATMs in central Bruges include Europabank at Vlamingstraat 13. There are also some at the train station.
Pharmacies Pharmacies are liberally distributed across the city centre, with late-night and weekend duty rotas

usually displayed in the window.
Post office The main post office is well to the west of the city centre at Smedenstraat 57 (Mon–Fri 9am–6pm, Sat 9am–3pm).

Ostend and the coast

The *Baedeker* of 1900 distinguished **OSTEND** as 'one of the most fashionable and cosmopolitan watering places in Europe'. Much of the gloss may be gone today, and the aristocratic visitors have certainly moved on to more exotic climes. Still, Ostend remains a likeable, liveable seaport and seaside resort, its compact centre a largely modern affair of narrow, straight streets shadowed by a battery of apartment blocks. Ostend's attractions include a clutch of first-rate seafood restaurants, a string of earthy bars, an enjoyable art museum and – easily the most popular – a long slice of gorgeous **sandy beach**.

Ostend also marks the midway point of the **Belgian coast**, which stretches for some 70km from Knokke-Heist in the east to De Panne in the west. The superb sandy **beach** that flanks Ostend extends along almost all of this coast, but the dunes that once backed onto it have largely disappeared, often beneath an unappetising covering of apartment blocks and bungalow settlements, a veritable carpet of concrete that can obscure the landscape and depress the soul. There are, however, one or two breaks in the aesthetic gloom, principally **De Haan**, a charming little seaside resort with easy access to a slender slice of pristine coastline; the substantial remains of the **Atlantikwall** built by the Germans to repel the Allies in World War II; and the enjoyable **Paul Delvaux Museum** in St-Idesbald. Exploring the coast by public transport could not be

2

easier as a fast and frequent **tram** – the **Kusttram** – runs from one end to the other (see box, page 123); you can also **cycle** from one end of the coast to the other along the seafront promenade/sea wall.

Brief history

The old fishing village of **Ostend** was given a town charter in the thirteenth century in recognition of its growing importance as a seaport for trade across the Channel. Flanked by an empty expanse of dunes, it remained the only important coastal settlement hereabouts until the construction of Zeebrugge six centuries later – the dunes were always inadequate protection against the sea, and precious few people chose to live along the coast until a chain of massive **sea walls** was completed in the nineteenth century. Like so many other towns in the Spanish Netherlands, Ostend was attacked and besieged time and again, winning the admiration of Protestant Europe in resisting the Spaniards during a **desperate siege** that lasted from 1601 to 1604. Later, convinced of the wholesome qualities of sea air and determined to impress other European rulers with their sophistication, Belgium's first kings, Léopold I and II, turned Ostend into a chichi **resort**, demolishing the town walls and dotting the outskirts with prestigious buildings and parks. Several of these have survived, but others were destroyed during **World War II** when the town's docks made it a prime bombing target. After the war, Ostend resumed its role as a major **cross-Channel port** until the completion of the Channel Tunnel in 1994 undermined its position. Since then, Ostend has had to reinvent itself, emphasising its charms as a seaside resort and centre of culture. There's some way to go – but Ostend is definitely on the up.

Visserskaai

With a string of restaurants on one side and fish stalls on the other, **Visserskaai** cuts a jaunty path up from near the train station and along the side of the **Montgomery Dok**, named after the British commander and formerly the main car-ferry dock. The **fish stalls** offer a wide range of fresh, cooked and dried fish partly supplied by Ostend's fishing fleet. Here also is the jetty for the passenger ferry that shuttles across the harbour to Fort Napoleon (daily: April–Sept 6.30am–9pm, every 30min–1hr; Oct–March 8am–6pm, hourly) and the fish market, the **Vistrap** (daily 7am–4pm). The north end of Visserskaai sports a large and somehow rather engaging piece of contemporary sculpture, the orange-red figures of *Rock Strangers* by Belgium's own Arne Quinze (b. 1971); beyond that, you can extend your stroll by walking out along the curving **mole**, an exhilarating experience if the wind is up.

MARVIN GAYE'S OSTEND

One of the greatest soul singers of all time, **Marvin Gaye** (1939–84), arrived in Ostend on 14 February 1981 and stayed here until the following year. A mightily troubled man, Gaye was struggling with both drug dependency and US tax demands when one of the few men he trusted, the Belgian music producer and club owner **Freddy Cousaert**, suggested he come to live with him and his family in his Ostend apartment. All in all, Gaye benefited enormously from his time here in Ostend, apparently more content than he had been for most of his life, and it was here that he wrote and recorded his biggest hit, 'Sexual Healing'. Capitalising on Gaye's stay here, the Ostend tourist office has assembled the outstanding '**Marvin Gaye Midnight Love Digital Tour**', an audio tour that guides you around every place with a Gaye connection, all to a great soundtrack, and takes a couple of hours to complete; the headphones and set can be collected from the tourist office (see page 121) and cost €6. As for Gaye himself, he returned to the States, where his life resumed its difficult trajectory, ending in bizarre circumstances in Los Angeles when his father shot him.

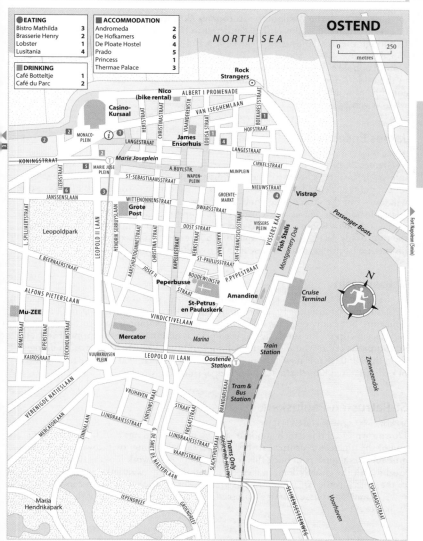

OSTEND

2

EATING
Bistro Mathilda	3
Brasserie Henry	2
Lobster	1
Lusitania	4

ACCOMMODATION
Andromeda	2
De Hofkamers	6
De Ploate Hostel	4
Prado	5
Princess	1
Thermae Palace	3

DRINKING
| Café Botteltje | 1 |
| Café du Parc | 2 |

0   250
metres

The seafront and beach

Casino Monacoplein • ⓦ casinooostende.be • **Kursaal** Monacoplein • ⓦ kursaaloostende.be

From the north end of Visserskaai, there are fine **coastal views** with the assorted moles and docks of the harbour in one direction, Ostend's main **beach** extending as far as the eye can see in the other. On sunny summer days, hundreds drive or train it into town to enjoy the **beach**, soaking up the sun, swimming and doing all the traditional seaside stuff – from sandcastle building to flying kites. Others amble or cycle along the **seafront promenade**, which runs along the top of the sea wall: part sea defence and part royal ostentation; the promenade was built to link the town centre with the **Wellington racecourse**, 2km west. It was – and remains – an intentionally grand walkway that pandered to the grandiose tastes of King Léopold II, though the first landmarks – the **casino** and adjoining **Kursaal** exhibition and concert centre – were added in the 1950s. To hammer home the original royal point, **Léopold's statue**, with fawning Belgians and Congolese at its base, still stands in the middle of a long line of columns towards the promenade's west end. These columns now adjoin the **Thermae Palace Hotel**, which was the epitome of luxury when it was added in the 1930s.

James Ensorhuis

Vlaanderenstraat 27 • Charge • ⓦ ensorhuis.be

The **James Ensorhuis**, footsteps from the seafront promenade, is of some specialist interest as the artist's home for the last thirty years of his life. It was from here that his aunt and uncle sold shells and souvenirs – hence the assorted knick-knacks in the window – but the shop is long gone, and the ground floor now exhibits a few Ensor-related incidentals, masks, etc. Upstairs, you'll find the painter's living room-cum-studio – the **Blue Room** – which has been returned to something like its appearance at the time of his death, a cluttered and somehow rather repressed room decorated with his intense paintings, though these aren't originals.

Wapenplein

At the centre of Ostend is the **Wapenplein**, a pleasant open space that zeros in on an old-fashioned bandstand. Typical of so much of Ostend, the square was once in the doldrums, but canny planning and sympathetic redevelopment have turned it into a very sociable spot. The south side of the square is dominated by the former **Feest-en Kultuurpaleis** (Festival and Culture Hall), a handsome vaguely Ruritanian building from the 1950s that is now a shopping centre. The Wapenplein is at the northern end of pedestrianised **Kapellestraat**, the principal shopping street.

St-Petrus-en-Pauluskerk

St-Petrus-en-Paulusplein • Free • ☎ 059 70 17 19

Downtown Ostend is largely modern, and its oldest buildings mostly date from the end of the nineteenth century. At first glance, the whopping, twin-towered **St-Petrus-en-Pauluskerk** appears to buck this trend, its fancy stonework looking distinctly Gothic, but the church does, in fact, date from the early twentieth century. At the back of the church is the last remnant of its predecessor, a massive sixteenth-century brick tower – the **Peperbusse** – with a canopied, distinctly morbid shrine of the Crucifixion at its base.

Léopold II-laan

Mercator Jan Piersplein 2 • Charge • ⓦ zeilschipmercator.be

The dead-straight boulevard of **Léopold II-laan** cuts past the little lakes, bandstand and mini-bridges of the **Léopoldpark**, a delightful and especially verdant park laid out in the 1860s. Across the boulevard, unmissable on Hendrik Serruyslaan, is the former post office, the **Grote Post**, a forceful 1950s building with a mighty statue of a messenger standing on a parapet to a design by Belgium's Gaston Eysselinck. Further down the boulevard, you reach the sailing ship **Mercator**, the old training vessel of the Belgian merchant navy, which has been converted into a marine museum holding a hotchpotch of items accumulated during her voyages.

Mu.ZEE

Romestraat 11 • Charge • ⓦ muzee.be

The **Mu.ZEE** (Kunstmuseum aan Zee), Ostend's capacious fine art museum, displays a wide selection of modern Belgian paintings drawn from its permanent collection alongside top-quality temporary exhibitions, mostly of modern and contemporary work. The layout of the museum is a tad puzzling. Still, it begins well on the **ground floor** with a show-piece permanent exhibition on the life and times of Ostend's two leading artists – Leon Spilliaert and James Ensor – who witnessed the transformation of Ostend from a garrison town and fishing village to a royal resort. The oldest of seven children and the son of a perfumer, **Leon Spilliaert** (1881–1946) was smitten by the land- and seascapes of his home town, using them in his work time and again – as in *De Windstoot* (*Gust of Wind*), with its dark, forbidding colours and screaming woman, and the comparable *Vertigo*. **James Ensor** (1860–1949), the son of an English father and Flemish mother, was barely noticed until the 1920s, spending nearly 89 years working in Ostend, but is now considered a pioneer of Expressionism. His first paintings were rather sombre portraits and landscapes, but in the early 1880s, he switched to brilliantly contrasting colours, most familiarly in his *Self-portrait with Flowered Hat*, a deliberate variation on Rubens' famous self-portraits. Less well known is his large and very bizarre *Christ's Entry into Brussels* and, from a later period, *The Artist's Mother in Death*, a fine, penetrating example of his preoccupation with the grim and macabre. The museum also exhibits a number of Ensor's etchings and gouaches, including a savage *The Gendarmes* with their bloodied bayonets.

Moving on, the museum's **first floor** is dedicated to temporary exhibitions, while the second floor offers a regularly rotated selection from the permanent collection. Highlights include works by Constant Permeke, Paul Delvaux's harsh Surrealism, and a number of paintings by the versatile and prolific **Jean Brusselmans** (1884–1953), most notably his stunningly beautiful *Thunderstorm* (*Het Onweder*).

Fort Napoleon

Vuurtorenweg • Charge • ⓦ fort-napoleon.be • Take the coastal tram to the 'Duin en Zee' stop, from where it's a (signed) 5–10min walk, or catch the free passenger ferry across the harbour from Montgomery Dok to Maritiemplein, a 10min walk from the fort

Completed in 1812, **Fort Napoleon** is one of the best-preserved Napoleonic fortresses in Europe, an impressive star-shaped structure whose concentric brick walls are planted amongst the dunes behind the seashore on the eastern side of Ostend's harbour. The careful design meant that potential attackers could be fired on from almost every angle, and the French were so confident of the fort's impregnability that the garrison never exceeded 260 men (and 46 cannon). It takes about twenty minutes to wander the fort's long, echoing galleries, but there's nothing much to see apart from the actual structure.

ARRIVAL AND INFORMATION   OSTEND

By train Ostend's grand and stately train station is on the east edge of the town centre, a 10min stroll from the tourist information office.

Destinations Bruges (every 20min; 15min); Brussels (hourly; 1hr 20min); Ghent (every 30min; 40min).

By bus The bus station is adjacent to the train station.

Destinations Diksmuide (Mon–Fri hourly, Sat & Sun every 2hr; 50min); Veurne (hourly; 1hr).

By coastal tram The coastal tram (see box, page 121) has two stops in central Ostend: at the train station and on

Marie Joséplein.

Destinations De Haan (every 15min in summer, every 30min in winter; 20min); De Panne (same frequency; 1hr 20min); Knokke (same frequency; 1hr); Nieuwpoort (same frequency; 40min).

Tourist information Ostend's excellent tourist office is across the street from the casino at Monacoplein 2 (daily: April–June 10am–6pm; July & Aug 9am–7pm; Sept–March 10am–5.30pm; ⓦ visitoostende.be).

2

GETTING AROUND

By bike One of the most reliable bike rental places is Nico, at Albert 1 Promenade 44A (July & Aug: daily 9am–8pm; rest of year times vary – ring ahead; ☎ 059 23 34 81, ⓦ nicokarts.be). They also do four-seater bikes and tandems.

By ferry There are currently no car ferries from the UK to Belgium.

By car Try Europcar at Zandvoordeschorredijkstraat 48 (☎ 059 50 12 18); tourist information has a complete list of local car rental agencies.

ACCOMMODATION
SEE MAP PAGE 119

The best option is a **beachside hotel**, but these are few and far between (most of the seashore is given over to apartment blocks), so you might plump instead for the area around **Léopoldpark** on the west side of the city centre, a pleasant district with a relaxed and easy air. There's also a good and centrally located **HI hostel**.

Andromeda Kursaal Westhelling 5 ⓦ andromedahotel. be. Smart and modern, four-star high-rise next door to the casino and overlooking the town's beach. Many rooms have balconies, sea views (for a surcharge of around €40), fitness facilities, and an indoor pool. €€€

★ **De Hofkamers** Ijzerstraat 5 ⓦ dehofkamers.be. A family-run, 27-room, three-star hotel whose somewhat dour exterior belies its cosy public areas, kitted out with all sorts of local bygones, and the comfortable bedrooms beyond. The nicest room, on the top (sixth) floor, has its mini-balcony with a view (albeit a somewhat distant one) of the sea. Excellent breakfasts, too. €€€

De Ploate Hostel Langestraat 72 ⓦ jeugdherbergen. be. Well maintained and occupying bright, modern premises, this HI hostel sits in the town centre and offers 49 en-suite rooms of varying sizes. There's free wi-fi, a bar and self-catering facilities plus a sociable TV room. The overnight fee includes breakfast. Reservations are strongly advised in summer. Dorms €, doubles €

★ **Prado** Léopold II-laan 22 ⓦ hotelprado.be. A very likeable three-star hotel with neatly furnished modern rooms, attentive staff, especially tasty breakfasts, and views over mini-park-cum-square, Marie Joséplein. Ask for a room at the front, overlooking the square – and a few floors up from the traffic. €€

Princess Boekareststraat 7 ⓦ hotelprincess.be. This family-owned 35-room hotel is in a modern block on a narrow side street a couple of minutes' walk from the beach. The rooms are neat and trimly decorated, and the best have mini-balconies. Minimum two- or three-night stay in peak periods. €€

Thermae Palace Koningin Astridlaan 7 ⓦ thermaepalace. be. Located a 10min walk west of the centre, this four-star hotel long enjoyed the reputation of being Ostend's best. The building is striking – think Art Deco extravagance, expansive public rooms and spacious bedrooms offering sea views – yet the place can't help but seem a little sorry for itself: there's just so much here to keep in good working order. €€€

EATING
SEE MAP PAGE 119

Ostend has scores of cafés, café-bars and **restaurants**, and seafood is the big gastronomic deal – as evidenced by the **seafood stalls** lining up along Visserskaai. The enterprising tourist board has led a campaign to encourage the use of less familiar fish, and the results are visible on many menus.

★ **Bistro Mathilda** Léopold II-laan 1 ⓦ bistromathilda. be. Smooth, slick and stylish restaurant in modern premises with attentive service and a wonderfully creative menu that's especially strong on seafood and lamb: try, for example, the Dover sole à la meunière or the lamb couscous. €€€

Brasserie Henry Albert I-promenade 65 ⓦ brasserie henry.be. Of all the many restaurants that line up along Ostend's elongated seafront, this is certainly one of the best, offering a classic Franco-Flemish menu of well-presented, home-cooked meals. Eat either inside or on the sheltered patio. Mussels are the house's speciality, but the steaks and salads are especially tasty, too. €€

Lobster Van Iseghemlaan 64 ⓦ lobster.be. There are no prizes for guessing the house speciality at this long-established restaurant, which deserves its reputation for reliability. Don't be put off by the rather dismal entrance, as the dining area is fine. The two-course 'Menu of the Month' can be an especially good deal. €€€

Lusitania Visserskaai 32 ⓦ restaurant-lusitania.be. Neat and trim modern restaurant opposite the Vistrap specialising in seafood: wet fish and shellfish. Does a particularly good whole Dover sole. €€€

DRINKING
SEE MAP PAGE 119

Ostend does well for cafés and restaurants, but the **bars** dotted across the city centre are harder to warm to, with the majority pretty rough and ready, or at least dark and gloomy.

Café Botteltje Louisastraat 19 ⓦ botteltje.be. This ersatz brown café has more character than most bars in downtown Ostend. Its deep, dark interior is equipped with a formidable selection of bottled and draught beers, of which there are usually sixteen.

Café du Parc Marie Joséplein 3 ⓦ brasserieduparc.be.

Old-fashioned café a short stroll from the beach, whose main claim to fame is its Art Deco furnishings and fittings – from the Tiffany glass down to the wooden chairs and leather benches. The drinks are fine, but it is perhaps best to avoid the food.

The coast east of Ostend

Heading **east** along the coast from Ostend, the undoubted highlight is **De Haan**, the prettiest and most appealing of the seaside resorts. Beyond lie kiss-me-quick **Blankenberge**, the heavily industrialised port of **Zeebrugge** and sprawling **Knokke-Heist**. The latter is not an immediately appealing place. Still, you might be drawn here by one of its many **festivals**, most notably the International Cartoon Festival (Ⓦcartoonfestival.be), which runs from early July to the middle of September.

De Haan

Flanked by empty dunes, **DE HAAN** is a leafy family resort with an excellent **beach** and a pleasant seafront promenade. It was established at the end of the nineteenth century, conceived as an exclusive seaside village in a rustic Gothic Revival style known as *Style Normand*. The building plots were irregularly dispersed between the tram station and the sea, with the whole caboodle set around a pattern of winding streets reminiscent of – and influenced by – contemporaneous English suburbs. The only formality was provided by a central circus with a casino plonked in the middle, though this was demolished in 1929. Casino apart, De Haan has survived pretty much intact – a welcome relief from the surrounding apartment block developments.

ARRIVAL AND INFORMATION — DE HAAN

By tram De Haan aan Zee coastal tram stop is a 5–10min walk from the beach.
Destinations Ostend (every 15min in summer, every 30min in winter; 20min); Knokke (same frequency; 40min).
Tourist information The tourist office is next door to the De Haan aan Zee tram stop (April–June, Sept & Oct: daily 9.30am–noon & 1.30–5pm; July & Aug: daily 9.30am–1pm & 1.30–6pm; Nov–March: Mon–Sat 9.30am–noon & 1.30–4pm, Sun 10am–2pm; Ⓦvisitdehaan.be). They issue a useful English-language leaflet describing local cycling routes.

ACCOMMODATION — SEE MAP PAGE 124

Auberge des Rois Beach Hotel Zeedijk 1 Ⓦbeachhotel.be. This smart, modern, medium-sized, four-star hotel has a splendid location, overlooking the beach and just a few metres from an undeveloped tract of dune. The guest rooms are spick and span and the best have wide sea views (attracting a modest premium). €€€
Hotel Rubens Rubenslaan 3 Ⓦhotel-rubens.be. In a tastefully decorated, cottage-like house, the guest rooms at this small, three-star hotel are spotless and cosy in equal measure. The hotel prides itself on its banquet breakfasts, which can be taken outside in the garden when the weather is good. There's also an outside pool. €€€
★ **Manoir Carpe Diem** Prins Karellaan 12 Ⓦmanoircarpediem.com. Chichi four-star hotel in a handsome *Style Normand* villa, which perches on a grassy knoll about 400m from the beach. It's all very period – from the Dutch gables, open fires and heavy drapes to the fifteen guest rooms, decorated in an attractive version of the country-house style. There's an immaculate garden and an outside pool, too. €€€

THE KUSTTRAM – THE COASTAL TRAM

Fast and efficient, the **Kusttram** (Ⓦdelijn.be/en/kusttram) travels the length of the Belgian coast from Knokke-Heist train station in the east to De Panne train station in the west, putting all the Belgian resorts within easy striking distance of each other. Services are **regular** in both directions, with trams departing every fifteen minutes or so in summer and about every half-hour in winter. **Tickets** can be bought from the ticket machines at major stops or from a De Lijn **ticket office** – there is one beside Ostend train station and another on Ostend's central Marie Joséplein. **Fares** are inexpensive: a flat-rate, single-journey ticket costs €2.50, or you can opt for unlimited tram travel for one day with the *dagpas* for €7.50.

2

DE HAAN

NORTH SEA

Beaches

N

■ ACCOMMODATION
Auberge des Rois Beach Hotel	1
Hotel Rubens	3
Manoir Carpe Diem	2

ZEEDIJK

DÜRERHELLING

ENSORLN

KONINKLIJKE BAAN

LEOPOLDPLEIN

GOETHEHELLING

KONINKLIJKE BAAN

VONDELAAN

DÜRERLAAN

MARIA-HENDRIKALN

MURILLOLAAN

HOLBEININ

GRACIALAAN

GOETHELAAN

GRACI ALAAN

TOLLENSLAAN

VAN MAERIANTLAAN

MURILLOLAAN

SHAKESPEARELAAN

VONDELLAAN

LEOPOLDLAAN

CLEMENINALAAN

MERCATORLAAN

JORDAERRSLAAN

PRINS BOUDEWIJNL

JEAN D'ARDENNELAAN

TENIERSLAAN

NORMANDIELAAN

SCHILLERLN

DANTELAAN

ALBERTLAAN

MARIA-HENDRIKALAAN

ORTELIUSLAAN

POPPLARN

RUBENSLAAN

VAN MAERIANTLAAN

MONTAIGNEIN

CAMOESLN

COLINELLAAN

BILDERDIJKLAAN

QUINTEN MATSIJSLAAN

LEOPOLDLAAN

MARIAHENDORIK LAAN

RUBENSLAAN

CARVERLN

RAFFAEILLAAN

NIEUWE RIJKSWEG

MEMLINGLAAN

VAN EYCKLN

De Haan Aan Zee
Tram Stop

DRIFTWEG

REMBRANDTLAAN

NIEUWE RIJKSWEG

MARKSTRAAT

STATIONSSTRAAT

WENUINESTEENWEG

●EATING
L'Espérance	2
Tearoom Beaufort	1

Ostend

0   100
metres

EATING   SEE MAP PAGE 124

L'Espérance Driftweg 1 ☏ 059 32 69 00. De Haan has a healthy supply of cafés and restaurants, and this is one of the more distinctive places. Small, smart and intimate, it offers classic French cuisine to a Michelin standard. Their three-course set meals are especially popular. Reservations are strongly advised. €€€€

Tearoom Beaufort Koninklijk Plein 6 ⓦbeaufort. be. This neat and trim modern café-cum-restaurant has a spacious terrace to soak up the sun and offers a good range of snacks and light meals. Pancakes are a house speciality. €

The coast west of Ostend

Travelling **west from Ostend**, the Kusttram (coastal tram) skirts the dunes of a long and almost entirely undeveloped stretch of coast dotted with the substantial military remains of the **Atlantikwall** (Atlantic Wall), built during the German occupation of World War II to guard the coast from Allied invasion. Beyond, the tram ploughs through a series of medium-sized resorts before cutting inland to round the estuary of the River Ijzer. It then scuttles through the small town of **Nieuwpoort**, the scene of some of the bloodiest fighting in World War I, before proceeding onto **St-Idesbald**, home to the intriguing **Paul Delvaux Museum**. After St-Idesbald comes **De Panne**, an uninspiring resort at the west end of the Belgian coast that is partly redeemed by its proximity to a pristine slice of beach and dune, the **Staatsnatuurreservaat De Westhoek**.

The Atlantikwall

Nieuwpoortsesteenweg • Charge • ⓦ raversyde.be • From the Raversijde Provinciedomein tram stop, take the conspicuous wooden stairway over the dunes and then follow the signs, a 5–10min walk

A slice of coast just to the west of Ostend has managed to dodge development. It's here you'll find the **Raversijde Provinciedomein**, a protected area where the most interesting attraction is the open-air **Atlantikwall**, a series of well-preserved gun emplacements, bunkers, pillboxes, tunnels, trenches and artillery pieces that line up along the dunes just behind the beach and the coastal tram line. The Germans had these elaborate fortifications constructed in World War II to forestall an Allied invasion, though, in the event, the Allies landed much further to the west in France. The remains are extensive and take well over an hour to explore.

Nieuwpoort

Nieuwpoort Stad tram stop

Nudging back from the canalised River Ijzer, a couple of kilometres inland from the coast, the little town of **NIEUWPOORT** hasn't had much luck. Founded in the twelfth century, it was besieged nine times in the following six hundred years, but this was nothing compared to its misfortune in World War I. In 1914, the first German campaign reached the River Ijzer, prompting the Belgians to open the sluice gates on the northeast edge of town. The water stopped the invaders in their tracks and permanently separated the armies, but it also put Nieuwpoort on the front line, where it remained for the rest of the war. Four years of shelling reduced the town to ruin, and most of what you see today, especially the attractive main square, the **Marktplein**, a five-minute walk south from the Nieuwpoort Stad tram stop, is the result of a meticulous restoration that lasted well into the 1920s.

Westfront Nieuwpoort Museum

Kustweg 2, 250m east of the Nieuwpoort Stad tram stop • Charge • ⓦ visit-nieuwpoort.be/en/westfront-nieuwpoort

A large and sombre **war memorial**, comprising of an Art Deco **stone rotunda** with an equestrian statue of King Albert I at its centre, stands on the east side of Nieuwpoort beside the old sluice gates. Beneath the rotunda is the fascinating, semi-subterranean **Westfront Nieuwpoort Museum**, whose single long gallery is divided into several distinct sections. One section holds a huge panoramic screen on which are projected scenes from World War I as it unfolded at Nieuwpoort, a second tracks through the German invasion of 1914 and a third, perhaps the most interesting, explores and explains the opening of the sluice gates and the flooding that followed – how it worked, whose idea it was and the bravery of the men who undertook it.

You can also take the lift up to the **walkway** at the top of the rotunda, from where there are expansive and sobering views over what was once the front line. Immediately behind the museum, a large and partly buried **concrete bunker** is a further reminder of the horrors of the war, and from here, it's the briefest of walks to the assorted **war memorials** that dot the ring of **sluice gates** that proved so crucial in stopping the German advance.

St-Idesbald: the Paul Delvaux Museum

Paul Delvauxlaan 42, off Pannelaan • Charge • W delvauxmuseum.com • From the Koksijde St-Idesbald tram stop, walk 100m west towards De Panne, turn left (away from the coast) down the resort's main street, Strandlaan, and keep going until you reach Albert Nazylaan, where you go right, following the signs to the museum; allow 15min

ST-IDESBALD, one hour by tram from Ostend, is an unassuming seaside town that would be of no particular interest were it not for the **Paul Delvaux Museum**, which occupies a handsome house purchased by the artist's foundation in the 1980s and subsequently remodelled and enlarged. The museum holds a comprehensive collection of paintings by **Paul Delvaux** (1897–1994), following his development from early Expressionist days to the Surrealism that defined his oeuvre from the 1930s onwards. Two of the artist's pet motifs were train stations, in one guise or another, and nude or semi-nude women set against a classical backdrop. His intention was to usher the viewer into the unconscious with dreamlike images where every perspective is exact, but despite the impeccable craftsmanship, there's something very cold about his vision. At their best, his paintings achieve an almost palpable sense of foreboding, good examples being *The Garden* of 1971 and *The Procession,* dating from 1963, while *The Station in the Forest* of 1960 has the most wonderful trees.

De Panne

From St-Idesbald, it only takes the tram a couple of minutes to slide into **DE PANNE**, sitting close to the French border and now one of the largest settlements on the Belgian coast – a mishmash of apartment blocks and second homes shunting up against the beach. As late as the 1880s, De Panne was a tiny fishing village of low white cottages nestling in the wooded hollow (*panne*) from which it takes its name. The town achieved ephemeral fame in World War I when it was part of the tiny triangle of Belgian territory that the German army failed to occupy, becoming the temporary home of King Albert's government.

Natuurreservaat De Westhoek

Main access point just to the west of De Panne on Schuilhavenlaan • Free • From De Panne Esplanade tram stop, proceed along Dynastielaan, which ends at a T-junction, where you turn left onto Schuilhavenlaan; the distance from the tram stop to the park entrance is 1.6km

On the western edge of De Panne – and the main reason to come this far – lies a chunk of coast protected in the **Natuurreservaat De Westhoek**, whose dunes, grasslands and scrub are fringed by a long sandy beach. It feels surprisingly wild here, and you can explore the reserve along a network of marked footpaths. In 1940, the retreating British army managed to reach these same dunes between De Panne and Dunkirk, 15km to the west, just in time for their miraculous evacuation back to England – in eight days, an armada of vessels of all sizes and shapes rescued over three hundred thousand Allied soldiers.

Veurne and around

Small-town Flanders at its prettiest, **VEURNE** is a charming little place whose clutch of ancient buildings, relaxed atmosphere and pavement cafés make for an enjoyable overnight stay. Founded in the ninth century as one of a chain of fortresses built to defend the region from the raids of the Vikings, Veurne was little more than an insignificant hamlet when **Robert II of Flanders** returned from the Crusades in 1099 with a piece of the True Cross. His ship was caught in a gale, and, in desperation, he vowed to offer the relic to the first church he saw if he survived. He did, and the lucky beneficiary was Veurne's **St-Walburgakerk**, which became an important centre of medieval pilgrimage for some two hundred years, a real fillip to the local economy. These days, Veurne's main attraction is its **Grote Markt**, one of the best-preserved town squares in Belgium, but it's also a useful base for exploring, preferably by bike, the **Veurne-Ambacht**, a flat agricultural region of quiet villages and narrow country lanes that stretches south of the town, encircled by the French border and the canalised River Ijzer. Of all the villages hereabouts, **Lo** is the most delightful, but the district also holds a sprinkling of World War I sights that lie dotted along the line of the **River Ijzer**, which formed the front line for most of the war; the most interesting of these are in the vicinity of the small town of **Diksmuide** (see page 129).

Grote Markt

All of Veurne's leading sights are located on or around the **Grote Markt**, beginning in the northwest corner with the **Stadhuis**, an engaging mix of Gothic and Renaissance styles built between 1596 and 1612 and equipped with a fine blue-and-gold decorated stone loggia projecting from the original brick facade. The Stadhuis connects with the more austere classicism of the **Gerechtshof** (Law Courts), whose symmetrical pilasters and long, rectangular windows now front the tourist information office but once sheltered the Inquisition as it set about the Flemish peasantry with gusto. The attached tiered and balconied **Belfort** (no public access) was completed in 1628; its Gothic lines culminate in a dainty Baroque tower from where carillon concerts ring over the town throughout the summer.

St-Walburgakerk

St-Walburgastraat • Free

Just off the Grote Markt stands **St-Walburgakerk**, a replacement for the original church that Robert II of Flanders caught sight of, which was burnt to a cinder in 1353. The new church was begun in style with a mighty, heavily buttressed choir, but the money ran out during construction, and the nave – a truncated affair if ever there was one – was only finished off in 1904. The interior has four highlights: the exquisite vaulting of the ceiling; the superb stonework of the tubular, composite columns at the central crossing; a handsome set of stained-glass windows, some Gothic, some neo-Gothic; and the ornately carved Flemish Renaissance choir stalls.

Spaans Paviljoen

Ooststraat 1, northeast corner of the Grote Markt • No public access

The **Spaans Paviljoen** (Spanish Pavilion) was built as the town hall in the mid-fifteenth century. However, it takes its name from its later adaptation as the officers' quarters of the Habsburg garrison. It's a self-confident structure. The initial square

---

VEURNE'S BOETEPROCESSIE (PENITENTS' PROCESSION)

In 1650, a young soldier by the name of Mannaert was on garrison duty in Veurne when he was persuaded by his best friend to commit a **mortal sin**. After receiving the consecrated wafer during Communion, he took it out of his mouth, wrapped it in a cloth, and returned to his lodgings where he charred it over a fire, under the illusion that by reducing it to powder he would make himself invulnerable to injury. The news got out, and he was later arrested, tried and executed, his friend suffering the same fate a few weeks later. Fearful of the consequences of this sacrilege in their town, the people of Veurne resolved that something must be done, deciding on a procession to commemorate the Passion of Christ. This survives as the **Boeteprocessie** (Penitents' Procession; ☻ boetprocessie.be), held on the last Sunday in July, whose leading figures dress up in the brown cowls of the Capuchins to carry wooden crosses that weigh anything up to 50kg through the streets. Until very recently, the procession was a serious-minded, macabre affair, but nowadays, many locals clamber into all manner of vaguely 'biblical' gear to join in, making it all rather odd.

2

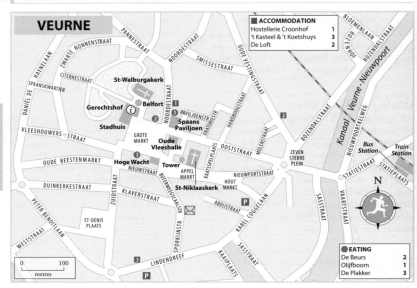

brick tower, with its castellated parapet, is extended by a facade of long, slender windows and flowing stone tracery in the true Gothic manner – an obvious contrast to the Flemish shutters and gables of the **Oude Vleeshalle** (Old Meat Hall) standing directly opposite.

Hoge Wacht

Grote Markt 9, southeast corner of the Grote Markt • No public access

Originally an inn and later the home of the town watch – hence its name – the **Hoge Wacht** displays a fetching amalgam of styles. Its brick gable is decorated with a small arcaded gallery, and brightly painted shutters guard its upper windows. It was here that Veurne's wealthier citizens once gathered to shoot the breeze, much, it is imagined, to the chagrin of the hard-pressed peasantry.

ARRIVAL AND INFORMATION   VEURNE

By train Veurne's train station is a 5–10min stroll from the Grote Markt.
Destinations De Panne (hourly; 10min); Diksmuide (hourly; 10min); Ghent (hourly; 1hr).
By bus Veurne's bus station is adjacent to the train station.

Destinations Ieper (hourly; 1hr); Lo (hourly; 25min); Ostend (hourly; 1hr).
Tourist information Grote Markt 29 (April to early Nov: Mon–Fri 9am–5pm, Sat & Sun 10am–5pm; early Nov to March: Mon–Fri 9am–5pm, Sat & Sun 1–5pm; ⓦveurne.be).

GETTING AROUND

By bike The most central bicycle rental outlet is at the *De Loft*   hotel; cycling maps are on sale at Veurne tourist information.

ACCOMMODATION   SEE MAP PAGE 128

Hostellerie Croonhof Noordstraat 9 ⓦcroonhof. be. This smart and well-cared-for three-star hotel, in an attractively converted old house just off the Grote Markt, has fourteen spotless rooms of modern demeanour. Reservations are advised in summer. €€

★ **'t Kasteel & 't Koetshuys** Lindendreef 5 ⓦkasteel

enkoetshuys.be. Housed in a sympathetically renovated Edwardian mansion, this family-run hotel boasts eight large and well-appointed guest rooms, each decorated in relaxing pastel shades with high ceilings and marble fireplaces. A sauna and hot tub complete the appealing picture. €€

De Loft Oude Vestingstraat 36 ⓦdeloft.be. This eight-room hotel is an inventive affair in a cleverly recycled industrial building, with a café, a kids' play area and a small art gallery. The guest rooms are kitted out in the full flush of modern style with lots of greys, creams and blues. Cycle rental is available, too. €€

EATING

SEE MAP PAGE 128

★ **De Beurs** Grote Markt 32 ⓦ debeursveurne.be. In every Belgian town, café-restaurants line up along the main square – and Veurne is no exception – but this popular spot, with its attractive pavement terrace, is exceptionally good, its imaginative salads delicious, its fish and meat dishes well prepared and presented. €€

★ **Olijfboom** Noordstraat 3 ⓦ olijfboom.be. Arguably the best restaurant in town, this chic and modern place has a well-considered French menu where the lobster (*kreeft*) and bouillabaisse are hard to beat. €€€

De Plakker Grote Markt 14 ☎ 058 31 51 20. Bistro-style restaurant with a wide-ranging menu from pasta to mussels and chips, home-made shrimp croquettes and beef stew, though its hallmark dish is grilled steak.

Lo

The agreeable little hamlet of **LO**, off the N8 some 15km southeast of Veurne, has one claim to fame: it was here that **Julius Caesar** tethered his horse to a yew on his way across Gaul, an event recalled by a plaque and a battered old tree beside what is now the **Westpoort**, whose twin turrets and gateway are all that remains of Lo's medieval ramparts. Less apocryphally, the village once prospered under the patronage of its Augustinian **abbey**, founded in the twelfth century and suppressed by the French Revolutionary Army. Today, it's the peace and quiet that appeals, with the village's old stone houses fanning out from the most pleasant of main squares.

ARRIVAL AND DEPARTURE

LO

By bus Buses pull in on the Oude Eiermarkt, footsteps from Lo's main square, the Markt.

Destinations Ieper (hourly; 35min); Veurne (hourly; 25min).

ACCOMMODATION

Hotel Stadhuis Markt 1 ⓦ stadhuis-lo.be. Right in the centre of the village, the old town hall – a much-modified sixteenth-century structure with a slender tower – has been converted into a small, two-star hotel. Its handful of bedrooms are neat, trim and comfortable, and the traditional ground-floor restaurant serves good-quality Flemish food in pleasant surroundings. Restaurant €€; Accommodation €€

Diksmuide

DIKSMUIDE, a pleasant little town about halfway between Ieper and Ostend, sits on the east bank of the River Ijzer – which turned out to be a particularly unfortunate location in World War I. In 1914, the German offensive across Belgium came to a grinding halt when it reached the river, which then formed the front line for the next four years. As a result, Diksmuide was shelled to pieces, so much so that by 1918, its location could only be identified from a map. Painstakingly rebuilt in the 1920s, the reconstruction works best in the **Grote Markt**, an attractive, spacious square flanked by a handsome set of brick gables in traditional Flemish style. Presiding over the square is a statue of a heroic-looking **Colonel Jacques** (1858–1928), a Belgian commander who did a great deal to delay the German advance of 1914 – and was subsequently made a baron as his reward. The Grote Markt is also within easy striking distance of two prime World War I sites, the **Ijzertoren**, a ten-minute walk away, and the **Dodengang**, 2km or so outside the town.

The Ijzertoren

Ijzerdijk • Charge • ⓦ museumaandeijzer.be • On the west bank of the River Ijzer, a 10min walk from the Grote Markt via General Baron Jacquesstraat & Ijzerlaan

2

The domineering, 84m high **Ijzertoren** is a massive war memorial and museum that rises high above the River Ijzer. The present structure, a brooding affair dating from the 1950s, bears the letters **AVV-VVK** – Alles voor Vlaanderen (All for Flanders) and Vlaanderen voor Kristus (Flanders for Christ) – in a heady mix of religion and nationalism. The tower is the second version: the original, erected in 1930, was blown up under mysterious circumstances in 1946. Belgium's French speakers usually blame Flemish fascists disappointed at the defeat of Hitler for its destruction, while the Flemings accuse French-speaking leftists, who allegedly took offence at the avowedly Flemish character of the memorial. In front of the Ijzertoren are a few incidental memorials, principally the **Pax gateway** of 1950, built of rubble from the original tower, a **crypt** holding the gravestones of a number of Belgian soldiers and a rather incongruous 20m long segment of replica World War I **trench**.

Museum aan de Ijzer

Inside the Ijzertoren, lifts whisk visitors up to the top, from where there are grand views out across West Flanders, and this is also where you start a visit to the **Museum aan de Ijzer**, one of the province's best war museums. Spread over a number of floors, each getting larger as you descend the tapering tower, the museum begins with a good section on the build-up to World War I and then traces the war's course with particular reference to the Belgian army. Included are a couple of re-created **trenches** – and very convincing they are, too – as well as a number of mini-sections on the likes of gas and gas masks, trench communications, and subterranean warfare. There's also an excellent section on the atrocities committed by the Germans during the invasion of 1914 and another on the unequal treatment dished out to the Flemings by the Belgian army's Francophone officer class. A later section explains how the original Ijzertoren became a focus of **Flemish nationalism** in the 1930s and even during World War II when many members of the Flemish Nationalist Movement collaborated with the Germans; several of its leaders, most notably **August Borms**, were shot for their treason after the war's end.

The Dodengang

Ijzerdijk 65, 1.5km north of the Ijzertoren • Charge • ⓦ dodengang.be

There's a second reminder of World War I north of the Ijzertoren along the river's west bank. The **Dodengang** (Trench of Death) was an especially dangerous slice of trench held by the Belgians throughout the war. Around 400m of the trench is viewable; the original sandbags have, of necessity, been replaced by concrete imitations, but it's all very well done. The attached **museum** fills in the military background.

ARRIVAL AND INFORMATION   DIKSMUIDE

By train & bus Diksmuide's train station is a 5min walk from the Grote Markt along L-shaped Stationsstraat; the bus station is adjacent.
Destinations by train De Panne (hourly; 20min); Ghent (hourly; 50min); Veurne (hourly; 10min).

Destinations by bus Ieper (hourly; 50min); Ostend (hourly; 50min).
Tourist information Diksmuide's tourist office is at Grote Markt 6 (April–Sept: daily 9am–5pm; Oct–March: Mon–Sat 10am–noon & 1–4pm; ⓦ tourism.diksmuide.be).

ACCOMMODATION AND EATING

Fijnbakkerij Vandooren Grote Markt 17 ⓦ fijnbakkerij vandooren.be. Cheerful modern café where the coffee is good and the cakes are better – try the mousses. €
De Groote Waere Vladslostraat 21 ⓦ degrootewaere. be. Easily the best accommodation hereabouts, this top-notch B&B is located on a farm about 4.5km from Diksmuide.

Breakfast is served in the attractively modernised farmhouse, and the barnlike annexe behind holds several comfortable, modern rooms with all mod cons. To get there, drive east from Diksmuide on the N35, take the Vladslo turning, and it's beside the road on the left. €€

Ieper and around

Engaging **IEPER**, about 30km southeast of Veurne, is one of the most interesting towns in Flanders, a calm and well-composed sort of place whose expansive main square is distinguished by the proud reminders of its medieval heyday as a centre of the cloth trade. Initial appearances are, however, deceptive, for all the 'old' buildings in the centre were built from scratch after World War I when Ieper – or **Ypres** as it was then known – was shelled to smithereens, the reconstruction a tribute to the determination of the town's citizens. Today, with its clutch of good-quality restaurants and hotels, Ieper is an enjoyable place to spend a night or two, especially if you're planning on exploring the assorted **World War I** cemeteries, monuments and memorials that speckle the town and its environs, the most famous of which are the **In Flanders Fields Museum**, the **Menin Gate** and **Tyne Cot**.

2

Brief history

Ieper's long and troubled history dates back to the tenth century when it was founded at the point where the Bruges–Paris trade route crossed the River Ieperlee. Success came quickly, and the town became a major player in the cloth trade. Its thirteenth-century population of some two hundred thousand shared economic control of the region with rivals Ghent and Bruges. Ypres was, however, the most precariously sited of the great Flemish cities, much too near the French frontier for comfort and too strategically important to be ignored by any of the armies whose campaigns crisscrossed the town's surroundings with depressing frequency. The city governors kept disaster at bay by reinforcing their defences and **switching allegiances** whenever necessary, fighting against the French at the Battle of the Golden Spurs in 1302 (see page 141) and with them forty years later at Roosebeke. The first major misjudgement came in 1383 when Ypres allied with France against Bruges, Ghent and an English army. Ypres was besieged for two long months, and although a French army finally appeared to save the day, the damage was done. Unable to challenge its two main competitors, many of its weavers upped sticks and migrated. The process of **depopulation** proved irreversible, and by the sixteenth century, the town had shrunk to a mere five thousand inhabitants.

World War I and after

In **World War I**, the first German thrust of 1914 left a bulge in the Allied line to the immediate east of Ypres. This **Salient** (see page 135) preoccupied the generals of both sides. Over the course of the next four years, a series of bloody and particularly futile offensives attempted to break the stalemate – with disastrous consequences for Ypres, which served as the Allied communications centre. Comfortably within range of the German artillery, Ypres was rapidly **reduced to rubble**, and its inhabitants were evacuated in 1915. After the war, the returning population decided to rebuild their town, a twenty-year project in which the most prominent medieval buildings – primarily the old **cloth hall** (the Lakenhalle) and the **cathedral** – were meticulously reconstructed. The result must once have seemed strangely antiseptic – old-style edifices with no signs of decay or erosion – but now, after a century or so, the brickwork has mellowed, and the centre looks authentically antique and rather handsome.

Lakenhalle

Grote Markt

A monument to the power and wealth of the medieval guilds, the magnificent **Lakenhalle** (Cloth Hall) dominates the Grote Markt, its long line of doors and pointed windows framed by a mighty, soaring belfry. The building is a 1930s copy of the thirteenth-century original, though today, many of the wooden doors that originally

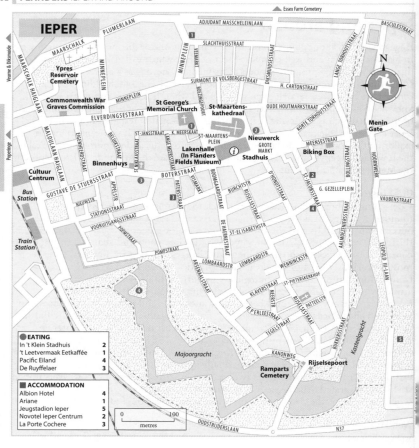

IEPER

EATING

In 't Klein Stadhuis	2
't Leetvermaak Eetkaffée	1
Pacific Eiland	4
De Ruyffelaer	3

ACCOMMODATION

Albion Hotel	4
Ariane	1
Jeugstadion Ieper	5
Novotel Ieper Centrum	2
La Porte Cochere	3

led into the selling halls lead nowhere in particular. The other major change from medieval times – though this happened long before the war – is at the west end of the building, where boats once sailed up the River Ieperlee to unload their cargoes until that is, the river was vaulted to flow underground.

In Flanders Fields Museum

Lakenhalle, Grote Markt • Charge • ⓦ inflandersfields.be

Inside the Lakenhalle, the outstanding **In Flanders Fields Museum** focuses on the experiences of those caught up in the war rather than the ebb and flow of the military campaigns, though these are sketched in, too. At the start, there is an excellent introduction to the origins of the war, followed by a detailed section on the German invasion of Belgium in 1914, describing the damage the invaders inflicted and the atrocities they committed. Thereafter, the museum outlines the creation of the **Ypres Salient** and the gruesome nature of trench warfare with discrete subsections on, for example, the evolution of mortars, the use of gas and tunnelling. Taken as a whole, the exhibits are wide-ranging and thoughtful, and the multilingual quotations are well chosen. But, above all, it's the photographs that steal the show: soldiers grimly digging trenches, the pathetic casualties of a gas attack, flyblown corpses in the mud, and panoramas of a blasted landscape. You can also clamber from the museum to the top of the adjoining **belfry** for the panoramic views.

The Nieuwerck

At its eastern end, the Lakenhalle is attached to the **Nieuwerck**, a fancy, pirouetting structure whose slender arches and gables were constructed in 1622 – though what you see today is a 1930s replica. The Nieuwerck began life as a customs and shipping control house but is now a modest museum tracing the history of Ieper.

St-Maartenskathedraal

St-Maartensplein • Free

To the rear of the Lakenhalle rises **St-Maartenskathedraal**, a 1920s copy of the thirteenth-century Gothic original. The church's cavernous nave is a formal, rather bland affair, but the rose window above the door in the south transept is a fine tribute to **King Albert I** of Belgium, its yellow, green, red and blue stained glass the gift of the British armed forces. Some of the British may have envied the Belgians: their commander Albert, realising that offensives always resulted in heavy casualties, repeatedly refused requests to lend his men to the French and the British when they were launching major attacks and, as a result, Belgian losses were by percentage far fewer than those of her main allies.

St George's Memorial Church

Elverdingsestraat 1 • Free • ⓦ stgeorgesmemorialchurchypres.com

The Anglican **St George's Memorial Church**, a modest brick building finished in 1929, lies just northwest of the cathedral. The interior is crowded with brass plaques honouring the dead of many British regiments, and almost all the chairs carry individual and regimental tributes. It's hard not to be moved, for there's nothing vainglorious in this public space, so consumed as it is with private grief.

Ypres Reservoir Cemetery

Plumerlaan • Free

From St George's, it's a brief walk to the silent graves of the **Ypres Reservoir Cemetery**, laid out to a pre-ordained plan (see page 135) and one of two British Commonwealth graveyards in the town centre. In use from 1915 onwards, just over 2,500 men are buried here, though only half were identified. Many were brought in from the Salient to die of their wounds in field hospitals, but others were killed in the town itself. Among the latter were sixteen men of the Duke of Cornwall's Light Infantry, who were billeted

---

FELINE TERRORS

During winter, **wool** was stored on the upper floor of the Lakenhalle and **cats** were brought in to keep the mice down. The cats may have had a good time in winter, but they couldn't have relished the prospect of spring when they were thrown out of the windows to a hostile crowd below as part of the **Kattenstoet** or Cats' Festival (ⓦ kattenstoet.be) the slaughter intended to symbolise the killing of evil spirits. The festival ran until 1817 and was revived in 1938 when the cats were (mercifully) replaced by cloth imitations. Since then, it's developed into one of Ieper's biggest shindigs, held every three years on the second Sunday in May. The main event is the **parade** – a large-scale celebration of all things catty, complete with dancers and bands and some of the biggest models and puppets imaginable.

in the vaults of the cathedral when they were interred by a giant, long-range German shell: they were not the only ones to be killed by what the soldiers grimly called the 'Ypres Express'. Here also are three graves of men **shot at dawn** for desertion by British firing squad – Ernest Lawrence, Charles Frederick McColl and Thomas Moles.

Menin Gate

East of the Grote Markt, the massive **Menin Gate** war memorial was built on the site of the old Menenpoort, which served as the main route for British soldiers heading for the front. It's a simple, brooding monument, towering over the edge of the town, its walls covered with the names of those fifty thousand British and Empire troops who died in the Ypres Salient but have no grave. The simple inscription above the lists of the dead has none of the victor's arrogance but rather a sense of great loss. Nevertheless, the self-justifying formality of the memorial did offend many veterans and prompted a bitter verse from **Siegfried Sassoon**:

Was ever an immolation so belied
As these intolerably nameless names?
Well might the Dead who struggled in slime
Rise and deride this sepulchre of crime.

Volunteers from the local fire brigade sound the **Last Post** beneath the gate each evening at 8pm. Sometimes, it's an extremely moving ceremony, especially when the fire brigade is joined by other bands, but at other times, it's noisy and really rather crass, with scores of schoolchildren milling around aimlessly.

The ramparts

Curiously, the seventeenth-century brick and earthen **ramparts** on either side of the Menin Gate were strong enough to survive World War I in good condition – the vaults even served as some of the safest bunkers on the front. These massive ramparts and their protective moat still extend right around the east and south of the town centre, and a pleasant **footpath** runs along the top amidst mature horse-chestnut trees to a second British Commonwealth graveyard, the small and tranquil **Ramparts Cemetery**, which slopes down towards the old moat.

ARRIVAL AND INFORMATION
IEPER

By train Ieper train station stands on the western edge of the centre, a 10min walk from the Grote Markt.
Destinations Ghent (hourly; 1hr); Kortrijk (hourly; 30min); Poperinge (hourly; 7min).
By bus Ieper bus station is next door to the train station.
Destinations Diksmuide (Mon–Fri 6 daily, Sat 4 daily; 50min); Veurne (Mon–Fri 4 daily; 1hr).

Tourist information The helpful and efficient tourist office is in the Lakenhalle on the Grote Markt (April to mid-Nov: Mon–Fri 9am–6pm, Sat & Sun 10am–6pm; mid-Nov to March: Mon–Fri 9am–5pm, Sat & Sun 10am–5pm; ⓦ toerismeieper.be). The attached shop has booklets and leaflets describing various car and cycle routes around the Salient and also sells a first-rate range of books on World War I.

GETTING AROUND

By bike There are at least six bike rental outlets in Ieper – tourist information has the full list. One handy option is the Biking Box, in the town centre at Menenstraat 15

(ⓦ bikingbox.be/en).
By car There are currently no car rental companies in Ieper.

ACCOMMODATION
SEE MAP PAGE 132

Tourist information's website (ⓦ toerismeieper.be) has comprehensive accommodation listings. There are nearly twenty B&Bs, though the majority are out in the sticks,

whereas most of Ieper's hotels are in the centre; there's a handily located campsite too.
★ **Albion Hotel** St-Jacobsstraat 28 ⓦ albionhotel.be.

This three-star hotel has stacks of appeal with eighteen large and well-appointed en-suite guest rooms decorated in a spick-and-span, unfussy modern style. The public areas are commodious, the breakfasts are good, and it's in a handy location, a brief stroll from the Grote Markt. €€

★ **Ariane** Slachthuisstraat 58 ⓦ ariane.be. Flanked by a prim and proper garden with a water fountain and pond, this ultramodern four-star hotel occupies a secluded location, a 5min walk north of the Grote Markt. The fifty en-suite rooms are large, well appointed and very comfortable. €€€

Jeugstadion Ieper Bolwerkstraat 1, off Karel Steverlyncklaan ⓦ jeugdstadion.be. Small campsite in a leafy location across the canal from the southeast end of town – and a 25min walk from the train station. There's bike rental, seventy tent pitches, twenty-odd tent and vehicle pitches, and three hikers' huts. March to mid-Nov. Pitches €, hikers' huts €

Novotel Ieper Centrum St-Jacobsstraat 15 ⓦ novotel. com. The building might be a bit of a modern bruiser, but the interior is surprisingly swish, and the hundred-odd rooms are all comfortably modern in true *Novotel* style. Fitness facilities and a sauna, too. €€€

La Porte Cochere Paterstraat 22 ⓦ laportecochere. com. This charming B&B occupies a handsome, three-storey house with grand double doors and a fancy fanlight in a pleasant location near the Grote Markt. Has three comfortable bedrooms with period touches. €€

EATING   SEE MAP PAGE 132

★ **In 't Klein Stadhuis** Grote Markt 32 ⓦ inhetklein stadhuis.be. In a convenient location, next to the Lakenhalle, this cosy and informal split-level restaurant is a popular spot. Its excellent Flemish menu features delights like Flemish stew and rabbit cooked in beer. €€

't Leetvermaak Eetkaffée Korte Meersstraat 2 ⓦ leetvermaak.be. This excellent café-restaurant sports a cosy interior and plays a smooth, jazzy soundtrack. The cuisine is largely Flemish, with a sprinkling of Italian and Spanish/Portuguese dishes adding interest. Cultural events are staged here, too. €€€

Pacific Eiland Eiland 2 ⓦ pacificeiland.be. In a superb wooded setting, flanked by the old city moat, this popular café-restaurant has a wide-ranging – perhaps too wide-ranging – menu featuring such delights as Norwegian smoked salmon and a mixed fish grill. €€€

★ **De Ruyffelaer** Gustave de Stuersstraat 11 ⓦ deruyffelaer.be. This homely, weekends-only restaurant is kitted out with all sorts of local trinkets and offers delicious home-made food, with Flemish dishes uppermost – the stews are outstanding. Wash it down with Hommel, the tangy local ale from the neighbouring town of Poperinge. €€€

The Ypres Salient

Immediately east of Ieper, the **Ypres Salient** occupies a basin-shaped parcel of land about 25km long and never more than 15km deep. For the commanders of World War I, the area's key feature was the long and low sequence of ridges that sweeps south from the hamlet of Langemark to the French border. These gave the occupants a clear view of Ieper and its surroundings, and consequently, the British and Germans spent the war trying to capture and keep them. The dips and sloping **ridges** that were then so vitally important are still much in evidence today. Still, the tranquillity of the landscape makes it difficult to imagine what the war was like. Most of what remains today – concrete pillboxes, craters from exploded mines, even the occasional segment of (restored) trench – only hint at what happened here, though three Salient '**Entry Points**' – of which **Entry Point South** is the most convincing – make a gallant attempt to remedy matters. Each of these Entry Points concentrates on the war as it evolved in their locality.

The British Commonwealth War Cemeteries

Across the Salient, the most resonant reminders of the blood-letting are the 160 or so **British Commonwealth War Cemeteries** that dot the landscape, each immaculately maintained by the Commonwealth War Graves Commission. Every cemetery, including the most famous, **Tyne Cot**, has a **Cross of Sacrifice** in white Portland stone, and the larger ones also have a sarcophagus-like **Stone of Remembrance** bearing the legend 'Their Name Liveth For Ever More', a quotation selected by Rudyard Kipling from Ecclesiasticus. The **graves** line up at precisely spaced intervals and, wherever possible, **headstones** bear the individual's name, rank, serial number, age and date of death, plus the badge of the relevant military unit or a national emblem, an appropriate

2

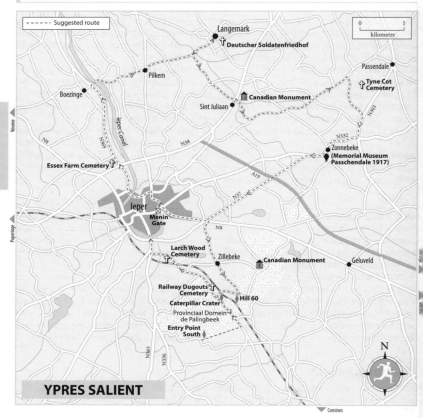

YPRES SALIENT

religious symbol and, at the base, an inscription chosen by relatives. All the graves are numbered, and at each cemetery, a **registry book** is kept in an alcove at the entrance recording alphabetically who is buried where – if, of course, the remains have been identified: thousands of gravestones do not carry any or all of these tags as the bodies were buried without anyone knowing who they were. If you are looking for someone's grave in particular, consult the **Commonwealth War Graves Commission**'s excellent website (ⓦcwgc.org).

GETTING AROUND   YPRES SALIENT

By car or bike You cannot explore the Ypres Salient by public transport, though there are guided tours. The best bet is by car or cycle. There are currently no car hire companies in Ieper, but there is cycle hire at Biking Box, in the town centre at Menenstraat 15 (ⓦbikingbox.be/en). The sites we have detailed below are both the pick of the bunch and

described in geographical order; all together, they comprise a comfortable, day-long tour. The route includes **Entry Point South but not the Sanctuary Wood Museum** (Hill 62), privately owned by the farmer's grandson, who reclaimed his land in 1919.

INFORMATION AND TOURS

Information and maps Ieper tourist information (see page 134) has a wide range of leaflets and booklets outlining cycling and driving tours of the Salient. They also

have detailed brochures on the three 'Entry Points' – South, North and East.

Guided tours Tours of the Salient beginning in Ieper

are provided by Flanders Battlefield Tours (@ipers-fbt. com), which offers 4hr and 2.5hr trips for €45 and €30, respectively. For tours beginning in Bruges, check out Quasimodo (see page 114).

Essex Farm Cemetery
Diksmuideseweg, 8900 Ieper • Free • 3km north of Ieper along the N369 (to Diksmuide), just beyond the flyover

Essex Farm Cemetery is where the dead were brought from the neighbouring battlefield. In the bank behind and to the left of the cemetery's Cross of Sacrifice are the remains of several British bunkers, part of a combined forward position and first-aid post dug into the west side of the canal. It was here that the Canadian **John McCrae** wrote the war's best-known poem, 'In Flanders Fields'. The second stanza speaks for the dead:

We are the Dead. Short days ago
We lived, felt dawn, saw sunsets glow,
Loved and were loved, and now we lie,
In Flanders fields.

Deutscher Soldatenfriedhof
Klerkenstraat, 8920 Langemark • Free • About 9km northeast of Essex Farm

On the northern edge of the hamlet of **LANGEMARK** is the Salient's only German war cemetery, the **Deutscher Soldatenfriedhof**. Nearly 45,000 German soldiers are buried here, mostly in communal graves, but others are interred in groups of eight with stone plaques above each tomb carrying the names of the dead (where known). The entrance gate is a squat neo-Romanesque structure whose style is continued by the basalt crosses dotting the rest of the site. Overlooking it all is a moving **bronze** of four mourning soldiers by the Munich sculptor Emil Krieger.

Tyne Cot
Vijfwegestraat, 8980 Zonnebeke • Free • About 8km from Deutscher Soldatenfriedhof

Tyne Cot is the largest British Commonwealth war cemetery in the world, containing no fewer than 11,956 graves as well as the so-called **Memorial to the Missing**, a semicircular wall inscribed with the names of a further 35,000 men whose bodies were never recovered. The soldiers of a Northumbrian division gave the place its name, observing that the Flemish house on the horizon looked like a Tyneside cottage as they tried to fight their way up the ridge. The house disappeared during the war, but the largest of the concrete **pillboxes** the Germans built to defend the ridge has survived, incorporated within the mound beneath the **Cross of Sacrifice** at the suggestion of George V – you can still see a piece of it where a slab of stone has been deliberately omitted. Strangely, the Memorial to the Missing at the back of the cemetery wasn't part of the original design: the intention was that these names be recorded on the Menin Gate, but there was not enough room. Beside the car park, the **visitor centre** gives further background information and displays World War I photos.

Passendale
About 1km from Tyne Cot

Tyne Cot cemetery overlooks the shallow valley that gently shelves up to the hamlet of **PASSENDALE**, known then as **Passchendaele**. This village was the British objective in the **Third Battle of Ypres**, but torrential rain and intensive shelling turned the valley into a giant quagmire. The whole affair came to symbolise the futility of the war and the incompetence of its generals: when Field-Marshal Haig's Chief of Staff ventured out of his HQ to inspect progress, he allegedly said, 'Good God, did we really send men to fight in that?'

Memorial Museum Passchendaele 1917
Berten Pilstraat 5, 8980 Zonnebeke • Charge • @ passchendaele.be • About 4.5km southwest of Passendale

2

Beside the main road in the middle of **Zonnebeke**, occupying a nineteenth-century château and its grounds is the **Memorial Museum Passchendaele 1917**, home to the region's largest collection of World War I artefacts. Displays are focused on the Third Battle of Ypres (see box, page 139), illustrating this desperately futile conflict with photos, military hardware and reconstructions of a trench and a dugout.

Ypres Salient: Entry Point South (The Bluff)

Palingbeekstraat, 8902 Zillebeke • Free • About 8km southwest of the Memorial Museum • ⓦ toerismeieper.be/entry-point-south

Of the three 'Entry Points' to the Salient, **Entry Point South** is the most diverting. A small pavilion at the entrance features a short (15min) **film** on the military comings and goings on this part of the Front. Afterwards, a marked, 4km long **hiking trail** follows the line of the trenches, taking in **The Bluff**, the much-mined **Hill 60** and **Caterpillar Crater**. You'll need a lively imagination to conceive of precisely what went on and where, but it's still a good way to understand the war, and information plaques will help you on your way.

Poperinge

Execution place Guido Gezellestraat 1 • Free

Flanked and fringed by hop fields, small-town **POPERINGE**, just 12km west of Ieper, has one major claim to fame – it managed to escape the German occupation of World War I. It was also out of range of all but the largest of German guns, and so it was here that thousands of British and Empire soldiers licked their wounds – both physical and mental. Many found solace at the **Talbot House**. But, Poperinge had a darker side, too, for it was here that many soldiers were **court-martialled** for a variety of offences, from cowardice and desertion to insubordination. A few were shot at dawn and, at the back of the Stadhuis, just off the Grote Markt, the **cells** where the condemned were incarcerated have been restored, as has the adjacent **execution place**, complete with a replica of the wooden stake to which the condemned men were tied.

Talbot House Museum

Gasthuisstraat 43 • Charge • ⓦ talbothouse.be

In late 1915, Philip 'Tubby' Clayton (1885–1972), a British army chaplain, played a key role in establishing the **Talbot House** as a rest and recreation centre for soldiers from the Front. Unusually, it was open to all ranks, and consequently, it soon became known as the **Every Man's Club**. Hundreds found comfort here in simple pleasures – sing-alongs and prayer – and after the war, Clayton pioneered **Toc H**, an international Christian movement for peace and reconciliation named after Talbot House – 'Toc' being 'T' in the signals alphabet of the time. Today, Talbot House looks something like it did in World War I – even the simple chapel in the loft has survived – and it's attached to a small **war museum**, which holds a series of intriguing displays on, for example, the exploitation of Chinese coolies, Tubby Clayton, R&R and the war in the air.

ARRIVAL AND DEPARTURE   POPERINGE

By train Poperinge train station is an 8min walk from the Grote Markt – straight down Ieperstraat.

Destinations Ieper (hourly; 7min); Kortrijk (hourly; 40min).

ACCOMMODATION

★**Talbot House** Gasthuisstraat 43 ⓦ talbothouse. be. In what was once the Every Man's Club, this distinctive, one-star guesthouse has seven cosy guest rooms decorated in appropriate period style – and with war art on the walls. Each room has a washbasin, but other facilities are shared. €

POINTLESS SLAUGHTER: THE YPRES SALIENT

The creation of the **Ypres Salient** was entirely accidental. When the German army invaded Belgium and launched the war in the west, they followed the military principles laid down by a previous chief of the German General Staff, **Alfred von Schlieffen**, who had died eight years earlier. The idea was simple: to avoid fighting a war on two fronts, the German army would outflank the French and capture Paris by attacking Belgium well before the Russians had assembled on the eastern frontier. But it didn't work, as the initial German offensive ground to a halt; two lines of opposing trenches were dug, which soon stretched from the North Sea to Switzerland.

No one knew quite what to do next, but attention focused on the two main bulges – or **salients** – in the line, one at Ieper, the other at Verdun in France. To the Allied generals, the bulge at Ieper – the **Ypres Salient** – was a good place to puncture the German lines and roll up their front; to the Germans, it represented an ideal opportunity to break the deadlock by attacking enemy positions from several sides at the same time. Contemporary **military doctrine** on both sides held that the way to win a war was first to destroy the enemy's strongest forces – a theory based on cavalry tactics, where a charge that broke the enemy's key formations brought victory. The consequence of this tactical similitude was that the salients attracted armies like magnets. The problem was that **technological changes** had shifted the balance of war in favour of defence: machine guns had become more efficient, barbed wire more effective, and the railways could shift defensive reserves faster than an advancing army could march. Another issue was **supply**. These vast armies couldn't live off the land, and once they advanced much beyond the reach of the railways, the supply problems were enormous. As the historian A.J.P. Taylor succinctly put it, 'Defence was mechanized; attack was not'.

The generals had no answer to the stalemate. They demonstrated amazing profligacy with the lives of their men – the British commander, Douglas Haig, even proposing a **war of attrition** in which Germany was bled to death, never mind the casualties on his side. It's true there were tactical innovations as the war progressed. Still, these were very limited, and indeed, two of the new techniques – gas attack and a heavy preliminary bombardment – often made matters worse: the **shells** forewarned the enemy of an offensive and churned the trenches into a muddy maelstrom where men, horses and machinery were engulfed; the **gas** was as dangerous to the advancing soldiers as it was to the retreating enemy. **Tanks** proved successful, but only on relatively good ground, and although explosive-packed **mines** were used to great effect, they were extraordinarily costly and time-consuming.

This was the background to the four years of war that raged in and around the Ypres Salient, producing **four major battles**. The first, in October and November of 1914, settled the lines of the bulge as both armies tried to outflank each other; the second was a German attack the following spring that moved the trenches a couple of kilometres west. The third, launched by British Empire soldiers in July 1917, was even more pointless, with thousands of men dying for an advance of only a few kilometres. It's frequently called the **Battle of Passchendaele**, but Lloyd George more accurately referred to it as the 'Battle of the Mud', a disaster that cost 250,000 British lives. The fourth and final battle, in April 1918, was another German attack inspired by General Ludendorff's desire to break the British army. Instead, it broke his own, leading to the **11 November Armistice**.

Kortrijk

KORTRIJK (Courtrai in French), just 8km from the French border, is the largest town in this part of West Flanders, a lively, busy sort of place with a couple of excellent hotels, several good places to eat and a smattering of distinguished medieval buildings. The town traces its origins back to a **Roman settlement** called Cortoriacum, but its salad days were in the Middle Ages when its burghers made a fortune producing linen and

2

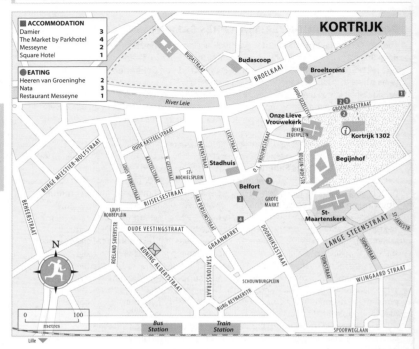

flax. The problem was its location: Kortrijk was just too close to France for comfort, and time and again, the town was embroiled in the wars that swept across Flanders – the landmark **Broeltorens**, the pair of conical towers that guard the River Leie today, witness this troubled history.

The Grote Markt

Heavily bombed during World War II, Kortrijk's **Grote Markt** is a comely but architecturally incoherent mixture of bits of the old and a lot of the new surrounding the forlorn, turreted **Belfort** – all that remains of what was once a splendid medieval cloth hall. At the northwest corner of the Grote Markt stands the **Stadhuis**, a sedate edifice with modern statues of the counts of Flanders on the facade. Inside, through the side entrance on the left, things pick up in the **Historisch Stadhuis** (free) with two fine sixteenth-century **chimneypieces**. The first is in the old **Schepenzaal** (Aldermen's Room) on the ground floor, a proud, intricate work decorated with municipal coats of arms and carvings of bishops, saints and the archdukes Albert and Isabella of Spain; the other, upstairs in the **Raadzaal** (Council Chamber), is a more didactic affair, ornamented by three rows of precise statuettes representing, from top to bottom, the virtues, the vices (to either side of the Emperor Charles V) and the torments of hell.

St-Maartenskerk

St-Maartenskerkstraat • Free

Just off the Grote Markt rises the heavyweight tower of **St-Maartenskerk**, whose gleaming white-stone exterior, dating from the fifteenth century, is distinguished by its slender artichoke spire. The outside of the church may be handsome, but the cavernous interior is a yawn, with the exception of the intricately carved, 6.5m high tabernacle tucked away among the columns of the nave near the high altar, dated to the sixteenth century.

Begijnhof

Begijnhofstraat • Free

Founded in 1238 by Joanna of Constantinople, the Countess of Flanders, the **Begijnhof** (see box, page 307) is an especially pretty corner of Kortrijk, its huddle of ancient whitewashed cottages flanking a network of narrow cobbled lanes. The Begijnhof's charm lies in its general appearance, but you can pop into the **chapel**, whose cream-painted walls are adorned by the most mawkish of religious paintings.

Onze Lieve Vrouwekerk

Deken Zegerplein • Free • ☎ 056 25 88 35

The **Onze Lieve Vrouwekerk** (Church of Our Lady) is a hulking grey structure that formerly doubled as part of the city's fortifications. In July 1302, the nave of the church was crammed with hundreds of spurs, ripped off the feet of dead and dying French knights at the **Battle of the Golden Spurs**, one of the most important military engagements of the period. These plundered spurs were all that remained of the army that Philip the Fair had sent to avenge the slaughter of the Bruges Matins earlier that year (see page 98). The two armies, Philip's heavily armoured cavalry and the lightly armed Flemish weavers, had met outside Kortrijk on marshy ground. Despising their low-born adversaries, the French knights made no reconnaissance and milled around in the mud like cumbersome dinosaurs. They were massacred, the first time an amateur civilian army had defeated mail-clad knights.

The interior

The spurs disappeared long ago, and today, the church's **interior** is a medley of styles, from the Gothic and the Baroque through to the Neoclassical. The gloomy and truncated north transept holds one splendid painting, **Anthony van Dyck**'s *Raising of the Cross*, a muscular, sweeping work with a pale, deathly Christ, completed just before the artist went to England. Across the church, the **Counts' Chapel** has an unusual series of somewhat crude nineteenth-century portraits painted into the wall niches. However, the highlight is a sensuous medieval alabaster **statue of St Catherine**, her left hand clutching a representation of the spiked wheel on which her enemies tried to break her (hence the 'Catherine wheel' firework).

Kortrijk 1302

Begijnhofpark, above tourist information • Free • ⓦ kortrijk1302.be

Hammering home the importance of the Battle of the Golden Spurs, the town's leading museum, **Kortrijk 1302,** provides a detailed account of the engagement and its historical context, culminating in a short feature film. Also on display are a number of original artefacts, most memorably the metal tips of the long pikes carried by the Flemings. This weapon was crucial to the success of the guildsmen who, with true gallows humour, named it the *Goedendag* (Good Day) because the French knights had to nod their heads when the pike was aimed at one of their weak spots – the gap between their helmet and breastplate. A later section explores how the battle served as propaganda: Flemish nationalists trumpeted the success of their forebears, and the French tried to gainsay their defeat by alleging that the Flemings disguised the marshy ground with brushwood – almost certainly untrue.

2

By train Kortrijk train station – and adjacent bus station – is a 5min walk from the Grote Markt.

Destinations Brussels (every 30min; 1hr 10min); Ghent (every 30min; 20min); Ieper (hourly; 30min); Oudenaarde (every 30min; 15min); Poperinge (hourly; 40min).

Tourist information Begijnhofpark, above Kortrijk 1302 (May–Sept: Mon–Fri 10am–6pm, Sat & Sun 10am–5pm; Oct–April: daily 10am–5pm; ⓦvisitkortrijk.be).

Damier Grote Markt 41 ⓦhoteldamier.be. With its handsome Neoclassical facade, this has been the town's prime luxury hotel for many years, and the approach – down through the old carriage archway – is suitably grand. Beyond is a warm and inviting wood-panelled foyer, which is rather charming. The guest rooms are similarly appealing; many make the most of their antique fittings. €€€

The Market by Parkhotel Graanmarkt 6 ⓦthe marketbyparkhotel.be. Medium-sized three-star hotel occupying a six-storey modern block in a handy location near the Grote Markt. There's nothing fancy about the rooms, but they're comfortable, and each is kitted out in a brisk, minimalist manner. €

★ **Messeyne** Groeningestraat 17 ⓦhotelmesseyne. be. Excellent four-star in a creatively modernised eighteenth-century mansion. There's a sauna, a health centre and 28 large, well-appointed rooms, most decorated in fetching creams and browns, some with timber-beam ceilings. €€€

Square Hotel Groeningestraat 39 ⓦsquarehotel.be/ en. Brisk and efficient three-star hotel with 26 trim, modern rooms designed with visiting business folk in mind. In a convenient location, too. €€

Heeren van Groeninghe Groeningestraat 36 ⓦheeren vangroeninghe.be. Set in a cleverly revamped eighteenth-century mansion, this popular bistro-style bar and restaurant does a fine line in Flemish and Italian dishes and is strong on salads. Eat inside or outside on the terrace. Reservations advised. €€€

Nata Grote Markt 4 ⓦnatakortrijk.be. Of all the café-bars that line up along the Grote Markt, this is probably the best, serving a good selection of Franco-Flemish dishes in bright, modern surroundings. A pleasant pavement terrace, too. €€

★ **Restaurant Messeyne** Groeningestraat 17 ⓦhotelmesseyne.be/en. Deluxe-meets-bijou at the *Hotel Messeyne*'s restaurant. The menu is extremely well chosen, and the French cuisine, the *jus* in particular, is delicious. €€€

Oudenaarde

Hugging the banks of the River Scheldt about 30km to the east of Kortrijk, **OUDENAARDE**, literally 'old landing place', is a beguiling sort of place, an easy-paced little town with a clutch of fascinating old buildings, a sprinkling of enjoyable bars and restaurants and a museum that features Oudenaarde's main claim to fame, its **tapestries** (see box, page 144). The town has a long and chequered history. Granted a charter in 1193, it concentrated on cloth manufacture until the early fifteenth century, when its weavers switched to tapestry-making, an industry that made its burghers rich and the town famous, with the best tapestries becoming the prized possessions of the kings of France and Spain. So far so good, but Oudenaarde became a key **military objective** during the religious and dynastic wars of the sixteenth to the eighteenth centuries. Attacked and besieged time and again, Oudenaarde found it impossible to sustain any growth, and the demise of the tapestry industry pauperised the town, rendering it an insignificant backwater in one of the poorest parts of Flanders – until recently, when the canny use of regional development funds has put the spring back in the municipal step.

Tacambaroplein war memorial

On the way into town from the train station, the only surprise is the romantic **war memorial** occupying the middle of **Tacambaroplein**. For once, it has nothing to do with either world war. Instead, it commemorates those who were daft or unscrupulous enough to volunteer to go to Mexico and fight for **Maximilian**, the Habsburg son-in-law of the Belgian king, Léopold I. Unwanted and unloved, Maximilian was imposed on the Mexicans by a French army provided by Napoleon III, who wanted to create his western empire while the eyes of the US were averted by their civil war. It was, however, all too fanciful, and the occupation rapidly turned into a fiasco. Maximilian paid for the adventure with his life in 1867, and precious few of his soldiers made the return trip. The reasons for this calamity seem to have been entirely lost on Maximilian, who declared, in front of the firing squad that was about to polish him off, 'Men of my class and lineage are created by God to be the happiness of nations or their martyrs … Long live Mexico, long live independence.'

Stadhuis

Markt

The airy and expansive **Markt** at the heart of Oudenaarde is overlooked by the **Stadhuis**, one of the finest examples of Flamboyant Gothic in the country. Built around 1525, its elegantly symmetrical facade spreads out on either side of a slender central tower, whose extravagant tiers, balconies and parapets are topped by the gilded figure of a knight, *Hanske de Krijger* (Little John the Warrior). Underneath the knight, the cupola is shaped like a crown, a theme reinforced by the two groups of cherubs on the dormer windows below, who lovingly clutch the royal insignia. Inside, a magnificent oak **doorway** forms the entrance to the old Schepenzaal (Aldermen's Hall). A stylistically influential piece of 1531, the **doorway** consists of an intricate sequence of carvings surmounted by miniature cherubs who frolic above three coats of arms and a 28-panel door.

Tourist information (see page 145) will be able to provide details of (sporadic) guided tours.

MOU

Markt • Charge • ⓦ oudenaarde.be/en/mou

Attached to the back of the Stadhuis, the thirteenth-century **Lakenhalle** now holds **MOU**, the town's principal museum. Spread over several floors, the museum begins with a modest history of Oudenaarde. It follows up with a large quantity of silverware. Still, the main event is a magnificent collection of **tapestries**, the pick of which are exhibited to fine effect in a capacious, high-ceilinged hall. Among the tapestries on display, look out for a trio of wonderful, late sixteenth-century classical pieces celebrating Alexander the Great – *Alexander is offered the Crown*; *Alexander before the high priest Iaddo*; and *The Army Camp beside the River Granikos*. Equally delightful is *Scipio and Hannibal*,

Map labels

OUDENAARDE

■ ACCOMMODATION	
La Pomme d'Or	1
Steenhuyse	2

● EATING	
De Cridts	2
Margaretha's	3
Wine & Dine Café	1

■ DRINKING	
Bieren Roman	1
De Carillon	2

0   200
metres

Train Station / Bus Station
STATIONSPLEIN
Old Train Station
STATIONSSTRAAT
BROEKSTRAAT
PAUWEL VANDERSCHELDENSTR
J. LACOPSSTRAAT
DIJKSTRAAT
Coupere
BEVERESTRAAT
GEVAERTSDREEF
GEN. PERSINGHSTR
DEVOSTR
TACAMBARO-PLEIN
WIJNGAARDSTR
ACHTER DEWACHT
MEINAERT
HOOGSTRAAT
CAPUCIJNENGANG
KATTESTRAAT
NEDERSTRAAT
WOEKER
Lakenhalle & Mou
Stadhuis
EINE STRAAT
LAPPERSFORT
KONINGSTR
MARKT
BROODSTRAAT
KREKEL PUT TUSSENBRUGGEN
GRACHT
VOORBURG
ST-WALBURGASTR
 RGASTR
BURGSCHELDE
St-Walburgakerk
LEVERENSTR
ACHTERBURG
Centrum Ronde Van Vlaanderen
Begijnhof
SMALLENDAM
KASTEELSTR
MARGARETHA VAN PARMASTRAAT
Scheldt
LOUISE MARIEKAAI
MAT. CASTEELSTRAAT
DE HAM
ZAKCE
O.L.V. Van Pamelekerk
SPEI
Park Liedts
PARKSTR
SIMON DE PAEPESTR
BEKSTRAAT
GENTIEL ANTHEUNISPLEIN
JEZUIETENPLEIN
REFUGESTR
MARLBOROUGHLAAN
N

Astra Bike Hire

2

where the border is decorated with medallions depicting the Seven Wonders of the World – though the Hanging Gardens of Babylon appear twice to create symmetry. Romanticised pastoral scenes were perennially popular too: the seventeenth-century *Landscape with Two Pheasants* frames a distant castle with an intricate design of trees and plants, while *La Main Chaude* (or *Pat-a-Cake* as it's labelled here) depicts a game of blind man's buff.

St-Walburgakerk

Markt • Free • ☎ 055 31 72 51

Soaring high above the town, **St-Walburgakerk** is a hulking, rambling mass of Gothic masonry that took a real hammering from the Protestants, who trashed almost all the original furnishings and fittings. Nowadays, gaudy Baroque altarpieces dot the yawning interior, but in the **choir**, there are several large, albeit very faded, tapestries, most memorably an exquisite *Calvary* in which two symbols of Christ's suffering – a spear and a stick with a sponge – are nailed to the Cross instead of Christ himself.

Centrum Ronde van Vlaanderen

Markt 43 • Charge • ⓦ crvv.be

Oudenaarde is home to a noteworthy special interest museum, the **Centrum Ronda Van Vlaanderen**. It has everything you could ever want to know about Belgium's premier professional cycling competition, the **Tour of Flanders**, including a film and cycling

---

APPLIED ART AT ITS FINEST: OUDENAARDE'S TAPESTRIES

Tapestry manufacture in Oudenaarde began in the middle of the fifteenth century. It was an embryonic industry that soon came to be based on a dual system of workshop and outworking, one with paid employees and the other with workers paid on a piecework basis. From the beginning, the town authorities took a keen interest in the business, ensuring its success through a rigorous quality control system, which soon gave Oudenaarde an international reputation for consistently well-made tapestries.

The first great period of the town's tapestry-making lasted until the middle of the sixteenth century, when **religious conflict** overwhelmed the town, and many Protestant-inclined weavers, who had come into direct conflict with their Catholic masters, migrated north. In 1582, Oudenaarde was finally incorporated into the Spanish Netherlands, precipitating a **revival of tapestry** production fostered by the king and queen of Spain, who were keen to support the industry and passed draconian laws banning the movement of weavers. Later, however, the French occupation and the shrinking of the Spanish market led to diminishing production, with the industry finally fizzling out in the late eighteenth century.

There were two significant types of tapestry: **decorative** – principally *verdures*, showing scenes of foliage in an almost abstract way (the Oudenaarde speciality) – and **pictorial**, which were usually variations on the same basic themes, particularly rural life, knights, hunting parties and religious scenes. Over the centuries, style changes were strictly limited, though the early seventeenth century saw an increased use of elaborate woven borders and an appreciation of perspective.

Standard-size Oudenaarde tapestries took **six months** to make and were produced exclusively for the wealthy. They were usually in yellow, brown, pale blue, and shades of green, with an occasional splash of red, though the most important clients would occasionally insist on using gold and silver thread. Some also insisted on employing the most famous artists of the day for the preparatory painting – **Pieter Paul Rubens** and Jacob Jordaens completed tapestry commissions.

simulators. Enthusiasts can also drop by the shop, where they sell cycling maps, books and equipment – including retro-style jerseys.

ARRIVAL AND INFORMATION OUDENAARDE

By train Oudenaarde train station is a 10min walk from the town centre; the bus station is adjacent. Incidentally, the present train station has usurped its neo-Gothic predecessor, which stands lonely and forlorn next door. Destinations Brussels (every 30min to hourly; 50min); Ghent (hourly; 35min); Kortrijk (every 30min; 15min).

Tourist information The tourist office occupies the same premises as the MOU museum, in the Lakenhalle at the back of the Stadhuis (April–Sept: daily 9.30am–5.30pm; Oct–March: Mon–Fri 9am–5pm, Sat 10am–5.30pm; ⓦ oudenaarde.be/en/tourism).

GETTING AROUND

By bike Bike rental is available from Asfra, a short walk southeast of the centre at Bergstraat 75 (ⓦ asfra.be). Tourist information sells cycling maps of the Vlaamse Ardennen (Flemish Ardennes), the ridge of low, wooded hills that rises from the Flanders plain a few kilometres to the south of town.

ACCOMMODATION SEE MAP PAGE 143

La Pomme d'Or Markt 62 ⓦ lapommedor.be. This ten-room, three-star hotel offers plain but perfectly adequate modern rooms in a large, good-looking old building on the main square. Try one of their splendid, advocaat-laced cappuccinos in the bar. €€

Steenhuyse Markt 37 ⓦ steenhuyse.be. This enjoyable four-star hotel occupies a tastefully modernised eighteenth-century mansion, whose handsome stone facade fronts the Markt. The seven large and well-appointed rooms come with all mod cons (rain showers and so forth). €€€

EATING SEE MAP PAGE 143

De Crids Markt 58 ☏ 055 31 17 78. Friendly, traditional, family-owned café-restaurant serving standard-issue but tasty Flemish dishes at very reasonable prices – the steaks are a speciality. €€

Margaretha's Markt 40 ⓦ margarethas.com. Oudenaarde tends to be low-key, so it's something of a surprise to find this extraordinarily lavish restaurant here, right bang in the centre of town. The place has the appearance of a stately home, and the cuisine is very French, with due prominence given to local, seasonal ingredients. Set meals are the order of the day, with lunches being a good deal less expensive than evening dinners. €€€

Wine & Dine Café Hoogstraat 34 ⓦ wine-dine.be. Nattily decorated café-restaurant offering a good choice of Franco-Flemish food served with style and panache. For example, try slow-cooked suckling pig chops with cabbage puree, pickles and mousseline. €€€

DRINKING SEE MAP PAGE 143

Bieren Roman Hoogstraat 21. The local Roman brewery rules the Oudenaarde roost, and this traditional neighbourhood bar is devoted to its products – try, for example, the Tripel Ename, a strong blond beer, or the Roman Dobbelen Bruinen, a snappy filtered stout.

De Carillon Markt 49 ⓦ decarillon.be. Old-fashioned café-bar that occupies an ancient brick-gabled building in the shadow of St-Walburgakerk. It's at its best in the summertime when the large pavement terrace heaves with drinkers (rather than eaters).

Ghent

Of all the cities in Belgium, it's hard to trump **GHENT**, a vital, vibrant metropolis whose booming restaurant and bar scene wends its way across a charming cityscape comprising a network of narrow canals overseen by handsome classical mansions and antique red-brick houses. If Bruges is a tourist industry with a town attached, Ghent is the reverse – a proudly Flemish city with a population of around 470,000, Belgium's third-largest conurbation. Evidence of Ghent's medieval pomp is to be found in a string of superb Gothic buildings, most memorably **St-Baafskathedraal**, whose principal treasure is Jan van Eyck's remarkable *Adoration of the Mystic Lamb*, one of the world's most important paintings. Supporting the cathedral are the likes of **St-Niklaaskerk**, with its soaring arches and pencil-thin turrets; the forbidding castle of the counts of

Dampoort Train Stations & Oktrooiplein (200m)

GHENT

2

DAMPOORTSTRAAT
HAGELANDKAAI
SCHOOLKAAI
L MUNICHSTR
SPANJAARDSTRAAT
St-Baafsabdij
FERDINAND LOUSBERGSKAAI
VOORHOUTKAAI
Leie
KOEPOORTKAAI
NIEUWE BOSSTR
NIEUWBRUGG VEERKAAI
NIEUWBRUG VEERKAAI
APOSTELHUIZEN
ST-ANNAPLEIN
ZUIDSTATIONSTR
Studio Skoop
GEBR D EYCKSTR
KEIZER KARELSTRAAT
ABEELSTR
GRAAF VAN VLAANDERENPLEIN
BELGRADOSTR
LANGE BOOMGAARDSTR
BRABANTDAM
VLAANDERENSTR
WILSONPLEIN
BAUDELOKAAI
STEENDAM
NIEUWPOORT VOLMOLENSTR
HOUTBRIEL
KWAADHAM
SEMINARIESTR
KUIPERSKAAI
FRANKRIJKPLEIN
BIBLIOTHEEKSTR
OTTOGRACHT
BAUDELOSTR
BEVERHOUTPLEIN
ST-JACOBSNIEWSTR
BARRESTRAAT
NEDERPOLDER
REEP
Duivelsteen
REEP
LAMMERSTR
Vooruit
ANSEELEPLEIN
BUS ST-JACOBS
VRIJDAGMARKT
BELFORTSTR
St-Baafskathedraal
LIMBURGSTR
HENEGOUWENSTR
WALPOORTSTR
KETELVEST
BAGATTENSTRAAT
Huis Van Alijn
PATERSHOL
OUDBURG
KRANLEI
ONDERSTRAAT
HOOGPOORT
DONKERSTEEG
Stadhuis
GOUDEN LEEUWPLEIN
Belfort & Lakenhalle
MAGELEINSTR
KOESTR
VOGEL-MARKT
KTE DAGSTEEG
KOUTER
Concertzaal Handelsbeurs
SCHOUWBURGSTR
SAIVANSTRAAT
GELDMUNT
ST-VEERLEPLEIN
Oude Vismijn
KORENMARKT
St-Niklaaskerk
ST-NIKLAASSTR
VOLDERSSTR
KORTE MEER
ZONNESTR
De Vlaamse Opera
NEDERKOUTER
HET PAND
GRASLEI
ST-MICHIELSBRUG
VELDSTRAAT
KOOP HANDELS-PLEIN
KETELBRUG
Het Pand
LINDENLEI
Het Gravensteen
GEWAD
ST-WIDOSTRAAT
BURGSTRAAT
J BREYDELSTR
POEL
DRABSTR
KORENLEI
ST-MICHIELSPLEIN
St-Michielskerk
ZWARTEZUSTERSSTR
ONDERBERGEN
AJUNLEI
GANDASTR
GEBR VANEYCKSTR
VANDERSTR
Justitiepaleis
IEPENSTRAAT
PRINSENHOF
SEE 'CENTRAL GHENT MAP' FOR DETAILS
RAMEN
OUDE HOUTLEI
HOOGSTRAAT
PEPERSTR
HOLSTRAAT
BRANDSTRAAT
ANNONCIADENSTR
RABOTSTRAAT
ST-ELIZABETH PLEIN
PROVENIERSTERSSTRAAT
BEGIJNENGR
THERESIANENSTR
CASINO-PLEIN
GALGENBERG
TWAALFKAMEREN
COUPURE RECHTS
COUPURE LINKS
G.JOHANNASTR
BEGIJNHOFDRIES
ST-ELIZABETH BEGIJNHOF
PROVENIERSTERSSTRAAT
BEGIJNENGR
MARIALAND
RASPHUISSTRAAT
PAPEGAAISTR
Coupure
COUPURE LINKS
COUPURE RECHTS
COUPURE LINKS
ROZEMARIJNSTR
B SPAELAAN
BIJLOKEVEST
MARTELAARSLAAN
COLPAERTSTG
N

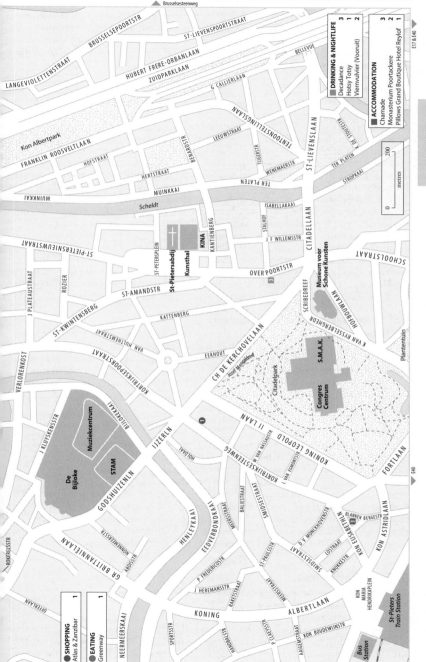

Brusselsesteenweg

DRINKING & NIGHTLIFE
Decadance	3
Hotsy Totsy	1
Viervuilver (Vooruit)	2

ACCOMMODATION
Chamade	3
Monasterium Poortackere	2
Pillows Grand Boutique Hotel Reylof	1

0 — 200 metres

E17 & E40

2

BRUSSELSEPOORTSTR

ST-LIEVENSPOORTSTRAAT

LANGEVIOLETTENSTRAAT

HUBERT FRERE-ORBANLAAN

ZUIDPARKLAAN

BELLEVUE

G CALLIERLAAN

Kon Albertpark

FRANKLIN ROOSVELTLAAN

HOEFSTRAAT

HERTSTRAAT

LEEUWSTRAAT

TENTOONSTELLINGSLAAN

TIJGERSTR

WENEMAERSTR

BENARDSTR

ST-LIEVENSLAAN

K DE STUYSTER

TER PLATEN

MUINKKAI

MUINKKAI

Scheldt

TER PLATEN

STROPKAAI

ISABELLAKAAI

STALHOF

CITADELLAAN

ST-PIETERSNIEUWSTRAAT

KINA

KANTIENBERG

St-Pietersabdij

Kunsthal

J F WILLEMSSTR

SCHOOLSTRAAT

ST-PIETERSPLEIN

OVERPOORTSTR

ROZIER

J PLATEAUSTRAAT

ST-AMANDSTR

SCRIBEDREEF

Museum voor
Schone Kunsten

ST-KWINTENSBERG

KATTENBERG

HOFBOUWLAAN

K VAN NYSSELBERGHEDR

VAN HULTHEMSTRAAT

EEKHOUT

VERLORENKOST

KORTRIJKSEPOORTSTRAAT

CH DE KERCHOVELAAN

Jozef Kluyskensstr

Citadelpark

S.M.A.K.

Plantentuin

J KLUYSKENSSTR

Muziekcentrum

BIJLOKEKAAI

IJZERLN

HOLDAAL

KONING LEOPOLD II LAAN

Congres
Centrum

FORTLAAN

De
Bijloke

STAM

GODSHUIZENLN

HENLEYKAAI

KORTRIJKSESTEENWEG

WIM V MASSAUSTR

WIM V EGMONTSTR

E40

NOKERELESSTR

NONNEMEERSSTR

ABDISSTR

EEDVERBONDKAAI

MEERSSTRAAT

BALLESTRAAT

SMIDSESTRAAT

ST-PAULUSSTR

A D MONCKHOVENSTR

BLANKEN BERGSTR

LOSTRAAT

KNOKKESTR

KON ELISABETHLN

KON ASTRIDLAAN

GR BRITTANNIELAAN

P FREDERICQSTR

J HEREMANSSTR

RAMEETSTRAAT

MEERSSTRAAT

KON BOUDEWIJNSTR

KON
MARIA
HENDRIKAPLEIN

OTTERLAAN

NEERMEERSKAAI

SPORTSTR

HANDBALSTR

KONING

P CLAESSTR

NAIGEMSTRAAT

ALBERTLAAN

St-Pieters
Train Station

Bus
Station

SHOPPING
| Atlas & Zanzibar | 1 |

EATING
| Greenway | 1 |

Flanders, **Het Gravensteen**; and the delightful medieval guild houses of the **Graslei**. These central attractions are supplemented by a trio of outlying museums within comfortable strolling distance of the Korenmarkt: **S.M.A.K**, an enterprising Museum of Contemporary Art; **STAM**, the city's main historical museum; and the fine art of the excellent **Museum voor Schone Kunsten** (MSK).

Brief history

The principal seat of the counts of Flanders and one of the largest towns in Western Europe during the thirteenth and fourteenth centuries, **Ghent** was once at the heart of the **Flemish cloth trade**. By 1350, the city boasted a population of fifty thousand, of whom no fewer than five thousand were directly involved in the industry, a prodigious concentration of labour in a predominantly rural Europe. Like Bruges, Ghent prospered throughout the Middle Ages, but it also suffered from endemic disputes between the count and his nobles (who supported France) and the cloth-reliant citizens (to whom friendship with England was vital). In the early sixteenth century, the relative decline of the cloth trade and the move into export-import did little to ease the underlying tension, as the people of Ghent were still resentful of their ruling class, from whom they were now separated by **language** – French against Flemish – and **religion** – Catholic against Protestant. The catalyst for conflict was usually **taxation**: long before the Revolt of the Netherlands, Ghent's merchants and artisans found it hard to stomach the financial dictates of their rulers – the Habsburgs after 1482 – and time and again they rose in revolt, only to be crushed and punished. In 1540, for example, the Holy Roman Emperor **Charles V** lost patience and stormed the town, abolishing its privileges, filling in the moat and building a new castle at the city's expense.

Incorporation within the Spanish Netherlands

In 1584, with the Netherlands well on the way to independence from Habsburg Spain, Philip II's armies captured Ghent. It was a crucial engagement: thereafter, Ghent proved too far south to be included in the United Provinces and was reluctantly pressed into the **Spanish Netherlands**. Many of its citizens fled north, and those who didn't may well have regretted their decision when the Inquisition arrived bent on hunting down the Protestants and the Dutch forced the Habsburgs to close the River Scheldt, Ghent's economic lifeline, as the price of peace in 1648.

Nineteenth century till today

In the centuries that followed, Ghent slipped into a slow decline from which it only emerged during the **industrial boom** of the nineteenth century, when it filled with factories, whose belching chimneys encrusted the old city with soot and grime, a disagreeable measure of the city's economic revival. Indeed, its entrepreneurial mayor, Emile Braun, even managed to get the **Great Exhibition**, showing the best in contemporary design and goods, staged here in 1913. Ghent remains an industrial city, but in the last twenty years, it has benefited from an extraordinarily ambitious programme of **restoration and refurbishment**, thanks to which the string of fine Gothic buildings that dot the ancient centre have been returned to their original glory.

St-Baafskathedraal

St-Baafsplein • **Cathedral** Free • **Adoration of the Mystic Lamb** Charge • ⓦ sintbaafskathedraal.be

The best place to start an exploration of the city is the mainly Gothic **St-Baafskathedraal** (St Bavo's Cathedral), squeezed into the eastern corner of St-Baafsplein. The third church on this site, and 250 years in the making, the cathedral is a tad lop-sided, but there's no gainsaying the imposing beauty of the **west tower**, with its long, elegant windows and perky corner turrets. Some 82m high, the tower was the last major part of the church to be completed, topped off in 1554 – just before the outbreak of the religious wars that were to wrack the country for the next hundred years. The cathedral is famous today as the home of the *Adoration of the Mystic Lamb* altarpiece (see page 150), which is now displayed in a separate area at the back of the church.

The nave, north transept and crypt

Inside the cathedral, the mighty, fifteenth-century **nave** is supported by tall, slender columns, which give the whole interior a cheerful sense of lightness. However, the Baroque marble screen spoils the effect by darkening the choir. The nave's principal item of interest is the Rococo **pulpit**, a whopping oak and marble affair, where the main timber represents the Tree of Life with an allegorical representation of Time and Truth at its base. Nearby, the **high altar** is a marble extravaganza featuring St Baaf (St Bavo) ascending to heaven on an untidy heap of clouds. Then it's on to the **north transept**, which now serves as the entrance to the *Adoration of the Mystic Lamb. A* visit to the altarpiece begins in the dank and capacious crypt, a survivor from the earlier Romanesque church, where you can don the appropriate gear for a virtual reality show on the painting before moving on upstairs to view the artwork itself.

The Adoration of the Mystic Lamb

Ghent's greatest treasure is a **winged altarpiece** known as *The Adoration of the Mystic Lamb* (*De Aanbidding van het Lam Gods*), a seminal work of the early 1430s, though of dubious provenance. Since the discovery of a Latin verse on its frame in the nineteenth century, academics have argued about who painted it. The inscription reads that **Hubert van Eyck**, 'than whom none was greater', began, and **Jan van Eyck**, 'second in art', completed the work, but as nothing else is known of Hubert, some art historians doubt his existence. They argue that Jan, who lived and worked in several cities (including Ghent), was entirely responsible for the painting and that only after Jan had firmly rooted himself in the rival city of Bruges did the citizens of Ghent invent 'Hubert' to counter his fame. No one knows the altarpiece's authorship for sure, but what is certain is that in his manipulation of the oil painting technique, the artist – or artists – was able to capture a needle-sharp, luminous realism that must have stunned his contemporaries.

The cover screens

The altarpiece is now displayed with its panels open, though originally, these were kept closed, and the painting was only revealed on high days and holidays. Consequently, it's best to examine the **cover screens first**, beginning with a beautiful Annunciation scene where the Archangel Gabriel's wings reach up to the timbered ceiling of a Flemish house, the streets of a town visible through the windows. In a brilliant coup of **lighting**, the shadows of the angel dapple the room, emphasising the reality of the apparition – a technique repeated on the opposite cover panel around the figure of Mary. Below, the **donor and his wife**, a certain Joos Vydt and Isabella Borluut, kneel piously alongside statues of the saints.

The upper level

By design, the restrained exterior was but a foretaste of what lies within – a striking, visionary work of art whose brilliant colours and precise draughtsmanship still take the breath away. On the **upper level** sit God the Father (some say Christ Triumphant), the Virgin and John the Baptist in gleaming clarity; to the right are musician-angels and a nude, pregnant Eve; and on the left is Adam plus a group of singing angels, who strain to read their music. The celebrated sixteenth-century Flemish art critic Karel van Mander argued that the singers were so artfully painted that he could discern the different pitches of their voices – and true or not, it is indeed the detail that impresses, especially the richly embroidered trimmings on the cloaks.

2

The lower central panel

In the **lower central panel**, the Lamb, the symbol of Christ's sacrifice, is depicted in a heavenly paradise – 'the first evolved landscape in European painting' suggested Kenneth Clark – seen as a sort of idealised Low Countries. The Lamb stands on an altar whose rim is minutely inscribed with a quotation from the Gospel of St John, 'Behold the Lamb of God, which taketh away the sins of the world' – hence the wound in the lamb from which blood issues into a gold cup. Four groups converge on the Lamb from the corners of the central panel. On the bottom right is a group of male saints, and up above them are their female equivalents; on the bottom left are the patriarchs of the Old Testament, and above them is an assortment of bishops dressed in blue vestments and carrying palm branches.

The side panels

On the **side panels**, approaching the Lamb across symbolically rough and stony ground, are more saintly figures. On the right-hand side are two groups, the first being St Anthony and his hermits, the second St Christopher, shown here as a giant with a band of pilgrims. On the left-hand side panel come the horsemen, the inner group symbolising the Warriors of Christ (including St George bearing a shield with a red cross), and the outer group showing the Just Judges, each dressed in fancy Flemish attire.

The Lakenhalle

Botermarkt • No public access except to visit the attached Belfort

Across from the cathedral, on the west side of St Baafsplein, stands the **Lakenhalle** (Cloth Hall), a sombre hunk of a building with an unhappy history. Work began on the hall in the early fifteenth century, but the cloth trade slumped before it was finished, and it was only grudgingly completed in 1903. Since then, no one has ever worked out what to do with the building – though its basement once served as the town prison – and today, it's little more than an empty shell. The entrance to the prison was round on the west side of the Lakenhalle through the **Mammelokker** (The Suckling), a grandiose Louis XIV-style portal of 1741 that stands propped up against the main body of the building. Part gateway, part warder's lodging,

GHENT'S MYSTIC LAMB

Despite appearances, the **Just Judges panel** is not authentic. It was added during the 1950s to replace the original, which was stolen in April 1934 and never recovered. The lost panel features in **Albert Camus**'s novel *The Fall*, whose protagonist keeps it in a cupboard, declining to return it for a complex of reasons, one of which is 'because those judges are on their way to meet the Lamb … [but] there is no lamb or innocence any longer'. Naturally enough, there has been endless speculation as to who stole the panel and why, with suspicion ultimately resting on a certain **Arsène Goedertier**, a stockbroker and conservative politician from just outside of Ghent, who made a deathbed confession in November 1934. Whether he was acting alone or as an agent for others is still hotly contested – other suspects have ranged from the ridiculous (the Knights Templar) to the conceivable (the Nazis), but no one really knows. The **theft** was just one of many **dramatic events** to befall the painting – indeed, it's remarkable that the altarpiece has survived at all. The Calvinists wanted to destroy it; Philip II of Spain tried to acquire it; Emperor Joseph II disapproved of the painting so violently that he replaced the nude Adam and Eve with a clothed version of 1784 (exhibited today in the crypt) and near the end of World War II, the Germans hid it in an Austrian salt mine, where it remained until American soldiers rescued it in 1945.

the Mammelokker is adorned with a bas-relief sculpture illustrating the classical legend of Cimon, whom the Romans condemned to death by starvation. Pero, his daughter, saved him by turning up daily to feed him from her breasts – hence the name.

The Belfort

Botermarkt • Charge • ⓦ belfortgent.be

The first-floor entrance on the south side of the Lakenhalle is the only way to reach the adjoining **Belfort**, a much-amended medieval edifice whose soaring spire is topped by a comically corpulent gilded copper dragon. Once a watchtower and storehouse for civic documents, the interior is now little more than an empty shell displaying a few old bells, a carillon drum or two and incidental statues alongside the rusting remains of a brace of antique dragons, which formerly perched on top of the spire. The belfry is equipped with a **glass-sided lift** that climbs up to the roof, where consolation is provided in the form of excellent views over the city centre.

The Stadhuis

Botermarkt • Charge • ⓦ visit.gent.be

Stretching along the west side of the Botermarkt is the **Stadhuis** (City Hall), whose discordant facade comprises two distinct sections. The later section, dating from the 1580s, frames the central stairway and is a fine example of Italian Renaissance architecture, its crisp symmetries faced by a multitude of black-painted pilasters. In stark contrast are the wild, curling patterns of the section to the immediate north, carved in Flamboyant Gothic style at the beginning of the sixteenth century to a design by one of the era's most celebrated architects, **Rombout Keldermans** (1460–1531). The whole of the Stadhuis was originally to have been built by Keldermans, but the money ran out when the wool trade collapsed, and the city couldn't afford to finish it until much later – hence today's mixture of styles.

Guided tours of the Stadhuis amble around a series of halls and chambers, the most interesting being the old Court of Justice or **Pacificatiezaal** (Pacification Hall), where the Pacification of Ghent was signed in 1576. A plaque commemorates this treaty, which momentarily bound the rebel armies of the Low Countries (today's Belgium and the Netherlands) together against their rulers, the Spanish Habsburgs. The hall's charcoal-and-cream **tiled floor** is designed as a maze. No one's quite sure why, but it's thought that more privileged felons (or sinners) had to struggle around the maze on their knees as a substitute punishment for a pilgrimage to Jerusalem – a good deal if ever there was one.

St-Niklaaskerk

Cataloniestraat • Free • ⓦ visit.gent.be

Just along the street from the Lakenhalle is **St-Niklaaskerk**, an architectural hybrid dating from the thirteenth century that was once the favourite church of the city's principal merchants. It's the shape and structure that pleases most, especially the arching buttresses and pencil-thin turrets, which, in a classic example of the early Scheldt Gothic style, elegantly attenuate the lines of the nave. Many of the original Baroque furnishings and fittings have been removed, and the windows have been unbricked, thus returning the church to its light and airy original appearance. One feature you can't miss is the giant-sized Baroque **high altar** with its mammoth representation of a muscular God the Father glowering down its back, blowing the hot wind of the Last Judgement from his mouth and surrounded by a flock of cherubs. The church is sometimes used for temporary **art exhibitions**.

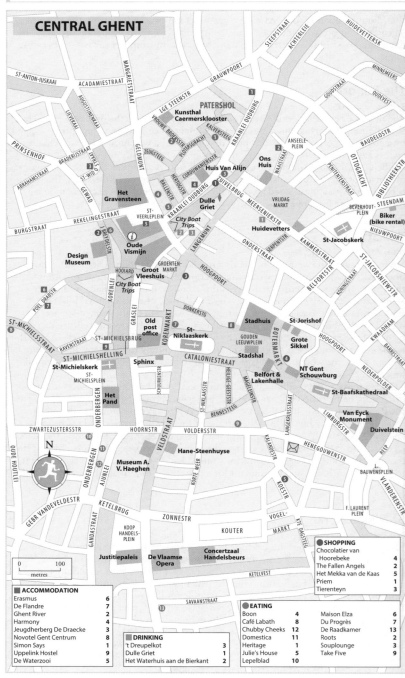

CENTRAL GHENT

ACCOMMODATION

Erasmus	6
De Flandre	7
Ghent River	2
Harmony	4
Jeugdherberg De Draecke	3
Novotel Gent Centrum	8
Simon Says	1
Uppelink Hostel	9
De Waterzooi	5

DRINKING

't Dreupelkot	3
Dulle Griet	1
Het Waterhuis aan de Bierkant	2

SHOPPING

Chocolatier van Hoorebeke	4
The Fallen Angels	2
Het Mekka van de Kaas	5
Priem	1
Tierenteyn	3

EATING

Boon	4	Maison Elza	6
Café Labath	8	Du Progrès	7
Chubby Cheeks	12	De Raadkamer	13
Domestica	11	Roots	2
Heritage	1	Souplounge	3
Julie's House	5	Take Five	9
Lepelblad	10		

The Korenmarkt

St-Niklaaskerk marks the southern end of the **Korenmarkt** (Corn Market), the traditional focus of the city, a long and wide cobbled area where the grain which once kept the city fed was traded after it was unloaded from the boats that anchored on the Graslei dock nearby (see page 153). The one noteworthy building here is the former **post office**, now a shopping centre, whose combination of Gothic Revival and neo-Renaissance styles illustrates the eclecticism popular in Belgium at the beginning of the twentieth century – the building was completed in 1909. The carved heads encircling the building represent the great and good of the time, including – curiously enough - Florence Nightingale. The Korenmarkt was also where the bourgeoisie rubbed uneasy shoulders with the workers – and the **street plan** of the city centre still reflects Ghent's ancient class and linguistic divide: the streets to the south of the Korenmarkt tend to be straight and wide, lined with elegant old mansions, the former habitations of the wealthier, French-speaking classes, while, to the north, Flemish Ghent is all narrow alleys and low brick houses.

St-Michielsbrug

Next to the old post office, **St-Michielsbrug** (St Michael's Bridge) offers fine views back over the towers and turrets that pierce the Ghent skyline. This is no accident: the bridge was built in 1913 to provide visitors to the Great Exhibition with a vantage point from which to admire the city centre. The bridge also overlooks the city's oldest harbour, the **Tussen Bruggen** (Between the Bridges), from whose quays – the **Korenlei** and the **Graslei** – boats leave for trips around the city's canals (see box, page 159).

St-Michielskerk

St-Michielsplein • Free • ⓦ visit.gent.be

Beside St Michielsbrug rises the bulky mass of **St-Michielskerk**, a heavy-duty Gothic edifice begun in the 1440s, which looks rather handsome despite its forlorn and clumsily truncated tower. The interior is even more enticing, the broad sweep of the five-aisled nave punctuated by tall and slender columns that shoot up to the arching vaults of the roof. Here also, in the north transept, is a splendidly impassioned *Crucifixion* by **Anthony van Dyck** (1599–1641). Trained in Antwerp, where he worked in Rubens' workshop, van Dyck made extended visits to England and Italy in the 1620s before returning to Antwerp in 1628. He stayed there for four years – during which he painted this *Crucifixion* – before migrating to England to become a portrait painter for Charles I and his court.

The guild houses of the Graslei

Ghent's boatmen and grain-weighers were crucial to the functioning of the medieval city, and they built a row of splendid **guildhouses** along the **Graslei**, each gable decorated with an appropriate sign or symbol. Working your way north from St Michielsbrug, the first building of distinction is the **Gildehuis van de Vrije Schippers** (Guild House of the Free Boatmen), at No. 14, where the weathered sandstone is decorated with scenes of boatmen weighing anchor plus a delicate carving of a caravel located above the door – caravels were the type of Mediterranean sailing ship used by Columbus. Medieval Ghent had **two boatmen guilds**: the Free, who could discharge their cargoes within the city, and the Unfree, who could not. The Unfree Boatmen were obliged to unload their goods into the vessels of the Free Boatmen at the edge of Ghent – an inefficient arrangement by any standard, though typical of the complex regulations governing the guilds.

Next door, the seventeenth-century **Cooremetershuys** (Corn Measurers' House), at Graslei 12–13, was where city officials weighed and graded corn behind a facade graced by cartouches and garlands of fruit. Next to this, at No. 11 stands the quaint **Tolhuisje**, another delightful example of Flemish Renaissance architecture, built to house the customs officers in 1698, while the adjacent limestone **Spijker** (Staple House), at No. 10 boasts a surly Romanesque facade dating from around 1200. The city stored its grain supply here for over five hundred years until a fire gutted the interior.

Finally, three doors down at No. 8, the splendid **Den Enghel** takes its name from the banner-bearing angel that decorates the facade; the building was originally the stonemasons' guild house, as evidenced by the effigies of the four Roman martyrs who were the guild's patron saints, though they are depicted in medieval attire rather than togas and sandals.

The Groentenmarkt

The jumble of old buildings at the **Groentenmarkt** (Vegetable Market) makes for one of the city's more diverting squares. The west side of the square is flanked by a long line of stone gables, which were once the retaining walls of the **Groot Vleeshuis** (Great Butchers' Hall), a covered market in which meat was sold under the careful control of the city council. The gables date from the fifteenth century but are in poor condition, and the interior is only of interest because of its intricate wooden roof.

The Korenlei

Across the **Grasbrug** bridge from the Graslei lies the **Korenlei**, where a series of expansive, Neoclassical merchants' houses, mainly from the eighteenth century, overlooks the western side of the old city harbour. It's the general ensemble that appeals rather than any particular building. Still, the **Gildehuis van de Onvrije Schippers** (Guild House of the Unfree Boatmen), at No. 7, does boast a fetching eighteenth-century facade decorated with whimsical dolphins and bewigged lions, all bulging eyes and rows of teeth.

Design Museum

Jan Breydelstraat 5 • Closed for refurbishment until 2026 • Charge • ⓦ designmuseumgent.be

Currently closed for a major overhaul, the **Design Museum** has long focused on Belgian decorative and applied arts, with its wide-ranging collection traditionally divided into two distinct sections. At the front, squeezed into what was once an eighteenth-century patrician's mansion, there has always been an attractive sequence of **period rooms**, mostly illustrating the Baroque and the Rococo. The original dining room is especially fine, from its fancy painted ceiling, ornate chandelier and Chinese porcelain to its intricately carved elm panelling. The second section, at the back of the mansion, has formerly comprised a **modern display** area used for temporary exhibitions and to showcase the museum's collection of applied arts, dating from 1880 onwards. This area will be expanded and refreshed during the refurbishment – and undoubtedly, due prominence will be given to the museum's outstanding collection of Art Nouveau material, especially the finely crafted furnishings of **Henry van der Velde** (1863–1957).

Het Gravensteen

St-Veerleplein • Charge • Ⓦ gravensteen.stad.gent

The cold, forbidding walls and unyielding turrets of **Het Gravensteen**, the castle of the counts of Flanders, look sinister enough to have been lifted from a Bosch painting. They were first raised in 1180 as much to intimidate the town's unruly citizens as to protect them, and, considering the castle has been used for all sorts of purposes since then (even a cotton mill), it has survived in remarkably good nick. The imposing **gateway** comprises a deep-arched, heavily fortified tunnel leading to a large **courtyard**, which is framed by protective battlements complete with ancient arrow slits and apertures for boiling oil and water.

Overlooking the courtyard are the castle's two main buildings: the **count's residence** on the left and the **keep** on the right, the latter riddled with narrow, interconnected staircases set within the thickness of the walls. A **self-guided tour** takes you through this labyrinth, the first highlight being a room full of medieval military hardware, from suits of armour, pikes, swords, daggers and early pistols to a pair of exquisitely crafted sixteenth-century crossbows. Beyond is a collection of instruments of torture; a particularly dank, underground dungeon (or oubliette); and the counts' vaulted session room – or council chamber. It's also possible to walk along most of the castle's encircling wall, from where there are pleasing views over the city centre.

St-Veerleplein

Public punishments ordered by the counts and countesses of Flanders were carried out in front of the castle on **St-Veerleplein**, now an attractive cobbled square, but with an ersatz punishment post plonked here in 1913 and topped off by a lion carrying the banner of Flanders. In case the citizenry became indifferent to beheading, it was here also that currency counterfeiters were thrown into boiling oil or water.

Oude Vismijn

At the back of St-Veerleplein, beside the junction of the city's two main canals, is the grandiloquent Baroque facade of the **Oude Vismijn** (Old Fish Market), in which Neptune stands on a chariot drawn by sea horses. To either side are allegorical figures representing the River Leie (Venus) and the River Scheldt (Hercules), the two rivers that spawned the city. After years of neglect, the Oude Vismijn has been redeveloped and is now home to the tourist office (see page 160).

Huis van Alijn Museum

Kraanlei 65 • Charge • Ⓦ huisvanalijn.be

The **Huis van Alijn** folklore museum occupies a series of pretty little almshouses set around a central courtyard. Dating from the fourteenth century, the **almshouses** were built following a major scandal reminiscent of *Romeo and Juliet*. In 1354, two members of the Rijms family murdered three of the rival Alijns when they were at Mass in St-Baafskathedraal. The immediate cause of the affray was jealousy – one man from each clan was after the same woman – but the dispute went deeper, reflecting the commercial animosity of two guilds, the weavers and the fullers. The murderers fled for their lives and were condemned to **death in absentia** but were eventually – eight years later – pardoned on condition that they paid for the construction of a set of almshouses, which was to be named after the victims. The result was the Huis van Alijn, which became a hospice for elderly women and then a workers' tenement until the city council snapped it up in the 1940s.

The **museum** consists of two sets of rooms on either side of the courtyard, depicting local life and work in the nineteenth and twentieth centuries. The duller rooms hold

2

reconstructed shops and workshops – a dispensary, a cobbler's and so forth – the more interesting are thematic, illustrating particular aspects of **traditional Flemish society**, popular entertainment and mourning, for example. The more substantial exhibits are explained in multilingual leaflets, available in the appropriate room, but generally, the labelling is very skimpy. One of the rooms on the right-hand side of the museum has a bank of **miniature TV screens** showing short, locally-made amateur films in a continuous loop. Some date back to the 1920s, but most are postwar, including a snippet featuring a local 1970s soccer team in terrifyingly tight shorts. Overlooking the central courtyard between the two sets of rooms is the **chapel**, a pleasantly gaudy affair built in the 1540s and now decorated with folksy shrines and votive offerings. When they aren't out on loan, the chapel is also home to a pair of '**goliaths**', large and fancily dressed wooden figures that are a common feature of Belgian street processions and festivals.

The Patershol

Kuntshal Caermersklooster Lange Steenstraat 14 • 'Pay What You Can' • ⓦ kunsthal.gent

Behind Kraanlei are the lanes and alleys of the **Patershol**, a tight web of brick-terraced houses dating from the seventeenth century. Once the heart of the Flemish working-class city, this thriving residential quarter had, by the 1970s, become a slum threatened with demolition. After much debate, the area was saved from the developers, and a restoration process began, resulting in today's gaggle of modernised terraced houses and apartments. The only specific attraction as such is the grand old Carmelite Monastery on Lange Steenstraat, now the **Kuntshal Caermersklooster**, which showcases regular exhibitions of contemporary art, photography, design and fashion.

Dulle Griet

From the Kraanlei, an antiquated little bridge leads over to **Dulle Griet** (Mad Meg), a lugubrious fifteenth-century **cannon** whose failure to fire provoked a bitter row between Ghent and the nearby Flemish town of Oudenaarde, where it was cast. In the 1570s, fearful of a Habsburg attack, Ghent purchased the cannon from Oudenaarde. As the region's most powerful siege gun, able to propel a 340kg cannonball several hundred metres, it seemed a good buy, but when Ghent's gunners tried it out, the barrel cracked on the first firing. The useless lump was then rolled to the edge of the Vrijdagmarkt, where it has stayed ever since – and much to the chagrin of the Ghent city council, Oudenaarde simply refused to offer a refund.

Vrijdagmarkt

A wide and open square, the **Vrijdagmarkt** was long the political centre of Ghent, the site of both public meetings and executions – sometimes at the same time. In the middle of the square stands a nineteenth-century **statue** of the guild leader **Jacob van Artevelde** (see box below), portrayed addressing the people in heroic style. Of the buildings flanking the Vrijdagmarkt, the most appealing is the old headquarters of the trade unions, the whopping **Ons Huis** (Our House), a sterling edifice built in eclectic style at the beginning of the twentieth century.

Bij St-Jacobs

St-Jacobskerk, Bij St-Jacobs • Free • ⓦ visit.gent.be

Adjoining the Vrijdagmarkt is **Bij St-Jacobs**, a sprawling and irregularly shaped square whose centrepiece is the whopping **St-Jacobskerk**. This glum-looking edifice partly dates from the twelfth century. From the outside, the church's proudest features are

JACOB VAN ARTEVELDE COMES TO A STICKY END

One of the shrewdest of Ghent's medieval leaders, **Jacob van Artevelde** (1290–1345), was elected captain of all the guilds in 1337. Initially, he steered a delicate course during the interminable wars between France and England, keeping the city neutral – and the **textile industry** going – despite the machinations of both **warring countries**. Yet, ultimately, he was forced to take sides, plumping for England, and this proved his undoing: in a burst of Anglomania, Artevelde rashly suggested that a son of Edward III of England become the new count of Flanders. This unpopular notion prompted a mob to storm his house and hack him to death. Artevelde's demise fuelled further outbreaks of communal **violence**, and a few weeks later, the Vrijdagmarkt witnessed a riot between the fullers and the weavers that left five hundred dead. This rumbling **vendetta** – one of several that plagued the city – was the backdrop to the creation of the Huis van Alijn.

its twin west towers and central spire. Inside, the vaulted nave is awash with Baroque decoration from the gaudy pulpit to the kitsch high altar, but as compensation, the acoustics are outstanding.

The Hôtel d'Hane-Steenhuyse

Veldstraat 55 • Free • ⓦ visit.gent.be /en/see-do/hotel-dhane-steenhuyse

The city's main shopping street, **Veldstraat**, leads south from the Korenmarkt, parallel to the River Leie. By and large, it's a fairly ordinary strip. Still, the grand eighteenth-century mansion at No. 55, the **Hôtel d'Hane-Steenhuyse**, is notable as the place where King Louis XVIII took refuge after Napoleon landed in France following his escape from Elba. While others did his fighting for him, Louis waited around gorging himself – his daily dinner lasted all of seven hours, and the bloated exile was known to polish off one hundred oysters at a sitting – but as soon as the coast was clear, one week after Waterloo, Louis rushed back to Paris. Here on Veldstraat, Louis' one-time hideaway has survived in excellent condition, the pediment of its grand facade sporting allegorical representations of Time and History. The interior is similarly grand, its expansive salons sporting a simply delightful sequence of romantic murals.

STAM

De Bijloke, Godshuizenlaan • Charge • ⓦ stamgent.be • Passenger boats to and from the city centre depart from the mini-jetty on the River Leie beside De Bijloke every 1hr 30min

Now a sprawling multi-use site just west of the River Leie, **De Bijloke** incorporates the substantial remains of an old Cistercian abbey, the **Bijlokeabdij**, which dates back to the thirteenth century. Today, the core of De Bijloke is **STAM**, a new museum that explores the city's history through paintings and a battery of original artefacts. Visits begin in a bright, new **cube-like structure** and continue in the former **abbey church and cloisters**, with one of the early highlights being the two delightful medieval wall paintings in the former refectory. Look out also for the medieval illuminated books, the incidental religious sculpture and the section on the city's guilds.

Citadelpark

A large chunk of greenery, **Citadelpark** takes its name from the fortress that stood here until the 1870s, when the land was cleared and prettified with the addition of grottoes and ponds, statues and fountains, a waterfall and a bandstand. These nineteenth-century niceties survive today, and, as a bonus, the park seems refreshingly hilly after the flatness of the rest of Ghent. In the 1940s, a large brick complex was built on the east side of the park, and after various incarnations, it now divides into two – a (disused) Conference Centre and the S.M.A.K. art gallery.

S.M.A.K.

Jan Hoetplein 1 • Charge • ⓦ smak.be

S.M.A.K, the Stedelijk Museum voor Actuele Kunst (Municipal Museum of Contemporary Art), is one of Belgium's most adventurous contemporary art galleries. It's primarily devoted to temporary displays of international standing, and these **exhibitions** are supplemented by a regularly rotated selection of sculptures, paintings and installations drawn from the museum's **permanent collection**. S.M.A.K possesses examples of all the major artistic movements since World War II – everything from Surrealism, the CoBrA group and Pop Art through to Minimalism and conceptual art – as well as their forerunners. Perennial favourites include the installations of the influential German **Joseph Beuys** (1921–86), who played a leading role in the European avant-garde art movement of the 1970s, and **Panamarenko**'s eccentric polyester zeppelin entitled *Aeromodeller*.

Museum voor Schone Kunsten (MSK)

Fernand Scribedreef 1 • Charge • ⓦ mskgent.be

The **Museum voor Schone Kunsten** (MSK; Fine Art Museum), just opposite S.M.A.K., holds the city's principal art collection and runs an ambitious programme of temporary exhibitions. It occupies an imposing Neoclassical edifice, and the paintings are well displayed, but the interior can be a tad confusing – be sure to pick up a floor plan at reception.

Early Flemish paintings

One highlight of the museum's small but eclectic collection of early Flemish paintings is **Rogier van der Weyden**'s (1399–1464) *Madonna with Carnation*. In this charming work, the proffered flower, in all its exquisite detail, symbolises Christ's passion. From the same period are two superb works by **Hieronymus Bosch** (1450–1516); his *Bearing of the Cross* shows Christ mocked by some of the most grotesque and deformed characters he ever painted. Among the grotesques, you'll spy a singularly wan penitent thief confessing to a monstrously ugly monk and St Veronica, whose cloak carries the imprint of Christ's face. This struggle between good and evil is also the subject of Bosch's *St Jerome at Prayer*, in the foreground of which the saint prays, surrounded by a brooding, menacing landscape.

Rubens and his contemporaries

From the seventeenth century, there's a powerful *St Francis* by **Rubens** (1577–1640), in which a very sick-looking saint bears the marks of the stigmata, while **Jacob Jordaens** (1593–1678), whom Rubens greatly influenced, is well represented by the whimsical romanticism of his *Allegory of Fertility*. Jordaens was, however, capable of much greater subtlety, and his *Studies of the Head of Abraham Grapheus* is an example of the high-quality preparatory paintings he completed, most of which were later recycled within larger compositions. In the same section, **Anthony van Dyck**'s (1599–1641) *Jupiter and Antiope* wins the bad taste award for its portrayal of the lecherous god with his tongue hanging out in anticipation of sex with a sleeping Antiope.

Dutch genre paintings

Elsewhere, there's a fine collection of seventeenth-century **Dutch genre paintings**, notably several works by Kortrijk's talented **Roelandt Savery** (1576–1639), who trained in Amsterdam and worked for the Habsburgs in Prague and Vienna before returning to the Low Countries. To suit the tastes of his German patrons, Savery infused many of his landscapes with the romantic classicism that they preferred – Orpheus and the

Garden of Eden were two favourite subjects – but the finely observed detail of his paintings was always in the true Flemish tradition as in his striking *Plundering of a Village*, where there's a palpable sense of outrage.

The eighteenth century onwards

The museum's eighteenth- and nineteenth-century collection includes a handful of romantic historical canvases, plus – and this is a real surprise – a superbly executed portrait of a certain *Alexander Edgar* by the Scot **Henry Raeburn** (1756–1823). Also displayed are several key paintings by Ostend's **James Ensor** (1860–1949), notably the ghoulish *Skeleton looking at Chinoiserie* and *Pierrot and Skeleton in Yellow Robe*. However, you have to take potluck with the museum's most famous Ensor, his much-lauded *Self-Portrait with Flower Hat*, as this is often out on loan. Other high points include a batch of Expressionist paintings by the likes of **Constant Permeke** (1886–1952) and **Gustave de Smet** (1887–1943), as well as several characteristically unsettling works by both **Paul Delvaux** (1897–1994) and **René Magritte** (1898–1967). Delvaux's *The Staircase*, with its unnatural light and expressionless central figure, and Magritte's *Perspective II. Manet's Balcony*, in which wooden coffins have replaced the figures from Manet's painting, are two cases in point.

St-Baafsabdij

Spanjaardstraat • ⓦ historischehuizen.stad.gent/en/st-bavos-abbey • Free • A 15min walk east of the cathedral

The extensive ruins of **St-Baafsabdij** (St Bavo's Abbey) ramble over a narrow parcel of land beside the River Leie in what was once a strategically important location. It was here, in 630, that the French missionary St Amand (584–675) founded an abbey, which flourished as a place of pilgrimage on account of its guardianship of the remains of St Bavo (622–659). In the ninth century, the abbey suffered a major disaster when the **Vikings** decided this was the ideal spot to camp while they raided the surrounding region. Still, order was eventually restored, another colony of monks moved in, and the abbey was rebuilt in 950. Emperor Charles V had most of this second abbey knocked down in the 1540s, and the monks decamped to St Baafskathedraal, but somehow the ruins managed to survive.

Tucked away behind a stone retaining wall, the abbey's **ruins** include the remnants of an ivy-covered Gothic cloister, whose long, vaulted corridors are attached to a distinctive, octagonal tower, comprising a toilet on the bottom floor and the storage room – the *sanctuarium* – for the St Bavo relic up above. Attached to the cloister is a substantial two-storey building, whose lower level holds all sorts of architectural bits and pieces retrieved from the city during renovations and demolitions. There's precious little labelling, but it's the skill of the carving that impresses and if you've already explored the city, one or two pieces are identifiable, principally the original lion from the old punishment post on St-Veerleplein (see page 155).

Close by, a flight of steps leads up to the Romanesque **refectory**, a splendid chamber whose magnificent, hooped timber roof dates remarkably from the twelfth century. The **grounds** of the abbey are small, but they are partly wild, a flurry of shrubs and flowers that are absolutely delightful – and perfect for a picnic.

GHENT BY BOAT

Throughout the season, **boat trips** explore Ghent's inner waterways. They depart from the Korenlei quay, just near the Korenmarkt, and from the Vleeshuisbrug, beside the Kraanlei (April–Oct: daily 10am–6pm). Trips last forty minutes and currently cost €9.50 per person. They leave every fifteen minutes or so, though the wait can be longer as boats often delay their departure until they are reasonably full.

2

ARRIVAL AND DEPARTURE

By train, Ghent has three train stations, but the one you're almost certain to arrive at is Gent St-Pieters, about 2km south of the city centre. From outside the station, tram No. 1 (destination Evergem, NOT Flanders Expo) runs up to the Korenmarkt in the city centre every few minutes.

Destinations Antwerp Centraal (every 30min; 50min); Bruges (every 20min; 20min); Brussels (every 20min; 30min); De Panne (hourly; 1hr 15min); Diksmuide (hourly; 50min); Kortrijk (every 30min; 20min); Mechelen (hourly; 50min); Ostend (every 30min; 40min); Oudenaarde (Mon–Fri hourly, Sat & Sun every 2hr; 35min); Veurne (hourly; 1hr 10min).

By car The E40, the Brussels-Ostend motorway, clips the southern edge of the city. There are lots of city-centre car parks, one of the most convenient being the 24hr one beneath the Vrijdagmarkt.

GETTING AROUND

By tram & bus Trams and buses are operated by De Lijn (@ delijn.be). A standard one-way fare costs €2.50. Tickets are valid for an hour and can be purchased at automatic ticket machines. A 24hr city transport pass, the Dagpas, costs €7.50. Note also that a Ghent CityCard (see page 153) includes public transport. Tourist information issues free maps of the transport system.

By bike Ghent is good for cycling: the terrain is flat, with cycle lanes on many roads and cycle racks dotted across the centre. Bike rental is available at St-Pieters train station with the municipal Blue-bike scheme (@ blue-bike.be).

By guided walking tour There are several different types of guided walking tours to choose from, but the standard tour is a 2hr jaunt around the city centre. Tickets are on sale at tourist information. Booking in person or online (at least a few hours ahead) is strongly recommended.

By taxi Try V-Taxi on @ 092 22 22 22.

INFORMATION

Tourist information Ghent's efficient tourist office is located in the Oude Vismijn, opposite Het Gravensteen on St-Veerleplein (daily: mid-March to mid-Oct 10am–6pm; mid-Oct to mid-March 9.30am–4.30pm; @ visit.gent.be).

ACCOMMODATION

SEE MAPS PAGES 146 AND 152

Ghent has around sixty **hotels** and a small army of **B&Bs**, with several of the most enjoyable places in the centre where you want to be. The city also has a couple of bright and cheerful **hostels**. The tourist office's website has comprehensive listings (@ visit.gent.be).

HOTELS

Chamade Koningin Elisabethlaan 3 @ chamade.be. Standard, three-star accommodation in bright, modern bedrooms at this family-run hotel. Occupies a distinctive, six-storey modern block, a 5min walk north of the train station. €€

Erasmus Poel 25 @ erasmushotel.be. Friendly, family-run, two-star in a commodious old townhouse a few metres away from the Korenlei. Each room is thoughtfully decorated and furnished in traditional style with lots of antiques. The breakfast is excellent, too. Reservations are strongly advised in summer. €€

De Flandre Poel 1 @ hoteldeflandre.be. Medium-sized, four-star hotel in a thoroughly refashioned, nineteenth-century mansion with a modern annexe at the back. The rooms vary considerably in size, style and comfort – and those towards the rear are much quieter than those on the Poel. Competitively priced. €€€

Ghent River Waaistraat 5 @ ghent-river-hotel.be. This four-star hotel's austere modern facade doesn't do it any favours, but persevere, the interior is much more appealing. Most of the guest rooms occupy the part of the building which was once a cotton mill – hence the bare-brick walls and industrial trappings. €€€

★ **Harmony** Kraanlei 37 @ hotel-harmony.be. Housed in an immaculately renovated old mansion, this deluxe four-star hotel's twenty-odd guest rooms are decorated in an attractive modern style: all wooden floors, strong pastel shades and photos of old Ghent. The best rooms are on the top floor and come complete with a mini-terrace, affording grand views over the city. €€€€

Monasterium Poortackere Oude Houtlei 56 @ monasterium.be. This unusual three-star hotel-cum-guesthouse occupies a rambling and somewhat spartan former nunnery and orphanage a 5min walk west of Veldstraat, with ageing brickwork dating from the nineteenth century. There's a choice of rooms, all en suite; the cheapest are the doubles in the former doctor's house, but those in the former nuns' quarters offer a slightly more authentic experience. Breakfast is taken in the old chapterhouse. €€

Novotel Gent Centrum Goudenleeuwplein 5 @ all. accor.com. The guest rooms at this brisk, three-star chain hotel are pretty routine, but the location – just near the cathedral – is hard to beat, the price is very competitive, and there's an outdoor swimming pool – a rarity in central Ghent and great if the sun is out. €€

★ **Pillows Grand Boutique Hotel Reylof** Hoogstraat 36 @ pillowshotels.com. This superb chain hotel occupies a spacious nineteenth-century mansion whose elegant, high-ceilinged foyer sets a perfect tone. Beyond, the 158 rooms vary in size and facilities, but most are immaculate, spacious and decorated in an appealing rendition of country-house style. The former coach house is now a spa, and there is a patio terrace. €€€€

B&BS

Simon Says Sluizeken 8 ⓦ simon-says.be. On the edge of the Patershol, in a good-looking building with an Art Nouveau facade, this combined coffee bar and B&B has just two guest rooms, both fairly small and straightforward modern en-suite affairs. Smashing breakfasts – be sure to try the croissants. €€

De Waterzooi St-Veerleplein 2 ⓦ dewaterzooi.be. Superbly renovated eighteenth-century merchants' house with a handful of handsome rooms that manage to make the most of their antique setting but are extraordinarily comfortable at the same time – the split-level attic room is the most ambitious. Wonderful views of Het Gravensteen; if the weather is good, you can have breakfast outside on the

garden patio. Minimum two- or sometimes three-night stay at peak periods. €€€

HOSTELS

Jeugdherberg De Draecke St-Widostraat 11 ⓦ jeugdherbergen.be/en. Well-equipped, HI-affiliated hostel that's just a 5min walk north of the Korenmarkt. It has 120 beds in two- to six-bunk, en-suite rooms, a library, bar and lounge. Reservations are advised, especially in summer. Breakfast included. Dorms €, doubles €

Uppelink Hostel St-Michielsplein 21 ⓦ hosteluppelink. com. A family-owned hostel in a prime location, occupying a rambling late-nineteenth-century building beside St-Michielsbrug (bridge). Some rooms have great views over the city centre, and the public areas have a fetching mix of antique fittings and boho-distressed furnishings. Laundry facilities, free luggage storage, and – more unusually – kayak rental (single kayak €29 for 3hr, twin kayak €39 for 3hr per person). Dorms have between six and fourteen bunk beds. Minimum two-night stay during the summer. Dorm beds €, doubles €.

EATING

SEE MAPS PAGES 146 AND 152

Ghent's multitude of **cafés**, **café-bars** and **restaurants** offer the very best Flemish and French food alongside an international cast of other cuisines, with prices that match every budget. Most restaurants close on **Sundays**.

CAFÉS

Boon Geldmunt 6 ⓦ boon.gent. Across the street from the castle, this neat and trim vegetarian restaurant offers a wide range of well-prepared dishes. The salads are particularly good – try the salad with kale, ricotta and carrots.

Café Labath Oude Houtlei 1 ⓦ cafelabath.com. Housed in neat, modern premises that attract a boho crowd, this specialist coffee house emphasises the quality of its beans (with good reason). It also serves snacks, soups and teas.

Greenway Nederkouter 42 ⓦ greenway.be. This straightforward café-cum-takeaway is decorated in a sharp modern style and sells a wide range of eco-friendly foods, from organic burgers to pasta, noodles and baguettes, all for just a few euros each.

Julie's House Kraanlei 13 ⓦ julieshouse.be. Squeezed into an ancient terrace house in one of the prettiest parts of the city, 'Baked with love, served with joy' is the boast here. It's a little OTT, but Julie's home-made cakes and patisseries are genuinely delicious. They also serve breakfasts (until 2pm) and pancakes.

Souplounge Zuivelbrugstraat 4 ⓦ souplounge.be. Big bowls of freshly made soup are the main event at this bright and cheerful self-service café, but sandwiches and salads, too.

Take Five Voldersstraat 10 ⓦ take-five-espressobar.be. This buzzy café-bar hits all the right notes: a cool soundtrack (jazz meets house), pleasing decor, a great range of

specialist bean coffees, a selection of teas, and delicious cakes and pastries.

RESTAURANTS

★ **Chubby Cheeks** Onderbergen 33 ⓦ chubbycheeks. be. This fabulous restaurant is food as an adventure with an ingenious menu featuring tapas-style dishes like Swiss chard and beetroot or the dark meat of Cecina de Leon. There's an open kitchen, so you can sit on a bar stool and watch or choose one of a handful of tables – the place is small and intimate. €€€

Domestica Onderbergen 27 ⓦ domestica.be. Smart and chic brasserie-restaurant serving up an excellent range of Belgian, French and Flemish dishes in nouvelle cuisine style. Has a garden terrace for good-weather eating. The fillet of lamb is especially delicious. €€€

Heritage Rodekoningstraat 12 ⓦ heritage.gent. Cosy, somehow rather rustic decor sets the scene for this enterprising restaurant, where there's no meat, just fish and vegetarian dishes with a strong Latin American influence. Try, for starters, the fennel, seitan and vegan cheese. The set three-course menu at lunchtime is very reasonably priced. €€€

Lepelblad Onderbergen 40 ⓦ lepelblad.be. A very popular restaurant with a heaving pavement terrace, where the ever-changing menu is inventive and creative with pasta dishes, salads and traditional Flemish cuisine to the fore – try, for example, the Ghent waterzooi. The arty decor is good fun, too. €€

Maison Elza Jan Breydelstraat 36 ⓦ maisonelza.be. Idiosyncratic, split-level café-restaurant liberally sprinkled with Edwardian bric-a-brac – you'll even spot some vintage models' dummies. They serve a tasty breakfast here (three days a week) as well as afternoon teas, and in the evening (currently two days a week), the menu offers a limited but well-chosen selection of freshly prepared meat and fish dishes: try, for example, the wood-pigeon risotto. The window tables overlook a canal; if the weather holds, you can eat out on the pontoon at the back. €€€

Du Progrès Korenmarkt 10 ⓦ duprogres.be. This long-established, family-owned café-restaurant is popular with tourists and locals alike. The house's speciality is steak, which is very tasty, too. Rapid-fire service and a handy central location. €€

★ **De Raadkamer** Nederkouter 3 ⓦ de-raadkamer.be. A family-run restaurant in neat, modern premises offering a short but well-conceived menu of Belgian favourites: try, for example, the turbot risotto with asparagus and lobster sauce. €€

Roots Vrouwebroersstraat 5 ⓦ rootsgent.be. This cool and collected Patershol haunt, hidden behind ancient brickwork, may have the simplest boho decor, but the menu is subtle and complex, always featuring local, seasonal ingredients. Pumpkin and parmesan with red gurnard give the flavour. Fixed menus are the order of the day here. €€€

DRINKING AND NIGHTLIFE
SEE MAPS PAGES 146 AND 152

Ghent's **bars** are an absolute delight, and some of the best (with a beer list long enough to strain any liver) are within easy strolling distance of the Korenmarkt. The **club** and **live music** scene is also first-rate, with Ghent's students leading the way, congregating at the string of bars and clubs that line Overpoortstraat, just south of St-Pietersplein.

Decadance Overpoortstraat 76 ⓦ decadance.be. Long a standard-bearer for the city's nightlife, this club, just near the university (hence the abundance of students), offers one of the city's best nights out, with either live music – most of Belgium's bands have played here at one time or another – or DJs. Three rooms – three styles of music.

't Dreupelkot Groentenmarkt 12 ⓦ dreupelkot.be. Located down a little alley leading off the Groentenmarkt and next door to *Het Waterhuis*, this cosy bar specialises in jenever (Belgian gin). It stocks more than two hundred brands, all kept at icy temperatures – the vanilla flavour is particularly delicious.

Dulle Griet Vrijdagmarkt 50 ⓦ dullegriet.be. A long, dark, and atmospheric bar with all manner of incidental objets d'art and an especially wide range of beers. One of their fortes is their range of Trappist beers.

★ **Hotsy Totsy** Hoogstraat 1 ☎ 092 24 20 12. Long

the gathering place of the city's intelligentsia, though less so today, this ornately decorated bar, with its Art Nouveau flourishes, has ranks of drinkers lining up along its long wooden bar. There are also regular live jazz and blues sessions.

Viernulvier (Vooruit) St-Pietersnieuwstraat 23 ⓦ viernulvier.gent/en. The Vooruit performing arts centre (see page 162) – now rebranded as Viernulvier – has a good claim to be the cultural centre of the city (at least for the under-40s), offering a wide-ranging programme of rock and pop through to dance. It also occupies a splendid building, a twin-towered and turreted former festival hall built for Ghent's socialists in an eclectic rendition of Art Nouveau in 1914. The café-bar is a sizeable barn-like affair that stays jam-packed until the small hours of the morning.

★ **Het Waterhuis aan de Bierkant** Groentenmarkt 9 ☎ 092 25 06 80. More than a hundred types of beer are available in this engaging canal-side bar, which is popular with tourists and locals alike. Be sure to try Stropken (literally 'noose'), a delicious local brew named after the time; in 1540, Charles V compelled the rebellious city burghers to parade outside the town gate with ropes around their necks.

ENTERTAINMENT

Ghent prides itself on its **performing arts** scene, with five first-rate venues, two very good art-house cinemas, a premier opera company (that it shares with Antwerp) and half a dozen theatre troupes. For upcoming **events**, consult the tourist information website (ⓦ visit.gent.be).

MAJOR VENUES

Concertzaal Handelsbeurs Kouter 29 ⓦ haconcerts. be/en. The city's primary concert hall has two auditoria and hosts a broad and diverse programme.

Muziekcentrum De Bijloke Godhuizenlaan 2 ⓦ bijloke. be. The old Bijloke abbey complex now holds the STAM historical museum (see page 157) and a Muziekcentrum, which includes a smart new concert hall.

NT Gent Schouwburg, Sint Baafsplein 17 ⓦ ntgent.

be. Right in the centre of the city, the municipal theatre accommodates the Nederlands Toneel Gent, the regional repertory company. Almost all of their performances are in Flemish, though they occasionally host touring English-language theatre companies.

Vlaamse Opera Gent Schouwburgstraat 3 ⓦ opera ballet.be. When not on tour, the city's opera company performs at this handsomely restored nineteenth-century opera house.

Viernulvier (formerly Vooruit) St-Pietersnieuwstraat 23 ⓦ viernulvier.gent. One of Ghent's leading venues for rock, pop and jazz concerts, with a lively on-site café-bar.

ART-HOUSE CINEMAS

Sphinx Sint-Michielshelling 3 ⓦ sphinx-cinema.be.

2

GHENT FESTIVALS

Ghent boasts a hatful of **festivals**, some an excuse for an alcoholic knees-up, others more demure (read cultural). To begin with, there's the prestigious **Festival van Vlaanderen** (Flanders Festival; ⓦgentfestival.be), a classical music event which runs from March to October with concerts in all of the major cities of Flanders, including Ghent. The **Gentse Feesten** (ⓦgentsefeesten.stad.gent), held in mid-to-late July (always including 21 July), brings ten days of partying, including all sorts of gigs. Last but not least, the **Ghent Film Festival** (ⓦfilmfestival.be), held over eleven days in October, is one of Europe's foremost cinematic events, showcasing around two hundred feature films from all over the world and screening Belgian films well before they hit the circuit.

Behind an old facade metres from the Korenmarkt, Sphinx focuses on foreign-language and art-house films, which are almost always sub-titled (rather than dubbed).

Studio Skoop Sint Annaplein 63 ⓦstudioskoop.be. The cosiest of the city's cinemas, but still with five screens and a café, located a 10min walk east from the city centre.

SHOPPING

SEE MAPS PAGE 146 AND 152

Ghent has the range of shops you would expect of a big city and does well in open-air markets. Amongst a number, there's a large and popular **flea market** (*prondelmarkt*) on Bij St-Jacobs and adjoining Beverhoutplein (Fri, Sat & Sun 8am–1pm); a daily **flower market** on the Kouter, just off Veldstraat, though this is at its best and busiest on Sundays (7am–1pm); and **organic foodstuffs** on the Groentenmarkt (Fri 7.30am–1pm).

★ **Atlas & Zanzibar** Kortrijksesteenweg 19 ⓦatlaszanzibar.be. An outstanding travel bookshop with a comprehensive range of (English-language) travel guidebooks and maps, not to mention well-informed staff to help you on your way – located some 2km south of the city centre.

★ **Chocolatier Van Hoorebeke** St-Baafsplein 15 ⓦchocolatesvanhoorebeke.be. Many locals swear that this independent, family-run chocolatier sells the best chocolates in town: mouthwatering, lip-smacking, taste-bud-satisfying stuff.

The Fallen Angels Jan Breydelstraat 29–31 ⓦthe-fallen-angels.com. A mother and daughter run these two adjacent shops, selling all manner of antique bric-a-brac, from postcards and posters to teddy bears and toys. They are intriguing at best and twee at worst but are a distinctive source of unusual gifts.

Het Mekka van de Kaas Koestraat 9 ⓦhetmekka vandekaas.be. Literally the 'Cheese Mecca', this small specialist shop offers a remarkable range of traditional and exotic cheeses – try some of the delicious Ghent goat's cheese (*geitenkaas*) – alongside a good range of wine.

Priem Zuivelbrugstraat 1 ☎092 23 25 37. One of the oddest shops in Ghent, Priem has an extraordinary range of vintage wallpaper dating from the 1950s. The main shop is at Zuivelbrugstraat, but there are three other neighbouring premises on the Kraanlei.

Tierenteyn Groentenmarkt 3 ⓦtierenteyn-verlent. be. This traditional shop, one of the city's most delightful, makes mustards – wonderful, tongue-tickling stuff displayed on shelves upon shelves of ceramic and glass jars. A small jar will set you back about €7.

DIRECTORY

ATMs are liberally distributed across the city centre. ING has ATMs at most branches, including Belfortstraat 18, and Europabank has one on the Groentenmarkt.

Pharmacies Two central pharmacies are at St Michielsstraat 15 and Nederkouter 123. Duty rotas detailing late-night opening pharmacies should be displayed in every pharmacy window.

Post office The main post office is at Lange Kruisstraat 55 (Mon–Fri 9am–6pm, Sat 9am–3pm).

Antwerp
and the
northeast

GROTE MARKT SQUARE, ANTWERP

Antwerp and the northeast

Stretching up to the border with the Netherlands, the provinces of Antwerp and Limburg and a chunk of Brabant constitute the Flemish-speaking northeast rim of Belgium. The main attraction here is the sprawling, intriguing city of Antwerp, which retains many reminders of its sixteenth-century golden age – expect splendid medieval churches and as fine a set of museums as you'll find anywhere in Belgium, with the stirring legacy of Rubens adding artistic élan. Antwerp also has a much-vaunted fashion scene built on the success of its home-grown designers. It incorporates one of Europe's biggest ports and is the international centre of the diamond trade. But these roles by no means define its character: for one thing, its centre has a range of bars and restaurants to rival almost any city in Northern Europe.

The city is also within easy striking distance of a string of old Flemish towns that make for ideal day-trips. In the **province of Antwerp**, the obvious targets are **Lier**, whose centre is particularly quaint and diverting, and **Mechelen**, the ecclesiastical capital of Belgium, which weighs in with its handsome Gothic churches, most memorably a magnificent cathedral. Southeast from here, over in **Vlaams-Brabant** (Flemish Brabant) – and just beyond the reaches of Brussels' sprawling suburbs – the magnet is the lively university town of **Leuven**, which boasts a cluster of fine medieval buildings and a vibrant atmosphere. Further to the east, the **province of Limburg** is seldom visited by tourists, unlike Antwerp, its low-key mixture of small towns and rolling farmland is rarely given due attention. Its capital, **Hasselt**, has some fascinating museums and a lovely Japanese garden, while pint-sized **Tongeren**, which claims to be the oldest town in Belgium, makes the most of its Gallo-Roman history and hosts one of Europe's largest weekly flea and antiques markets every Sunday. With Tongeren as a base, you can cycle off into the surrounding countryside, where the village of **Zoutleeuw** is distinguished by its medieval church – the only one in Belgium that managed to avoid the assorted depredations of Protestants, iconoclasts and invading armies.

Antwerp

Some 50km north of Brussels, **ANTWERP**, Belgium's second city, lays claim to being the de facto capital of Flemish Belgium, boosting its credentials with an animated cultural scene, an internationally renowned fashion industry, a batch of beautiful old buildings and more top-ranking cafés and restaurants than you could sample – quite enough to keep anyone busy for a few days if not more. The city fans out carelessly from the east bank of the **Scheldt**, its nucleus a rough polygon formed and framed by its enclosing boulevards and the river. The **centre** is a hectic and immediately likeable place, with a dense concentration of things to see, not least the magnificent Gothic **Onze Lieve Vrouwekathedraal**, home to a quartet of paintings by Rubens. There's also the fascinating old printing house of Christopher Plantin, a UNESCO World Heritage Site and now the **Museum Plantin-Moretus**, the sinuous Baroque **St-Pauluskerk**, a pair of small but superb collections of paintings at the **Rockoxhuis** and the **Museum Mayer van den Bergh**, and **ModeNatie**, a large-scale celebration of the city's fashion industry, incorporating a brilliant museum, **MoMu**.

To the **east of the centre**, the star turns are the **Rubenshuis**, the one-time home and studio of Rubens, and the cathedral-like **Centraal Station**, which abuts the **diamond**

REUBENSHUIS

Highlights

❶ Antwerp cathedral This supreme example of the Gothic is both magnificent and stunningly beautiful. See page 173

❷ Antwerp's MoMu Antwerp's first-class fashion museum has an international reputation for the quality of its temporary exhibitions. See page 178

❸ Rubens Don't leave Antwerp without viewing at least some of Rubens' paintings, most stirringly inside the cathedral and at the KMSKA

museum. Don't miss Reubenshuis, his former home and studio. See pages 179 and 182

❹ Antwerp at night The city boasts a mouthwatering selection of restaurants and bars, more than enough for the pickiest of gourmands and the strongest of livers. See page 186

❺ Tongeren An amiable, traditional kind of place which hosts Belgium's largest weekly flea and antiques market. See page 204

HIGHLIGHTS ARE MARKED ON THE MAPS ON PAGES 168, 170 AND 174

district. The area to the **south of the centre**, **Het Zuid**, is of interest too, a long-neglected but now resurgent residential district whose wide boulevards, with their long vistas and geometrical roundabouts, were laid out at the end of the nineteenth century. The obvious targets here are **M HKA** (the Museum of Contemporary Art) and **KMSKA**, the wide-ranging **Koninklijk Museum voor Schone Kunsten** (Fine Art Museum). Finally, **north of the centre** lies **Het Eilandje** (the Little Isle), where the city's old docks and wharves have been rejuvenated and deluxe apartments shoehorned into former warehouses, the whole caboodle overseen by the soaring modernism of the **MAS** (Museum Aan de Stroom).

Brief history

In the beginning, **Antwerp** wasn't much desired: it may have occupied a prime river site, but it was too far east to be important in the cloth trade and too far west to be on the major trade routes connecting Germany and Holland. However, in the **late fifteenth century**, it benefited from a general movement of commerce to the west and the decline of the Anglo-Flemish cloth trade. Within just 25 years, many of the great trading families of Western Europe had relocated here, and a deluge of splendid new mansions and churches, docks and harbours transformed the tiny old fortified settlement of yesteryear. In addition, the new masters of the region, the **Habsburgs**, had become frustrated with the turbulent burghers of Flanders, and both the emperor **Maximilian** and his successor **Charles V** patronised the city at the expense of its Flemish rivals, underwriting its success as the leading port of their expanding empire.

Religious turmoil

Antwerp's **golden age** lasted less than a hundred years, prematurely stifled by Charles V's son **Philip II**, who inherited Spain and the Low Countries in 1555. Fanatically Catholic, Philip viewed the reformist stirrings of the Low Countries with horror, and his sustained attempt to bring his Protestant subjects to heel was to bring war and pestilence to the region for decades. In Antwerp, where Protestantism had taken root early, it didn't take long for Philip's religious intentions to become all too clear, and the city seethed with discontent. The spark that lit the rioting was the **Ommegang** of 18 August 1566, when priests carting the image of the Virgin through the city's streets insisted that all should bend the knee as it passed. The parade itself was peaceful enough, but afterwards, the city's Protestant guildsmen and their apprentices smashed the inside of the cathedral to pieces – the most extreme example of the '**iconoclastic fury**' that then swept the whole region.

Catholic reaction

Philip responded by sending an army of occupation, which sought to intimidate the local citizenry from a brand-new citadel built on the south side of town. Nine years later, it was this same garrison that sat unpaid and underfed in its fortress, surrounded by the wealth of what the predominantly Catholic soldiers regarded as a 'heretical' city. Philip's mercenaries **mutinied**, and at dawn on 4 November 1576, they stormed Antwerp, running riot for three long days, plundering public buildings and private mansions, and slaughtering some eight thousand of its inhabitants in the '**Spanish fury**', a catastrophe that finished the city's commercial supremacy. More disasters were to follow. Philip's soldiers were driven out after the massacre, but they were back in 1585, laying siege outside the city walls for seven months, their success leading to Antwerp's ultimate incorporation within the **Spanish Netherlands**. Under the terms of the capitulation, Protestants had two years to leave town, and a flood of skilled workers poured north to the relative safety of Holland, further weakening the city's economy.

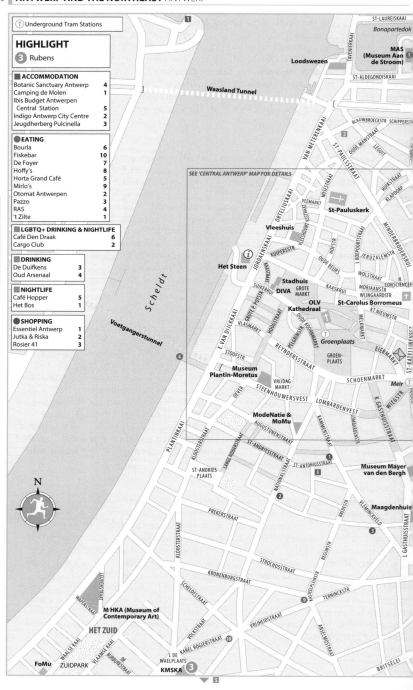

ⓣ Underground Tram Stations

HIGHLIGHT
③ Rubens

■ ACCOMMODATION
Botanic Sanctuary Antwerp	4
Camping de Molen	1
Ibis Budget Antwerpen Central Station	5
Indigo Antwerp City Centre	2
Jeugdherberg Pulcinella	3

● EATING
Bourla	6
Fiskebar	10
De Foyer	7
Hoffy's	8
Horta Grand Café	5
Mirlo's	9
Otomat Antwerpen	2
Pazzo	3
RAS	4
't Zilte	1

■ LGBTQ+ DRINKING & NIGHTLIFE
Café Den Draak	6
Cargo Club	2

■ DRINKING
De Duifkens	3
Oud Arsenaal	4

■ NIGHTLIFE
Café Hopper	5
Het Bos	1

● SHOPPING
Essentiel Antwerp	1
Jutka & Riska	2
Rosier 41	3

3

SEE 'CENTRAL ANTWERP' MAP FOR DETAILS

Decline and resurgence

In the early seventeenth century, there was a modest recovery, but the Dutch, who were now free of Spain, controlled the waterways of the **Scheldt** and were determined that no neighbouring Catholic port would threaten their trade. Consequently, in 1648, under the **Peace of Westphalia**, which finally wrapped up the Thirty Years' War, they forced the closure of the Scheldt to all non-Dutch shipping. This ruined Antwerp, and the city remained firmly in the doldrums until the French army arrived in 1797, **Napoleon** declaring it to be 'little better than a heap of ruins ... scarcely like a European city at all'. The French rebuilt the docks and reopened the Scheldt to shipping, and the city revived to become independent Belgium's **largest port**, a role that made it a prime target during both world wars.

Modern times

In 1914, the invading German army overran Antwerp's outer defences with surprising ease, forcing the Belgian government – which had moved here from Brussels a few weeks before – into a second hasty evacuation, along with Winston Churchill and the Royal Marines, who had only just arrived. During **World War II**, both sides bombed Antwerp, but the worst damage was inflicted after the liberation when the city was hit by hundreds of **Hitler's V1 and V2 rockets**. After the war, Antwerp quickly picked up the pieces, becoming one of Europe's major **seaports** and, more recently, acting as a cultural and political focus for those Flemish speakers looking for greater independence within (or without) a federal Belgium. It has also consolidated its position at the heart of the worldwide **diamond** trade and developed an international reputation for innovative **fashion designers**, from the so-called 'Antwerp Six' to talents such as Tim Van Steenbergen, A.F. Vandevorst and Christian Wijnants.

Grote Markt

The centre of Antwerp is the **Grote Markt**, at the heart of which stands the 1887 **Brabo Fountain**, a haphazard pile of roughly sculpted rocks surmounted by a bronze of legendary Roman soldier Silvius Brabo, depicted flinging the hand of the prostrate giant Antigonus into the Scheldt. Legend asserts that Antigonus extracted tolls from all passing ships, cutting off the hands of those who refused to pay. He was eventually beaten by the valiant Brabo, who tore off his hand and threw it into the river, giving the city its name, which means 'hand-throw'. There are more likely explanations of the city's name, but this is the most colourful, and it certainly reflects Antwerp's early success at freeing the river from the innumerable taxes levied on shipping by local landowners. The north side of the Grote Markt is lined with daintily restored **guild houses**, their sixteenth-century facades decorated with appropriate reliefs and topped by finely cast gilded figures basking in the afterglow of the city's Renaissance lustre. No. 7, the **House of the Crossbowmen**, with its figures of St George and the dragon, is the tallest and most distinctive; it stands next to the **Coopers' House**, with its barrel motifs and statue of St Matthew.

Stadhuis

Grote Markt 1 • Charge • ⓦ experienceantwerp.be/en

Presiding over the square, the **Stadhuis** was completed in 1566 by Cornelis Floris de Vriendt in an innovative design, though several modifications have been made. The building's pagoda-like roof gives it a faintly oriental appearance. Still, apart from the central gable, it's pretty plain, with a long pilastered facade of short and shallow Doric and Ionic **columns**. These, along with the windows, lend it a simple elegance, in contrast to the purely decorative **gable** (no roof behind it). Here, the niches at the top contribute to the self-congratulatory aspect of the building, with a statue of the

Virgin Mary set above representations of *Justice* and *Wisdom*, virtues the city burghers reckoned they had in plenty.

DIVA Museum
Suikerrui 17-19 • Charge • ⓦ divaantwerp.be

Footsteps from the Stadhuis is the **DIVA Museum**, whose carefully curated displays celebrate the city's diamond, gold and silver working industries. There are temporary exhibitions plus a permanent collection that explores these related industries from mine to the finished product, beginning in the Raw Materials Room and ending in the (self–explanatory) 'Room of Wonder' via the **Dining Room**, the **Trading Room**, and the **Atelier**. It's all a little self-conscious, but drop by if diamonds and precious metals take your fancy.

Handschoenmarkt

Leaving the Grote Markt by its southeast corner, you'll soon come to the triangular **Handschoenmarkt** (the former Glove Market), an appealing little square with the cathedral on one side and an attractive ensemble of antique gables on the other two. The conspicuous **stone well** in the corner of the Handschoenmarkt is adorned with a graceful iron canopy and bears the legend 'It was love connubial taught the smith to paint' – a reference to the fifteenth-century painter **Quinten Matsys** (1465–1530), who learned his craft so he could woo the daughter of a local artist: at the time, marriage between families of different guilds was strongly discouraged.

Onze Lieve Vrouwekathedraal
Handschoenmarkt • Charge • ⓦ dekathedraal.be

One of the finest Gothic churches in Belgium, the **Onze Lieve Vrouwekathedraal** (Cathedral of Our Lady) is a forceful, self-confident structure that mainly dates from the middle of the fifteenth century. Its graceful, intricate **spire** dominated the skyline of the medieval city. It has long been a favourite with travellers – William Beckford, for instance, fresh from spending millions on his own house in Wiltshire in the early 1800s, was particularly impressed, writing that he 'longed to ascend it that instant, to stretch myself out upon its summit and calculate, from so sublime an elevation, the influence of the planets'.

The interior
Inside, the seven-aisled **nave** is breathtaking, if only because of its sense of space, an impression reinforced by the bright, light stonework. The religious troubles of the sixteenth century – primarily the Iconoclastic Fury of 1566 (see page 310) – polished off the cathedral's early furnishings and fittings, so what you see today are largely Baroque embellishments, most notably four early paintings by **Pieter Paul Rubens** (1577–1640). The *Descent from the Cross*, a triptych painted after the artist's return from Italy in 1612 and hung just to the right of the central crossing, is undoubtedly the most beautiful, displaying an uncharacteristically moving realism derived from Italian Baroque painters. Christ languishes in the centre in glowing white, surrounded by mourners tenderly struggling to lower him. As was standard

ANTWERP CITY PASS
The **Antwerp City Pass** (ⓦ visit.antwerpen.be/en) gives free access to almost all major sites, various supplementary discounts and free public transport. It costs €45 for 24 hours, €55 for 48 hours and €65 for 72 hours; it's on sale online and at the tourist office (see page 184).

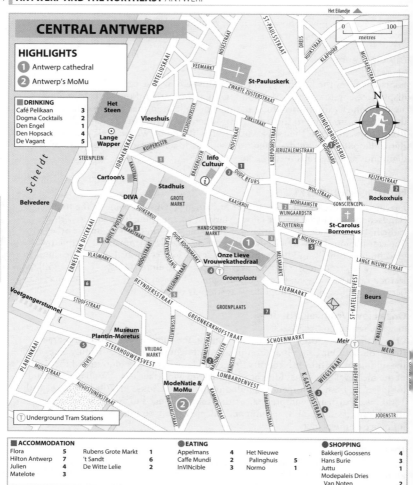

CENTRAL ANTWERP

HIGHLIGHTS
1 Antwerp cathedral
2 Antwerp's MoMu

DRINKING	
Café Pelikaan	3
Dogma Cocktails	2
Den Engel	1
Den Hopsack	4
De Vagant	5

T Underground Tram Stations

ACCOMMODATION				EATING				SHOPPING	
Flora	5	Rubens Grote Markt	1	Appelmans	4	Het Nieuwe		Bakkerij Goossens	4
Hilton Antwerp	7	't Sandt	6	Caffe Mundi	2	Palinghuis	5	Hans Burie	3
Julien	4	De Witte Lelie	2	InVINcible	3	Normo	1	Juttu	1
Matelote	3							Modepaleis Dries	
								Van Noten	2

practice at the time, collaborators in Rubens' studio worked on the painting, among them the young **Anthony van Dyck**, who completed the face of the Virgin and the arm of Mary Magdalene.

Above the **high altar** is a second Rubens painting, the *Assumption*, a swirling Baroque scene painted in 1625, full of cherubs and luxuriant drapery, while on the left-hand side of the central crossing, the same artist's *The Raising of the Cross* is a grandiloquent canvas full of straining, muscular soldiers and saints; this triptych was painted in 1610, which makes it the earliest of the four. On the right-hand side of the ambulatory in the **second chapel** along, there's the cathedral's fourth and final Rubens, the *Resurrection*, painted in 1612 for the tomb of his friend, the printer Jan Moretus, showing a strident, militaristic Christ carrying a red, furled banner.

Groenplaats

Flanked by some of the busiest cafés in town, **Groenplaats**, the expansive open square behind the cathedral, actually started as the municipal graveyard, though presumably the bodies were moved before today's underground car park was constructed. In the middle of the square stands a rather uninspiring **statue of Rubens**, the work of the prolific Willem Geefs (1806–60), one of King Léopold II's favourite sculptors.

Museum Plantin-Moretus

Vrijdagmarkt 22 • Charge • Ⓦ museumplantinmoretus.be

The intriguing **Museum Plantin-Moretus** occupies the old mansion of the printer Christopher Plantin, who rose to fame and fortune in the second half of the sixteenth century. Born in Tours in 1520, Plantin moved to Antwerp when he was 34 to set up a small bookbinding business, but in 1555, he was forced to give up all heavy work when, in a case of mistaken identity, he was wounded by revellers returning from the carnival. Paid to keep quiet about his injuries, Plantin used the money to start a printing business. He was phenomenally successful, and his fortune was assured when King Philip II granted him the monopoly of printing missals and breviaries for the **Spanish Empire**. On Plantin's death, the business passed to his son-in-law, Jan Moerentorf, who Latinized his name following the fashion of the day, to Moretus, as did his son, Balthasar, a close friend of Rubens. The family sold their mansion to the city in 1876.

The collection

A signed route takes visitors through most of the house's rooms from the **entrance**, set around a pretty central courtyard. The mansion is worth seeing in itself, its warren of small, dark rooms equipped with mullioned windows and lockable wooden window shutters, plus a brace of handsome libraries and oodles of **leather wallpaper** in the Spanish style (from Room 10 onwards). As for the exhibits, they provide a marvellous insight into how Plantin and his descendants conducted their business with the tools of their trade – printing presses, typesets, woodcuts, copper-plate engravings, etc – exhibited beside the books they created. Particular **highlights** include a painting of Plantin by Rubens in Room 2, the world's two oldest surviving printing presses at the far end of Room 14, and, in Room 31, the world's second oldest printed Bible (1461), the 36-line version printed by **Johannes Gutenberg** (1398–1468), the inventor of moveable type printing.

From the Vrijdagmarkt to the waterfront

Across Vrijdagmarkt from the museum is **Leeuwenstraat**, a narrow little street flanked by some old terraced houses. At the end, turn left and then first right for **Pelgrimstraat**, which provides one of the best views of the cathedral, with a sliver of sloping, uneven roofs set against the majestic lines of the spire behind. By No. 6, an ancient alley called **Vlaeykensgang** (Pie Lane) is a surviving fragment of the honeycomb of narrow lanes that made up medieval Antwerp. Today, it twists a quaint route through to **Oude Koornmarkt**, which soon leads west into **Suikerrui**, a wide street connecting the Grote Markt with the east bank of the Scheldt, clearly separated from the town since Napoleon razed the riverside slums and constructed proper wharves in the early 1800s.

Vleeshuis Museum

Vleeshouwersstraat 38 • Charge • Ⓦ museumvleeshuis.be

Conspicuous amid the narrow side streets just north of the Grote Markt are the tall, turreted gables of the **Vleeshuis** (Meat Hall), a strikingly attractive building of 1504, whose alternating layers of red brick and cream stone resemble rashers of bacon – appropriately enough, as this was where the guild of butchers (see box, page 176) had their headquarters. Inside, the vaulted brick hall that comprises the ground floor now holds the **Klank van de Stad** (Sound of the City), an ambitious if not entirely successful exhibition on **music and dance** in the city over the last six hundred years. The museum does hold an excellent range of sixteenth- and seventeenth-century musical instruments, most memorably a platoon of primly decorated **clavichords** and **harpsichords**, some of which were produced locally in the Ruckers workshop. You can learn about the most important exhibits and hear them being played via a free digital guide from the ticket desk.

Veemarkt

The narrow streets around the Vleeshuis and the neighbouring **Veemarkt**, home to St Pauluskerk, were badly damaged by wartime bombing, leaving a string of bare, open spaces edged by some of the city's worst slums. However, the area has largely been rebuilt and revamped in the last decade or two. The sex workers who once congregated here have moved north to Verversrui, near the Willemdok, and the crumbling terraces have been replaced by cosy modern houses, whose pinkish brick facades imitate the style of what went before – **urban renewal** at its best.

St-Pauluskerk

Veemarkt • Free • ⓦ sintpaulusantwerpen.be/en/

Entered via an extravagant Baroque portal on the Veemarkt, **St-Pauluskerk** is one of the city's most delightful churches, an airy, dignified, late Gothic structure built for the Dominicans in the early sixteenth century. The monks were expelled when the Calvinists looted the church in 1578. Still, less than a decade later, after the Spanish recaptured the city, they were restored to their property. They proceeded to refashion St-Pauluskerk in a **Baroque** style that was designed to glorify the Catholic Church, thereby grinding salt into the wounds of the defeated Protestants. To hammer home the ecclesiastical point, the **Dominicans** commissioned a series of **paintings** to line the nave's north aisle wall. Dating from 1620, this series, which depicts the 'Fifteen Mysteries of the Rosary', has survived intact, a remarkable snapshot of Antwerp's artistic talent with works by the likes of Cornelis de Vos (1584–1651) – *Nativity* and *Presentation at the Temple*; David Teniers the Elder (1582–1649) – *Gethsemane*; van Dyck (1599–1641) – *The Bearing of the Cross*; and Jordaens (1593–1678) – *The Crucifixion*. But it is **Rubens**' contribution – the *Scourging at the Pillar* – that stands out as a brilliant, brutal canvas showing Jesus clad in a blood-spattered loincloth. There's more Rubens close by – at the far end of

---

THE BUTCHERS' BLUNDER

The **Vleeshuis** (see page 175) was built as the grand headquarters of the **guild of butchers**, one of the most powerful of Antwerp's medieval guilds. It was here in 1585, with the Spanish army approaching, that the butchers made a fateful decision: they opposed the opening of the dykes along the River Scheldt as advised by the Protestant commander, **William the Silent**, who realised that the best way to defend the city was by flooding its immediate surroundings. The butchers were, however, more worried about the safety of their sheep, which grazed the threatened meadows, so they sent a deputation to the city magistrates to object. The magistrates yielded, and the consequences were disastrous – the Spaniards were able to close the Scheldt and eventually force the town to **surrender**, a defeat that placed Antwerp firmly within the Spanish Netherlands. Protestant butchers hightailed it north to the Netherlands.

the Mysteries series – in the *Adoration of the Shepherds*, an early work of 1609 which has a jaunty secular air, with a smartly dressed Mary imperiously lifting the Christ Child's bedsheet to the wonder of the shepherds.

Look out for **Our Lady of the Rosary**, an early sixteenth-century polychromed wood statuette stuck to a pillar next to the nave's north aisle. It's a charming effigy, with the Virgin robed in the Spanish manner – it was the Spaniards who first introduced dressed figurines to Flemish churches. The two unusual bas-relief **medallions** to either side are just as folksy, telling a Faustian story of a rich woman gulled by the devil, shown here as a sort of lion with an extremely long tail. The first panel sees the woman entrapped by the devil's letter; the second shows the good old Dominicans coming to the rescue and the devil being carted off by an angel.

Calvarieberg

Glued to the exterior buttresses of the south transept, just off the passageway linking the Baroque portal and the church, is the **Calvarieberg**, a curious **mound of rock and slag** decorated with statues of angels, prophets and saints beneath a crucified Christ. It was built during the eighteenth century at the behest of the Pilgrims of Jerusalem, a society keen to encourage the devout to visit the Holy Land. Writing in the nineteenth century, the traveller Charles Tennant got things about right when he described it as 'a more striking instance of religious fanaticism than good taste'.

Snijders & Rockoxhuis

Keizerstraat 10–12 • Charge • ⓦ snijdersrockoxhuis.be/en

The **Snijders & Rockoxhuis** holds a small but highly prized collection of fine art, which is mainly displayed in what was once the townhouse of Nicolaas Rockox (1560–1640), friend and patron of Rubens, though a handful of additional paintings are shown in the house next door, which was formerly the home of the painter Frans Snijders (1579–1657). Highlights of the collection include a gentle *Holy Virgin and Child* by Quinten Matsys (1465–1530), several dramatic genre paintings by Snijders, and a *St Christopher Bearing the Christ Child*, a typical work by Quentin's collaborator **Joachim Patenier** (1485–1524). Born in Dinant, Patenier moved to Antwerp, where he became the first Flemish painter to emphasise the landscape of his religious scenes at the expense of its figures – which he reduced to compositional elements within expansive, sweeping vistas. The gallery also owns several works by **Rubens**, most memorably the small and romantic *Virgin in Adoration Before the Sleeping Christ Child*, which depicts the Virgin with the features of Rubens' first wife and models Jesus on the artist's son. Antwerp's own **Joachim Beuckelaer** (1533–73) chimes in with a restrained *Flight into Egypt*, revealing a bustling river bank where – in true Mannerist style – the Holy Family are hard to spot, and there's also **Pieter Bruegel the Younger's** (1564–1638) *Proverbs*, an intriguing folksy work, one of several he did in direct imitation of his father, a frenetic mixture of the observed and imagined set in a Flemish village. The meaning of many of the pictured proverbs has been the subject of lengthy debate – and the museum fills in the details on the adjacent touch screen – but there's little doubt about the meaning of the central image with an old man dressed in the blue, hooded cape of the cuckold at the suggestion of his young wife.

St-Carolus Borromeus

Hendrik Conscienceplein • Charge

One of the most agreeable piazzas in central Antwerp, tiny Hendrik Conscienceplein – named for the prolific nineteenth-century Flemish novelist – has all the Baroque pomp and circumstance of the Jesuits, for it was here that they set up their Antwerp headquarters in the 1620s. Presiding over the square is the church of St-Carolus

Borromeus, whose finely contrived facade may well have been based on designs by Rubens. Much of the barrel-vaulted interior, including 39 ceiling paintings by Rubens, was destroyed by fire in 1718; the ornate Mariakapel (Chapel of Maria), on the right-hand side of the nave, happily avoided the flames, its stucco ceilings and luxurious mix of marbles a fancy illustration of the High Baroque. Streaky, coloured marble was a key feature of the original design, and here in this side chapel, it serves as the background for a series of tiny pictures placed on either side of the high altar.

ModeNatie

Nationalestraat 28

Spread over several floors, **ModeNatie** is a lavish and extraordinarily ambitious fashion complex, which incorporates both the fashion department of the Royal Academy of Fine Arts and the Flanders DC (District of Creativity). As such, it reflects the international success of local designers, beginning in the 1980s with the so-called 'Antwerp Six' – including Dries van Noten, Ann Demeulemeester and Marina Yee – and continuing with younger designers like A.F. Vandevorst, Christian Wijnants and Tim Van Steenbergen; all are graduates of the academy.

MoMu

Nationalestraat 28 • Charge • Ⓦ momu.be

Part of the Modenatie building has been converted into a fashion museum, **MoMu** (Mode Museum). Its adventurous, brilliantly presented, and thought-provoking temporary displays cover a lot of ground – everything from the walking stick as a fashion statement to the evolution of the trench coat and the use of plumes and feathers in fashion from the 1920s to the present day. Each **temporary exhibition** lasts for around five months, and many exhibits are drawn from MoMu's massive stock of fashion-related items.

Museum Mayer van den Bergh

Lange Gasthuisstraat 19 • Charge • Ⓦ museummayervandenbergh.be

The appealing **Museum Mayer van den Bergh** comprises the art collection of Fritz Mayer van den Bergh, a member of a wealthy merchant family who gave his artistic hoard to the city in the early twentieth century. Very much a connoisseur's collection, it offers a superb sample of **Netherlandish paintings** and examples of many branches of the **applied arts**, from tapestries and sculptures to ceramics, silver, illuminated manuscripts and furniture. For decades, the collection has been crowded into the house that the family had built here in the style of a sixteenth-century mansion in 1904, but a thoroughgoing reorganisation is about to commence. High points of the collection include several incredibly charming children's portraits; an arresting *Jesus carrying the Cross* by Hieronymus Bosch (1450–1516); and a stunning *Crucifixion* triptych by **Quinten Matsys** (1465–1530), with the unidentified donors painted on the wings. Intriguingly, the female donor is pictured alongside one of the family's patron saints, Mary of Egypt, a repentant prostitute who spent her final years in the desert miraculously sustained by three little loaves.

The museum's most celebrated painting is **Pieter Bruegel the Elder**'s (1525–69) *Dulle Griet* (*Dull Gret*) or *Mad Meg*, one of his most Bosch-like works. Experts have written volumes on the painting's iconography, but in broad terms, there's no disputing it's a misogynistic allegory in which a woman, weighed down with possessions, stalks the gates of hell in a surrealistic landscape of monsters and pervasive horror. The title refers to the archetypal shrewish woman who, according to a Flemish proverb, 'could plunder in front of hell and remain unscathed'. The van Berghs took a shine to the

Bruegels – the museum holds several more of their paintings, most notably **Pieter the Elder**'s *Twelve Proverbs,* in which a sequence of **miniatures** illustrates popular Flemish aphorisms, including an old favourite – the man in a blue, hooded cape, the symbol of the cuckold.

The Bourlaschouwburg and Stadsschouwburg

Fringed with pleasant pedestrianised streets and squares, the **Bourlaschouwburg** (Bourla Theatre) – home to the city's municipal theatre company, Toneelhuis – is an elegant nineteenth-century rotunda with a handsomely restored interior. Just beyond, at the end of the Graanmarkt, lurks its modern concrete and steel equivalent, the huge and rather brutal **Stadsschouwburg** (Municipal Theatre; see page 187), which is attached to a large glass and metal roof that shelters **market** traders on Saturdays and Sundays (see page 188).

Maagdenhuis

3

Lange Gasthuisstraat 33 • Charge • ⓦ maagdenhuis.be/en

Formerly a hospital and orphanage for children of the poor, the **Maagdenhuis** (Maidens' House) is now partly occupied by a small **museum**. Created in the mid-sixteenth century, the original orphanage was strictly run, its complex rules enforced by harsh punishments. On the other hand, those children left here were fed and taught a skill, and desperate parents felt that they could at least retrieve their children if their circumstances improved. To ensure their offspring could be identified (in an illiterate age), they were given **tokens**, usually irregularly cut playing cards or images of saints – one part was left with the child, the other kept by the parent. If the city fathers didn't encourage this practice, they certainly accepted it, and several municipal buildings even had specially carved **alcoves** on their facades where **foundlings** could be left under shelter, certain to be discovered in the morning.

Inside the **museum**, particular highlights in the chapel to the right of the entrance include a cabinet of foundling tokens, three seventeenth-century paintings depicting the orphan girls at work and a number of colourful, sixteenth-century majolica porridge bowls. In the five rooms across from the chapel, several **paintings** are worth seeking out, including, in the end room on the right, **Anthony van Dyck**'s (1599–1641) mournful *St Jerome* and **Jacob Jordaens**' (1593–1678) profound study of Christ in his *Descent from the Cross*.

East of the centre

Meir, Antwerp's pedestrianised main shopping street, connects the city centre with Centraal Station, some fifteen minutes' walk away to the **east**. Taken as a whole, this part of the city lacks any particular character – being an indeterminate medley of the old and the new – but there's no disputing the principal sight, the **Rubenshuis**, the former home and studio of Rubens (1577–1640), though note that the house is closed until 2028. Rubens was buried nearby in **St-Jacobskerk**, a good-looking Gothic church that deserves a visit. Still, the architectural highlight hereabouts is the neo-Baroque **Centraal Station**, a sterling edifice dating from 1905. The station presides over Koningin Astridplein, a large, busy square that adjoins the city's excellent **zoo**.

Rubenshuis

Wapper 9 • Closed until 2028 • Charge • ⓦ rubenshuis.be

Not so much a house as a mansion, the Rubenshuis was where the great man lived for most of his adult life, but it was only acquired by the city in 1937, at which time it was little more than a shell. Skilfully restored, the Rubenshuis opened as a **museum** in 1946 but is now undergoing a complete refit, which involves the creation of a new reception building. The intention is for this reception area to set the artistic scene before visitors move over to the **mansion**, which comprises two main sections – the gabled Flemish house where he lived on the left and his classical studio to the right. Rubens had an enviably successful career, spending the first years of the seventeenth century studying the Renaissance masters in Italy before settling here in 1608. Soon afterwards, he painted two wonderful canvases for the cathedral (see page 173), and his fame spread, both as a painter and diplomat, working for Charles I in England and receiving commissions from all over Europe.

The interior

When the Rubenshuis reopens, an arrowed tour is anticipated to begin by twisting its way through the neatly panelled and attractively furnished domestic interiors of the **Flemish house** where Rubens lived. Beyond, at the back – and in contrast to the cramped living quarters – visitors will be able to amble through the elegant **art gallery**, an Italianate chamber where Rubens displayed his favourite pieces to a chosen few in a scene comparable to that portrayed in Willem van Haecht's *The Gallery of Cornelis van der Geest* (which will be displayed here), after that will come the **great studio**, which is overlooked by a narrow observation gallery and is equipped with a special high door to allow the largest canvases to be brought in and taken out with ease. Several of Rubens' **paintings** will be displayed here, including a playful *Adam and Eve*, an early work in which the couple flirt while the serpent slithers back up the tree, and a more characteristic piece, the *Annunciation*, where you can sense the drama of the angel Gabriel's appearance to Mary, who is shown in her living room complete with wicker basket and a sleeping cat. Behind the house, the **garden** is laid out in the formal style of Rubens' day – the Baroque portico might be familiar from the artist's Medici series on display in the Louvre.

St-Jacobskerk

St-Jacobstraat 9 • Free • ⓦ sintjacobantwerpen.be

Rubens died in 1640 and was buried in **St-Jacobskerk**, a short walk north from the Rubenshuis. Very much the church of the Antwerp nobility, who lie interred in its multiple vaults and chapels, St-Jacobskerk is a mighty Gothic structure whose construction ground from 1491 to 1659. This delay means that much of its Gothic splendour is hidden by an overly decorative **Baroque interior**, the soaring heights of the nave flattened by heavy marble altars and a colossal marble rood screen.

The Rubens chapel

Nine chapels radiate out from the ambulatory, including the **Rubens chapel** directly behind the high altar, where the artist and his immediate family are buried beneath the tombstones in the floor, with a lengthy Latin inscription giving details of Rubens' life and honours. The **chapel's altar** was the gift of Helena Fourment, Rubens' second wife, and shows one of his last works, *Our Lady and the Christ Child Surrounded by Saints* (1634), in which he is thought to have painted himself as St George, his wives as Martha and Mary, and his father as St Jerome. Incidentally, the chapel next to – and north of – the Rubens tomb is worth a peek for its religious ironies. The chapel's dark and gaudy canvas – *St Charles Borromeo Pleading with the Virgin on Behalf of those Stricken by the Plague* – was completed by Jacob Jordaens, a committed Protestant, but commissioned by a fervent and very reactionary Catholic, the Archbishop of Milan. Chances are the archbishop didn't realise.

Centraal Station

Heading east from the Rubenshuis, De Keyserlei offers a fine view of **Centraal Station**, a magnificent neo-Baroque structure whose medley of spires and balconies, glass domes and classical pillars was completed in 1905 to a design by **Louis Delacenserie**, who had made his reputation as a restorer of Gothic buildings in Bruges. By any standard, the station is an extraordinary edifice, a well-considered blend of earlier architectural styles and fashions – particularly the Gothic lines of the main body of the building and the **ticket hall**, which has all the darkened mystery of a medieval church – yet displays all the self-confidence of the new age of industrial progress. The station also proved large enough to adapt to modern use, with the Belgians digging away until they created the extra **subterranean platforms** that exist today.

The diamond district
The anonymous streets just to the southwest of Centraal Station, along and around **Lange Kievitstraat** and pedestrianised **Schupstraat/Hoveniersstraat**, are home to the largest **diamond market** in the world. Behind these indifferent facades, precious stones pour from every continent to be cut or re-cut, polished and sold. There's precious little indication that all this is going on – no show of wealth, no grand bazaar, nor could any tax collector ever keep track of the myriad deals which make the business hum; the only exception is the string of **diamond shops** that fill up the outer precincts of Centraal Station beside **Pelikaanstraat**. Although it used to be **Orthodox Jews** who ran the diamond trade in Antwerp, these days, it's mostly Jain Indians running the show. They act as middlemen in a chain that starts in the producer countries, especially South Africa, with no less than **85 percent** of the world's rough diamonds and half the total supply of cut diamonds traded here in Antwerp.

Antwerp ZOO
Koningin Astridplein 20 • Charge • ⓦ zooantwerpen.be
Metres from Centraal Station, **Antwerp ZOO**, is one of the oldest zoos in the world, dating back to 1843. In recent decades, it has kept ahead of the animal welfare curve, enlarging and improving its assorted **compounds**. There are around thirty separate areas today, including a 6m high 'skywalk' for great views, a savannah with African buffaloes, a butterfly garden, an aquarium, a special 'valley' for gorillas and a hippo pool.

South of the centre: Het Zuid
Fanning out from **Léopold de Waelplaats**, the wide avenues and symmetrical squares of **Het Zuid** (The South), a couple of kilometres south of the centre – and reachable by tram from Groenplaats – were laid out at the end of the nineteenth-century on the site of the **old Spanish citadel**, of which nothing now remains. The district hit the skids in the 1960s, with many of its grand French-style mansions left to decay, but it's bounced back to become one of Antwerp's more **fashionable** residential quarters. Setting aside the district's cafés and bars, the obvious targets here are **KMSKA** (Koninklijk Museum voor Schone Kunsten Antwerpen; the Royal Museum of Fine Arts Antwerp), Antwerp's principal art gallery with a fine collection of Belgian/Low Countries art from the fifteenth to the twentieth century; the enterprising **M HKA** (Museum van Hedendaagse Kuns Antwerpen; Museum of Contemporary Art); and **FoMu** (Fotomuseum Antwerpen; Photo Museum Antwerp), which is well known for the quality of its photography exhibitions.

BUYING DIAMONDS IN ANTWERP

Tourists are often reluctant to **buy diamonds** in Antwerp, scared of being cheated or conned. To combat this reticence, several private and public bodies have combined to launch a quality-control label called **Antwerp's Most Brilliant** (ⓦ antwerpsmostbrilliant.be). Diamond sellers must pass a rigorous inspection scheme to be accepted onto the label.

KMSKA

Leopold de Waelplaats 1 • Charge • ⊕ kmska.be • Reached by tram No. 4 from Groenplaats – Museum stop

Antwerp's most prestigious art gallery, **KMSKA** occupies an immense and rather grand Neoclassical edifice dating from the 1880s. The museum's permanent collection spreads over two large floors with the paintings displayed by theme rather than artist – hence 'Suffering', 'Entertainment', and so forth; there's also ample room for an ambitious programme of temporary exhibitions. The gallery's early Flemish works include two tiny but incredibly delicate works by **Jan van Eyck** (1390–1441), a florid *Madonna at the Fountain* and a *St Barbara*, where a palm and prayer book, representing her faith and self-sacrifice, has replaced the usual symbol of the saint's imprisonment – a miniature tower held in the palm of her hand. Behind, a full-scale Gothic tower looms over her – a much more powerful indication of her confinement.

Look out also for **Rogier van der Weyden**'s (1400–64) *Triptych of the Seven Sacraments*, painted for the Bishop of Tournai in 1445 and graced by an inventive frame, which merges with the lines of the Gothic architecture inside. Weyden's *Portrait of Philippe de Croy* is here, too, the artist blending a dark background into the lines of his subject's cloak, a simple technique to emphasise the shape of the nobleman's angular face and his slender hands. KMSKA has two paintings by **Hans Memling** (1433–94), the *Portrait of Giovanni de Candida* and the *Angels Singing and Playing Instruments*. Neither is among his most distinguished works, but they have that finely textured quality for which he is famous. There are also two-panel paintings by **Gerard David** (1460–1523), each cool and meticulous, though the finer is the evocative *Pilate and the High Priests*, whilst **Jean Fouquet** (1425–80), the most influential French painter of his day, chimes in with a *Madonna and Child* in which orange-red, latex-like angels, surround a chubby Jesus, who looks away from a pale, bared breast.

Rubens

The museum owns a platoon of enormous canvases by **Pieter Paul Rubens** (1577–1640). Amongst them is an inventive *Last Communion of St Francis* (1619), showing a very sick-looking saint equipped with the marks of the stigmata, a faint halo and a half-smile. Despite the sorrowful ministrations of his fellow monks, Francis can't wait for salvation. Also from 1619 is *Christ Crucified Between the Two Thieves*, which, with its muscular thieves and belligerent Romans, possesses all the high drama you might expect but is almost overwhelmed by its central image – you can virtually hear the tearing of Christ's flesh as the soldier's lance sinks into him. From 1624 comes the outstanding *Adoration of the Magi*, a beautifully free and very human work apparently finished by Rubens in a fortnight. No doubt he was helped by his studio where one of the major figures was **Jacob Jordaens**' (1593–1678), responsible here for the striking *Martyrdom of St Apollonia*; the saint's head cruelly jerked back, her tongue attacked with what look like a pair of pliers.

Modern Belgian art

KMSKA's bountiful collection of modern Belgian paintings is regularly rotated. Still, you can expect to see a good sample of the work of **James Ensor** (1860–1949), whose subdued, conservative beginnings, such as *Afternoon at Ostend* (1881), contrast with his piercing later works – for instance, *Intrigue* and *Skeletons Fighting for the Body of a Hanged Man*. Also likely to be on show is **Paul Delvaux**'s (1897–1994) much-praised *The Pink Bows*, showing a classical city in the process of disintegration, and several canvases by **René Magritte** (1898–1967), most memorably the macabre *Madame Recamier* and *Storm Cape*. Look out for **Constant Permeke** (1886–1952), a leading member of the artistic coterie who first congregated at the village of Sint Martens-Latem near Ghent just before World War I. Dark and broody, Permeke's works are mostly Expressionistic studies of rural Flemish life, his style typified by *The Coffee Drinkers*, *Man with the Vest*, and *The Farmer*.

M HKA
Leuvenstraat 32 • Charge • ⓦ muhka.be

Het Zuid once had its **dock** between Vlaamse Kaai and Waalsekaai, but this was filled years ago, becoming today's wide and open square. There are two museums on the west side of this square, FoMu and **M HKA**, which occupies a cumbersome functionalist building that backs up towards the River Scheldt. M HKA specialises in large-scale, **avant-garde exhibitions** – a delight for some, obscurantism gone mad for others.

FoMu
Waalsekaai 47 • Charge • ⓦ fomu.be

Housed in a big old warehouse near the River Scheldt, **FoMu** owns a massive collection of **photographic images** relating to the evolution of Antwerp in particular and Belgium in general. A regularly rotated selection of these images is on display here, but the museum is better known for its temporary photographic exhibitions by international figures.

North of the centre: Het Eilandje

Antwerp has always been reliant on its sea trade and the assorted docks and wharves of **Het Eilandje** (The Little Isle), just to the north of the city centre, abutting the River Scheldt, was the city's economic hub for many decades. Work on these maritime facilities began in the sixteenth century. However, the economic collapse following the **Spanish Fury** (see page 311) stopped the digging in its tracks, and it was only much later, in the 1860s, that work resumed in earnest. After that, the docks of this district were crowded with vessels from every corner of the globe, and its quays were lined with warehouses, sheds, offices and factories. But the boom times were short-lived. The docks could not accommodate the larger vessels built after World War II. Het Eilandje went into free fall in the late 1950s, becoming a neglected, decaying corner of the city – until forty years later when, in the manner of dockside developments across Western Europe, plans were laid to rejuvenate the whole district. It's still a work in progress, but a stroll around the area is a pleasant way to while away a couple of hours, with the obvious targets being **MAS** (Museum aan de Stroom; Museum by the Stream) and the **Red Star Line Museum**, as well as the new cafés and bars in the renovated warehouses on the waterfront, though you can also explore more of the docks on a boat trip (see page 184).

Bonapartedok and Willemdok

Approaching from the south via **Falconplein**, where seamen once hung out in numbers, you soon reach the **Bonapartedok** and the **Willemdok**, the first of a chain of docks that extends north for many kilometres. Created in the nineteenth century, these two docks were the first to be protected from the River Scheldt tides by locks. Both are now **marinas** – albeit in a low-key way – and the warehouses that overlook them have been turned into apartments. Apart from the Museum aan de Stroom, plonked on the jetty between the docks, the one notable old building is the **Loodswezen**, a grand neo-Gothic edifice of 1885 that once housed the city's river pilots and tugboat crews.

MAS and the Havenhuis
Hanzestedenplaats • Charge • ⓦ mas.be

The striking, reddish-brown Cubist building that rises high above the Willemdok and the Bonapartedok is a flashy home for **MAS** (Museum aan de Stroom), a museum whose collection is anchored in Antwerp's seafaring history via themed permanent and temporary exhibitions. It's not a bad idea to start on the tenth-floor viewing terrace from where you can spy – just to the east – Zaha Hadid's jaw-dropping 2016 silver roof extension to the **Havenhuis** (Harbour House). Otherwise, the museum's collection is vast, with well over half a million artefacts, and includes everything from pre-Columbian art to a 'visible storeroom' on the second floor where you can look at exhibits waiting to be displayed. There are also sections on all manner of maritime activity, from inland navigation to life on the waterfront and shipbuilding.

Red Star Line Museum

Montevideostraat 3 • Charge • ⓦ redstarline.be • 15min walk north of MAS

Opened in 2013, the **Red Star Line Museum** tells the story of the eponymous shipping company whose transatlantic passenger liners carried more than two million emigrants from Antwerp, via Southampton and Liverpool in the UK, to the United States between 1873 and 1934. Housed in the company's former warehouse, the fascinating two-floor exhibition shows the different stages of the journey, from booking tickets to arriving at Ellis Island. However, the collection's strength lies in the uplifting and moving stories of some of RSL's passengers, who included Albert Einstein and Irving Berlin.

ARRIVAL AND DEPARTURE   ANTWERP

By train Antwerp has two main train stations, Berchem, 4km southeast of downtown, and Antwerpen Centraal, about 2km east of the city centre (a 15min walk from the main sights). For train timetables, consult ⓦ belgianrail.be.

Getting to the centre from Centraal Station Trams from Centraal Station to the city centre depart from the Diamant stop (Nos 5, 9 or 15, direction Linkeroever); get off at Groenplaats. That said, it's easy enough to walk via Leysstraat and then Meir (15min).

Destinations from Antwerp Centraal Station Amsterdam (every 30min; 2hr); Bruges (every 30min; 1hr 30min);

Brussels (every 20min; 45min); Ghent (every 30min; 1hr); Hasselt (every 30min; 1hr 30min); Lier (every 15min; 15min); Leuven (every 15min; 50min); Mechelen (every 15min; 18min); Tongeren (hourly; 1hr 50min).

By bus Most long-distance buses, including FlixBus, arrive at the bus station on Franklin Rooseveltplaats, a 5min walk from Centraal Station.

By plane Antwerp's tiny airport (ⓦ luchthaven-antwerpen. com) is located about 6km southeast of the city centre in the suburb of Deurne. Regular buses run from the airport into the city centre.

GETTING AROUND

By bus and tram Operated by De Lijn (ⓦ delijn.be), a first-rate tram and bus system serves the city and its suburbs from two main hubs, Groenplaats and Centraal Station (Diamant). A standard single fare within the city centre costs €2.50 (valid for 1hr); a 24-hour unlimited day pass, called a *dagpas*, costs €7.50, €15 for three days. Advance tickets are sold everywhere, but most conveniently at tram stations with multilingual ticket machines. You must validate the ticket in the machine on the bus or tram.

By bike The city operates a bike rental scheme, Velo Antwerpen (ⓦ velo-antwerpen.be), with racks liberally distributed across the centre. There's a modest registration fee and a charge after the first half-hour. After registration, you receive a user code and select a self-chosen passcode.

Payment can be made by credit card, and bikes can be returned to any rack.

By boat Flandria (ⓦ flandria.nu/en) operates two- or three-hour Antwerp port/harbour cruises (€22–26) daily for most of the year. Passengers embark at the Asiadok-Oostkaai, about 2km (25min walk) northeast of the MAS museum.

By car Among many car rental companies, Europcar has a branch in the bowels of Centraal Station at Pelikaanstraat 3 (ⓦ europcar.be), while Sixt is at the airport (ⓦ sixt.be). As of 2017, Antwerp city centre is a Low-Emission Zone, which means that your car must meet the conditions for admission. To find out more see ⓦ slimnaarantwerpen.be/en/lez.

By taxi There is a taxi rank outside Centraal Station. Antwerp Taxi is on ☎ 032 38 38 38.

INFORMATION

Tourist information The main tourist office, at Steenplein 1, is in the old fortress by the riverside (daily 10am–6pm; ⓦ visit.antwerpen.be). Parts of the fortress date back to

the thirteenth century, and it's here, alongside the tourist office, that the *Antwerp Story* (charge) explores the city's past, present and future.

ACCOMMODATION   SEE MAPS PAGES 170 AND 174

Antwerp has the range of **hotels** you'd expect of Belgium's   second city, a limited supply of **B&Bs** and several **hostels**.

Consequently, finding accommodation is rarely difficult, although surprisingly few places in the centre are the best spots to soak up the city's atmosphere.

HOTELS

Botanic Sanctuary Antwerp Lange Gasthuisstraat 45 ⓦ botanicantwerp.be. This luxury hotel occupies a sympathetically modernised former monastery and its gardens – indeed, one of its pleasures is the quiet, almost secluded setting. The hotel bills itself as a destination in itself, a reasonable enough claim given it has every facility: three top-notch restaurants, a congress/conference area and a spa. €€€€

Flora Korte Nieuwstraat 12 ⓦ hotelflora.be/en. This small, deluxe hotel occupies ancient premises hidden away behind the narrowest and most charming Baroque gateways. The guest rooms are flamboyantly decorated in the brightest and boldest of colours with a multitude of retro flourishes. €€€€

Hilton Antwerp Groenplaats 32 ⓦ hilton.com/en. Good points: central location, the handsome, nineteenth-century facade, the fitness centre and the rooftop terrace. Not-so-good points: decoratively predictable modern rooms and part of an international chain. €€€

Ibis Budget Antwerpen Centraal Station Lange Kievitstraat 145 ⓦ all.accor.com. In an unassuming tower block about a 10min walk south of Centraal Station, this bright and breezy chain hotel has around 145 basic, modern rooms sleeping up to three people. €€

Indigo Antwerp City Centre Koningin Astridplein 43 ⓦ ihg.com. Good-value, boutique-style chain hotel near Centraal Station, where the stripped-back guest rooms are equipped with amenable touches like Nespresso machines and bathrobes. The buffet breakfast is very good. €€

Julien Korte Nieuwstraat 24 ⓦ hotel-julien.com. Deluxe boutique hotel with just 22 rooms and lots of stylish flourishes, from rain-showers and flat-screen TVs to vintage details and oodles of greys, creams and browns. There's also a spa. €€€€

Matelote Haarstraat 11A ⓦ hotel-matelote.be. Decorated in a crisp, modernist style, this small and really rather handsome hotel occupies intelligently revamped and remodelled old premises on a narrow street a (long) stone's

throw from the Grote Markt. The rooms vary in size, but the best are large and well-appointed. €€

★ **Rubens Grote Markt** Oude Beurs 29 ⓦ hotelrubens antwerp.be. Arguably the most agreeable hotel in town, this four-star establishment has just 36 large guestrooms in a mix of styles, though the default button is modern. It occupies a smashing downtown location on a quiet side street a few minutes' walk from the Grote Markt. It has a dinky little courtyard overseen by an ancient brick tower, evidence that the building started as a medieval mansion. €€€

★ **'t Sandt** Zand 13 ⓦ hotel-sandt.be. Near the river, in a tastefully converted, centrally located, seventeenth-century mansion, this four-star hotel has 29 stylish rooms and suites decorated in an appealing mixture of modern-meets-country-house style. Tasty breakfasts plus a pleasant garden patio out the back. €€€

De Witte Lelie Keizerstraat 16 ⓦ dewittelelie.be. Immaculate four-star – one of the city's ritziest – with just ten charming rooms in a handsomely renovated seventeenth-century merchant's house, a 5min walk from the Grote Markt. With prices like these, you'd expect each room to be different – and they are, from duplexes with wood-beam ceilings through to the Louis XIV-style 'Presidential Suite'. €€€€

HOSTELS AND CAMPSITES

Camping de Molen Jachthavenweg 6 ⓦ citycamping antwerp.be/en/. This straightforward camping and caravan site (also offering cabins holding up to four people) occupies what amounts to a field on the left-hand side of the River Scheldt – it's roughly opposite the Red Star Line Museum and a short stroll from the slab of shingly sand that passes for the city beach. To get there from the centre on foot or by bike, use the Voetgangerstunnel under the Scheldt from St-Jansvliet. Reservations are recommended. No cash. Mid-March to mid-Oct. Camping €, cabins €

Jeugdherberg Pulcinella Bogaardeplein 1 ⓦ jeugdherbergen.be. Well-equipped HI-affiliated hostel in a bright modern block just on the south side of the city centre. Has 162 beds in two- four- and six-bed en-suite rooms. A bar and restaurant serve lunch and dinner, free wi-fi and a bicycle shed. Breakfast included. Dorms €, doubles €

EATING   SEE MAPS PAGES 170 AND 174

Antwerp's busy, bustling centre is liberally sprinkled with cafés, café-bars and restaurants, with standards generally high. The default option is **Flemish cuisine**, but as you would expect in a big city, there are lots of alternatives, with Italian and French restaurants leading the way. There's an appealing **informality** about eating in Antwerp, too, with smart (read stuffy) places thin on the ground, but note that many places close early in the week from Sunday or Monday through Wednesday.

CAFÉS

★ **Caffe Mundi** Oude Beurs 24 ⓦ caffemundi.be/en. Just off the Grote Markt, this friendly little café serves what many regard as the best coffee in town – from the roastery next door and both single origin and blends. Home-made cakes, too, if you are feeling peckish. €

De Foyer Komedieplaats 18 ⓦ cafefoyer.be. The grand foyer of the elegant Bourla theatre is now a tearoom. You can pop in for a drink or light lunch on Saturday, enjoy a copious brunch or sample one of their *pistolets* (sandwiches). €̄

Hoffy's Lange Kievitstraat 52 ⓦhoffys.be. Reliable, simply decorated traditional Jewish/Yiddish kosher restaurant and takeaway near Centraal Station. Very reasonable prices. Try the *gefillte fisch*. €̄

Mirlo's Verbondstraat 1 ⓦmirlos.be. Friendly little café where they offer tasty breakfasts, lunches and snacks from neat and modern premises. Lots of the goodies are home-made and organic where possible, from cakes and sandwiches to lemonade. €̄

Normo Minderbroedersrui 30 ⓦnormocoffee.be. A short walk to the northwest of the Rockoxhuis, this cool, boho café and roastery, with its bare brick walls, makes some of the best coffee in town. There is great music and atmosphere, and some squashy sofas, too. Try an affogato (espresso poured over vanilla ice cream. €̄

RESTAURANTS

★ **Appelmans** Papenstraatje 1 ⓦbrasserieappelmans. be. Although this buzzy brasserie by the cathedral is open for lunch, it's a great place to spend an evening – an absinthe and cocktail bar (open until late) and DJs on Fri and Sat evenings. Mains, like beef stew with fries. €€€

Bourla Graanmarkt 7 ⓦbourla.be. A mixed bag of a place with an extensive outside terrace and an antique interior – think leather banquettes, big old mirrors, chandeliers and lots of Art Nouveau flourishes. The menu concentrates on Flemish dishes, with the beef stew nigh-on perfect, and when the kitchen closes, it morphs into a bar. €€

Fiskebar Marnixplaats 11, Het Zuid ⓦfiskebar.be. This fashionable place, with its tiled interior and simple furnishings, has dispensed with unnecessary fripperies to concentrate on the seafood – and it's generally reckoned to be one of the best fish restaurants in Antwerp. Mains average around €35, but a whole lobster will rush you €145. Reservations advised. €€€€

Horta Grand Café Hopland 2 ⓦgrandcafehorta.be/en. In 1965, Brussels allowed one of Victor Horta's magnificent buildings to be demolished. Still, some bright spark in Antwerp saw an opportunity and saved its splendid – and splendidly large – iron rafters, and these now frame the airy and glassy *Horta Grand Café*, which spreads over several levels. The menu is ambitious, and portions are substantial. Opt for seafood dishes, say, halibut with zucchini, celery, savoy, and potatoes. €€€

InVINcible Haarstraat 9 ⓦinvincible.be. Flashy little restaurant near the Grote Markt, where you're best off perched on a bar stool in full view of the chef. The menu is short but extremely well-considered, giving prominence to seasonal ingredients – spring chicken in tarragon or fried veal liver. Reservations advised. €€€

Maritime Suikerrui 4 ⓦrestaurantmaritime.be. In a great location between the Grote Markt and the river, this long-established restaurant is particularly good for seafood – try, for example, the Dover sole. It's a fairly small restaurant, so booking is advised. €€€

★ **Het Nieuwe Palinghuis** St-Jansvliet 14 ⓦhet nieuwepalinghuis.be. Many locals think this is the best seafood restaurant in town, a lovely place with a mishmash of nautical furnishings. It serves an outstanding shell and wet fish selection – try the poached ray with butter and capers. On one of the city's most agreeable squares, the Art Deco tower holds the wooden escalators leading down to the old pedestrian tunnel under the River Scheldt. €€€

★ **Otomat Antwerpen** Van Schoonbekeplein 11, Het Eilandje ⓦotomat.be. A couple of streets south of the MAS, this is the hippest and arguably the best pizza place. From a vegan option with carrots and broccoli to blue cheese and pear, not to mention the Nutella and strawberry dessert version, all have crusts made with Duvel beer. €€

Pazzo Oude Leeuwenrui 12, Het Eilandje ⓦpazzo.be. Well-regarded restaurant featuring inventive cooking – roast fillet of lamb with goat's cheese, peppers, aubergine and olive crumble gives the idea. A great selection of wines and a jazz soundtrack are further pros. Has a separate wine bar on the first floor. €€€

RAS Ernest van Dijckkai 37 ⓦras.today/en. With its whimsical Art Deco references, the appealing building that houses the RAS restaurant is part of a long-term effort to brighten the city's riverfront. The restaurant offers views across the river, slick modern decor and an imaginative menu. For example, try the Spanish salad with mango, brava wedges and yoghurt dressing. €€

't Zilte Hanzestdenplaats 5, Het Eilandje ⓦtzilte.be. On the ninth floor of the MAS, this Michelin-star restaurant is the perfect spot to celebrate a special occasion. The three-course lunch, which changes daily, is good value, but the evening meal will singe your pocketbook. Choosing some bread might take you a while – there are fifteen kinds. €€€€

DRINKING AND NIGHTLIFE

SEE MAPS PAGES 170 AND 174

Antwerp is a great place to **drink**. There are lots of bars in the city centre, mostly dark and tiny affairs exuding a cheerful vitality, a few lively live music. The favourite local tipple is *De Koninck*, a light ale drunk in a *bolleke*, or small, stemmed glass. The **club scene** is in rude health, with a handful of boisterous places dotted around the peripheries of the city centre, both gay and straight.

They get going around midnight, and admission fees are typically modest, except when big-name DJs are in. There's a competent **jazz** scene, too.

BARS

Café Pelikaan Melkmarkt 14 ☎032 84 04 05. There's nothing smart and touristy about the *Pelikaan*, a packed and somewhat battered-looking bar metres from the cathedral where (an occasionally confused and raucous set of) locals get down to some serious drinking. Daily 9am till late.

Dogma Cocktails Wijngaardstraat 5 ⓦdogmacocktails. be. If you're tired of swimming in a sea of Belgian beer, drop by this lively cocktail bar, which occupies pleasantly refurbished premises near Hendrik Conscienceplein.

De Duifkens Graanmarkt 5 ☎032 25 10 39. This old-style Antwerp café-bar with its wood-panelled interior has long been a favourite haunt of the city's actors, who hunker down here after appearing at one of the nearby theatres. The range of beers is a little limited (by Belgian standards), but it's a convivial spot, and when the weather is good, customers spill out onto the lovely terrace.

★ **Den Engel** Grote Markt 3 ⓦcafedenengel.be. This is a traditional bar with an easy-going, occasionally anarchic atmosphere. It occupies the ground floor of a guild house on the northwest corner of the main square and attracts a bubbly mix of business people and locals from the residential enclave around the Vleeshuis. Late-night dancing (of no particular merit) too.

Den Hopsack Grote Pieter Potstraat 24 ⓦdenhopsack. be. A postmodern bar with all wood and Spartan fittings, it offers highbrow conversation and an amenable, low-key atmosphere. The venue also hosts all sorts of special events, from live music to poetry readings.

Oud Arsenaal Maria Pijpelincxstraat 4 ⓦdorstvlegel. be. No one could accuse the *Oud Arsenaal* of bending the knee to gentrification, but this traditional brown café, with its vintage bric-a-brac and ageing decor, is great for the atmosphere. It also offers a well-chosen selection of beers – from Rodenbach to gueuze and beyond. Metres

from the Rubenshuis.

De Vagant Reyndersstraat 25 ☎0473 91 16 60. Something of a rarity, this small and homely bar specialises in Belgian and Dutch jenever, served ice cold and a popular drink with Flemish workers from time immemorial. There is a baffling range to choose from – ask, and all will be revealed. There is a small pavement terrace, too.

CLUBS AND LIVE MUSIC

Café Hopper Léopold de Waelstraat 2, Het Zuid ⓦcafehopper.be. Featuring regular live bands, this high-ceilinged café with a funky retro interior, next to the Museum of Fine Art, is the best jazz joint in town.

★ **Het Bos** Ankerrui 5–7 ⓦhetbos.be. Antwerp's hippest venue is a cultural centre in a former office block north of the city. The eclectic programme includes up-and-coming bands, art exhibitions, films, theatre, food festivals and much more. See website for details.

LGBTQ+

Café Den Draak Draakplaats 1 ⓦdendraak.be. If there is a centre to Antwerp's gay and lesbian scene, it's this busy café-bar, which is part of a larger gay and lesbian project called Het Roze Huis (ⓦhetrozehuis.be). Draakplaats is a 15min walk south from Centraal Station: take Pelikaanstraat and its continuation Simonsstraat/Mercatorstraat, turn left down Grote Hondstraat, and it's at the end of the street.

Cargo Club Lange Schipperskapelstraat 11–13 ⓦcargo club.be. Formerly called *Red & Blue*, this gay club attracts partygoers from far and wide with different theme nights and guaranteed floor-filling disco and house music. It is busy from around 1am.

ENTERTAINMENT

Antwerp has a vibrant **cultural scene** with regular performances by Flemish ballet, various theatre and opera companies and by the internationally acclaimed Antwerp Symphony Orchestra (ⓦantwerpsymphonyorchestra.be), which mainly plays at Koningin Elisabethzaal on Koningin Astridplein. The city also possesses a first-rate **art-house cinema**, where – as is usual in Flemish Belgium – English-language films are subtitled (as opposed to dubbed). For **upcoming events**, ask at a tourist information centre or check their website (ⓦvisitantwerpen.be)

THEATRES AND CONCERT HALLS

deSingel Desguinlei 25 ⓦdesingel.be. Major arts centre and performance venue on the southern edge of the city. Occasional performances by the Antwerp Symphony Orchestra.

Koningin Elisabethzaal Koningin Astridplein 26 ⓦkoninginelisabethzaal.be/en/. This concert hall by Centraal Station offers a wide-ranging programme of music and is the main home of the Antwerp Symphony Orchestra

(ⓦantwerpsymphonyorchestra.be).

Stadsschouwburg Theaterplein 1 ⓦstadsschouwburg-antwerpen.be. A big bruiser of a modern building not far from the Rubenshuis, it has an eclectic programme that includes popular music concerts, opera, ballet and musicals.

Toneelhuis Komedieplaats 18 ⓦtoneelhuis.be. This handsomely restored nineteenth-century theatre – the Bourlaschouwburg – is the city's premier venue for theatre as performed by the Toneelhuis repertory company.

De Vlaamse Opera Frankrijklei 1 ⓦoperaballet.be/en. The excellent Vlaamse Opera (Flemish Opera) mostly performs here at this grand, early twentieth-century building on the ring road, about halfway between the Grote Markt and Centraal Station.

CINEMA

Cartoon's Kaasstraat 4, off Suikerrui ⓦcinemacartoons. be. The most distinctive downtown cinema, Cartoon's shows mainstream and art-house films in several auditoria. *Bar Kino* is a nice wine and beer bar for drinks before and after a movie.

3

BAARLE-HERTOG: A LEG IN EACH COUNTRY

Filling out the **northeast corner of Belgium**, just beyond Antwerp, are the flat, sandy moorlands of the **Kempen**. Once a barren wasteland dotted with the poorest of agricultural communities – and punctuated by tracts of acid heath, bog and deciduous woodland – the Kempen's more hospitable parts were first cultivated and planted with pine by pioneering **Cistercian monks** in the twelfth century. The monks helped develop and sustain a strong regional identity and dialect, which survives in good order today, though the area's towns and villages are uniformly drab. The Kempen was also the subject of endless territorial bickering during the creation of an independent Belgium in the 1830s, a particular point of dispute being the little town of **Baarle-Hertog**, about 35km northeast of Antwerp. The final compromise verged on the ridiculous: Baarle-Hertog was designated as being part of Belgium, but it was surrounded by Dutch territory, and the international border between it and the adjoining (Dutch) town of **Baarle-Nassau** cut through houses, never mind dividing streets. If you're eager to have one leg in the Netherlands and another in Belgium, here's the spot.

SHOPPING
SEE MAPS PAGES 170 AND 174

Antwerp loves its **open-air markets**. There are lots to choose from, but three of the best are the **antique and jumble** market in the city centre on Sint-Jansvliet (Easter–Oct Sun 9am–5pm); the Bio Market, an **organic foods** market on the Falconplein (Sun 8am–4pm); and the large, **general market** on Theaterplein and its surroundings (Sun 8am–1pm). The city is also a hub of the diamond trade (see box, page 181) and a popular place for fashion shopping (ⓦfashioninantwerp.be), with a particular concentration of shops and stalls within easy striking distance of the ModeNatie complex (see page 178).

Bakkerij Goossens Korte Gasthuisstraat 31 ⓦbakkerij goossens.nl. Join the queue at the best bakery in town, founded in 1884. It sells a superb range of breads, cakes, and tarts.

Essentiel Antwerp Kammenstraat 56 ⓦessentiel-antwerp.com. Founded in 1999 with a collection of T-shirts, this men's and women's casual clothing company is now an international brand. Its flagship store is in Antwerp, Huidevettersstraat 57–59.

Hans Burie Nationalestraat 2 ⓦburie-chocolade pralines-antwerpen.be. Belgians love their chocolates, and although it's a matter of hot debate, many reckon this to be the best chocolatier in town – three cheers (or chocs) for Hans.

Jutka & Riska Nationalestraat 87 ⓦjutkaenriska.com. This women's clothes shop sells vintage pieces and items by young designers. Expect to pay around €60 for a dress.

Juttu Meir 19 ⓦjuttu.be. Concept/lifestyle store featuring a good selection of stylish, little-known Belgian and European brands – at affordable prices.

Modepaleis Dries Van Noten Nationalestraat 16 ⓦdriesvannoten.be. Amongst the string of fashion shops near ModeNatie, one good and classy bet for both men and women is this large outlet featuring the work of one of the city's most celebrated designers.

Rosier 41 Rosier 41 ⓦrosier41.be. This large store sells a raft of Belgian and international designers, from established names to the up-and-coming. It also gets discounted clothes straight from designers' showrooms.

DIRECTORY

Pharmacy Apotheek Melkmarkt is at Melkmarkt 33 (Mon–Fri 8.30am–6.30pm, Sat 9.30am–5.30pm ☎032 26 08 97). Details of 24hr pharmacies are available from the tourist office; duty rotas should also be displayed on all pharmacists' windows or doors.

Post office The main post office is at Eiermarkt 33–35 (Mon–Fri 9am–6pm, Sat 9am–3pm).

Lier

An ideal day-trip destination, likeable **LIER**, just 17km southeast of Antwerp, has an amenable, small-town air, its pocket-sized centre boasting a particularly pretty **Grote Markt** and a cluster of handsome medieval buildings, especially **St-Gummaruskerk**. Lier was founded in the eighth century, but despite its ancient provenance, the town has never managed to dodge the shadow of its much larger neighbour,

Antwerp – even when **Felix Timmermans**, one of Belgium's best-known writers, lived here. All the same, Timmermans did add a certain local sparkle – and it may have been needed: other Belgians have been referring to Lier's citizens as 'sheepheads' (*schapenkoppen*) ever since the fifteenth century, when – so the story goes – the locals opted to have an animal market here rather than a university. Well-known street artist **Joachim** hails from Lier, and you can see a number of his works around the town (pick up a leaflet at the tourist office; see page 191).

Grote Markt

Central Lier's ancient streets and alleys are encircled and bisected by the waterways that mark the course of its old harbours and moat. At the centre is the **Grote**

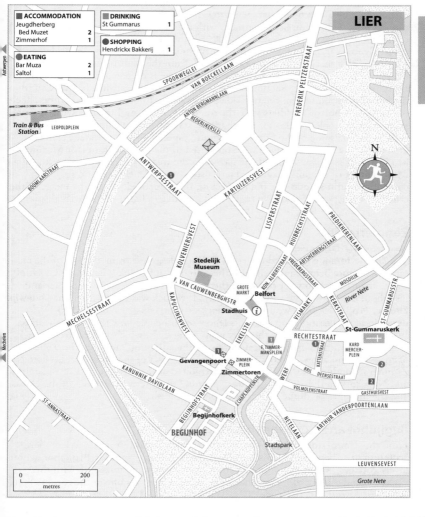

Markt, where pride of place goes to the turreted fourteenth-century **Belfort**, an attractively spikey affair incongruously attached to the classically elegant **Stadhuis**, which was built to replace the medieval cloth hall in 1740. Otherwise, the square is an attractive medley of 'neos', with neo-Gothic, Neoclassical and even neo-Romanesque buildings, mostly dating from the 1920s, jostling for space and attention.

St-Gummaruskerk

Kardinaal Mercierplein • Partly closed for repairs until 2029 • Free • ⓦ visitlier.be/en

Lier's ecclesiastical highlight is **St-Gummaruskerk**, which takes its name from a courtier of the king of France who, repenting of his sinful ways, settled in Lier as a hermit in the middle of the eighth century. Dating from 1425, the church is a fine illustration of the Flamboyant (or Late) Gothic style, its sturdy buttresses surmounted by a tiered and parapeted tower. Chunky pillars rise to support a vaulted roof, whose simplicity contrasts with the extraordinary intricacy of the conspicuous stone rood screen below. Close by, the **high altar** is topped off with an especially fine carving, a fourteenth-century wooden altarpiece whose inside panels are alive with a mass of finely observed detail, from the folds of the bed linen to the pile of kindling underneath Abraham's son as he is prepared for sacrifice. The church's most interesting **painting** is the triptych in the chapel just behind and to the left of the rood screen: the two side panels are by Rubens, but the central panel is a copy – Napoleon's soldiers stole the original Rubens, and the French have never given it back. Look out also for the **chancel**'s **stained-glass windows**, which are reckoned to be some of the finest in Belgium, especially the five stately, elongated ones above the high altar; these were presented to the town by Emperor Maximilian in 1516. A passageway leads off the nave into the **treasury** (*Schatkamer*), a tiny affair with a clutter of religious artefacts. Here also is an extremely rare and very early copy of the **Turin Shroud**, the old linen cloth that supposedly bears the image of the crucified Christ – it's incredibly fragile and sensitive to light, so it's rarely displayed.

Zimmertoren

Zimmerplein • Charge • ⓦ zimmertoren.be

The **Zimmertoren**, a medieval tower on Zimmerplein, was formerly part of the city ramparts before being equipped with the colourful **Jubelklok** (Centenary Clock), whose many dials show the phases of the moon, the zodiac, the tides of Lier and just about everything else you can think of. The clock was the work of one **Lodewijk Zimmer** (1888–1970), a wealthy city merchant who constructed it in 1931 to dispel local superstition and show his fellow townspeople how the cosmos worked. Inside the tower, you can see the bevy of rotating dials, which make the clock tick, along with Zimmer's astronomical studio. In the adjoining museum, the *Time and Space* exhibition allows visitors to learn about the start of the universe; also here is Zimmer's **Wonderklok** (Wonder Clock), exhibited at the World's Fairs of Brussels and New York in the 1930s. A **guide** explaining the internal workings of the clocks and the meaning of all the dials is available in English.

Begijnhof and Gevangenpoort

From the Zimmertoren, **Schapekoppenstraat** leads southwest past a wry modern **sculpture** of a shepherd and his metal sheep to a side gate into the **Begijnhof**, whose lovely cottages, which date from the thirteenth century, are mixed up with the slightly grander terraced houses that were inserted later. It's one of the region's best-preserved *begijnhoven* (see page 307), its narrow cobbled lanes stretching as far as the earthen bank that marks the line of the old city wall. On the far side of the Begijnhof, Begijnhofstraat leads back to the Zimmerplein through the arches of the **Gevangenenpoort** – the fortified medieval gate which served as the town's prison for many years.

Stadsmuseum

Florent van Cauwenberghstraat 14 • Charge • ⓦ stadsmuseumlier.be

Lier's enjoyable **Stadsmuseum** concentrates on all things to do with its home town, adopting an informal, thematic approach as it does so. The museum has a small but significant collection of paintings, including two works by Pieter Bruegel the Younger (1564–1638), namely *St John the Baptist Preaching to a Crowd*, who are dressed in an idiosyncratic mix of rural Flemish and imaginary Middle Eastern attire, and a *Flemish Proverbs* (*Vlaamse Spreekwoorden*), illustrating over eighty proverbs satirising every vice and foolery imaginable. There's also a pious preparatory sketch of *St Theresa* by Rubens (1577–1640), a cruelly drawn *Brawling Peasants* by Jan Steen (1626–79), and several works by David Teniers the Younger (1610–90), who made a small fortune by churning out earthy peasant scenes such as his *Jealous Wife* and *The Backgammon Players*.

The museum also pays tribute to the town's most famous inhabitants, the writer Felix Timmermans (1886–1947) and the painter Isidore Opsomer (1878–1967), two friends who considered themselves custodians of Flemish culture. The Stadsmuseum has a permanent collection of a large selection of Opsomer's paintings, including a number of appealing rural scenes, such as the Expressionistic *Middelburg*, but also a large and laughable, pseudo-religious painting entitled *Christ Preaches in Lier*. The churn of this Flemish nativism seems to have caught Timmermans out. He went from writing about traditional village life, most memorably in the earthy humour of his *Pallieter*, to editing a right-wing Flemish newspaper during World War II and having regular dealings with the governing regime, leading, not surprisingly, to a chorus of accusations of German collaboration.

ARRIVAL AND INFORMATION   LIER

By train and bus From Lier's train and adjoining bus station, it's a 10min walk southeast to the Grote Markt.
Destinations by train Antwerp (every 15min; 15min); Hasselt (every 20min; 1hr); Leuven (every 30min; 40min); Mechelen (direct trains hourly; 15min).

Tourist information On the first floor of the Stadhuis, on the Grote Markt (April–Oct: Mon–Fri 9am–4.30pm, Sat & Sun 9am–12.30pm & 1–4pm; Nov–March: Mon–Fri 9am–12.30pm & 1.30–4.30pm; ⓦ visitlier.be).

ACCOMMODATION   SEE MAP PAGE 189

Jeugdherberg Bed Muzet Volmolenstraat 65 ⓦ jeugdherbergen.be/en/lier. In a wing of a renovated convent, this newish youth hostel is aimed at groups wanting to undertake cultural activities but offers accommodation to individuals too. Breakfast is included in the price, but not towels. Meals in *Bar Muza*. Dorms €̄, doubles €̄

Zimmerhof Begijnhofstraat 2 ⓦ zimmerhof.be. Lier is too small (and too near Antwerp) to have much to offer in terms of accommodation. With 23 smart, modern rooms, this appealing hotel occupies a sympathetically updated early twentieth-century courtyard complex next to the Gevangenpoort and is a refreshing and enjoyable place to stay. €€€

EATING   SEE MAP PAGE 189

Bar Muza Gasthuisvest 52 ⓦ bar-muza.be. Modern, airy café next to the town's music school and opposite the new youth hostel, serving tasty and unfussy lunches and dinners – the prawn croquettes are especially delicious. There's a decent selection of beers, which can be enjoyed in the garden on fine days. €̄

Salto! Rechtestraat 18 ⓦ saltolier.be. Smart, minimalist gourmet bistro run by young chef Joris Duys, who trained at one of the best catering schools in Belgium. Mains include his takes on traditional specialities such as vol-au-vent and a creamy chicken and mushroom casserole. €€€€

St Gummarus Felix Timmermansplein 2 ☎ 034 88 17 21. This traditional small-town pub by the river with a cosy interior and a pleasant pavement terrace offers a good range of bottled beers, including the local brew, Caves, based on a sixteenth-century recipe. €

Hendrickx Bakkerij Antwerpsestraat 130 ☎ 034 80 03 61. Lier's most famous product is a Liers *vlaaike*: a small, round, spiced cake whose recipe dates back several hundred years and has been granted a protected status (IGP) by the EU. This bakery is the best place to get them, and they also sell other local products, including Caves beer.

Mechelen and around

Midway between Antwerp and Brussels, **MECHELEN**, the home of the Primate of Belgium and the country's ecclesiastical capital, is an ancient and intriguing city of just 87,000 inhabitants. In recent years, a well-conceived municipal plan to freshen up the centre has worked wonders, resulting in today's pleasant and appealing town. The key sights – primarily a cache of **medieval churches**, including a splendid **cathedral** – are easily seen on a day-trip from either of its neighbours, but spend the night here, and you'll give the place the attention it deserves. One scar on Mechelen's history was its use by the Germans as a transit camp for Jews in World War II: the **Kazerne Dossin museum** recalls these terrible times, and a short train ride or drive away, is **Fort Breendonk**, a one-time Gestapo interrogation centre.

Brief history

Mechelen's Christian past dates back to **St Rombout**, an Irish evangelist who converted the locals in the seventh century. Little is known about Rombout, but legend asserts he was the son of a powerful chieftain who gave up his worldly possessions to preach to the heathens – not that it did him much good: after publicly criticising a stonemason for adultery, the ungrateful wretch chopped him up with his axe and chucked the body into the river. In the way of such things, Rombout's remains were retrieved and showed no signs of decay, which was easily enough justification for constructing a **shrine** in his honour. Rombout proved a popular saint, and pilgrims flocked here, ensuring Mechelen had steady revenue. By the **thirteenth century**, Mechelen had become one of the more powerful cities of medieval Flanders, and it entered a brief golden age after 1473, when the Burgundian prince, **Charles the Bold**, decided to base major parts of his administration here. Charles died four years later, and his redoubtable widow, **Margaret of York**, moved to Mechelen, where she formed one of the most famous courts of the day with her stepdaughter, **Mary of Burgundy**. Mary died in 1482, and Margaret followed in 1503, but Mary's daughter – and Margaret's great-stepdaughter – **Margaret of Austria** returned to Mechelen in 1507 to become Habsburg governor of the Low Countries and guardian of the future emperor, Charles V. It was during the governorship of Margaret of Austria that Mechelen peaked again, with artists and scholars drawn here from all over Flanders, attracted by the Renaissance pomp and ceremony, with enormous feasts in fancy clothes in fancy buildings. For the men, two particular peccadilloes were **pointed shoes** (whose length – up to about 60cm – reflected social status) and bright, two-colour hose. This glamorous facade camouflaged serious political intent: surrounded by wealthy, independent merchants and powerful, well-organised guilds, Margaret – as well as Mary and Margaret of York before her – realised they had to impress and overawe as a condition of their survival. Margaret of Austria died in 1530, and the capital moved to Brussels. Mechelen was never quite the same, though many of its older buildings survived the **industrial boom** of the nineteenth century and emerged intact today.

Grote Markt

As always, the town centre is the **Grote Markt**, an exceptionally handsome and expansive affair offering a superb view of the cathedral. It's flanked on its eastern side by the **Stadhuis**, whose bizarre and incoherent appearance does it no favours: the left-hand side of the building, comprising an ornate arcaded loggia fronting a fluted, angular edifice, was commissioned by Margaret of Austria and designed by Rombout Keldermans. The plan was to extend the Stadhuis further along the Grote Markt. However, the money ran out after Margaret's death, and the **plain stonework** and

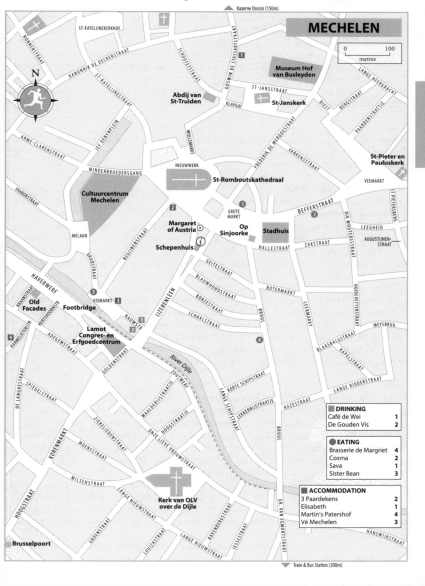

MECHELEN

0   100
metres

Kazerne Dossin (150m)

ST-KATELIJNEKERKHOF

NOMBERSTRAAT

KANUNNIK DE DECKERSTRAAT

ST-KATELIJNESTRAAT

SCHOUTESTRAAT

GOSWIN DE STASSARTSTRAAT

Museum Hof
van Busleyden

LANGE HEERGRACHT

ST-JANSSTRAAT

Abdij van
St-Truiden

KLAPGAT

St-Janskerk

BIEST

BERGSTRAAT

PAARDENSTRAATJE

FREDERIK DE MERODESTRAAT

VARENSSTRAAT

ARME-CLARENSTRAAT

IJZERMARKT

JEF DENYNPLEIN

WOLLMARKT

NIEUWWERK

MINDERBROEDERSGANG

St-Pieter en
Pauluskerk

IMABORSTRAAT

Cultuurcentrum
Mechelen

St-Romboutskathedraal

VEEMARKT

ST-PIETERSBERG

BEFFERSTRAAT

RIK WOUTERSSTRAAT

LEEGHEID

MELAAN

BEGIJNENSTRAAT

Margaret
of Austria

Op
Sinjoorke

GROTE
MARKT

Stadhuis

ZAKSTRAAT

AUGUSTIJNEN-
STRAAT

Schepenhuis

HALLESTRAAT

DRABSTRAAT

GEITESTRAAT

HAVERWERF

Old
Facades

VISMARKT

Footbridge

BLAUWHONDSTRAAT

BORZESTRAAT

BOTERMARKT

BRUUL

LEERMARKT

HUIDEVETTERSSTRAAT

MEYSBRUG

KRAMSTRAAT

HERTSHOORNSTR

NAUWSTR

IJZERENLEEN

SCHAALSTRAAT

KARMELIETENSTR

KAMMELEENSTR

ADEGEMSTRAAT

Lamot
Congres- en
Erfgoedcentrum

BLAASBALGSTRAAT

KAPELSTRAAT

DE LANGHESTRAAT

SPIEGELSTRAAT

GULDENSTRAAT

River Dijle

ZIEKELIEDENSTRAAT

COUTMBR

MAALDERIJSTRAATJE

HOOGSTRAAT

KORTE SCHIPSTRAAT

LEKKERBEETSTRAATJE

LANGE SCHIPSTRAAT

HAZESTRAAT

LANGE RIDDERSTRAAT

BRUUL

GR. VAN EGMONTSTRAAT

KORENMARKT

MOENSSTRAAT

ONZE LIEVE VROUWSTRAAT

MILSENSTRAAT

HOOGSTRAAT

Kerk van OLV
over de Dijle

LANGE NIEUWSTRAAT

GROENSTRAAT

RAVENBERGSTRAAT

LOUIZASTRAAT

LANGE NIEUWSTRAAT

IESSESTRAAT

HANSWIJKSTRAAT

Brusselpoort

Train & Bus Station (300m)

DRINKING
Café de Wei	1
De Gouden Vis	2

EATING
Brasserie de Margriet	4
Cosma	2
Sava	1
Sister Bean	3

ACCOMMODATION
3 Paardekens	2
Elisabeth	1
Martin's Patershof	4
Vé Mechelen	3

3

MECHELEN MEN

Once a generalised symbol of male irresponsibility, the effigy of **Op Sinjoorke** and its forebears enjoyed a variety of names – *vuilen bras* (unfaithful drunkard), *sotscop* (fool) and *vuilen bruidegom* (disloyal husband) – until the events of 1775 redefined its identity. Every year, it was customary for the dummy to be paraded through Mechelen and tossed up and down in a sheet. In 1775, however, a young man from Antwerp attempted to steal it and was badly beaten for his pains: the people of Mechelen were convinced he was part of an Antwerp plot to rob them of their cherished mascot. The two cities were already fierce **commercial rivals**, and the incident soured relations even further. Indeed, when news of the beating reached Antwerp, there was sporadic **rioting** and calls for the city burghers to take some revenge. Refusing to be intimidated, the people of Mechelen derisively renamed the doll after their old nickname for the people of Antwerp – 'Op Sinjoorke', from 'Signor', a reference to that city's favoured status under earlier Spanish kings. It was sweet **revenge** for an incident of 1687 that had made Mechelen a laughing stock: staggering home, a drunk had roused the town when he thought he saw a fire in the cathedral. The 'fire' was moonlight, earning the Mechelaars the soubriquet '**Maneblussers**' (Moondousers).

---

simple gables of the rest of the building were only added several centuries later. In front of the Stadhuis is a modern sculpture of **Op Sinjoorke** (see box below), the town's mascot, being tossed in a blanket.

St-Romboutskathedraal

Grote Markt • **Cathedral** Free • **Tower** Charge • ⓦ visit.mechelen.be/en

St-Romboutskathedraal dominates the town centre just as it was supposed to. The cathedral's mighty square tower takes the breath away. It is a wonderful, almost imperial Gothic structure with soaring, canopied pinnacles and extraordinarily long and slender apertures. It's matched below by heavy-duty buttressing, which supports a sequence of high-arched pointed windows that encircle the nave and the choir, rising to the delicate fluting of a stone balustrade. The **construction** of the church was not without its problems. Work began with draining the marshes on which it was to be built in 1217, but the money ran out before the tower was erected, and the initial design had to be put on hold until the fifteenth century. In 1451, the pope obligingly provided the extra funds when he put St Rombout's on a list of specified churches where pilgrims could seek absolution for their sins without visiting Rome. The money rolled in, and the tower was completed by 1546 – just before the outbreak of the religious wars that would undoubtedly have stymied the whole project.

Nave

Inside the cathedral, the thirteenth-century **nave** has all the cloistered elegance of the Brabantine Gothic style. However, an unfortunate series of seventeenth-century statues of the Apostles spoil the original lines. Between the arches lurks an extraordinary Baroque **pulpit**, a playful mass of twisted and curled oak dotted with carefully camouflaged animal carvings – a squirrel, a frog and a snail here, a salamander and a pelican there. The main scene shows **St Norbert** being thrown from his horse, a narrow escape that convinced this twelfth-century German prince to give his possessions to the poor and dedicate his life to the church. At the far end of the nave, look at the elaborate doors of the **high altar**, which hide the gilt casket containing the remains of St Rombout. They are only opened on major religious festivals, principally during the **Hanswijkprocessie**, held in May, when the reliquary is paraded through the town centre.

The nave's other curiosity, in the side chapel next to the north transept, is the **tomb** of Mechelen's **Cardinal Mercier** (1851–1926), plus a plaque, presented by the Church of England, commemorating his part in coordinating the **Mechelen (or Malines) Conversations**. These investigated the possibility of reuniting the two churches of England and Rome from 1921 until Mercier's death but with little result. Mercier is more often remembered in Belgium for his staunch opposition to the German occupation of World War I. His pastoral letters, notably 'Patriotism and Endurance', proclaimed loyalty to the Belgian king, paid tribute to the soldiers at the front and condemned the invasion as illegal and un-Christian.

South transept

The **south transept** displays the cathedral's most distinguished painting, **Anthony van Dyck**'s dramatic *Crucifixion*, which portrays the writhing, muscular bodies of the two thieves in the shadows to either side of Christ, who is bathed in a bluish-white light of extraordinary clarity. The painting is part of a heavy, marble Baroque **altarpiece** carved for the guild of masons. Still, it was only installed here after the French Revolutionary Army razed the church where the painting was originally displayed.

Ambulatory

In the **ambulatory** are 25-panel **paintings** relating to the legend of **St Rombout**. Such devotional series were comparatively commonplace in medieval Flanders, but this is one of the few to have survived, painted by several unknown artists between 1480 and 1510. As individual works of art, the panel paintings are not perhaps of the highest order, and some are in poor condition. Still, the cumulative attention to detail – in the true Flemish tradition – is quite remarkable, with all manner of **folksy minutiae** illuminating what would otherwise be a predictable tale of sacrifice and sanctity. The panels are exhibited (and numbered) in chronological order, beginning with Rombout's appointment as bishop (Panel 1) and continuing, via assorted miracles, to Rombout's arrival in Mechelen (Panel 7) and finally, the Brotherhood of St Rombout honouring its patron saint (Panel 25). Two of the most interesting scenes are those where Rombout publicly admonishes a local stonemason for adultery (Panel 12) and the saint's **martyrdom** at the hands of the same man while his workmate picks Rombout's pockets (Panel 13).

THE BELLS, THE BELLS

During the fourteenth century, bells were first used in Flemish cities to regulate the working day, reflecting the development of a **wage economy** – employers were keen to keep tabs on their employees. Bells also served as a **public-address system**: pealing bells, for example, announced good news; tolling summoned the citizens to the main square; and a rapid sequence of bells warned of danger. By the early fifteenth century, a short peal marked the hour, and from this developed the **carillon** (*beiaard*), in which the ringing of a set of bells is triggered by the rotation of a large drum with metal pegs; the pegs pull wires attached to the clappers in the bells, just like a giant music box. Later, the mechanics were developed so that the carillon could be played using a keyboard, giving the **player** (*beiaardier*) the chance to improvise.

Carillon playing almost died out in the nineteenth century when it was dismissed as too folksy for words. Still, it's on the rebound, and several Flemish cities – including Bruges and Mechelen – have their municipal carillon player. Mechelen's **cathedral tower** (see page 194) has Belgium's finest carillon, a fifteenth-century affair of 49 bells, and the city is also home to the renowned **Koninklijke Beiaardschool** (Royal Carillon School; ⓦ beiaardschool.mechelen.be), which attracts students from right around the world. Mechelen's carillon resounds over town on high days and holidays, and there are also regular, hour-long **performances** on Saturdays (11.30am), Sundays (3pm), and from June through to mid-September on Monday evenings (8.30pm). In 2014, **Belgian Carillon Culture** was added to UNESCO's list of Intangible Cultural Heritage, with Mechelen's school being an example of best practices to safeguard the tradition.

3

Tower

The energetic can now clamber up **St-Romboutstoren**, an exhausting 538-step climb that leads past assorted bell and carillon chambers (see box below) to the observation platform right at the top. As you might expect, there are panoramic views from the platform and on a clear day, you can spy the Brussels Atomium (see page 78), but mostly you'll realise just how flat this part of Belgium is.

St-Janskerk

St-Janstraat • Free • Ⓦ visit.mechelen.be/sint-janskerk

With its imposing tower and handsome high-pointed windows, **St-Janskerk** is a fine illustration of the Gothic style, mostly dating from the fifteenth century. Inside, almost everything is on a grand scale, from the massive pulpit and the whopping **organ** to two large and unusual canons' pews. But the Baroque high altarpiece grabs the attention, a suitably flashy setting for a flashy but wonderful painting – **Rubens'** *Adoration of the Magi*. Painted in 1619, the central panel, after which the triptych is named, is an exquisite example of the artist's use of variegated lighting – and also features his first wife portrayed as the Virgin. The side panels are rotated, so on the left-hand side, you'll either see Jesus baptised by John the Baptist or John the Baptist's head on a platter; to the right, it's St John the Evangelist on Patmos or the same saint being dipped in boiling oil.

Museum Hof van Busleyden

Frederik de Merodestraat 65 • Charge • Ⓦ hofvanbusleyden.be

Mechelen's principal museum, the **Museum Hof van Busleyden**, occupies a large and particularly attractive Renaissance complex built for the wealthy Busleyden family in the sixteenth century. This palatial complex was home to the Berg van Barmhartigheid (Mountain of Charity), which provided interest-free loans to Mechelen's poor for many years. Severely damaged in World War I, the building was subsequently passed to the city. Recently revamped, the museum's wide-ranging collection features fine and applied art. However, the emphasis is very much on Mechelen's Burgundian salad days at the end of the fifteenth century. Highlights include a medieval Mechelen choir book, a striking, seventeenth-century bust of Hercules and Omphale, a whopping tapestry depicting the 1535 Battle of Tunis and an exquisite Portrait of Margaret of Austria by Bernard van Orley.

Kazerne Dossin

Goswin de Stassartstraat 153 • **Memorial** Free • **Museum** Charge • Ⓦ kazernedossin.eu

During the **German occupation**, Nazi officials chose **Mechelen** as a staging point for Belgian and refugee Jews destined for the concentration camps of Eastern Europe. Their reasoning was relatively straightforward: most of Belgium's Jews were in either Antwerp or Brussels, and Mechelen was halfway between the two – with the result that over 25,000 Jews passed through Mechelen between 1942 and 1944; most ended up in Auschwitz and only 1,200 survived.

These desperate times are recalled at the **Kazerne Dossin**, which divides into two distinct parts, beginning with the large, eighteenth-century **barracks** used for temporary internment during the war. Most of the barracks have been turned into apartments, but one part has been left as a **memorial** to those who died or passed through here with a string of bleak, bare and sombre rooms. The personal testimonies and accompanying photos displayed can't help but be harrowing, and some bring a deep chill to the soul, none more so than the pleading letters and postcards thrown from deportation trains.

The new building across the street from the barracks holds a **museum** that widens the focus, its several floors divided thematically in an attempt to tie in what happened to the Jews with broader issues of human rights, racism and oppression. **Floor 1** sets the scene and looks at Jewish life in Belgium in the 1930s; **Floor 2** investigates the sliding scale of cooperation, collaboration and resistance as applicable to Belgium; and **Floor 3**, titled 'Death', details the fate of most of the Jews temporarily interned here.

South of the Grote Markt

The innocuous **statue of Margaret of Austria** on the south side of the Grote Markt dates from 1849, but it was only moved here from the centre of the square a few years ago. Behind the statue stands the **Schepenhuis** (Aldermen's House), a fetching Gothic structure from 1374 that now holds the tourist office (see page 197) and marks the start of the **Ijzerenleen**, the focus of one of the region's best Saturday **food markets** (8am–1pm). At the far end of Ijzerenleen, turn right down **Nauwstraat** for the cluster of bars at the heart of Mechelen's drinking scene. Here also, a footbridge spans the river, leading over to **Haverwerf** (Oats Wharf), where the old Lamot brewery has been turned into the architecturally predictable, very modern **Lamot Congres- en Erfgoedcentrum** (Lamot Conference & Heritage Centre; ⓦlamot-mechelen.be), where they host conferences and put on special events.

Haverwerf facades

Near the Lamot conference centre, three old and contrasting **facades** overlook **Haverwerf**. On the right is **Het Paradijske** (The Little Paradise), a slender structure with fancy tracery and mullioned windows that takes its name from the Garden of Eden reliefs above the first-floor windows. Next door, the all-timber **De Duiveltjes** (The Little Devils), a rare survivor from the sixteenth century, is also named after its decoration, this time for the carved satyrs above the entrance. Finally, on the left and dating to 1669, is **St-Jozef**, a graceful example of the Baroque merchant's house, where the fluent scrollwork swirls over the top of the gable and camouflages the utilitarian, upper-storey door: trade goods were once pulled up the front of the house by pulley and shoved in here for safekeeping. A **pontoon walkway** extends southeast along the river from Haverwerf, making a pleasant stroll en route to the Kerk van Onze Lieve Vrouw over de Dijle.

Kerk van Onze Lieve Vrouw over de Dijle

Onze-Lieve-Vrouwestraat • Free • ⓦ visit.mechelen.be/church-of-our-lady-across-the-dyle

The **Kerk van Onze Lieve Vrouw over de Dijle** (Church of Our Lady across the River Dijle) is a massive pinnacled and turreted affair that was begun in the fifteenth century and finally completed two hundred years later – hence the mix of late Gothic and Baroque features. Apart from its sheer size, the interior is rather mundane, its mediocrity only redeemed by **Rubens**' *Miraculous Draught of Fishes*, an exquisite triptych painted for the fishmongers' guild in 1618 and displayed in the south transept. The central panel has all the usual hallmarks of Rubens in his pomp – note the fishermen's thick, muscular arms – but it's the glistening and wriggling fish that inspire.

ARRIVAL AND INFORMATION   **MECHELEN**

By train and bus Mechelen's train and bus stations are a 15min walk from the town centre, straight ahead down Hendrik Consciencestraat and its continuation Graaf van Egmontstraat and Bruul. Do not take Léopoldstraat, the more obvious road leading from the stations.
Destinations by train Antwerp (every 15min; 18min); Brussels (every 15min; 20min); Ghent (every 15min; 1hr);

Leuven (every 15min; 30min); Lier (direct trains hourly; 15min).

Tourist information Mechelen's tourist office is in the Schepenhuis, just off the Grote Markt, at Vleeshouwersstraat 6 (April–Oct: Mon–Fri 10am–5pm, Sat & Sun 10am–4pm; Nov–March: Mon–Sat 10am–4pm, Sun 12.30–4pm; ⓦvisitmechelen.be).

ACCOMMODATION
SEE MAP PAGE 193

3 Paardekens Begijnenstraat 3 ⓦ3paardekens.com. Down a narrow side street within shouting distance of the cathedral, this medium-sized, three-star hotel has 33 pleasantly modern rooms with bare faux-wood floors and big beds. The roof-top breakfast room has smashing views of the cathedral. €€

Elisabeth Goswin de Stassartstraat 28 ⓦelisabeth-hotel.be. Bright, modern and cheerful, three-star hotel with spick and span rooms in various shades of cream and brown. It has a central location, good breakfasts and a pleasant swimming pool. €€

★ **Martin's Patershof** Karmelietenstraat 4 ⓦmartins hotels.com. One of a small chain, this deluxe four-star hotel occupies an immaculately and imaginatively renovated nineteenth-century church with original stained-glass windows and neo-Gothic arches. The seventy or so rooms – both in the church and in a side building – are divided into five categories, from the 'Cosy' to the 'Exceptional'; all decor is über-modern. Very good breakfasts are served in the former choir. €€€

Vé Mechelen Vismarkt 14 ⓦhotelve.com. This enjoyable and distinctive four-star hotel occupies two intelligently recycled former 1920s factories – an old fish smokery at the front and a cigar-making factory at the back. Some thought has gone into the decor, with pride of place going to a large tubular sculpture, and the clean, modern rooms are well-appointed. The only fly in the ointment is the night-time noise from the square in front in summer – request a room at the back. There's also an on-site spa and fitness centre. €€

EATING
SEE MAP PAGE 193

Brasserie de Margriet Bruul 52 ⓦdemargriet.be. Popular and enjoyable brasserie in one wing of a former seminary; though this part of the building has been rehashed with standard-issue modern furnishings, only the odd flourish hints at what went before. The menu covers all the Flemish bases, but there are a few surprises, notably a local delicacy, the *Mechelse Koekoek* (Mechelen cuckoo), a particularly succulent variety of chicken. Courtyard eating in the summertime, too. €€

Cosma Befferstraat 24 ⓦcosma.be. Smart, contemporary deli brasserie, short walk east of Grote Markt, with refined versions of Belgian and French staples. They serve a particularly tasty steak tartare (raw minced beef), while the blackberries marinated in gin are a winner for dessert. Alternatively, you can have a snack from the deli to take out. €€

Sava Grote Markt 13 ⓦsavamechelen.be. Bright and attractive café with a stylish (very wooden) interior and a pavement terrace. Offers a good range of wines and local beers to wash down a small but tasty range of authentic tapas – try the meatballs. Tapas include a good range of vegetarian dishes. €€

★ **Sister Bean** Vismarkt 26 ⓦsisterbean.be. Unsurprisingly run by sisters, this is a great little café for breakfast, lunch, coffee and delicious home-made cake. The menu consists of soups, salads and quiches, with vegetarian options. €

DRINKING
SEE MAP PAGE 193

Mechelen has a band of busy **bars** down on the **Vismarkt**, which is the focus of the night-time action. While you are here, try one local beer: **Gouden Carolus** (Golden Charles). This delicious dark-brown or blond barley beer was once the favourite tipple of Emperor Charles V (or so they say); it's still brewed here in town.

Café de Wei Nauwstraat 6 ⓦcafedewei.com. This lively, vaguely dishevelled watering hole serves a first-rate selection of beers – including all the Trappist brews – and filling bar food, too.

De Gouden Vis Nauwstraat 7 ⓦdegoudenvis.be. This laid-back, arty 'brown café' with a boho, vaguely Art Nouveau interior and an outside terrace overlooking the river offers a great selection of beers, including the dark and malty Corsendonk Pater.

Fort Breendonk

Brandstraat 57, Willebroek, 16km west of Mechelen • ⓦbreendonk.be • Train from Mechelen to Willebroek (every 30min; 10min); the fort is on the edge of town, a 1.9km walk from the train station; by car, the fort is a stone's throw from the A12 linking Antwerp and Brussels, and well signposted

Built as part of the circle of fortifications that ringed early twentieth-century Antwerp, **Fort Breendonk** became notorious as a Gestapo interrogation centre during World War II. The fort's surly concrete buildings were originally encased in a thick layer of sand, but the Germans had this carted away by their prisoners in 1940. After the war, Breendonk was preserved as a **national memorial** in honour of the four thousand men and women who suffered or perished in its dark, dank tunnels and cells. As you might expect, it's a powerful, disturbing place to visit, with a marked tour taking you through the SS tribunal room, poignantly graffitied cells, the prisoners' barrack room and the bunker that was used as a torture chamber. There's also a **museum** dealing with the German occupation of Belgium, prison life and the postwar trial of Breendonk SS criminals and their collaborators.

Leuven

Half an hour by train from both Mechelen and Brussels, **LEUVEN** offers an easy and enjoyable day-trip from either. The town is the seat of Belgium's oldest **university** (see box, page 199), whose students give the place a lively, informal air – and sustain an army of inexpensive bars and cafés. There are also a couple of notable medieval buildings, the splendid **Stadhuis** and the imposing **St-Pieterskerk**, which is home to three wonderful early Flemish paintings, and in the **Oude Markt** Leuven possesses one of the region's most personable squares. Otherwise, the centre is not much more than an undistinguished tangle of streets with a lot of the new and few remnants of the old. Then again, it's something of a miracle that any of Leuven's ancient buildings have survived at all since the town suffered badly in both world wars: in 1914, much of Leuven was razed during the first German offensive; thirty years later, the town was heavily bombed. Today, it's best known internationally as the home of the Stella Artois brewery.

The Stadhuis

Grote Markt • Charge • ⓦ visitleuven.be/stadhuis

Overlooking the **Grote Markt** is Leuven's magnificent fifteenth-century **Stadhuis**, an extraordinarily light and lacy confection crowned by soaring pinnacles and a dainty, high-pitched roof studded with dormer windows. The 236 statues on the exterior date from the 1850s when the hall was restored, while the niche bases supporting them are exuberantly medieval, depicting biblical subjects in a free, colloquial style and adorned by a panoply of grotesques. The town hall is now mainly used for weddings and functions (the city council meets elsewhere), and you can visit its sumptuous rooms on a daily guided tour.

LEUVEN: ACADEMIC TEARS AND TRAVAILS

The university's history isn't particularly happy, though everything began rosily enough. Founded in 1425, it soon became one of Europe's most prestigious educational establishments: the cartographer Mercator (see page 330) was a student here, and it was here that the religious reformer **Erasmus** (1466–1536) founded the Collegium Trilingue for the study of Hebrew, Latin and Greek, as the basis of a liberal (rather than Catholic) education. However, in response to the rise of **Lutheranism**, the authorities changed tack, insisting on strict **Catholic orthodoxy** and driving the university into an educational retreat. In 1797, the French suppressed the university. Then, when Belgium fell under Dutch rule, William I replaced it with a **Philosophical College** – one of many blatantly anti-Catholic measures which fuelled the Belgian Revolution. Re-established after independence as a bilingual Catholic institution, the university became a hotbed of **Flemish Catholicism**, and French and Flemish speakers were long locked in a bitter nationalist dispute. In 1970, a separate, French-speaking university was founded at **Louvain-la-Neuve**, just south of Brussels – a decision that propelled Leuven into its present role as a bastion of **Flemish thinking**, wielding considerable influence over the region's political and economic elite.

3

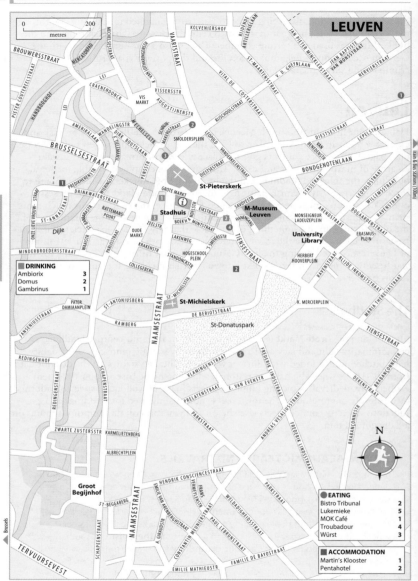

St-Pieterskerk

Grote Markt · **Church** Free · **Chancel** Charge · ⓦ visitleuven.be/sint-pieterskerk

Across the square from the Stadhuis, **St-Pieterskerk** is a rambling, heavily buttressed late Gothic pile whose western facade defeated its architects – hence its stumpy appearance. Work began on the present church in the 1420s and continued until the start of the sixteenth century when the Romanesque towers of its western facade, the last remaining part of an earlier church, were pulled down to make way for a grand replacement. It didn't work out – the foundations proved too weak – and finally, another hundred years on, the unfinished second-attempt towers were capped, creating the truncated, asymmetrical versions that rise above the west entrance today.

Inside, the church is distinguished by its soaring **nave**, whose enormous composite pillars frame a fabulous **rood screen**, an intricately carved piece of stonework surmounted by a wooden Christ. The nave's Baroque **pulpit** is also striking, with a weighty wooden extravagance that shows St Norbert being thrown off his horse by lightning, a dramatic scene set beneath spiky palm trees. This brush with death persuaded Norbert, a twelfth-century German noble, to abandon his worldly ways and dedicate himself to the Church, on whose behalf he founded a devout religious order, the Premonstratensian Canons, in 1120.

The chancel

In the **chancel**, the ambulatory holds three important paintings dating from the fifteenth century. There's a copy of **Rogier van der Weyden**'s marvellous triptych, the *Descent from the Cross*, and two of the few surviving paintings by Weyden's apprentice **Dieric Bouts** (*c.*1415–75), who worked for most of his life in Leuven, ultimately becoming the city's official painter. Bouts' carefully contrived paintings are inhabited by stiff and slender figures in religious scenes almost devoid of action – a frozen narrative designed to stir contemplation rather than strong emotion. Of the **two triptychs** on display here, the gruesome *Martyrdom of St Erasmus*, which has the executioners extracting the saint's entrails with a winch, is less interesting than the *Last Supper*, showing Christ and his disciples in a Flemish dining room; the two men standing up, as well as the couple peeping through the service hatch, are the rectors of the fraternity who commissioned the work. It was customary for Judas to be portrayed in a yellow robe, the colour of hate and cowardice; however, Bouts broke with tradition and made Judas almost indistinguishable from the others – he's the one with his face in shadow and his hand on his left hip. The change of emphasis, away from the betrayal to the mystery of the Eucharist, is continued on the **side panels**: to the left, Abraham is offered bread and wine above a Jewish Passover; to the right, the Israelites gather manna and, below, the prophet Elijah receives angelic succour.

M-Museum Leuven

Léopold Vanderkelenstraat 28 • Charge • ⓦ mleuven.be

Big, flashy and rather groovy, the **M-Museum** (Museum Leuven) occupies a strikingly modern building that's been squeezed into the grounds of an old mansion. There are three main floors here, two devoted to temporary exhibitions, often of modern art, and one to the permanent collection; the museum also hosts gigs and special events and opens a popular rooftop bar in summer. Highlights of the **permanent collection** include medieval sculpture, vestments, porcelain, silver and glassware, plus a good showing for Belgian nineteenth-century sculptors and painters, especially **Constantin Meunier** (see page 73). There are medieval paintings too, most memorably two works by **Rogier van der Weyden**, an exquisite *Seven Sacraments* and a *Holy Trinity*, though this has, at some point, actually been altered: if you look closely at Christ's shoulder, you'll spot a pair of bird's feet. Originally, these were the feet of the dove that represented the Holy Spirit, but somewhere along the line, someone decided that God the Father and the Son would suffice.

The Oude Markt and Groot Begijnhof

The **Oude Markt**, a large cobblestoned square just to the south of the Grote Markt, is the boisterous core of Leuven's nightlife, its assorted bars and cafés occupying a handsome set of tall gabled houses that mostly date from the nineteenth century.

To the immediate east of Oude Markt, **Naamsestraat** leads south towards the **Groot Begijnhof**, a labyrinthine enclave of tall and rather austere red-brick houses tucked away beside the River Dijle. Once home to around three hundred *begijns* – women living as nuns without taking vows – the Begijnhof was bought by the university in 1962, since when its mostly seventeenth-century buildings have been painstakingly restored as **student residences**, and very nice they are too.

ARRIVAL AND INFORMATION
LEUVEN

By train and bus From the train and adjacent bus station, it's an easy 10min walk west along Bondgenotenlaan to the Grote Markt.

Destinations by train Antwerp (every 15min; 50min); Brussels (every 15min; 25min); Hasselt (every 30min;

40min); Lier (every 30min; 40min); Mechelen (every 15min; 30min); Tongeren (every 15min; 1hr 20min).

Tourist information Available at the side of the Stadhuis at Naamsestraat 3 (daily 10am–5pm; ⓦ visitleuven.be).

ACCOMMODATION
SEE MAP PAGE 200

★ **Martin's Klooster** Onze-Lieve-Vrouwstraat 18 ⓦ martinshotels.com. The town's most distinctive hotel by a long chalk, this smooth and polished place occupies an immaculately renovated former monastery with mullioned windows and handsome brick gables. The hundred-odd rooms are tastefully decorated, with beiges and creams predominant, and the location is central, too. Part of a

medium-sized chain. €€€

Pentahotel Alfons Smetsplein 7 ⓦ pentahotels.com. Stylish, modern boutique hotel set over five floors, just off Tiensestraat. They even have a suite for gamers. The cool bar and restaurant on the ground floor serves burgers and the like. Excellent breakfast buffet. €€€

EATING
SEE MAP PAGE 200

With all those students to feed and water, the centre of Leuven heaves with **fast-food joints**, though there's a gaggle of more up-market **restaurants** too – and indeed, Leuven has its own 'restaurant streets', Muntstraat and Tiensestraat.

★ **Bistro Tribunal** Vaartstraat 9 ⓦ bistrotribunal.be. Popular with the legal crowd from the nearby law courts, this is the place to go for an excellent steak, although there's something to please most palates, including salads and pasta. Great cocktails, too. Neat and appealing decor. €€

Lukemieke Vlamingenstraat 55 ⓦ lukemieke.be. Long-established vegetarian café housed in attractive premises and with a good line in daily specials. Verdant garden terrace for outside eating, too. €

MOK Café Diestsestraat 165 ⓦ mokcoffee.be. This café and micro-roastery east of the Grote Markt serves the best coffee in town. The cakes and snacks, including healthy salads, are top-notch, too. €

Troubadour Tiensestraat 32 ⓦ troubadour. This formal, even slightly old-fashioned restaurant offers all the Belgian classics and an excellent range of seafood. Mussels, served every which way, are the house's speciality. €€

Würst Margarethaplein 1 ⓦ wurstdogs.be. Jeroen Meus, Belgium's answer to Jamie Oliver, serves up 'haute dogs' at his café on the northwest corner of St-Pieterskerk. There are vegetarian options, but most people go for the likes of the 'Memphis Soul' – cornbread, coleslaw, pulled beef, würst, sweet relish, Texas honey, fried onion and jalapenos. €

DRINKING
SEE MAP PAGE 200

Ambiorix Oude Markt 3 ☎ 0473 29 50 73. There was a time when all the bars on this square attracted students by the score, but today, the scene is more varied, and this is one of the last student bars left. It has a rough and ready decor and a lively/boisterous clientele.

Domus Tiensestraat 8 ⓦ domusleuven.be. If not the best bar in town, it is undoubtedly the most distinctive. Spreading

over two large floors with ancient beamed ceilings, old bygones on the walls, and a small brewery out the back, it offers an excellent range of ales and a (competent) bar menu.

Gambrinus Grote Markt 13 ☎ 016 20 12 38. The food may not be inspiring, but this handsome old café, with its 1890s leather banquettes, chandeliers and murals, beats all its rivals for decor.

Hasselt

HASSELT, the capital of the province of **Limburg**, is a busy, modern town that acts as the administrative centre for the surrounding region. A pleasant place with stylish shops, the roughly circular city centre fans out from a series of small **interlocking squares**, with surprisingly few old buildings as evidence of its medieval foundation. The city is famous for its **street art**, with around one hundred works by local and international artists at last count; you can pick up a leaflet for a self-guided tour at the tourist office or look online (ⓦstreetartcities.com). Hasselt holds a full complement of museums, including two dedicated to fashion and contemporary art, but the **Jenevermuseum** probably has the most mainstream appeal, not to mention the largest authentic **Japanese garden** in Europe.

Jenevermuseum

Witte Nonnenstraat 19, about 500m north of the Grote Markt • Charge • ⓦ jenevermuseum.be

The **Jenevermuseum** occupies an attractively restored nineteenth-century distillery, and its assorted displays explore the history of Belgium's favourite liquor, jenever, a type of gin. The museum is stuffed with jenever-related artefacts – from stone jars and shot glasses through to advertising posters and brand labels – and provides lots of interesting details: how in good times it was made from corn, in bad times from molasses, and how the government was periodically concerned with the effect it had on the efficiency of the average Belgian worker. The museum makes a couple of its jenevers, and you can taste them in the bar, which is open to the public.

Japanese Tuin

Gouverneur Verwilghensingel 15, 25min walk east of the Grote Markt partly via Koning Boudewijnlaan • Charge •
ⓦ visithasselt.be/en/japanse-tuin

In 1985, Hasselt twinned with the Japanese city of Itami, and to cement their friendship, Hasselt gave Itami a carillon, and Itami helped Hasselt build the **Japanese Tuin**. This peaceful garden, set over 6 acres and open in spring, summer and autumn, provides a glimpse into Japanese culture, with traditional buildings, waterfalls and pools of koi carp. There are Japanese-themed festivals, regular tea-making ceremonies and Ikebana courses (flower art) throughout the year. April is the perfect time to visit, as the cherry blossoms are in bloom.

ARRIVAL AND INFORMATION   HASSELT

By train and bus Hasselt's train and adjoining bus station are a 10min walk from the Grote Markt: turn right out of the train station and proceed down Stationsplein/Bampslaan to the inner ring road; here, cross the road, veer to the right and follow Ridder Portmansstraat and its continuation, Havermarkt.
Destinations by train Antwerp (every 30min; 1hr 30min); Leuven (every 30min; 40min); Liège (hourly; 50min); Lier (every 20min; 1hr); Sint Truiden (hourly; 15min); Tongeren (every 30min; 25min).

Tourist information To the east of the Grote Markt at Maastrichterstraat 59 (April–Oct: Mon–Fri 9am–6pm, Sat 10am–6pm, Sun 10am–6pm; Nov–March: Mon–Fri 9am–6pm, Sat 10am–6pm, Sun 10am–4pm; ⓦvisithasselt.be). They sell a HasPas (€18), which gives access to the museums and a host of excellent benefits such as free or discounted coffee and cake.

ACCOMMODATION AND EATING

SmaakSalon Maastrichterstraat 61 ⓦsmaaksalon.be. This buzzy brasserie is housed in a gorgeous, high-ceilinged, nineteenth-century building next to the tourist office. Dishes are made with local, seasonal ingredients, such as asparagus and watercress; the quiches are particularly delicious. €€

YUP Thonissenlaan 52, 10min walk northwest of tourist office ⓦ yuphotel.com. This novel boutique hotel features strong, blocked colours, and rooms are like ships' cabins. There's an Italian restaurant, a cocktail bar and vending machines serving artisan coffee. A massive piece of street art graces the exterior back wall. €€

SHOPPING

Boon Paardsdemerstraat 13 ⓦchocoladehuisboon. be. Pralines are the name of the game here; their flavours change with the seasons. There's also a tearoom where you can enjoy a yummy hot chocolate.

La Bottega Paardsdemerstraat 9 ⓦlabottega.be. lifestyle store sells clothes and accessories for men, women
Housed in a former jenever factory, this hip concept/ and children and stocks more shoes than you've ever seen.

Tongeren

Engaging **TONGEREN**, about 20km southeast of Hasselt, is a small and amiable
market town on the border of Belgium's language divide. It's also – and this is its
main claim to fame – the oldest town in Belgium, built on the site of a **Roman
camp** that guarded the road to Cologne. Its early history was plagued by misfortune
– destroyed by the Franks and razed by the Vikings – but it did modestly prosper

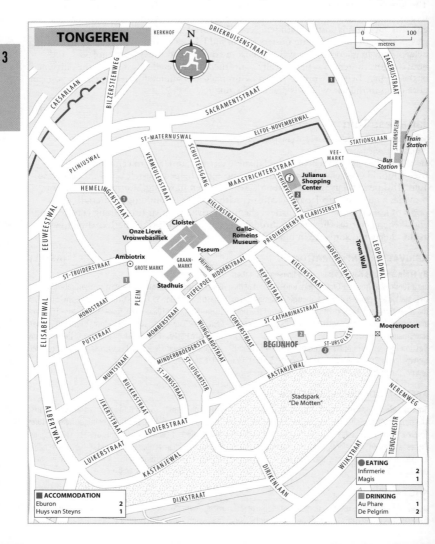

during the Middle Ages as a dependency of the bishops of Liège. Nowadays, it's hard to imagine a more relaxing town, quiet for most of the week except on Sunday mornings (from 7am), when the area around Léopoldwal and the Veemarkt is taken over by the stalls of a vast **flea and antiques market**, probably the largest weekly market of its kind in Belgium.

Onze Lieve Vrouwebasiliek

Grote Markt • Free • ⓦ visittongeren.be/onze-lieve-vrouwebasiliek

Shadowing the Grote Markt, the mostly Gothic **Onze Lieve Vrouwebasiliek** (Basilica of Our Lady) towers over the town with an impressive symmetrical elegance, its assorted gargoyles, elaborate pinnacles and intricate tracery belying its piecemeal construction: it's the eleventh- to sixteenth-century outcome of an original fourth-century foundation, which was the first church north of the Alps to be dedicated to the Virgin. Still very much in use, the yawning interior, with its high, vaulted **nave**, has preserved an element of Catholic mystery, its holiest object a bedecked medieval walnut statue of **Our Lady of Tongeren** – the '**Mariabeeld**' – which stands in the transept surrounded by candles and overhung by a gaudy canopy.

Teseum

Museumkwartier 2, Graanmarkt • Charge • ⓦ teseum.be

Round the side of the church, off the Graanmarkt, is the **Teseum**, the town's successfully revamped treasury and one of the region's most interesting, crowded with reliquaries, monstrances and reliquary shrines from as early as the tenth century. Three artefacts stand out: a beautiful sixth-century **Merovingian buckle**; a pious, haunting eleventh-century **head of Christ**; and an intricate, bejewelled, thirteenth-century reliquary shrine of the **martyrs of Trier**, celebrating a large group of German Christians killed at the hands of the Romans in the third century AD. Visitors can also climb the church tower, stroll the medieval cloister, and peek at the archaeological site, which traces how the church has developed over the past two thousand years

Gallo-Romeins Museum

Kielenstraat 15 • Charge • ⓦ galloromeinsmuseum.be

In a large and beetling modern building, the ambitious **Gallo-Romeins Museum** tracks through the history of Tongeren from prehistoric times to the fall of the Roman Empire. The displays are almost exclusively in Flemish, but a scholarly, English-language guide to the exhibits is available for free at reception. Perhaps inevitably, some sections are light on original artefacts – and here they have opted for dioramas (with mixed results) – but the **best section**, dealing with the culture, attitudes and beliefs of **Roman Tongeren**, is supported by all manner of remains, from pottery, glassware and coins through to tombstones, a mosaic or two and chunks of carved stonework. There's also a very nice café here.

Grote Markt

Presiding over the **Grote Markt** is a haughty statue of **Ambiorix**, with his tumbling locks, bushy moustache and winged helmet. Erected in the middle of the nineteenth century, the statue commemorates a local chieftain who gave the Romans a drubbing here in 54 BC – but whatever he looked like, he surely didn't look much like this, his 'noble savage' visage owing more to Belgian nationalism than historical accuracy. On the Grote Markt is also the eighteenth-century

Stadhuis, whose graceful lines are nicely balanced by an external staircase. The whole caboodle is imitative of the town hall in Liège.

The Begijnhof and Moerenpoort

From the Grote Markt, it's a five-minute stroll to the pretty cottages and terraced houses of the **Begijnhof**, which was founded in the thirteenth century. You can learn more about them at the small Begijnhofmuseum (Onder de Linde 12; Charge; ⓦbegijnhofmuseumtongeren.be). The Begijnhof abuts the **Moerenpoort**, one of Tongeren's six medieval gates, now anchoring a surviving stretch of the medieval city wall, which extends up towards Clarissenstraat.

ARRIVAL AND INFORMATION TONGEREN

By train and bus Tongeren's train and adjoining bus station are a 10min walk from the Grote Markt.
Destinations by train Antwerp (hourly; 1hr 50min); Hasselt (every 30min; 25min); Liège (hourly; 30min); Leuven (every 15min; 1hr 10min); Sint Truiden (hourly; 55min).
Tourist information Tongeren's tourist office is at via

Julianus 2, off Maastrichterstraat (April–June & Sept: Mon–Fri 8.30am–noon & 1–5pm, Sat & Sun 9.30am–5pm; July & Aug: Mon–Fri 8.30am–5pm, Sat & Sun 9.30am–5pm; Oct–March: Mon–Fri 8.30am–noon & 1–5pm, Sat & Sun 10am–4pm; ⓦvisittongeren.be).

GETTING AROUND

By bike Marco's Veloshop at Maastrichterstraat 99 (ⓦmarcosveloshop.be) rents out city bikes electric bikes.

ACCOMMODATION SEE MAP PAGE 204

Eburon De Schiervelstraat 10 ⓦeburonhotel.be. This is a slightly self-conscious boutique hotel with lots of bells and whistles, from flatscreen TVs to rainforest showers. The design is firmly modernist, with acres of white and grey intercepted by streaks of red and brown, all shoehorned into a grand eighteenth-century building that started as a convent. **€€**

★ **Huys van Steyns** Henisstraat 20 ⓦhuysvansteyns. be. Classy boutique hotel in a distinctive nineteenth-century house, 5min walk from the train station. The seven rooms are stylishly furnished, with large, comfortable beds, wooden floors and a scattering of vintage furnishings – such as the grand chandeliers. Excellent breakfasts, too. **€€**

EATING SEE MAP PAGE 204

★ **Infirmerie** St Ursulastraat 11 ⓦinfirmerie.be. Set in the Begijnhof's old hospital, this modern brasserie serves dishes made with local, seasonal products in the chic dining room or the gorgeous courtyard garden. **€€**
Magis Hemelingenstraat 23 ⓦrestaurantmagis.

be. Smart and well-regarded Michelin-star restaurant in a sympathetically modernised nineteenth-century mansion with a garden terrace out the back. The menu is international; the tendency is nouvelle. Particularly strong on local produce. **€€€€**

CYCLING THE HASPENGOUW AND ZOUTLEEUW

Filling out the southern part of the **province of Limburg**, between Tongeren and Sint Truiden, is the **Haspengouw**, an expanse of gently undulating land whose fertile soils are especially suited to fruit growing. The area is at its prettiest during **cherry blossom** time. Still, at any time of the year, its quiet lanes, cycle routes and tiny villages make for a pleasant detour, with **Tongeren** the obvious base, especially as bicycles can be rented from the town's Marco's Veloshop (see page 206). As for particular targets, the cream of the crop is **Zoutleeuw**, some 30km from Tongeren and 7km west of Sint Truiden. This tiny hamlet on the periphery of the Haspengouw boasts the splendid, pre-Reformation **St-Leonarduskerk** (April–Sept Tues–Sun 2–5pm; free; ⓦtoerismevlaamsbrabant.be), which somehow managed to avoid the attentions of both the Protestants and the Napoleonic army. The church is crammed with the accumulated treasures of several hundred years, from reliquaries and religious paintings to **medieval carvings**, including a statue of St Catherine of Alexandria, shown merrily stomping on the Roman Emperor Maxentius, who had her put to death.

DRINKING

SEE MAP PAGE 204

Au Phare Grote Markt 21 ⓦ auphare.be. Nothing seems to have changed here for decades – as of yore, there are ornamental plates on the pelmet and rugs on the tables. The beer menu is wide-ranging (150 at last count) – try *La Cress*, made from local watercress. €

De Pelgrim Brouwersstraat 9 ⓦ herbergdepelgrim.be. This infinitely cosy bar-cum-café occupies antique, wood-beamed premises in the Begijnhof. It offers a good range of bottled beers and tasty sandwiches at lunchtime. €

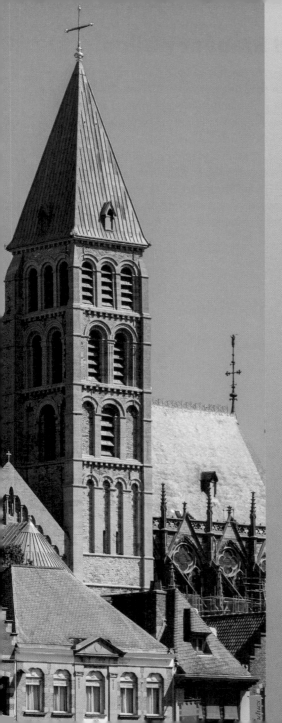

Hainaut and Brabant Wallon

CHARMING TOURNAI

Hainaut and Brabant Wallon

South of Brussels, the western reaches of Wallonia comprise the province of Hainaut and the French-speaking portion of Brabant, Brabant Wallon. The area has its moments, with plenty of rolling farmland and wooded hills dotted across the entire region. Still, industry sets the general tone, especially between Mons and Charleroi. However, even here, the landscape is green and pleasant and puckered with grassed-over spoil tips from the region's coal-mining heyday. In the western part of the province, close to the French border, Tournai is the main highlight. Once part of France, it is now a vibrant, unpretentious town with several decent museums, some tasty restaurants and a magnificent cathedral.

East of Tournai, the vibrant town of **Mons**, with its charming main square, is a pleasant and useful base for further explorations of Hainaut, whose scattered attractions include the zoo at **Pairi Daiza** and the industrial heritage of Grand-Hornu. East again, **Binche** is a humdrum place best known for its explosive February carnival and its carnival museum, while to the north, in Brabant Wallon, the star turn is the battlefield sights of **Waterloo**, though there's also the fabulous Musée Hergé in the otherwise undistinguished town of **Louvain-la-Neuve**; the Romanesque abbey of Ste-Gertrude in Nivelles; and the elegiac ruins of the **Abbaye de Villers**, in a wooded valley on the edge of tiny Villers-la-Ville.

Further east, back in Hainaut, the industrial and engineering centre of **Charleroi** is the area's biggest city. Few would call it pretty, but it is gallantly attempting to reinvent itself, and there are a couple of worthwhile attractions on its southern outskirts – namely, an excellent museum of photography and the mining museum of Bois du Cazier. South of Charleroi, the rural **Botte du Hainaut** is an extension of the Ardennes and is named for its shape, as it juts boot-like into France; most of the 'boot' is part of Hainaut, but it also incorporates a narrow slice of Namur province. Largely bypassed by the Industrial Revolution, the area is a quiet corner of the country, its undulating farmland and forests dotted with the smallest country towns. Among them, Chimay, with its castle and pretty old centre, is the most diverting and is well endowed with facilities for holidaymakers since hundreds of vacationing Belgians hunker down in cottages in the surrounding countryside.

Tournai

Charming **TOURNAI** has a population of just over fifty thousand inhabitants. It is by far Wallonia's most interesting and enjoyable town, its ancient centre latticed by narrow cobbled streets and straddling the black-green, canalised River L'Escaut (Scheldt in Dutch). The town's pride and joy is, of course, its magnificent medieval cathedral, Cathédrale Notre-Dame, arguably the country's most beautiful cathedral. However, there's more: the town centre also holds a brigade of handsome eighteenth-century **mansions** constructed in the French manner. These stately structures feature double doors, stone lower and brick upper storeys and, more often than not, fancy balconies and a pretty central courtyard. Add to this a handful of museums and several decent **restaurants** worthy of a lingering meal and you've reason enough to stay in Tournai for a night or two, especially as tourism here remains distinctly low-key, with barely a tour bus in sight.

Highlights

❶ Cathédrale Notre-Dame, Tournai One of Belgium's most stunningly beautiful cathedrals. See page 214

❷ Binche Carnival Almost certainly the liveliest, most colourful carnival in the country. See page 224

❸ Abbaye de Villers The ruins of this Cistercian abbey comprise one of the region's most evocative sights. See page 226

❹ Memorial 1815, Waterloo Everything you ever wanted to know about this crucial battle – in dramatic detail. See page 229

❺ Bois du Cazier Perhaps the best insight into the region's coal-mining heritage. See page 232

❻ Chimay A charming country town with a picture-postcard Grand-Place. See page 235

HIGHLIGHTS ARE MARKED ON THE MAP ON PAGE 212

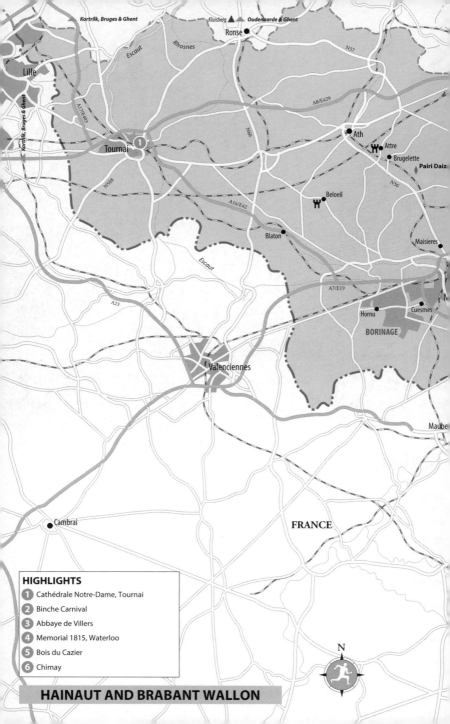

HIGHLIGHTS

1 Cathédrale Notre-Dame, Tournai
2 Binche Carnival
3 Abbaye de Villers
4 Memorial 1815, Waterloo
5 Bois du Cazier
6 Chimay

HAINAUT AND BRABANT WALLON

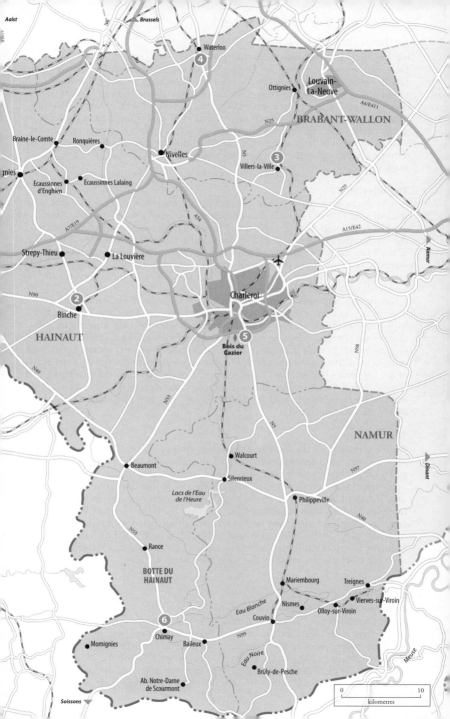

Cathédrale Notre-Dame

pl de l'Evêché 1 · **Cathedral** Free · **Treasury** Charge · ⓦ cathedrale-tournai.be

Dominating the skyline with its distinctive five towers, Tournai's Cathédrale Notre-Dame was built on the profits of the wool and stone trades – and is a seminal construction whose stirring amalgamation of Romanesque and early Gothic styles was much imitated all along the Escaut valley. The present UNESCO World Heritage-listed cathedral is the **third church** on this site, most of it completed in the latter half of the twelfth century, although the choir was reconstructed a century later and is in the Gothic style. It's a stunningly beautiful building that's slowly emerging from a thorough but authentic restoration scheduled to carry on for another five years, maybe more.

The interior

Inside, the twelfth-century nave is a sterling illustration of the Romanesque, as are the intricately carved capitals that distinguish the lowest set of columns, though the vaulted roof is eighteenth-century. Beyond, the **choir** was the first manifestation of the Gothic style in Belgium, and its too-slender pillars later had to be reinforced at the base: the whole choir still leans slightly to one side due to the unstable soil beneath. In front of the choir, the Renaissance rood screen is a flamboyant marble extravaganza by Cornelis Floris (1514–75), embellished by biblical events such as Jonah being swallowed by the whale.

The majestic late twelfth-century **transepts** are, however, the cathedral's most impressive – and most beautiful – feature, imparting a lovely diffuse light through their many windows, some of which (in the south transept) hold superb sixteenth-century stained glass depicting semi-mythical scenes from far back in Tournai's history. Opposite, in the north transept, is an intriguing twelfth-century **mural**, a pockmarked cartoon strip relating the story of St Margaret, a shepherdess martyred on the orders of the Emperor Diocletian. Its characters are set against an exquisite blue background reminiscent of – and influenced by – Byzantine church paintings. Take a look, too, at **Rubens'** characteristically bold *The Deliverance of Souls from Purgatory*, which hangs beside the adjacent chapel.

The treasury

A little dowdy from the outside, the treasury occupies a suite of ecclesiastical rooms, most memorably a splendid wood-panelled, eighteenth-century meeting room and a chapel hung with a rare, albeit faded, example of a medieval **Arras tapestry** made up of fourteen panels depicting the lives of St Piat and of St Eleuthère, the first bishop of Tournai. Elsewhere, amongst the assorted vestments, reliquaries and religious baubles, look out for two magnificent, thirteenth-century silver and gilded copper *châsses*: one, the *châsse de Notre-Dame*, is festooned with relief figures clothed in fluidly carved robes and was completed in 1205 by Nicolas de Verdun. Equally exquisite is a wonderful early sixteenth-century *Ecce Homo* by Quentin Matsys, showing Christ surrounded by the most monstrous of faces.

Le Beffroi

rue Vieux Marché-aux-Poteries 14 · Charge · ⓦ visittournai.be

A short stroll from the cathedral, virtually on the corner of the Grand-Place, Le Beffroi (the Belfry) is the oldest such structure in Belgium, its lower portion dating from 1200. The bottom level once held a prison cell, and the minuscule **balcony** immediately above was where public proclamations were announced. Climb the 257 steps to the top, where the carillon tower has been subjected to architectural tinkering from the sixteenth through to the nineteenth century – hence its ungainly appearance – but the views compensate.

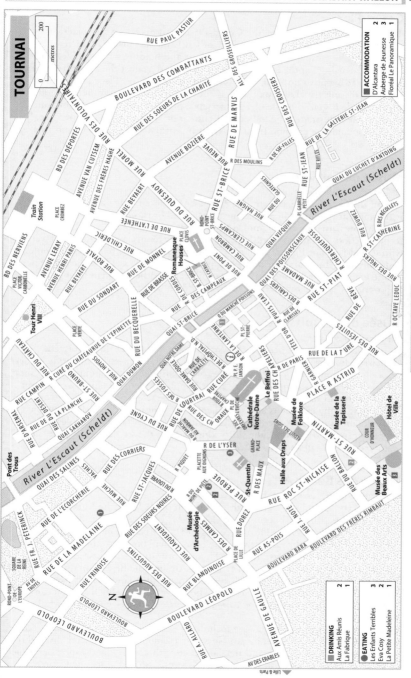

TOURNAI

0 — 200 metres

ACCOMMODATION
D'Alcantara · 2
Auberge de Jeunesse · 3
Floréal Le Panoramique · 1

DRINKING
Aux Amis Réunis · 2
La Fabrique · 1

EATING
Les Enfants Terribles · 3
Eva Cosy · 2
La Petite Madeleine · 1

Train Station

Romanesque Houses

Tour Henri VIII

Pont des Trous

River L'Escaut (Scheldt)

Le Beffroi

Cathédrale Notre-Dame

Musée de Folklore

Musée de la Tapisserie

Hôtel de Ville

Halle aux Draps

Musée d'Archéologie

St-Quentin

Musée des Beaux Arts

▲ Lille & Paris

Grand-Place

A few steps west of Le Beffoi, the Grand-Place is an open and airy piazza, the middle of which is occupied by a statue of Christine de Lalaing, depicted in a heroic 'to the ramparts' pose, clad in armour and holding a hatchet. A local aristocrat, Lalaing led the locals in a last-ditch stand against the Spanish Habsburg army in 1581, but to no avail. The south side of the Grand-Place holds the seventeenth-century Halle aux Draps (Cloth Hall), a crisply symmetrical edifice whose facade is graced by slender Renaissance pilasters and a row of miniature lions on the balustrade. The bulk of the church of St-Quentin, an impressive, bare stone, Romanesque creation from the twelfth century, anchors the Grand Palace's western tip.

Musée de Folklore

réduit des Sions 36 • Charge • ⓦ mufim.tournai.be

Just off the Grand-Place, the amiable **Musée de Folklore** is one of the city centre's better museums, housed in an antique high-gabled brick mansion known as the Maison Tournaisienne and crammed with a treasure-trove of objects. There are reconstructions of various workshops and domestic rooms, a mock-up of a tavern with its old-fashioned *jeu de fer* game (a sort of cross between billiards and boules), and exhibits of Tournai's blue and white pottery. Look also at the replica **cloister** on the first floor, where one of the cells exhibits the pathetic tokens left by those impoverished parents forced to leave their children with the nuns.

Musée de la Tapisserie

pl Reine Astrid 9 • Charge • ⓦ tamat.be

Handily located just southeast of the Grand-Place, the **Musée de la Tapisserie** (Tapestry Museum) features a small selection of antique tapestries alongside modern work on the ground floor – with temporary exhibitions and a restoration workshop above. Tournai was among Belgium's most important pictorial tapestry centres in the fifteenth and sixteenth centuries, producing characteristically massive works juxtaposing many characters and several episodes of history. The pick of the vintage tapestries on display here are the trio recounting Homer's tale of Hercules and his dealings with Laomedon, the shifty king of Troy; they're richly coloured and crammed with detail and wry observation.

Musée des Beaux Arts

rue de l'Enclos, St–Martin 3 • Charge • ⓦ mba.tournai.be

Sitting pretty behind the eighteenth-century Hôtel de Ville, the Musée des Beaux Arts (Fine Arts Museum) occupies an elegant Art Nouveau edifice designed by no less a figure than Victor Horta (see page 73). The central hall and radiating rooms provide a suitably attractive setting for a small but enjoyable collection of mainly Belgian paintings, from the Flemish primitives to the twentieth century. The works here are regularly rotated, though the first room on the left is usually devoted to the nineteenth-century medievalist **Louis Gallait** (whose statue is in the gardens outside), two of whose vast and graphic historical canvases – the *Plague of 1092* and the *Abdication of Charles V* – cover virtually a whole wall each.

Other notable works you may see include an exquisite *Virgin and Child* by Rogier van der Weyden; *St Donatius* by Jan Gossaert; a winter scene by Pieter Bruegel the Younger; a variety of French and Belgian nineteenth-century landscapes; paintings by impressionists Manet and Monet and post-impressionist works by Georges

Seurat; drawings by Vincent Van Gogh, as well as gritty working-class scenes by Constantin Meunier.

Musée d'Archéologie

rue des Carmes 8 • Closed for refurbishment at time of writing • Charge • Ⓦ tournai.be

Inhabiting a rambling old brick building with a splendid tower, the **Musée d'Archéologie** displays a hotchpotch of local archaeological finds, including a heavy-duty Gallo-Roman lead sarcophagus downstairs and, upstairs, a smattering of rare **Merovingian** artefacts, from weapons to brooches and bee-shaped jewellery. The latter is thought to have come from the tomb of the Merovingian king Childeric, which was accidentally unearthed in 1653 on place Clovis, just north of the river. Interestingly, Napoleon adopted the Merovingian bee as his symbol in preference to the **fleur-de-lys**.

ARRIVAL AND INFORMATION | TOURNAI

By train Tournai's train station is located on the northern edge of town, a 10min walk from the centre; the bus station is handily right next door. Tournai is just 28km from Lille, in France.

Destinations Ath (every 30min–1hr; 20min); Brussels (every 30min–1hr; 1hr); Lille – Flandres station (hourly; 30min); Mons (every 30min–1hr; 40min).

Tourist information The tourist office is opposite the cathedral at pl Paul-Emile Janson 1 (April–Oct: Mon–Fri 9am–12.30pm & 1–6pm, Sat & Sun 10am–12.30pm & 1–6pm; Nov–March: Mon–Fri 9am–12.30pm & 1–5pm, Sat 10am–12.30pm & 1–5pm, Sun 1–5pm; Ⓦ visittournai.be). They show a free, 20min film about the cathedral.

ACCOMMODATION | SEE MAP PAGE 215

★ D'Alcantara rue des Bouchers, St-Jacques 2 Ⓦ hotelalcantara.be. Friendly, family-run hotel in an ingeniously converted old mansion, with 25 modern rooms squeezed in behind its eighteenth-century brick and stone façade. D'Alcantara has a pleasant courtyard garden and terrace, and some parking. Light sleepers should avoid the rooms overlooking busy placette aux Oignies at the back. It's by far the best option in town, so book early to avoid disappointment. €€

Auberge de Jeunesse rue St-Martin 64 Ⓦ lesauberges dejeunesse.be. Occupying an attractive old mansion, a couple of minutes' walk from the Grand-Place, this is a well-cared-for, friendly hostel. It has around one hundred beds,

the majority in dormitories of five or six, though there are also a handful of two- and four-bunk rooms. The restaurant serves breakfast, lunch and dinner. Dorms €, doubles €€

Floréal Le Panoramique pl du Mont Saint-Aubert 2 Ⓦ florealgroup.be. Situated on top of a hill – yes, a hill! – and about 8km north of Tournai, this neat and trim, modern hotel is flanked by old cottages and next door to a lugubrious-looking church: the hill concerned – the 149m high Mont St-Aubert – was long the focus of all sorts of pagan shenanigans until the Catholic Church adopted it. The hotel's main selling point is the pleasant views over the countryside – hardly breathtaking, perhaps, but still a welcome change. €€

EATING | SEE MAP PAGE 215

Les Enfants Terribles rue de l'Yser 35 Ⓦ enfants-terribles.be. Just off the Grand-Place, this popular, good value brasserie-style restaurant serves up good steaks, brochettes and salads in a contemporary, minimalist setting. €€

Eva Cosy rue Piquet 6 ☎ 069 77 22 59. Delightful café-restaurant that's the perfect spot for breakfast, lunch or afternoon tea, with many different teas and coffee, home-

made cakes, pasta dishes and outstanding salads on the menu. €

★ La Petite Madeleine rue de la Madeleine 19 Ⓦ lapetitemadeleine.be. Chic and smart restaurant offering a well-considered – and well-presented – menu with seasonal ingredients to the fore. For example, try the chicken with braised onions and tarragon. €€€

DRINKING | SEE MAP PAGE 215

Aux Amis Réunis rue St-Martin 89 ☎ 069 55 96 59. Dating back to 1911, this traditional Belgian bar has a good range of domestic beers on tap and bottled, and its wood-panelled walls and antique feel make it one of the town's most agreeable watering holes. It also has a table for *jeu de fer* - a traditional game originating from Tournai that is somewhat a

cross between billiards and boules (see page 216).

La Fabrique quai du Marché aux Poissons 13b ☎ 069 21 66 72. With a riverside terrace where you can sip away to your heart's content, this large and boisterous bar is one of Tournai's best places for a drink. It has a charming Art Nouveau facade, too.

4

Mons

One of Hainaut's most appealing towns, **MONS** spreads up and over the hill, giving the settlement its name and strategic significance – an obvious place for a key Roman fortress. The town's other military associations are more accidental, for it was here, by happenstance, that the British army fought its first battle in **World War I**. In 1967, after Charles de Gaulle had expelled NATO from Paris, it was here that NATO's SHAPE (Supreme Headquarters Allied Powers in Europe) resited itself, moving to the suburbs of Mons, where it continues to employ hundreds of Americans and other NATO nationals. For visitors today, Mons has several modest attractions and a platoon of good restaurants, with a particular concentration in and around the main square. It also has a couple of decent places to stay, making it a **good base** for exploring much of the region: railways and roads radiate out from the town in all directions, putting most of Hainaut's key attractions within easy reach and making for several enjoyable day-trips (see page 221).

Grand-Place

Mons zeroes in on its Grand-Place, a long, elegant square flanked by terrace cafés and framed by a medley of substantial stone merchants' houses, both old and new. The fifteenth-century **Hôtel de Ville** dominates the square, a considerably altered building whose tiny cast-iron **monkey** on the front wall is reputed to bring at least a year of happiness to all who stroke him with their left hand – hence his bald, polished crown. The porch of the double-doored gateway on the front of the Hôtel de Ville carries several commemorative plaques recalling the town's involvement in past wars: one is for the food sent to the town by the Americans at the end of World War II, another recalls the Canadian brigade who liberated Mons in 1918, and yet another – the most finely executed – honours the bravery of the Irish Lancers, who defended the town in 1914. The tunnel on the far side of the courtyard brings you to a small enclosed **garden**, a peaceful retreat from the buzz of the square, and home to the Musée du Doudou, devoted to the town's most colourful annual event.

Musée du Doudou

Jardin du Mayeur & rue du 11 Novembre • Charge • ⓦ museedudoudou.mons.be

Every year, in late May or early June, on the weekend of Trinity Sunday, Mons hosts the festival of the Ducasse de Mons or **Doudou**. This kicks off with a solemn

---

THE ANGELS OF MONS

Mons has figured prominently in both world wars. At the start of **World War I**, in August 1914, the British forces found themselves outnumbered by the advancing Germans to about twenty to one. The subsequent **Battle of Mons** began on 26 August, and the British – despite grand heroics (the first two Victoria Crosses of the war were awarded here) – were inevitably forced to retreat. The casualties might have been greater had the troops not been hard-bitten professional soldiers. Meanwhile, back in England, the horror-story writer and part-time mystic **Arthur Machen** (1863–1947) wrote an avowedly fictional tale for the *Evening News* in which the retreating troops were assisted by a host of bowmen, the ghosts of Agincourt. Within weeks, rumour had transmogrified Machen's bowmen into the **Angels of Mons**, which had supposedly hovered overhead just at the point when the Germans were about to launch their final attack, causing them to fall back in fear and amazement. Machen himself was amazed at this turn of events, but the angel story was unstoppable, taking on the status of legend, and those soldiers lucky enough to return home obligingly reported similar tales of supernatural happenings on the battlefield. There's a **painting** of the angelic event by Marcel Gillis in the Mons Hôtel de Ville.

ceremony on Saturday in the church of Ste-Waudru when the casket holding the saint's remains is given to the city's mayor and assorted dignitaries. On Sunday morning, the casket is processed around the town in a golden carriage – the **Car d'Or** – accompanied by a thousand-odd costumed participants, with everyone joining in to push the carriage back up the hill to the church with one huge shove: failure to get it there in one go brings bad luck.

After the relics are safely back in the church, chaos erupts on the Grand-Place, with a lively re-enactment battle – known here as 'Lumeçon' – between St George and the Dragon. St George and his 38 helpers slug it out with the dragon and his entourage – it's considered good luck to grab a hair or ribbon from the dragon's tail, which the crowd does its best to do as it whips through the air just above their heads. Inevitably, George and crew emerge victorious. The festival's origins, background information on the saint and the dragon and film clips of the Doudou are featured here in the enjoyable **Musée du Doudou** – nothing beats seeing the festival in person, but this is the next best thing.

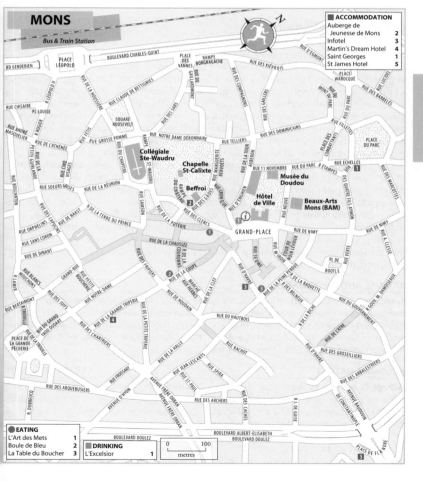

Beaux-Arts Mons (BAM)

rue Neuve 8 • Charge • ⦿ bam.mons.be

Around the corner from the Hôtel de Ville, **Beaux-Arts Mons** (BAM) occupies a slick and stylish modern building with two main floors for temporary exhibitions of modern and contemporary art. Many exhibitions focus on local themes – for example, *Van Gogh in the Borinage* and *Mons, from reality to legend*. Others have a more international dimension – for instance, *Andy Warhol: Life, Death and Beauty*.

Beffroi

Rampe du Chateau • Charge • ⦿ beffroi.mons.be

A hop, step, and a jump from the Grand-Place, at the end of a steep lane, the town's Baroque **Beffroi** is a splendid structure that rises high above a miniature park that's a favourite picnic spot. Completed in 1699, the belfry long served as a watchtower – as the modest exhibitions inside now explain. From the top, there are also expansive views over the town and its surroundings.

Collégiale Ste-Waudru

Rue du Chapitre • **Church** Free • **Treasury** Charge • ⦿ waudru.be

Near the belfry, the **Collégiale Ste-Waudru** is a massive and majestic church whose heavily buttressed nave and choir are a fine illustration of the Gothic with a superb set of gargoyles to round things off. The church is named after Ste Waudru (St Waltrude), a virtuous seventh-century aristocrat who dedicated much of her life to the church and founded a small religious community in Mons. The elaborate, eighteenth-century Car d'Or, used to transport her casket around town in the annual Doudou festival (see page 218), can be seen in the nave, though much more interesting is the work of the local sixteenth-century sculptor, architect and builder **Jacques du Broeucq**. The latter's glorious alabaster rood loft was broken up by French Revolutionary soldiers in 1797, but thankfully, much of it was saved, and pieces are now spread around different parts of the church, especially in the transepts. These high-relief carvings are wonderful, designed to explain the story of Christ to a largely illiterate congregation: the north transept holds the reliefs of the *Resurrection*, the *Ascension* and the *Descent of the Holy Ghost*; the **south transept** has the *Flagellation of Christ* and the *Bearing of the Cross*, as well as Broeucq's memorial plaque; chapels in the ambulatory display other fragments, including an exquisite *Last Supper*. The church **treasury** is also of some mild interest with a battery of vestments, reliquaries and statuettes shown alongside items associated with, or dedicated to, Ste Waudru.

ARRIVAL AND INFORMATION   MONS

By train The train station (and adjacent bus station) is on the western edge of the town centre, fronting onto pl Léopold. From here, it's a 10min walk up the hill to the Grand-Place.
Destinations Ath (hourly; 30min); Brussels (every 30min–1hr; 1hr); Charleroi-Sud (every 30min; 35min); La Louvière-Sud (hourly; 15min); Tournai (every 30min–1hr; 40min).

Tourist information The tourist office is handily located at Grand-Place 27 (April–Oct: daily 9.30am–5.30pm; Nov–March: Mon–Sat 9.30am–5.30pm, Sun 9.30am–4.30pm; ⦿ visitmons.be).

ACCOMMODATION   SEE MAP PAGE 219

Auberge de Jeunesse de Mons rampe du Château 2 ⦿ lesaubergesdejeunesse.be. Well-equipped, modern HI hostel in a great location, metres from the Grand-Place and the belfry. There are self-catering facilities, a café-bar and parking, plus over one hundred beds spread over double rooms and four-berth dorms. Dorms €̄, doubles €̄
Infotel rue de Havré 32 ⦿ hotelinfotel.be. Set in a

refurbished old house with a modern extension, this oddly named but very friendly hotel has twenty-odd spick and span modern rooms. Great location, just 100m from the Grand-Place, and free parking. €̄€̄
Martin's Dream Hotel rue de la Grande Triperie 17 ⦿ martinshotels.com/en. It is an ingenious conversion of a church – to the extent that, apart from the Gothic window

tracery and giant columns, you might not even realise you're in a church. This is Mons' designer hotel, with spacious black, white, and grey rooms with flatscreen TVs, walk-in showers, and bespoke carpets with signature graffiti. There's a bar serving cocktails, a brasserie and a more upscale restaurant downstairs. Comfy and convenient. €€

★ **Saint Georges** pl du Parc 32 ⓦ hotelsaintgeorges. be. Easily the best hotel in town, this privately-owned establishment occupies a splendid eighteenth-century mansion (and a more modern annexe) with lots of period details – from the big wooden doors and mosaic floor to the high ceilings and long, shuttered windows. There are fifteen

comfortable studio apartments here, all with kitchenettes and a large garden with sofas; a tasty breakfast is served in your room. In an enjoyable part of town, a 5min walk from the Grand-Place, but don't turn up on spec – arrange to meet the owner-manager at a set time. €€

St James Hotel pl de Flandre 8 ⓦ hotelstjames.be. This small hotel in a solid stone-and-brick eighteenth-century house is the closest Mons gets to 'boutique', with very comfortable rooms in a modernist style, either in the main building or an equally well-appointed garden annexe. Free parking, too. A 10min walk east of the Grand-Place. €€

EATING

SEE MAP PAGE 219

L'Art des Mets rue des Clercs 9 ⓦ artdesmets.be. Classic Franco-Belgian restaurant with a rather traditional air where the emphasis is on the set menus – their lunches are the most economical. A sample main course would be sliced lobster with truffle and mhamsa risotto. Family run and a short walk from the Grand-Place. €€€

★ **Boule de Bleu** rue de la Coupe 46 ⓦ bouledebleu. com. Good organic soups, huge salads and filled focaccia

alongside a wide selection of teas and organic wines and beers. Coffee desserts served in glasses with ice cream are especially popular. The interior is rustic and inviting, with a covered courtyard at the back. €€

La Table du Boucher rue d'Havré 49 ⓦ latableduboucher. be. This smart, modern restaurant with banquette seats offers perfectly cooked steaks, lamb and veal dishes, and a fish of the day. Prices are moderate to high. €€€

DRINKING

SEE MAP PAGE 219

4

L'Excelsior Grand-Place 29 ☎ 065 36 47 15. There's no shortage of bars on the main square, but this establishment's

leather benches and wooden panelling give it a warm and welcoming feel. Like its neighbours, it has a pavement terrace.

Around Mons

Mons is a convenient base for seeing some of the best of **Hainaut**, with a central position in the province and good transport connections. The town also stands on the eastern edge of the Borinage. This densely populated working-class area was, until recently, one of Belgium's three main **coalfields**, an ugly jigsaw of mining villages and spoil tips. Here, a young Van Gogh, the Protestant pastor, spent two years ministering to the locals and, more memorably, drawing some of them too. As late as 1957, there were 65,000 colliers in the Borinage, but a decade or two later, the mines had all closed, though at least the one-time spoil tips dotting the landscape have since been greened and wooded. There are a couple of attractions to tempt you out into this post-industrial sprawl, specifically a house that **Vincent van Gogh** once lived in and the Grand-Hornu, a very real remnant of the region's industrial past.

North of Mons towards Ath is the excellent zoo-cum-theme park of Pairi Daiza – worth a special trip. Beyond it are the handsome chateaux of Beloeil and Attre – though these are best visited with your own transport. Finally, to the northeast of Mons, there's the Canal du Centre and its fantastic boat lifts, a UNESCO World Heritage Site that is perhaps the most tangible working manifestation of the region's salad days.

Vincent van Gogh house

rue du Pavillon 3, 7033 Cuesmes, 5km southwest of Mons • Charge • ⓦ maisonvangogh.mons.be • Several local buses run from Mons bus station to the Cuesmes Grand Marais stop, a 4min walk from the Van Gogh House; route planning on ⓦ letec.be

On the southern outskirts of Mons, the former pit village of CUESMES was home to Vincent van Gogh from 1879 until the following year, and the tidily restored two-storey **brick house** where he lodged is open to the public. Van Gogh was sent to the Borinage as a missionary, choosing to live in acute poverty and helping the villagers in their fight for social justice. Here, he started drawing seriously, taking his inspiration from the hard life of the miners – 'I dearly love this sad countryside of the Borinage and it will always live with me,' he said. Unfortunately, despite this emotional bond, there's very little to recall his time here – merely a couple of **period rooms** and no original artwork.

Grand-Hornu

rue Saint-Louise 82, B-7301 Hornu, 13km west of Mons • Charge • ⓦ cid-grand-hornu.be • Bus Nos 7 or 9 from Mons bus station (every 15min; 20min); the Grand-Hornu bus stop is on the main road – rue de Mons – from where it's a 500m walk

In the village of **HORNU**, between 1810 and 1830, the French industrialist Henri De Gorge set about building the large complex of offices, stables, workshops, foundries and furnaces that comprise **Grand-Hornu**. De Gorge owned several collieries in the area, so the project made economic sense. He opted to build an elegant version of the Neoclassical style and constructed more-than-adequate workers' houses just outside, which survive to this day. This progressiveness did not necessarily win the workers' affection – in 1830, they came close to lynching him during an industrial dispute over wages – but De Gorge's mines, as well as Grand-Hornu itself, remained in operation until 1954. After that, the complex fell into disrepair but was revived in the 1990s. With its large elliptical **courtyard** and derelict workshops, it remains a compelling slice of nineteenth-century industrial history. The old office buildings on one side now hold the **Musée des Arts Contemporains** (ⓦ mac-s.be), which has established a reputation for the quality of its temporary contemporary art exhibitions. There's a bookshop, further exhibition areas (one devoted to design) and a nice café.

Pairi Daiza

Domaine de Cambron, B7940 Brugelette, 20km north of Mons, just off the N56 • Charge • ⓦ pairidaiza.eu • Cambron-Casteau train station, on the Mons–Ath line, is a 10min walk away

A large private zoo founded among the ruins of a Cistercian monastery, **Pairi Daiza**, is justifiably popular. The name means 'walled garden' or 'paradise' in ancient Persian and features a lake, beautiful **gardens** and a series of deftly created habitats – you could happily spend a whole day and not see anything twice. One zone is dotted with oriental temples and streams crossed by bridges and has a rope walkway that gives views over the entire park; it's also home to the park's star pair of **pandas**, Hao Hao and Xing Hiu. There's a savannah habitat, with elephants, rhinos, lions, cheetahs, and giraffes you can pet while they're feeding, and an 'Indian Kingdom of Ganesha', where Indian elephants are treated to the most sumptuous of enclosures and a swimming pool. There's also a **reptile house** fashioned out of a beached container ship, which you can reach via a fabulous 'African village' on stilts. Predictably, places to eat and shop abound, but overall, Paira Daiza is what it sets out to be – a *jardin des mondes* that feels quite apart from the world outside and is worth a day of anyone's time, with kids or without.

Beloeil

rue du Chateau 11, Beloeil, 25km northwest of Mons • Charge • ⓦ chateaudebeloeil.com • Best visited by car, though you can get there by train and bus from Mons; the fastest routing (around 1hr) departs every 2hr (consult ⓦ belgiantrain.be/en)

The **château de Beloeil**, about halfway between Mons and Tournai, broods over the village that bears its name, its long brick and stone facades redolent of the enormous wealth and power of the **Ligne family**, regional bigwigs since the fourteenth century. This aristocratic clan began by strengthening the medieval fortress built here by their predecessors, turning it into a commodious **moated castle** that was later remodelled and refined on several occasions. The wings of the present structure date from the late seventeenth century, while the main body, though broadly compatible, was rebuilt after a fire in 1900. Without question, a stately building, it has a somewhat gloomy air. However, the lavish interior is stuffed with tapestries, paintings and furniture – the collected indulgences (and endless portraits) of various generations of Lignes. Despite all this grandeur, only one member of the family – **Charles Joseph** (1735–1814) – cuts much historical ice: a diplomat, author and field marshal in the Austrian army, Joseph's pithy comments were much admired – and often repeated - by his fellow aristocrats. Several of Beloeil's rooms contain paintings of Charles' life and times, and there's also a small selection of his personal effects, including the malachite clock given to him by a fellow reactionary, the tsar of Russia. Otherwise, the best parts are the **library**, which contains twenty thousand volumes, many ancient and beautifully bound, and the eighteenth-century formal gardens, probably the largest in the country, whose lakes and flower beds stretch away from the house to a symmetrical design by Parisian architect and decorator Jean-Michel Chevotet.

Château d'Attre

Av du Château 8, Attre, 21km north of Mons • Charge • ⓦ attre.be • Best visited by car; the nearest station is Mevergnies-Attre, just over 1km south of the château and on the Mons–Ath line

Completed in 1752, the elegant, Neoclassical **Château d'Attre**, just to the northeast of Beloeil, was built on the site of a distinctly less comfortable medieval fortress on the orders of the Count of Gomegnies, chamberlain to Emperor Joseph II. It soon became a favourite haunt of the ruling Habsburg elite – especially the Archduchess Marie-Christine of Austria (1742–98), the two-time governor of the Austrian Netherlands.

The château

The château's original, carefully selected furnishings and decoration have survived pretty much intact, providing an insight into the tastes of the time – from the **sphinxes** framing the doorway and the silk wrappings of the Chinese room through to the extravagant parquet floors, the ornate moulded plasterwork and the archducal room hung with the first hand-painted wallpaper ever to be imported into the country (it dates to about 1760). There are also excellent silver, ivory and porcelain pieces, as well as **paintings** by Frans Snyders, a friend of Rubens, and the Frenchman Jean-Antoine Watteau, whose romantic, idealised canvases epitomised early eighteenth-century aristocratic predilections. Neither is the castle simply a display case: it's well cared for and has a lived-in, human feel, in part created by the arrangements of freshly picked flowers chosen to enhance the character of each room.

The park

The surrounding park straddles the River Dendre and holds several curiosities, notably a 24m high **artificial rock** with subterranean corridors and a chalet-cum-hunting lodge – all to tickle the fancy of the archduchess. The ruins of a tenth-century **tower**, also in the park, may have pleased her risqué sensibilities too; it was reputed to have been the hideaway of a local villain, a certain Vignon who, disguised as a monk, robbed passing travellers.

Canal du Centre

To the northeast of Mons lies one of the quietest corners of Hainaut. In this pocket-sized district, drowsy little villages and whitewashed farmhouses interrupt a bumpy landscape patterned by a maze of narrow country lanes. The area is perhaps best known for the **Canal du Centre**, which has flowed through this region since its inception in 1888 to connect the rivers Meuse and Scheldt – a distance of around 20km. Classified as a **UNESCO World Heritage Site**, the canal climbs up 23m using six locks before reaching a 7km stretch, negotiated by a series of four historic hydraulic boat lifts – each covering a change in level of 15–16m. All four are in working order but were retired from commercial use in 2002 with the opening of the gargantuan Strépy-Thieu Boat-Lift.

Strépy-Thieu Boat-Lift

rue Raymond Cordier 50, Strépy-Thieu, 15km northeast of Mons • Charge • Ⓦ canalducentre.be

The tallest boat lift in Europe, the **Strépy-Thieu Boat-Lift**, took twenty years to construct (1982–2002). You can admire it from the outside, but if you have any interest in engineering, it's worth taking the one-hour self-guided tour – you can watch a film showing how the lift was built and how it works, not to mention take a peek at the engine room.

Binche

A sleepy little town halfway between Mons and Charleroi, **BINCHE** jolts into life every year when it hosts perhaps the country's best and most renowned carnival (see box, page 224). Inevitably, the carnival provides the main reason for a visit – but not just when it's on, as Binche also holds a fascinating **museum** dedicated to this particular festival. The museum is at the far end of Binche's Grand-Place, a spacious square edged by the onion-domed **Hôtel de Ville**, built in 1555 by Jacques du Broeucq to replace a version destroyed by the French the previous year. Close by, a small park marks the site of the town's medieval **ramparts**, which curve impressively around most of the town centre, complete with 22 towers.

Musée International du Carnaval et du Masque

rue de Saint-Moustier 10 • Charge • Ⓦ museedumasque.be

Housed in a former school, the delightful **Musée International du Carnaval et du Masque** is signalled by a statue of a Gille – one of the figures that dance through the city streets during carnival. Naturally, the museum's emphasis is on the Binche festivities, and they do a good job explaining the event with the help of a free **audio guide**, wall-mounted screens and photos that convey how central carnival is to the town and its people. Costumes and various objects complete the picture and are complemented by a wide assortment of masks and fancy dresses from other carnivals worldwide.

CARNIVAL IN BINCHE

Carnival has been celebrated in Binche since the fourteenth century. The festivities last several weeks, starting in earnest on the Sunday before **Shrove Tuesday** when thousands turn out in costume. During the main events on **Shrove Tuesday**, the traditional **Gilles** – males born and raised in Binche – appear in clogs and embroidered costumes from dawn onwards, banging drums and stamping on the ground. In the morning, they wear 'green-eyed' **masks**, dancing in the Grand-Place carrying bunches of sticks to ward off evil spirits. In the afternoon, they don their plumes – a mammoth piece of headgear made of ostrich feathers – and throw oranges at the crowd as they pass through town in procession. The rituals of the carnival date back to pagan times, but the Gilles were probably inspired by the fancy dress worn by Mary of Hungary's court at a banquet held in honour of Charles V in 1549: Peru had recently been added to the Habsburg Empire, and the courtiers celebrated the conquest by dressing up in (their version of) **Inca gear**.

ENCIRCLING BRUSSELS: VLAAMS BRABANT

The Flemings claim the lion's share of the Brabant province, and **Vlaams Brabant** (Flemish Brabant) encircles Brussels, thinning down to a narrow corridor of Flemish-speaking communities to the immediate south of the capital – the cause of much inter-communal (Walloon v Fleming) wrangling (see pages 319 and 322). The highlights of Vlaams Brabant, the pick of which is **Leuven** (see page 199), are covered in 'Chapter 3'.

ARRIVAL AND INFORMATION BINCHE

By train Binche is the only station on a short branch line, which intersects with the Mons/Charleroi main line at La Louvière-Sud; connections between the main and the branch lines are not especially good. In Binche, the train station is a 10min walk from the Grand-Place: take rue Gilles Binchois from the square in front of the station building and keep straight until you reach the end of rue de la Gaieté, where you turn left.

Destinations La Louvière-Sud (hourly; 15min).

Tourist information Binche's tourist office is in the Hôtel de Ville on the Grand-Place (Mon–Fri 10am–noon & 1–5pm, Sat & Sun 2–6pm; ⓦ binchetourisme.be).

Brabant Wallon

To the northeast of Mons, you cross the border into **Brabant**, whose southern, French-speaking districts – known as **Brabant Wallon** – form a band of countryside that rolls up to and around Waterloo, the site of the famous battle and the location of two outstanding museums that examine the conflict and its historical context. En route, **Nivelles** is the obvious target, an amiable, workaday town worth a visit for its interesting church as well as its proximity to the beguiling ruins of the Cistercian abbey at Villers-la-Ville, a short car ride away (train travellers have to make the trip via Charleroi). The **Musée Hergé**, meanwhile, is the highlight of the otherwise entirely missable new town of **Louvain-la-Neuve**.

Nivelles

Now a small industrial town, **NIVELLES** grew up around its **abbey**. It was founded in the seventh century and flourished to become one of the most powerful religious houses in Brabant until its suppression by the French Revolutionary Army in 1798. Today, the abbey is recalled by the town's only significant sight, the giant bulk of the Collégiale Ste-Gertrude.

Collégiale Ste-Gertrude

Grand-Place • Free • ⓦ collegiale.be

The **Collégiale Ste-Gertrude** was erected as the abbey church in the tenth century, a vast edifice dominating the Grand-Place at the heart of Nivelles. Built in the Ottonian style (the forerunner of Romanesque), with a transept and chancel at each end of the nave, the church is a beautiful and unusual construction. The west chancel represents imperial authority, and the east papal is an architectural illustration of the tension between the pope and the emperor that plagued Western Europe during the reign of the East Frankish king Otto I (912–73) and his immediate successors. The simple **interior** is long and lofty, with a nave supported by sturdy pillars, between which sits a flashy oak and marble pulpit by the eighteenth-century Belgian artist Laurent Delvaux, who also executed the statues at the western end of the nave and in the apse.

The heavily restored, fifteenth-century **wooden wagon** kept in the church is used to carry Ste Gertrude's silver casket in procession through the fields around Nivelles in the autumn. Little is known of Gertrude, but legend asserts that she was the first abbess of Nivelles, a gentle, miracle-making goodie who offered succour to travellers and protection against rats and mice – her symbol is a pastoral staff with a mouse running along it.

ARRIVAL AND INFORMATION   NIVELLES

By train From Nivelles' train station, it's a 10min walk west along rue de Namur to the L-shaped Grand-Place.
Destinations Brussels (every 30min; 30min); Charleroi (every 20min; 30min); Mons (every 20min; 1hr 20min with one change); Waterloo (every 30min; 15min).
Tourist information Nivelles' tourist office is at rue des Saintes 48 (daily 9am–5pm; ⓦ tourisme-nivelles.be), a signed, 5min walk up from the Grand-Place.

EATING AND DRINKING

Dis Moi Où? rue Ste-Anne 5 ⓦ dis-moiou.be. Just off the northeastern corner of the main square, this inviting French restaurant serves top-notch food, including mains such as cod in a mousseline sauce. The decor is brisk, modern, and rather appealing.

Le P'tit Gabriel square Gabrielle 11 ⓦ leptitgabriel.be. Just a few metres from the *Dis Moi* restaurant, this fab little place serves excellent traditional Burgundian fondues – accompanied by chips, salads and various sauces. €€

Abbaye de Villers

rue de l'Abbaye 55, 1495 Villers-la-Ville, 20km east of Nivelles • Charge • ⓦ villers.be • Trains run to Villers-la-Ville from Charleroi to the south and Ottignies to the north (Mon–Fri hourly; Sat & Sun every 2hr); the abbey is 1.6km from Villers-la-Ville station: follow the sign to Monticelli, head up and over the gently sloping cobbled street until, after about 100m, you reach a T-junction; turn right and follow the road round until you see the ruins ahead

The ruined Cistercian **Abbaye de Villers** nestles in a lovely wooded dell on the edge of pint-sized **VILLERS-LA-VILLE** and is one of the most haunting and evocative sights in Belgium. The first monastic community – an abbot and twelve monks – settled here in 1146. From these humble beginnings, the abbey became a wealthy local landowner, managing a domain of several thousand acres, with numbers rising to about a hundred monks and three hundred lay brothers. A healthy annual income funded the construction of an extensive **monastic complex**, most erected in the thirteenth century. The less austere structures, such as the Abbot's Palace, rose in a second spurt of activity some four hundred years later. In 1794, the French Revolutionary Army ransacked the monastery, and later, a railway was ploughed through the grounds. Still, more than enough survives – albeit in various states of decay – to pick out Romanesque, Gothic and Renaissance features and make some mental reconstruction of abbey life possible.

From the **entrance**, a path crosses the courtyard in front of the Abbot's Palace to reach the warming room (*chauffoir*), the only place in the monastery where a fire would have been kept going all winter – it still has its original chimney. The fire provided a little heat to the adjacent rooms: on one side, the monks' workroom (*salle des moines*), used for reading and studying; on the other, the sizeable Romanesque-Gothic refectory (*réfectoire*), lit by ribbed twin windows topped with chunky rose windows. Next door is the **kitchen** (*cuisine*), which contains a few remnants of the drainage system that once piped waste to the river and a central hearth, whose chimney helped air the room. The most spectacular building, however, is the church (*église*), which fills out the north corner of the complex. With pure lines and elegant proportions, it displays the change from Romanesque to Gothic – the transept and choir are the first known examples of **Brabantine Gothic**. The building has the dimensions of a cathedral, 90m long and 40m wide, with a majestic nave whose roof was supported on strong cylindrical columns. An unusual feature is the series of bull's-eye windows lighting the transepts. Of the original twelfth-century cloister (*cloître*) adjoining the church, a pair of twin windows is pretty much all that remains, flanked by a two-storey section of the old monks' quarters.

Musée Hergé

rue du Labrador 26, Louvain-la-Neuve, 15km northeast of Villers-la-Ville & 40km southeast of Brussels • Charge (includes audio guide in English) • ⓦ museeherge.be • The museum is about 400m from Louvain-la-Neuve train station, connecting with Brussels (hourly; 1hr)

Established in the 1970s as a French-speaking rival to the Flemish university town of Leuven (see page 199), new-town **LOUVAIN-LA-NEUVE** is hardly prepossessing, but it does hold one notable attraction: the **Musée Hergé**, honouring perhaps the most famous Belgian of them all, Georges Remi (better known as **Hergé**), the creator of *Tintin* (see box, page 227). The museum, the brainchild of Hergé's second wife, Fanny Rodwell, concentrates on his life and work, but his most celebrated creation inevitably grabs attention. A couple of rooms take you through Hergé's 'dreary but happy' childhood, his early cartoon creations, and work in advertising and design, while later ones examine the inception of the *Tintin* stories in detail, with displays on each of the principal characters as well as Hergé's influences in creating them – foreign travel, science and cinema among them. It's all made accessible and entertaining by **audio guides**, which provide excellent commentary and background. However, whether Hergé was quite the towering creative genius the museum makes him out to be is debatable. Nonetheless, it's all brilliantly done and enjoyable whether you're a fan of the man and his quiffed reporter.

Waterloo

WATERLOO is no more than a run-of-the-mill suburb of Brussels. Still, the name has a resonance far beyond its size, and its battlefield is easily the most popular attraction in Brabant Wallon, drawing scores of day-trippers from the capital. On 18 June 1815, at this small crossroads town on what was once the main route to Brussels from France, **Wellington** masterminded the battle that ended Napoleon's imperial ambitions. The engagement turned out to have far more significance than even its generals realised. Not only was this the last throw of the dice for the formidable army born of the French Revolution, but it also marked the end of France's prolonged attempts to dominate Europe militarily.

4

Nevertheless, the historical importance of Waterloo has not saved the **battlefield** from interference – a motorway cuts right across it – and if you do visit, you'll need a lively imagination to picture what happened and where – unless that is, you're around to see one of the re-enactments, which take place in June every year (the big ones occur every five years, with the next scheduled for 2025). Otherwise, the best place to start a visit is

---

TINTIN

Tintin was the creation of Brussels-born **Georges Remi** (1907–83) under his pen name **Hergé**. Remi's first efforts (pre-*Tintin*) were sponsored by a right-wing Catholic journal, *Le XXième Siècle*, and in 1929, when this same paper produced a kids' supplement – *Le Petit Vingtième* – Remi was given his first big break. He was asked to create a two-page comic strip, and the result was *Tintin in the Land of the Soviets*, a didactic tale about the evils of Bolshevism. His titular character's Soviet adventure lasted until May 1930, and to round it all off, the director of *Le XXième Siècle* decided to stage a PR-stunt reception to celebrate his return from the USSR. Remi – along with a Tintin lookalike – hopped on a train just east of Brussels, and when they pulled into the capital, they were mobbed by scores of excited children; the rest, as they say, is history.

Remi immediately decided on the famous **quiff**, but other features – the mouth and expressive eyebrows – only came later. His popularity was – and remains – quite **phenomenal**: *Tintin* has been translated into sixty languages, and over **twenty million copies** of the comic *Le Journal de Tintin*, Remi's independent creation first published in 1946, have been sold – and that's not mentioning all the *Tintin* TV cartoon series.

the fascinating **Musée Wellington** in Waterloo itself, after which it's a 4km trip south to the battlefield, where the Memorial 1815 comprises an excellent museum as well as the **Butte de Lion**, a huge earth mound – part viewpoint, part commemoration – and the nearby Hougoumont farm, where some of the fiercest fighting took place.

Musée Wellington

ch de Bruxelles 147 • Charge (included in Pass 1815, see page 230) • ⓦ museewellington.be

The **Musée Wellington** occupies the old inn where Wellington slept the nights before and after the battle. It's an intriguing affair, whose displays detail the build-up to – and the course of – the battle via plans and models, alongside an engaging hotchpotch of personal effects. Room 4 holds the bed where Alexander Gordon, Wellington's principal aide-de-camp, was brought to die, and here also is the artificial leg of Lord Uxbridge, another British commander: 'I say, I've lost my leg' Uxbridge is reported to

---

THE BATTLE OF WATERLOO

In 1814, at what must have seemed like the end of the **Napoleonic Wars**, France finally admitted defeat, and **Emperor Napoleon** was sent into exile on the Italian island of Elba. But he didn't stay there long: on 26 February 1815, he escaped imprisonment, landing at Cannes three days later. After that, he moved swiftly north, entering Paris on 20 March just as his unpopular replacement – the slothful **King Louis XVIII** – high-tailed it to Ghent. Thousands of Frenchmen rallied to Napoleon's colours, and with little delay, Napoleon marched northeast to fight the two armies that threatened his future. Both were in Belgium: one, an assortment of British, Dutch and German soldiers, was commanded by the **Duke of Wellington**; the other was a Prussian army led by **Marshal Blücher**. At the start of the campaign, Napoleon's army was about 130,000 strong, larger than each opposing army but not big enough to fight them both simultaneously. Napoleon's strategy was to stop Wellington and Blücher from joining together – and to this end, he crossed the Belgian frontier near Charleroi to launch a quick attack. On 16 June, the French hit the Prussians hard, forcing them to retreat and giving Napoleon the opportunity he sought. Napoleon detached a force of thirty thousand soldiers to harry the retreating Prussians while he concentrated his main army against Wellington, hoping to deliver a knockout blow. Meanwhile, Wellington had assembled his troops at **Waterloo**, on the main road to Brussels.

At **dawn on Sunday, 18 June**, the two armies faced each other. Wellington had some 68,000 men, about one-third British, and Napoleon had around five thousand more. The armies were deployed just 1,500m apart, with Wellington on the ridge north of – and uphill from – the enemy. It had rained heavily during the night, so Napoleon delayed his first attack to give the ground a chance to dry. At **11.30am**, the battle began when the French assaulted the fortified farm of Hougoumont, which was crucial for the defence of Wellington's right. The assault failed, and at approximately **1pm**, there was more bad news for Napoleon when he heard that the Prussians had eluded their pursuers and were closing fast. To gain time, he sent fourteen thousand troops off to impede their progress, and at **2pm**, he tried to regain the initiative by launching a large-scale infantry attack against Wellington's left. This second French attack also proved inconclusive, so at **4pm**, Napoleon's cavalry charged Wellington's centre, where the British infantry formed into squares and managed to keep the French at bay. This desperate engagement cost hundreds of lives. By **5.30pm**, the Prussians had begun to reach the battlefield in numbers to the right of the French lines and, at **7.30pm**, with the odds getting longer and longer, Napoleon made a final bid to break Wellington's centre, sending in his Imperial Guard. These were the best soldiers Napoleon had but slowed down by the mud churned up by their cavalry, the veterans proved easy targets for the British infantry, and they were beaten back with significant loss of life. At **8.15pm**, Wellington, who knew victory was within his grasp, rode down the ranks to encourage his soldiers before ordering the decisive large-scale counterattack.

have said during the battle, to which Wellington replied, 'By God, sir, so you have!' After the battle, Uxbridge's leg was buried here in Waterloo, but it was returned to London when he died to join the rest of his body. Such insouciance was not uncommon among the British ruling class, and neither were the bodies of the dead soldiers considered sacrosanct: **tooth dealers** roamed the battlefields of the Napoleonic Wars pulling out teeth, which were then stuck on two pieces of board with a spring at the back – primitive dentures known in England as 'Waterloos'.

In **Wellington's bedroom**, Room 6, there are copies of the messages Wellington sent to his commanders during the battle, curiously formal epistles laced with phrases such as 'Could you be so kind as to …'. Finally, an **extension** at the back of the museum reprises what has gone before, albeit on a slightly larger scale, with more models, plans and military paraphernalia, plus a lucid outline of the immediate historical background.

Church of St Joseph
ch de Bruxelles • Free • ⓦ sjoseph.be

Across the street from the Musée Wellington, the **church of Saint Joseph** is a curious affair, its over-large, domed and circular portico of 1689 built as part of a larger chapel on the orders of a Habsburg governor in the hope that it would encourage God to grant King Charles II of Spain an heir. It didn't, but the plea to God survives in the Latin inscription on the tympanum. The portico holds a bust of Wellington and a monument to all those British soldiers who died at Waterloo, plus there's an assortment of British **memorial plaques** at the back of the chapel beyond. They are, however, a somewhat jumbled bunch as they were plonked here unceremoniously when the original chapel was demolished in the nineteenth century to be replaced by the substantial building of today. Most of the plaques were paid for by voluntary contributions from the soldiers who survived – the British state rarely coughed up for any but the most aristocratic of its veterans.

The Battlefield: Memorial 1815
rte du Lion 1815 • Charge (included in Pass 1815; see page 230) • ⓦ waterloo1815.be

Beginning some 4km south of town, the **Waterloo** battlefield is a landscape of rolling farmland, interrupted by a couple of main roads and more pleasingly punctuated by the odd copse and farmstead. The ridge where Wellington once marshalled his army now holds the outstanding **Memorial 1815**, a lavish, subterranean museum whose several displays explore every aspect of the battle – from its historical context to the course of the fighting and the nature of the armaments. Original artefacts are, perhaps inevitably, thin on the ground, but there are four soldiers' skulls and a skeleton, though the most popular feature is a dramatic 4-D film of the battle.

Panorama de la Bataille

Adjoining the museum, and also part of Memorial 1815, is the enjoyable **Panorama de la Bataille**, where a circular, naturalistic painting of the battle, on a canvas no less than 110m in circumference, is displayed in a purpose-built, rotunda-like gallery – to a thundering soundtrack of bugles, snorting horses and cannon fire. Panorama painting is extremely difficult – controlling perspective is always a real problem – but it was very much in vogue when the Parisian artist Louis Dumoulin began this effort in 1912. Precious few panoramas of this kind have survived, and this one is a bit past its best, but it does at least give a sense of the battle.

Butte de Lion

The third part of Memorial 1815 is the 100m high Butte de Lion, built by local women with soil from the battlefield. The Butte marks where Prince William of Orange – one of Wellington's commanders and later King William II of the Netherlands – was wounded. It was only a nick, so goodness knows how high it would have been if William had been seriously injured, but the mound is certainly a commanding monument, surmounted by a regal **28-tonne lion** atop a stout plinth. From the viewing platform, there's a panoramic view over the battlefield, and a plan identifies which army was where.

Hougoumont farm

From the museum, it's a 1,200m walk south (or a quick and free shuttle bus ride) to Hougoumont Farm, a partly fortified and partly whitewashed compound that witnessed some of the fiercest fighting of the battle. Inside, exhibitions and a multimedia show flesh out the military details.

ARRIVAL AND DEPARTURE   WATERLOO

By train & bus There are direct trains to Waterloo from Brussels' three main stations (every 30min; 25min), as well as from Braine l'Alleud (every 20min; 4min) and Nivelles (every 20min; 15min) to the south. From Waterloo train station, it's an easy 15min walk to Waterloo's tourist office and the Musée Wellington in the town centre – turn right outside the station building, then take the first left along rue de la Station. After you've finished at the museum, you can take bus W (every 30–40min) from across the street – the ch de Bruxelles – to the battlefield. The bus stops beside the Esso gas station about 500m from Memorial 1815 – ring the bell when the bus reaches the first traffic island. After visiting the memorial, backtrack to the bus stop and catch bus W to Braine-l'Alleud train station, from where there are frequent trains to Waterloo and Brussels.
By car Take the Brussels Ring east, and come off at junction 26.

INFORMATION

Tourist office Waterloo's tourist office is handily located in the centre of town, opposite the Musée Wellington at ch de Bruxelles 218 (daily: June–Sept 9.30am–6pm; Oct–May 10am–5pm; ⚹ waterloo-tourisme.com). They issue free town maps and sell a combined ticket, the Pass 1815 (€23), for all the key attractions; the Pass 1815 is also on sale at the Musée Wellington and Memorial 1815.

ACCOMMODATION AND EATING

Most visitors to Waterloo are **day-trippers**, but the tourist office has details of several local hotels.
Hotel Le 1815 rte du Lion 367 ⚹ hotel1815.com. This comfortable three-star hotel has rooms in an attractive modern style and couldn't be more convenient for the battlefield – it's located about 500m east of the Butte de Lion. €€

Le Pain Quotidien ch de Bruxelles 125 ⚹ lepain quotidien.com. A pleasant, modern café – part of a chain – where they serve a good line of sandwiches, soups and pastries, though the main event is perhaps the range of bread; it's located just along the street from the Musée Wellington. €

Charleroi

Arriving by train, **CHARLEROI**'s industrial – and post-industrial – peripheries are hardly tempting. Still, they witness the city's key role in Wallonia's steel and coal industries, once the driving force of the Belgian economy. Heavy industry hereabouts hit the skids in the 1970s; however, Charleroi has battled on as best it can, becoming the home of Belgium's second **airport** (see page 233) and, more recently, creating the sprawling Rive Gauche **shopping centre** opposite the train station – though whether this is such a good idea is hard to say: Rive Gauche may well end up destroying the 'retail offering' in the rest of the city centre. Nosing around Charleroi is an agreeable way to spend an hour or two; allow a few more if you plan to visit the city's museums.

The Lower Town

Charleroi's main train station – **Charleroi Sud** – is a handsome and rather grand affair, built in a sort of French Empire style, and in front is the pedestrianised Pont

Roi Baudouin, connecting the station with the **Lower Town**. The bridge sports two statues of workers by Constantin Meunier, championing the working class, and spans the green-black waters of the River Sambre. The latter was crucial to the region's industrialisation before the railways took the lead, its canalised course once crowded with coal and iron-ore barges. It was in this same river, albeit further to the west, that René Magritte's mother, Régina, drowned herself in 1912 with such dramatic effects on her young son.

On the far side of the bridge from the station, **place Emile Buisset** leads to the heart of the Lower Town and the Passage de la Bourse – an attractive covered arcade whose late

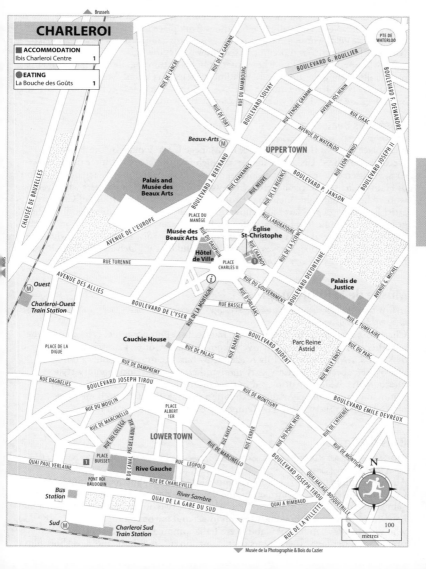

nineteenth-century, wooden-framed shops have survived in fine fettle. Beyond, cobbled **rue de la Montagne** clambers up towards the Upper Town, though frankly, it has seen better days, and the only thing to look for is the *sgraffiti* decorating the facade of No. 38, the work of one of Belgium's most talented Art Nouveau painters and architects, Paul Cauchie (1875–1952).

The Upper Town

Rue de la Montagne emerges onto the circular **place Charles II**, the centre of the **Upper Town**, formerly the site of a substantial seventeenth-century fortress. Nothing remains of the stronghold today, but the neighbourhood's gridiron street plan recalls its presence. Several especially fine buildings flank place Charles II, beginning with the **Hôtel de Ville**, whose imposing façade is a creative mix of Neoclassical and Art Nouveau features. Even more impressive, however, is the Église St Christophe (free), a real whopper of a building whose interior holds a stunning 200m2, gold-leaf apse mosaic illustrating the Book of Revelation in all its fiery detail. Wallonia's Jean Ransy (1910–91) completed the mosaic in 1957, and the artist's close connections with the Surrealists are self-evident when you examine the work.

Musée des Beaux Arts

pl du Manège 1 • Free • Ⓦ charleroi-museum.be

Near place Charles II, the busy place du Manège is overlooked by the striking Art Deco lines of the Palais des Beaux-Arts, which incorporates the Musée des Beaux-Arts, accessed by the glass extension on the right. The museum has a good collection of Hainaut artists, supplemented by the work of other Belgian painters who lived or worked here. Highlights include the romantic, Neoclassical paintings of Charleroi artist François Joseph Navez and the stern naturalism of Constantin Meunier, whose grim vision of industrial life was balanced by the heroism he saw in the working class. There are also several canvases by the talented Expressionist Pierre Paulus, whose oeuvre takes up where Meunier's leaves off, and a handful by Paul Delvaux, Felicien Rops and Magritte, as in his *Liberty of the Spirit*.

Musée de la Photographie

av Paul Pastur 11, about 4km southwest of the train station • Charge • Ⓦ museephoto.be • Buses Nos 70, 71 or 170 from Charleroi-Sud bus station to pl de Mont-sur-Marchienne

Charleroi's best museum, the inventive **Musée de la Photographie**, is located on the outskirts of town in the imaginatively renovated neo-Gothic Carmelite monastery of Mont-sur-Marchienne. Easily reachable by bus, the museum holds a thought-provoking collection of nearly sixty thousand creative and **documentary-style photographs**, which are displayed in rotation. It also has a well-organized and reasonably interesting permanent exhibition that takes you through the history of photography to the present day. Temporary exhibitions are staged regularly, too.

Bois du Cazier

rue du Cazier 80, 4km south of Charleroi Sud • Charge • Ⓦ leboisducazier.be • Buses Nos 1 or 3 from Charleroi-Sud bus station to square Buisset, Marcinelle, then a 10min walk

Almost as compelling as – and more unusual than – the photography museum, Charleroi's other outlying attraction, the **Bois du Cazier**, is a former coal mine which gained tragic notoriety in August 1956 when over two hundred miners died in a fire here. Most of the **mine buildings** remain intact and are both a memorial to those who died (more than half of whom were Italian immigrants) and a memorable piece of industrial heritage. There is lots of information in English, including a short film about the 1956 catastrophe, and the outbuildings hold a host of related objects and exhibitions, most interestingly a museum of industry full of obsolete heavy machinery. However, the most intriguing exhibits are those original to the mine: the showers where the miners ended their shifts or the punch clocks where they would begin them.

ARRIVAL AND INFORMATION
CHARLEROI

By plane The city's international airport – rather cheekily called Brussels South Charleroi – is 11km north of town; there are regular buses from the airport to Charleroi bus station; Ryanair flies here from the UK and Ireland (see page 23).

By train Charleroi has two train stations, Charleroi-Sud by the River Sambre, where you're most likely to arrive, and the less important Charleroi-Ouest, on the west side of the city centre.

Destinations (Charleroi-Sud) Brussels (every 30–50min; 50min); Couvin (Mon–Fri hourly, Sat & Sun every 2hr; 1hr); La Louvière-Sud (every 30min; 20min); Mons (every 30min; 35min); Namur (every 30min; 40min); Nivelles (every 30min–1hr; 25min); Villers-la-Ville (Mon–Fri hourly, Sat & Sun every 2hr; 30min); Walcourt (Mon–Fri hourly, Sat & Sun every 2hr; 30min).

Tourist office The tourist office is at pl Charles II, 20 (Mon–Sat 9am–6pm, Sun 10am–3pm; ⓦ cm-tourisme.be/en).

GETTING AROUND

By métro Charleroi-Sud train station is the hub of the city's pocket-sized métro, whose trams circle the centre.

ACCOMMODATION
SEE MAP PAGE 231

Ibis Charleroi Centre Quai Paul Verlaine 12 ⓦ all.accor. com. Of the chain hotels dotting the centre of Charleroi, this is probably the best bet – a proficient place with neat and tidy rooms in an old and good-looking block right in the centre of town – near the train station. €€

EATING
SEE MAP PAGE 231

La Bouche des Goûts rue Vauban 14 ⓦ labouchedes gouts.be. This small, cosy, family-run restaurant dishes up French cuisine with Alsatian flourishes; expect delights such as frogs' legs, snails and duck. €€

Botte de Hainaut

A tongue of land jutting south into France, the **Botte de Hainaut** (Boot of Hainaut) is a natural extension of the Ardennes range further east, if a little flatter and less wooded. It's mostly visited for its gentle scenery and country towns, among which Walcourt and **Chimay** are the most appealing – the former graced by a handsome basilica, the latter by a charming château and one of the prettiest main squares in the whole of Wallonia. The Boot's only **train** line runs south from Charleroi to Walcourt and, ultimately, Couvin, with **local buses** filling in most of the gaps, but really, the best way to get around is with your own car. The other complication is that, apart from campsites, **accommodation** is thin on the ground – Chimay is your best bet by a country mile.

Walcourt: the Basilique Ste-Materne

Grand-Place • Free • ⓦ walcourt.be

The hillside settlement of **WALCOURT**, about 20km from Charleroi, is a pleasant old town whose pride and joy is its medieval, artichoke-domed **Basilique Ste-Materne**, which dominates the town from its hilltop location at the top of the Grand-Place. The church is an imperious building from the outside, very dark and atmospheric within, distinguished by a marvellous Gothic rood-screen adorned by a flurry of Renaissance decoration. The screen was presented to the church by Emperor Charles V on the occasion of a pilgrimage he made to the **Virgin of Walcourt**, a silver-plated wooden statue that now stands in the north transept. An object of considerable veneration even today, the statue is believed to have been crafted in the tenth century, making it one of the oldest such figures in Belgium. The late medieval choir stalls are equally fascinating, sporting a wealth of naturalistic detail: centaurs and griffins, rams locking horns, and acrobats alongside biblical scenes.

ARRIVAL AND DEPARTURE   **WALCOURT**

By train From Walcourt train station, it's a good – and partly steep – 1,200m walk to the church: turn right outside the station building, left down the short access road, turn right at the T-junction and then follow the road as it curves round and then up.

Destinations Charleroi (Mon–Fri hourly, Sat & Sun every 2hr; 30min); Couvin (Mon–Fri hourly, Sat & Sun every 2hr; 30min).

Couvin and around

COUVIN, 30km south of Walcourt, was one of the first settlements in Hainaut to be industrialised, its narrow streets choked by forges and smelting works as early as the eighteenth century. As it turned out, Couvin was soon marginalised by the big cities further north, but it has battled gainfully on as a pint-sized manufacturing centre. Tourism has also had an impact, as the town lies at the heart of a popular holiday area, a quiet rural district whose forests and farmland are liberally sprinkled with country cottages and second homes. Long and slim and bisected by the River Eau Noire, Couvin is short on specific sights. However, it does possess a good-looking if small **old** quarter, set on top of a rocky hill high above the river and main road, where you'll also find the boringly modern main square, **place du Général Piron**.

Grottes de Neptune

rue de l'Adujoir 24, B-5660 Couvin • Charge • ⓦ grottesdeneptune.be

About 3km north of Couvin, in a lovely spot that's difficult to reach without private transport, the Grottes de Neptune are the big local attraction. This small network of **caverns** can be partially explored by boat on an underground river – a journey enhanced by some dramatic and accomplished music and light shows.

Forty-five-minute guided tours run from late February to October on a complex schedule, starting from as early as 10.15am and as late as 1pm (see website for times).

ARRIVAL AND DEPARTURE   **COUVIN**

By train Couvin train station is on the north side of the town centre, a 5min walk from the main square, pl du Général Piron.

Destinations Charleroi (Mon–Fri hourly, Sat & Sun every 2hr; 1hr); Walcourt (Mon–Fri hourly, Sat & Sun every 2hr; 30min).

EATING

Brasserie des Fagnes 26 rte de Nismes, Couvin ⓦ brasseriedesfagnes.com. Just outside Couvin, signed from the main road north (to Mariembourg), this is one of the best places to eat hereabouts – a fabled and very popular brewery-cum-restaurant which does delicious, crispy pizza-breads topped with cheeses and ham and serves them with its beer, Super des Fagnes – there are no fewer than five hundred varieties, from the usual brown, blond and cherry brews to daily specials such as coriander and orange-flavoured ale. €€

Brûly-de-Pesche

Abri d'Hitler pl St Meen, Brûly-de-Pesche • Charge • ⓦ bdp1940.be/en

Heading south from Couvin on the N5, it's a couple of kilometres to the 5km long byroad that weaves its way up through wooded hills to the small village of **BRÛLY-DE-PESCHE**, where Hitler had his advance headquarters for three weeks during the invasion of 1940. The Germans commandeered the entire village, drawing up the terms of the French surrender in the church, and Hitler himself held sway in the so-called **Abri d'Hitler**, a complex whose scant remains – essentially a decrepit concrete bunker or two – lie in a wooded park nearby. There are a couple of rebuilt huts here as well, showing a film on the 1940 campaign and a display on the local Resistance.

Chimay

It may be best known for the beer brewed by local Trappists, but the small and ancient town of **CHIMAY**, 14km west of Couvin, is a charming old place in its own right, governed for several centuries by the de Croy family, a clan of influential bigwigs whose dynastic tentacles once stretched over much of Europe. Many of the de Croy family were interred in the Collégiale des Sts **Pierre et Paul** (free), a mostly sixteenth-century limestone pile with a high and austere vaulted nave that squeezes into the town's slender main square. This square, the **Grand-Place**, is an exceedingly pretty little piazza, and it surrounds the dinky Monument des Princes, a water fountain erected in 1852 in honour of – you guessed it – the de Croys. Incidentally, one of Chimay's most delicious specialities is **Bernadins de Chimay** biscuits, made with almonds, honey and brown sugar; you can buy them at the Pâtisserie Hubert, Grand-Place 32.

Château des Princes de Chimay
rue du Château • Charge • ⓦ chateaudechimay.be

The town's main sight is the **Château des Princes de Chimay**, just off the main square in the town centre. A considerably altered structure; it was originally built in the fifteenth century, reconstructed in the seventeenth, then severely damaged by fire and partly rebuilt to earlier plans in the 1930s. Today, the main body of the building is fronted by a long series of rectangular windows edged by a squat turreted tower. Inside, tours explore a fair portion of the castle, with the highlight being the carefully restored **theatre** modelled on the Louis XV theatre at Fontainebleau.

ARRIVAL AND INFORMATION

By bus There are no trains to Chimay, but there is a good bus service from the nearest train station at Couvin. In Chimay, most buses pull in on pl Froissart, a few minutes' walk from the Grand-Place.
Destinations Couvin (hourly; 1hr).

Tourist office The tourist office is a few paces south of the Grand-Place at rue de Noailles 6 (July & Aug: daily 9am–6pm; Sept–June: Mon–Fri 9am–5pm, Sat & Sun 10am–5pm; ⓦ visitchimay.be).

ACCOMMODATION

L'Auberge de Poteaupré rue de Poteaupré 5, 6464 Bourlers ⓦ chimay.com. Simple modern rooms in a rural setting above the eponymous restaurant. The rooms are decorated in the reds and blues of the Chimay monks and equipped with en-suite bathrooms. €€

★ **Le Petit Chapitre** pl du Chapitre 5 ⓦ lepetitchapitre. be. A delightful B&B comprising a handful of period rooms in attractive old premises, metres from the Grand-Place. All rooms have en-suite baths, TVs and wi-fi. The price includes breakfast. €€

EATING AND DRINKING

★ **L'Auberge de Poteaupré** rue de Poteaupré 5, 6464 Bourlers ⓦ chimay.com. About 10km from Chimay, this busy restaurant is owned by the Trappist monks of the Cistercian Order of the Strict Observance, who live about 500m away along the main road in the Abbaye N-D de Scourmont. The restaurant is an informal affair that serves some of the best food in the region with a bit of something for everyone: a tasting menu of goodies to have with Chimay's various cheeses and beers, a short menu of Belgian 'tapas' and a full menu of classic Belgian mains, not

to mention, a fabulous fondue. There are rooms here, too.
La Charlotte pl Froissart 8 ☎ 060 21 21 00. This small modern café-restaurant is one of the best places to eat in Chimay, serving excellent home-cooked food, including *escavèche*, a mix of either eel or trout with onions, white wine and vinegar that's a speciality of the Botte. €€
Queen Mary Grand-Rue 22 ☎ 0470 61 57 14. Chimay's nicest option for a drink, this cosy and popular bar, is decked out to look like an English pub. Chimay Tripel is often on tap. €

The Ardennes

BOUILLON CHATEAU, WALLONIA

5

The Ardennes

Belgium's southernmost region – known as the Ardennes – is a striking contrast to the crowded, industrial cities of the north, the flat polders morphing into rugged landscapes of rolling hills and forests. The Ardennes begin in France and stretch east across Luxembourg and Belgium before continuing into Germany, covering three Belgian provinces en route: Namur in the west, Luxembourg in the south and Liège in the east. The highest part, lying in the German-speaking east of the country, is the Hautes Fagnes (the High Fens), an expanse of windswept heathland that extends from Eupen to Malmedy.

The region's major towns – **Namur** and the capital **Liège** – have a quaint charm, with the latter boasting several interesting museums and a lively student scene, while the former's atmospheric Old Town lies under the watchful eye of an impressive citadel. But the Ardennes' most attractive and popular areas are found further south, around **Dinant**, **La Roche-en-Ardenne** and **Bouillon**. Characterised by river valleys and high green peaks, this is the ideal kayaking territory, and there are good caving opportunities around the **Meuse**, **Ourthe** and **Lesse** valleys. Several ski resorts in the region's northeast offer a range of winter activities. Generally, travelling about the Ardennes feels less frenetic than in Flanders. Instead of ticking off UNESCO-listed sites and ogling one gilded Grand-Place after another, the Ardennes region is more about meandering through ancient hilltop villages, enjoying French-style food and savouring the distinctly laid-back mood. Finally, make a literary pilgrimage to bookish **Redu** or dip in **Spa**'s thermal waters for Ardennes-style relaxation of a slightly different order.

Namur and around

Just 60km southeast of Brussels, **NAMUR** is a logical gateway to the Ardennes and is refreshingly clear of the industrial belts of Hainaut and Brabant. Strategically sited at the confluence of the Sambre and Meuse **rivers**, it was the quintessential **military town** from the sixteenth century until 1978, when the Belgian army finally moved out. Now, it's best known as the home of Wallonia's parliament. Namur's pride and joy is its massive, mostly nineteenth-century hilltop **citadel** – once one of the mightiest fortresses in Europe – but its quaint **Old Town**, down below, also musters a handful of decent museums – notably the **Trésor d'Oignies** – plus some very good restaurants and stylish clothes shops. Visit at the end of May, and you can join the four-day Namur en Mai (ⓦnamurenmai.be) celebrations when jugglers, stilt-walkers and street entertainment descend upon the city. Namur is within easy striking distance of the assorted pleasures of Dinant (see page 260), and the road there passes by the delightful **Jardins d'Annevoie**.

The citadel

Citadel rte Merveilleuse, a circuitous 4km south of Namur train station • Free general access • ⓦ citadelle.namur.be • Namer cable car (charge; ⓦ telepheriquedenamur.be) from pl Maurice Servais or the tourist train from the Terra Nova Visitor Centre (April–Sept; charge; ⓦ citadelle.namur.be)

The result of centuries of military endeavour, Namur's **citadel** is an immense complex which extends across the steep and craggy hill that rises high above the confluence of

Highlights

❶ **Trésor d'Oignies, Namur** A unique collection of exquisitely crafted, jewel-encrusted metalwork from the thirteenth century. See page 244

❷ **Stavelot Carnival** One of Belgium's most flamboyant festivals – watch out for the Blancs Moussis, with white robes and long red noses. See page 256

❸ **Hautes Fagnes** Belgium's highest terrain, with genuinely wild walking across windy moorland and through deep forests. See page 259

❹ **Kayaking and rafting** Take your pick from the rivers, but the River Lesse is hard to beat. See page 263

❺ **Redu** This quaint hamlet serves as the country's official 'book town'. See page 266

❻ **Bouillon Château** The best-preserved medieval castle in the country. See page 268

HIGHLIGHTS ARE MARKED ON THE MAP ON PAGE 240

BRUSSELS

Waterloo

BRABANT-WALLON

Ottignies

N25

Nivelles

Villers-la-Ville

Gembloux

N29

N5

A15/E42

A4/E411

Strepy-Thieu

N40

Charleroi

Binche

Floreffe

Namur ①

NAMUR

N69

Méhai

N80

N97

Huy

N90

HAINAUT

N53

Jardins d'Annevoie

Godinne

N5

Maredret

Maredsous

Walcourt

Falaën

Moliignée Valley

Dinant

Beaumont

Silenrieux

N97

Anseremme

Vêves

Celles

Lacs de l'Eau de l'Heure

Hastière-par-Delà

Château de Frëyr ④

Gendron Celles

Philippeville

Waulsort

N40

Houyet

Rochefort

Jeme

BOTTE DU HAINAUT

Agimont

Lessive

Han-sur-

Givet

Lavaux Sainte Anne

Mariembourg

Treignes

A4/E411

Nismes

Viervés-sur-Viroin

N99

Couvin

Olloy-sur-Viroin

N5

Lesse

St-Hu

Baileux

Redu ⑤

Euro Space Center

Brûly-de-Pesche

Meuse

Rochehaut

Bert

Frahan

Dohan

Herbe

Poupéhan

Bouillon ⑥

Semois

Charleville-Mézières

A34/E46

Sedan

Meuse

FRANCE

HIGHLIGHTS

① Trésor d'Oignies, Namur
② Stavelot Carnival
③ Hautes Fagnes
④ Kayaking and rafting
⑤ Redu
⑥ Bouillon Château

the rivers Sambre and Meuse. It's a curious mixture of styles and periods: during the medieval period, a succession of local counts made elaborate additions to each other's fortifications, which were gradually abandoned when the section near the top of the hill – now loosely known as the **Château des Comtes** – was incorporated into a partly subterranean fortress, the **Médiane**, whose ramifications occupy the eastern portion of the present citadel.

This part of the fortress was always the most vulnerable to attack. For two hundred years, successive generations of military engineers, including Vauban and the Dutchman Van Coehoorn, tried to work out the best way to protect it. The surviving structure reflects this preoccupation, with the lines of defence becoming more complex and extensive the further you go. To further strengthen the defences, the Spanish completed the **Terra Nova** bastion at the west end of the citadel in the 1640s, separating the two with a wide **moat**; this made Namur one of the strongest fortresses in Europe, but didn't stop Louis XIV besieging the town in 1692. The Dutch rebuilt the citadel between 1816 and 1825, and much of today's remains date to this period.

The **views** from the citadel, over the town and the surrounding countryside, are fantastic, and the information office at the Terra Nova Visitor Centre can provide details of **walking trails** of varying lengths. The centre also sells various Citadelle PASS bundles.

Many events take place here throughout the year, including a local wine festival in February and a food festival in July.

Atelier de Parfumerie Guy Delforge
rte Merveilleuse 60 • Charge • ⓦ delforge.com

At the **Atelier de Parfumerie Guy Delforge**, the award-winning scent maker crafts his unique creations in the citadel's cellars and sells them in the smart shop. A fifty-minute guided (or audio guide) **tour** gives a glimpse into the alchemy behind the creation of the perfumes.

Terra Nova Visitor Centre
rte Merveilleuse 64 • Charge • ⓦ citadelle.namur.be

Housed in a former barracks, the **Terra Nova Visitor Centre** contains a fascinating and well-put-together multimedia exhibition on Namur's urban and military history. It's best to rent an audio guide to get the most out of your visit. There's a lovely café, too.

Underground casemates
rte Merveilleuse • Charge • ⓦ citadelle.namur.be

Dubbed 'The Termite Nest of Europe' by Napoleon, the **underground casemates** stretch for 7km under Terra Nova and Médiane and are the largest such network in Europe. Guided tours run just shy of an hour and a half long and, with sound and visual accompaniment, tell you about the labyrinth's 500-year-old history and how it was used during World War II.

Halle Al' Chair (Musée Archéologique)
rue du Pont 21 • Free • ⓦ namurtourisme.be

Right on the river by the Pont du Musée, the red-brick **Halle Al' Chair** is one of the stand-out buildings of Namur's Old Town. Built by the Spanish in the sixteenth century and originally a meat market, it now houses the tourist office (see page 245) and Namur's small **archaeological museum**, with local finds from prehistory to the Merovingian era, including a fine collection of personal items from a late Roman cemetery.

Musée Félicien Rops

rue Fumal 12 • Charge • W museerops.be

In a handsome old mansion down a narrow lane, the **Musée Félicien Rops** is devoted
to the life and work of cartoonist, painter, graphic artist and illustrator Félicien Rops
(1833–98), a native of Namur who settled in Paris in the 1870s and went on to fame
and fortune by illustrating the works of the likes of Baudelaire. Rops had contempt

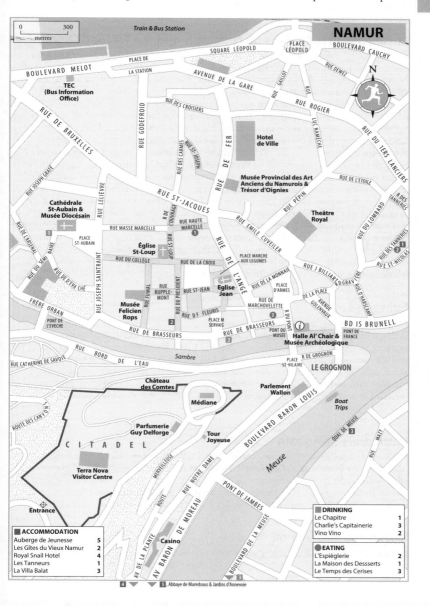

NAMUR

0 — 300 metres

Train & Bus Station

SQUARE LÉOPOLD

PLACE LÉOPOLD

BOULEVARD CAUCHY

PLACE DE LA STATION

BOULEVARD MELOT

RUE DEWEZ

AVENUE DE LA GARE

RUE GALLOT

RUE JULIE

RUE ROGIER

UC NAMECHE

RUE DU TERS LANCIERS

TEC (Bus Information Office)

RUE DE BRUXELLES

RUE DES CROISIERS

RUE GODEFROID

Hotel de Ville

RUE DE FER

RUE DES CARMES

RUE ST-JOSEPH

RUE DE L'ÉTOILE

R DES TANNERIES

RUE JOSEPH GRAFÉ

Cathédrale St-Aubain & Musée Diocésain

RUE LELIÈVRE

RUE ST-JACQUES

Musée Provincial des Art Anciens du Namurois & Trésor d'Oignies

RUE PÉPIN

Théâtre Royal

RUE DU LOMBARD

RUE DES TANNERIES

RUE DE L'ARSENAL

PLACE ST-AUBAIN

RUE MASSE MARCELLE

RUE DE L'OUVRAGE

RUE HAUTE MARCELLE

RUE EMILE CUVELIER

RUE ST-NICOLAS

RUE DU SEMINAIRE

RUE DE D'EVA CHÉ

RUE JOSEPH SAINTRAINT

Église St-Loup

RUE DU COLLÈGE

RUE ST-LOUP

RUE DE LA CROIX

RUE DE L'ANGE

PLACE MARCHE AUX LEGUMES

RUE J BILLIARD

ED GRAV ÈRE

BLVD D'HARSCAMP

FRÈRE ORBAN

RUE FUMAL

RUE RUPPLE-MONT

RUE DU PRÉSIDENT

RUE ST-JEAN

Église Jean

RUE DE LA MONNAIE

PLACE D'ARMES

RUE DE MARCHOVELETTE

DE LA PLACE

AVENUE GOLENVAUX

PONT DE L'EVECHE

Musée Félicien Rops

RUE D F FLEURIS

PLACE M SERVAIS

BD IS BRUNELL

RUE DE BRASSEURS

RUE DE BRASSEURS

PONT DU MUSÉE

Halle Al' Chair & Musée Archéologique

PONT DE FRANCE

RUE CATHERINE DE SAVOIE

RUE BORD DE L'EAU

Sambre

PLACE ST-HILAIRE

R DE GROGNON

LE GROGNON

Château des Comtes

Parlement Wallon

Boat Trips

ROUTE DES CANTONS

Médiane

Parfumerie Guy Delforge

Tour Joyeuse

BOULEVARD BARON LOUIS

QUAI DE MEUSE

RUE MALY

C I T A D E L

Terra Nova Visitor Centre

MERVEILLEUSE

RUE NOTRE DAME

Meuse

Entrance

PONT DE JAMBES

ROUTE

Casino

AV DE LA PLANTE

AV BARON DE MOREAU

BOULEVARD DE LA MEUSE

ACCOMMODATION

Auberge de Jeunesse	5
Les Gîtes du Vieux Namur	2
Royal Snail Hotel	4
Les Tanneurs	1
La Villa Balat	3

DRINKING

Le Chapitre	1
Charlie's Capitainerie	3
Vino Vino	2

EATING

L'Espièglerie	2
La Maison des Dessserts	1
Le Temps des Cerises	3

5

for the bourgeois family values that went down well with so many Parisian artists, though not so well with his long-suffering wife, who objected to his affairs, one of which involved two sisters and their mother. Rops is probably best known for his erotic and macabre **drawings**, of which there is a good selection on display here: skeletons, nuns and priests depicted in oddly compromising poses or old men serviced by young, partially clad women. Some are just perverse, but the wit in his work is hard to deny – check out his famous *Pornocrates* on the second floor.

Musée des Arts Anciens du Namurois and the Trésor d'Oignies

rue de Fer 24 • Charge • ⓦ museedesartsanciens.be

The impressive **Musée Provincial des Arts Anciens du Namurois** is housed in one of Namur's finest eighteenth-century mansions. The collection includes an enjoyable sample of devotional **metalwork** from the Mosan, most memorably, the dinky geometrics of dozens of brass enamels. It also includes medieval sculptures and painted wooden panels. Of the many **paintings**, the most distinguished are those by **Henri Blès**, an early sixteenth-century local artist who favoured panoramic landscapes populated by tiny figures. However, the museum's pride and joy is the **Trésor d'Oignies** (Oignies Priory Treasury), a unique hoard of the exquisitely beautiful gold- and silverwork of **Brother Hugo d'Oignies**, one of the region's most gifted medieval metalworkers. From the eleventh to the thirteenth centuries, the Meuse Valley was famous for the skill of its artisans, and Hugo was an innovator in the art of **filigree**, raising the decoration from the background so that the tiny human figures and animals seem to be suspended in space. The pieces here are elaborately studded with precious and semiprecious stones and display an exquisite balance between ornament and function, depicting, for example, minute hunting scenes with animals leaping convincingly through delicate foliage. Look out for the dazzling **reliquary cover** for St Peter's rib, the charming songbird and goblet of St Marie of Oignies, and a magnificent cover for a Gospel book.

Église St-Loup

rue du Collège 17 • Free • ⓦ eglise-saint-loup.be

Perhaps the pick of Namur's many churches, the **Église St-Loup** is a Baroque extravagance built for the Jesuits between 1621 and 1645, with a fluently carved facade and a sumptuous interior of marble walls and sandstone vaulting. The **high altar** is wood painted to look like marble – the ship carrying the last instalment of Italian marble sank, and the Jesuits had to finish the church with this imitation. Free organ recitals are held here most Saturdays (11.30am–noon), and there is a classical music festival in July.

Cathédrale St-Aubain

pl du Chapitre 4 • **Cathedral** Free • ⓦ namurtourisme.be • pl du Chapitre 1 • **Musée Diocésain** Charge • ⓦ musee-diocesain.be

The elaborate Neoclassical **Cathédrale St-Aubain** is decorated with acres of creamy white paint, and its choir groans with melodramatic **paintings** by Jacques Nicolai, one of Rubens' less talented pupils. Attached is the **Musée Diocésain**, which contains sculptures, paintings, silver pieces, textiles and manuscripts gathered from churches across Namur province.

ARRIVAL AND INFORMATION   **NAMUR**

By train Namur's train station is at pl de la Station, 500m north of the town centre.

Destinations Arlon (hourly; 1hr 35min); Brussels (every 30min; 1hr); Charleroi (hourly; 30–40min); Dinant (hourly;

30min); Liège (hourly; 45min); Luxembourg City (hourly; 1hr 40min).

By bus The square beside the train station is the terminus for local and regional buses. These are operated by TEC (ⓦletec.be), which has an information office close by at bd Ernest Mélot 15. The Maison du TEC can provide information about bus services across French-speaking Belgium.

Tourist information The tourist office is in the Halle Al' Chair (see page 242), beside the river at rue du Pont 21, a 15min walk from the train station (daily 9.30am–6pm; ⓦnamurtourisme.be). Staff issue free town maps and brochures, give details of guided tours – including guided walking tours of Namur's pedestrianised Old Town – and provide information on what's on in the town and its environs.

GETTING AROUND

By bike Libia Velo (ⓦen.libiavelo.be) is a municipal rental scheme with stations dotted around town. The charge is an initial €1 per day or €3 per week paid by bank card; the first half-hour is free. You can also rent electric bikes from the tourist office.

By water taxi Les Namourettes (June & Sept Sat & Sun; July & Aug daily; €1 one-way; ⓦnamurtourisme.be) ferry passengers around town via the Sambre and Meuse rivers.

ACCOMMODATION   SEE MAP PAGE 243

Namur has several top-notch hotels and one large hostel, but **book ahead** if you plan to visit during mid- or late-summer as it gets very busy.

Auberge de Jeunesse av Félicien Rops 8 ⓦlesauberges dejeunesse.be. Offers twins and three-, four- and five-bed dorms in a listed Mosan villa. There's a bar with a terrace overlooking the river, a communal kitchen, another serving breakfast and evening meals, a TV room, free wi-fi and laundry. It's 3km from the train station: walk along the river or take bus Nos 3 or 4 from the bus station. Sheets and breakfast included. Dorms €̄, doubles €̄

Les Gîtes du Vieux Namur rue du Président 32 ⓦlesgitesduvieuxnamur.be. Live like a local in an old townhouse in one of four stylish, contemporary gîtes. Each one sleeps two people; *La Citadelle*, on the third floor, has great views over said fortress and rooftops. The welcome basket featuring coffee, tea and biscuits is a nice touch. Minimum stay of two nights. €̄€

Royal Snail Hotel av de la Plante 23 ⓦtheroyalsnail. com. Namur's first boutique hotel sits in the shadow of the impressive citadel. It boasts clean, white rooms with pops of colour, gastronomic delights at *Le Table du Royal Snail*, a slim-line pool and a wellness centre offering massages. €̄€̄€

★ **Les Tanneurs** rue des Tanneries 13 ⓦtanneurs. com. Right in the town centre, this hotel occupies a lavishly and imaginatively renovated seventeenth-century building, with fifteen characterful rooms in the old building and 32 modern rooms in an extension. There's (limited) parking and two good restaurants. €̄€

La Villa Balat quai de Meuse 39 ⓦvillabalat.be. Housed in a striking, early twentieth-century villa next to the Meuse, this B&B offers two traditionally furnished bedrooms named after Belgian artists and a suite recalling the celebrated architect Alphonse Balat (thought to have designed the house). Breakfast is taken in the waterside dining room, and there's a garden, too. Secure parking is also available (€10/night). €̄€̄€

EATING   SEE MAP PAGE 243

Namur has a good selection of **cafés and restaurants**. Like the rest of Belgium, food is generally of high quality wherever you eat.

★ **L'Espièglerie** rue des Tanneries 13 ⓦtanneurs.com. This smart, gourmet restaurant, housed in the beamed dining room of *Hotel Les Tanneurs*, is one of the best deals in town, with local ingredients turned into creative French dishes. Prices are higher in the evening. €̄€̄€

La Maison des Desserts rue Haute Marcelle 17 ⓦmaison-des-desserts.be. This third-generation *pâtisserie* in a pretty seventeenth-century townhouse is a must for those with a sweet tooth. They also serve snacks and salads in an attractive dining room. €̄

Le Temps des Cerises rue des Brasseurs 22 ⓦcerises. be. This intimate, cherry-coloured, cherry-themed restaurant offers a quality French menu with a Belgian touch. €̄€

DRINKING   SEE MAP PAGE 243

Namur has a first-rate selection of **bars**, many clustered on and around the quaint, pedestrianised squares just west of rue de l'Ange – especially Marché-aux-Légumes.

Le Chapitre rue du Séminaire 4 ☎0489 18 41 73. An unassuming bar with an extensive beer list – try local brews Houppe and Blanche de Namur. Popular with students, it is a busy and convivial place for a late-evening drink.

Charlie's Capitainerie bd de la Meuse 38, 5100 Jambes ☎04 76 23 31 42. A waterside bar where you can hire SUPs to explore the river. They regularly hold events, including musical entertainment.

Vino Vino rue des Brasseurs 61 ⓦvinovino.be. This small, contemporary wine bar is the place to sample Belgian wines accompanied by cheese and charcuterie.

5

Les Jardins d'Annevoie

rue des Jardins d'Annevoie 37A, Annevoie-Rouillon; 18km south of Namur • Charge • Ⓦ annevoie.be • Hourly Namur–Dinant trains stop at Godinne, 2km east of the gardens; bus No. 21 Namur-Maredsous (2–3 daily; 30min; Ⓦ letec.be) stops just outside the gardens

A highly recommended stop on the road between Namur and Dinant (see page 260), **Les Jardins d'Annevoie** is reckoned to be among Belgium's finest gardens. The estate – both manor house and gardens – has been in the hands of the Montpelliers since 1675, and one of the clan, a certain Charles Alexis, turned his hand (or rather those of his gardeners) to garden design in the 1770s. Widely travelled, Charles picked up tips in France, Italy and England, which he then rolled into one homogeneous creation. From the French came **formal borders**, from the Italians the romance of mossy banks and arbours, while the English influence is most apparent in the **grotto of Neptune**. They are architectural rather than flower gardens; the common denominator is water. Fountains, jets and mini-waterfalls are everywhere you look, all worked by natural pressure from the tree-lined Grand Canal immediately above the gardens. There's a pleasant café, the *Orangerie*, above the shop, offering views over the garden and the local Maredsous beer on tap.

Abbaye de Maredsous and St-Joseph visitor centre

rue de Maredsous 11, Denée; 12km west of Annevoie • Free • Ⓦ tourisme-maredsous.be • Bus No. 21 from Namur bus station (2–4 daily; 50min) or bus No. 35 from Dinant train station (2–3 daily; 35min); both stop at or near the Abbaye de Maredsous; route planning on Ⓦ letec.be

Founded in the 1870s, the neo-Gothic **Abbaye de Maredsous** in **Denée** is renowned for its beers even though they haven't been brewed here since 1963 – Duvel Moortgat bought the licence and recipes. You're free to wander around the **monastery** and abbey **gardens**. As guided tours (arranged at the visitor centre) are only available in French or Dutch, most people head to the **St-Joseph visitor centre**, a complex containing a café, bookshop and shop. The shop does a roaring trade in Maredsous produce, notably the abbey's cheese and various beers – they make a blond, a bruin and a strong tripel.

Huy and around

Midway between Namur and Liège and easily accessible by train from either, the bustling town of **HUY** spreads across both sides of the River Meuse. One of the oldest settlements in Belgium and a flourishing market town for a long time, the place was badly damaged by Louis XIV in the late seventeenth century and was mauled by several passing armies. Consequently, little remains of the old town, but Huy is worth a brief stop, mainly for its splendid **church** and dramatic **citadel**.

The Grand-Place and around

The central **Grand-Place** features an ornate bronze fountain dating from 1406 – decorated with four saints and, at the top, a hornblower as a symbol of the city; the wrought-iron and stone vats were added in the eighteenth century. The square is flanked by the **Hôtel de Ville**, a self-confident, château-style edifice dating from the 1760s, behind which is tiny **place Verte**, overlooked by an attractive Gothic church and lying at the start of a pretty maze of narrow lanes and alleys that stretch north to rue Vankeerberghen.

Collégiale Notre-Dame et Saint-Domitien

Parvis Théoduin de Bavière • **Church** Free • **Treasury** Charge • Ⓦ visithuy.be

Down by the river, the imposing Gothic bulk of the **Collégiale Notre-Dame et Saint-Domitien** dominates the town, towering over the banks of the River Meuse with the high cliffs and walls of the citadel behind. Built between 1311 and 1536, the church's interior is decked with fine stained glass, especially the magnificent **rose window**. On the right side of the nave as you enter, stairs lead down to a Romanesque **crypt** and **trésor** (treasury), where the relics of Huy's patron saint, St Domitian, were once venerated, and whose original twelfth-century shrine is on display, along with three other large shrines crafted by the Mosan gold- and silversmiths for which Huy was once famous. They're somewhat faded, but the beauty and skill of their execution shine through. Outside, on the side of the church facing the town centre, look out for the **Porte de Bethléem**, topped by a mid-fourteenth-century arch decorated with scenes of the Nativity.

Fort de Huy

ch Napoléon • Charge • ⓦ visithuy.be • Accessible from quai de Namur by taking the signed footpath up to the left

There's been a fortress here since the ninth century, though the medieval castle that once occupied the site was demolished in 1717; the present **Fort de Huy**, partly hewn out of solid rock, was erected by the Dutch in the early nineteenth century. The fort is a massive complex, and although much of it can be visited, the most compelling and coherent section is the dozen or so rooms used by the Germans as a **prison** during World War II, when no fewer than seven thousand prisoners passed through this bleak place. The cells, dormitories and interrogation chambers are grim enough, but the mountain of press cuttings, photos and personal effects pertaining to the Resistance and, in particular, to the **concentration camps** is simply harrowing; it's a relief to emerge into the daylight of the central courtyard, from where you can climb up onto the top for what are, predictably, stunning **views** over Huy and the countryside around.

ARRIVAL AND INFORMATION   HUY

By train Huy's train station is on the opposite (west) side of the river from the town centre, a 15min walk: head straight out of the station down to the river, turn right and cross the Pont Roi Baudouin to reach the Collégiale Notre-Dame.
Destinations Liège (every 30min; 20min); Namur (every 20min; 25min).

Tourist information The tourist office is right by the river at quai de Namur 1 (April to mid-Sept: Mon–Fri 9.30am–5.30pm, Sat & Sun 10am–5pm; mid-Sept to March: Mon–Fri 9.30am–4pm, Sat & Sun 10am–4pm; ⓦ terres-de-meuse.be).

ACCOMMODATION AND EATING

Les Augustins rue des Augustins 28 ⓦ lesaugustins.be. Cosy B&B in a former convent dating from the eighteenth century. The spacious attic room sleeps two people, and a separate gîte sleeps three people (minimum two nights). There is a lovely garden and secure parking. €€

Les Caves Gourmandes pl St Séverin 5a ⓦ lescaves gourmandes.be. Handily located down by the river, beautifully presented French cuisine is on the menu in this restaurant and wine bar in a vaulted cellar. Delicious lobster. Booking advised. €€€

Liège

The capital of the Ardennes and its province, **LIÈGE**, straddling the River Meuse, is an underdog among Belgian towns. It has struggled to shake off its reputation as a large, grimy, **industrial city**. Still, these days, thanks to urban regeneration, internationally acclaimed architecture (Santiago Calatrava's Guillemins train station), vibrant cultural life and a rocking bar scene, Liège seems to have found its mojo. The city is steeped in folkloric romance – locals know it as **La Cité Ardente** (The Passionate City) – and it has a strong culinary identity with a growing band of **excellent restaurants**, as well as several interesting museums, including the new fine arts hub **La Boverie**, all of which warrant at least a day's exploration. Winter is a good time to visit: the wooden chalets of the **Christmas markets** line the squares throughout December and, at the end of

5

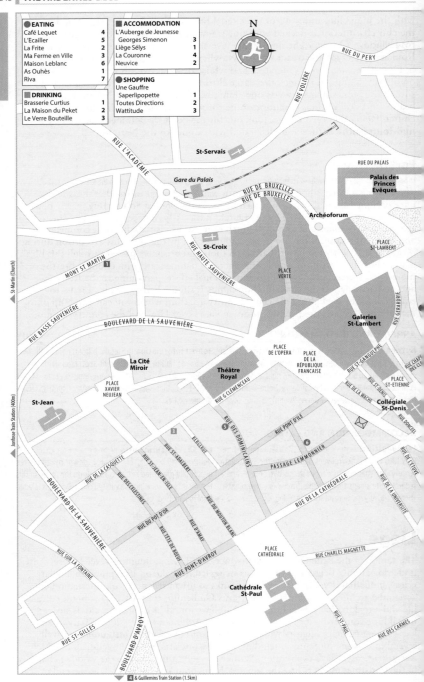

EATING
Café Lequet	4
L'Ecailler	5
La Frite	2
Ma Ferme en Ville	3
Maison Leblanc	6
As Ouhès	1
Riva	7

DRINKING
Brasserie Curtius	1
La Maison du Peket	2
Le Verre Bouteille	3

ACCOMMODATION
L'Auberge de Jeunesse Georges Simenon	3
Liège Sélys	1
La Couronne	4
Neuvice	2

SHOPPING
Une Gauffre Saperlipopette	1
Toutes Directions	2
Wattitude	3

N

RUE DU PERY
RUE VOLLÈRE
RUE L'ACADÉMIE
St-Servais
RUE DU PALAIS
Gare du Palais
RUE DE BRUXELLES
RUE DE BRUXELLES
Palais des Princes Evêques
Archéoforum
PLACE ST-LAMBERT
St-Croix
RUE HAUTE SAUVENIÈRE
PLACE VERTE
MONT ST MARTIN
St-Martin (Church)
RUE BASSE SAUVENIÈRE
BOULEVARD DE LA SAUVENIÈRE
RUE GÉRARDRIE
Galeries St-Lambert
PLACE DE L'OPERA
PLACE DE LA RÉPUBLIQUE FRANCAISE
RUE ST-GANGULPHE
RUE CHAP DES CLE
La Cité Miroir
PLACE XAVIER NEUJEAN
Théâtre Royal
RUE ST-DENIS
PLACE ST-ETIENNE
RUE DE LA WACHE
St-Jean
Jonfosse Train Station (400m)
RUE G. CLÉMENCEAU
Collégiale St-Denis
RUE DONCEL
RUE DES DOMINICAINS
RUE PONT D'ILE
RUE DE LA CASQUETTE
RUE ST-ADALBERT
BERGERUE
RUE ST-JEAN-EN-ISLE
RUE DES CELESTINES
PASSAGE LEMMONNIER
RUE DE L'ETUVE
RUE DE LA CATHÉDRALE
RUE DE LA UNIVERSITÉ
RUE DU POT D'OR
RUE DU MOULON BLANC
BOULEVARD DE LA SAUVENIÈRE
RUE D'AMAY
RUE FÊTE DE BREUE
PLACE CATHÉDRALE
RUE CHARLES MAGNETTE
RUE SUR LA FONTAINE
RUE PONT-D'AVROY
Cathédrale St-Paul
RUE ST-PAUL
BOULEVARD D'AVROY
RUE ST-GILLES
RUE DES CARMES
& Guillemins Train Station (1.5km)

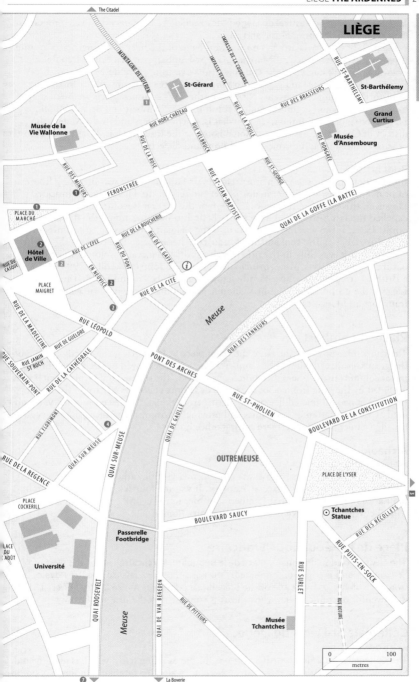

LIÈGE

The Citadel

MONTAGNE DE BUEREN

IMPASSE DE LA COURONNE

RUE ST-BARTHÉLEMY

St-Gérard

St-Barthélemy

RUE DES BRASSEURS

RUE DE LA POILE

Grand
Curtius

RUE HORS-CHÂTEAU

Musée de la
Vie Wallonne

RUE VELBRUCK

Musée
d'Ansembourg

RUE HONGRÉE

RUE DE LA ROSE

RUE ST-GEORGE

RUE DES MINEURS

FERONSTRÉE

RUE ST-JEAN-BAPTISTE

QUAI DE LA GOFFE (LA BATTE)

PLACE DU
MARCHÉ

RUE DE LA BOUCHERIE

RUE DE L'ÉPÉE

RUE DE LA GAFFE

RUE DU
CASQUE

Hôtel
de Ville

RUE DU PONT

EN NÉUVICE

PLACE
MAIGRET

RUE DE LA CITÉ

Meuse

QUAI DES TANNEURS

RUE DE LA MADELEINE

RUE LÉOPOLD

RUE DE GUELDRE

RUE SOUVERAIN-PONT

RUE JAMIN
ST ROCH

RUE DE LA CATHÉDRALE

PONT DES ARCHES

RUE ST-PHOLIEN

BOULEVARD DE LA CONSTITUTION

RUE FLORIMONT

QUAI DE GAULLE

QUAI SUR MEUSE

OUTREMEUSE

PLACE DE L'YSER

RUE DE LA REGENCE

QUAI SUR-MEUSE

PLACE
COCKERILL

Passerelle
Footbridge

BOULEVARD SAUCY

Tchantches
Statue

RUE DES RECOLLETS

PLACE
DU
AOÛT

RUE PUITS-EN-SOCK

Université

QUAI ROOSEVELT

QUAI DE VAN BEEKDEN

RUE DE PITTEURS

RUE SURLET

RUE ROTURE

Meuse

Musée
Tchantches

0   100

metres

La Boverie

January, the biennial **Festival de Liège** (ⓦfestivaldeliege.be) puts on a lively programme of contemporary theatre, music and dance.

The bulk of the city centre lies on the west bank of the river and congregates around three main **squares**: place du Marché, place St-Lambert and place de la République Française. What's known as the **Old Town** runs east from place du Marché, with Féronstrée as its spine, and is home to most of the city's museums and a smattering of historic buildings. The livelier **New Town**, the city's commercial centre, with shops, bars, restaurants and nightlife, nudges south from St-Lambert and de la République Française. To the east of the river, on what is, in effect, an island in the Meuse, the district of Outremeuse is the traditional home of the true Liégeois. It harbours a cluster of bars, restaurants and distinctive traditions and dialects.

Brief history

Independent for most of its history, **Liège** was famous as the seat of a long line of **prince-bishops**, who were major power brokers in the Holy Roman Empire. However, this ended abruptly in 1794 when the French Revolutionary Army expelled the last bishop, torching his cathedral to hammer home the democratic point. Later, Liège was incorporated into the Belgian state, rising to prominence as an industrial city. The **coal and steel** industries hereabouts date back to the twelfth century, but it was only in the nineteenth century that real development of the city's natural resources took place, principally under one **John Cockerill** (1790–1840), a British entrepreneur whose family name you still see around town. These days, Liège is the economic capital of Wallonia, and its main activities are centred around transport and logistics.

Place St-Lambert

The true centre of Liège, the large and open **place St-Lambert**, was formerly the site of the great Gothic cathedral of St-Lambert, which was destroyed by the French in 1794; metal columns mark where the church once stood. The square's only real distinction is provided by the long frontage of the **Palais des Princes Evêques** (Palace of the Prince-Bishops), a neo-Gothic edifice mostly dating from the mid-nineteenth century. It's now used as a combination of law courts and provincial government offices, and you can usually wander into its **courtyard** during office hours.

Archéoforum

pl St-Lambert • Charge • ⓦ archeoforumdeliege.be

You can visit the excavated site of the city's former Gothic cathedral in the **Archéoforum**, underneath place St-Lambert. It was the fourth successor to a church built at the supposed site of St Lambert's murder in the eighth century and is mixed up with the remains of an extensive second-century **Roman villa**.

Place de la République Française

The city's second main square, **place de la République Française**, sits to the west of place St-Lambert and is edged on one side by the shed-like Neoclassical **Théâtre Royale**, in front of which stands a statue of the Liège-born composer **André Grétry** (1741–1813), the inventor of comic opera, whose heart is contained in the urn just below.

Collégiale St-Denis de Liège

rue de la Cathédrale 64 • Free

The **Collégiale St-Denis** is worth a visit not for the building itself, which is gloomy and formless, but for a striking early sixteenth-century **wooden retable**, standing a good 5m

5

high, displayed in the south transept. The top (and principal) section has six assertively carved panels, a dramatic rendition of the Passion of Christ. The bottom set of panels is later and gentler in style, with smaller figures telling the story of St Denis from baptism to decapitation.

Cathédrale St-Paul

pl Cathédrale • Free • ⓦ cathedraledeliege.be

The imposing grey steeple of the **Cathédrale St-Paul** makes it a useful city landmark. The church was promoted to cathedral status in 1794 after the French destroyed the city's former cathedral. Inside are some swirling ceiling paintings from 1570 and a late thirteenth-century polychrome *Madonna and Child* at the base of the choir.

Trésor de Liège

rue Bonne-Fortune 6 • Charge • ⓦ tresordeliege.be

In neighbouring premises, the cathedral's **Trésor de Liège** features a mammoth 90kg bust reliquary of St Lambert, the work of a goldsmith from Aachen, dating from 1512; it contains the skull of the saint and depicts scenes from his life: the miracles he performed as a boy, his burial in Maastricht and the relocation of his body from Maastricht to Liège by St Hubert, who succeeded him as bishop. There are also some lovely **ivory works** from the eleventh century and a similarly dated missal stained by the waters of a 1920s flood that once inundated the cathedral.

Place du Marché

The northern side of the tree-lined **place du Marché** is flanked by a row of atmospheric bars and restaurants, behind which looms the curiously Russian-looking onion dome of the **Église Saint-André**. The south side of the square is occupied by the run-of-the-mill eighteenth-century **Hôtel de Ville**, while in the middle stands **Le Perron**, a grandiose symbol of civic independence comprising a fancy water fountain surmounted by a long and slender column.

The Old Town

From place du Marché, **Féronstrée** heads east to form the backbone of the **Old Town**, a historic, much quieter part of town – except on Sunday mornings, when the vigorous **La Batte market** takes over the nearby riverbank. For an impressive, panoramic view over the whole of Liège, make for **rue Hors-Château**, from where 374 steps ascend the very steep **Montagne de Bueren** up to the **citadel**, which is now little more than a set of ramparts enclosing a modern hospital. Well worth the genuinely lung-wrenching trek, the views are superlative, looking right out over the city and the rolling countryside beyond.

RESURRECTION OF THE CITY POOL

Opened in 2014, **La Cité Miroir Liège** (pl Xavier Neujean 22; ⓦ citemiroir.be) is the new incarnation of Liège's much-loved public swimming pool(s). The building was designed by local Modernist architect **Georges Dedoyard** (1897–1988), inspired by the Bauhaus movement to create this 'oversized cruise ship'. Originally opened in 1942, the baths closed in 2000 for health and safety reasons. Today, it houses two permanent exhibitions, one dedicated to Nazi concentration camps and the other to workers' struggles and social solidarity (both in French and Dutch), as well as an auditorium, a restaurant on the ground floor, a bookshop and a second-floor café.

5

LIÈGE VISIT PASS

The **Liège Visit Pass** (ⓦ visitezliege.be/en) grants free entry to thirteen museums, costs €18 and is valid for 48 hours. It can be bought online and from tourist information (see page 253).

Musée de la Vie Wallonne

cours des Mineurs • Charge • ⓦ provincedeliege.be/en/viewallonne.

Devoted to Walloon culture, the **Musée de la Vie Wallonne** is housed in a beautifully restored former Franciscan friary. It's a nostalgic collection with lots of assorted items from past eras, including **carnival masks** and puppets, children's toys and old brands of soap and cigarettes, all displayed with a contemporary and serious touch. A series of room tableaux illustrate the changing fashions and technologies of the past century, and there are also displays examining **Walloon militancy** and separatism, as well as the decline of local industry (particularly the mines). Look out for the occasional puppet show featuring **Tchantchès** (charge; see box, page 253). The on-site café, run by a social enterprise to get people back into work, serves regional specialities and beer.

Musée d'Ansembourg

Féronstrée 114 • Charge • ⓦ lesmuseesdeliege.be/ansembourg

Occupying a grand eighteenth-century mansion, the **Musée d'Ansembourg**'s interior is distinguished by its sweeping wooden staircase, stucco ceilings and leather wallpaper. This provides a suitably lavish setting for a **sumptuous collection** of period furniture, Delftware, a selection of clocks (including a unique six-faced specimen by Hubert Sarton from 1795), and portraits of various local bigwigs – including several of Liège's prince-bishops – in various stages of self-importance.

Grand Curtius

Féronstrée 136 • Charge • ⓦ grandcurtius.be

Set in three grand mansions dating from the sixteenth to the eighteenth century, the vast, three-storey **Grand Curtius** is a chronological romp through history, studiously covering all ages from prehistoric times to Art Nouveau. Collections include archaeology, decorative arts, religious and Mosan art, and internationally significant collections of arms and glassware; they are all beautifully displayed, with info panels in English. The **Mosan religious art** is a standout, especially Prince-Bishop Notger's ivory and silver bible and the eleventh-century Évégnée Virgin, which bears an uncanny resemblance to former French president François Mitterrand. Recover in the ground-floor bistro with its shady courtyard garden when you've had enough.

Collégiale St-Barthélemy

pl St-Barthélemy • Charge • ⓦ st-barthelemy.be

Originally a Romanesque edifice dating back to the twelfth century, the interior of the **Collégiale St-Barthélemy** was entirely re-equipped six centuries later. Of most significance is the magnificent Romanesque bronze **baptismal font** of 1118 (sculptor unknown); it rests on ten oxen, who bend their heads and necks as if under the weight of the great bowl.

Outremeuse

Across the River Meuse, **Outremeuse** is an old working-class quarter that's said to be the home of the true Liégeois. The district's inhabitants were long known for their forthright radicalism, rioting against their rulers on many occasions and refusing, during the German occupation of World War I, to keep the city's small-arms factories in production. Their appointed guardian was the folkloric figure known as **Tchantchès** (see box, page 253), and the quarter was also the childhood home of acclaimed writer **Georges Simenon** (1903–89), creator of Inspector Maigret – the tourist office has details of a tour entitled 'Following Simenon's Footsteps'.

Musée Tchantchès
rue Surlet 56 • Charge • ⓦ tchantches.be

Also known as the Royal Theatre, the **Musée Tchantchès** is dedicated to Outremeuse's cheeky mascot and displays various costumes and child-size marionettes sculpted by puppet-maker Denis Bisscheroux. From October to April, puppet shows are performed on the beautiful old stage – great for kids.

The Guillemins-La Boverie-Médiacité Axis

Running down two banks of the River Meuse south of the Pont du Roi Albert, complete with walking/cycling tracks, is the **Guillemins-La Boverie-Médiacité Axis**. Calatrava's striking Guillemins train station on the west bank is linked by the La Belle Liégeoise footbridge to La Boverie island, where you'll find the Médiacité shopping centre and ice rink, a park and the fine arts museum, La Boverie.

La Boverie
Parc de la Boverie • Charge • ⓦ laboverie.com

Opened in 2016, **La Boverie** is housed in a rather grand 1905 building with a new glass wing designed by Rudy Ricciotti. The gallery showcases Wallonian modern and contemporary art and has developed a glowing reputation for the quality of its temporary exhibitions. Walloon art is boosted by the work of international luminaries such as Van Gogh, Monet, Picasso, Magritte and Tapiès. The café has a delightful terrace overlooking the park and river.

ARRIVAL AND INFORMATION   LIÈGE

By train Liège has three train stations: all trains stop at the stunningly redesigned main terminal, Guillemins, about 2km south of the centre. Most services also call at Liège's other two stations: Carre, not far from boulevard de la Sauvenière, just west of the centre, and St-Lambert in the city centre. Note, however, that most express trains from Brussels and Luxembourg City only stop at Guillemins. To get to the centre of town from Guillemins station, take the train to St-Lambert.

Destinations from Liège-Guillemins Brussels (hourly; 1hr); Coo (every 2hr; 50min); Eupen (hourly; 40min); Huy (every 20min; 20–30min); Jemelle (hourly; 1hr 30min); Luxembourg City (hourly; 2hr 30min); Melreux-Hotton (hourly; 1hr); Namur (hourly; 45min); Spa, via Pepinster (hourly; 55min).

Tourist information The city tourist office is located southeast of pl St-Lambert at quai de la Goffe 13 (daily 9am–5pm; ⓦ visitezliege.be), in a former meat market dating from the sixteenth century. It's said to be the city's oldest public building.

GETTING AROUND

Water taxi La Navette Fluviale (April–Oct 10am–6pm; ⓦ navettefluviale.be) makes several stops hourly, including quai de Maestricht by Grand Curtius and quai de Rome by La Boverie.

Bike rental You can rent bikes from the tourist office.

TCHANTCHÈS

Tchantchès (Liège slang for 'François'), the so-called 'Prince of Outremeuse', is an earthy, independent-minded, brave but drunken fellow who is said to have been born between two Outremeuse paving stones on 25 August 760. Later in life, legend claims, he was instrumental in Charlemagne's campaigns, thanks to the use of his enormous nose(!). Nowadays, Tchantchès can be seen in action in traditional Liège **puppet shows** (see page 253); he's also represented in a **statue** on place l'Yser, the traditional place of his death.

5

ACCOMMODATION
SEE MAP PAGE 248

L'Auberge de Jeunesse Georges Simenon rue Georges Simenon 2 ⓦlesaubergesdejeunesse.be. This modern, well-equipped hostel with 215 beds is housed in a pleasant old building in the heart of Outremeuse, a 10min walk from St-Lambert. Has self-catering facilities, a café, internet access and a laundry. Dorms €, doubles €

Liège Sélys Mont Saint Martin 9 ⓦhotelselys.be. Occupies a pair of sixteenth-century townhouses that were painstakingly restored and now offer ultra-modern, luxurious rooms, a stunning vaulted-ceiling bar, spa,

brasserie with an impressive terrace and a restaurant. €€€

La Couronne pl des Guillemins 11 ⓦhoteldelacouronne. be/en. Crisp, Italian-style three-star right opposite Guillemins station. It caters to businessfolk, but the 24hr bar and epic breakfast buffet appeal to all. €€

★ **Neuvice** En Neuvice 45 ⓦhotelneuvice.be. Smooth and slick, modern boutique-style options spread through three historic buildings on one of the oldest streets in town. *Neuvice* boasts ten spacious rooms and a library, and breakfast is served in a restored fifteenth-century cellar. €€

EATING
SEE MAP PAGE 248

Liégeois cuisine is deliciously **hearty** rather than refined – in particular, look out for *boulets avec sirop de Liège* (meatballs drizzled in a sweet local syrup).

Café Lequet quai sur-Meuse 17 ⓦcafe-lequet.com. An authentic bygone-era restaurant that serves arguably the best Boulet-frites – meatballs doused in sweet *sirop de Liège* – in the city. It attracts people from far and wide, plus it's cheap. Also, the chocolate mousse is to die for. €

L'Écailler rue des Dominicains 26 ⓦlecailler.be. Behind the Théâtre Royale, this cosy, old-fashioned, bistro-style joint is a long-term favourite and does great oysters and seafood platters. €€€

La Frite rue de la Cité 5 ⓦlafrite.be. This chip shop serves yummy fries and a choice of burgers (including a vegetarian option). Eat in or take away. €

Ma Ferme en Ville rue Souverain Pont 34 ⓦmaferme enville.be. This bright, charming 'farm in town' is open for breakfast and lunch, serving dishes made with local

products and seasonal fruit and vegetables. €

Maison Leblanc rue Lulay des Fèbres 5 ⓦmaison leblanc.be. This butcher's shop, established in 1873, has a restaurant with a blood-red interior. Steak from around the world, including Wagyu, is on the menu. Try the 250g Belgian White Blue. €€€

★ **As Ouhès** pl du Marché 21 ☎04 223 32 25. This traditional restaurant with an outside terrace in the city's liveliest square is a good place to try Liégeois and Belgian food – meatballs, vol-au-vent (creamy chicken casserole) and chicory wrapped in ham. End your meal with a café liégeois – sweet, creamy coffee. €

Riva Esplanade Albert 1er 7 ⓦriva-brasserie.com. A 15min walk northeast of Guillemins station, *Riva* is Liège's only restaurant with a proper riverside terrace. In the minimalist dining room, you can tuck into Belgian, French or Italian mains or stick to nibbles. €€

DRINKING
SEE MAP PAGE 248

The grid of streets in the New Town running north from rue Pont d'Avroy to rue de la Casquette (known locally as 'le carré') is the hub of the city's nightlife, with loads of good, largely **student-oriented bars** that can get very raucous later on. There's a clutch of more sedate venues on **pl du Marché**.

★ **Brasserie Curtius** impasse des Ursulines ⓦbrasseriec.com. Award-winning beer Curtius is brewed in this seventeenth-century convent next to the Montagne de Bueren (see page 251). Try some in the upstairs bar or on one of the terraces in summer. €

La Maison du Peket rue de l'Epée 4 ⓦmaisondupeket. be. The place to taste the local drink *peket* – a type of gin – in 250 varieties, from guava and mango in the fruit section to the old bottles on the vintage shelves. €

Le Verre Bouteille rue de la Casquette 13 ⓦleverre bouteille.be. Contemporary wine bar run by two young guys, stocking six hundred wines from thirty countries. Dim lighting and candles create a cosy atmosphere when it gets dark, while ham and cheese platters should quell hunger pangs. €

SHOPPING
SEE MAP PAGE 248

★ **Une Gaufrette Saperlipopette** rue des Mineurs 7 ☎04 222 37 13. Liège is famous for its crisp, sweet waffles; this is the best place to get them. They also sell delicious traditional biscuits and pastries.

Toutes Directions rue de la Violette 3 ☎04 262 20 64. This travel and food bookshop has a good selection of

English publications, including Rough Guides. You can also have coffee here.

Wattitude rue Souverain-Pont 7 ⓦwattitude.be. This boutique sells hip clothes, accessories, arts, and crafts, primarily made in Wallonia.

Spa

SPA, about 40km southeast of Liège, was the world's first health resort, established in the sixteenth century. Pliny the Elder knew of the healing properties of the waters here, and Henry VIII was an early visitor, but Peter the Great clinched the town's fame, heralding it as 'the best place to take the waters'. Since then, the town has given its name to thermal resorts worldwide, reaching a height of popularity in the eighteenth and nineteenth centuries, when it was known as the 'Café of Europe', being graced by monarchs, statesmen, intellectuals and aristocrats from every corner of the continent. Later, the town went into slow decline – when the poet Matthew Arnold visited in 1860, he claimed it 'astonished us by its insignificance' – but nowadays, Spa has regained some of its chicness thanks, in part, to the modern thermal complex, **Les Thermes de Spa**, on the hill overlooking the town. It also makes a good base for excursions into the **Hautes Fagnes** (see page 259), a short drive to the south and southeast.

The **town centre** has a certain faded elegance, mostly thanks to a cluster of grand Neoclassical buildings presided over by the towering steeples of the church of the 1880s Notre-Dame et St-Remacle. Chief among these neighbours is Spa the casino, perhaps the oldest in the world. It was founded in 1763 under the improbable auspices of the prince-bishop of Liège, though the current building dates only from 1919. It hosts the annual Francofolies festival in July, where established and emerging Belgian-French artists celebrate their music (ⓦ francofolies.be).

Pouhon Pierre-le-Grand and other springs

rue du Marché 1A • Pouhon Pierre-le-Grand • Charge

In the town centre is Spa's main mineral spring, the **Pouhon-Pierre-le-Grand**, where you can drink the cloudy waters, allegedly beneficial for lung and heart ailments and rheumatism. The spring is housed in a barnlike Neoclassical pavilion – also home to the tourist office (see page 256) – and is named after Peter the Great, who appreciated the therapeutic effects of its waters and visited often. Spa's **other springs** – notably Tonnelet, Barisart, Géronstère and Sauvenière – are open year-round and are free to enter.

Musée de la Ville d'Eaux

av Reine Astrid 77 • Charge • ⓦ spavillaroyale.be

Five minutes' walk west of the town centre, situated in the former mansion of Queen Marie-Henriette, the **Musée de la Ville d'Eaux** tells the story of Spa with original documents, rare objects and videos. The stables next door have been turned into the **Musée du Cheval**, exhibiting all things equine.

Les Thermes de Spa

Colline d'Annette et Lubin • Charge • ⓦ thermesdespa.com • Take the funicular from pl Royale or follow the path through the woods just to the side

On the hill immediately above central Spa stands the town's leading attraction, **Les Thermes de Spa**, a thermal complex offering a multitude of treatments. On arrival, you can sample three different types of Spa spring water: Reine, Clementine and the iron-rich Marie-Henriette. There is an outdoor and indoor **pool** with water-massage jets and hot tubs galore. Upstairs is reserved for saunas, steam rooms, a relaxation area with chill-out music and a **panoramic view** of the valley below. You must book massages, mud wraps or water treatments in the famous retro copper baths in advance.

5

ARRIVAL AND INFORMATION

SPA

By train Spa has two train stations, but the one you want for the town centre is Spa-Géronstère, a 5min walk south of the casino.

Destinations Liège, via Pepinster (hourly; 50min); Namur (hourly; 2hrs with two changes).

Tourist office Situated inside the Neoclassical pavilion, which houses the Pierre-le-Grand spring fountain at rue du Marche 1A (Nov–June: Tues–Sun 9.30am–5.30pm; July–Aug: daily 9.30am–5.30pm; ⓦ visitspa-hautesfagnes. be). There are 21 walking routes around the surrounding countryside, and the office sells a map detailing them all.

GETTING AROUND

By cliff railway A funicular running up and down the hillside connects the Thermes de Spa with the lower town; tickets cost just a few cents.

ACCOMMODATION

Camping Spa d'Or Stockay 17, 4845 Sart-les-Spa ⓦ campingspador.be. This four-star campsite is 4km northeast of town, beside the small Wayai River. As well as camping spots, travellers can rent mobile homes and cabins. Also on site is a large open-air, heated swimming pool, a restaurant, a bar, a well-stocked shop and wi-fi in the main building. Children's entertainment activities are organised during summer. Mid-April to Sept. €

★ **L'Écrin d'Ô** rue de la Sauvenière 108 ⓦ lecrin-do.be. Utterly charming chalet-style hotel on the hillside above Spa. The seven rooms are decorated in a contemporary style, with an elegant lounge and a terrace. Spa packages are available. €€€

Radisson Blu Palace pl Royale 39 ⓦ radissonhotels. com. Seated at the base of the hill in the centre of town, this hotel's winning feature is its private funicular railway to Les Thermes de Spa, so guests (who receive discounts) can travel to and fro in their dressing gowns. See the website for packages. €€

La Villa des Fleurs rue Albin Body 31 ⓦ villadesfleurs. be. Right in the centre of town, this is Spa's most characterful and comfortable option, a handsome old townhouse dating from 1912, with just a dozen or so large guest rooms decorated in a modern version of period style – and with a nice private garden, too. €€

EATING

La Belle Époque pl du Monument 15 ⓦ la-belle-epoque-spa.be. As the name suggests, this place has a beautiful interior with oodles of wood panelling, and a hatful of Art Nouveau flourishes. It serves excellent fish mains, and its mussels are famous for miles around. €€

Source de la Géronstère rte de la Géronstère 119 ⓦ lageronstere.be. In a peaceful woodland location next to the Géronstère spring, this restaurant specialises in grilled meats and traditional Belgian food, but it also does an excellent line in salads. €€

★ **La Table de Spa** rue Delhasse 23 ⓦ latabledespa. be. Neat and modern little café-restaurant with a pavement terrace, serving, for example, *Croque Végétarien* with home-made tapenade, mushrooms and mozzarella. Other specialities include Ardennes trout and prawns. €€

Stavelot

The small and tranquil town of **STAVELOT** rambles up the hill from the River Amblève. It grew up around its **abbey**, which ran the area as an independent principality until the French Revolutionary Army ended its privileges at the end of the eighteenth

---

SPA-FRANCORCHAMPS

Spa-Francorchamps, 10km southeast of Spa, is renowned as one of the most scenic and historic venues in the **Motorsports** world. The highlight by far is the **Belgian Grand Prix**. The circuit is busy almost every day between March and November, hosting all kinds of events, some of which are free. Anyone can visit, and most of the time, there's free access to the paddock, pit lane and the panoramic top-floor brasserie. It's also possible to see more of the circuit – the media centre and **race control room**, for example – through a **guided tour** (charge; ⓦ spa-francorchamps.be). You can also book a drive around the track (charge).

century. The town was also the scene of fierce fighting during the Ardennes campaign of World War II, and some of the Germans' worst atrocities in Belgium were committed there.

These days, it's a pleasant old place, the pretty streets of its **tiny centre** flanked by a battery of half-timbered houses that mostly date from the eighteenth century. The best time to be here is for its renowned annual **carnival**, the **Laetare**, first celebrated here in 1502 and held on the third weekend before Easter, from Saturday to Monday evening; the main protagonists are the **Blancs Moussis** – white-robed, masked figures with obscenely long red noses – of which you'll see depictions adorning various Stavelot houses. There are also theatre and music **festivals** in July and August, respectively, with performances in the abbey buildings.

Abbaye de Stavelot

Cour de l'Abbaye 1, Stavelot • Charge • ⓦ abbayedestavelot.be

The **Abbaye de Stavelot's** sprawling complex of mainly eighteenth-century buildings sits in front of the stumpy foundational columns of the former abbey. Today, the abbey buildings house the **tourist office** (see page 257) and **three modern museums**.

Musée Historique de la Principauté de Stavelot-Malmedy

The multimedia layout here traces the **principality's history** from the seventh century to the present through religious artefacts, town crafts and folkloric exhibits. There are also interesting **3D creations** of what the original walled abbey would have looked like.

Musée du Circuit de Spa-Francorchamps

The **museum** (ⓦ musee-circuit.be) in the abbey's vaulted cellars holds a collection of racing cars and motorcycles from the nearby **racetrack** (see box, page 256) – home of the Belgium Formula 1 Grand Prix – including the 1974 Lotus of Belgian ace Jackie Ickx.

Musée Guillaume Apollinaire

The second-floor museum is dedicated to **Guillaume Apollinaire** (1880–1918), the influential French writer and poet who spent the summer of 1899 in Stavelot (he left without paying his bill, apparently). Apollinaire wrote many poems about the town and the Ardennes before his early death in Paris during the influenza epidemic of 1918.

Église St-Sebastien

ol du Vinâve • Free • ⓦ openchurches.eu

The angular **Église St-Sebastien** is home to the wonderfully intricate thirteenth-century **shrine of St Remacle**, the seventh-century founder of Stavelot abbey, who is said to have built the abbey with the aid of a wolf he tamed for the purpose. The Romanesque shrine is made of gilt and enamelled copper with filigree and silver statuettes, though you can usually only view it from a distance.

ARRIVAL AND INFORMATION   STAVELOT

By train and bus Take the train to Trois-Ponts on the Liège-Luxembourg line, and then catch the bus (every 2hr; 10min) outside Trois-Ponts train station; alight at 'Stavelot: Place E Grandprez'

Tourist information Stavelot's tourist office is in the glass-window corridor of Stavelot abbey (daily 10am–1pm & 1.30–5pm; ⓦ tourismestavelot.be).

ACCOMMODATION AND EATING

Friterie Sébastien av F. Nikolay 15 ⓦ friterie-sebastien. be. Popular with young locals, this is a great place for a quick, cheap snack and yummy fries in the beamed dining room or on the roadside terrace. €

5

Hôtel-Restô ô Mal Aimé rue Neuve 12 ⓦomalaime.
be. Apollinaire famously stayed at this lively little place.
Its eight spotless rooms, painted in bright, happy shades
of blue, lime green and pink, have bags of character. As do
the restaurant and public areas, decorated with quirky art.
Restaurant €€; accommodation €€

Romantik Hotel Le Val d'Amblève rte de Malmédy 7
ⓦ levaldambleve.be. This family-run option is just 200m
from the centre, with 24 excellent rooms: four in the main
building and the rest in a separate section nearby. Romantic
restaurant with views of the garden and small wellness
centre too. €€€

Coo and around

Just west of Stavelot, perched above the banks of the Amblève, **COO** is a nice enough
village. Still, the real action is down by the river, where the modest **waterfalls** have
given birth to a thriving resort area made up of a cluster of hotels and restaurants in
Petit Coo and, in **Grand Coo** on the other side of the river, the unfortunately named
Plopsa Coo, an adventure and theme park aimed at families.

Plopsa Coo

Grand Coo 4 • Charge • ⓦ plopsacoo.be

For families, the **Plopsa Coo** theme park is an ideal day's distraction, particularly as
you can wander around for free and only have to buy a ticket if you try out any of the
rides. These include the mildly terrifying 'Mega Mindy Flyer', while 'Monkey Island',
Smurfer (a ride through a Smurf-themed forest) and 'Animal Farm' will delight little
ones. You can ride down a dry bobsleigh, go go-karting, take a chair lift for vertiginous
views or do other activities.

Grottes de Remouchamps

rue de Louveigné 3, Remouchamps • Charge • ⓦ lesgrottes.be

About 25km from Coo, the **Grottes de Remouchamps** are the country's second-largest
caves after Han (see page 264) and have been open to visitors since 1828. **Tours** last
over an hour and take you some 800m through the heart of the cave system, which is
6km in length overall, before punting you back 700m to the entrance by the **river** – a
head-ducking and somewhat claustrophobic journey, but one not to be missed. The
ticket gives access to the (missable) museum.

Malmedy and around

About 8km northeast of Stavelot, the bustling resort of **MALMEDY** is a popular
tourist destination, its attractive streets flanked by lively restaurants, smart shops
and cheap hotels. The town itself is thin on sights – most people come for the
surrounding scenery – but it's a pleasant place to spend a night or two and makes a
relatively inexpensive base for the **Hautes Fagnes** (see page 259). Malmedy is also
home to the **Cwarmê**, one of Belgium's most famous festivals, held over the four
days leading up to Shrove Tuesday. The main knees-up is on the Sunday, during
which roving groups of masked figures in colourful velvet robes and plumed hats
– the so-called **Haguètes** – wander around town seizing people with long wooden
pincers derived, it's thought, from the devices that were once used to give food to
lepers. Malmedy was also caught up in the Battle of the Bulge (see page 273),
during which 84 American prisoners of war were murdered in cold blood by their
German captors just 4km or so southeast of Malmedy at the **Baugnez crossroads**, a
simple **memorial** – and an American flag – now stand beside the **roundabout** at the
crossroads recalling this savage event.

Malmundarium

pl du Châtelet 10 • Charge • ⓦ malmundarium.be

Housed in the ancient Malmedy monastery – most of which dates from the early eighteenth century – the **Malmundarium** museum is the pride and joy of the town. It displays items originating from the eighteenth-century cathedral treasury and has rooms that explain local **carnival folklore** and the dual traditions of making paper and leather.

ARRIVAL AND INFORMATION

MALMEDY

By bus, Bus No. 745 (every 2hr; 25min) departs from outside Trois-Pont station on the Liège–Luxembourg line and drops you off at the tourist office, stop 'Malmedy: Place Albert 1er'.

Tourist information The well-equipped tourist office, on pl Albert 1er (low season: Wed–Sat 10am–6pm; high season: daily 9am–6pm; ⓦ ostbelgien.eu/en), has truckloads of information on the town and its environs.

ACCOMMODATION AND EATING

Albert 1er pl Albert 1er 40 ⓦ hotel-albertpremier.be. These six rooms, situated above a good restaurant, might not be anything special, but they're well looked after and right in the centre. €€
Au Petit Chef pl de Rome 5–6 ⓦ aupetitchef.be. This straightforward brasserie/restaurant serves tasty and inexpensive Belgian and French dishes, plus mussels cooked a million ways. It has a *friterie* tacked onto its right-

hand side. €
Auberge de Jeunesse Hautes Fagnes rte d'Eupen 36 ⓦ lesaubergesdejeunesse.be. Rustic chalet-style youth hostel that can help arrange activities such as beer-tasting and orienteering; they also rent out mountain bikes and have a café-restaurant serving a bargain plat du jour. Beside the main road, a couple of kilometres north of Malmedy. Dorms €, doubles €

The Hautes Fagnes

The high plateau that stretches north of Malmedy up as far as Eupen (see box, page 260) is known as the **Hautes Fagnes** (in German, the Hohes Venn, or High Fens) and is now protected as a national park. This area marks the end of the Ardennes proper and has been twinned with the Eifel hills to form the sprawling **Deutsch-Belgischer Naturpark**. The Hautes Fagnes accommodates Belgium's highest peak, the **Signal de Botrange** (694m), but the rest of the area is boggy heath and woods, windswept and rather wild – excellent **hiking** country and great for cross-country skiing in winter.

Centre Nature Botrange

rte de Botrange 131, 7km north of Robertville, on the road to Eupen • ⓦ botrange.be • Bus No. 390 runs to the centre from Verviers station (4 daily; 30min) or bus No. 394 (7 daily; 20min) runs from Eupen station (see box, page 260); otherwise, you'll need a car to get there

The **Centre Nature Botrange** provides a focus for explorations of the national park. Its **museum** describes the flora and fauna of the area and explains how the *fagnes* were created and how they have been exploited. The centre also rents out **electric bikes** and, in winter, **cross-country skis**; it also sells a map, 'Ronde de Botrange', so that you can explore the accessible parts of the fens on foot (some of the footpaths run along the edges of the protected areas). The rustic *Fagn'eteria* café serves hot meals and beers.

Signal de Botrange

Just a 3km walk up the main N676 road is the **Signal de Botrange**, Belgium's highest point at 694m. However, the Hautes Fagnes' high plateau means it doesn't feel very high at all. A **tower** marks the summit, offering a good panorama over the *fagnes*, and there's a restaurant popular with coach parties and walkers alike.

5

EUPEN

The pleasant but unexceptional little town of **EUPEN** is the capital of the German-speaking region of Belgium, or **Deutschsprachige Gemeinschaft Belgiens**, a pint-sized area pushed tight against the German border that's home to around 78,000 people and enjoys the same federal status as the other two linguistic areas of the country. Once part of **Prussia**, the area was ceded to Belgium by the Treaty of Versailles at the end of World War I. It has a distinctive Rhineland feel, but that aside, there's precious little reason to visit. Direct **trains** to Eupen depart from Liège-Guillemins station (hourly; 40min). Travelling from Spa takes slightly longer and requires a change of station.

Dinant and around

Pretty little **DINANT**, some 30km south of Namur, strings along the River Meuse beneath craggy green cliffs, its onion-domed **Notre-Dame church** looming over the barges and tourist cruise boats that ply these calm waters. Dinant is a lovely town to wander around for a few hours and, although the scenery is not nearly as wild as you'll find deeper in the Ardennes, there are compensations, notably a **citadel** and the **Maison Leffe** – Leffe beer was invented here in the thirteenth century. There are also a couple of minor sites associated with Dinant's most famous son, **Adolphe Sax** (see box, page 261), the inventor of the saxophone, and there are plentiful kayaking and hiking opportunities in the surrounding villages of **Anseremme**, **Gendron** and **Houyet**.

Brief history

The Romans were the first to put the place on the map, occupying the settlement and naming it after **Diana**, the goddess of the hunt. Still, the town's heyday came much later, in the fourteenth century, when it boomed from the profits of the **metalworking** industry, turning copper, brass and bronze into ornate jewellery known as dinanderie. Local counts slugged it out for possession of the town until, in 1466, Charles the Bold decided to settle his Dinant account by simply razing it to the ground. One result of all this medieval blood and thunder was the construction of an imposing **citadel** on the cliff immediately above Dinant. Although the town was sacked on several subsequent occasions and badly damaged in both world wars, the fortress survived and became the town's principal attraction.

Collégiale Notre-Dame de Dinant

pl Reine Astrid • ⓦ doyennededinant.com

Dinant's most distinctive landmark, the **Collégiale Notre-Dame de Dinant** church, is topped with a distinctive bulbous spire featured on all the tourist brochures. Rebuilt on several occasions, and lastly in the 1820s, there's not much of interest to see inside except the stained-glass windows and an unfinished painting by one of Dinant's most famous sons, the nineteenth-century artist **Antoine Wiertz**. Situated on the right of the ambulatory, it's a mawkish affair dedicated to his parents and entitled *We'll Meet Again in Heaven*.

The citadel

pl Reine Astrid 3–5 • Charge • ⓦ citadellededinant.be • A daily cable car ferries visitors up to the top during high season (weekends and school hols in low season); on foot, it's a 400-odd step slog

Next to Notre-Dame church lies the entrance to **Dinant's citadel**, which mostly dates from the Dutch occupation of the early nineteenth century – after the French destroyed the medieval castle in 1703. The citadel saw heavy **fighting** in both world wars: in 1914, having struggled to dislodge French soldiers from the stronghold, German troops took revenge on the locals, executing over six hundred and deporting several hundred more before torching the town; the Germans captured the citadel again in 1940, and it was the scene of even worse fighting when the Allies took Dinant in 1944. There's a memorial to those who gave their lives here, a **historical museum** with models re-creating particular battles and the Dutch occupation, plus a section with weapons from the Napoleonic era to the last world war. You can also see the wooden beams which supported the first **bridge** in Dinant, built nine hundred years ago by monks and found again by accident in 1952, as well as **dungeons** and the kitchen and bakery of the Dutch fortress.

Maison Leffe

Charreau des Capucins 23 • Charge • ⓦ leffe.com

In the chapel of the former convent that is now *Hotel La Merveilleuse* (see page 262), the **Maison Leffe** explores the story of Dinant's most famous export – Leffe beer. The monks started brewing at the Abbaye de Leffe in 1240, but after a turbulent history, which saw the building destroyed by floods and war, the beer is now brewed in Leuven by a multinational conglomerate. During the multimedia exhibition, you can find out how the nine varieties are made and how to pair them with food, which includes a tasting.

Grotte la Merveilleuse

rte de Philippeville 142, on the far side of the river about 750m from the bridge • Charge • ⓦ exploremeuse.be

One of Belgium's most beautiful cave systems, the **Grotte la Merveilleuse**, was discovered in 1904 during the construction of a railway. It's not the largest of the Ardennes cave complexes by any means, but the fifty-minute **tours** take you some 40m below ground and give a good grounding in the science of stalagmites and stalactites, rock formations and caves in general.

ARRIVAL AND INFORMATION   DINANT

By train Dinant's train station is 300m from the bridge that spans the River Meuse to Notre-Dame church.
Destinations Brussel-Zuid/Bruxelles-Midi (hourly; 1hr 50min with 1 change); Liège (every 30min; 1hr 40min with 1 change); Namur (every 30min; 30min).
Tourist information The tourist office is located at av

Cadoux 8 (April–June, Sept & Oct: Mon–Fri 9am–5pm, Sat 9.30am–5pm, Sun 10am–4.30pm; July & Aug: Mon–Fri 9am–5.30pm, Sat 9am–5.30pm, Sun 10am–4.30pm; Nov–March: Mon–Fri 9am–5pm, Sat 9.30am–4pm, Sun 10–3pm; ⓦ exploremeuse.be).

ACCOMMODATION

Camping Devant-Bouvignes quai du Camping 1 ☎ 082 22 40 02. Small, two-star, family-friendly campsite next to the Meuse with sixty tent pitches. There's also a modern sanitary block and a kids' playground. It's a 20min walk into

town. Mid-March to mid-Nov. €
Ibis Dinant Rempart d'Albeau 16 ⓦ all.accor.com. Chain hotel in a conspicuous brick block, 1km or so south of the town bridge. There are no points for originality, but at least

---

SAX APPEAL

Dinant's most famous son is **Adolphe Sax** (1814–94), the inventor of the saxophone. Saxophiles will want to have a look at the musician's old home, right in the centre at rue Adolphe Sax 35 (daily 9am–7pm; free), marked by a commemorative **plaque** and a neat stained-glass mural of a man blowing his horn, along with a statue of the king of cool reclining on a bench outside.

5

its neat, trim, modern rooms look out over the water. €€
Le Freyr ch des Alpinistes 22, Anseremme ⓦ lefreyr.be.
Set in a good-looking older building close to the Meuse,
about 4km south of Dinant, this very comfortable, chalet-
style hotel in Anseremme offers a handful of rooms and a
first-rate restaurant. €€

★ **La Merveilleuse** Charreau des Capucins 23
ⓦ infiniti-resort.be. Perched on a hill overlooking the
town, this neo-Gothic nineteenth-century nunnery was
transformed into a hotel in 2008 with nineteen rooms
that range from fairly spartan to luxurious, plus there's an
adjoining high-tech spa with a pool and fine restaurant. €€

EATING

Catering for Dinant's passing tourist trade is big business,
which means that **run-of-the-mill cafés** and **restaurants**
are ten-a-penny. That said, there are still a few quality places
worth mentioning.

La Broche rue Grande 22 ⓦ labroche.be. One short block
from the river, on Dinant's old main street, this smart and
well-regarded French restaurant has an excellent line of set
meals and an à la carte menu. €€€

Café Leffe rue Adolphe Sax 2 ⓦ cafeleffe-dinant.be. Crisp,
modern and trim riverside café with a good selection of beers
plus Belgian, Italian and Moroccan food on the menu. €
Patisserie Jacobs rue Grande 147 ☎ 082 22 21 39.
Patisserie with a small café section at the back that,
among other things, sells *couques de Dinant*, a honey-flour
combination that's better admired than consumed unless
you have the teeth of a horse. €

Château de Freÿr

Freÿr 12, Hastière, 6.5km south of Dinant • Charge • ⓦ freyr.be

South of Dinant and a short walk from the village of Anseremme, the solitary
Château de Freÿr is a crisply symmetrical, largely eighteenth-century brick mansion
pushed up against the main road and the river. Once the summer home of the
dukes of Beaufort-Spontin, it's still privately owned and immaculately maintained.
The opulent rooms are distinguished by their period furniture and thundering
fireplaces. The adjoining gardens parallel the river, laid out in the formal French
style, spreading over three terraces and including a **maze** and 300-year-old **orange
trees**. A pavilion at the highest point provides a lovely view over the château
and river.

Rochefort and around

One of the Ardennes' most beautiful regions lies a scenic 33km southeast of Dinant,
a thickly wooded terrain of plateaux, gentle hills and valleys, with quiet roads perfect
for cycling. At its centre is the tourist resort of **ROCHEFORT**, which, though short on
specific sights, is one possible base for rural wanderings – especially as it attracts fewer
crowds than neighbouring **Han-sur-Lesse**.

Castle of the Counts

rue Jacquet • Charge • ⓦ chateaurochefort.be

Once the largest fortress in the area, all that remains of Rochefort's medieval **Castle of
the Counts** – perched atop a rocky outcrop off to the right of rue Jacquet – are the old
walls, a couple of **wells** and, in the small **park** just below the entrance, the eighteenth-
century arcades that were added to prop up the château's fashionable formal **gardens**. It
does, however, afford superb views of the town below.

Château de Lavaux-Ste-Anne

rue du Château 8, Lavaux-Ste-Anne • Charge • ⓦ chateau-lavaux.com

Roughly 16km southwest of Rochefort, the pretty and moated **Château de Lavaux-Ste-
Anne** holds no fewer than three **museums**: the first depicts the everyday life of locals

ACTIVITIES AROUND DINANT

With access to two **rivers** – the broad and sluggish **River Meuse** and the prettier **River Lesse** – and surrounded by steep, wooded cliffs, Dinant is the ideal base to try some outdoor sports.

RIVER MEUSE CRUISES

A range of boat tours depart from Avenue Winston Churchill, the main stretch of street next to Dinant's citadel. Regardless of the company you choose, prices and itineraries are pretty consistent.

Les Croisières Mosanes rue Daoust 64 ⓦ croisieres-mosanes.be. Offers cruises to Anseremme (April to mid-Sept: hourly 10.30am–6.30pm; return trip 45min) and to Freÿr (May–Aug: daily 2.30pm; return trip 2hr).

Dinant Evasion pl Albert 1er (pontoon) or rue du Vélodrome 15 ⓦ dinant-evasion.be. This outfit runs a similar set-up to Les Croisières Mosanes, with cruises to Anseremme (April to mid-Sept: hourly 10.30am–6.30pm; return trip 45min) and to Freÿr (May to mid-Sept: 2.30pm; return trip 2hr). The company also rents out electric boats, which can hold up to seven people (April to mid-Sept: noon–6pm).

KAYAKING ALONG THE RIVER LESSE

Wilder and prettier than the River Meuse, the **River Lesse**, which spears off the Meuse in Anseremme, is open to kayakers from April to September. Visitors travelling by train can make for the villages of **Gendron or Houyet** and pick up a kayak at either – but remember to reserve them in advance. Gendron-Celles and Houyet train stations are metres from the river – and the boats. Driving travellers can park their cars, buy tickets at Anseremme, and then take the train to either Gendron for a 12km two-and-a-half-hour paddle or to Houyet for a longer 21km five-hour paddle. Both routes cross two gentle, 50cm deep **rapids**. The Lesse itself is wild and winding, with incredible scenery running past the rocky **Les Aiguilles de Chaleux** cliffs, though be warned that it sometimes gets so packed that there's a veritable canoe log jam. Consequently, it's a good idea to set out as early as possible to avoid the worst of the crush.

Dinant Evasion Lesse Kayaks pl Baudouin 1er 2, Anseremme ⓦ dinant-evasion.be. Dinant Evasion rents out one- and two-seater kayaks and three-person canoes. They also offer packages that include kayaks, train tickets to Houyet and Gendron, and ultra-light paddles.

HIKING AND BIKING

The Dinant tourist office (see page 261) sells the *Carte Dinant*, which shows several signposted **walks** in the Dinant area, as well as several **mountain-biking** routes between 20km and 35km long.

Moss'Bikes! rue de Sûre 108, Dréhance ⓦ www.mossbikes-dinant.be. Mountain bikes can be rented for four hours or five days, with a deposit depending on the length of the rental. Helmets cost extra.

during the nineteenth and early twentieth centuries; the second shows how the lords of Lavaux lived in comparison; and the third is a nature museum. Nearby, a revived **marshland** has been created to encourage nature back into the area – lovely for a walk. There's a brasserie on site, too, in case tummies start to rumble.

ARRIVAL AND INFORMATION   ROCHEFORT

By train and bus Access by public transport is easiest from Namur; take the train to Jemelle (hourly; 40min), from where it's about 4km west to Rochefort by bus (ⓦ letec.be). Buses pull in on Rochefort's main street, rue de Behogne.

Tourist information The well-organised tourist office is at rue de Behogne 5 (Easter–June & Sept: Mon–Fri 8am–5pm, Sat & Sun 9.30am–5pm; July & Aug: Mon–Fri 8am–6pm, Sat & Sun 9.30am–5pm; Oct–Easter: Mon–Fri 8am–5pm, Sat 10am–5pm, Sun 10am–4pm; ⓦ visitardenne.com).

It has multilingual staff, free wi-fi and sells walking maps.

Outdoor pursuits Crisscrossed by rivers, the handsome countryside around Rochefort provides lots of opportunities for walking, canoeing and mountain biking. **Walkers** need the *Rochefort et ses villages* guide (on sale at local tourist offices), which lists thirty numbered walks and six routes for **mountain bikers** and four for **cyclists**.

Cyclesport rue de Behogne 59, Rochefort ⓦ cyclesport.be Rents mountain, trekking and electric bikes.

5

ACCOMMODATION

La Malle Poste rue de Behogne 46 ⓦmalleposte. net. An attractively restored old coaching inn with large, handsomely finished rooms and expansive public spaces. Its rates are high for Rochefort, but there are loads of facilities, including an indoor pool, fitness centre and garden. €€€

EATING

Couleur Basilic pl Albert 1er 25 ⓦcouleurbasilic.be. Hip restaurant with a cocktail and champagne bar. The Belgian-French menu features classic Mediterranean dishes, some with an Asian accent (though there are burgers, grills and pasta, too). €€

★ **La Gourmandise** rue de Behogne 24 ⓦla-gourmandise.be. Opposite the tourist office, this place has a big menu of local dishes, wood-fire grills and an excellent selection of beers, including the famous local Trappist brew named after the town. €€

Han-sur-Lesse

Just 6km southwest of Rochefort, **HAN-SUR-LESSE** sits – as the name suggests – on the banks of the River Lesse. It is a popular summer resort, a neat, trim, and rural little place with a well-known cave system that draws in day-trippers by the coachload.

Grottes de Han

Grottes de Han rue J Lamotte 2 · Charge · ⓦgrotte-de-han.be · Complimentary trams run from the ticket office in the centre of the village to the caves; the return journey on foot takes 5–10min

Discovered at the beginning of the nineteenth century, the **Grottes de Han** are a series of limestone galleries carved out of the hills by the River Lesse millions of years ago. **Tours** of the caves are well worth it, although you visit only a small portion of the 8km cave system, taking in the so-called **Salle du Trophée**, the site of the largest **stalagmite**; the **Salle d'Armes**, where the Lesse reappears after travelling underground for 1km; and the massive **Salle du Dôme** – 129m high – which contains a small **lake**. Amongst several potential add-ons, tickets also cover entry to the 2.5-square-kilometre **wildlife reserve** that sits above the cave system and is home to European bison, Przewalski's horses, wolf and lynx – follow the 2km forest path or join a safari bus tour.

ARRIVAL AND DEPARTURE

HAN-SUR-LESSE

By bus and train Take the train to Jemelle and catch the No. 29 bus, which connects Jemelle, Rochefort and Han.
Tourist information Han's tourist office is on the central square at pl Théo Lannoy 2 (daily 9.30/10am–4/5pm; ⓦrochefort.be). They rent out mountain and electric bikes, among other services.

ACCOMMODATION AND EATING

Camping le Pirot rue Charleville ⓦcamping shansurlesse.be. Just 100m from the village centre and seated by the river's edge, this workaday site has washing and barbecue facilities. April–Oct. €

Mercure Han-sur-Lesse rue Joseph Lamotte 18 ⓦall. accor.com. In the centre of the village, this chain hotel occupies a substantial modern building with a pool and guest rooms decorated in a vintage style. Filling buffet breakfasts in the morning. €€€

La Stradella rue d'Hamptay 59 ☎084 38 82 96. Proficient Italian restaurant serving wood-fired pizzas and pasta; good mussels and game in season.

St-Hubert and around

ST-HUBERT, about 20km southeast of Rochefort, is another popular Ardennes resort perched on a plateau and surrounded by **forest**. It's a small town with just under six thousand inhabitants, but it has a star attraction – a splendid **basilica** – and is also a good base for hiking out into the surrounding woods. Curiously, American writer Ernest Hemingway stayed here at the former *Hôtel de l'Abbaye* (place du Marché 18) in December 1944 while serving as a war correspondent. Travellers with children can take their budding scientists to the **Euro Space Center** on the outskirts of town, while

5

would-be writers will be right at home in the official 'book town' of **Redu**, a short journey west of St-Hubert.

Basilique St-Hubert

pl de l'Abbaye 1 • Free • ⓦ basilique-sainthubert.be

The **Basilique St-Hubert** is easily the grandest religious edifice in the Ardennes. It has been an important place of pilgrimage since the eponymous saint's thigh bones were moved here in the ninth century. **St Hubert** (*c*.656–727 AD) was, according to legend, formerly Count Hubert, a Frankish noble whose love of hunting culminated in a vision of Christ between the antlers of a stag, after which – in the way of such things – he gave his money away and dedicated his life to the church. Later, he was canonised as the patron saint of hunters and trappers. The first **abbey** here predated the cult of St Hubert, but after the saint's relics arrived, the abbey – as well as the village that grew up in its shadow – was named in his honour. In medieval times, the abbey was one of the region's most prosperous and a significant landowner. Suppressed by the French in the 1790s, the abbey church was back in ecclesiastical action by the early 1800s, replacing St-Gilles (rue St-Gilles; worth a look in its own right) as the parish church and rising to the rank of minor basilica in 1927.

From the outside, the basilica's outstanding feature is the Baroque **west facade** of 1702, made of limestone and equipped with twin pepper-pot towers, a clock and a carving on the pediment depicting the miracle of St Hubert. Inside, the clear lines of the Gothic nave and aisles have taken an aesthetic hammering from both an extensive Baroque refurbishment and a heavy-handed neo-Gothic makeover in the 1840s. Consequently, the basilica is impressive more for its size than for any particular features. However, spare a look for the **choir stalls**, typically Baroque and retelling the legend of St Hubert (on the right-hand side) and St Benedict (on the left). Look out also for the elaborate **tomb of St Hubert**, on the left at the beginning of the ambulatory, carved in the 1840s (King Léopold I, a keen huntsman, picked up the bill). Above the tomb is the only stained-glass **window** to have survived from the sixteenth century, a richly coloured, wonderfully executed work of art.

Musée Redouté

rue Redouté 11 • Charge • ⓦ museepjredoute.be/en

Only open during the summer months but worth a visit if you're artistically inclined, the intimate **Musée Redouté** gallery showcases the work of Pierre-Joseph Redouté. A St-Hubert native born in 1759, Redouté was famous for his watercolours of **roses**. He was well known during his lifetime and taught a host of royalty, including Queen Marie-Antoinette.

ARRIVAL AND INFORMATION
ST-HUBERT

By train There are frequent trains from Namur to Poix St-Hubert (hourly with one change; 1hr 10min). Poix St-Hubert station is 7km west of the town. Bus No. 5 (Mon–Fri; ⓦ letec. be) leaves Poix station for St-Hubert every few hours.

Tourist information The tourist office is at pl du Marché 15 (daily 9am–5.30pm; ⓦ foretdesainthubert-tourisme. be). They sell local artisanal beers, including La Saint-Hubert Cuvée du Borq and Le Semeur, and have a list of local B&Bs.

ACCOMMODATION AND EATING

La Touratte B&B rue St–Michel 40 ⓦ latouratte.be. This charming and distinctive old house on the northern edge of St-Hubert offers three guest rooms, each of which is attractively decorated and complete with vintage furnishings. Tasty breakfasts, too. €€

Le Val de Poix rue des Ardennes 18, 6870 Poix St-

Hubert ⓦ levaldepoix.com. Near Poix station, this welcoming hotel has attractive, contemporary rooms, some of which overlook the river. Its 'Slow Food' restaurant, *Les Gamines*, is renowned for its excellent regional dishes. Restaurant €€€; Accommodation €€€

5

Fourneau St-Michel

8km north of St-Hubert • Charge • ⓦ fourneausaintmichel.be

One of the walks recommended by the St-Hubert tourist office is the two-to-three-hour trek up to **Fourneau St-Michel**, an outdoor **museum** of rural life in Wallonia spread across 200 acres of beautiful green valley. Its most important and interesting section is made up of old buildings brought from all over the county – bakeries, farmhouses, forges, chapels, schools – reassembled here according to region and linked by paths that give the impression of strolling from one village to another. There are a couple of **cafés**, but it's a lovely place to picnic.

Euro Space Center

Devant les Hêtres 1, Libin • 12km west of St-Hubert, right by the E411 (Exit 24) • Charge • ⓦ eurospacecenter.be

The **Euro Space Center** is a hugely popular attraction, easily identified by the space rocket parked outside. Its hangar-like premises house a hi-tech **museum** about space travel and the applications of space and satellite technology, with many buttons for kids to press in the interactive displays and full-scale models of the space shuttles and the Mir space station. You can also try a Moon/Mars walk, visit the Planetarium and gasp at the breathtaking 5D space show. There's an on-site café for snacks and drinks.

Redu

Twinned with the UK's Hay-on-Wye, **REDU**, 18km west of St-Hubert, is Belgium's official 'book town' (ⓦ redu-villagedulivre.be). As such, the hamlet features a quaint cluster of **bookshops**, where travellers can watch book-binding and paper-making demonstrations and illustrators showing off their talents at the annual **Fête du Livres** in April. Most of the books are in French or Flemish, but several have a reasonable selection of **English titles**: try De Eglantier (rue Transinne 34) and De Griffel (rue Transinne 34a). Note that some bookshops insist on cash. The region is also renowned for its **raspberries**, and you can buy locally made jams, vinegar and spirits at café-cum-shop La Framboiseraie (rue de Daverdisse 66; ⓦ wallux.com/la-framboiseraie-de-redu).

ARRIVAL AND INFORMATION   REDU

By train and bus or taxi Catch the train as far as Libramont-Chevigny, then take TEC bus No. 61 to 'Redu Eglise' (Mon–Fri every 2–3hr; 1hr). Arriving from St-Hubert, you'll have to arrange a taxi.

Tourist information The tourist office is located at pl de l'Esro 60 (daily: March–Oct 9am–6pm; Nov–Feb 9.30am–4.30pm; ⓦ visitwallonia.com).

ACCOMMODATION AND EATING

Au Clocher rue de St-Hubert 17B ⓦ auclocher.be. A cosy restaurant in a stone house with an outside terrace serving traditional regional dishes such as local trout and delicious home-made desserts. You can call in for tea and cake, too. €€

Le Fournil pl de l'Esro 58 ⓦ le-fournil.be. Sitting pretty in the heart of the village, this small hotel has a dozen modern and unassuming guest rooms above its respected restaurant (which has an excellent beer selection). Book a 'comfort' double if you can: they're larger, have a bath and sitting room, a Nespresso coffee machine, and offer dressing gowns and slippers. Breakfast included. €€

La Roche-en-Ardenne and around

About 25km northeast of St-Hubert, hill-hidden **LA ROCHE-EN-ARDENNE** is amazingly picturesque, crowned by romantic **castle ruins** and boasting some of the wildest scenery in the Ardennes. The secret of its beauty has spread, though, and come summer high season, the town is teeming with people. Most come for the superb **outdoor activities** – from kayaking and rafting along the **River Ourthe** to hiking, biking, horse riding and caving.

The château

rue du Purnalet • Charge • ⓦ chateaudelaroche.be • To get to the castle, take the steps that lead up from pl du Marché, at the south end of the high street

5

The ninth-century **château** was destroyed in the late eighteenth century on the orders of the Habsburgs to stop it from falling into the hands of the French. However, its ruins still command sweeping views over the valley and the surviving fragments of the curtain wall that once enclosed the town. During the summer, medieval activities and **falconry shows** are organised.

Musée Bataille des Ardennes

rue Chamont 5 • Charge • ⓦ batarden.be

One of the best of the Ardennes battle museums, the **Musée Bataille des Ardennes** offers a homespun but effective collection foraged from the surrounding hills, including anti-tank guns and light weaponry, medical supplies and ancient unopened cigarette packs, all displayed by way of well-thought-out dioramas and tableaux. Curiously enough, the corner of the high street and rue de la Gare, a few metres to the north of the museum, is the spot where US and British soldiers met on 11 January 1945, as their respective armies converged on the Bulge, a **commemorative plaque** depicts the wintry scene.

ARRIVAL AND INFORMATION

LA ROCHE-EN-ARDENNE

By train and bus La Roche is not on the rail network; the nearest train stations are Marloie and Melreux on the Liège-Jemelle line, both around half an hour away. Buses run roughly bi-hourly – catch the No. 13 from Melreux (25min) or the No. 15 from Marloie (1hr) – and drop passengers off in the town centre; route planning on ⓦ letec.be.

Tourist information The tourist office is at pl du Marché 15 (daily 9.30am–5pm; July & Aug: until 6pm; ⓦ coeurde lardenne.be). They have details of B&Bs and sell a selection of walking and cycling maps.

Tourist train Le P'tit Train (Easter–Nov: hourly 11am–

5/6pm; charge; ⓦ la-roche-tourisme.com/en/le-petit-train) runs 40min tours of the town and surroundings. Trains depart from pl du Bronze.

Outdoor activities The wild terrain surrounding La Roche-en-Ardenne is an outdoor enthusiast's dream: a wide range of sports is on offer, from kayaking to caving. **Ardennes Aventures** rue de la Gare 4 ⓦ ardenne aventures.com/en. The leading local operator, they offer long (5hr) and short (1hr 30min) kayak trips year-round (leaving hourly in high season); mountain biking (4hr); horse riding (2hr); and rafting (Jan–April, Nov & Dec; 1hr 30min).

ACCOMMODATION

Camping Club Benelux rue de Harzé 24 ⓦ club-benelux.be. Large, leafy site spread along a curve in the Ourthe River. There's a shop and a brasserie; a local company organises outdoor activities. Easter to Oct. €

Camping de l'Ourthe rue des Echavées ⓦ camping delourthe.be. Situated 700m from the town centre, this family-orientated riverside site has a kids' corner, wi-fi and a shop. Mid-March to Oct. €

La Claire Fontaine rue Vecpré 64 ⓦ clairefontaine.be. About 2km outside La Roche on the road to Marche-en-Famenne, this lovely hotel restaurant is the best option if

you have a car; set in an extensive garden, the old lodge is strewn with antiques and boasts extremely well-appointed rooms. Sauna and massages are also available. Breakfast included. Accommodation €€; Restaurant €€

Moulin de la Strument Petite Strument 62 ⓦ strument. com. Located about 800m south of the town centre along the Val du Bronze, this hotel offers eight simple rooms, a cosy on-site restaurant and a huge campsite with a picturesque stream-side setting. Breakfast included. Campsite Easter–Oct. Doubles €€, camping €

EATING

Chez Henri rue Chamont 8 ⓦ restaurantardennais. be. This rustic restaurant with wood-panelled walls serves traditional Ardennais cuisine; try the *Grande Assiette Ardennaise* featuring local ham, cured sausage, venison and foie gras. €€

La Stradella pl du Marché 2 ☎ 084 41 11 34. The decor may be garish, but the handcrafted, wood-fired Italian pizza is very tasty. You'll find Belgian and French dishes on the menu too. Forget the beer; it's all about gin here. €

5

Durbuy

Tucked into a narrow ravine beside the River Ourthe, a circuitous 25km northwest of La Roche, **DURBUY** is inordinately pretty, its picturesque old buildings set below bulging wooded hills. Perhaps inevitably, such a lovely little place attracts more than its fair share of day-trippers, difficulties in getting here notwithstanding – you'll need your own transport. That said, Durbuy's immaculately maintained huddle of seventeenth- and eighteenth-century **stone houses**, set around a cobweb of cobbled lanes, show to best advantage out of season or late in the evening.

INFORMATION AND GETTING AROUND   DURBUY

Tourist information Durbuy's tourist office is on the main square at pl aux Foires 25 (Mon–Fri 9am–12.30pm & 1–5pm, Sat & Sun 10am–6pm; ⓦ durbuytourisme.be).

Tourist train A seasonal, canvas-roof mini train (ⓦ adventure-valley.be/activites/petit-train) takes tourists to Belvedere, Durbuy's panoramic viewpoint.

ACCOMMODATION AND EATING

Azur en Ardenne rue de Jastrée 31, Barvaux-sur-Ourthe ⓦ azurenardenne.be. About 8km east of Durbuy along the N833 then N831, this four-star resort hotel is situated in a rural setting with wonderful views. The fifty-odd rooms are decorated in an elegant, contemporary style; there is a well-appointed cottage, too. It's a great base for outdoor activities, and there's a wellness centre, pool and gourmet restaurant. Accommodation €€€; Restaurant €€€

Clos des Récollets rue de la Prévôté 9 ⓦ closdesrecollets. be. A charming stonewalled house right in the centre that has slick, modern and very comfortable rooms with large bathrooms. Their popular restaurant does fancy French cuisine in a classic manner with both set menus and à la carte: try, for example, the mackerel with beetroot, smoked yoghurt and quinoa. Accommodation €€€; Restaurant €€€

Grottes de Hotton

2km from the centre of Melreux-Hotton village • Charge • ⓦ grottesdehotton.be • The caves are well signposted from Melreux-Hotton but only reachable on foot or by car; from the main riverside rue de la Roche, follow route de Speleo Club de Belgique

The deepest of the Ardennes cave systems, the **Grottes de Hotton**, are well worth the short trip from La Roche. **Tours** last a little over an hour and take you 75m underground, where a fast-flowing river pours through a canyon almost 40m deep and just a few metres wide – a stupendous sight. Stalactites and **stalagmites** galore, including patches of rare and peculiar specimens that grow horizontally from the rock. Outside, there's a lovely garden with panoramic views over the countryside.

Bouillon and the Semois river valley

Beguiling **BOUILLON**, close to the French border on the edge of the Ardennes, is a good-looking resort town, enclosed in a loop of the River Semois and crowned by an outstanding **castle**. Be sure to mingle with the locals at the **weekly market** held every Sunday morning from April to October on boulevard Heynen and, if visiting in summer, at the **medieval market** held in August. The town makes an excellent base for exploring the wildly dramatic scenery of the countryside, particularly the **Semois river valley** to the west, with quiet country roads climbing into wooded hills before careering down to the riverside. Holidaying Belgians descend on this beautiful area in their hundreds, with many **old farmhouses** turned into gîtes and a wealth of opportunities for **outdoor activities**. You'll need wheels – car or bike – to get around, or, for **Poupehan**, simply hop in a canoe.

Bouillon château

esplanade Godefroid 1 • Charge • ⓦ chateaudebouillon.com

Bouillon's highlight is its impossibly picturesque **castle** on a long, craggy ridge high above the town. The castle was originally held by a succession of independent dukes who controlled most of the land. There were five of these, all called **Godfrey de Bouillon**, the fifth and last of whom left on the First Crusade in 1096, selling his dominions (partly to raise the cash for his trip) to the prince-bishop of Liège and capturing Jerusalem three years later, when he was elected the Crusaders' king. However, he barely had time to settle himself before he became sick – either from disease or, as was suggested at the time, because his Muslim enemies poisoned him, and he died in Jerusalem in 1100. Later, Louis XIV got his hands on the old dukedom and promptly had the castle refortified to the design of his military architect **Vauban**, whose handiwork defines most of the fortress today.

It's an intriguing old place, with three **drawbridges** to enter and then paths winding through most of its **courtyards**, along the battlements and towers, and through dungeons filled with weaponry and instruments of torture. Most visitors drive to the entrance, but walking there is easy enough either via rue du Château or, more strenuously, by a set of steep steps that climbs up from rue du Moulin, one street back from the river. Among the highlights, the thirteenth-century **Salle de Godfrey**, hewn out of the rock, contains a large wooden cross sunk into the floor and sports carvings illustrating the castle's history; there's also the **Tour d'Autriche** (Austrian Tower) at the top of the castle, with fabulous views over the Semois valley.

Musée Ducal

rue Petit 1–3 • Charge • Ⓦ museeducalbouillon.be

Below the castle and accessible across the car park, the **Musée Ducal** exhibits a wide-ranging collection neatly displayed in an attractive eighteenth-century mansion. As you'd expect, there are lots of artefacts relating to Godfrey (see page 269), plus assorted weaponry, exhibits on medieval daily and religious life and a large-scale model of the town as of 1690.

Archéoscope Godefroid de Bouillon

quai des Saulx 14 • Charge • Ⓦ archeoscopebouillon.be

The **Archéoscope Godefroid de Bouillon** should ideally be visited before exploring the castle. Its exhibitions on the Crusades and Arab culture, a multimedia show on the duke, and a half-hour film laying out the castle's history help to put everything in context, so when you come to do your castle visit, you can thoroughly soak up the atmosphere.

Poupehan

Heading west from Bouillon along the N810, it's just 12km to **POUPEHAN**. This inconsequential village straggles the banks of the River Semois and as such it is along the route of the extremely popular **canoe trips** paddling out from Bouillon (see box, page 270). Poupehan's handful of cafés and restaurants earn a healthy living from its many visitors, who come to enjoy the peace and quiet and, of course, mess around on the river.

Rochehaut

From Poupehan, it's a steep 4km drive up through the woods to **ROCHEHAUT**, a beguiling hilltop village whose rustic **stone cottages** amble across a gentle dip between two sloping ridges. Nowadays, most visitors come here to **hike** (see box, page 270), exploring the locality's steep forested hills and the valley down below using a network of marked trails. There are superb views over the Semois from the village.

ARRIVAL AND INFORMATION

By train and bus Catch the train to Libramont on the Namur–Luxembourg line, then take bus No. 8 (hourly; 50min; ⓦletec.be) to Bouillon, which departs from outside the station. No buses or trains run from Bouillon to Rochehaut, so a car or taxi is required.

BOUILLON AND THE SEMOIS RIVER VALLEY

Tourist information Bouillon's tourist office is centrally located at quai des Saulx 12 (Mon–Sat daily 10am–5pm; ⓦpaysdebouillon.be). They have a list of B&Bs and sell local hiking maps.

ACCOMMODATION

BOUILLON

Auberge de Jeunesse de Bouillon rte du Christ 16 ⓦlesaubergesdejeunesse.be. Large and well-equipped HI hostel with dorm beds, family rooms, kitchen, laundry and café. It's east across the river from the castle, on the hill opposite – a long walk by road, but there is a shortcut via the steps leading up from rue des Hautes Voies, just above place St Arnould. Reservations advised. Mid-Feb to Dec. Dorms €, doubles €

Camping Halliru rte de Corbion 1 ☎061 46 60 09. Nicely situated and reasonably well-equipped riverside campsite, some 1.5km southwest of the town centre on the road to Corbion. It's an easy walk – go through the tunnel by the *Auberge d'Alsace*, turn left and follow the path by the river. April–Sept. €

Hotel Cosy rue Au-Dessus de la Ville 23 ⓦhotelcosy. be. Perched on a hill overlooking the old town, the exterior of this place looks a little kitsch, but its eleven individually designed boutique-style rooms have bags of character – some have castle views, others a hot tub – as does the on-site restaurant and terrace. Check their website for weekend deals. €€

ACTIVITIES AROUND BOUILLON AND THE SEMOIS RIVER VALLEY

The **River Semois** snakes its way across much of southern Belgium, rising near Arlon and then meandering west until it finally flows into the Meuse in France. The most impressive part of the **river valley** lies just to the west of Bouillon, the river wriggling beneath steep wooded hills and ridges – altogether some of the most sumptuous scenery in the whole of the Ardennes and ripe territory for an active day out.

WALKS

Before setting out, **walkers** should get hold of the *Promenades du Randonnée* (on sale at Bouillon's tourist office), with nine circular walks – ranging from 12km to 25km – that begin and end in town. The routes are well-marked but study the map carefully to avoid walking on major or minor roads. The marked river crossings are not bridges, so be prepared to get your feet your feet wet. The tourist office also sells a map detailing suggested **cycling** routes and **mountain bikes** can be rented from *Semois Kayaks*.

There's also a **half-day circular hike** from Rochehaut to Poupehan. From Rochehaut, take the path out of the village's southern end, which leads into thick forests high above the river, from where a series of fixed ladders help you negotiate the steep slopes down to the water. This is by far the most challenging part of the walk, and once you're at the bottom, you can follow the easy path to Poupehan; from there, take the path that follows the river north back up to a **quaint bridge** over the river to the hamlet of **Frahan**, a huddle of stone houses draped over a steep hillock and surrounded by meadows. From here, various paths will deliver you back up to Rochehaut on its perch high above.

CANOEING

The riverscape is gentle and sleepy, the Semois slow-moving and meandering – and the whole shebang is less oversubscribed than, say, Dinant. Bouillon has two main **canoe** rental companies, both providing transport to the departure point or from the destination.

Les Epinoches Faubourg de France 29 (by the Pont de France) ⓦkayak-lesepinoches.be. Les Epinoches rents kayaks and canoes to go down to Saty (7km; 2hr), Dohan (14km; 3hr) and Cugnon (28km; 5hr).

Semois Kayaks bd Vauban ⓦsemois-kayaks.be. Semois oversees routes in the other direction down to Poupehan (15km; 3hr 30min) and from Poupehan to Frahan (4km; 1hr). Reservations are strongly advised.

5

★ **Hôtel Panorama** rue Au-Dessus de la Ville 25 ⊚ panoramahotel.be. A four-star hotel and restaurant that lives up to its name, with sweeping views of the Semois valley and Bouillon castle from each of its 22 high-spec rooms and terrace bar. There's also a small wellness centre. Breakfast included. Accommodation €€€; Restaurant €€€

Hôtel de la Poste pl St Arnould 1 ⊚ hotelposte.be. There's been a hotel here, right by the Pont de Liège, since the 1730s. The present incarnation has some characterful rooms with contemporary decor, and it's pretty good value for what you get. There are great views of the castle from one side of the hotel, so be sure to get a west-facing room, preferably high up in the hotel tower. The restaurant has a waterside terrace. Accommodation €€; Restaurant €€

POUPEHAN

Auberge le Vieux Moulin rue du Pont 18 ⊚ aubergele vieuxmoulin.be/en. There's a rustic feel to this unassuming, two-star hotel where the guest rooms are rather spartan. However, the *Auberge*'s traditional Ardennes restaurant is a real plus, serving tasty home-made meals at very reasonable prices. Accommodation €€; Restaurant €€

ROCHEHAUT

Auberge l'An 1600 rue du Palis 7 ⊚ an1600hotel.be. A first-rate alternative to the *Auberge Rochehaut* with a small platoon of smart chalet-style rooms. There's also a top-quality restaurant in a charming stone cottage dating from the seventeenth century; the trout is especially delicious. Accommodation €€€; Restaurant €€€

Auberge de Rochehaut rue de la Cense 12 ⊚ aubergede rochehaut.com/en. Offers a range of comfortable rooms in a tastefully modernised old stone inn with outbuildings and a modern annexe. There's also an excellent restaurant (although you can eat more informally – and just as well – in the bar). Hot tubs throughout. Accommodation €€€; Restaurant €€€

EATING

For a place of its size and popularity, Bouillon is surprisingly light on good places to **eat**. The three places below represent the best of a rather uninspiring bunch. A couple of the accommodation options listed for **Rochehaut** and **Poupehan** also offer good eating.

Le Roy de la Moule quai du Rempart 42 ☎ 061 46 62 49. A local favourite, famed for its steaming pots of mussels cooked 35 different ways. Wash them down with a glass of Ciney blonde beer. €€€

La Table des Sépulcrines quai des Saulx 10 ☎ 061 32 07 63. Housed in a former seventeenth-century convent, this brasserie focuses on French food enhanced by international flavours – the menu changes monthly. €€

La Vieille Ardenne Grand-rue 9 ☎ 061 46 62 77. This slightly old-fashioned restaurant near the Pont de Liège specialises in regional dishes. It also has an extensive beer menu. €

Abbaye d'Orval

rue Orval, Villers-devant-Orval • Charge • ⊚ orval.be • If driving, Orval is 8km from Florenville, in the direction of Virton; alternatively, take the train to Florenville (direction Bertrix and Virton), then catch TEC bus No. 24 (⊚ letec.be) from the station and alight at 'Orval Carrefour'

Around 30km southeast of Bouillon, the **Abbaye d'Orval** is a place of legendary beginnings. It was founded, so the story goes when Countess Mathilda of Tuscany lost a gold ring in a lake. A fish recovered it for her, prompting the countess to donate the surrounding land to God for the construction of a monastery – a fish with a golden ring is still the emblem of the monastery and can be seen gracing the **bottles of beer** for which Orval is most famous these days. By the time the French Revolutionary Army got to it in 1793, much of the medieval abbey had already disappeared during an eighteenth-century revamp. Left in tatters by the French, the abbey lay abandoned until 1926, when the **Trappist order** acquired the property and built on the site to the eighteenth-century plans, creating an imposing new complex complete with a monumental statue of the Virgin.

Of the original twelfth- and thirteenth-century buildings, only remnants survive. You can see the ruins of the Romanesque-Gothic **church of Notre-Dame**, with the frame of the original rose window and Romanesque capitals in the nave and transept, and its attached **cloister** and surrounding buildings, including the almost-intact chapterhouse and the eighteenth-century **cellars**, which hold a small **museum** and models and photos of the site over the years. The abbey has always been, first and foremost, a **working community**, making beer and cheese (samples of which are on sale in the abbey shop); unfortunately, the main, modern part of the complex isn't accessible to the public, and it is only possible to visit the **brewery** on open days – see website for listings.

272 THE ARDENNES ARLON

5

ACCOMMODATION AND EATING   ABBAYE D'ORVAL

Orval Guesthouse ⓦorval.be. It is possible to stay in the abbey's guesthouse, which has a mixture of simple single and double rooms, but you'll need to bring towels and sheets or a sleeping bag. Guests can stay for two to seven days and are invited to participate in prayers or seek guidance from the brothers. The free, thrice-daily communal meals are taken in silence with background music. Alternatively, you can camp (an exceptionally cheap option); you'll need to bring everything with you, although it's possible to pay a little for a fridge. Note that the use of the shower costs extra. **€**

Arlon

The capital of Luxembourg province, **ARLON** is one of the oldest towns in Belgium – a trading centre for the Romans as far back as the second century AD. These days, it's an amiable country town, perhaps a little down on its luck, but with a relaxed and genial atmosphere that makes for a pleasant break on any journey – although there's not a lot to see. The modern centre is **place Léopold**, with the clumping Palais de Justice at one end and a World War II tank in the middle, commemorating the American liberation of Arlon in September 1944. A couple of minutes' walk from place Léopold, up a flight of steps, is the diminutive **Grand-Place**, where there are fragments from Roman times, namely the **Tour Romaine** (no public access), formerly part of the third-century ramparts. The principal sites are the **Musée Archéologique** (rue des Martyrs 13; charge; ⓦmuseearcheologiquearlon.be), which is situated behind the Palais de Justice and has a good collection of Roman finds from the surrounding area, and the **Musée Gaspar** (rue des Martyrs 16; charge; ⓦmuseegaspar.be), which displays the works of nineteenth-century sculptor Jean-Marie Gaspar (1861–1931), a native of Arlon, who specialised in animal carvings.

ARRIVAL AND INFORMATION   ARLON

By train Arlon train station is on the south side of the town centre, roughly a 10min walk from the Musée Archéologique.
Destinations Jemelle (every 30min; 50min); Luxembourg City (every 25min; 20min); Namur (hourly; 1hr 40min).
Tourist information The tourist office is just off the main square at rue des Faubourgs 2 (Mon–Fri 8.30am–5pm, Sat & Sun 9am–5pm; ⓦvisitarlon.be/en).

Faubourg 101 rue des Faubourgs 101 ⓦfaubourg-101. be. Chic and slick brasserie-cum-lounge bar with an invariably delicious plat du jour, exceedingly good pasta and dainty slivers of steak and duck. **€€**
★ **Hostellerie du Peiffeschof** chemin du Peiffeschof 111 ⓦpeiffeschof.be. Set in a quiet location about 4km northeast of the town, this lovely little hotel has just nine rooms. The guest rooms are neat, trim and very modern. The excellent hotel restaurant emphasises French dishes made with local produce: try, for example, the roasted veal kidneys with rice. Accommodation **€€**; Restaurant **€€€**

Bastogne

BASTOGNE, some 35km north of Arlon, is a brisk modern town and important road junction whose strategic position has attracted the attention of almost every invading army that has passed this way. Indeed, the town is probably best known for its role in World War II, when the Americans held it against a much larger German force in December 1944 – a key engagement of the Battle of the Ardennes, or **Battle of the Bulge** (see box, page 273). The American commander, General Anthony McAuliffe's response to the German demand for surrender was 'Nuts!' – one of the war's more quotable rallying cries. Nowadays, there's no strong reason to stay overnight here, but there are several interesting sights connected with the events of 1944.

Place McAuliffe

As a token of appreciation for the Americans holding the town during the Battle of the Ardennes, the town renamed its main square after **General McAuliffe** and plonked an American **tank** here to hammer home the point. Broad and breezy, the square is the most agreeable part of town and very much the social focus, flanked by a string of busy cafés.

Église St-Pierre

pl St-Pierre • Free

From the northeast corner of the central square, **Grand-rue**, the long main street, trails off to Place St-Pierre, where the **Église St-Pierre** sports a sturdy Romanesque tower topped by a timber gallery. Inside, and more unusually, the vaulting of the well-proportioned Gothic nave is decorated with splendid, brightly coloured frescoes painted in the 1530s and depicting biblical scenes, saints, prophets and angels. Also of note are a finely carved Romanesque baptismal font and a flashy Baroque pulpit.

Bastogne War Museum and American Memorial

Colline du Mardasson 5, 2km northeast of town • Charge • ⓦ bastognewarmuseum.be

The first-rate **Bastogne War Museum** relates the events of World War II with a particular focus on the Battle of the Bulge. Similar in setup and style to Ieper's In Flanders Fields Museum (see page 132), it's a dynamic layout of artefacts, interactive videos, sound pods, and 3D displays. Flanking the museum is the star-shaped **American Memorial**, inscribed with the names of all the American states. Side panels recount different episodes from the battle. With its three altars, the **crypt** is suitably sombre, and it's possible to climb onto the **roof** for a windswept look back at Bastogne.

THE BATTLE OF THE BULGE

The **Battle of the Bulge** – also known as the **Battle of the Ardennes** – was the site of some of the fiercest fighting in the latter stages of World War II. By September 1944, the Allies had liberated most of Belgium, after which they concentrated on striking into Germany from Maastricht in the north and Alsace in the south, leaving a lightly defended central section whose **front line** extended across the Ardennes from Malmedy to Luxembourg's Echternach. In December 1944, **Hitler** embarked on a desperate plan to change the course of the war by breaking through this part of the front, his intention being to sweep north behind the Allies, capture Antwerp and force them to retreat. It was virtually the same plan he had applied with such great success in 1940, but this time, he had fewer resources – especially fuel oil – and the Allied air force ruled the skies. **Von Rundstedt**, the veteran German general in command, was acutely aware of these weaknesses – indeed, he was against the operation from the start – but he hoped to benefit from the wintry weather conditions which would limit Allied aircraft activity. Carefully prepared, Von Rundstedt's offensive began on **16 December 1944**, and one week later had created a 'bulge' in the Allied line that reached the outskirts of Dinant (the Germans famously reached the so-called Rocher de Bayard, which still marks the spot today). The American 101st Airborne Division held firm around Bastogne. The operation's success depended on rapid results, so Von Rundstedt's inability to reach Antwerp meant failure. Montgomery's forces from the north and Patton's from the south launched a counterattack, and by the end of January, the Germans had been forced back to their original position. The **loss of life** was colossal, however: 75,000 Americans and over 100,000 Germans died in the battle.

5

101st Airborne Museum

av de la Gare 11, on the southwest side of the town centre • Charge • ⊚ 101airbornemuseumbastogne.com

The **101st Airborne Museum** occupies a 1930s Belgian Army officers' mess that the Germans used during World War II. The museum displays the belongings of the 101st Airborne Division and other units involved in the Battle of Bastogne via dioramas. The **basement** has been converted into a 'bombing experience' bunker – parents might want to check it out first before coming in with children, as it can be pretty noisy.

ARRIVAL AND INFORMATION   BASTOGNE

By train and bus Bastogne is off the train network, but there are connecting buses (⊚ letec.be) from the nearest train station at Libramont; these stop at McAuliffe. TEC buses also run between Arlon and Bastogne.
Destinations Arlon (every 30min; 1hr); Libramont (hourly; 50min).

Tourist information The tourist office is at pl McAuliffe 60 (daily: mid-June to mid-Sept 9am–12.30pm & 1–6pm; mid-Sept to mid-June daily 9.30am–12.30pm & 1–5.30pm; ⊚ paysdebastogne.be). It issues free town maps and has a variety of brochures on the Battle of the Bulge.

ACCOMMODATION AND EATING

Brasserie Lamborelle rue Lamborelle 19 ⊚ brasserie lamborelle.be. It's all about meat cooked on a hot stone in this popular brasserie, but you'll also find pasta, salads and croque monsieurs. More than a hundred ales are on the menu; adventurous sorts might like to try the house special: 'flaming beer'. €€

Léo At Home rue du Vivier 4–8 ⊚ wagon-leo.com. Just off the central place McAuliffe, this establishment has twelve cheerful and spacious – if unremarkable –

modern rooms. However, the lively wood-panelled *Wagon Léo* restaurant, inside something akin to an old 1940s train carriage, is a real experience. Accommodation €€; Restaurant €€

Motel Le Merceny chaussée d'Arlon 4 ⊚ lemerceny. be. This three-star motel holds eight crisp, modern, soundproofed rooms with a/c and free wi-fi. They only serve a breakfast buffet, and there's no on-site restaurant, but nonetheless, it's great value for money. €

Luxembourg

VIANDEN'S HILLTOP CASTLE

Luxembourg

The Grand Duchy of Luxembourg is one of Europe's smallest sovereign states, a mere 85km from tip to toe. As a country, it's relatively neglected by travellers, which is a pity considering its varied charms, from pretty hilltop villages and castles galore (over 130) to deep forested valleys ideal for hiking and rivers ripe for canoeing. Add to this its proud culinary traditions, delicious home-produced Moselle Valley wines, top-notch public transport system and a UNESCO-listed capital, and you'll understand why this ultra-clean, efficient and well-maintained duchy is well worth a week of anyone's time.

The obvious place to start a visit is **Luxembourg City**, one of Europe's most spectacularly sited capitals and home to a fifth of Luxembourg's population. Segments of its massive bastions and zigzag walls have survived in good shape, while its deep winding valleys and steep hills have restricted development, making the city feel more like a grouping of disparate villages than the world financial centre and administrative focus for the EU that it is. It's true that there is not an overabundance of sights here, but there's compensation in the excellent restaurants and plush hotels.

Moving on, the country's southeast corner, within easy striking distance of the capital, is famous for its **vineyards** that line up along the west bank of the **River Moselle**, which forms the border with Germany. Tours and tastings of the wine cellars (*caves*) are the big deal here and best arranged in **Remich**. Further afield, the northeast corner of the duchy boasts a patch of spectacular scenery known as **La Petite Suisse Luxembourgeoise**. The inviting town of **Echternach**, which boasts a fine old abbey, is easily the best base hereabouts.

Further to the north, in the **Luxembourg Ardennes**, is **Vianden**, a popular resort famous for its glowering castle. Between the two, more humdrum **Diekirch** has a competent museum dedicated to the Battle of the Bulge (much of which took place in the northern part of the country). Also worth visiting are the imposing castle of **Bourscheid** and the quaint village of **Esch-sur-Sûre**, clasped in the horseshoe bend of its river.

Brief history

Before **Napoleon** rationalised much of Western Europe, **Luxembourg** was just one of several hundred small kingdoms dating back to medieval times. Perhaps the most

---

LUXEMBOURG'S LINGUISTIC MIX

Luxembourg has three **official languages**: French, German and **Luxembourgish** (Lëtzebuergesch), a Germanic language derived from the Rhineland. **French** is the official language of the government and judiciary, but most Luxembourgians speak **German** with equal ease, and **English** is also widely understood and spoken. Incidentally, attempts by visitors to speak Lëtzebuergesch are well received – though sometimes locals are just too surprised to seem exactly pleased.

Moien Good morning/hello
Äddi or a'voir Goodbye
Merci (villmols) Thank you (very much)
Pardon Sorry
Entschëllegt Excuse me

Wann-ech-glift (pronounced as one word) Please
Ech verstin lech nët I don't understand you
Ech versti kee Lëtzebuergesch I don't understand any Luxembourgish

THE MULLERTHAL TRAIL

Highlights

❶ Chemin de la Corniche This panoramic walkway offers fabulous views over the capital's bastions and bulwarks. See page 287

❷ Esch-sur-Sûre A postcard-perfect hamlet snuggled in a bend of the Sûre River. See page 293

❸ Vianden Site of an inordinately pretty castle atop a steep, wooded hill. See page 294

❹ Clervaux Home to *The Family of Man* – one of Europe's most famous and moving photographic exhibitions. See page 297

❺ Moselle Valley Lined with vineyards producing sparkling crémant – Luxembourg's affordable and delicious alternative to champagne. See page 298

❻ Echternach A lovely little town within easy striking distance of some excellent hiking in the surrounding wooded hills and valleys. See page 299

❼ Mullerthal Trail A scenic walking trail through Luxembourg's 'Little Switzerland' region, home to castles and staggering rock formations. See page 302

HIGHLIGHTS ARE MARKED ON THE MAP ON PAGE 280

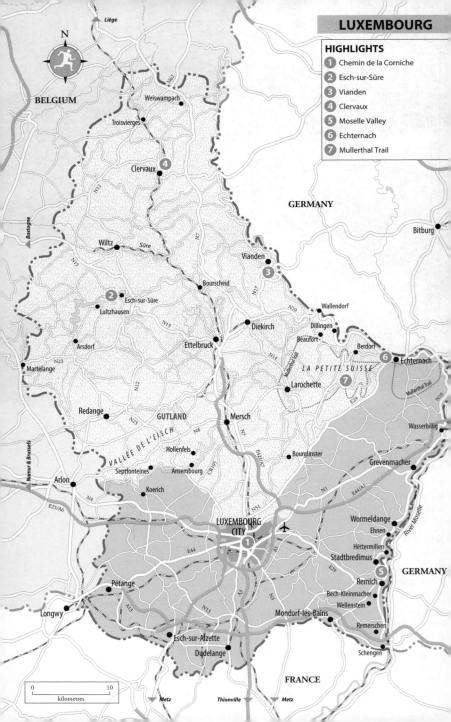

LUXEMBOURG

HIGHLIGHTS

1. Chemin de la Corniche
2. Esch-sur-Sûre
3. Vianden
4. Clervaux
5. Moselle Valley
6. Echternach
7. Mullerthal Trail

N

BELGIUM

Liège

Weiswampach

Troisvierges

Clervaux **4**

GERMANY

Bitburg

Wiltz

Sûre

Vianden **3**

Bourscheid

N17

Wallendorf

2 Esch-sur-Sûre

Lultzhausen

N15

Diekirch

Dillingen

Beaufort

Berdorf

6 Echternach

Arsdorf

N23

Ettelbruck

N14

LA PETITE SUISSE

Mullerthal Trail

Martelange

Larochette

7

Redange

N12

GUTLAND

Mersch

Wasserbillig

N8

Bourglinster

VALLÉE DE L'EISCH

Hollenfels

Grevenmacher

Septfonteines

Ansembourg

Arlon

Koerich

E25/A6

N4

Wormeldange

Ehnen

River Moselle

LUXEMBOURG CITY

1

Hettermillen

Stadtbredimus

E29

5 Remich

GERMANY

Pétange

Bech-Kleinmacher

Wellenstein

Longwy

Mondorf-les-Bains

Remerschen

Esch-sur-Alzette

Schengen

Dudelange

FRANCE

0   10

kilometres

Metz   Thionville   Metz

Namur & Brussels

Bastogne

surprising thing about the modern state is that it exists at all: You'd certainly think that Luxembourg, perilously sandwiched between France and Germany, would have been gobbled up by one or the other – and but for some strange quirks of history, it would have been.

Romans and counts

The **Romans** incorporated the region into their empire, colonising 'Luxembourg' after Julius Caesar had conquered Gaul (including present-day Belgium) in 58–52 BC. Roman control lasted until the middle of the fifth century when the Germanic **Franks** overran most of France and the Low Countries to create the **Merovingian** and the **Carolingian** Empire, whose most successful ruler was Charlemagne (742–814). The subsequent disintegration of the Frankish state left a power vacuum with middle Europe breaking up into dozens of small principalities, and one of them was Luxembourg, established by **Count Siegfried of Lorraine** when he fortified the site of what is now Luxembourg City in 963. Siegfried and his successors ensured that Luxembourg City remained – as it had been under the Romans – a major staging point on the trade route between German Trier and Paris, its strategic importance enhanced by its defensibility, perched high above the sheer gorges of the Pétrusse and Alzette rivers. These counts ruled the area first as independent princes and then as (nominal) vassals of the Holy Roman Emperor; however, in the early fourteenth century, dynastic shenanigans temporarily united Luxembourg with **Bohemia**.

Medieval Luxembourg

By 1354, Luxembourg was independent again, this time as a **duchy**, and its first duke – **Wenceslas** – extended his lands up to Limburg in the north and down to Metz in the south. This state of affairs was also short-lived; in 1443, Luxembourg passed to the dukes of Burgundy and then, forty years later, to the **Habsburgs**. After that, its history mirrors that of Belgium, successively becoming part of the Spanish and Austrian Netherlands before occupation by **Napoleon**.

A bid for independence

Things got complicated in the early nineteenth century. In 1814, at the tail end of the Napoleonic Wars, the **Congress of Vienna** decided to create the **Grand Duchy of Luxembourg**, nominally independent but ruled by **William I** of Orange-Nassau, who doubled as the newly appointed king of the newly created United Kingdom of the Netherlands (including Belgium). This arrangement proved deeply unpopular in Luxembourg, and when the **Belgians rebelled** in 1830, the Luxembourgers joined in. It didn't do them much good. The Great Powers recognised an independent Belgium but declined to do the same for Luxembourg, which remained in the clutches of William. Even worse, the Great Powers were irritated by William's inability to keep his kingdom in good nick, so they punished him by giving a chunk of Luxembourg's Ardennes to Belgium – now that country's *province* of Luxembourg. By these means, however, Luxembourg's survival was assured: neither France nor Germany could bear to let the duchy pass to its rival, and London ensured the duchy was **declared neutral**. Luxembourg City was **demilitarised** in 1867, and most of its fortifications were torn down. It remained the property of the Dutch monarchy until 1890, when the ducal crown passed to the **House of Nassau-Weilburg** – a (separate) Germanic branch of the House of Orange. The late nineteenth century also witnessed the industrialisation of a large slice of Luxembourg, and by the 1890s, the duchy had one of the largest **steel industries** in Europe.

World Wars I and II

In the **twentieth century**, the Germans overran Luxembourg twice, first in 1914 and then again in 1940, when the royal family and government fled to Britain and the US. The second occupation was predictably traumatic. At first, the Germans were comparatively benign, but later, they banned the Luxembourgish language, dispatched forced labourers to the Russian front and took savage reprisals against any acts of resistance. **Liberation** by US forces led by General Patton (see box, page 292) came in September 1944, but in December of that year, the Germans launched an offensive through the Ardennes between Malmédy in Belgium and Luxembourg's Echternach. The ensuing **Battle of the Bulge** (see box, page 273) engulfed northern Luxembourg: hundreds of civilians were killed, and a great swathe of the country was devastated – events recalled today by several museums and many roadside monuments.

Modern-day Luxembourg

In the **postwar period**, Luxembourg adopted a shrewd policy of industrial diversification, which helped make it one of the most prosperous parts of Europe. It also discarded its prior habit of neutrality, joining **NATO** and becoming a founding member of the EU. It remained a **constitutional monarchy**, currently ruled by Grand Duke Henri (b.1955), who succeeded his long-serving father, Jean, in 2000. Politically and constitutionally stable, the duchy's favourable tax regime has, however, resulted in it acquiring an unenviable reputation as a **tax haven** for multinational corporations. In late 2014, just days after former finance minister (1989–2009) and prime minister (1995–2013) **Jean-Claude Juncker** became European Commission president (2014–19), the **LuxLeaks scandal** broke, exposing the duchy's role in dodgy tax avoidance schemes. Two years later, the whistleblowers were convicted and punished, but lo and behold, no one else was. Journalists continue to complain about political corruption to this day, with **Xavier Bettel**, who succeeded Juncker as prime minister (2013–23), accused – amongst other things – of appointing his chums to lucrative jobs.

Luxembourg City

One of Europe's most spectacularly sited capitals, **LUXEMBOURG CITY** spreads across a series of sandstone plateaus high above the deep and leafy gorges carved by the rivers Alzette and Pétrusse. These gorges were once key to the city's defences, and today, they parcel up the city into clearly defined districts (*quartiers*), easily the most diverting of which is the **Old Town** (*La Vieille Ville*), on the north side of the Pétrusse valley and the location of almost all of the key sights. Encircling the Old Town are the modern **business districts** established to house EU institutions and the international banking headquarters that have brought the city much wealth. Compact and relatively easy to navigate, the Old Town's charms soon become apparent: smashing views over river gorges, smart hotels, prime museums and a platoon of great restaurants.

GETTING AROUND AND THE LUXEMBOURG CARD

Operated by CFL (ⓦcfl.lu), Luxembourg's efficient **rail network** bisects the country with its one and only main line running south-north from Luxembourg City to Clervaux and on into Belgium; there are also two small branch lines – one to Wiltz, another to Diekrich. Where the trains won't take you, **buses** will, and there's also a **tram** line in Luxembourg City. A helpful website lists all the various **timetables** (ⓦmobiliteit.lu). All public transport within the duchy is **free** – and you may be able to reduce the costs of a visit further by buying the **Luxembourg Card** (ⓦvisitluxembourg.com). This provides free access to over **sixty nationwide attractions**. The card is valid for one (€13), two (€20) or three days (€28).

LUXEMBOURG CITY ORIENTATION

Luxembourg City has **four main districts** (*quartiers*), each of which can be explored on foot; the Old Town and the Grund are the most interesting by far.

Old Town (La Vieille Ville) No more than a few hundred metres across, the Old Town sits on a tiny plateau forged by the valleys of the rivers Alzette and Pétrusse, which meet here. All the city's major sights are located here, and the area is largely pedestrianised.

Grund (Lower Town) Situated at the base of the river valley, this attractive village-like enclave once housed the city's working class but is now largely gentrified. It features an engaging mix of old stone houses, medieval fortifications and parkland and can be most readily accessed from the Old Town via a lift (see page 287).

Clausen Located north of the Grund, this district is an expat hotspot. The Rives de Clausen nightlife 'village' teems with bars, clubs and restaurants.

Kirchberg The city's fourth major part, lies northeast of the Old Town, on the far side of the Alzette valley. It is reached by the imposing modern span of the Pont Grand-Duchesse Charlotte, usually known as the 'Red Bridge' for obvious reasons. Kirchberg accommodates a battery of high rises, including the Centre Européen, home to several EU institutions, and two museums, one art and one history.

6

Old Town

Protected by its river gorges, the **Old Town** plateau was first fortified by the Romans and then strengthened and refortified by a succession of medieval rulers. In 1554, a huge gunpowder explosion razed most of the medieval city, which was then rebuilt. The Spanish made more wholesale modifications in the seventeenth century, constructing a series of encircling bastions and ramparts. The latter was partly demolished when the city was **demilitarised** in 1867 – boulevards Royal and Roosevelt are built on their foundations, whereas the more **easterly fortifications** have survived pretty much intact. The latter gives a clear sense of the city's once formidable defensive capabilities.

Place d'Armes

At the centre of the Old Town is **place d'Armes**, a shaded oblong fringed with pavement cafés and the sturdy **Palais Municipal** of 1907 – now a convention and exhibition centre. It's a delightful spot, and throughout the summer, there are frequent free concerts – everything from jazz to brass bands – and a small (and expensive) **flea market** every second and fourth Saturday of the month. Near the square are the city's principal **shops**, concentrated along Grand-rue and rue des Capucins to the north, rue du Fossé to the east, and rue Philippe II running south.

Place Guillaume II

A passage from the southeast corner of place d'Armes leads through to the larger and less immediately picturesque **place Guillaume II**, in the middle of which is a jaunty-looking equestrian statue of William II. The square, the site of a sizeable fresh-food **market** (Wed & Sat), is flanked by pleasant old townhouses and the solid Neoclassical **Hôtel de Ville**, adorned with a pair of gormless copper lions. There's also a modest stone water fountain bearing a cameo of the Luxembourg poet and writer **Michel Rodange** (1827–76), who created something of a stir with his best-known work, *Rénert the Fox*, a satirical exploration of the character of his fellow countrymen.

Cathédrale Notre-Dame

rue Notre-Dame • Free • ⓦ luxembourg-city.com/en

On rue Notre-Dame, an ornate Baroque portico leads into the **Cathédrale Notre-Dame**, whose slender spires dominate the city's puckered skyline. It is, however, a real mess of a building: dating to the 1930s, the transepts and truncated choir are

6

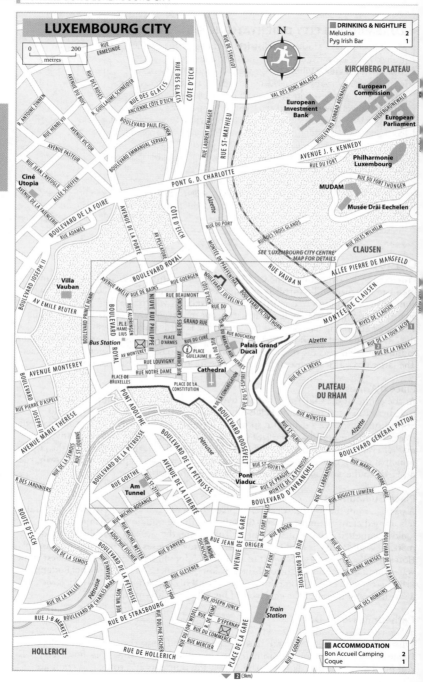

LUXEMBOURG CITY

0   200
metres

N

KIRCHBERG PLATEAU

European
Commission

European
Investment
Bank

European
Parliament

AVENUE J. F. KENNEDY

Philharmonie
Luxembourg

PONT G. D. CHARLOTTE

MUDAM

Musée Dräi Eechelen

Ciné
Utopia

CLAUSEN

SEE 'LUXEMBOURG CITY CENTRE'
MAP FOR DETAILS

Villa
Vauban

Bus Station

Palais Grand
Ducal

Cathedral

PLACE DE LA
CONSTITUTION

PLATEAU
DU RHAM

Am
Tunnel

Pont
Viaduc

Train
Station

HOLLERICH

2 (3km)

in a clumping Art Deco style and have been glued onto the (much more appealing) seventeenth-century nave. Items of interest are few and far between. Still, there is a **plaque** in the nave honouring those priests killed in World War II, and the likeable, seventeenth-century Baroque **gallery** at the back of the nave is graced by alabaster angels and garlands of flowers. In the apse is the country's most venerated **icon**, *The Comforter of the Afflicted*, a seventeenth-century lime-wood effigy of the Madonna and Child, which is frequently dressed up in all manner of lavish gear with crowns and sceptres, lace frills and gold brocade.

6

The crypt

A door on the west side of the chancel leads through to the side entrance of the cathedral. Here, stairs lead down to the **crypt** and a barred chapel containing a number of ducal tombs. Here, you'll spy the Baroque **tomb** of John the Blind (Jean l'Aveugle), which depicts the Entombment of Christ in a mass of mawkish detail. John was one of the most successful of Luxembourg's medieval rulers until he came a cropper at the Battle of Crécy in 1346.

Casemates de la Pétrusse

pl de la Constitution • Charge • ⓦ luxembourg-city.com/en

Near the cathedral, **place de la Constitution** sits on top of one of the old bastions, whose subterranean depths – the **Casemates de la Pétrusse** – are entered via a stone stairway. Dug by the Spaniards in the 1640s, these artillery chambers make for a dark and dank visit.

Palais Grand-Ducal

rue du Marché aux Herbes 17 • Charge • ⓦ monarchie.lu/en/visit-grand-ducal-palace

Originally built as the town hall but adopted by the Luxembourg royals as their winter residence in the nineteenth century, the **Palais Grand-Ducal** has been remodelled on several occasions. The exterior, with its dinky dormer windows and spiky little spires, reveals a Moorish influence. The interior is lavish in the extreme, with dazzling chandeliers, Brussels tapestries, frescoes and acres of richly carved wood panelling. To the right of the palace, an extension of 1859 houses the Luxembourg Parliament, the **Chambre des Députés**, in slightly plainer but still very comfortable surroundings.

The Luxembourg City Tourist Office organises guided tours (1hr 15min) of the palace in the summer months. Tickets can be purchased online or in person at the tourist office; see page 289).

Musée d'Histoire de la Ville de Luxembourg

rue du St-Esprit 14 • Charge • ⓦ citymuseum.lu

Converted from four historic houses, the first-rate **Musée d'Histoire de la Ville de Luxembourg** features a series of wooden models of the city through the ages, plus displays on the city's royal dynasty and government, industry and contemporary life. The highlight, though, is the **360-degree panorama** showing city life in 1655 – it's a perfect example of a trompe-l'oeil, making you feel slightly giddy when you stand in the middle.

Musée National d'Histoire et d'Art

pl du Marché aux Poissons • **Permanent collection** Free • **Temporary exhibitions** Charge • ⓦ nationalmusee.lu

The large and lavish **Musée National d'Histoire et d'Art** has a wide-ranging permanent collection, beginning in the basement with a **prehistoric** section and then working its way up chronologically to the **Middle Ages** and **Renaissance**. Above are two floors devoted to **fine art**, mostly from Luxembourg and Belgium, stretching from medieval times to the early twentieth century. There's also a floor dedicated to **temporary exhibitions**.

6

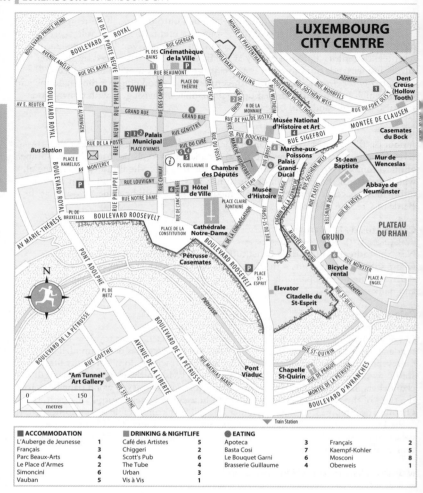

▪ ACCOMMODATION		▪ DRINKING & NIGHTLIFE		● EATING			
L'Auberge de Jeunesse	1	Café des Artistes	5	Apoteca	3	Français	2
Français	3	Chiggeri	2	Basta Cosi	7	Kaempf-Kohler	5
Parc Beaux-Arts	4	Scott's Pub	6	Le Bouquet Garni	6	Mosconi	8
Le Place d'Armes	2	The Tube	4	Brasserie Guillaume	4	Oberweis	1
Simoncini	6	Urban	3				
Vauban	5	Vis à Vis	1				

The Gallo-Roman collection

The basement's extensive **Gallo-Roman** section is a particular highlight. Southern Luxembourg has proved particularly rich in Roman artefacts, with archaeologists unearthing truckloads of bronzes and terracottas, glassware, funerary objects, busts and mosaics. In particular, look for a fine (albeit weathered) marble bust of Emperor Septimius Severus and a magnificent mosaic from Vichten.

The fine art galleries

On the top floors, the museum's wide-ranging **fine art** collection includes works by Lucas Cranach and Jan Bruegel as well as more modern paintings by the likes of Paul Cézanne and Pablo Picasso, who is well represented by the eerie twistings of his *Paysage de Cannes au Crépuscule*. There is also a comprehensive selection of paintings by Luxembourg artists, few of whom are well known internationally, though you might look out for the forceful Expressionism of Joseph Kutter (1894–1941). One real surprise is a delightful *View of Luxembourg* by J. M. W. Turner, who made two extended visits to the duchy – the first in 1825 and the second in 1834.

Rocher du Bock

In 963, a powerful local lord, a certain Count Siegfried of Lorraine, decided to build a castle on the **Rocher du Bock**, a sandstone outcrop rising high above the River Alzette just to the east of today's Marché aux Poissons. Luxembourg City originated with this stronghold, but precious little survives of Siegfried's construction – it was incorporated into the much larger **fortifications** built around the city from the seventeenth century onwards. The only significant piece of masonry to survive from the original construction is the so-called **Dent Creuse** (Hollow Tooth) stone tower on the north side of the rue Sigefroi/Montée de Clausen. This same road, which now links the Old Town with the suburb of Clausen, makes it difficult to appreciate the layout of the original castle, which in medieval times was connected to the Marché aux Poissons by a drawbridge. That said, the **views** of the spires, outer fortifications, and aqueducts of the Alzette valley are superb. The Montée de Clausen also acts as the starting point for the **Pétrusse Express** (see page 289).

Casemates du Bock

Montée de Clausen • Charge • ⓦ luxembourg-city.com/en

In the seventeenth century, the Spaniards began digging beneath the site of Siegfried's castle, eventually creating the **Casemates du Bock**, a honeycomb of tunnels and galleries within which they placed bakeries, kitchens, stables and all the other amenities necessary to support a garrison. At the entrance to the *casemates* is an archaeological crypt housing the bits and pieces surviving from Luxembourg's **first castle**, and then another flight of steps leads you down into the *casemates* themselves, though only a small portion of the 23km long network of tunnels can be visited.

Chemin de la Corniche

From just above the Casemates du Bock on rue Sigefroi, you can follow the pedestrianised **chemin de la Corniche** along the ramparts that once marked the eastern perimeter of the main fortress. The views are spectacular, and there's no better way to get a sense of the strength of the city's defences. Several major European powers added to them over the decades, most notably the French and the Spanish. By the 1690s, Luxembourg City was one of the continent's most strongly defended citadels – the so-called 'Gibraltar of the north'. A few minutes' walk along the *chemin* brings you to place St-Esprit and more fortifications in the form of the **Citadelle du St-Esprit**, a colossal, stone-faced bastion built in 1685. On the far side of the square, you'll find the main **elevator** down to Grund (see box, page 287).

Alzette river valley and Grund

Below and to the east of the Old Town, the **Alzette river valley** is dotted with ancient, pastel-painted houses and the battered remains of the outer fortifications – with the walls of the main citadel rising steeply above. The most illuminating walking route is via Montée de Clausen and then **rue de La Tour Jacob**, which takes you past the needle-thin spire of the **Église St-Jean** en route to **Grund**, a partly gentrified former working-class

---

THE LIFT BETWEEN THE UPPER AND LOWER TOWNS

You can reach the Pétrusse and Alzette river valleys from the Old Town by road, steps or **elevator**: the main elevator runs from place St-Esprit, near the Palais de Justice, to Grund (daily 7am–2am; free).

6

district that strings along the river for a few hundred metres. Grund zeroes on its chunky little **bridge** and close by, on the west side of the river, the **markers** at **rue St-Ulric 14** show how high the river has risen in flood years (the worst inundation was in 1756).

Pétrusse river valley

The pathway of **rue St-Quirin**, which links with rue St-Ulric, weaves its way west through the wooded parkland of the **Pétrusse river valley**. One obvious sight here is the mostly fourteenth-century **Chapelle St-Quirin**, a tiny chapel chiselled out of the rock face and equipped with a dinky little spire. Further along the valley, paths clamber up to both ends of the **Pont Adolphe**, from where it's the briefest of walks back into the Old Town.

Am Tunnel Art Gallery

rue Ste-Zithe 16 • Free • ⓦ visitluxembourg.com/en

Tucked away underground, just to the west of the Pont Adolphe and beneath a branch of the Banque et Caisse d'Epargne de l'Etat Luxembourg, the **Am Tunnel Art Gallery** houses the bank's private contemporary art collection. Some one hundred Luxembourgish artists are featured, as well as photos by **Edward Steichen**, the man behind the world-famous *The Family of Man* exhibition in Clervaux (see page 297).

Kirchberg

For several decades, the **Kirchberg district**, on a plateau a couple of kilometres to the northeast of the Old Town, was nothing more than an administrative centre for a battery of European institutions built on either side of avenue John F. Kennedy. In the 1990s, however, the Luxembourg government decided to prime and pump a large-scale urban development programme featuring new office blocks designed by eminent architects and all appearing at break-neck speed – the overall aim being to consolidate and confirm the duchy's leading role in the financial world. Capitalist eye-catchers now dot the district – Gottfried Böhm's **Deutsche Bank** being a case in point – which may not sound too tempting. Still, the district is also home to two good **museums** in a matching pair of outlying fortifications just to the south of avenue John F. Kennedy.

Musée Dräi Eechelen

Park Dräi Eechelen 5 • Charge • ⓦ m3e.public.lu • The T1 links the Old Town with Kirchberg, get off at 'Philharmonie/MUDAM'

Housed in the handsomely restored, round-towered Fort Thüngen, the **Musée Dräi Eechelen** traces the duchy's history using over six hundred items, from historical photographs, paintings, and costumes to original documents. A detailed **audio guide** in English explains everything, and there's also a film to help set the scene.

Musée d'Art Moderne Grand-Duc Jean (MUDAM)

Park Dräi Eechelen 3 • Charge • ⓦ mudam.com • For buses, see under Musée Dräi Eechelen

Metres from the Musée Dräi Eechelen, the **Musée d'Art Moderne Grand-Duc Jean** (MUDAM) occupies a large, striking, glassy structure designed by the architect I.M. Pei (more famous for the Louvre pyramid). The museum has a far-reaching and wide-ranging collection of **modern and contemporary art**, displayed through a programme of rotating temporary displays alongside regular visiting exhibitions.

ARRIVAL AND DEPARTURE   **LUXEMBOURG CITY**

BY PLANE

Luxembourg's international airport (ⓦ lux-airport. lu) is located 8km northeast of the city on the road to

Grevenmacher. There are a number of ways of getting into town: at the moment, the best is to take the No. 16 bus (Mon–Fri 5.30am–11pm every 10min, Sat 5.25am–11.05pm every

20min, Sun 6am–11pm every 30min) to either the main train station or the bus station, but this will change in late 2024 when a new tramway will connect the airport to the city centre. All public transport within Luxembourg is free.

BY TRAIN
Luxembourg City's main train station – Gare Centrale – is on the city's south side, a 15min walk from the Old Town. All public transport within Luxembourg is free.
Destinations Brussels (hourly; 3hr); Clervaux (every 30min;

1hr); Ettelbruck (every 20min; 30min); Liège (hourly; 2hr 30min); Namur (hourly; 2hr).

BY BUS
Most long-distance buses stop in the vicinity of the train station, as do most local city buses. The latter mostly proceed to the city's bus station in the Old Town on pl E. Hamilius.
Destinations Echternach (hourly; 1hr); Mondorf-les-Bains (hourly; 25min); Remich (hourly; 45min).

6

GETTING AROUND

BY BUS AND TRAM
Luxembourg City has an excellent public transport system (ⓦmobiliteit.lu), with buses from every part of the city and its surroundings converging on the bus station in the Old Town on pl E. Hamilius. Usefully, most services are also routed via the train station. There's also a tram (T1) which connects Kirchberg with the Old Town, the train station, and, at some point, the airport. Public transport within Luxembourg is free.

BY TOURIST TRAIN
The **Pétrusse Express** sightseeing train runs city tours (April–Oct daily 10am–6pm; 50min) with departures every 30min or so from Montée de Clausen, near the Casemates du Bock (see page 287). Tickets cost €15 for adults.

BY WALKING TOUR
The city's tourist office organises a series of guided walks, starting from their premises on pl Guillaume II. Options include a 'City Promenade' around the Old Town (2hr) and the excellent 'Wenzel Walk' (2hr 30min–3hr), which takes you right around the fortifications on the east side of the Old Town. In both cases, booking – at least a couple of hours beforehand – is advised.

BY BICYCLE
If you're pretty fit – there are lots of hills – cycling can be a good way to get around the city, which has well-marked cycling trails.
Municipal bike rental Velóh (ⓦmyveloh.lu/en/) is a municipal bike-rental scheme whereby you can pick up and drop off a bike at over seventy stations dotted around town and join the scheme at any station.

BY CAR
Driving around the centre of Luxembourg City can be a real hassle as many of the streets are very narrow, and the one-way system can be baffling. The best bet is to either plump for one of the free P+R car parks on the main approach roads or use one of the car parks.
Car parks There are a handful of underground car parks in the Old Town, though spaces can still be hard to find.

BY TAXI
Before collapsing into a taxi, bear in mind that they are expensive – for example, the 8km trip from the airport to the Old Town will set you back around €35.

INFORMATION

Tourist office The Luxembourg City Tourist Office (LCTO) is bang in the centre of town at pl Guillaume II 30 (April–Sept: Mon–Sat 9am–7pm, Sun 10am–6pm; Oct–March: Mon–Sat 9am–6pm, Sun 10am–6pm; ⓦluxembourg-city.com). They supply free city maps, issue all manner

of glossy leaflets and have details of – and take bookings for – guided walking tours. For more general information on Luxembourg, consult the Luxembourg National Tourist Office's excellent website (ⓦvisitluxembourg.com).

ACCOMMODATION   SEE MAPS PAGES 284 AND 286

HOTELS
Coque rue Léon Hengen 2 ⓦcoque.lu; T1 departs from Luxembourg Central train station. Part of one of Europe's best sports centres with 36 spacious, fresh, woodland-themed rooms, this enjoyable wild-card option is located in the Kirchberg district east of the city centre. Added perks include free access to an Olympic-size pool and discounted access to the Centre de Détente spa. €€

Français pl d'Armes 14 ⓦhotelfrancais.lu. This attractive and central three-star has 24 smart and spotless rooms in a crisp, modern style. Not surprisingly, the rooms at the back are a lot quieter than those at the front. It has a pleasant café, too. €€€
★ **Parc Beaux-Arts** rue Sigefroi 1 ⓦparcbeauxarts. lu. Housed in one of the city's oldest mansions, right in the centre, this four-star hotel has eleven fresh and bright

6

rooms and suites, each decorated with unique artwork. Some rooms have period features, such as stone fireplaces and parquet floors. €€€€

Le Place d'Armes pl d'Armes 18 ⓦ hotel-leplacedarmes. com. Situated in the heart of the Old Town, this deluxe five-star's tasteful rooms are a seamless blend of modern and traditional decor. A gourmet restaurant, brasserie, two wine bars and a snug wellness centre are on site. The website invariably has offers and online-only discounts. €€€€

★ **Simoncini** rue Notre-Dame 6 ⓦ hotelsimoncini.lu. Sleek boutique hotel bang in the centre of the Old Town, just off pl Guillaume II. The 36 rooms are cool and stylish, the service is good, and the modern art in the public rooms is appealing. Good weekend deals, but not overpriced in any case. €€€

Vauban pl Guillaume 10 ⓦ hotelvauban.lu. On one of the city's busiest squares, opposite the town hall, this good-value option has sixteen small but spotlessly clean and entirely functional rooms with wooden floors and white bed linens. €€€

HOSTEL AND CAMPING

L'Auberge de Jeunesse rue du Fort Olisy 2 ⓦ youth hostels.lu; bus Nos 9 or 14 from the train station, get off at the 'Plateau Altmunster' stop. This modern, well-equipped, HI-affiliated hostel is located below the Bock fortifications, 1km from the centre and 3km from the train station. It has 240 beds in four- to six-bunk rooms, mostly en suite. Facilities include laundry, bar/café and 24hr reception. Non-members pay a small surcharge. Dorms €, doubles €

Bon Accueil Camping rue du Camping 2, Alzingen ⓦ camping-alzingen.lu; several buses, including bus No. 194 from the train station. Just 10km south of the city centre with a nice location on the banks of the River Alzette, off route d'Echternach in the village of Alzingen. April to mid-Oct. €

EATING
SEE MAP PAGE 286

The **Old Town** is crowded with cafés and restaurants, including **inexpensive places** where a filling plat du jour can cost as little as €15. **French cuisine** is popular, and traditional **Luxembourgish dishes** are found on many menus too, mostly meaty affairs such as neck of pork with broad beans (*judd mat gaardebounen*), black sausage (*blutwurst*) and chicken in Riesling (*hahnchen im Riesling*), not to mention freshwater fish from the River Moselle. Keep an eye out also for *gromperenkichelchen* (potato cakes, usually served with apple sauce) and, in winter, stalls and cafés selling **glühwein** (hot wine mulled with cloves). One of the great Luxembourg traditions is **coffee and cakes** in a salon or one of the city's numerous patisseries. As in Belgium, **pavement cafés** are thronged in the summertime, pl d'Armes being the centre of the outdoor scene.

★ **Apoteca** rue de la Boucherie 12 ⓦ apoteca.lu. Perhaps the most fashionable restaurant in town, solidly booked at weekends, with two floors of dining and a nightclub-like bar downstairs. The menu is wide-ranging and imaginative, with a fondness for Italian flavours. Ask for the wine list, and you'll receive the key to the cellar, where bottles range from the entirely affordable to the hideously expensive. €€€

Basta Cosi rue Louvigny 10 ⓦ bastacosi.lu. The traditional Italian menu at this stylish restaurant features all the classics, such as lasagne, saltimbocca and bruschetta. €€

Le Bouquet Garni rue de l'Eau 32 ⓦ lebouquetgarni. lu. Polished restaurant with old-beamed ceilings, exposed stone walls and starched tablecloths. The French cuisine, which features local ingredients, regularly wins a Michelin star, and there's an excellent wine cellar too. €€€€

Brasserie Guillaume pl Guillaume II 12–14 ⓦ brasserie guillaume.lu. This bright, modern brasserie is beloved for its lobster and carpaccio dishes. It's very affordable, too, with plats du jour being a real bargain at lunchtime. Reserve at weekends. €€

Français pl d'Armes 14 ⓦ hotelfrancais.lu. The pavement café of the *Hôtel Français* offers tasty salads, an extensive menu including several Luxembourgish standbys, and sweet treats such as ice creams and pancakes. €€

★ **Kaempf-Kohler** pl Guillaume 18 ⓦ kaempff-kohler. lu. This smooth and polished, upmarket deli-cum-café, with a terrace overlooking the square, offers all manner of tasty sandwiches and other picnic goodies, such as fancy cheeses and the like. €

Mosconi rue Münster 13 ⓦ mosconi.lu. Decorated in lavish style, this smart and sleek Italian place down by the river in Grund is regularly awarded Michelin stars. It's not a budget option, but the set lunch menus can be a reasonably good deal, and it's a fine spot for a special night out. Reservations required. €€€€

Oberweis Grand-rue 16 ⓦ oberweis.lu. There's a café-restaurant upstairs here, but the real deal is the mouthwatering patisserie section full of cakes, chocolates and tarts – famous across the duchy. Also, there are great sandwiches and wraps and an outside terrace to enjoy it all. The most central of the several *Oberweis* dotted across Luxembourg City. €

DRINKING AND NIGHTLIFE
SEE MAPS PAGES 284 AND 286

Luxembourg City has a lively **bar and club** scene. Hotspots include pl d'Armes and its surroundings: the streets around the train station, rue de Hollerich south of the city, and the Rives de Clausen bar/club 'village' east of the centre. Opening hours are pretty elastic, but bars usually stay open until around 1am and clubs until 3am. Wherever you

6

FESTIVALS IN LUXEMBOURG CITY

Luxembourg City offers a long series of high-quality concerts and events, especially – but not exclusively – during the warm spring and summer months.

Luxembourg City Film Festival ⓦ luxfilmfest.lu. A ten-day run of films and documentaries made in or about Luxembourg from late February to early March.

Summer in the City ⓦ luxembourg-city.com/en/summer-in-the-city. An annual programme of free music concerts, fashion shows and parades held from late June to September.

Blues'n Jazz Rallye ⓦ visitluxembourg.com/event/blues-n-jazz-rallye. This one-day annual jazz event in late July attracts fifty local and international bands who play on ten open-air city-centre stages.

Schueberfouer ⓦ fouer.lu. Held over the last week in August and the first two weeks of September, this is the city's main knees-up, featuring one of the biggest mobile fairs in Europe.

---

go, you'll encounter the duchy's three most popular beers: Mousel, Diekirch and Bofferding.

Café des Artistes Montée du Grund 22 ⓦ cafedes artistes.lu. Charming café-bar close to the bridge in Grund. They lay on regular chanson with piano accompaniment to a mixed and boozy crew.

Chiggeri rue du Nord 15 ⓦ chiggeri.lu. This cool first-floor bar in Old Town serves light bites and good wines to a mixed clientele beneath a funky painted ceiling. It also has a smarter restaurant on the ground floor.

Melusina rue de la Tour Jacob 145, Clausen ⓦ melusina. lu. This is an expat favourite, with varied sounds from local and international DJs, plus a hectic bar.

Pyg Irish Bar rue de la Tour Jacob 19, Clausen ☎ 26 00 82 42. This raucous Irish bar, down in the depths of Clausen, serves all the Emerald Isle classics, including Guinness and

Kilkenny.

Scott's Pub Bisserweg 4 ⓦ scotts.lu. By the bridge in Grund, this pubby English bar is where expats congregate for draught Guinness and bitter.

The Tube rue Sigfroi 8 ⓦ thetube.lu. Named after the London Underground, this youthful bar/nightclub features live DJs who play varied sounds from techno to soul most nights. Sports events (including Formula 1) are screened here, too, plus there are occasional quiz nights.

★ **Urban** rue de la Boucherie 2 ⓦ urban.lu. This bar-brasserie is popular with expats and local business folk for its retro-chic interior, good burgers and impressive cocktail list.

Vis à Vis rue Beaumont 2 ☎ 46 03 26. This laid-back, comfortable bar with old posters and a relaxed feel is a good option for a drink or snack anytime.

ENTERTAINMENT

Cinémathèque de la Ville de Luxembourg pl du Théâtre 17 ⓦ vdl.lu. As you might expect, Luxembourg City has several cinemas, but this is the pick of the bunch: an art-house cinema offering a wide-ranging and adventurous cinematic programme. It is conveniently located in the Old Town.

Philharmonie Luxembourg pl de l'Europe 1, Kirchberg ⓦ philharmonie.lu. Out in Kirchberg, the duchy's sleek and modern concert hall is a striking building that looks something like a classical Greek temple. Its annual programme showcases Luxembourg's Philharmonic Orchestra concerts, as well as performances by visiting classical and jazz musicians.

DIRECTORY

Embassies Belgium, rue des Girondins 4 ☎ 442 74 61; Ireland, rte d'Arlon 28 ☎ 450 61 0; Netherlands, rue Ste-Zithe 6 ☎ 22 75 70; UK, bd Joseph II, 5 ☎ 22 98 64; USA, bd E. Servais 22 ☎ 46 01 23 00.

Emergencies Fire and ambulance ☎ 112; police ☎ 113.
Pharmacies Central pharmacies include Goedert, pl d'Armes 5 (☎ 222 39 91; Mon–Sat 9am–5.30pm). Duty rotas are displayed in pharmacy windows.

The Luxembourg Ardennes

The rolling, thickly forested hills north of Luxembourg City are known as the **Luxembourg Ardennes** (D'Éisléck in Luxembourgish), and they spread across the border into France, Belgium and Germany. It's an intensely pretty and peaceful region dotted with ancient hilltop castles and quaint villages ensconced within river bends. Its forests and rivers are ideal for **sports**, with plentiful kayaking, hiking and biking opportunities. Particular highlights include postcard-pretty **Esch-sur-Sûre**,

6

the handsome scenery and castle at **Vianden**, the hilltop town of **Wiltz** and **Clervaux**'s UNESCO-listed photography exhibition, **The Family of Man**.

Ettelbruck

ETTELBRUCK, just 35km north of Luxembourg City, is a workaday crossroads town at the confluence of the rivers Alzette and Sûre. Badly damaged in the fighting of 1944, Ettelbruck has only one significant sight, dedicated to **General George Patton** (see box, page 292), the American general who liberated the town on Christmas Day 1944.

Musée Général Patton
rue Dr Klein 5 • Charge • ⓦ patton.lu

A relatively dry affair, the **Musée Général Patton** focuses on the eponymous general's involvement in the **Battle of the Bulge** (see box, page 273), with a wide range of photographs displayed alongside weapons and arms. A **statue of Patton**, presented to Ettelbruck by his son, sits just outside town on the N7 as it heads off to Diekirch.

ARRIVAL AND INFORMATION   **ETTELBRUCK**

By train Ettelbruck train station is on the south side of the town centre – about 200m from the Musée Général Patton. | **Destinations** Diekirch (every 30min; 10min); Luxembourg City (every 20min; 30min).

Bourscheid

North of Ettelbruck, two equally appealing country roads – the CR348 and the CR349 – worm their way 10km through forested hills to the trio of villages known collectively as **BOURSCHEID**. Rambling along the bony ridge is Bourscheid village, and down in the valley are Bourscheid-Moulin and Bourscheid-Plage. High on a hill above these is the massive **Château de Bourscheid.**

Château de Bourscheid
rue du Château • Charge • ⓦ castle-bourscheid.lu

Perched high above the River Sûre, the **Château de Bourscheid** has a fairy-tale appearance, its mighty turrets and thick towers enclosed within an extended curtain wall and eleven watchtowers. It appears as if the Romans were the first to fortify the

---

A BELLICOSE BELLIGERENT: GENERAL GEORGE S. PATTON

Born in California to an affluent family with a strong military tradition, **General George S. Patton** (1885–1945) entered the Virginia Military Institute at 18, transferring to the United States Military Academy a year later before seeing service in France during **World War I**. Badly wounded when a bullet ripped through his upper thigh, he would later joke about being a '**half-assed general**' but regularly over-egged the pudding by dropping his pants to prove it.

Charismatic and immaculately groomed, Patton was a first-rate field commander and, at the head of the US 3rd Army, it was he who drove the Germans out of Luxembourg in the later stages of the **Battle of the Bulge** (see box, page 273), a skilled operation that demonstrated Patton's military prowess to fine advantage. Yet, his **compulsiveness** was disruptive: he repeatedly berated British Commander Field Marshal Bernard **Montgomery** for being too cautious and, in an incident that almost wrecked his career, **slapped the face** of a battle-fatigued GI he was visiting in hospital, accusing him of cowardice. By comparison with his tumultuous life, Patton's **death** can't help but seem anticlimactic – he died from injuries sustained in a car accident. It was perhaps a blessing in disguise: peace could hold little for a man who declared, 'Compared to war, all other forms of human endeavour shrink to insignificance …God how I love it.'

site, but the building began in earnest around AD 1000 and continued, off and on, for several hundred years. By comparison, the interior is disappointing, with precious little to see. However, the gabled **Stolzembourg house** gamely displays a ragbag of artefacts unearthed during archaeological digs, alongside occasional exhibitions of local artists' work.

ARRIVAL AND DEPARTURE
BOURSCHEID

By bus A reasonably frequent bus service links Ettelbruck train station with Bourscheid (hourly; 20min); from the Bourscheid Kirch bus stop, it's a 1.7km (20min) walk up to the castle.

Esch-sur-Sûre

From Bourscheid-Moulin, you can follow the River Sûre west along the N27 for about 20km to reach **ESCH-SUR-SÛRE**. This little place has a reputation out of all proportion to its size – mainly because of its gorgeous situation, with the village draped over a hill within an **oxbow loop** in the river. Specific sights are in short supply, but wandering the village's old cobbled streets, lined with good-looking stone houses, is delightful, and you can scramble around the hilltop ruins of its medieval **château** (open access; free) and/or follow the walking trail off rue de Kaundorf for the panoramic views.

ARRIVAL AND INFORMATION
ESCH-SUR-SÛRE

By train and bus Trains from Luxembourg City travel as far as Ettelbruck (every 20min; 30min), from where local buses (every 30min; 30min) will take you to Esch-sur-Sûre.
Tourist information The tourist office is in the Naturpark, a 10min walk from town along the south side of the river at rte de Lultzhausen 15 (April–Oct: Mon–Fri 10am–noon & 2–6pm, Sat & Sun 2–6pm; Nov–March: Mon–Fri 10am–noon & 2–5pm, Sat & Sun 2–5pm; ⊚ esch-sur-sure.lu).

ACCOMMODATION

Hôtel de la Sûre rue du Pont 1 ⊚ hotel-de-la-sure.lu. Full of character, this warren-like four-star hotel has fourteen standard and ten luxury rooms, the latter with either a hot tub or private hammam. There is a real charm to the place, especially in the country-house-style public areas, and there's also a bar and a first-rate restaurant, where they highlight seasonal offerings – in April, for example, it's trout and asparagus. Restaurant €€€, Accommodation €€

Diekirch

The compact centre of **DIEKIRCH**, just 8km from Ettelbruck, hugs the north bank of the River Sûre, its encircling boulevard marking the route of the long-demolished medieval walls. The town took a pounding in 1944 – hence the modern buildings that characterise the centre – but bits and pieces of the old have survived. Diekirch is at its most agreeable on the main pedestrianised shopping street, **Grand-rue**, which cuts a cosy route along to the main square, **place de la Libération**, but frankly, the town is nowhere near as appealing as other Luxembourgish towns nearby and an hour or two's stroll does it justice.

Musée National d'Histoire Militair
Bamertal 10 • Charge • ⊚ mnhm.net

One of the better World War II museums in the region, the **Musée National d'Histoire Militaire**, provides a thorough historical survey of the Battle of the Bulge (see box, page 273), with particular emphasis on the US forces that liberated Diekirch. There's plenty of equipment on display, but the **photographs** are the main draw, showing both sets of troops in action and at leisure, some recording the appalling freezing conditions of December 1944, others the horrific state of affairs inside the medics' tents. There's also a series of dioramas and a display entitled '**Veiner Miliz**', detailing the activities of the Luxembourg resistance movement based in Vianden, plus a room devoted to **Tambow**, where the Soviets incarcerated many Luxembourgers whom the Germans had drafted to the Eastern Front as forced labour.

ARRIVAL AND DEPARTURE   DIEKIRCH

By bus Diekirch's combined bus and train station is a 5–10min walk southwest of the centre on av de la Gare. Many buses also stop at or near the pl Guillaume, on the northern edge of the centre.

Destinations Echternach (hourly; 30min); Ettelbruck train station (every 30min; 10min); Vianden (every 30min; 20min).

INFORMATION

Tourist information In the centre, at pl de la Libération 3 (July & Aug: Mon–Fri 10am–12.30pm & 1–6pm, Sat 10am–12.30pm & 1–5pm, Sun 10am–2pm; Sept–June: Mon 2–5pm, Tues–Sat 10am–12.30pm & 1–5pm; ⓦ visit-diekirch.lu/en).

ACCOMMODATION AND EATING

Hôtel Du Parc av de la Gare 28 ⓦ hotel-du-parc. lu. Housed in a rather glum-looking modern building, facing a small park that, in turn, abuts the River Sûre, this spick-and-span, three-star hotel offers pleasant enough if undemanding rooms decorated in creams and whites. €€

Restaurant du Commerce rue du Marché 1 ❶ 26 80 37 74. This central option serves tasty, traditional Luxembourgish dishes at reasonable prices. €€

Vianden

Tucked away in a deep fold in the landscape, beneath bulging forested hills, pocket-sized **VIANDEN**, with its famous hilltop castle, is the most strikingly sited of all Luxembourg's smaller towns. The castle and the scenery have made Vianden a popular tourist destination – exactly as the writer Victor Hugo (1802–85) predicted during his exile here in the 1870s when it was a remote and isolated little place. Orientation couldn't be easier: the main street, **Grand-rue**, begins at the **bridge** and sweeps some 500m up a steep hill flanked by ageing, pastel-painted buildings before curling beneath the **castle** (château). Wherever else you go in the duchy, be sure to come here.

The bridge

Vianden's pint-sized **bridge** spans the River Our. It is crowned with a statue of St John Nepomuk, a fourteenth-century Bohemian priest who was thrown into the River Vltava for refusing to divulge the confessional secrets of his queen. This untimely end was to make him the patron saint of bridges. Also on the bridge is a fine bust of **Victor Hugo**, who was expelled from France for supporting the French Revolutionaries of 1848 and spent almost twenty years in exile. He visited Vianden four times and spent the summer of 1871 here.

Musée Littéraire Victor Hugo

rue de la Gare 37 • Charge • ⓦ victor-hugo.lu

Hugo's former summerhouse, at the east end of the bridge, has been turned into the **Musée Littéraire Victor Hugo** to commemorate the writer's stay here. Spread over several small floors, the displays are mildly diverting and include a selection of the great man's letters, poems and manuscripts, most memorably his laudatory *Discourse on Vianden*, and a few sketches of local places of interest – the castles at Beaufort and Larochette, for example. Perhaps inevitably, few of Hugo's other possessions have survived, with the notable exception of some bedroom furniture, including his bed.

Église des Trinitaires

Grand-rue 55 • Free • ❶ 83 42 57

Strolling up Grand-rue from the bridge, look for the **Église des Trinitaires**, a handsome Gothic church dating from the thirteenth century. The heavily vaulted interior is distinguished by its fanciful Rococo high altar, added in the 1740s. The adjoining **cloître** (cloister) is also in the Gothic style, as exemplified by the subtle, sinuous tracery of the windows.

Musée Histoire de la Ville
Grand-rue 96 • Charge • ☎ 83 45 91

The **Musée Histoire de la Ville** occupies an old, distinguished-looking building up the street from the church. It holds an enjoyable hotchpotch of rural **furniture**, fancy fire-backs and old clothes, plus a sprawling display of dolls; on the top floor, a small room is devoted to old photographs of the town and castle.

The castle
Montée du Château • Charge • ⓦ castle-vianden.lu • The obvious, albeit strenuous, approach is along the short access road at the top of Vianden's main street; the easier alternative is to take the télésiège (chairlift; see page 295), whose upper terminal is a 5–10min walk from the castle

Vianden's principal sight is its inordinately picturesque **castle**, perched high above the town. The Romans were the first to fortify the site, but what you see today mainly dates from the eleventh century, though bits and pieces were added later – hence the mixture of Romanesque, Gothic and Renaissance features. The castle was originally the home of the **counts of Vianden**, who ruled the town and much of the surrounding area from the twelfth to the early fifteenth century when the House of Luxembourg swallowed them up. The castle remained the property of the grand dukes until it was bequeathed to the state in 1977.

The interior
A sprawling complex, the castle has a platoon of **rooms** furnished in an approximation of period style – the **Salle des Banquets** (Banqueting Hall) being a case in point – while others display suits of armour and suchlike. Of particular architectural merit are the long **Galerie Byzantine** (Byzantine Room), with its high trefoil windows, and the **Chapelle Supérieure** (Upper Chapel) next door, surrounded by a narrow defensive walkway. For a bit of authentic mustiness, peek down the **well** just off the Grand Kitchen, its murky darkness lit to reveal profound depths in which, legend maintains, a former count can be heard frantically playing dice to keep the devil at bay and avoid being dragged off to hell.

ARRIVAL AND DEPARTURE — VIANDEN

By bus Vianden's bus station is a 5min walk or so east of the town bridge along rue de la Gare and its continuation, rue de la Frontière.
Destinations Diekirch (every 30min; 20min); Ettelbruck (every 30min; 30min); Luxembourg City (bus to Ettelbruck, then take the train; 1hr).
Tourist information The tourist office is on the castle side of the river, at rue du Vieux Marché 1A (Mon–Fri 10am–noon & 1–5pm, Sat & Sun 10am–3pm; ⓦ visit-vianden.lu). They issue hiking maps and sell a helpful booklet describing around thirty walks in the vicinity of Vianden, ranging from a short ramble along the river to more energetic hauls up into the surrounding hills.

GETTING AROUND

By télésiège (chairlift) The duchy's only chairlift (April to mid-Oct: daily 10am–5pm; ⓦ visit-vianden.lu) departs from rue du Sanatorium 39, on the east side of the river, about 400m north of the town bridge; the upper terminus is on one of the hills on the west side of the river; from here, an easy footpath leads round to the castle in about 5min.

ACCOMMODATION

Accommodation isn't usually a problem in Vianden – virtually every other building seems to be a hotel or guest house – but you would be well advised to reserve in advance during the high season.
Auberge de Jeunesse Montée du Château 3 ⓦ youth hostels.lu. Set back from the road at the top of Grand-rue, on the left, near the castle, this modern hostel offers ten rooms (all with shared facilities) and an on-site kitchen that can prepare inexpensive, packed lunches and evening meals; non-members pay a little extra. Beware the check-in time of 5pm. Dorms €, doubles €
★ **Auberge de l'Our** rue de la Gare 35 ⓦ aubergede lour.com. This riverside option offers smart and stylish contemporary rooms with wet-room bathrooms in an immaculately modernised old building close to the bridge. The better rooms, like the hotel's delightful waterside

terrace, provide attractive views. €€

Camping de l'Our rte de Bettel 2 ⓦ camping-vianden. lu. Situated 1km south of town by the river, this top-notch campsite has every conceivable facility, including free wi-fi, mini-golf, a restaurant, a shop and washing machines. Easter to mid-Oct. €

★ **Hôtel Heintz** Grand-rue 55 ⓦ hotel-heintz.lu. A traditional, family-owned hotel, its elegant facade is an appropriate prelude to the thoroughly alpine interior: lots of wood panelling and oodles of local bygones. The rooms are comfortable and well-appointed; some have private balconies with views over the river. €€

EATING AND DRINKING

Ancien Cinema Café Club Grand-rue 23 ⓦ ancien cinema.lu. Quirky café-bar filled with books, old cinema chairs and a large screen at the back (for occasional film nights). It has a tasty please-all menu of pizza, pasta and tortillas, fifty kinds of organic tea and a luscious array of cakes. €€

Veiner Stuff rue de la Gare 26 ⓦ veistuff.lu. An upmarket restaurant that takes real pride in serving traditional Luxembourgish food made only with seasonal produce. The menu changes weekly and features three options for starters and mains. There's also an excellent-value two-course lunch menu. Reservations required. €€

Wiltz

The approach to the pleasant hilltop town of **WILTZ**, 26km northwest of Ettelbruck, is a delight, with the road threading its way up through the forests while offering glimpses of quiet valleys down below. Remote as Wiltz may seem today, it's witnessed more than its fair share of bloodshed ever since the local count built a castle here in the thirteenth century: the town was savaged by the French, raided by the Burgundians and, last but not least, was caught up in the Battle of the Bulge in 1944 (see box, page 273), with both sides using its airfield as the front line moved back and forth. Today, the town still clusters around its elegant Renaissance-style **castle**, which now serves as the impressive venue for the three-week-long annual summer **Wiltz Festival** (ⓦ festivalwiltz.lu), which combines theatre performances with classical music concerts.

Wiltz Castle
rue du Château 35 • Charge • ⓦ visitwiltz.lu/en

Work began on **Wiltz Castle** in the thirteenth century, but over the centuries, the counts of Wiltz replaced the original stone fortress with a capacious Renaissance complex, with the last bits and pieces – a chapel and a monumental staircase – added in the 1720s. In the event, the counts didn't enjoy their palace for long – the last of the line fled for his life as the French Republican Army approached in 1793 – and, after a period of dereliction, the castle passed to the state in 1951. Today, access is restricted to some areas of the castle, but three museums are inside.

Battle of the Ardennes Museum
This mildly diverting museum focuses on the bloody **Battle of the Bulge** (see box, page 273) that raged from 16 December 1944 to 21 January 1945. Collections of photos, uniforms, documents and other military paraphernalia sit alongside a few mock-ups.

Tannery Museum
The **Tannery Museum** examines Wiltz's long association with leather. From small beginnings in late medieval times, the town developed a large leather industry. By the middle of the nineteenth century, there were around thirty tanneries here; the last one, Lambert, closed its doors in 1953.

National Brewery Museum
Located inside the castle's former stables, the **National Brewery Museum** covers the 6,000-year-old history of brewing in Luxembourg, but of more interest is the attached wooden-floored **estaminet** and **microbrewery**, which produces just fifty litres of beer a year, making it the world's smallest – or so they claim.

ARRIVAL AND INFORMATION

By train Wiltz train station is on av de la Gare, on the south side of the river; from here, it's a 15min (800m) walk east to the castle.
Destinations Ettelbruck (every 30min; 40min with one change); Luxembourg City (every 30min; 1hr with one change).

Tourist office The tourist office is located inside the castle at rue du Château 35 (July & Aug: daily 9am–6pm; Sept–June: Mon–Sat 9am–noon & 2–5pm; ⓦ visitwiltz.lu/en).
Bike rental Mountain bikes can be rented from *Camping Kaul*.

ACCOMMODATION AND EATING

Aux Anciennes Tanneries Am Bongert 18 ⓦ aux tanneriesdewiltz.com. North of the river, this friendly three-star hotel has seventeen Mediterranean-style rooms, a leafy terrace and an atmospheric breakfast room/restaurant set beneath a vaulted stone ceiling. €€
Camping Kaul Campingstrooss 60 ⓦ kaul.lu. Excellent four-star campsite on the north side of the river offering

wooden Hobbit-style pods, two-bed cabins for families and camping pitches. A heated open-air swimming pool with a slide and bike rental are just some of the perks. April–Oct. Pitches €, pods €, cabins €€
Le Croquant rue Grande-Duchesse Charlotte 4 ⓦ le croquant.lu. A simple affair, close to the castle, this café serves a tasty array of freshly prepared sandwiches. €

Clervaux

Tiny **CLERVAUX**, northern Luxembourg's most interesting town, snuggles into a tight, forested loop of the River Clerve, its jangle of slate-grey roofs set against green surroundings. Clervaux's most notable building is its **castle**, and inside is the town's pride and joy, **The Family of Man** photography exhibition.

Château de Clervaux

Mont du Château • Charge • ⓦ clervaux.lu • ⓦ steichencollections.lu

Plonked on a hill in the heart of the town, the white walls and perky turrets of the **Château de Clervaux** dominate proceedings. The castle sustained considerable damage in World War II but has been carefully restored, its 'oldest' sections being the twelfth-century west wing and the impressive 'Witch Tower' in the main courtyard. However, the main reason to visit is **The Family of Man**, a remarkable collection of 503 photographs compiled by **Edward Steichen** (1879–1973) as a manifesto for peace and to celebrate 'how marvellous people are'. Steichen, formerly Director of Photography at the Museum of Modern Art in New York, where the show was first exhibited in 1955, made his selection from no fewer than two million entries, with the final cut depicting life, love and death as captured by 273 photographers from 68 countries. They range from TIME magazine covers to snapshots by little-known photographers, but the overall collection is very raw and moving. Steichen bequeathed it to the country of his birth in his will, and in 2003, **UNESCO** classified it as a 'Memory of the World'.

ARRIVAL AND INFORMATION

By train Clervaux is on the main Belgium–Luxembourg train line. From the train station, it's a good 10min walk south into the town centre, straight down rue de la Gare and its continuation, Grand-rue.
Destinations Liège (every 2hr; 1hr 40min); Luxembourg

City (every 30min; 1hr).
Tourist information The tourist office is in the town centre, close to the castle at Grand-rue 11 (daily 10am–noon & 2–4pm; ⓦ visit-clervaux.lu). It has details of local accommodation and issues free town maps.

ACCOMMODATION

Le Clervaux Grand-rue 9 ⓦ le-clervaux.excellence-group.lu. Chic and central boutique hotel occupying a handsomely renovated old building. It has some 22 opulent suites, each kitted out in a contemporary version of country-house style. Big, comfortable beds and some rooms have

great views over the town. €€€
Koener Grand-rue 14 ⓦ koener.excellence-group. lu. Behind a handsome façade, this smart four-star establishment has crisp, modern rooms and an on-site sauna, pool and fitness studio. €€€

EATING

Au Chocolat Grand-rue 13 ⓦauchocolat.lu. This pleasant café serves indulgent home-made cakes, crêpes, and ice creams with good coffee. It also has a lovely terrace to sit on when the weather is warm enough. €̄

Rhino Steakhouse & Pizzeria Grand-rue 10 ⓦexcellence-group.lu. The liveliest spot in town, this trim modern restaurant rustles up sizzling steaks of various cuts and sizes as well as stone-baked pizzas. €€̄

The Moselle River Valley

6

The small towns and villages east of Luxembourg City spread out as far as the **Moselle River**, whose gentle curves form the border with Germany. The river's fertile banks hold a string of **vineyards** – this is a prime wine-producing region – and, amongst a number of riverside settlements, **Remich** is the best base if you're after a leisurely sampling of the local vintages. These are sold at the numerous *caves* (wine cellars) that dot the **route du Vin** (the N10), which tracks along the west bank of the Moselle from one end of the duchy to the other.

Remich

REMICH, some 25km east of Luxembourg City, is a likeable riverside town and the tourist hub of the Moselle Valley. Germany lies just across the bridge, and **cruise boats** (see box, page 298) ply the Moselle River from Easter to October, connecting Remich with points north and south. Several local **wineries** offer tours and tastings (see box, page 300).

By bus Remich bus station is down by the river near the bridge and just off the Esplanade.

Destinations Luxembourg City (every 30min; 50min); Ehnen (hourly; 15min); Grevenmacher (hourly; 30min).

ACCOMMODATION AND EATING

Hôtel St-Nicolas Esplanade 31 ⓦsaint-nicolas.lu. This nicely turned-out four-star hotel occupies a good-looking older building dating back to the 1880s. Forty neat and trim modern rooms, plus a spa and fitness suite. The hotel also has a good French restaurant serving such delights as poached turbot in a mousseline sauce. Restaurant €€̄; Accommodation €€€̄

Ehnen

Tiny **EHNEN**, just 10km north of Remich, is at its prettiest beside the two little streams that roll down through the old centre of the village with antique stone dwellings to either side. The river bank has been conserved as a municipal park with a better-than-average adventure playground.

By bus Buses to Ehnen stop down by the river. Destinations Grevenmacher (hourly; 15min); Remich (hourly; 15min).

CRUISING THE MOSELLE RIVER

From mid–April to late September, once daily in each direction, the *Princesse Marie-Astrid* **cruise boat** sails along a fair old slice of the **River Moselle** at a leisurely pace, stopping at most of the settlements on the way, including Remich, Stadtbredimus and Grevenmacher. The vessel is owned and operated by **Entente touristique de la Moselle** (ⓦentente-moselle.lu); as a sample fare, a single from Remich to Grevenmacher costs €16 (€23 return).

TAKING THE WATERS: MONDORF-LES-BAINS

The old spa town of **Mondorf-les-Bains**, about 8km southwest of Remich, has attracted health tourists since the 1840s when an underground spring was discovered here. Visitors still come from all around to wallow in the mineral waters of the **Domaine Thermal** (av des Bains 52; ⓦ mondorf.lu), a series of indoor and outdoor **pools** heated to 36ºC alongside no fewer than nine themed **saunas**. There's also an on-site **spa** offering all manner of treatments and massages. Costs vary enormously, depending on the wellness/treatment package you opt for, but if you stick to taking the waters, you can keep costs down to a minimum.

6

Grevenmacher

GREVENMACHER, about 20km upriver from Remich, is the pint-sized capital of the Luxembourg Moselle. It's a pleasant old town with a comely set of stone houses, but the main pull is the Bernard Massard **winery** (see box, page 300).

ARRIVAL AND INFORMATION   GREVENMACHER

By bus Grevenmacher's main bus station is centrally located, 50m or so back from the river and just off the main road (N10).
Destinations Echternach (hourly; 40min); Ehnen (hourly;

15min); Remich (hourly; 30min).
Tourist office rte du Vin 10 (Mon–Fri 8am–5pm; mid-May to Aug: Mon–Fri 8am–5pm, Sat 10am–3pm; ⓦ visit maacher.lu).

Echternach and around

Tucked tight against the German border, pocket-sized **ECHTERNACH** grew up around an abbey founded here in 698 by the energetic **St Willibrord**, a Northumbrian missionary monk whose magic touch was said to cure epilepsy and cattle diseases. Such balanced skills went down a treat with the locals, and nowadays, Willibrord is commemorated by a renowned, day-long **dancing procession**, held annually on Whit Tuesday, in which the participants, holding white handkerchiefs, cross the town centre in leaps and jumps (to signify epilepsy) to the accompaniment of polka music. Heavily damaged during World War II, Echternach was painstakingly restored to an approximation of its former appearance. Today's aesthetic highlight is the **place du Marché**, whose finest building is the late-medieval **Palais de Justice**, or Denzelt (Law Courts), a striking, turreted structure with an elegant Gothic arcade. Echternach also possesses a narrow stone bridge over the River Sûre to Germany and sits on the edge of the forested valleys and open uplands of **La Petite Suisse Luxembourgeoise**, whose handsome landscapes support a plethora of outdoor activities (see box, page 302) and holds a pair of medieval **castles** at Beaufort and Larochette.

Basilique St-Willibrord

Parvis de la Basilique • Free • ⓦ basilika.lu/en

At the heart of Echternach is the **Basilique St-Willibrord**, a forceful edifice equipped with two sets of turreted towers. The church has had a long and chequered history. The first structure, built in 706, was a relatively modest affair, but as the Benedictine monastery grew more affluent, the monks extended it, stuffing it with all sorts of holy treasures. This made it a tempting target for the French Revolutionary Army, who sacked the abbey and expelled the monks in 1797. After that, the monastery was turned into a pottery factory, but the Benedictines returned a few years later and promptly restored the abbey to its medieval layout. There was more trouble during the Battle of the Bulge when the abbey was bombed. Still, the monks persevered, rebuilding the abbey yet again, and today's basilica has all the feel of a medieval

6

LUXEMBOURG'S WINERIES

Whether or not the Romans introduced **wine** to the Luxembourg region is still the subject of debate, but one thing is sure: the fertile banks of the **Moselle River** have nourished the vine for a very long time. Rivaner and **Elbling** (one of the oldest wines in the world) used to dominate the area, but nowadays, **Riesling, Auxerrois, Pinot Gris** and **Pinot Blanc** have a particularly strong presence. Standards are generally very high, so it's a little unfair that those of France and Germany largely overshadow the duchy's wines. Luxembourg's champagne-like sparkling wine – **crémant** – is particularly praiseworthy and costs half the price of the French stuff.

Caves Bernard Massard rte du Vin 22, 6794 Grevenmacher ⓦ bernard-massard.lu. Bernard Massard is known for its sparkling *méthode champenoise* wine. Visitors usually see the modern production process, making the tour less interesting (and shorter)

than it might otherwise be. A brief introductory film and a tasting in the slick hospitality suite are included. The *cave* is down by the river, next to the bridge.

★ **Caves St Martin** rte de Stadtbredimus 53, just north of Remich ⓦ cavesstmartin.lu. The house speciality is sparkling wine, and the tours and tastings are arguably the pick of the bunch, showcasing the traditional *méthode champenoise* process in which the bottles are turned by hand every other day. The caves are a 15min walk north along the river from the centre of Remich, on the left of the main road (the N10). Reservations for the guided tours (45min) are advised.

Domaines Vinsmoselle rte du Vin 12, 5450 Stadtbredimus, just north of Remich ⓦ vinsmoselle. lu. Founded in 1966, Vinsmoselle is a cooperative for wine cellars in five surrounding towns famous for their crémant. Their main showroom is the Caves du Sud, 32 Waistrooss, 5440 Remerschen.

---

church, most notably in its yawning, dimly lit **nave**. That said, the furnishings are pretty pedestrian, and the only significant piece to have survived the bombing is a part of the exquisite **crucifix** on the nave's left-hand wall. Downstairs, the **crypt** dates back to the original eighth-century foundation and accommodates the primitive **coffin** of St Willibrord, though this is enclosed within a hideously sentimental marble canopy of 1906.

Musée de l'Abbaye

Parvis de la Basilique 11 • Charge • ⓦ abteimuseum.org

The expansive **abbey complex** spreads out beyond the church, its crisply symmetrical, mainly eighteenth-century buildings now used as offices, including the tourist office (see page 301). Here also, next door to the church, in the vaulted cellars of the former Abbot's Palace, is the **Musée de l'Abbaye**, which displays a fine collection of **illuminated manuscripts**. The manuscripts are organised chronologically so visitors can examine their artistic evolution from the eighth century to the scriptorium's eleventh-century, German-influenced heyday. Two of the finest are the tenth-century *Codex Caesareus Upsaliensis* and the book of pericopes (a selection of biblical texts) made for the Holy Roman Emperor Henry III (1017–56). Many of the manuscripts are illustrated and explained at some length (in French and German), though all are facsimiles. The rest of the museum holds a few incidental bits and pieces, notably a couple of seventh-century **sarcophagi**.

The Roman villa

rue des Romains 47 • Free • ⓦ mnaha.lu • 850m walk southwest of the town centre

In 1975, in the grassy fields on the southwest side of town, builders accidentally unearthed the remains of what proved to be a sprawling **Roman villa** dating from AD 70. At its peak, the villa had seventy rooms on the ground floor along with porches, courtyards, mosaic tiling and under-floor heating, and today visitors can stroll the surviving foundations.

Beaufort Castle

rue du Château, Beaufort • Charge • ⓦ beaufortcastles.com • Local buses link Echternach with Beaufort (every 2hr; 25min); from the nearest bus stop, it's 1km or so to the castle; timetables on ⓦ mobiliteit.lu

Pretty country roads lead to **BEAUFORT**, a humdrum agricultural village that strings across a narrow, open plateau just 14km northwest of Echternach. In the wooded valley on the west side of the village is the settlement's only claim to fame, its rambling, mostly medieval **castle**, whose stern walls and bleak towers roll down a steep escarpment. The most impressive part of a visit is the climb up the **stone stairway** into the fortress, past a series of well-preserved gateways. There's not much to look at inside. However, the torture chamber is suitably grim, and the stinky old well is a reminder that, by the fourteenth century, castles were as likely to surrender because of the stench of the sanitation as they were from attack and assault.

6

Larochette Castle

Montée du Château, Larochette • Charge • ⓦ visitlarochette.lu • Local buses link Echternach with Larochette (every 2hr; 45min); from the nearest bus stop, it's 2.1km to the castle; timetable on ⓦ mobiliteit.lu

Sprawling along a rocky ridge high above its village, the substantial ruins of **Larochette Castle** are located a scenic 20km west of Echternach and 12km southwest of Beaufort. There's been a fortress here since the tenth century, but the most significant remains date from the fourteenth century, when the local lords controlled a whole swathe of Luxembourg. Allow thirty minutes to explore the fortress before popping down to the **village**, whose attractive medley of old houses strings along the valley below.

ARRIVAL AND INFORMATION   ECHTERNACH

By bus The bus station is 500m from the main square, pl du Marché, straight down rue de la Gare.
Destinations Beaufort (every 2hr; 25min); Diekirch (hourly; 30min); Ettelbruck (hourly; 40min); Grevenmacher (hourly; 40min); Larochette (every 2hr; 45min); Luxembourg City (hourly; 1hr); Wasserbillig (hourly; 30min).

Tourist information The tourist office is metres from the basilica at Parvis de la Basilique 9–10 (Mon–Fri 10am–4pm, Sat 10am–noon; ⓦ visitechternach.lu). It supplies free town maps and sells the Mullerthal trail hiking map (see box, page 302).

ACCOMMODATION

L'Auberge de Jeunesse rue Grégoire Schouppe 100 ⓦ youthhostels.lu. In a striking modern building of adjoining cubic blocks, this sporty hostel – with an indoor climbing wall and bike rental – has over one hundred beds in two- to six-bunk, en-suite rooms. Situated about 1.5km (a 20min walk) southwest of the town centre, this is a popular spot, so book well ahead. Note double/family rooms are often only available with a sports booking. Dorms €̄, doubles €̄
Bel-Air, Sport & Wellness 1 rte de Berdorf, 6409 Echternach ⓦ hotel-belair.lu. Perhaps surprisingly,

Echternach is short of good places to stay, but this substantial resort-like hotel does something to fill the gap. Set beside the road, about 2km northwest of Echternach, the main body of the hotel is in a pleasant old building in the French style, and both the guest rooms and the suites are briskly modern – and are mostly an adjunct to the spa treatments. €̄€̄
Le Petit Poète pl du Marché 13 ⓦ lepetitpoete.lu. Bang in the centre of town, behind a demure facade, this straightforward hotel has around a dozen plain but perfectly adequate modern rooms above a café on the main square. €̄€̄

EATING AND DRINKING

Café De Philo'soff rue de la Gare 31 ☎ 26 72 03 11. Student bar serving light bites beyond an Art Nouveau-style entrance and with a leafy terrace and a tank of terrapins out the back. Live bands, too. It's hectic on the weekend.
GriMouGi rue du Pont 34 ⓦ grimougi.com. Opposite the river and the old customs tollhouse, this lively, attractively kitted out restaurant is very popular with locals, particularly

for the inventive salads, good fish dishes and brochettes. €̄€̄€̄
Oktav Amadeus rue de la Gare 56 ⓦ oktav-amadeus. lu. Italian restaurant with smartly turned-out waitstaff, a pleasant outdoor terrace and a neat and trim interior dining room. The menu comprises authentic Italian classics, notably wood-fired pizzas and tasty pasta. €̄€̄

ACTIVITIES AROUND ECHTERNACH

HIKING

Echternach is the heart of Luxembourg's **La Petite Suisse** (Little Switzerland) region. It makes an excellent base for tackling the scenic 112km long **Mullerthal Trail**, commonly split into three shorter routes: a 38km trail that loops east, starting and finishing in Echternach, leads walkers through open meadows and forest; a 37km trail that loops west from Echternach, taking in the **Wolfsschlucht** (Wolves Canyon) and the striking **Goldfralay** and **Goldkaul rock formations**; and another 37km trail that starts and ends not in Echternach but in the town of **Mullerthal** and encompasses **Hallerbauch Valley**, **Larochette Castle** (see page 301) and more rock formations. The trail is steep in places, but paths are well-marked and suitable for children. **Maps** can be picked up from the Echternach tourist office (see page 301) or ordered in advance via email (w mullerthal-trail.lu).

The Mullerthal Trail map details other **local walks**. One popular, much shorter route, taking in some fine, rugged scenery, is the 6km walk west from Echternach to the plateau hamlet of **Berdorf**, up the dramatic **Gorge du Loup**. At the top of the gorge are grottoes – which may have been where the Romans cut millstones – and an open-air theatre. There's a reasonably frequent bus service between Berdorf and Echternach, or you can extend the hike by returning down the next valley to the south, with the path weaving through the **woods** across the valley from the N11, the main road back into Echternach.

CYCLING

Three official **cycling routes** depart from Echternach: Echternach–Luxembourg City (37km), Echternach–Wasserbillig (22km), and the Echternach–Vianden/Diekirch option (30km). The tourist office can supply more information.

Bike Mëllerdall w rentabike-mellerdall.lu. Bike Mëllerdall rents mountain and trekking bikes from a number of bike stations dotted around the region. In Echternach, they can be picked up from the youth hostel (see page 301).

CANOEING AND KAYAKING

You can **kayak or canoe** down the River Sûre to Echternach from Dillingen. In the high season (mid-July to Sept), the Dillingen–Echternach route is 14km; in the low season, you can choose a 12km or a 16km route.

Outdoor Freizeit rue de la Sûre 10, Dillingen w outdoorfreizeit.lu. Outdoor Freizeit rents out single and double kayaks and Canadian canoes. Booking is essential.

WORLD WAR I, BELGIAN 'GUIDES' OFF TO THE FRONT, 1914

Contexts

History

Jumbled together throughout their history, the countries now known as Belgium, Luxembourg and the Netherlands didn't define their present frontiers until 1830. Before then, their borders were continually being redrawn following battles, treaties and alliances, a shifting pattern that makes it impossible to provide a history of one without frequent reference to the others. To make matters more convoluted, these three countries were – and still are – commonly lumped together as the 'Low Countries' because of their topography, though given the valleys and hills of southern Belgium and Luxembourg, this is more than a little unfair. Even more confusing is that the Netherlands is frequently called 'Holland' when Holland is a province of the Netherlands. In the following account, we've used 'Low Countries' to cover all three countries and 'Holland' to refer to the province. In addition, we've termed the language of the northern part of Belgium 'Flemish' to save confusion, though 'Dutch' and even 'Netherlandish' are sometimes the preferred options among Belgians themselves.

Beginnings

Little is known of the **first** inhabitants of the Low Countries, whose various tribes only began to emerge from the prehistoric soup after Julius Caesar's conquest of Gaul (broadly France) in 57–50 BC. The **Romans** found three tribal groupings living in the region: the mainly Celtic **Belgae** (hence the nineteenth-century term 'Belgium') by the rivers Rhine, Meuse and Waal to the south and, further north, two Germanic peoples, the **Frisians** and the **Batavi**. The Romans conquered the Belgae and incorporated their lands into the imperial province of **Gallia Belgica**, but the territory of the Batavi and Frisians was not considered worthy of colonisation. Instead, these tribes were granted the status of allies, a source of recruitment for the Roman legions and curiosity for imperial travellers. In AD 50, Pliny observed, 'Here a wretched race is found, inhabiting either the more elevated spots or artificial mounds … When the waves cover the surrounding area they are like so many mariners on board a ship, and when again the tide recedes their condition is that of so many shipwrecked men.'

The **Roman occupation** continued for nigh on five hundred years until the legions were pulled back to protect the heartland of the crumbling empire. Yet, despite the length of their stay, there's a notable lack of material evidence to indicate their presence, two important exceptions being the odd stretch of the city wall and the Gallo-Romeins Museum in Tongeren (see page 204), one of the principal Roman settlements.

c.1750 BC	c.750 BC	c.50 BC
Beginnings of the 'Belgian' Bronze Age.	'Belgian' Iron Age kicks off with dramatic improvements in tools.	The Romans conquer the lands of the Belgae.

The Merovingians

As the Roman Empire collapsed in chaos and confusion, the Germanic **Franks**, who had been settling within Gallia Belgica since the third century, filled the power vacuum to the south and, along with their allies, the Belgae, established a **Merovingian** kingdom based around their capital in Tournai. A great swathe of forest extending from the Scheldt to the Ardennes separated this predominantly Frankish kingdom from the more confused situation to the north and east, where other tribes of Franks settled along the Scheldt and Leie – a separation which came to delineate the ethnic and linguistic division that survives in Belgium to this day. North of the Franks of the Scheldt were the **Saxons**, and finally, the north coast of the Netherlands was settled by the **Frisians**.

Towards the end of the fifth century, the Merovingians extended their control over much of what is now north and central France. In 496, their king, **Clovis**, was converted to **Christianity**. This faith slowly filtered north, spread by energetic missionaries like St Willibrord, the first bishop of Utrecht from about 710, and St Boniface, who was killed by the Frisians in 754 in a final act of pagan resistance before they too were converted. Meanwhile, after the death of the last distinguished Merovingian king, Dagobert, in 638, power passed increasingly to the so-called 'mayors of the palace', a hereditary position whose most outstanding occupant was **Charles Martel** (*c*.690–741). Martel ruled a large but all too shambolic kingdom whose military weakness he determined to remedy. Traditionally, the Merovingian (Frankish) army comprised a body of infantry led by a small group of cavalry. Martel replaced this with a largely mounted force of trained knights, who bore their military expenses in return for land – the beginnings of the **feudal system**.

The Carolingians

Ten years after Martel's death, his son, Pepin the Short, formally usurped the Merovingian throne with the blessing of the pope, becoming the first of the **Carolingian** dynasty, whose most famous member was **Charlemagne**, king of the west Franks from 768. In a dazzling series of campaigns, Charlemagne extended his empire south into Italy, west to the Pyrenees, north to Denmark and east to the Oder, his secular authority bolstered by his coronation as the first **Holy Roman Emperor** in 800. The pope bestowed this title on him to legitimise the king's claim to be the successor of the emperors of imperial Rome – and it worked a treat. Based in Aachen, Charlemagne stabilised his kingdom, and the Low Countries benefited from a trading boom that utilised the region's principal rivers. However, unlike his Roman predecessors, Charlemagne was subject to the divisive **inheritance laws** of the **Salian** tribe of Franks. After he died in 814, his kingdom was divided between his grandsons into three roughly parallel strips of territory, the precursors of France, the Low Countries and Germany.

The growth of the towns

The **tripartite division** of Charlemagne's empire put the Low Countries between the emergent French- and German-speaking nations, a particularly dangerous place to be – and one that has defined much of their history. This was not, however, apparent amid the cobweb of local alliances that defined early feudal Western

AD 406	450	496
Barbarians cross the River Rhine in numbers; the Roman Empire contracts.	Merovingian kingdom coalesces around Tournai.	The Merovingian king, Clovis, becomes a Christian; the new faith filters north.

> ## NOT AS BAD AS A NUNNERY: THE BEGUINAGES
>
> One corollary of the urbanisation of the Low Countries was the establishment of **beguinages** (**begijnhoven** in Flemish) in almost every city and town. These were semi-secluded communities where widows and unmarried women – the **Beguines** (*begijnen*) – lived together, the better to do pious acts, especially caring for the sick. In **construction**, beguinages followed the same general plan, with several streets of whitewashed, brick-terraced cottages hidden away behind walls and gates and surrounding a central garden and chapel. The **origins** of the Beguine movement are somewhat obscure, but the initial impetus seems to come from a twelfth-century Liège priest, a certain **Lambert le Bègue** (the Stammerer). The main period of growth came a little later when several important female nobles established new beguinages, such as the ones in Kortrijk, Ghent and Bruges. Beguine communities differed from convents in that the sisters did not have to take **vows** and had the right to return to the secular world. At a time when hundreds of women were forcibly shut away in convents for all sorts of reasons (primarily financial), this element of choice was crucial.

Europe in the ninth and tenth centuries. French kings and German emperors exercised general authority over the Low Countries during this period, but power was effectively in the hands of **local lords** who, remote from central control, brought a degree of local stability. From the twelfth century, feudalism slipped into a gradual decline, the intricate pattern of localised allegiances undermined by the increasing strength of certain lords, whose power and wealth often exceeded that of their nominal sovereign. Preoccupied by territorial squabbles, this streamlined nobility was usually willing to assist the growth of towns by granting charters, which permitted a certain amount of autonomy in exchange for tax revenues and military and labour services. The first major cities were **the cloth towns of Flanders**, notably Ghent, Bruges and Ieper, which grew wealthy from manufacturing cloth, their garments exported far and wide and their economies dependent on a continuous supply of good-quality wool from England. Meanwhile, the smaller towns north of the Scheldt concentrated on trade, exploiting their strategic position at the junction of several of the major waterborne trade routes of the day.

The **economic interests** of the urbanised merchants and guildsmen often conflicted with those of the local lord. This was especially true in **Flanders**, where the towns were anxious to preserve a good relationship with the king of England, who controlled the wool supply, whereas their count was a vassal of the king of France, whose dynastic aspirations often clashed with those of his English rival. As a result, the history of thirteenth- and fourteenth-century Flanders is punctuated by endemic conflict, as the rival kings and the guildsmen slugged it out. Though the fortunes of war oscillated between the parties, the underlying class conflict was never resolved.

The Burgundians

By the late fourteenth century, the political situation in the Low Countries was pretty clear: five lords controlled most of the region, paying only nominal homage to their French or German overlords. Yet things began to change in 1419, when **Philip the Good**, Duke of Burgundy, succeeded to the countship of Flanders and, by a series of

768	1200s	1302
Charlemagne becomes the king of the Franks and subsequently extends his control over the whole of the Low Countries.	Growth of the cloth towns of Flanders.	French knights come a cropper against the Flemings outside Kortrijk at the Battle of the Golden Spurs.

adroit political moves, gained control over a large tract of territory including Antwerp, Brabant and Limburg to the north, and Namur and Luxembourg to the south. Philip consolidated his power by establishing a strong central administration based in Bruges and by curtailing the privileges granted in the towns' charters. Less independent it may have been, but **Bruges** benefited greatly from the duke's presence, becoming an emporium for the **Hanseatic League**, a mainly German association of towns that acted as a trading group and protected its interests with a system of trading tariffs.

Philip died in 1467 to be succeeded by his son, **Charles the Bold**, who was killed in battle ten years later, plunging his father's carefully crafted domain into turmoil. The French took the opportunity to occupy Arras and Burgundy. Before the people of Flanders would agree to fight the invading French, they kidnapped Charles's successor, his daughter **Mary**, forcing her to sign a charter that restored the civic privileges removed by her grandfather.

The Habsburgs

After her release, Mary married the **Habsburg Maximilian of Austria** (1459–1519), who assumed sole authority when Mary was killed in a riding accident in 1482. A sharp operator, Maximilian continued where the Burgundians had left off, whittling away at the power of the cities with considerable success. When Maximilian became Holy Roman Emperor in 1494, he transferred control of the Low Countries to his son, **Philip the Handsome**, and then – after Philip's early death – to his grandson **Charles V** (1500–58), who subsequently became king of Spain and Holy Roman Emperor in 1516 and 1519 respectively. Charles ruled his vast kingdom with skill and energy, but having been born in Ghent, he was very suspicious of the turbulent Flemish burghers. Consequently, he favoured **Antwerp** at their expense. That city became the greatest port in the Habsburg Empire, part of a general movement that took trade and prosperity away from Flanders to the cities further north. As part of the process, the Flemish cloth industry had, by the 1480s, begun its long decline, undermined by England's new-found cloth manufacturing success.

By sheer might, Charles V systematically bent the merchant cities of the Low Countries to his will. However, despite this display of force, a spiritual trend was emerging that would soon question the rights of the emperor and rock the power of the Catholic Church.

The Reformation

An alliance of church and state had dominated the medieval world: popes and bishops, kings and counts were supposedly the representatives of God on Earth, and they worked together to crush religious dissent wherever and whenever it appeared. Much of their authority depended on the ignorance of the population, who were entirely dependent on their priests to interpret holy scripture. The **Reformation** was a religious revolt that stood sixteenth-century Europe on its head. There were many complex reasons for it, but certainly, the development of **typography** was a crucial element. For the first time, printers could produce relatively cheap Bibles in quantity, and the religious texts were no longer the exclusive property of the priesthood. The first

1419	c.1430	1482
Philip the Good, Duke of Burgundy, consolidates his control over most of the Low Countries, including 'Belgium'.	Van Eyck completes *The Adoration of the Mystic Lamb*.	Mary of Burgundy is killed in a riding accident; the Habsburg Empire absorbs Belgium and Luxembourg.

ERASMUS, THE ITINERANT GENIUS

By any measure, **Desiderius Erasmus** (1466–1536) was a remarkable man. Born in Rotterdam, the illegitimate son of a priest, he was orphaned at the age of 13 and defrauded of his inheritance by his guardians, who forced him to become a monk. He hated monastic life and seized the first opportunity to leave, becoming a student at the University of Paris in 1491. Throughout the rest of his life, Erasmus kept on the move, travelling between the Low Countries, England, Italy and Switzerland, and everywhere he went, his rigorous scholarship, sharp humour and strong moral sense made a tremendous impact. He attacked the abuses and corruptions of the Church, publishing scores of polemical and **satirical essays**, which were read all over Western Europe. He argued that most monks had 'no other calling than stupidity, ignorance … and the hope of being fed'. These attacks reflected Erasmus' determination to reform the Church from within by rationalising its doctrine and rooting out hypocrisy, ignorance and superstition. He employed other methods, too, producing translations of the New Testament to make the scriptures more widely accessible and coordinating the efforts of like-minded Christian humanists. The Church authorities periodically harassed Erasmus, but generally, he was tolerated, not least for his insistence on the importance of Christian unity. Luther was less indulgent, bitterly denouncing Erasmus for 'making fun of the faults and miseries of the Church of Christ instead of bewailing them before God'. The quarrel between the two reflected a growing schism among the reformers on the brink of the Reformation.

stirrings of the Reformation were in the welter of debate that spread across much of western Europe under the auspices of theologians like **Erasmus of Rotterdam** (1465–1536; see box, page 309), who wished to cleanse the Catholic Church of its corruptions, superstitions and extravagant ceremony; only later did many of these same thinkers – principally **Martin Luther** (1483–1546) – decide to support a breakaway Church. In 1517, Luther produced his Ninety-five Theses against indulgences, rejecting – among other things – Christ's presence in the sacrament of the Eucharist and denying the Church's monopoly on the interpretation of the Bible. There was no way back, and when Luther's works were disseminated, his ideas gained a European following among reforming groups branded as **Lutheran** by the Church, while other reformers were drawn to the doctrines of **John Calvin** (1509–64). Luther asserted that the Church's political power was subservient to that of the state; Calvin emphasised the importance of individual conscience and the need for redemption through the grace of Christ rather than the confessional.

These **Protestant** seeds fell on fertile ground among the merchants of the Low Countries, whose wealth and independence had never been easy to accommodate within a rigidly hierarchical society. Similarly, their employees, the guildsmen and apprentices, had a long history of opposing arbitrary authority and were easily convinced of the need to reform an autocratic, venal Church. In 1555, **Charles V abdicated**, possibly due to poor health, transferring his German lands to his brother Ferdinand and his Italian, Spanish and Low Countries territories to his son, the fanatically Catholic **Philip II**. In the short term, the scene was set for a bitter confrontation, while the dynastic ramifications of the division of the Habsburg Empire were to complicate European affairs for centuries.

1517	**1555**	**1566**
Luther posts his Ninety-five Theses against the sale of indulgences by the Catholic Church; the Reformation begins.	The resolutely Catholic Philip II of Spain prepares to weed out his Protestant subjects in the Low Countries.	Rebellious Protestants smash up hundreds of Catholic churches in the Iconoclastic Fury.

The Revolt of the Netherlands

After his father's abdication, **Philip II** (1527–98) decided to teach his heretical subjects a lesson they wouldn't forget. He garrisoned the towns of the Low Countries with Spanish mercenaries, imported the **Inquisition** and passed a series of anti-Protestant edicts. However, other pressures on the Habsburg Empire forced him into a tactical withdrawal, and he transferred control to his sister **Margaret of Parma** in 1559. Based in Brussels, the equally resolute Margaret implemented her brother's policies with gusto. In 1561, she reorganised the Church and created fourteen new bishoprics, a move construed as a wresting of power from civil authority and an attempt to destroy the local aristocracy's powers of religious patronage. Protestantism – and Protestant sympathies – spread among the nobility, who now formed the '**League of the Nobility**' to counter Habsburg policy. The league petitioned Philip for moderation but was dismissed out of hand by one of Margaret's Walloon advisers, who called them *ces gueux* (French for 'those beggars'), an epithet to be enthusiastically adopted by the rebels.

The Iconoclastic Fury

In 1565, a harvest failure caused a winter famine among the urban workers across the region. After years of repression, they struck back when a Protestant sermon in the tiny Flemish textile town of Steenvoorde incited the congregation to purge the local church of its papist idolatry. The crowd smashed up the church's reliquaries and shrines, broke the stained-glass windows and terrorised the priests, thereby launching what became known as the **Iconoclastic Fury**. The rioting spread like wildfire, and within ten days, churches had been ransacked from one end of the Low Countries to the other, nowhere more so than in Antwerp. The ferocity of this outbreak shocked the upper classes into renewed support for Spain, and Margaret regained the allegiance of most nobles – with the principal exception of the country's greatest landowner, Prince William of Orange-Nassau, known as **William the Silent** (1533–84). Of Germanic descent, he was raised a Catholic, but the excesses and rigidity of Philip had caused him to side with the Protestant movement. A firm believer in religious tolerance, William became a symbol of liberty for many. However, after the Iconoclastic Fury had revitalised the pro-Spanish party, he prudently slipped away to his estates in Germany.

The Duke of Alva and the Sea Beggars

Philip II was keen to capitalise on the increase in support for Margaret following the Iconoclastic Fury, and in 1567, he dispatched the **Duke of Alva** (and an army of ten thousand men) to the Low Countries to suppress his religious opponents absolutely. Margaret was not at all pleased by Philip's high-handed decision, so when Alva arrived in Brussels, she resigned in a huff, initiating what was, in effect, military rule. One of Alva's first acts was to set up the Council of Troubles, which was soon nicknamed the '**Council of Blood**' after its habit of executing those it examined. No fewer than twelve thousand citizens were polished off, mostly for participating in the Fury.

Initially, the repression worked: in 1568, when William the Silent attempted an invasion from Germany, the towns, garrisoned by the Spanish, offered no support. William waited and conceived other means of defeating Alva. In April 1572, a band of privateers entered **Brielle** on the Meuse and captured it from the

1567	1576	1579
Philip II establishes the Council of Troubles in Brussels to punish his Protestant subjects; locals rename it the 'Council of Blood'.	In the Spanish Fury, Antwerp's Spanish garrison turns on the city, slaughtering thousands.	Seven northern provinces break away from Habsburg Spain.

Spanish. This was one of several commando-style attacks by the so-called **Waterguezen** or **Sea Beggars**, who were at first obliged to operate from England, although it was soon possible for them to secure bases in the Netherlands, whose citizens had grown to loathe Alva and his Spaniards.

Luis de Resquesens, the Spanish Fury and the Union of Brussels
After the success at Brielle, the revolt spread rapidly: by June, the rebels controlled the province of Holland and William was able to take command of his troops in Delft. Alva and his son Frederick fought back but were frustrated by William's superior naval power and a mightily irritated Philip replaced Alva with **Luis de Resquesens**. Initially, Resquesens had some success in the south, where the Catholic majority were more willing to compromise with Spanish rule than their northern neighbours. However, the tide of war was against him – most pointedly in William's triumphant relief of Leiden in 1574. Two years later, Resquesens died, and the (unpaid) Habsburg garrison in Antwerp mutinied and attacked the town, slaughtering some eight thousand of its inhabitants in what was soon known as the **Spanish Fury**. The massacre alienated the south and pushed its inhabitants into the arms of William, whose troops now swept into Brussels, the heart of imperial power. Momentarily, it seemed possible for the whole region to unite behind William when all signed the **Union of Brussels**, which demanded the departure of foreign troops as a condition for accepting a diluted Habsburg sovereignty. This was followed, in 1576, by the **Pacification of Ghent**, a regional agreement that guaranteed freedom of religious belief, a necessary precondition for any union between the largely Protestant north (the Netherlands) and the predominantly Catholic south (Belgium and Luxembourg).

The United Provinces break free
Despite the precariousness of his position, Philip II was not inclined to compromise, especially after he realised that William's Calvinist sympathies were giving his new-found Walloon and Flemish allies the jitters. The king bided his time until 1578 when, with his enemies arguing among themselves, he sent another army from Spain to the Low Countries under the command of Alessandro Farnese, the **Duke of Parma**. Events played into Parma's hands. In 1579, tiring of all the wrangling, seven northern provinces agreed to sign the **Union of Utrecht**, an alliance against Spain that was to be the first unification of the Netherlands as an identifiable country – the **United Provinces**. The assembly of these United Provinces was known as the **States General** and met at The Hague. The role of **Stadholder** was the most important in each province, roughly equivalent to that of a governor, though the same person could occupy this position in any number of provinces. That same year, representatives of the southern provinces signed the **Union of Arras**, a Catholic-led agreement that declared loyalty to Philip II and counter-balanced the Union of Utrecht in the north. Parma used the south as a base to recapture Flanders and Antwerp, which fell after a long and cruel siege in 1585. But Parma was unable to advance any further north, and the Low Countries were, de facto, divided into two – the Spanish Netherlands and the United Provinces – beginning a separation that would lead, after many changes, to the creation of three modern countries.

1584	1599	1604
A Catholic fanatic assassinates the Protestant hero, William the Silent.	Anthony van Dyck is born in Antwerp.	Spanish forces lay siege to Ostend.

The Spanish Netherlands (1579–1713)

With his army firmly entrenched in the south, Philip was now prepared to permit some degree of economic and political autonomy, exercising control over the **Spanish Netherlands** through a governor in Brussels. Still, he was not inclined to tolerate his newly recovered Protestant subjects. As a result, thousands of weavers, apprentices and skilled workers – the bedrock of Calvinism – fled north to escape the new Catholic regime, thereby fuelling an economic boom in Holland. It took a while for this migration to take effect in the Spanish Netherlands. For several years, the region had all the trappings – if not the substance – of success, its mini-economy sustained by the conspicuous consumption of the Habsburg elite. Silk weaving, diamond processing, tapestry and lace-making were particular beneficiaries, and a new canal was cut linking Ghent and Bruges to the sea at Ostend. This commercial restructuring underpinned a brief flourishing of artistic life in Antwerp, centring on **Rubens** and his circle of friends – including Anthony van Dyck and Jacob Jordaens – during the first decades of the seventeenth century.

Habsburg failure

Months before his death in 1598, Philip II had granted his daughter and her husband control of the Spanish Netherlands, appointing them the **Archdukes Isabella and Albert**. Failing to learn from experience, the ducal couple continued prosecuting the war against the Protestant north, but with such little success that they were obliged to make peace – the **Twelve-Year Truce** – in 1609. When the truce ended, the new Spanish king, **Philip IV**, proved equally foolhardy, bypassing Isabella – Albert was dead – to launch his campaign against the Protestant Dutch. This was part of the **Thirty Years' War** (1618–48), a devastating conflict that spread across most of Western Europe in a mix of dynastic rivalry and religious (Catholic against Protestant) hatred. The Spanish were initially successful, but the war with France and Dutch sea power weakened them. From 1625 onwards, the Spaniards suffered a series of defeats on land and at sea, and in 1648, were compelled to accept the humiliating terms of the **Peace of Westphalia**. This general treaty ended the Thirty Years' War, and its terms both recognised the independence of the United Provinces and closed the Scheldt estuary, an action designed to destroy the trade and prosperity of Antwerp. By these means, the commercial pre-eminence of Amsterdam was assured.

The Spanish Netherlands paid dearly for its adherence to the Habsburg cause. In the course of the Thirty Years' War, it had teetered on the edge of chaos – highwaymen infested the roads, trade had almost disappeared, the population had been halved in Brabant, and acres of fertile farmland lay uncultivated – but the peace was perhaps as bad. Denied access to the sea, Antwerp was ruined and simply withered away, while the southern provinces as a whole spiralled into an **economic decline** that pauperised its population. Yet the country's ruling families seemed proud to appear to the world as the defenders of the Catholic faith; those who disagreed left.

The Counter-Reformation

Politically dependent on a decaying Spain, economically ruined and deprived of most of its more independent-minded citizens, the Spanish Netherlands turned in on itself, sustained by the fanatical Catholicism of the **Counter-Reformation**. Religious worship became strict and magnificent, medieval carnivals were transformed into

1609	1610 onwards	1648
Rubens sets out his artistic stall in Antwerp.	A veritable army of Jesuit priests settles in the Spanish Netherlands.	The Dutch secure the closure of the River Scheldt; Antwerp hits the economic skids.

exercises in piety, and penitential flagellation became popular, all under the approving
eyes of the **Jesuits**. Indeed, the number of Jesuits was quite extraordinary: in the whole
of France, there were only two thousand, but the Spanish Netherlands had no fewer
than 1,600. It was here that they wrote their most important works, exercised their
greatest influence and owned vast tracts of land. Supported by draconian laws that
barred known Protestants from public appointments, declared their marriages illegal
and forbade them municipal assistance, the Jesuits and their fellow Catholic priests
overwhelmed the religious opposition; in the space of fifty years, they transformed this
part of the Low Countries into an introverted world shaped by a mystical faith, where
Christians were redeemed by the ecstasy of suffering.

The visible signs of the change were all around, from extravagant Baroque churches
to crosses, calvaries and shrines scattered across the countryside. Literature disappeared,
the sciences vegetated and religious orders multiplied. In **painting**, artists – principally
Rubens – were used to confirm the ecclesiastical orthodoxies, their canvases full of
muscular saints and angels, reflecting a religious faith of mystery and hierarchy; others,
such as David Teniers and the later Bruegels, retreated into minutely observed realism.

French interference

The **Peace of Westphalia** (see page 312) in 1648 freed the king of France from his
fear of Germany, and the political and military history of the Spanish Netherlands
after that was dominated by **Louis XIV**'s efforts to add the country to his territories.
Fearful of an over-powerful France, the United Provinces, England and Sweden, among
others, determinedly resisted French designs and, to preserve the so-called balance of
power, they fought a long series of campaigns beginning with the **War of Devolution**
in 1667 and ending in the **War of the Spanish Succession**. The latter was sparked by
the death in 1700 of **Charles II**, the last of the Spanish Habsburgs, who had willed his
territories to the grandson of Louis XIV of France. An anti-French coalition refused to
accept the settlement, and there ensued a haphazard series of campaigns that dragged
on for eleven years, marked by the spectacular victories of the **Duke of Marlborough**
– Blenheim, Ramillies, Malplaquet and Oudenaarde. Many of the region's cities were
besieged and badly damaged during these wars, and only with the **Treaty of Utrecht**
of 1713 did the French temporarily abandon their attempt to conquer the Spanish
Netherlands. The latter were now passed to the Austrian Habsburgs in the shape of
Emperor Charles VI.

The Austrian Netherlands (1713–94)

The country's transfer from Spanish to **Austrian control** made little appreciable
difference. There were more wars and invasions, and a remote central authority
continued operating through Brussels. In particular, the **War of the Austrian Succession**
(1740–48), fought over the right of Maria Theresa to assume the Austrian Habsburg
throne, prompted the French to invade and occupy much of the Austrian Netherlands
in 1744. However, the **Treaty of Aix-la-Chapelle** restored Habsburg control four years
later. Perhaps surprisingly, these dynastic shenanigans had little effect on the Austrian
Netherlands' agriculture, which survived the various campaigns and became more
productive, leading to a marked increase in the rural population, especially after the

1700	1708	1713
Charles II of Spain dies without issue ending the Spanish Habsburg dynasty.	The Duke of Marlborough wins a spectacular victory over the French at Oudenaarde.	Austrian Habsburg Charles VI claims sovereignty over the Spanish Netherlands.

introduction of the **potato**. But intellectually, the country remained vitrified and stagnant – only 3 percent of the population was literate, workers were forbidden to change towns or jobs without obtaining permission from the municipal authorities, and skills and crafts were tied to particular families. As **Voltaire** quipped:

In this sad place wherein I stay,
Ignorance, torpidity,
And boredom hold their lasting sway,
With unconcerned stupidity;
A land where old obedience sits,
Well filled with faith, devoid of wits.

Progress at last

This sorry state of affairs began to change in the middle of the eighteenth century as the Austrian oligarchy came under the influence of the **Enlightenment**, that belief in reason and progress – as against authority and tradition – that had first been proselytised by French philosophers. In 1753, the arrival of a progressive governor, the **Count of Cobenzl**, signified a transformation of Habsburg policy. Eager to shake the country from its torpor, Cobenzl initiated an ambitious programme of public works. New canals were dug, old canals deepened, new industries were encouraged, and public health was at least discussed, one result being regulations forbidding burial inside churches and the creation of new cemeteries outside the city walls. Cobenzl also took a firm line with his clerical opponents, who took a dim view of all this modernising and tried to encourage the population to thwart him in his aims and ambitions.

The Brabant Revolution

In 1780, **Emperor Joseph II** came to the throne, determined, as he put it, to 'root out silly old prejudices' by imperial decree. His reforming zeal was not matched by any political nous, and the deluge of edicts he promulgated managed to offend all of the country's major groups – from peasants, clerics and merchants to the nobility. Opposition crystallised around two groups – the liberal-minded **Vonckists**, who demanded a radical, republican constitution, and the conservative **Statists**, whose prime aim was maintaining the Catholic status quo. Pandemonium ensued, and in 1789, the Habsburgs dispatched an army to restore order. Against all expectations, the two political groups swallowed their differences to combine and defeat the Austrians near Antwerp in what became known as the **Brabant Revolution**. The rebels promptly announced the formation of the United States of Belgium. However, the uneasy alliance between the Vonckists and Statists soon broke down, not least because the latter were terrified by the course of the revolution that had erupted across France's border. Determined to keep the radicals at bay, the Statists raised the peasantry to arms and, with the assistance of the priests, encouraged them to attack the Vonckists, who were killed in their hundreds. The Statists now had the upper hand, but the country remained in turmoil. When Emperor Joseph died in 1790, his successor, **Léopold**, quickly withdrew many reforming acts and sent in his troops to restore imperial authority.

1794	1812	1815
The French Revolutionary Army occupies the Austrian Netherlands.	French control of Belgium disintegrates; local leaders slug things out.	William I becomes king of the United Kingdom of the Netherlands.

French rule and its aftermath (1794–1830)

The new and repressive Habsburg regime was short-lived. French Republican armies brushed the imperial forces aside in 1794, and the Austrian Netherlands was annexed the following year, an annexation that was to last until 1814. The **French** imposed radical reforms: the Catholic Church was stripped of much of its worldly wealth; feudal privileges and guilds were abolished; and a consistent legal system was formulated. **Napoleon**, in control from 1799, carried on modernisation, rebuilding the docks of Antwerp and forcing the Netherlanders, whose country the French had also occupied, to accept the reopening of the Scheldt. Unrestricted access to French markets boosted the local economy, kick-starting the mechanisation of the textile industry in Ghent and Verviers and encouraging the growth of the coal and metal industries in Hainaut. Nonetheless, except for a radical minority, the French occupation remained unpopular with most of the populace: **looting** by French soldiers was commonplace, especially in the early years, but it was the introduction of **conscription** which stirred the most resistance, provoking a series of (brutally repressed) peasant insurrections.

The United Kingdom of the Netherlands (1815–30)

French rule in the Low Countries evaporated after Napoleon's disastrous retreat from Moscow in 1812. It had all but disappeared long before Napoleon's final defeat just outside Brussels at the **Battle of Waterloo** in June 1815. At the **Congress of Vienna**, called to settle Europe at the end of the Napoleonic Wars, the primary concern of the Great Powers – including Great Britain and Russia – was to create a buffer state against any possible future plans the French might have to expand to the north. With scant regard for the feelings of those affected, they decided to establish the **United Kingdom of the Netherlands**, which incorporated both the old United Provinces and the Spanish (Austrian) Netherlands. Frederick William of Orange was placed on the throne and crowned **King William I**. The Great Powers also decided to give Frederick William's German estates to Prussia and, in return, presented him with the newly independent **Grand Duchy of Luxembourg**. This was a somewhat confusing arrangement. The duchy had previously been part of both the Spanish and Austrian Netherlands, but now it was detached from the rest of the Low Countries constitutionally and pushed into the German Confederation at the same time as it shared the same king with the old United Provinces and Austrian Netherlands.

Given the imperious way the new Kingdom of the Netherlands had been established, considerable **royal tact** was required to make things work. William lacked this in abundance; indeed, some of his measures seemed designed to inflame his French-speaking (Belgian) subjects. He made Dutch the official language of the whole kingdom, and in a move against the Catholics, he tried to secularise all Church-controlled schools. Furthermore, each of the two former countries had the same number of representatives at the States General even though the population of the old United Provinces was half that of its neighbour. There were **competing economic interests**, too. The north relied on commerce and sought free trade without international tariffs; the industrialised south wanted a degree of protectionism. William's refusal to address any of these concerns united his opponents in the south, where both industrialists and clerics now clamoured for change.

1815	1830	1860s onwards
Wellington defeats Napoleon at Waterloo.	Belgian declares independence from the Netherlands.	Belgium becomes a major industrial power, but one with striking inequalities.

Independent Belgium: 1830–1900

The **revolution** against King William began in the Brussels opera house on 25 August 1830, when the singing of the duet, 'Amour Sacré de la Patrie', hit a nationalist nerve, and the audience poured out onto the streets to raise the flag of Brabant in defiance of the king. At first, the revolutionaries only demanded a scaling down of royal power and a separate 'Belgian' administration. However, negotiations soon broke down, and in late September, the insurrectionists proclaimed the **Kingdom of Belgium**. William prepared for war, but the liberal governments of Great Britain and France intervened to stop hostilities. In January of the following year, they recognised an independent Belgian state at the **Conference of London**. The caveat – and this was crucial to the Great Powers given the trouble the region had caused for centuries – was that Belgium should be classified as a '**neutral**' state outside any other sphere of influence. To bolster this new nation, they ceded to it the western segments of the Grand Duchy of Luxembourg and dug out **Prince Léopold of Saxe-Coburg** to present with the crown. William retained the northern part of his kingdom and received the remainder of Luxembourg as his personal possession, but he still hated the settlement, and there was a further bout of sabre-rattling before he finally caved in and accepted the new arrangements in 1839.

Léopold I

Shrewd and capable, **Léopold I** (1790–1865) was careful to maintain his country's neutrality and encouraged an industrial boom that saw coal mines developed, iron foundries established and the rapid expansion of the railway system. One casualty, however, was the traditional linen-making industry of rural Flanders. The cottagers who spun and wove the linen could not compete with the mechanised mills, and their pauperisation was compounded by the poor grain harvests and potato blight of 1844–46. Their sufferings were, however, of only mild concern to the country's political representatives, who were elected on a strictly limited franchise, which ensured the domination of the middle classes. The latter divided into two loose groups, the one attempting to undermine Catholic influence and control over such areas as education, the other profoundly conservative in its desire to maintain the status quo. Progressive elements within the bourgeoisie coalesced into the anti-clerical and pro-free trade **Liberal Party** and conservatives into the **Catholic Party**, which formed in opposition. In its retreat from the industrialised and radicalised cities, the political twist was that the Catholic Party began to identify with the plight of rural Dutch-speaking Belgians – as against the French-speaking ruling and managerial classes.

Léopold II

Léopold II's long reign (1865–1909) saw the emergence of Belgium as a major industrial power. The 1860s and 1870s also witnessed the first significant stirrings of a type of **Flemish nationalism** which felt little enthusiasm for the unitary status of Belgium, divided as it was between a French-speaking majority in the south – the Walloons – and the minority Dutch-speakers of the north. There was also industrial unrest towards the end of the century, the end results being a body of legislation improving working conditions and, in 1893, the extension of the **franchise** to all men over 25. The Catholic party also ensured that, under the Equality Law of 1898, Dutch was ratified as an official language, equal in status to French – the forerunner of many long

1885	1907	1908
Léopold II seizes the Congo Free State as his personal possession,	Georges Prosper Remi, the future Hergé – and creator of *Tintin* – is born in a suburb of Brussels.	Léopold II relinquishes control of the Congo Free State to the Belgian government after human rights abuses are exposed.

and difficult debates. Another matter of concern was the **Belgian Congo**. Determined to cut an international figure, Léopold II had decided to build up a colonial empire. The unfortunate recipients of his ambition were the Africans of the Congo River basin, who were effectively given to him by a conference of European powers in 1885. Ruling the Congo as a personal fiefdom, Léopold established an extraordinarily cruel colonial regime – so cruel in fact that even the other colonial powers were appalled, and the Belgian state was obliged to end the embarrassment (if not the brutal exploitation of the Congolese) by taking over the region – as the Belgian Congo – in 1908.

The twentieth century to 1939

At the beginning of the twentieth century, Belgium was an industrial powerhouse with a booming economy and a rapidly increasing workforce – 934,000 in 1896 and 1,176,000 in 1910. The country was also determined to keep on good terms with all the Great Powers but could not prevent itself from getting caught up in **World War I**. Indifferent to Belgium's proclaimed neutrality, the **Germans** had decided as early as 1908 that the best way to attack France was via Belgium, and this is precisely what they did in 1914. They captured almost all of the country except for a narrow strip of territory around De Panne. Undaunted, **King Albert I** (1909–34) and the Belgian army manned the northern part of the Allied line, and the king's refusal to surrender made him a national hero. The **trenches** ran through western Flanders, and all the towns and villages lying close to them – principally Ieper (Ypres) and Diksmuide – were simply obliterated by artillery fire. Belgium also witnessed some of the worst of the slaughter in and around a bulge in the line, which became known as the **Ypres Salient** (see page 135). The destruction was, however, confined to a narrow strip of Flanders, and most of Belgium was relatively unscathed, though the local population did suffer during the occupation from lack of food and outbursts of cruel treatment from the occupying army, while hundreds of Belgians were forced to work in German factories.

Political change in the 1920s and 1930s

After World War I, under the terms of the **Treaty of Versailles**, Belgium was granted extensive reparations from Germany and some German territory – the slice of land around Eupen and Malmédy and, in Africa, Rwanda and Burundi. Domestically, the Belgian government extended the franchise to all men over 21, a measure that ended several decades of **political control** by the Catholic Party. The latter was now only able to keep power in coalition with the Liberals – usually with the Socialists, the third major party, forming the backbone of the opposition. The political lines were, however, increasingly fudged as the Catholic Party moved left, becoming a Christian Democrat movement that was keen to cooperate with the Socialists on such matters as social legislation. The political parties may have been partly reconciled, but the **economy** staggered from crisis to crisis even before the effects of the Great Depression hit Belgium in 1929.

The political class also failed to appease those **Flemings** who felt discriminated against. There had been a widespread feeling among the Flemish soldiers of World War I that they had borne the brunt of the fighting. Now, an increasing number of Flemings came to believe – not without justification – that the Belgian government was

1914	1918	1940
Germany invades Belgium; Belgian forces withdraw behind the line of the River Yser.	Germany signs the Armistice and evacuates occupied territory in Belgium.	Germany invades the Low Countries; Léopold III surrenders the Belgian forces to the Germans without his government's consent.

A ROYAL MISCELLANY: BELGIUM'S KINGS

Léopold I (1790–1865; king 1831–65). Foisted on Belgium by the Great Powers, Léopold, the first king of the Belgians, was imported from Germany, where he was the prince of Saxe-Coburg – and the uncle of Queen Victoria. Despite lacking a popular mandate, Léopold made a reasonably good fist of things, keeping the country neutral as the Great Powers had ordained.

Léopold II (1835–1909; king 1865–1909). Energetic, crafty and forceful, Léopold II – son of Léopold I – encouraged the urbanisation of his country and promoted its importance as a major industrial power. He was also the man responsible for landing Brussels with such grandiose monuments as the Palais de Justice and for the imposition of a particularly barbaric colonial regime on the peoples of the Belgian Congo (now the Democratic Republic of the Congo).

Albert I (1875–1934; king 1909–34). The nephew of Léopold II and the father of Léopold III, Albert's determined resistance to the German invasion of World War I made him a national hero, and his untimely death in a climbing accident traumatised the nation.

Léopold III (1901–83; king 1934–51). In contrast to his father, Léopold III had the dubious honour of becoming one of Europe's least popular monarchs. His first wife died in a suspicious car crash; he nearly lost his kingdom by remarrying (then anathema in a Roman Catholic country); and he was badly compromised during the German occupation of World War II. During the war, Léopold remained in Belgium rather than face exile, fuelling rumours that he was a Nazi collaborator – though his supporters maintained that he prevented thousands of Belgians from being deported. After several years of heated postwar debate, during which the king remained in exile, the issue of Léopold's return was finally put to a referendum in 1950. Just over half the population voted in his favour, but there was a clear French/Flemish divide, with opposition to the king concentrated in French-speaking Wallonia. Mercifully for Belgium, Léopold abdicated in 1951 in favour of his son, Baudouin.

Baudouin I (1930–93; king 1951–93). Baudouin did much to restore the monarchy's popularity within Belgium, not least because he was generally thought to be even-handed in his treatment of French and Flemish speakers. He also hit the headlines in April 1990 by standing down for a day so that an abortion bill (which he, as a Catholic, had refused to sign) could be passed. His Congolese subjects were less impressed: in 1960, at the ceremony proclaiming the independence of the Congo, Baudouin referred to the end of Belgium's 'civilising mission' there, which infuriated the assembled Congolese – with every justification. Childless, Baudouin was succeeded by his younger brother, Albert.

Albert II (b.1934; king 1993–2013). Impeccably royal, from his Swiss finishing school to his aristocratic Italian wife, Queen Paola, Albert proved a safe pair of hands. He became a national figurehead in the manner of his predecessor and steered a diplomatic course through the shoals of Flemish-Wallonian antagonisms. Albert abdicated in 2013 due to poor health and old age, though his decision may have been influenced by a long-running paternity suit that dogged his last years as king. He was succeeded by his son Philippe.

Philippe I (b.1960; king 2013–). With his father's banker-like looks but not the avuncular air (few would accuse him of being charismatic), Philippe I's carefully assembled CV, including international education, military training, marriage to Mathilde, a Walloon aristocrat, and four children, has ticked most of the 'Belgian Royal' boxes. However, the country has never really taken to him – and, given his reputation for awkward aloofness, there's no certainty it ever will.

1944–45	1946	1950–1951
Allied forces liberate Belgium and Luxembourg piece by piece between September 1944 and February 1945.	Belgium convicts 57,000 Belgians of collaborating with the Nazis and executes 250, including Flemish nationalist August Borms.	Léopold III's return to Belgium sparks violent protests, forcing him to abdicate in favour of his son, Baudouin.

overly Walloon in its sympathies. Only reluctantly did the government make Flanders and Wallonia legally unilingual regions in 1930, and even then, the linguistic boundary was left unspecified in the hope that French speakers would come to dominate central Belgium. Furthermore, changing expectations fuelled these **communal tensions**. The Flemings had accepted the domination of the French speakers without much protest for several centuries. Still, as their region became more prosperous and their numbers increased in relation to the Walloons, they grew in self-confidence, becoming increasingly unhappy with their social and political subordination. Perhaps inevitably, some of this discontent was sucked into **Fascist** movements, which drew some 10 percent of the vote in both the Walloon and Flemish communities, though for very different reasons: the former for its appeal to a nationalist bourgeoisie, the latter for its assertion of 'racial' pride among an oppressed group.

World War II

The Germans invaded again in **May 1940**, launching a blitzkrieg that overwhelmed both Belgium and the Netherlands in short order. This time, there was no heroic resistance by the Belgian king, now **Léopold III** (1934–51), who ignored the advice of his government and surrendered unconditionally and in such great haste that the British and French armies were, as their commander-in-chief put it, 'suddenly faced with an open gap of twenty miles between Ypres and the sea through which enemy forces might reach the beaches'. It is true that the Belgian army had been badly mauled and that a German victory was inevitable. Still, the manner of the surrender infuriated many Belgians, as did the king's refusal to form a government in exile. At first, the occupation was relatively benign, though most of the population waited apprehensively to see what would happen next. The main exception – setting aside the king, who at best played an ambivalent role – was the right-wing edge of the **Flemish Nationalist movement**, which cooperated with the Germans and (unsuccessfully) sought to negotiate the creation of a separate Flemish state. Popular opinion hardened against the Germans in 1942 as the occupation became more oppressive. The Germans stepped up the requisitioning of Belgian equipment, expanded its forced labour schemes, obliging thousands of Belgians to work in Germany, and cracked down hard on any sign of opposition. By the end of the year, a **Resistance** movement was mounting acts of sabotage against the occupying forces and this, in turn, prompted more summary executions of both Resistance fighters and hostages.

The summer of 1942 witnessed the first roundups of the country's **Jews**. In 1940, there were approximately fifty thousand Jews in Belgium, mostly newly arrived refugees from Hitler's Germany. Much to their credit, many Belgians did their best to frustrate German efforts to transport the Jews out of the country, usually to Auschwitz: the Belgian police did not usually cooperate, Belgian railway workers left carriages unlocked and/or sidelined trains, and many other Belgians hid Jews in their homes for the duration. The result was that the Germans had, by 1944, killed about half the country's Jewish population, a much lower proportion than in most other parts of occupied Europe.

With the occupation hardening, the vast majority of Belgians were delighted to hear of the D-Day landings in June 1944. The **liberation** of Belgium began in

1960	**1962**	**1980**
Belgium pulls out from the Congo, which becomes an independent state, amid bloody chaos and confusion.	The 'Language Frontier' is formally drawn.	Belgium adopts a federal form of government with three regions: the Flemish north, Walloon south and bilingual Brussels.

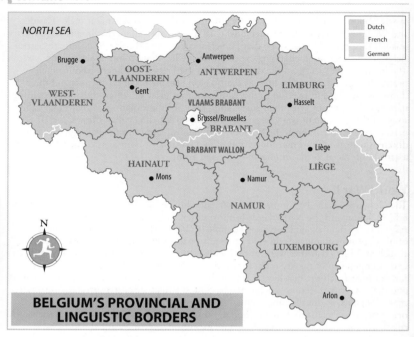

BELGIUM'S PROVINCIAL AND LINGUISTIC BORDERS

September with American troops in the south. It continued with British and Canadian divisions sweeping across Flanders in the north. However, the **Battle of the Bulge** (see page 273) did provide an unwelcome – and bloody – blip in the Ardennes in December of that same year.

1945–2010

After the war, the Belgians set about the task of economic **reconstruction**, helped by aid from the United States but hindered by a divisive controversy over the wartime activities of **King Léopold III**. Inevitably, the complex shadings of collaboration and forced cooperation were hard to disentangle, and the debate continued until 1950, when a **referendum** narrowly recommended Léopold's return from exile as king. His return was, however, marked by rioting across Wallonia, where the king's opponents were concentrated, and Léopold soon decided to **abdicate** in favour of his son, **Baudouin**.

Otherwise, the development of the **postwar Belgian economy** followed the pattern of most of Western Europe: boom in the 1960s, recession in the 1970s, retrenchment in the 1980s and 1990s, and a severe jolt during the financial crash of 2008. Significant events included the belated extension of the **franchise to women**

1992	1993	1996
Belgium ratifies the Maastricht Treaty on European Union.	Prince Albert is sworn in as king following the death of his brother Baudouin.	A series of failures in the Marc Dutroux case mires Belgium's law enforcement in scandal.

in 1948; an ugly, disorganised and hasty evacuation of the Belgian Congo in 1960 and of Rwanda and Burundi in 1962; and the transformation of Brussels from one of the lesser European capitals into a major player when it became the home of the EU and NATO – after the latter was ejected from France on the orders of de Gaulle in 1967. There was also acute **labour unrest** in the Limburg coalfield in the early 1980s, following plans to close most of the pits; a right royal pantomime when Catholic King Baudouin abdicated for the day while the law legalising **abortion** was ratified in 1990; and public outrage in 1996 when the Belgian police proved itself at best hopelessly inefficient, at worst complicit, in the gruesome activities of the child murderer and pornographer **Marc Dutroux**, who finally received a life sentence in 2004. The euro currency was introduced in 2002; the legalisation of **same-sex marriages** came in 2003, and the same year saw the government formally opposing the invasion of Iraq; 2005 witnessed a nationwide strike over proposals to reform pensions; and in 2008, the government felt obliged to invest vast sums of public money in shoring up the banking sector, thereby increasing the public debt from 84 percent of GDP in 2007 to 99.6 percent in 2012. Finally, in 2010, the official **Adriaenssens Commission** published a detailed report outlining several hundred cases of alleged child abuse by Catholic priests – a body blow to the church's reputation from which it may well never recover.

Communal tensions take centre stage

Above all, however, the postwar period was dominated by increasing **communal tension** between the Walloons and the Flemings, a state of affairs that was entangled with the economic decline of Wallonia, formerly the home of most of the country's heavy industry, as compared with burgeoning Flanders. One result of the tension was that every **national institution** became dogged by the prerequisites of bilingualism, and at the same time, all the main political parties created separate Flemish- and French-speaking sections. This communal rivalry also transformed **regional government**. The country had long been divided into provinces, but superimposed on this, in 1962, was the **language divide** (see box, page 322), which recognised three linguistic communities – French-, Flemish- and German-speaking. To complicate matters further, this was supplemented in 1980 by dividing the country into three **regions**, one each for the French and Flemish, with Brussels, the third, designated a bilingual region. The transfer of major administration areas from the centre to the regions followed.

By these means, it was hoped that communal tensions would dissolve – or at least dilute – but they did nothing of the sort. A pivotal moment came in 2007 when a bitter conflict between French- and Flemish-speaking politicians erupted over the electoral arrangements pertaining to **Brussels-Halle-Vilvoorde** (BHV for short). This extraordinarily complex dispute sapped the strength of the national government, and after the **federal elections of 2007**, no politician was able to construct a ruling coalition, and Belgium was left rudderless for several months. Neither was the instability at the heart of the national government short-lived – after the **federal elections of 2010**, it took the politicians over a year to hammer out a governing coalition, and in the federal elections four years later, amidst yet another carousel of resignations and changing party alliances, it took a dreary five months to broker a deal.

2002	2008	2010
Out with the Belgian franc – in with the euro.	Fortis, Belgium's largest bank, collapses amid a worsening financial crisis, forcing a government bail-out.	Explosive Adriaenssens report details hundreds of cases of systematic child abuse by Belgian's Catholic clergy.

THE BELGIAN LANGUAGE DIVIDE

There are almost twelve million Belgians divided into two main groups. The **Flemings** (Dutch or Flemish speakers) are concentrated in the north of the country and form nearly 60 percent of the population; to the south are the **Walloons**, French speakers, who account for around 40 percent. In the far east of the country, there are also a few pockets of **German speakers** around the towns of Eupen and Malmédy.

The Flemish–French **language divide** has troubled the country for decades, its significance rooted in deep class and economic divisions. When the Belgian state was founded in 1830, its ruling and middle classes were predominantly French-speaking, and they created a new state in their linguistic image: French was the official language, and Flemish was banned in schools. This Francophone domination was subsequently reinforced by the way the economy developed, with Wallonia becoming a major coal-mining and steel-producing area while Flanders remained a predominantly agricultural, rural backwater. There were nationalist stirrings among the Flemings from the 1880s onwards. Still, it was only after World War II – when Flanders became the country's economic powerhouse as Wallonia declined – that the demand for linguistic and cultural parity became irresistible. In the way of such things, the Walloons read Flemish 'parity' as 'domination', setting the scene for all sorts of inter-communal hassle.

In response to this burgeoning animosity, the **Language Frontier** was formally drawn across the country in 1962, cutting the country in half from west to east. The aim was to distinguish between the French- and Flemish-speaking communities, thereby defusing tensions, but it didn't work. In 1980, this failure prompted another attempt to rectify matters with the redrafting of the constitution and the creation of a **federal system**, with three separate **communities** – the Flemish north, the Walloon south and the German-speaking east – responsible for their own cultural and social affairs and education. At the same time, Belgium was divided into **three regions** — the Flemish north, the Walloon south and bilingual Brussels, with each regional authority dealing with matters like economic development, the environment and employment.

In hindsight, the niceties of this partition have done little to calm troubled waters. Right across Belgium, discontent on almost any matter – but especially pay, immigration and unemployment – smoulders within (or seeks an outlet through) the framework of this linguistic division; even individual neighbourhoods can be paralysed by language disputes, with **Brussels-Halle-Vilvoorde** (BHV; see page 321) being a case in point. All this said, it would be wrong to assume that Belgium's language differences have gone much beyond the level of personal animosity and institutionalised mutual suspicion. Belgian **language extremists** have been imprisoned over the years, but very few, if any, have died in the fight for supremacy. Suggesting a more measured approach to many a Belgian is often useless, but the casual visitor will rarely get a sniff of these tensions. It's probably better to speak English rather than Flemish or French in the 'wrong' part of Belgium, but if you make a mistake, the worst you'll get is a look of glazed indifference.

Belgium today

Given the current balance of political forces, Belgians anticipate that any foreseeable national election will be followed by murky political dealing as party leaders scrabble to construct ruling alliances – some of which may well be fragile, others positively

2013	2016	2020
King Albert abdicates in favour of his son Philippe.	Jihadist attacks on Brussels airport and metro station kill 32 people and injure over 300.	COVID-19 pandemic reaches Belgium in February.

unlikely: at the time of writing, the national government is comprised of seven political parties with contrasting agendas under the leadership of Alexander De Croo. These shifting political sands reflect deep inter-communal tensions. In essence, the (left-leaning) **Walloons** fear that the wealthier and more numerous (right-leaning) Flemings will come to dominate the state, and indeed, they may make this a self-fulfilling prophecy with their reluctance to learn Flemish – bilingualism being a prerequisite for any national job. On the other hand, the Flemings want political and cultural recognition, and many bristle at what they perceive as Wallonian cultural and linguistic arrogance. Even worse, compromise has been made harder by the emergence of a right-wing, Flemish, nationalist/separatist party, Vlaams Belang (VB), who regularly notch up between 10 and 20 percent of the vote. One touchstone for their relative success has been increasing concern over immigration, an issue which is often conflated with the several terrorist attacks Belgium has suffered: the worst, a trio of bombings organised by Islamic State in Brussels in 2016, resulted in the death of 32 and injury to over three hundred people. There was further disquiet when it turned out that Belgium had more nationals fighting for jihadist forces as a proportion of its population than any other Western European country. As elsewhere, concern over immigration has favoured the political right, who have been in power in Belgium since 2014. In this last decade, a series of conservative-friendly administrations has emphasised the need for a balanced budget – and austerity – rather than large-scale federal investment and pushed through legislation to make the labour market more 'flexible'.

These inter-communal tensions can, however, be exaggerated. Most polls indicate that a large majority of Belgians want their country to survive, though few would give the same reason as the country's most popular writer, **Hugo Claus** (1929–2008), who wrote, 'I insist on being Belgian. I want to be a member of the pariah nationality, the laughing stock of the French and the object of contempt of the Dutch. It's the ideal situation for a writer.'

The Grand Duchy of Luxembourg from 1830

At the Congress of Vienna in 1815, Luxembourg had been designated a **grand duchy** by the Great Powers and given (as personal property) to King William I of Orange-Nassau, the ruler of the United Kingdom of the Netherlands (see page 315). After Belgium broke away from William's kingdom in 1830, Luxembourg remained the property of the Dutch monarchy until 1890, when the ducal crown passed to another (independent) branch of the Nassau family, who have ruled there ever since. In 1867, the Great Powers made further decisions about Luxembourg: the **Treaty of London** reaffirmed the duchy's territorial integrity and declared it neutral in perpetuity, thereby – it was hoped – protecting it from the clutches of Germany and France. Following this declaration, Luxembourg City's fortifications were largely demolished.

The second half of the nineteenth century saw Luxembourg's agricultural economy transformed by the discovery and mining of **iron ore deposits**. This led to the foundation of what was soon one of Europe's largest steel industries. In 1914, the duchy confirmed its neutrality. However, it was still occupied by the Germans – as it was again in **World War II** when the Luxembourgers put up a stubborn resistance, leading to many brave acts of defiance and considerable loss of life. In particular, the

2022	2023
Belgian government returns the tooth of murdered Congolese leader Patrice Lumumba to his children. The symbolic righting of a colonial wrong?	Belgium's biggest-ever criminal trial begins in Brussels with 125 defendants accused of drugs and arms trafficking, kidnapping, extortion, forgery and money laundering.

Battle of the Bulge (see page 273) was a major disaster for Luxembourg – and when the war ended in 1945, one-third of the country's farmland lay uncultivated, the public transport system was in ruins, and some sixty thousand people were homeless.

In the **postwar years**, reconstruction was rapid. However, there was a major crisis in the mid-1970s when the iron and steel industry hit the economic buffers, obliging the government to pursue a policy of industrial diversification, with the main areas of growth being the **financial sector**, which now accounts for almost one-third of the duchy's tax revenues. Luxembourg also forsook its policy of neutrality, opting to join both NATO and the EC (EU), where it has often played a conciliatory role between the larger countries. In striking contrast to its neighbour, the duchy has also been extremely politically stable, with the **Christian Social People's Party** (CSV) the dominant force from 1945 until 2013, when the leader of the CSV, **Jean-Claude Juncker**, who had been prime minister since 1995, managed to lose the election: a scandal involving SREL, the duchy's intelligence service, and its cavalier attitude to legality (especially in the matter of wire-tapping). Although the CSV remained the largest party, it lost power to a three-party coalition. The coalition repeated its electoral success in 2018; however, the CSV returned to power in 2023 with **Luc Frieden** appointed prime minister on a right-wing ticket – the usual stuff of cutting red tape and opening up more healthcare to the private sector.

Belgian art

From medieval times onwards, the Low Countries and its successor states – the Netherlands, Belgium and Luxembourg – have produced some of Europe's finest artists, whose work has been digested and analysed in countless art books, some of which are reviewed in the 'Books' section on page 329. This guide doesn't have the space to cover the subject in any great detail, but the text below provides some background on ten of the country's most important painters. You'll see their work in museums across Belgium, especially in Antwerp, Ghent, Brussels and Bruges. The one major omission here is René Magritte (see box, page 65).

Jan van Eyck (1335–1441)

Medieval Flanders was one of Europe's most artistically productive parts, with each cloth town, especially Bruges and Ghent, trying to outdo its rivals with the quality of its religious art. Today, the works of these early Flemish painters, known as the **Flemish Primitives**, are highly prized and excellent examples are displayed in Ghent, Bruges and Brussels. **Jan van Eyck** is generally regarded as the first of the Flemish Primitives and has even been credited with the invention of oil painting itself – though it seems more likely that he simply perfected a new technique by thinning his paint with (newly discovered) turpentine, thus making it more flexible. His fame partially stems from the fact that he was one of the first artists to sign his work – an indication of how highly his contemporaries regarded his talent. Van Eyck's most celebrated work is *The Adoration of the Mystic Lamb*, a stunningly beautiful altarpiece displayed in St-Baafskathedraal in Ghent (see page 148). The painting was revolutionary in its realism, for the first time using elements of the native landscape in depicting biblical themes. It is underpinned by a complex symbolism which has generated analysis and discussion ever since.

Rogier van der Weyden (1400–64)

Apprenticed in Tournai and a one-time official painter to the city of Brussels, **Rogier van der Weyden** turned his hand to both secular and religious subjects with equal facility. His serene portraits of the bigwigs of his day were much admired across a large swathe of Western Europe, their popularity enabling him to set up a workshop manned by apprentices and assistants, who helped him with his work (and have often made authentication of his paintings problematic). In 1450, van der Weyden seems to have undertaken a pilgrimage to Rome. Although contact with his Italian contemporaries does not appear to have had much effect on his paintings, it did bring him several rewarding commissions. Perhaps, above all, it's his religious works that are of special appeal: warm and emotional, sensitive and dramatic, as in *St Luke painting the Portrait of Our Lady*, now displayed in Bruges (see page 104).

Hans Memling (1440–94)

Born near Frankfurt but active in Bruges, **Hans Memling** was almost certainly a pupil of Rogier van der Weyden, from whom he learnt an exquisite attention to detail. Memling is best remembered for his landscapes' pastoral charm and the quality of his **portraiture**, producing restrained and impeccably crafted works that often survive on the rescued side panels of triptychs. His **religious paintings** are similarly delightful, formal compositions that still pack an emotional punch – as exemplified by his *Moreel Triptych* (see page 104). The Memling collection in Bruges (see page 108) has a wonderful sample of his work.

Hieronymus Bosch (1450–1516)

One of the most distinctive of the early Netherlandish painters, **Hieronymus Bosch**, lived in the southern Netherlands for most of his life, though his style is linked to that of his Flemish contemporaries. About forty examples of his work survive, but none is dated, so no accurate chronology can be made. Nonetheless, it seems likely that his more conventional religious paintings, such as *The Crucifixion* in the Musées Royaux in Brussels (see page 62), were completed early on. Bosch is, however, much more famous for his **religious allegories** – frantic, frenetic paintings filled with macabre visions of tortured souls and grotesque beasts. At first glance, these works seem almost unhinged, but it's now thought they are visual representations of contemporary sayings, idioms and parables. While their interpretation is far from resolved, Bosch's paintings draw strongly on subconscious fears and archetypes, giving them a lasting, haunting fascination.

Quentin Matsys (1464–1530)

Following Flanders' decline at the end of the fifteenth century, the leading artists of the day migrated to the booming port of Antwerp, where they began to integrate the finely observed detail that characterised the Flemish tradition with the style of the Italian painters of the Renaissance in what is sometimes called the **Antwerp School**. A leading light of this school was **Quentin Matsys**, who was born in Leuven but spent most of his working life in Antwerp. Matsys introduced florid classical architectural details and intricate landscapes to his work, perhaps influenced by Leonardo da Vinci. As well as religious pieces, he also painted portraits and **genre scenes**, all of which have recognisably Italian facets and features, thereby paving the way for the Dutch genre painters of later years.

Pieter Bruegel the Elder (c.1525–69)

The greatest Netherlandish painter of the sixteenth century, **Pieter Bruegel the Elder**, is a shadowy figure, but he was likely born in Breda in the Netherlands. He certainly travelled widely, visiting France and Italy (where he was impressed by the Alps rather than the Italian painters) and worked in both Antwerp and Brussels. Many of his early works were landscapes, but in the 1560s, he turned his skills to the gruesome **allegories** (and innovative interpretations) of religious subjects for which he is now most famous – as in *The Fall of the Rebel Angels* and *The Fall of Icarus* (see page 63). Pieter also turned out a number of finely observed **peasant scenes** genre paintings that influenced generations of Low Country artists. Bruegel's two sons, **Pieter Bruegel the Younger** (1564–1638) and **Jan Bruegel** (1568–1625), were lesser painters: the former produced somewhat insipid copies of his father's work, but Jan developed a distinctive style, producing delicately rendered flower paintings and genre pieces that earned him the nickname 'Velvet'.

Pieter Paul Rubens (1577–1640)

Easily the most important exponent of the Baroque in northern Europe, **Rubens** was born in Siegen, Westphalia, but raised in Antwerp, where he entered the painters' guild in 1598. Two years later, he travelled to Italy and became court painter to the Duke of Mantua, who took a real shine to him. For the next eight years, he travelled extensively in Italy, absorbing the classical architecture and art of the High Renaissance. Consequently, by his return to Antwerp in 1609, Rubens had acquired an enormous artistic vocabulary, with the paintings of **Caravaggio** being a powerful influence. His first major success was *The Raising of the Cross*, painted in 1610 and displayed today in Antwerp cathedral (see page 173). A large, dynamic work which caused a sensation at the time, establishing Rubens' reputation and leading to a string of commissions. *The Descent from the Cross*, his next major work (also in Antwerp cathedral), consolidated this success, allowing him to set up a **studio** where he gathered a team of talented artists (among them **Anthony van Dyck** and **Jacob Jordaens**). The subsequent division of labour ensured a high productivity rate and a degree of personal flexibility; the degree to which Rubens personally worked on a canvas would vary and determine its price. From the early 1620s onwards, Rubens turned his hand to many themes and subjects – religious works, portraits, tapestry designs, landscapes, mythological scenes, ceiling paintings – each handled with supreme vitality and virtuosity. From his Flemish antecedents, he inherited an acute sense of light, using it not to dramatise his subjects (a technique favoured by Caravaggio and other Italian artists) but in association with colour and form. The drama in his works comes from the vigorous animation of his characters. His **large-scale allegorical works** are packed with heaving, writhing figures that appear to tumble out from the canvas. The energy of Rubens' paintings was reflected in his **private life**. In addition to his career as an artist, he undertook diplomatic missions to Spain and England. He used these opportunities to study the works of other artists and – as in the case of Velázquez – to meet them personally. In the 1630s, gout began to hamper his activities, and from this time, his painting became more domestic and meditative. **Hélène Fourment**, his second wife, was the subject of many portraits and served as a model for characters in his allegorical paintings, her figure epitomising the well-rounded women found throughout his work.

Anthony van Dyck (1599–1641)

Anthony van Dyck worked in Rubens' studio for two years from 1618, often taking on the depiction of religious figures in his master's works – the ones, that is, which required particular sensitivity and pathos (or so he claimed). Like Rubens, van Dyck was born in Antwerp and travelled widely in Italy, though Rubens influenced his initial work much more than his Italian contemporaries. Eventually, van Dyck developed his distinct style and technique, establishing himself as a court painter to Charles I in England in 1632 and creating **portraits** of a nervous elegance that would influence portraiture there for the next hundred and fifty years. Most of his great portrait paintings remain in England, but his best religious works – such as the *Crucifixions* in Mechelen cathedral (see page 194) and Ghent's St-Michielsbrug (see page 153) – can be found in Belgium.

Adriaen Brouwer (1605–38)

In the early seventeenth century, right across the Low Countries, another style emerged that was very different from the Baroque creations of Rubens and his acolytes – **genre painting**. Often misunderstood, the term was initially applied to everything from animal paintings and still life to historical works and landscapes. It later came to be applied only to scenes of everyday life. In the Spanish Netherlands, the most skilful practitioner was Oudenaarde's **Adriaen Brouwer**, whose peasant figures matched those of the much more famous **Jan Steen** in the Netherlands. Brouwer's output was unsurprisingly small given his short life – he died from either

LES XX

Founded in 1883, **Les XX** (*Les Vingt*) was an influential group of twenty Belgian painters, designers and sculptors keen to bring together all the different strands of their respective crafts. They staged an annual exhibition showcasing domestic and international talent for ten years: Cézanne, Manet and Gauguin all exhibited here at the beginning of their careers. With members as diverse as Ensor (see page 328) and the architect-designer Henri van de Velde, Les XX never professed to be united by the same artistic principles. However, several of its members, including Ghent's Theo van Rysselberghe (1862–1926), were inordinately impressed by the Post-Impressionism of Seurat, whose pointillist *The Big Bowl* created a sensation when it was exhibited by Les XX in 1887.

Les XX – and the other literary-artistic groupings that succeeded it – were part of a general **avant-garde** movement that flourished in Brussels at the end of the nineteenth century. This avant-garde was deeply disenchanted with Brussels' traditional salon culture, not only for artistic reasons but also because of its indifference to the plight of the Belgian working class. Such political views nourished close links with the fledgling **socialist/communist movement**, and Les XX even ran the slogan 'Art and the people have the same enemy – the reactionary bourgeoisie'. Indeed, the Belgian avant-garde came to see art (in all its forms) as a vehicle for liberating the Belgian worker, a project regularly proclaimed in *L'Art Moderne*, its most authoritative mouthpiece.

the plague or his drinking, maybe both – but his riotous tavern scenes and tableaux of everyday life are deftly done and were well received in their day, collected by, among others, Rubens and Rembrandt.

James Ensor (1860–1949)

Born to an English father and a Belgian mother, **James Ensor** lived in Ostend for almost all of his long life and was one of Belgium's most original artists. His early works were bourgeois in tone and content, a mixed bag of portraits and domestic interiors that gave little hint as to what was to follow. In the 1880s, he was snubbed by the artistic elite in Brussels, and this seems to have prompted a major rethink, for shortly afterwards, he picked up on the subject matter which was to dominate his paintings – macabre, disturbing works of skeletons, grotesques and horrid **carnival masks**, whose haunted style can be traced back to Bosch and Bruegel. As such, Ensor was a formative influence on the Expressionists and was claimed as a forerunner by several leading Surrealists.

Marcel Broodthaers (1924–76)

Born in Brussels, **Marcel Broodthaers** is one of Belgium's most celebrated modern artists, a witty and multitalented man who doubled as a filmmaker and journalist. He also tried his hand as a poet. In 1964, after twenty largely unsuccessful years, he gave up, symbolically encasing fifty unsold copies of his poetry in plaster and thereby, somewhat accidentally, launched himself as an artist. Initially, Broodthaers worked in a **Surrealist** manner with found objects and collages, but he soon branched out, graduating from cut-paper geometric shapes into the plastic arts and the sharp and brightly coloured **paintings** of everyday artefacts, especially **casseroles brimming with mussels**, for which he became famous.

Broodthaers summed himself up like this: 'I wondered whether I could not sell something and succeed in life … Finally the idea of inventing something insincere crossed my mind and I set to work straight away.'

Books

Most of the books listed below are in print and available as paperbacks, and those that are out of print (o/p) should still be easy enough to track down. Titles marked with the ★ symbol are especially recommended. Popular Belgian authors in print, but not in English, include Serge Delaive and Guy Goffette.

TRAVEL AND GENERAL

Derek Blyth *The 500 Hidden Secrets of Ghent.* British-born but a long-time Belgian resident, Blyth knows his Flemish turnips from its onions – and this intriguing and well-researched book delves deep into its subject. By the same author and in the same series is *The 500 Hidden Secrets of Antwerp* (2021), *500 Hidden Secrets of Flanders Fields* (2014) and *500 Hidden Secrets of Brussels* (2021). That's an awful lot of secrets, for sure!

Noah Charney *Stealing The Mystic Lamb* (o/p). Ghent's *Mystic Lamb* altarpiece (see page 149) has had a wild, weird and wonderful history, with parts or all of it being stolen time and again. This easy-to-read book charts its many adventures, though the story is a tad tarnished by some lacklustre writing and the occasional dubious assertion.

Hilde Deweer & Jaak van Damme *All Belgian Beers.* This is the most comprehensive guide on the market, covering its subject in extravagant (alphabetical) detail. Everything you ever wanted to know about Belgian beer and then some: first printed in 2008, a second updated edition was published in 2011.

Barry Forshaw *Simenon: The Man, The Books, the Films.* Forshaw makes sense of the books (some four hundred novels and a thousand short stories), films and controversial personal life of Georges Simenon (1903–89) in this entertaining primer.

Bruce McCall *Sit!: The Dog Portraits of Thierry Poncelet.* This strange and idiosyncratic book features the work of Belgian Thierry Poncelet, who raids flea markets and antique shops for ancestral portraits, then restores them and paints dogs' heads over the original faces.

Patrick McGuinness *Other People's Countries: A Journey into Memory.* This slim, thought-provoking book nudges into Bouillon (see page 268), a once-remote country town where the author spent much of his childhood.

Philip Mosley *The Cinema of the Dardenne Brothers:* *Responsible Realism.* The brothers Jean-Pierre (b.1951) and Luc (b.1954) Dardenne are arguably the finest Belgian filmmakers of today, composing hard-hitting, emotionally charged films set amid the post-industrial landscape of Wallonia. Mosley analyses the brothers' career from documentary beginnings to their six major films, from *The Promise* (1996) to *The Kid with a Bike* (2011). By the same author, there is also the authoritative *Split Screen: Belgian Cinema and Cultural Identity*, which tracks the development of Belgian cinema in lucid detail; the 'Split Screen' refers to the Walloon/Flemish cinematic/cultural division.

Lucy Sante *The Factory of Facts* (o/p). Born in Belgium in 1954 but raised in the US, Lucy Sante – formerly Luc Sante - returned to her native land for an extended visit in 1989 at 35. Her book is primarily a personal reflection, but she also uses this as a base for a thoughtful exploration of Belgium and the Belgians – from art to food and beyond.

Jeremi Szaniawiski & Marcelline Block *Directory of World Cinema: Belgium.* Published in 2014, this detailed book (320 pages) gives the low-down on the big names in Belgian cinema.

Marianne Thys *Filmography of Belgian Movies, 1896–1996* (o/p). This authoritative hardback volume reviews every Belgian film made within the stipulated dates. Published in 1999, it's 992 pages long and costs an arm and a leg.

★ **Tim Webb** *Good Beer Guide Belgium.* Belgium produces the best beers in the world; Webb is one of the best beer writers in the world – and the result is the best book on its subject on the market: cheeky, palatable and sinewy, with just a hint of fruitiness. Belgium's best bars, beers and breweries are covered in loving, liver-corroding detail (though bear in mind, it was published in 2014). Webb's *100 Belgian Beers to Try Before You Die!* (2008) is similarly excellent.

TINTIN

Michael Farr *Tintin: The Complete Companion.* This immaculately illustrated book – written by one of the world's leading Tintinologists – explores every aspect of Hergé's remarkably popular creation. It's particularly strong on the real-life stories that inspired Hergé, but you do have to be seriously interested in *Tintin* to really enjoy it. Farr (b.1953) has written a string of books on *Tintin*, and this one was published in 2011.

Hergé *The Calculus Affair* and *Tintin: Explorers on the Moon.* *Tintin* comic strips come in and out of print at a rapid rate, usually in anthologies; there's a wide selection of DVDs, too. Farshore (ⓦ farshore.co.uk), which publishes a veritable platoon of *Tintin* comic strips in different forms, is as good a place as any to start.

Benoit Peeters *Tintin and the World of Hergé: An Illustrated History* (o/p). Examines the life and career of Hergé, particularly the development of *Tintin*, and the influences on his work, with no fewer than three hundred illustrations.

HISTORY AND POLITICS

J.C.H. Blom (ed) *History of the Low Countries*. Belgian history books are thin on the ground, so this incisive, well-balanced volume is very welcome. A series of historians weigh in with their specialities to build a comprehensive picture of the region from the Celts and Romans through to the 1980s. It's hardly deckchair reading, but it's highly recommended nonetheless.

Nicholas Crane *Mercator: The Man who Mapped the Planet*. Arguably the most important map-maker of all time, Gerard Mercator, was born in Rupelmonde near Antwerp in 1512. This book details every twist and turn of his life and provides oodles – perhaps too many – of background material on the Flanders of his time.

Pieter Geyl *The Revolt of The Netherlands 1555–1609*. Geyl presents a detailed account of the Netherlands during its formative years, chronicling the uprising against the Spanish, the formation of the United Provinces and the creation of the Spanish Netherlands (the Belgium of today). First published in 1932, it has long been regarded as the classic text on the subject, though it's a hard and ponderous read.

★ **Samuel Humes** *Belgium: Long United, Long Divided*. This concise and well-considered account of Belgium from early times, with special reference to the Walloon–Flemish schism that troubles the country today, is a welcome addition to the limited number of books on the subject.

Lisa Jardine *The Awful End of Prince William the Silent*. The title alone is almost reason enough to read this intriguing book by the late and lamented Professor Jardine on the premature demise of one of the Low Countries' most acclaimed Protestant heroes. William led the revolt against Habsburg Spain and was assassinated in 1584 for his pains. The tale is told succinctly, but – unless you have a particular interest in early firearms – there is a bit too much information on guns.

Bart van Loo *The Burgundians: A Vanished Empire*. Burgundy and its assorted dukes and duchesses played a key role in the evolution of the Low Countries in the fourteenth and fifteenth centuries. Van Loo engages with his subject enthusiastically – and the book has gone down a storm in Belgium.

Philip Mansel *Prince of Europe: the Life of Charles Joseph de Ligne (1735–1814)* (o/p). The Habsburg aristocracy, which dominated the Austrian Netherlands (Belgium) in the eighteenth century, has rarely come under the historical spotlight, but this weighty tome partly remedies the situation. This particular aristocrat, the priapic Charles Joseph, was a multifaceted man, a gardener and a general, a curious traveller and a diplomat and the owner of the château de Beloeil (see page 222). Mansel explores his life and milieu thoroughly and entertainingly.

Geoffrey Parker *The Dutch Revolt* (o/p). Parker's compelling account of the struggle between the Netherlands and Spain is quite the best thing you can read on the subject. His rather academic-sounding *The Army of Flanders and the Spanish Road 1567–1659* gives a fascinating insight into the Habsburg army that occupied the Low Countries for well over a hundred years: how it functioned, was fed and moved from Spain to the Low Countries along the so-called Spanish Road.

Michael Pye *Antwerp: the Glory Years*. This lively and inventive book explores and investigates Antwerp's sixteenth- and early seventeenth-century Golden Age. Thematic rather than chronological, it can be a tad confusing.

Andrew Wheatcroft *The Habsburgs: Embodying Empire*. Wheatcroft's excellent and well-researched trawl through the dynasty's history, from its eleventh-century beginnings to its eclipse at the end of World War I, makes for enjoyable background reading.

THE BELGIAN CONGO

Neal Ascherson *The King Incorporated: Leopold the Second and the Congo*. Belgium's King Léopold II was responsible for one of the cruellest of colonial regimes, a murderous system of repression and exploitation that devastated the Belgian Congo. Ascherson details it all.

★ **Adam Hochschild** *King Leopold's Ghost*. This is a harrowing account of King Léopold's savage colonial regime in the Congo, explaining, exploring, and assessing all its gruesome workings. It is particularly good on Roger Casement, the one-time British consul to the Congo, who publicised the cruelty and helped bring it to an end. Hochschild's last chapter, 'The Great Forgetting', is a stern criticism of the Belgians for failing to acknowledge their brutal colonial history.

Jules Marchal *Lord Leverhulme's Ghosts: Colonial Exploitation in the Congo*. In his later years, Marchal, a Belgian diplomat in the Congo, became incensed by the suppression of information on the cruelties inflicted by his compatriots on the Congolese. After he retired in 1989, he spent fourteen years researching this colonial history, producing seven extremely detailed books on the subject, four on the Léopold regime and three on forced labour from 1910 to 1945. Only one has been translated into English, and this is it, with the spotlight falling on the

British entrepreneur Lord Leverhulme, who came to the Congo to exploit its rubber and was perfectly happy to take advantage of King Léopold's system of forced labour. Marchal died in 2003.

David van Reybrouck *Congo*. Born in Bruges in 1971, Reybrouck has travelled extensively in the Congo. This well-composed and very detailed book examines the country's troubled history, with special reference to the hundreds of Congolese the author has interviewed over the years. It was published in 2015.

Ludo De Witte *The Assassination of Lumumba*. The abrupt and poorly managed ending of colonial rule in the Belgian Congo in 1960 led to chaos. The new Prime Minister, Patrice Lumumba, attempted to bring some degree of cohesion, but both the Belgians and the Americans feared he would take the country into the Soviet camp. So they (appear to have) had him executed. De Witte, a well-respected Belgian writer and left-wing political activist tells the shoddy tale.

WATERLOO

Malcolm Balen *A Model Victory: Waterloo and the Battle for History* (o/p). Some twenty years after Waterloo, the British government asked Lieutenant William Siborne, a great fan of the Duke of Wellington, to prepare a scale model of the battle. They assumed that he would depict the start of the engagement, but he chose the crisis instead – and this is where he came unstuck. Based on interviews with scores of Waterloo veterans, Siborne's model had the Prussian army arriving on the battlefield earlier than the duke claimed, thereby taking some of the glory from the British army. Siborne felt the full fury of Wellington's ire – and this much-praised book details it all.

Bernard Cornwell *Waterloo: The History of Four Days, Three Armies and Three Battles*. Among a platoon of books published to commemorate the bicentenary of Waterloo, this is perhaps the most lucid: a galloping yomp through the campaign following Napoleon's return from exile. Cornwell is best known for his historical novels – hence the flamboyant and informal style.

★ **Christopher Hibbert** *Waterloo*. For many years, Hibbert (who died in 2008) was one of Britain's leading historians, an astute commentator who wrote in a fluent and easily accessible style. This book examines Napoleon's rise to power, the state of the British and Prussian armies and the battle itself. Hibbert also edited *The Wheatley Diary*, the journal and sketchbook of a young English officer who fought across Europe during the Napoleonic Wars.

Basil Henry Liddell Hart (ed) *The Letters of Private Wheeler 1809–1828*. A veteran of World War I, Liddell Hart writes with panache and clarity, marshalling the letters penned by the eponymous private as he fought Napoleon and the French across a fair slice of Europe. Wheeler fought at Waterloo, but the section on the battle is surprisingly brief. As a whole, the letters are a delight, a witty insight into the living conditions and attitudes of Wellington's infantry.

WORLD WAR I

★ **Ian Connerty et al** *At the Going Down of the Sun: 365 Soldiers from the Great War* (o/p). It is a curious - and curiously effective – book with a soldier's death described for each and every day of a year: some deaths are accidental, some heroic, others just odd. All the deaths recorded are in Flanders, and almost all are British or Empire soldiers.

William Allison & John Fairley, *The Monocled Mutineer* (o/p). An antidote to all those tales of soldiers dying for their country in World War I, this little book recounts the story of one Percy Toplis, a Nottinghamshire lad turned soldier, mutineer, racketeer and conman who was finally shot by the police in 1920. It includes an intriguing account of the large-scale mutiny that broke out along the British line in 1917.

Paul Fussell *The Great War and Modern Memory*. Fussell's intriguing take on World War I gives prominence to the rants, epistles, poems and letters of the British soldiers caught up in it – and, by implication, the effect it had on British society as a whole.

Basil Henry Liddell Hart *The History of the First World War*. No armchair general, Liddell Hart (1895–1970) fought in the trenches in World War I – and had the wounds to prove it. After the war, he became a well-known military expert, and he always claimed (with some justification) that he foresaw the potential importance of tanks – a voice crying in the British military wilderness before Hitler unveiled his blitzkrieg on, among many others, the poor old Belgian army. First published in 1930 and last republished in 2014, Hart's *History of the First World War* is lucidly written, well researched and good on military strategy and tactics. If you take a shine to it, you can also try Hart's *The History of the Second World War*. See also *The Letters of Private Wheeler 1809–1828*.

Nick Lloyd *Passchendaele*. Of all the battles in World War I, Passchendaele came to epitomise the senselessness of it all among the British – men struggling in a sea of mud for meagre (if any) territorial gains. Lloyd tells the tale with aplomb.

Janet Morgan *The Secrets of Rue St Roch*. This intriguing account of British spy operations in occupied Luxembourg during World War I is drawn from the assorted documents of a certain Captain George Wellington, a Paris-based intelligence officer who ran several agents, including a Belgian soldier who began by landing behind enemy lines in a balloon.

★ **David Olusoga** *The World's War: Forgotten Soldiers of Empire*. A wide-ranging account of the 'Babylon of races' that became entangled in World War I – from Indians in Flanders to the Kaiser's attempts to foment jihad in the Middle East. There's also a fascinating account of the campaign in East Africa and its disastrous effect on thousands of Africans.

Hew Strachan *The First World War: A New History*. Predictably, the centenary of World War I produced a veritable flood of books, many of which cover specific aspects of the conflict (see several titles above). This is probably the pick of the new general histories, a thoughtful and well-composed volume (400 pages) written by one of the UK's leading military historians.

★**A.J.P. Taylor** *The First World War: An Illustrated History*. First published in 1963, this superbly written and pertinently illustrated history offers a penetrating analysis of how the war started and why it went on for so long, including a fine section on events in the Ypres Salient. Many of Taylor's deductions were controversial at the time, but the power of his arguments was such that much of what he said is now mainstream history.

ART AND ARCHITECTURE

Alexander Adams *Magritte: Masters of Art*. Perhaps surprisingly, given the artist's popularity, there have been very few good books on Magritte in English – until recently, that is when there's been something of a flurry. This book, at 112 pages long, serves as a helpful introduction to its subject and is clearly written and attractively illustrated.

Stijn Alsteens *Van Dyck: The Anatomy of Portraiture*. Whether or not van Dyck justifies a book of this considerable length (just over 300 pages) is a moot point, but he did have an interesting life and certainly thumped out a fair few (exquisite) portraits. This volume explores every nook and cranny of every portrait he ever did.

Till-Holger Borchert *Van Eyck*. Not much is known about van Eyck, but Borchert has done his best to root out every detail in this nicely balanced and attractively illustrated 96-page Taschen book of 2008. Borchert has also written *Van Eyck to Dürer: The Influence of Early Netherlandish Painting on European Art, 1430–1530*, a beautifully illustrated tome, which covers its subject with academic rigour (it's 552 pages long). Published in 2010, this second book is already something of a collector's item and can be extremely expensive. The same caution applies to Borchert's similarly detailed *Bruegel: The Complete Paintings, Drawings and Prints*, which he co-authored with Manfred Sellink.

Walter Bosing *Bosch: The Complete Paintings*. One of the Taschen art series, this attractive little book covers its subject in just the right amount of detail (96 pages long). Well conceived and well illustrated, it was published in 2022.

Nils Büttner *Hieronymus Bosch: Visions and Nightmares*. A studious and immaculately researched book that digs deep into the archives to discover all that is known about Bosch, the most allegorical of painters.

Aurora Cuito (ed) *Victor Horta* (o/p). Concise and readily digestible guide to the work of Victor Horta, Belgium's leading exponent of Art Nouveau (see page 73). Since its publication in 2002, the book has become something of a collector's item, so unless you have a special interest, you'll probably want to settle for a secondhand copy.

David Dernie et al *Victor Horta: The Architect of Art Nouveau*. Detailed and beautifully illustrated book of 2018 tracking through the assorted schemes of that architectural pioneer Victor Horta (see page 73).

★**Rudi H. Fuchs** *Dutch Painting* (o/p). As complete an introduction to the subject as you could wish for in just a couple of hundred pages. Particularly good on the early Flemish masters. It was published in the 1970s, so an update would be welcome.

Suzi Gablik *Magritte* (o/p). Gablik lived in Magritte's house for six months in the 1960s, and this personal contact informs the text, which is lucid, perceptive and thoughtful. Most of the illustrations are, however, black and white. At 208 pages, it's also very manageable – and very readable.

Rachel Haidu *Absence of Work*. Haidu, an American art professor, clearly has a real respect for the Belgian artist Marcel Broodthaers and it shows in this detailed exploration of his life and times, work and philosophy.

David Helbich *Belgian Solutions*. Starting out as a collection of weird, wild and wonderful photos that Helbich posted on Facebook, there is now a series of books – three volumes with three hundred photos in each – and counting. Bizarre and entertaining in equal proportions.

Stephan Kamperdick *Rogier van der Weyden: Masters of Netherlandish Art*. Van der Weyden is something of a shadowy figure, but Kamperdick does well to muster what information there is – and the analysis of the paintings is first-rate.

Mark Lamster *Master of Shadows: The Secret Diplomatic Career of Peter Paul Rubens*. Detailed investigation of Rubens' work as a spy and diplomat – it's a wonder he ever got around to the painting.

Alfred Michiels *Hans Memling*. Thorough and very workmanlike investigation of the life and times of Hans Memling by a nineteenth-century history. The chapter on Memling's major works is particularly good. Extensively illustrated.

Jürgen Müller *Bruegel. The Complete Paintings*. Thoughtfully written account investigating one of the greatest of all the Netherlandish painters, Pieter Bruegel the Elder. Extensively illustrated and thoroughly researched. Published in 2022.

Susie Nash *Northern Renaissance Art*. Erudite, 368-page book which examines how art was made, valued and viewed in northern Europe from the late fourteenth to the early sixteenth centuries. All the leading Netherlandish figures are examined – van Eyck, Memling, van der Weyden and so forth – and by these means, Nash argues that these painters, rather than the Italians, set the artistic tone of the Europe of their day. Published in 2008.

Gilles Neret *Rubens* Amongst a limited range of books on Rubens, this Taschen art book is the best, a well-composed, concise and lovingly illustrated introduction to the great man, his times and his art.

Luc Tuymans & Adrian Locke *James Ensor*. One of Belgium's finest painters, though often neglected, Ostend's James Ensor is given due attention in this extensively illustrated scholarly work, which delves into his life, times, and artistic output.

Norbert Wolf *The Golden Age of Dutch and Flemish Painting*. A veteran art critic, Wolf brings his keen eye to his subject with illustrations that seem to be aimed at making a gallery visit unnecessary. All in all, 272 pages of artistic delight. Published in 2019.

LITERATURE

★ **Bernardo Atxaga** *Seven Houses in France*. This simply wonderful novel is set in the Congo among the members of its Force Publique (gendarmerie) in 1903. The enigmatic Chrysostome joins the garrison of a remote town, leading to a series of puzzling encounters and weird events. Rarely has the cruel brutality of the Belgian Congo been thrown into sharper/subtler relief – with never an anti-colonial rant in sight. Perhaps surprisingly, the author (real name Joseba Garmendia) is a Spaniard.

Mark Bles *A Child at War: The True Story of Hortense Daman* (o/p). This powerful book describes the tribulations of Hortense Daman, a Belgian girl who joined the Resistance at the tender age of 15. Betrayed to the Gestapo, Daman was sent to the Ravensbruck concentration camp, where she was used in medical experiments but remarkably survived. This is her story, though the book would have benefited from editorial pruning.

Louis Paul Boon *Chapel Road* Born in Aalst, Boon (1912–79) was a major literary figure in Belgium – second only to Hugo Claus. This is his finest work, a strange and mysterious tale woven around an eccentric group of friends and set alongside the retelling of myths and rumours.

Hugo Claus *The Sorrow of Belgium*. Claus (1929–2008) was generally regarded as Belgium's foremost Flemish-language novelist, and this was his finest novel, charting the growing maturity of a young boy living in Flanders under the German occupation. Claus's style is dense, to say the least, but the book gets to grips with the guilt, bigotry and mistrust of the period and caused a minor uproar when it was first published in the early 1980s. His *Swordfish* is a story of an isolated village rife with ethnic and religious tensions which precipitate a boy's descent into madness, while *Desire* is a strange and disconcerting tale of two drinking buddies who, on an impulse, abandon small-town Belgium for Las Vegas, where both of them start to unravel.

Stefan Hertmans *War and Turpentine*. Inspired by his grandfather's diaries, this eloquent mix of biography, autobiography, novel and history combs through Belgium's evolution from World War I onwards. Hertmans (b.1951) hails from Ghent.

Barbara Kingsolver *The Poisonwood Bible: A Novel*. In 1959, an American Baptist missionary and his family set out to convert souls in the jungly depths of the Belgian Congo. They are unprepared for the multiple disasters that befall them – from giant, stinging ants to irregular Congolese soldiers. An American, Kingsolver (b.1955) spent part of her childhood in the Congo – but as the daughter of a doctor rather than a missionary.

Caroline Lamarche *The Memory of the Air*. Since its recent publication, this powerful novel has garnered much attention, not least for its unflinching commentary on domestic violence and abuse.

Tom Lanoye *Speechless*. A moving account of the speechlessness that afflicted Lanoye's mother after a stroke – and her slow disintegration thereafter. In caring for her, Lanoye is forced to reflect on his boisterous childhood. Lanoye (b.1958) is one of Flanders' most widely read writers – a novelist, playwright, poet and columnist.

Amelie Nothomb *Hygiene and the Assassin*. English-language translations of modern Belgian books are a rarity, but Nothomb (b.1966), one of Belgium's most popular novelists, has made the linguistic leap. *Hygiene and the Assassin* deals with a terminally ill prize-winning author who grants deathbed interviews to five journalists. A deeply unpleasant man, the protagonist is only unpicked by his last interviewer – to stunning effect. Other Nothomb novels in translation include the controversial *Sulphuric Acid*, where a Big Brother–style show turns into a blood-fest in the manner of a concentration camp – hence the furore; *The Stranger Next Door*, featuring weird and disconcerting happenings in the Belgian countryside; and *Strike your Heart* set around the troubled relationship between a mother and a daughter.

Jean Ray *Malpertuis*. This spine-chilling Gothic novel was written in 1943 by Ghent's own Raymundus de Kremer, who adopted the pen name Jean Ray for his novels. He also turned out comic strips under the guise of John Flanders. *Malpertuis* is set in Flanders, where the suffocating Catholicism of the Inquisition provides a suitably atmospheric backdrop.

★ **Georges Rodenbach** *Bruges la Morte*. First published in 1892, this slim and subtly evocative novel is all about love and obsession – or rather, a highly stylised, decadent view of them. It's often credited with starting the craze to visit Bruges, the 'dead city' where the action unfolds.

Georges Simenon, *The Hanged Man of Saint-Pholien*; *Pietr the Latvian*. There can be no dispute that Simenon (1903–89) was Belgium's most famous crime writer, his main creation being the Parisian detective Maigret. There are dozens of books to choose from – and these two (recently reprinted) well-crafted, ripping yarns can get you started, though this author's personal favourite is *The Carter of La Providence*, translated by David Coward.

Hilde Vandermeeren *The Scorpion's Head*. Vandermeeren is an up-and-coming Flemish thriller writer – and this book, her first to be translated into English, cuts a dramatic and gory path with her hitman Michael leading things on at pace.

Dimitri Verhulst *The Latecomer*. Inventive novel in which an ageing former librarian has put himself into a home for the elderly because he is losing his mind, though actually he isn't – he has another agenda altogether. Much to his surprise, he soon realises other residents are playing the same game of pretence.

Emile Zola *Germinal*. First published in 1885 and the inspiration for a whole generation of Belgian radicals, Germinal exposed the harsh conditions of the coal mines of northeast France. It was also a rallying cry to action, with the protagonist, Etienne Lantier, organising a strike. This is a vivid, powerful work; Zola had a detailed knowledge of mines (how they were run and worked) and makes passing reference to the coalfields of southern Belgium, where conditions and working practices were almost identical.

Flemish and French

Throughout the northern part of Belgium, in the provinces of East and West Flanders, Antwerp, Limburg and Flemish Brabant, the principal language is Dutch, which is spoken in a variety of distinctive dialects commonly (if inaccurately) lumped together as Flemish. Flemish speakers have equal language rights in the capital, Brussels, where the majority of Belgians speak a French dialect known as Walloon, as they do in the country's southern provinces, known logically enough as Wallonia. Walloon is almost identical to French; you'll be readily understood if you know the language. French is also the most widely spoken language in Luxembourg, along with German – although most Luxembourgers also speak a local and distinctive German dialect, Lëtzebuergesch (see page 278).

Flemish

Flemish, or Dutch, is a Germanic language, and although Flemish speakers are at pains to stress the differences between the two, if you know any German, you'll spot many similarities. Many Flemish speakers also speak English to varying degrees of excellence, especially in the larger cities, and partly as a result, any attempt you make to speak Flemish may be met with bewilderment – though this can have as much to do with pronunciation (Dutch is very difficult to get right) as their surprise that you're making an effort. The following words and phrases serve as an introduction to the language, and we've included a basic **food and drink glossary**. Menus are often multilingual; where they aren't, ask, and one will almost invariably appear. We have also included a quick guide to some of **Belgium's best beers** (see box, page 343).

Pronunciation

Flemish is **pronounced** much the same as English. However, a few Dutch sounds are absent from English, which can be difficult to get right without practice.

Consonants

Double-consonant combinations generally keep their separate sounds in Flemish: **kn**, for example, is never like the English 'knight'. Note also the following consonants and consonant combinations:

j is an English y, as in yellow

ch and **g** indicate a throaty sound, as at the end of the Scottish word loch. The Dutch word for canal – gracht – is especially tricky since it has two of these sounds

– it comes out along the lines of khrakht. A common word for hello is Dag! – pronounced like daakh

ng as in bring

nj as in onion

y is not a consonant, but another way of writing **ij**

Vowels and diphthongs

A good rule of thumb is that doubling the letter lengthens the vowel sound.

a is like the English apple

aa like cart

e like let

ee like late

o as in pop

oo in pope

u is like the French tu if preceded by a consonant; it's like wood if followed by a consonant

uu is the French tu

au and **ou** like how

ei and ij as in fine, though this varies enormously from region to region; sometimes, it can sound more like lane

oe as in soon

eu is like the diphthong in the French leur

ui is the hardest Dutch diphthong of all, pronounced like how but much further forward in the mouth, with lips pursed (as if to say 'oo').

WORDS AND PHRASES

THE BASICS

ja yes
nee no
alstublieft please
(nee) dank u or **bedankt** (no) thank you
hallo, dag or **hoi** hello
goedemorgen good morning
goedemiddag good afternoon
goedenavond good evening
tot ziens goodbye
tot straks see you later
Spreekt u Engels? Do you speak English?
Ik begrijp het niet I don't understand
vrouwen/mannen women/men
kinderen children
heren/dames men's/women's toilets
Ik wil ... I want ...
Ik wil niet ... (+verb) I don't want to ...
Sorry sorry

TRAVEL, DIRECTIONS AND SHOPPING

Hoe kom ik in ...? How do I get to ...?
Waar is ...? Where is ...?
Hoe ver is het naar ...? How far is it to...?
Wat kost ...? How much is ...?
ver/dichtbij far/near
links/rechts left/right
luchthaven airport
postkantoor post office
postbus postbox
geldwisselkantoor money exchange
kassa cash desk
spoor or **perron** railway platform
loket ticket office
hier/daar here/there
goed/slecht good/bad
groot/klein big/small
open/gesloten open/closed
duwen/trekken push/pull
nieuw/oud new/old
goedkoop/duur cheap/expensive
heet or **warm/koud** hot/cold
met/zonder with/without
noord north
zuid south
oost east
west west

SIGNS AND ABBREVIATIONS

alle richtingen all directions (road sign)
A.U.B. alstublieft: please
BG Begane grond: ground floor
geen toegang no entry
gesloten closed
ingang entrance
K kelder: basement
let op! attention!
heren/dames men's/women's toilets
open open
rechtdoor straight ahead
T/M Tot en met: up to and including
toegang entrance
uitgang exit
V.A. vanaf: from
Z.O.Z. please turn over (page, leaflet, etc)

USEFUL CYCLING TERMS

band tyre
fiets cycle
fietspad cycle path
kapot broken
ketting chain
lek puncture
pomp pump
rem brake
stuur handlebars
trapper pedal
wiel wheel

DAYS OF THE WEEK

zondag Sunday
maandag Monday
dinsdag Tuesday
woensdag Wednesday
donderdag Thursday
vrijdag Friday
zaterdag Saturday
gisteren yesterday
vandaag today
morgen tomorrow
morgenochtend tomorrow morning
week week
dag day

MONTHS

jaar year
maand month
januari January
februari February
maart March
april April
mei May
juni June
juli July

augustus August
september September
oktober October
november November
december December

TIME

uur hour
minuut minute
Hoe laat is het? What time is it?

NUMBERS

When saying a number, Dutch speakers generally transpose the last two digits: for example, €3.25 is *drie euro vijf en twintig*.

nul 0
een 1
twee 2
drie 3
vier 4
vijf 5
zes 6
zeven 7
acht 8
negen 9
tien 10
elf 11
twaalf 12
dertien 13
veertien 14
vijftien 15
zestien 16
zeventien 17
achttien 18

negentien 19
twintig 20
een en twintig 21
twee en twintig 22
dertig 30
veertig 40
vijftig 50
zestig 60
zeventig 70
tachtig 80
negentig 90
honderd 100
honderd een 101
twee honderd 200
twee honderd een 201
vijf honderd 500
vijf honderd vijf en twintig 525
duizend 1000

A FLEMISH MENU READER

BASIC TERMS AND INGREDIENTS

belegd as in **belegde broodjes** filled or topped, (bread rolls topped with cheese, etc)
boter butter
boterham/broodje sandwich/roll
brood bread
dranken drinks
eieren eggs

gerst barley
groenten vegetables
honing honey
hoofdgerechten main courses
kaas cheese
koud cold
nagerechten desserts
peper pepper

FRITES

They may be known almost everywhere as **French fries**, but **frites** are a Belgian invention, and nowhere in the country are you far from a *frietkot* or *friture* stall. To be authentic, *frites* must be made with Belgian potatoes and parboiled before deep-fried. They're also not quite the same unless eaten with a wooden fork from a large paper cone, preferably with a large dollop of **mayonnaise** on top – or one of the many different **toppings** available, ranging from **curry** to **goulash** sauce.

sla/salade salad
stokbrood french bread
suiker sugar
vegetarisch vegetarian
vis fish
vlees meat
voorgerechten starters/hors d'oeuvres
vruchten fruit
warm hot
zout salt

COOKING TERMS
doorbakken well-done
gebakken fried/baked
gebraden roasted
gegrild grilled
gekookt boiled
geraspt grated
gerookt smoked
gestoofd stewed
half doorbakken medium-done
rood rare

STARTERS AND SNACKS
erwtensoep/snert thick pea soup with bacon or
  sausage
huzarensalade potato salad with pickles
koffietafel light midday meal of cold meats, cheese,
  bread, and perhaps soup
patat/friet chips/French fries
soep soup
uitsmijter ham or cheese with eggs on bread

MEAT AND POULTRY
biefstuk (hollandse) steak
biefstuk (duitse) hamburger
eend duck
fricandeau roast pork
fricandel frankfurter-like sausage
gehakt mince
ham ham
kalfsvlees veal
kalkoen turkey
karbonade a chop
kip chicken
kroket spiced veal or beef in hash, coated in
  breadcrumbs
lamsvlees lamb
lever liver
ossenhaas beef tenderloin
rookvlees smoked beef
spek bacon
worst sausages

FISH AND SEAFOOD
forel trout
garnalen prawns
haring herring
kabeljauw cod
makreel mackerel
mosselen mussels
oesters oysters
paling eel
schelvis haddock
schol plaice
tong sole
zalm salmon
zeeduivel monkfish

VEGETABLES
aardappelen potatoes
bloemkool cauliflower
bonen beans
champignons mushrooms
erwten peas
hutspot mashed potatoes and carrots
knoflook garlic
komkommer cucumber
prei leek
rijst rice
sla salad, lettuce
stampot andijvie mashed potato and endive
stampot boerenkool mashed potato and cabbage
uien onions
wortelen carrots
zuurkool sauerkraut

SWEETS AND DESSERTS
appeltaart/appelgebak apple tart or cake
gebak pastry
ijs ice cream
koekjes biscuits
pannenkoeken pancakes
pepernoten Dutch ginger biscuits
poffertjes small pancakes/fritters
(slag)room (whipped) cream
speculaas spice- and cinnamon-flavoured biscuit
stroopwafels waffles
taai-taai spicy Dutch cake
vla custard

FRUITS AND NUTS
aardbei strawberry
amandel almond
appel apple
appelmoes apple purée
citroen lemon
druiven grape

FLEMISH SPECIALITIES

hutsepot – a winter warmer consisting of various bits of beef and pork (including pigs' trotters and ears) casseroled with turnips, celery, leeks and parsnips

konijn met pruimen – rabbit with prunes

paling in 't groen – eel braised in a green (usually spinach) sauce with herbs

stoemp – mashed potato mixed with vegetable and/or meat purée

stoofvlees – cubes of beef marinated in beer and cooked with herbs and onions

stoverij – stewed beef and offal (especially liver and kidneys), slowly tenderised in dark beer and served with a slice of bread covered in mustard

waterzooi – a delicious, filling soup-cum-stew, made with either chicken (*van kip*) or fish (*van riviervis*)

framboos raspberry
hazelnoot hazelnut
kers cherry
kokosnoot coconut
peer pear
perzik peach
pinda peanut
pruim plum/prune

DRINKS

anijsmelk aniseed-flavoured warm milk
appelsap apple juice
bessenjenever blackcurrant gin
chocomel chocolate milk
warme chocolade melk hot chocolate
citroenjenever lemon gin
droog dry

frisdranken soft drinks
jenever Dutch gin
karnemelk buttermilk
koffie coffee
koffie verkeerd coffee with warm milk
kopstoot beer with a jenever chaser
melk milk
met ijs with ice
met slagroom with whipped cream
pils Dutch beer
proost! cheers!
sinaasappelsap orange juice
thee tea
tomatensap tomato juice
vruchtensap fruit juice
wijn (wit/rood/rosé) wine (white/red/rosé)
vieux Dutch brandy

French

Most **Walloons** (French-speaking Belgians) working in the business and tourist industries have at least some knowledge of English, but beyond that, and especially in Wallonia's small towns and villages, you'll need at least a modicum of **French** to have any sort of conversation at all. Differentiating words is the initial problem in understanding **spoken Walloon** – it's very hard to get people to slow down. If, as a last resort, you get them to write it down, you'll probably find you know half the words anyway – French and English share many words. We've also included a simple French **food and drink glossary** and a guide to **Belgium's top-tasting beers** (see box, page 343).

Pronunciation

Consonants

Consonants are pronounced much as in English, except:

c is softened to the **s** sound when followed by an 'e' or 'i' or when it has a cedilla (ç) below it

ch is always **sh**

g is softened to a French **j** sound when followed by e or i (eg gendarme)

h is silent

j is like the **s** sound in 'measure' or 'treasure'

ll is like the **y** in yes

qu is usually pronounced like a **k** as in **k**ey (eg quatre)

r is growled (or rolled).

th is the same as **t**

w is **v**

Vowels

These are the hardest sounds to get right. Roughly:

a as in h**a**t   **i** as in mach**i**ne
e as in g**e**t   **o** as in h**o**t
é between g**e**t and g**a**te   **o, au** as in **o**ver
è between g**e**t and g**u**t   **ou** as in f**oo**d
eu like the **u** in h**u**rt   **u** as in a pursed-lip version of **u**se

More awkward are the combinations below when they occur at the ends of words or are followed by consonants other than *n* or *m*:

in/im like the an in an**x**ious
an/am, en/em as in d**on** when said with a nasal accent
on/om like the d**on** in D**on**caster said by someone with a heavy cold
un/um like the u in **un**derstand.

WORDS AND PHRASES

BASICS
oui yes
non no
s'il vous plaît please
(non) merci (no) thank you
bonjour hello
comment allez-vous?/ça va? how are you?
bonjour good morning
bonjour good afternoon
bonsoir good evening
bonne nuit good night
au revoir goodbye
à bientôt see you later
maintenant/plus tard now/later
pardon, Monsieur/Madame, je m'excuse sorry
parlez-vous anglais? do you speak English?
je (ne) comprends (pas) I (don't) understand
femmes women
hommes men
enfants children
je veux I want
je ne veux pas I don't want
d'accord OK/agreed

TRAVEL, DIRECTIONS AND SHOPPING
comment est-ce que je peux arriver à ...? how do I get to ?
où est ...? where is ...?
combien y a-t-il jusqu'à ...? how far is it to ...?
c'est combien ...? how much is ...?
quand? when?
loin/près far/near
à gauche/à droite left/ right
tout droit straight ahead
voie de traversée through traffic only
aéroport airport
la poste post office
timbre(s) stamp(s)
bureau de change money exchange

la caisse cashier
quai quay, or (railway) platform
gare railway station
le guichet ticket office
ici/là here/there
derrière behind
bon/mauvais good/bad
grand/petit big/small
pousser/tirer push/pull
nouveau/vieux new/old
bon marché/cher cheap/expensive
chaud/froid hot/cold
avec/sans with/without
beaucoup/peu a lot/a little
est East
nord North
occidental West
sud South

SIGNS AND ABBREVIATIONS
acces interdit no entry
Attention! attention!
entrée entrance
étage floor (of a museum, etc)
fermé closed
fermeture closing period
hommes/femmes men's/women's toilets
ouvert open
sortie exit
S.V.P. S'il vous plaît: please

USEFUL CYCLING TERMS
bicyclette cycle
cassé broken
chaîne chain
frein brake
guidon handlebars
pédale pedal
pneu crevé puncture

pneu tyre
pompe pump
roue wheel

DAYS OF THE WEEK
lundi Monday
mardi Tuesday
mercredi Wednesday
jeudi Thursday
vendredi Friday
samedi Saturday
dimanche Sunday
matin morning
après-midi afternoon
soir evening
nuit night
hier yesterday
aujourd'hui today
demain tomorrow
demain matin tomorrow morning
jour day
semaine week

MONTHS
mois month
année year
janvier January
février February
mars March
avril April
mai May
juin June
juillet July
août August
septembre September
octobre October
novembre November
décembre December

TIME
minute minute
heure hour
Quelle heure est-il …? What time is it?

NUMBERS
zéro 0
un 1
deux 2
trois 3
quatre 4
cinq 5
six 6
sept 7
huit 8
neuf 9
dix 10
onze 11
douze 12
treize 13
quatorze 14
quinze 15
seize 16
dix-sept 17
dix-huit 18
dix-neuf 19
vingt 20
vingt-et-un 21
trente 30
quarante 40
cinquante 50
soixante 60
soixante-dix (local usage is septante) 70
quatre-vingts 80
quatre-vingt-dix (local usage is nonante) 90
cent 100
cent-et-un 101
deux cents 200
cinq cents 500
mille 1000

A FRENCH MENU READER

BASIC TERMS AND INGREDIENTS
beurre butter
chaud hot
crème fraîche sour cream
dessert dessert
dégustation tasting (wine or food)
escargots snails
frappé iced
fromage cheese
froid cold
gibier game

hors d'oeuvres starters
légumes vegetables
oeufs eggs
pain bread
poisson fish
poivre pepper
riz rice
salade salad
sel salt
sucre/sucré sugar/sweet (taste)
tourte tart or pie

WALLOON AND BRUSSELS SPECIALITIES

carbonnades de porc Bruxelloise – pork with a tarragon and tomato sauce
chicorées gratinées au four – chicory baked with ham and cheese
fricadelles à la bière – meatballs in beer
fricassée Liègeois – fried eggs, bacon and sausage or blood pudding
le marcassin – young wild boar, served either cold and sliced or hot with vegetables
pâté de faisan – pheasant pâté
truite à l'Ardennaise – trout cooked in a wine sauce

tranche slice
viande meat

COOKING TERMS
á point medium done
au four baked
bien cuit well done
bouilli boiled
frit/friture fried/deep fried
fumé smoked
grillé grilled
mijoté stewed
pané breaded
rôti roast
saignant rare (meat)
sauté lightly cooked in butter

STARTERS AND SNACKS
assiette anglaise plate of cold meats
bisque shellfish soup
bouillabaisse fish soup from Marseilles
bouillon broth or stock
consommé clear soup
croque-monsieur grilled cheese and ham sandwich
crudités raw vegetables with dressing
potage thick soup, usually vegetable
un sandwich/une baguette... a sandwich...
de jambon with ham
de fromage with cheese
de saucisson with sausage
à l'aïl with garlic
au poivre with pepper
oeufs... eggs...
au plat fried eggs
à la coque boiled eggs
durs hard-boiled eggs
brouillés scrambled eggs
omelette... omelette...
nature plain
au fromage with cheese
salade de... salad of...
tomates tomatoes
concombres cucumbers

crêpes... pancakes...
au sucre with sugar
au citron with lemon
au miel with honey
à la confiture with jam

MEAT AND POULTRY
agneau lamb
bifteck steak
boeuf beef
canard duck
cheval horsemeat
cuisson leg of lamb
côtelettes cutlets
dindon turkey
foie liver
gigot leg of venison
jambon ham
lard bacon
porc pork
poulet chicken
saucisse sausage
veau veal

FISH AND SEAFOOD
anchois anchovies
anguilles eels
carrelet plaice
crevettes roses prawns
hareng herring
lotte de mer monkfish
maquereau mackerel
morue cod
moules mussels
saumon salmon
sole sole
truite trout

VEGETABLES
aïl garlic
asperges asparagus
carottes carrots
champignons mushrooms

BELGIAN BEER: TOP BREWS

These tasting notes should help you navigate the (very pleasurable) maze of Belgian beer—after all, many bars in this country have their **beer menus**.

Brugse Zot (Blond 6%, Brugse Zot Dubbel 7.5%) Brouwerij De Halve Mann, a small brewery in the centre of Bruges, produces zippy, refreshing ales with a dry, crisp aftertaste. Their Blond is a light and tangy pale ale, whereas the Bruin – Brugse Zot Dubbel – is a classic brown ale with a full body.

Bush Beer (7.5% and 12%) A Walloon speciality. At 12%, the original version is claimed to be the strongest beer in Belgium. It's more like a barley wine, with a lovely golden colour and an earthy aroma. The 7.5% Bush is a tasty pale ale with a hint of coriander.

Chimay (red top 7%, blue top 9%) Made by Trappist monks in southern Belgium, Chimay beers are among the best in the world. Of their several brews, these two are the most readily available. They are fruity, strong, deep in the body, and somewhat spicy, with a hint of nutmeg and thyme.

La Chouffe (8%) Produced in the Ardennes, this distinctive beer is instantly recognisable by the red-hooded gnome *chouffe* on its label. It's a refreshing pale ale with a peachy aftertaste—very palatable indeed, but also very strong.

Gouden Carolus (8%) Named after – and allegedly the favourite tipple of – the Habsburg emperor Charles V, Gouden Carolus is a full-bodied dark brown ale with a sour and slightly fruity aftertaste. It is brewed in the Flemish town of Mechelen.

Hoegaarden (5%) The role model for all Belgian wheat beers, Hoegaarden, from near Leuven, is light and highly refreshing despite its cloudy appearance. It's brewed from equal parts wheat and malted barley, ideal for a hot summer's day.

De Koninck (5%) Antwerp's leading brewery, De Koninck, is something of a Flemish institution. Its standard beer is a smooth pale ale that's very drinkable, has a sharp aftertaste, and is better on draught than in the bottle.

Kriek (Cantillon Kriek Lambic 5%, Belle Vue Kriek 5.2%, Mort Subite Kriek 4.3%) A type of beer rather than a particular brew, Kriek is made from a base lambic beer to which are added cherries or, in the case of the more commercial brands, cherry juice and perhaps even sugar. Other fruit beers are available too – such as Framboise – but Kriek is probably the happiest blend,

and the better versions (including the three mentioned above) are not too sweet and taste simply wonderful. Kriek should be decanted from a bottle with a cork, like a sparkling wine.

Lambic (Cantillon Lambic 5%) One of the world's oldest styles of beer manufacture, Brussels' **lambic** beers are tart brews made with at least 30 percent raw wheat with malted barley. **Wild yeast** is used in their production, a spontaneous fermentation process in which the yeasts – specific to the air of Brussels – gravitate down into open wooden casks for two to three years. Draught lambic is rare, but the bottled varieties are more commonplace. **Cantillon Lambic** is perhaps the most authentic, an excellent drink with a lemony zip; it's the best you'll find. **Gueuze** is a blend of old and new lambics in a bottle, a little sweeter and fuller bodied than straight lambic, with an almost cider-like aftertaste. Try Belle Vue Gueuze (5.2%), Timmermans Gueuze (5.5%) and/or Lindemans Gueuze (5.2%)

Orval (6.2%) One of the world's most distinctive malt beers, Orval is made in the Ardennes at the Abbaye d'Orval, founded in the twelfth century by Benedictine monks from Calabria. Refreshingly bitter, the beer is a lovely amber colour and makes a great aperitif.

Rochefort (Rochefort 6 7.5%, Rochefort 8 9.2%, Rochefort 10 11.3%) Produced at a Trappist monastery in the Ardennes, Rochefort beers are typically dark and sweet and come in three main versions: Rochefort 6, Rochefort 8 and the extremely popular Rochefort 10, which has a deep reddish-brown colour and a delicious fruity palate.

Rodenbach (Rodenbach 5% and Rodenbach Grand Cru 6.5%) Located in the Flemish town of Roeselare, the Rodenbach brewery produces a reddish-brown ale in several forms, with the best brews aged in oak containers. Their widely available Rodenbach (5%) is a tangy brown ale with a hint of sourness. The much fuller – and sourer – Rodenbach Grand Cru is a tad more difficult to get hold of but delicious.

Westmalle (Westmalle Dubbel 7%, Tripel 9%) The Trappist monks of Westmalle, just north of Antwerp, claim their beers not only cure loss of appetite and insomnia but reduce stress. Whatever the truth, the prescription certainly tastes good. Their most famous beer, Westmalle Tripel, is creamy and aromatic, while the Westmalle Dubbel is dark and supremely malty.

---

choufleur cauliflower
concombre cucumber
genièvre juniper
laitue lettuce

oignons onions
petits pois peas
poireau leek
pommes (de terre) potatoes

tomate tomato

SWEETS AND DESSERTS
crêpes pancakes
crêpes suzettes thin pancakes with orange juice and liqueur
glace ice cream
madeleine small, shell-shaped sponge cake
parfait frozen mousse, sometimes ice cream
petits fours bite-sized cakes or pastries

FRUITS AND NUTS
amandes almonds
ananas pineapple
cacahouète peanut
cérises cherries
citron lemon
fraises strawberries
framboises raspberries
marrons chestnuts
noisette hazelnut
pamplemousse grapefruit

poire pear
pomme apple
prune plum
pruneau prune
raisins grapes

DRINKS
bière beer
café coffee
eaux de vie spirits distilled from various fruits
jenever Dutch/Flemish gin
lait milk
orange/citron pressé fresh orange/lemon juice
thé tea
vin ... wine ...
rouge red
blanc white
brut very dry
sec dry
demi-sec sweet
doux very sweet

Glossary

FLEMISH TERMS

Abdij Abbey.

Begijnhof Convent occupied by Christian lay sisterhood (begijn; see box, page 307).

Beiaard Set of tuned church bells, either operated by an automatic mechanism or played by a keyboard.

Belfort Belfry.

Beurs Stock exchange.

Botermarkt Butter market.

Brug Bridge.

Burgher Member of the upper or mercantile classes of a town, usually with certain civic powers.

Gemeente Municipal, as in *Gemeentehuis* (town hall).

Gerechtshof Law Courts.

Gilde Guild.

Gracht Canal.

Groentenmarkt Vegetable market.

(Grote) Markt Central town square.

Hal Hall.

Hof Courtyard.

Huis House.

Jeugdherberg Youth hostel.

Kaai Quay or wharf.

Kapel Chapel.

Kasteel Castle.

Kerk Church; eg Grote Kerk – the principal church of the town.

Koning King.

Koningin Queen.

Koninklijk Royal.

Korenmarkt Corn market.

Kunst Art.

Lakenhal Cloth Hall: medieval commercial building where cloth would be weighed, graded, stored and sold.

Molen Windmill.

Onze Lieve Vrouwekerk or **OLV** Church of Our Lady.

Paleis Palace.

Plaats A square or open space.

Plein A square or open space.

Polder An area of land reclaimed from the sea.

Poort Gate.

Raadhuis Town hall.

Rijk State.

Schatkamer Treasury.

Schepenzaal Alderman's Hall.

Schone Kunsten Fine arts.

Schouwburg Theatre.

Sierkunst Decorative arts.

Stadhuis Town hall.

Stedelijk Civic, municipal.

Steeg Alley.

Stichting Institute or foundation.

Straat Street.

Toren Tower.

Tuin Garden.

Vleeshuis Meat market.

Volkskunde Folklore.

Weg Way.

FRENCH TERMS

Abbaye Abbey.

Auberge de jeunesse Youth hostel.

Beaux arts Fine arts.

Beffroi Belfry.

Beguinage Convent occupied by Christian lay sisterhood (Beguines; see box, page 307).

Bourse Stock exchange.

Chapelle Chapel.

Château Mansion, country house or castle.

Cour Court(yard).

Couvent Convent, monastery.

Église Church.

Fouilles Archaeological excavations.

Gîte d'étape Dormitory-style lodgings in relatively remote parts of the country housing anywhere between ten and one hundred people per establishment.

Grand-place Central town square.

Halle aux draps Cloth Hall: medieval commercial building where cloth would be weighed, graded, stored and sold.

Halle aux viandes Meat market.

Halles Covered, central food market.

Hôpital Hospital.

Hôtel Hotel or mansion.

Hôtel de ville Town hall.

Jardin Garden.

Jours feriés Public holidays.

Maison House.

Marché Market.

Moulin Windmill.

Municipal Civic, municipal.

Musée Museum.

Notre Dame Our Lady.

Palais Palace.

Place Square, marketplace.

Pont Bridge.

Porte Gateway.

Quartier District of a town.

Roi King.

Reine Queen.

Rue Street.

Syndicat d'initiative Tourist office/information.

Tour Tower.

Trésor Treasury.

ART AND ARCHITECTURAL TERMS

Ambulatory Covered passage around the outer edge of the choir of a church.

Apse Semicircular or polygonal recess, especially at the east end of a church.

Art Deco Geometrical style of art and architecture popular in the 1920s and 1930s.

Art Nouveau International style in architecture and design characterised by long sinuous lines and organic shapes based on vegetal forms, most popular between 1890 and 1910.

Baroque Boldly ornamented and theatrical style of architecture and art prevalent in Europe between the late sixteenth and early eighteenth centuries.

Carillon Set of tuned church bells, either operated by an automatic mechanism or played by a keyboard.

Chancel The eastern part of a church containing the altar, choir and ambulatory, often separated from the nave by a screen (see 'Rood screen').

Classical Architectural style incorporating Greek and Roman elements: pillars, pilasters, domes and colonnades; at its height in the seventeenth century and revived as Neoclassical in the eighteenth and nineteenth.

Diptych Carved or painted work on two panels, commonly used as an altarpiece, both static and portable.

Expressionism Artistic style popular at the beginning of the twentieth century.

Genre painting In the seventeenth century, the term 'genre painting' was applied to everything from animal paintings and still life to historical works and landscapes. In the eighteenth century, the term came to be applied only to scenes of everyday life.

Gothic Architectural style of the thirteenth to sixteenth centuries, characterised by pointed arches, rib vaulting, flying buttresses and a general emphasis on verticality.

Misericord A ledge projecting from the underside of a choir stall's hinged seat to provide support when the occupant is standing.

Nave Main body of a church.

Neoclassical: A revival architectural style inspired by classical antiquity practised throughout Europe in the mid-eighteenth and early nineteenth centuries (see 'Classical' above).

Neo-Gothic A style of architecture using Gothic forms and motifs popular in the late eighteenth and nineteenth centuries.

Pediment Low-pitched ornate gable in classical architecture; a decorative triangular structure built above a door or window.

Pilaster A shallow rectangular column projecting, but only slightly, from a wall.

Renaissance A transitional period in Europe during the fourteenth, fifteenth and sixteenth centuries, characterised by an increase in classical scholarship, geographical discovery, the rise of secular values and the growth of individualism; the style of art and architecture of this era.

Retable Altarpiece.

Romanesque Early medieval architecture, distinguished by squat, heavy forms, rounded arches and naive sculpture.

Rood loft Gallery (or space) on top of a rood screen.

Rood screen Decorative screen separating the nave from the chancel.

Transept Arms of a cross-shaped church at right angles to the nave and chancel.

Triptych Carved or painted work on three panels, often used as an altarpiece.

Small print and index

A ROUGH GUIDE TO ROUGH GUIDES

Published in 1982, the first Rough Guide – to Greece – was a student scheme that became a publishing phenomenon. Mark Ellingham, a recent graduate in English from Bristol University, had been travelling in Greece the previous summer and couldn't find the right guidebook. With a small group of friends he wrote his own guide, combining a contemporary, journalistic style with a thoroughly practical approach to travellers' needs.

The immediate success of the book spawned a series that rapidly covered dozens of destinations. And, in addition to impecunious backpackers, Rough Guides soon acquired a much broader readership that relished the guides' wit and inquisitiveness as much as their enthusiastic, critical approach and value-for-money ethos. These days, Rough Guides include recommendations from budget to luxury and cover more than 120 destinations around the globe, from Amsterdam to Zanzibar, all regularly updated by our team of roaming writers.

Browse all our latest guides, read inspirational features and book your trip at **roughguides.com**.

Rough Guide credits

Editor: Kate Drynan
Cartography: Carte
Picture editor: Piotr Kala
Picture Manager: Tom Smyth

Layout: Ankur Guha
Head of DTP and Pre-Press: Rebeka Davies
Head of Publishing: Sarah Clark

Publishing information

Eighth edition 2024

Distribution

UK, Ireland and Europe
Apa Publications (UK) Ltd; sales@roughguides.com
United States and Canada
Ingram Publisher Services; ips@ingramcontent.com
Australia and New Zealand
Booktopia; retailer@booktopia.com.au
Worldwide
Apa Publications (UK) Ltd; sales@roughguides.com

Special Sales, Content Licensing and CoPublishing
Rough Guides can be purchased in bulk quantities
at discounted prices. We can create special editions,
personalised jackets and corporate imprints tailored to
your needs. sales@roughguides.com.
roughguides.com

Printed in Czech Republic

This book was produced using **Typefi** automated
publishing software.

Help us update

We've gone to a lot of effort to ensure that this edition of
The Rough Guide to Belgium & Luxembourg is accurate
and up-to-date. However, things change – places get
"discovered", transport routes are altered, restaurants and
hotels raise prices or lower standards, and businesses
cease trading. If you feel we've got it wrong or left
something out, we'd like to know, and if you can direct us
to the web address, so much the better.

Please send your comments with the subject line
"Rough Guide Belgium & Luxembourg Update" to mail@
uk.roughguides.com. We'll acknowledge all contributions
and send a copy of the next edition (or any other Rough
Guide if you prefer) for the very best emails.

Acknowledgements

Phil Lee would like to thank his editor, Kate Dynan, for her patient efficiency during the preparation of this new edition of
the Rough Guide to Belgium and Luxembourg. There are other people I would like to thank too, including the ever-helpful
Anita Rampall of Visit Flanders; Ann Plovie of Visit Bruges for her information and updates; Lynn Meyvaert of Visit Gent for
her tips and hints; Sylvia Van Craen for smoothing matters in Antwerp; and Erwin van de Wiele, also of Visit Gent, for his
advice and opinions. Finally, thanks to my two grandchildren - the irrepressible Marnie and Laurie Rees-Tyas.

ABOUT THE AUTHOR

Phil Lee has been writing for Rough Guides for well over twenty years and has a special liking
for both Belgium and Luxembourg. His other books in the series include Norway, Norfolk &
Suffolk, Amsterdam, Mallorca & Menorca and The Netherlands. He lives in Nottingham, where
he was born and raised.

Photo credits
(Key: T-top; C-centre; B-bottom; L-left; R-right)

Index

N

O

P

Map symbols

The symbols below are used on maps throughout the book

▬▬ ▪ ▪ International boundary	▬▬▬ Wall	♦ Point of interest	☦ Christian cemetery
▬ ▬ ▬ Provincial boundary	▬▬▬ Railways	ⓘ Information office	🍺 Brewery
▬▬ ▬▬ Chapter boundary	—Ⓣ— Tram line & stop	⊠ Gate	♜ Castle
▬▬▬ Motorway	◄— One way	⊙ Statue	↔ Church
▬▬▬ Main road	Ⓜ Metro	▲ Mountain peak	Building
▬▬▬ Minor road	✈ Airport	🏁 Race circuit	Park
▬▬▬ Pedestrianized road	★ Bus stop	♟ Museum	Beach
▥▥▥ Steps	Ⓟ Parking	🏛 Abbey	Cemetery
▬ ▬ ▬ Path	✉ Post office	🏛 Monument	

Listings key

■ Accommodation

● Eating

■ Drinking/nightlife/lgbt

● Shopping

YOUR TAILOR-MADE TRIP
STARTS HERE

Tailor-made trips and unique adventures crafted by local experts

Rough Guides has been inspiring travellers with lively and thought-provoking guidebooks for more than 35 years. Now we're linking you up with selected local experts to craft your dream trip. They will put together your perfect itinerary and book it at local rates.

Don't follow the crowd – find your own path.

HOW ROUGHGUIDES.COM/TRIPS WORKS

STEP 1

Pick your dream destination, tell us what you want and submit an enquiry.

STEP 2

Fill in a short form to tell your local expert about your dream trip and preferences.

STEP 3

Our local expert will craft your tailor-made itinerary. You'll be able to tweak and refine it until you're completely satisfied.

STEP 4

Book online with ease, pack your bags and enjoy the trip! Our local expert will be on hand 24/7 while you're on the road.

BENEFITS OF PLANNING AND BOOKING AT ROUGHGUIDES.COM/TRIPS

PLAN YOUR ADVENTURE WITH LOCAL EXPERTS

Rough Guides' English-speaking local experts are hand-picked, based on their experience in the travel industry and their impeccable standards of customer service.

SAVE TIME AND GET ACCESS TO LOCAL KNOWLEDGE

When a local expert plans your trip, you save time and money when you book, even during high season. You won't be charged for using a credit card either.

MAKE TRAVEL A BREEZE: BOOK WITH PIECE OF MIND

Enjoy stress-free travel when you use Rough Guides' secure online booking platform. All bookings come with a money-back guarantee.

WHAT DO OTHER TRAVELLERS THINK ABOUT ROUGH GUIDES TRIPS?

Trip to Spain

This Spain tour company did a fantastic job to make our dream trip perfect. We gave them our travel budget, told them where we would like to go, and they did all of the planning. Our drivers and tour guides were always on time and very knowledgable. The hotel accommodations were better than we would have found on our own. Only one time did we end up in a location that we had not intended to be in. We called the 24 hour phone number, and they immediately fixed the situation.

Don A, USA

Trip to Morocco

Our trip was fantastic! Transportation, accommodations, guides – all were well chosen! The hotels were well situated, well appointed and had helpful, friendly staff. All of the guides we had were very knowledgeable, patient, and flexible with our varied interests in the different sites. We particularly enjoyed the side trip to Tangier! Well done! The itinerary you arranged for us allowed maximum coverage of the country with time in each city for seeing the important places.

Sharon, USA

PLAN AND BOOK YOUR TRIP AT ROUGHGUIDES.COM/TRIPS